ALSO BY GERRI HIRSHEY

*We Gotta Get Out of This Place: The True, Tough Story
of Women in Rock*

Nowhere to Run: The Story of Soul Music

Not Pretty Enough

Not Pretty Enough

THE UNLIKELY TRIUMPH OF
HELEN GURLEY BROWN

GERRI HIRSHEY

SARAH CRICHTON BOOKS   FARRAR, STRAUS AND GIROUX   NEW YORK

Sarah Crichton Books
Farrar, Straus and Giroux
18 West 18th Street, New York 10011

Library of Congress Cataloging-in-Publication Data
Names: Hirshey, Gerri, author.
Title: Not pretty enough : the unlikely triumph of Helen Gurley Brown / Gerri Hirshey.
Description: First edition. | New York : Sarah Crichton Books ; Farrar, Straus and Giroux,
    2016. | Includes bibliographical references and index.
Identifiers: LCCN 2016007143 | ISBN 9780374169176 (Hardback) | ISBN 9780374712235 (Ebook)
Subjects: LCSH: Brown, Helen Gurley. | Periodical editors—United States—Biography. |
    Editors—United States—Biography | BISAC: BIOGRAPHY & AUTOBIOGRAPHY /
    Women. | BIOGRAPHY & AUTOBIOGRAPHY / Editors, Journalists, Publishers.
Classification: LCC PN4874.B768 H57 2016 | DDC 070.5/1092 [B] —dc23
LC record available at https://lccn.loc.gov/2016007143

Designed by Abby Kagan

Our books may be purchased in bulk for promotional, educational, or business use. Please
contact your local bookseller or the Macmillan Corporate and Premium Sales Department at
1-800-221-7945, extension 5442, or by e-mail at MacmillanSpecialMarkets@macmillan.com.

www.fsgbooks.com
www.twitter.com/fsgbooks • www.facebook.com/fsgbooks

10 9 8 7 6 5 4 3 2 1

For Mark

"I have always thought her pretty—not strikingly pretty—but 'pretty enough,' as people say; a sort of beauty that grows on one."

—JANE AUSTEN, *Mansfield Park*

Contents

Part Three ❧ New York

Preface:
The Trouble with Helen

I embrace the label of bad feminist because I am human. I am messy. I'm not trying to be an example. I am not trying to be perfect. I am not trying to say I have all the answers. I am not trying to say I'm right. I am just trying—trying to support what I believe in, trying to do some good in this world, trying to make some noise with my writing while also being myself . . .

—Roxane Gay, *Bad Feminist*

BEFORE I BEGAN THIS PROJECT, I was conflicted at best, dismissive at worst of the Helen Gurley Brown oeuvre and her golden-thighed creation of tall ambitions and bigger hair, "that *Cosmo* Girl." I did not read *Cosmopolitan* magazine as a young woman, though I do recall my mother canceling her subscription in the late sixties because "that woman" had gone and sexed it up.

As a young writer apprenticing at a frowsy if well-intentioned women's magazine, I longed to *be* Nora Ephron, who was gleefully tipping sacred cows like the food establishment and pan-searing Erich Segal's treacly bestselling weeper, *Love Story*, for *Esquire*. How I envied the detached Ray-Ban cool of Joan Didion, hanging out with the Doors for *Life*. I had no idea at the time that both writers had already tangled with Helen Gurley Brown, with results hilarious, grudgingly tender, and icily cutting. She had that sort of effect on people.

To escape the Casserole Gulag of granny-square quilts and "man-pleasing" meals, I needed to scare up some writing assignments elsewhere. I wangled a meeting with an assignment editor at *Cosmopolitan*. I had heard that the boss lady kept a thick binder full of article ideas. There was no need to come up with queries; HGB's was a singular Vision. And so it turned out: the gentleman who oversaw the articles list set the binder between us with a thud.

We settled on a seven-hundred-word piece on how to buy the right cat, on spec. I researched Abyssinians, Persians, and rescue tabbies; I studied hair-ball propensities and scratch-pole requisites. I turned the article in, and it came back swiftly, rejected. No kill fee, no do-over. The single comment, scrawled in a strong but loopy hand I have come to recognize so well: "Not sexy enough!"

Of course, Helen was right and I remain grateful that she showed me the door. Things worked out just fine elsewhere. Along my way, I had a couple of light brushes with HGB. The editor Clay Felker set me to the fun task of parodying the *Cosmo* Girl ethos during his brief tenure at the New York *Daily News*. Over the years, I would see Helen in restaurants favored by media types, generally leaning toward a young male lunch date held rapt by her laser gaze. I interviewed her once, for a story about marriage proposals. She was a reporter's dream, dispensing chewy quotes like chocolate truffles; she was charming, self-deprecating, and, above all, helpful.

I thought I knew who she was. Silly rabbit. How she has astonished me. I have found her in the strangest and most intriguing places, a Zelig in Pucci frocks: Long before she was famous, in her years as a striving "mouseburger," there was Helen, watching her ad agency boss help craft his friend Dick Nixon's strategy against JFK, Helen putting calls through from Eisenhower and E. F. Hutton and meeting after hours with the mysterious emissaries of Howard Hughes. I found Miss Gurley in a Beverly Hills Hotel bungalow, chilling with a war-hero general during a time when the general was lobbying President Truman, successfully, for "the Super," or hydrogen bomb, program. And there she was again, captured in the glare of flashbulbs at Los Angeles's storied Mocambo club. Helen was on the arm of a prizefighter twice her age;

he was dubbed "the Manassa Mauler," a brawler of such renown that his last championship fight took up half the front page in *The New York Times*.

How'd she do *that*?

The deeper I looked, the more delicious it was. Hers was such an epic and tragic family story, her rise out of poverty attained with so many jobs and so very many men, all vastly different. She was the unlikeliest of sirens: "not pretty enough" in her own estimation, yet formidable men were fools for her. The composer Irving Berlin so adored Helen that he faced down the famously dour waiters at Peter Luger Steak House to get Helen's pricey filet charred. (Quoth HGB, "Girls from Little Rock don't eat rare meat.") Though her knees knocked with hostess anxiety, she charmed her dinner guest the poet Carl Sandburg and discussed her lifelong struggles with depression with fellow sufferers Mike Wallace and Art Buchwald on Martha's Vineyard.

Helen could also get her crazy on. I turned up a few breathtaking examples of public and private tantrums—even an airport arrest—that sprang from a deep channel of molten rage; given her miserable family travails, she was devoted to and dependent upon psychotherapy from age twenty-two on. Few Brown familiars knew that. Over and over, I heard a version of this disclaimer from her friends: "I adored her, but I can't say as I really knew her."

She led an active public life, sailed on Malcolm Forbes's yacht, and walked the Oscars red carpet on the arm of her movie producer husband, David Brown, but she kept a good deal to herself. In public, she sketched a broad, sometimes burlesqued version of her "hillbilly" roots. But Helen's Depression childhood held a series of staggering tragedies that make her achievements more astonishing and, in a way, more understandable. Most of her closest New York friends were unaware of a piercing family grief cloaked in silence and, it seems, obscured by nameless fixers. It was the source of a deep and lasting sadness closely held within her half-century marriage.

Becoming HGB was a journey through three American cities and nearly a century of turbulent eras, from Jim Crow through the Information Age. It began in the Ozark Mountains of Green Forest, Arkansas, and in Little Rock, landlocked, segregated, and caught in the grips of the Depression. Helen escaped to make her stand in two land's-end cities. Los Angeles and New York would be the making of her, places with endless vistas east and west and fertile, forgiving urban centers, where reinvention of self is welcomed, even expected. As they defined and shaped Helen's life, those three places give this book its structure.

Let it be understood at the outset: sex has imbued the soft core, hard times, and glory days of this story—sex surrendered, sex wielded, lavished, and reveled in, sex merely endured and sometimes coolly transactional, sex reimagined, promised, and packaged on glossy magazine covers for global dissemination in the still-emerging foreign editions of *Cosmopolitan* magazine—sixty-four at last count. They appear in thirty-five languages and are sold in more than one hundred countries.

The young women in hijabs now reading *Cosmo* in Kazakhstan may never have heard of Helen Gurley Brown. The same goes for American women clicking into *Cosmo* online. But Helen, who never got the hang of using a computer, would crow at the digital/global deployment of her vision. Today's *Cosmopolitan*, using its "mega DAM," an asset management system that serves as a digital library of a magazine's images, articles, and covers, will soon be able to put up digital editions from Mongolia to Botswana. Current "connectivity" to today's young women in print, digital, and social platforms: 68 million, making *Cosmopolitan* the largest young women's magazine in the world.

It is all because of a little woman who could. And when other girls didn't dare, she would. With pleasure. Helen was the first to suggest to single women, without shame and very publicly, "Perhaps you will reconsider the idea that sex without marriage is dirty." Sex propelled Helen Gurley Brown into the pop/publishing legend "HGB" when she loosed her incendiary bestseller *Sex and the Single Girl* in 1962, then turned a moribund general-interest magazine, *Cosmopolitan*, into one very hot women's book that rescued the huge and foundering Hearst Corporation. Sex secured Helen's advantageous marriage to David Brown and kept it "frisky" for half a century; sex built her wealth and shaped her public persona. Behind closed doors, sex thrilled and sustained Helen well into her eighth decade. As the late Joan Rivers told me, when it came to conversations about sex, anywhere, anytime, "Helen leaned right in. She was always *interested*."

Helen's impressive ascent from the Ozark hollers to her pink-and-faux-leopard command post at *Cosmopolitan* was also shaped by the maddening tenacity of sexism; it bedeviled her in its many degrading forms, from her first grubby secretarial jobs to the boardrooms of ad agencies and the tower of the patriarchal, privately held Hearst Corporation. It follows that the entrenched sexism of the 1940s and '50s, her vaunted Single Girl years, turned young Helen Gurley into a determined and flexible contortionist. The systemic abuse and injustice she took for granted is jaw-dropping. Her wily and often over-the-top coping strategies won her the admiration of millions of grateful women and got her picketed by others who saw her seductive, girlie, "man-trapping" ways as pandering to the patriarchal status quo.

A bad feminist? A traitor to her sex? A retro geisha? Aw, pippy-poo, as Helen would say. In her view she was merely being realistic; as a very poor and traumatized child of the Depression, she grew into a practical woman who simply, resolutely "did not want to go down the drain." She scrabbled like crazy and held on for dear life. What some saw as character flaws and thorny contradictions, she saw as perfectly viable coping mechanisms. Helen's business ethos was a less funky variant of soul man James Brown's tribute to enterprising women: "Hot Pants, Part 1: She Got to Use What She Got to Get What She Wants."

There is no question that she made some devastatingly bad choices, personally and in her editorial pages. The "gaucheries" that mortified her as a young woman of limited education and means continued, magnified by her stature and visibility. So, if you want to know Helen Gurley Brown, you must have a strong tolerance for messy contradictions. What else is a woman's life?

I came to this biography as neither an apologist nor an antagonist. I do find much of the revisionist analysis and HGB meta-dissection to be tedious, solipsistic, and drearily beside the point. It is a common misfortune of some American masters of self-invention who outlive their own revolutions—just ask Elvis. I have little patience for the latter-day "third- and fourth-wave" feminists, those who never knew life before the convenience of pantyhose and the NuvaRing, scrapping online about Helen's heroism and/or betrayal of the sisterhood. Helen didn't sell little girls down the river to objecthood any more than Madonna or Miley has. She was always about *choices*. (Though, as a tango fanatic, she'd take a dim view of twerking, I'm sure.)

Context is essential here; one must take a long and careful walk in her tiny shoes. Helen's sincere and underrated feminism was somewhat case-specific; it played out and evolved over ninety years of women's history. It was very personal; she watched her mother's dreams crushed by a father who damned women's suffrage and made his wife give up the work she loved. At bottom, Helen's narrative is just too good a *story* to be circumscribed by gender politics. As a biographer, I am far less concerned, then, with What Helen Gurley Brown Meant for Women than I am with the reasons she could and did make her audacious stand, against impossible odds. As a sucker for true, amazing (and, yes, somewhat crackpot) American stories, I set out looking for answers to the very question Helen asked herself aloud one day when she was trying (unsuccessfully) to hammer out a Broadway play about her extraordinary life:

"How did *I* get to be this *global* editor?"

I wanted to know, too: How *did* she pull it off?

There is a map of sorts. To watch the progress of "little Helen" across the march of history, particularly during the rise of the age of advertising, is to watch the obvious and the subliminal perform a fascinating and seductive pas de deux. As an ad copywriter and a magazine editor, Helen Gurley Brown was one strong and canny persuader. In its demand for women's equality in the bedroom and the boardroom, Helen's message was inherently feminist. But her Single Girl cri de coeur would have been drowned out or ignored in buttoned-down 1962 if she hadn't had the skills to pitch it, hard and fast and right over the plate.

Helen was always the first to say she couldn't have done it alone. She was a die-hard champion of the single woman, but she also believed in marriage and in pleasing and standing by her man. Her union with David Brown was unlikely but lasting, outwardly glamorous yet remarkably, devotedly bourgeois—right down to the diet Jell-O and Lean Cuisine dinners à deux in their majestically towered Manhattan aerie. Conspiring together, the Browns became media titans, two who left an indelible mark on popular culture, from the birth of the summer block-buster with *Jaws* to saving the once-mighty Hearst empire by reviving its sinking property, *Cosmopolitan*, with a fizzy hormonal infusion of what *Forbes* magazine termed "do-me feminism."

They did it all together—he wrote the outrageous *Cosmo* cover lines, she did the shameless logrolling for David's films in her magazine. She was the more visible, intriguing, and quotable of the two; he didn't mind being "the guy married to Helen Gurley Brown." They lived a rich, exciting life, compiled a fortune in the hundreds of millions, and left it all to educational programs and institutions. Any serious por-trait of Helen requires a tight close-up on that marriage.

Helen Gurley Brown died in August 2012 at the age of ninety, but as I researched this book, she was having a bit of a moment. In the fall of 2015, full-page ads in *The New York Times* ballyhooed the fiftieth an-niversary of Helen's *Cosmo*. And her legacy as pop/cult muse was also finding more traction. In New York's Museum of the Moving Image, a copy of *Sex and the Single Girl* was enshrined under glass, along with Betty Friedan's *The Feminine Mystique*, *The Stories of John Cheever*, and David Ogilvy's *Ogilvy on Advertising*. They were key period refer-ences used by Matthew Weiner as he envisioned and wrote the hit cable series *Mad Men*, about the advertising business in the sixties and sev-enties. Lena Dunham, the star and creator of the HBO series *Girls*, had a bestseller with her own single-gal memoir, *Not That Kind of Girl*, which cited HGB's 1982 book, *Having It All*, as an inspiration. Dunham bought it at a thrift store for its kitsch value but found herself fascinated. Yes, some of Helen's ideas were "bananas," as Dunham said, but she had a bead on certain Essential Girls' Truths. Enough, one can assume, to help carry Dunham's next HBO series, *Max*, based on a character trying to rise in the world of women's magazines in 1963. An HGB movie and a Broadway play were also in the works.

There is a relatively new "beauty" phenomenon afflicting young girls of the digital age that would have broken Helen's heart. Her own physical insecurities made "Not Pretty Enough" a natural title for this book. I wish I could say such obsession with female standards of beauty belonged to her unenlightened Depression-era upbringing, safely in the past. But within a year of Helen's death, girls aged nine to fourteen began flooding YouTube with self-produced "POU" videos of themselves inviting anyone to judge them: "Am I pretty or ugly?" A study in the online magazine *Slate* estimated that half a million POU videos had gone online by 2013, calling it "a new form of self-mutilation." I also found that, particularly in teen categories, there are quite a few book titles similar to this one. The problem persists and goes viral; the selfie-stick can be a vicious cudgel.

Though she never published a formal autobiography, Helen Gurley Brown told us everything she thought we *should* know about her, and then some. Half a century before any Real Housewife or loudly ovulating Kardashian inflamed the medium cool, HGB was the doyenne of oversharing. Her star winked out before Snapchat and Instagram, but, given the stunning volume, range, and verve of her typed correspondence, it's a bit terrifying to think of her on social media. She wrote as she spoke, with italic *emphasis.*

In conversation and as a writer, Helen was a spewer. After *Sex and the Single Girl*, she published more than a dozen books and anthologies, most of them rather slapdash remixes of earlier memoirs and breezy advice tomes. She best described her own literary style: "Smatterings and Spatterings." Untold thousands of words sit in the Helen Gurley Brown Papers held by the Sophia Smith Collection at Smith College in Northampton, Massachusetts.

Thrilled by the invitation from a Seven Sisters college, Helen donated everything from unpublished 1940s fiction to consignment shop receipts, book drafts, and her handwritten New Year's resolutions—from 1939. She wrote to her mother, Cleo Sisco Bryan, of her pride in being archived at Smith: "I'm so happy I'm there." Despite the existence of that rich trove, this has been a most problematic biography to research and write; the reasons bear some explanation here.

Helen's collection at Smith contains a slim typed manuscript, the treatment for a Broadway musical based on her life. Her attached note to the archivists explains the project's fate: "Several people considered—nobody bought!"

Having paged through the failed treatment, I turned to the accompanying material, a small box of cassette tapes with yellowing labels. Helen made the recordings over several months in 1970–71 in a series of conversations with her friend and longtime *Cosmo* writer Lyn Tornabene, who, by mutual agreement, recorded and kept her own set of tapes. This was their plan: Tornabene would interview Helen in long and detailed sessions to get the basics and "turning points" of her life story. They would brainstorm on production numbers and song titles; then Tornabene would write the treatment, to be shown to agents and prospective theater angels. She was never compensated for this speculative work. The payoff, they both hoped, would be boffo at the Broadway box office.

The aged and brittle listening copies of the tapes at Smith were largely inaudible. I ordered digital transfers of the originals. Transcribing them, I realized what revelatory documents they are. Helen is speaking with an honesty and self-awareness completely unlike her coquettish media mien; this is not the coy HGB who held forth on foreplay and sexy underwear on *The Tonight Show*. Her soliloquy has humor, pain, mortification, anger, and regrets. It speaks to the damnable loneliness of her journey. This is the real deal, the unedited truth about events and relationships only hinted at or veiled in all those memoirs and advice books. It is the Rosetta stone of HGB in terms of translating her habitual printed-word euphemisms—"a man I was dating," and "a woman I know"—into flesh and blood, with names. It's all delivered in Helen's own soft, expressive, and sometimes gleefully profane voice.

Listening to Helen's recitation is alternately laugh-inducing, touching, and infuriating, especially in its detailed anecdotes of the brutish sexism in the offices she worked in as a secretary. Pared down and delivered by a strong actress or HGB herself, with just a spotlight and a mike, it could have made a riveting, lambent one-woman show.

Ideally, a biographer would present some of this extraordinary material verbatim. What better and more accurate delivery system than in Helen's own unfettered, purring syntax? She had placed the tapes, and all of her writings, correspondence, photos, and mementos, in the Smith archives, with no restrictions. Helen granted permission to quote material for an earlier biography by Jennifer Scanlon, published while she was alive. But, despite Helen's clear intentions in making her papers available—and her plan to set those taped recollections on a Broadway stage—they have been effectively held captive since her death. Smith College has physical possession of the material, and serious researchers may have access to it. But permission for quoting from the Helen Gurley Brown Papers verbatim and at length is now tightly controlled by Helen's coexecutor, Eve Burton, an executive of the Hearst Corporation, which publishes *Cosmopolitan*.

Officers of the privately held corporation who worked closest and longest with Helen did not respond to my repeated requests for interviews about her. That's their prerogative, of course. But other colleagues of Helen's still at Hearst were forbidden to participate in interviews for this book. Helen, who believed vehemently in free speech, would have flipped at the gag order. No reason was given; no communication of mine or from my publisher, e-mailed and hand-delivered, was ever acknowledged. Every Hearst employee who was forced to withdraw his or her help because of this blanket prohibition expressed bafflement and regret. Their reactions were all along these lines: We adored Helen. What are they afraid of?

Helen was particularly pleased that her papers are housed in the Sophia Smith Collection's excellent journalism section—along with those of Gloria Steinem. David Brown began his career as a journalist and an editor. A draft of the Browns' early will, dated 1964, indicates their intent to donate much of their estate to his alma maters, Stanford and Columbia Universities. And so it came to pass: $30 million built an impressive, cutting-edge journalism institute now shared by those two universities.

How incongruous, then, that working journalists may not directly cite the freely donated papers of a woman who willed these grand journalism bequests. Many questions have been raised about the current restrictions put into effect by Eve Burton, also Hearst's general counsel and vice president. "I am the keeper of the brand," Ms. Burton said in a 2015 *New York Times* article investigating the questionable fate of Helen's legacy.

Some of Helen's letters and internal memos at Smith refer to efforts of earlier Hearst executives to rein her in on occasion, but the horse had long ago left the barn, and the digital age has loosed some corkers. Helen still prattles online in a daffy instructional recording from the 1960s on how to catch a man "if you're not pretty enough." There is YouTube footage of her pantomiming for an off-camera interviewer how to self-administer a protein-rich semen facial. Her 2000 essay for *Newsweek*, "Don't Give Up on Sex After 60," began, "I had sex last night. I'm 78 and my husband, movie producer David Brown, is 83."

One simply can't out-Helen Helen. So why muzzle that extraordinary voice?

This was always meant to be a heavily reported biography; I had never intended to rely solely on Helen's archives, of course. But I was not about to give up on those tapes. I needed firsthand testimony from a live participant in those conversations to comment on the experience and verify facts. As it happened, I had already interviewed Lyn Tornabene a few times at the outset of my research, long before I knew of the tapes. Lyn, now in her mid-eighties, had proved to be an invaluable source with excellent recall and a wicked sense of humor.

"There's just so much," she told me. "You'd better come on out."

Toting a three-hundred-page transcript of the tapes, I went to visit Lyn at her mountainside home in the Sonoran desert. I left her alone with the two fat notebooks for a day or so.

Lyn thought she had embarked on another glamorous adventure—Broadway!—when she and Helen sat down at the Tornabene home in Greenwich, Connecticut, and at the Browns' apartment in New York, with their twin recorders whirring and Helen's Siamese cat, Samantha, yowling in the background. Forty years later, with Lyn's magisterial corgi, Britannia, clicking across the Spanish tiles in her den, we sat down to go through it all. On the wall above us: a framed photo of Helen in jeans and cowboy boots astride a swaybacked horse that looks hugely pregnant, probably taken at one of the Hearst family ranches. It was not easy for Lyn; she still misses her old boss and friend. She adored those *Cosmo* glory days, when an assignment would land her on a movie set with the ingénue Goldie Hawn, or downing blinis at the Russian Tea Room with a swoon-worthy troika: Richard Burton, Sidney Poitier, and Harry Belafonte. She answered my questions gamely, confirming and elucidating the substance of her conversations with Helen, with the recall and the sharp discernment that made her one of Helen's first "must-have" writers at the magazine.

Many more people stepped up to help. Upon learning of the difficulties with Hearst, other writers and archives generously shared HGB interview material. Though I turned up many obituaries in searching for Helen and David Brown's contemporaries, I did find scores of people to interview, from writers to editors, hairdressers, supermodels, film producers, restaurateurs, funeral home directors, attorneys, screenwriters, secretaries, photographers, financiers.

And, oh, the women. This is very much a book about women's friendships. Talking with Helen's friends was a constant and unexpected joy. They loved her dearly, even though she often drove them bonkers. Their voices help animate the narrative here; it is a chorus of tremendous range, from Helen's business school sorority sister Yvonne Rich to well-known women such as Gloria Vanderbilt, Joan Rivers, Barbara Walters, Judith Krantz, and more. If there is a godmother to this book, it's the writer Liz Smith, one of Helen's closest friends, who offered up nearly a half century of their correspondence. The box weighed eighteen pounds.

The sheer volume of HGB's editorial output is daunting, amounting to three decades of articles in issues that often ran from three to four hundred pages each. It was clear that I could expect no help from Hearst in verifying Helen's financial success, sales figures, and readership data. So I was madly grateful to discover a thorough and absorbing work by James Landers, professor of journalism and media studies at Colorado State University. For his 2010 history, *The Improbable First Century of* Cosmopolitan *Magazine*, Landers read and closely analyzed a century's worth of issues.

His book answers some intriguing questions: When did Helen first dare put the word "orgasm" on her cover and, as she put it, "welcome the penis" in her copy? Exactly how sexy was *Cosmo*, and how soon? There are some surprising answers. Landers studied Helen's article mix by subject and "periodicity"—that is, seen in the context of the times in which the articles appeared. Using a model he first applied to a study of news reportage on the Vietnam War, he pored over 216 back issues of Helen's *Cosmo*, from her first, in July 1965, through July 1986, inputting terms such as "birth control," "penis," "vagina," "abortion," and "orgasm" into his model. Thanks to his efforts, it's possible to separate *Cosmo*'s actual sexiness from the public perception of it.

Helen was impressed and intrigued by Landers's labors, enough to grant him one of her final substantive interviews. Landers told me that the Hearst Corporation did not welcome or address many of his questions, particularly about Helen's impressive revenues and sales figures. Helen, proud of her track record for the company, quietly took care of business: a plain manila envelope with no return address arrived at his home, containing a sheaf of the requested material. Landers's research and his generosity in speaking about his HGB experience were invaluable in giving her wild editorial run some essential context.

Toward the end of my research, I was also given access to the private papers of the late Charlotte Kelly Veal, Helen's boon companion, confidante, and Single Girl co-adventuress, beginning in 1949, when they were secretaries in adjoining cubicles at a Los Angeles ad agency. The Helen–Charlotte papers constitute a pink blizzard of letters, thank-you notes, poems, speeches, and billets-doux between girlfriends who shared *everything*—including old lovers. Helen wrote a poem about her best friend, about their wilder days and containing a few startling lines about Charlotte's sudden firing as head of PR for all Hearst magazines, at age fifty-five. A segment of that sweet-and-spicy verse appeared in the program for Charlotte Veal's November 2013 memorial service, which I attended. Some of the verse had to be censored, deemed a bit de trop in a consecrated church. They were both great *dames*, and incorrigible to the end.

Biography is often a pointillist exercise; one must search out and map contacts until a cogent portrait begins to show itself. Helen touched so very many lives, on such an immense canvas, that I had to indulge in the occasional broad stroke. The willful and puzzling erasure of a family member's existence occasioned some detective work through birth, death, and prison records. I slipped on a red herring or two. There were also ghostly shadow images to contend with. Helen presented *versions* of herself and often wrote for the public in a private code of pseudonyms and shifting points of view—for her pleasure as well as her protection. Despite the flamboyant public image, she was a deeply private woman who knew the comfort and safety conferred by genteel dissembling and camouflage.

On my longest research trip to Smith College, a compassionate archivist noticed a certain decline in energy on my part by about day six. She placed before me an oversized storage box from the Brown collection.

"Thought you might like to see this."

I opened it to find HGB's faux-leopard hat and boa, and was instantly revived. I picked up the pillbox-style hat. I could visualize her in the whole kit, fishnet stockings sagging, tight little skirt six inches above those skinny knees. It brought to mind the Bob Dylan classic "Leopard-Skin Pill-Box Hat." Darned if it doesn't speak to the biographer's nosy impulse:

> Yes I see you got your brand-new leopard-skin pillbox hat
> Well, you must tell me, baby,
> How your head feels under somethin' like that.

Not Pretty Enough

Prologue: That Woman

THE HOUSE THAT RANDY HIGH'S parents rented to an elderly school-teacher named Cleo Sisco Bryan in 1966 was not a handsome or comfortable structure, even when it was new. He would just as soon not direct a visitor to the site. About half a century ago, some wrongheaded speculator—a stranger to this part of northwestern Arkansas—tried to build and sell a bunch of flat-roofed houses in the town of Green Forest. It was lunacy to try to defy the pitiless rains and snows of the Ozark Mountains, where spring runoff can arrive with a biblical roar. No one was surprised when some of those flat roofs looked as bowed as swaybacked plow horses. The High family lived in one as a starter house; Randy High says his parents were very glad to finally build a new home and rent out the old hulk.

Tearing around outside on his Big Wheel trike as a young boy, High often saw the tiny woman who drove up monthly in an ancient black car to pay her rent. Cleo had returned to her home place—she was born in nearby Alpena—after decades away in Little Rock and Los Angeles.

She had been widowed and had two grown daughters from her first marriage, to Ira Gurley, a schoolteacher from Green Forest.

Randy High is a native son of Carroll County, and he knows the whole sad and rather ghastly story of Ira and Cleo Gurley, as well as the spectacular trajectory of their infamous younger daughter, Helen Gurley Brown. He is also paid to know folks' business. As genial curator of the Carroll County Historical Museum, High welcomes visitors and assists with land-grant, cemetery, and genealogy searches in the 1880 former courthouse building that fronts the town square in the county seat of Berryville. As a funeral assistant and "pre-need" counselor for the Nelson Funeral Service—the same family firm that buried poor Ira Gurley after the tragedy—High is familiar with generations of local families and their troubles.

Few are still subsistence farming, as they were when Cleo Gurley bore her daughters, Mary and Helen, here. Now Tyson, Butterball, and Walmart are the big employers in the area; vast modern poultry barns squat along the winding country roads amid signs that say "Let's Have Church!" and "When 1% of the church shows up Abortion in Arkansas shuts down."

Cleo Bryan didn't chitchat when she handed over the rent money. High remembers her always looking the same: "Plain dark dress that reached to the top of her shoes. Dark stockings. She always had those shoes old ladies wore—laced to the ankle, with round toes and a two-inch heel. Her white hair was pulled back in a little bun, very severe. She always wore this flat, kind of squashed dark hat. She never smiled. Never."

Cleo had taken a teaching job nearby and lived alone in the rented house. She had returned to Carroll County in the early 1950s and lived quietly until, midway through 1962, a certain unwelcome notoriety flapped in and roosted on her narrow shoulders. The scandalous news electrified even this remote corner of Arkansas, which is approached through towns and hamlets with evocative place names: Toad Suck. Possum Trot. Pickles Gap. Gobbler. Lake of No Return.

The details of Cleo's mortification spread quickly: "Did you know? She's the mother of *that woman*."

And: "Her daughter wrote *that book*."

Cleo's was a rugged cross to bear, especially for a respectable school-teacher in a small town. *That book* was titled *Sex and the Single Girl*, and its author, *that woman*, was Cleo's younger daughter, Helen Gurley Brown.

On July 6, 1971, *that woman* had the nerve to return to her home place as some sort of big-deal celebrity. The local press had been alerted, likely by Helen herself, and Cleo had made herself ready. She forswore her drab everyday dress when she went to Boone County Regional Airport, near Harrison, to meet her famous daughter's flight. A photo accompanying the front-page article in the *Harrison Daily Times* shows Cleo wearing a light-colored blouse with a jaunty bow and her flat little hat. The glamorous Mrs. Brown had just flown in from Hollywood for a visit. A reporter for the *Daily Times*, J. E. Dunlap, Jr., filed a dispatch bristling with barely contained righteousness. He noted: "Mrs. Brown now lives in New York where she is busy with her work as editor of the Cosmopolitan magazine . . . Mrs. Brown started putting sex into the Cosmopolitan and its circulation has risen from 750,000 copies monthly when she first became editor to 1,446,000 and the price has been increased four times. It is now 75 cents an issue."

Interviewing this wildly successful native daughter—Helen was born just up the road, in Green Forest—J.E. got right to it: "What do you think of today's sexual revolution?"

Cleo bore up as Helen answered: "I think it's splendid . . . It's a happy, comfortable, pleasant, pleasurable thing—sex—and I don't see any reason for making it something wicked and guilty and feel uneasy about."

After the airport event, mother and daughter drove north to Osage, to the house Cleo was raised in. There would still be many aunts and uncles and cousins to receive her, good people whom Helen had called hillbillies in press interviews—an unthinking, hurtful slur that she would eventually repent of. They would be waiting with some of the family's historically dreadful corn bread, a substance so viscous that, as a child, Helen had used globs of it as bookmarks. There would likely be some creditable fried chicken and ever so many questions. Helen always sent Cleo all her press clippings, rural delivery.

Their mother-daughter relationship was close and fraught and at the very heart of the insecurities that drove Helen Gurley Brown up and away from her past but sometimes left her trembling in the dark. When she answered questions in *Vanity Fair*'s "Proust Questionnaire" at age eighty-five, Helen said that her greatest regret in life was "that I never sat down with my mother and asked her to talk to me about her life . . . I should have persuaded her to talk as I do my girlfriends. She had nobody else to do that with."

This might have proved problematic, given that Helen had declared elsewhere that Cleo "had about as much insight as a waffle." Cleo's childhood hardships would inform her own motherhood deeply. Helen opened a remembrance of her mother with a pointed question: Just how neurotic could a mother be "and not louse up her children's lives?"

Despite Helen's global reach, the home place is where her story, and Cleo's, begins and ends. During an interview for this book, a New York friend of Helen's, herself once a desperately poor child trying to survive war-ravaged Paris, offered a bit of advice. Simone Levitt grew into a stunning French beauty and went on to unthinkable riches as the wife of Bill Levitt, the man who famously built the postwar American suburb of Levittown; the Levitts took Helen and David Brown cruising off Monaco on their enormous yacht, *La Belle Simone*. Helen danced with film stars and princes under the Mediterranean moon, but in the quiet hours, when the two women talked, they recognized the immutable effects of their origins, and how their unlovely beginnings still informed so very many aspects of the women they had become.

La Belle Simone, who sometimes lectures about her astonishing life to passengers on the ocean liner *Queen Mary 2*, pointed a bejeweled finger and said softly, "You can't understand a single thing about Helen unless you go there, to where and what she came from. Look hard. Listen. She never changed from that girl and she never forgot. And that is what made her, I promise you."

PART ONE

Arkansas

I'm sure this is very clichéd, but nothing is more beautiful than Eureka Springs and the Ozark Mountains in the fall. It's so satisfying, very different from what one usually sees in the world.

—HGB in *Somewhere Apart*: *"My Favorite Place in Arkansas"*

Cleo's Lament

It was a terrible life.
—HGB on the misfortunes of her mother, Cleo Sisco Bryan

THIN, TINY CLEO SISCO was hardly the only little girl in the Ozark Mountains of northwest Arkansas to have a baby on her hip at age four; it's just that she would have so many of them, in succession, to care for. Born in 1893, Cleo Fred Sisco was the first of ten children welcomed by Alfred Burr Sisco and Jennie Denton Seitz Sisco. Jennie, born in 1876, was a robust twenty years younger than her husband. For a time, Alfred ran the general store his father, Granville Sisco, had built in Alpena, a hamlet of a few dozen souls; he is also listed as a farm laborer in the Osage Township records. Alfred and Jennie lived in Alpena Pass (now Alpena), then moved to nearby Osage. Over the next twenty-five years, the babies kept coming. The last, and Cleo's favorite baby brother, Jack Harvey Sisco, was born in 1918.

It was understood that the eldest child would take care of the youngest baby, so Cleo was kept busy with child care until the blessed day that she was old enough to go to school herself. Even then, she was expected to get straight to her chores when she got home. Cleo's best chance to act like a child was during visits to her maternal grandparents, Isabella and Lawson Seitz, who pampered her with attention and oatmeal cookies. At home, Cleo was afforded none of the playtime that her siblings enjoyed. Instead, Helen wrote, "she was nursemaid." Gladys, the Siscos' second child, was as blond and beautiful as Cleo was plain; Gladys was smothered with attention by family members and later by adoring classmates and beaux. The injustice would gnaw at Cleo for decades. Once she had her own daughters, Cleo would deliver ominous warnings on the unfair advantages of pretty girls.

Not long after Gladys clambered down off her older sister and started walking, she was also given nursery duties—until she dropped the infant she had been carrying. ("Smart kid," Helen cracked.) From then on, the weight of child care rested primarily on Cleo's slight frame. The strain on still-growing bones had a lasting effect: Cleo's right hip was permanently higher, from hitching it up to support the succession of wiggly babies. Cleo concocted an escape plan. Most of her contemporaries had only an eighth-grade education; there were few high schools. At fifteen, Cleo wangled a miraculous reprieve when her uncle, a well-to-do dry goods merchant, and aunt agreed to let her live with them in Green Forest, twenty-two miles northwest of Osage, so that she could attend the high school there.

Green Forest was a teeming metropolis compared with Osage. For the two years she was with her aunt and uncle, Cleo shone in high school. As graduation approached, in the spring of 1913, one of her teachers, Jim Birney, hectored her skeptical parents into letting her enroll in the University of Arkansas in Fayetteville. He told them that she was a brilliant student who deserved the chance, and pleaded Cleo's case again and again, until they finally let her go.

In later life, Cleo would tell her daughters every detail of her spring of 1914 semester at the university, over and over. She would remember it as her happiest, most hopeful time. She had only herself to look after, and she quickly made a close friend there, Miss Ola Stephenson. Though Cleo was a shade under five feet tall, she was an aggressive stealth player on the basketball court, darting below the taller girls' elbows to steal the ball. It was all so exciting and audacious for a daughter of Osage.

Then, after just a semester, it was over. While Cleo was home for the summer, Alfred and Jennie thought of a new way for their eldest child to help out. Given the less rigorous teaching certifications acceptable in isolated rural schools and Cleo's claim to some college education, she would be eligible to teach, earn a salary of about thirty dollars a month, and help feed all those Sisco mouths. There would be no more college.

Summoning what became a lifelong habit of resignation, Cleo accepted her lot. She loved teaching; it was what she had wanted to study in college. Every weekday morning at seven, regardless of what sort of weather the Ozark Mountains might fling at her, twenty-year-old Cleo got up with the sun and saddled the family mare. Daisy was a small chestnut horse suited to Cleo's tiny frame; the animal was patient and docile and much beloved by Cleo for the sense of freedom and escape she represented. For the rest of her life, Cleo would have a fondness for horses.

The two settled into the clop-clop cadence of their long, all-weather commute up the winding road to the schoolhouse in Rule, on the northern side of Osage Creek. Rule wasn't much of a town. There was just the school, a church, a post office, and a graveyard; students came from nearby farms. Given the wild mood swings of the area's rivers and creeks, the poor mountain roads, and the distances, many teachers would board in homes near their one-room schools. But more often than not, Cleo and Daisy made the weekday trek, about two hours' ride.

They headed northwest, away from the rising sun. Disappearing behind them in the morning mist was the small, unlovely, and very crowded Sisco house, where the wail of the newest infant regularly sounded reveille through the quiet Ozark dawn. Cleo was relieved to become a career girl, although they didn't call it that. "Schoolmarm," "teacher"—the title didn't matter. This job was sweet deliverance. At least, during those long days in a one-room schoolhouse with a privy out back, she was free of the domestic drudgery she had endured for as long as she could remember.

She was content to have her own classroom domain, where she juggled six grades. Her students numbered ten to fifteen on any given day, depending on who was needed at home. Their teacher understood the absences all too well. No note was necessary, just the terse explanation that they had been kept home to "hep out" with planting, mowing, milking, feeding chicken and cattle, and child care. Most students preferred to be in school, with the gentle Miss Sisco teaching them history, reading, geography, math, and the few extras she could manage. She colored Easter eggs for them, an unheard-of frivolity, and carefully carried these to school aboard Daisy.

The bigger boys listened for Daisy's tread in the morning and took her reins as Cleo dismounted. They fed and watered the little horse. In cold weather, the older children chopped wood and tended a small woodstove. School lunches, toted from home, were basic and portable: a roasted yam, a chunk of bread or pone. Discipline was rarely a problem in Miss Sisco's class. Though some of the bigger boys towered over her, they were respectful. Helen had a couple of photographs of her mother in those days, prim and unsmiling in a starched white blouse and an ankle-length cotton skirt—"a solemn girl-woman," she observed.

Hard times and reversals of fortune had long plagued Cleo's maternal ancestors, who had been on this land bordering both sides of Osage Creek for nearly a century. Jennie Seitz's family had seen some boon times for a couple of decades before the Civil War. Her grandfather Charles Sneed—Helen's great-great-grandfather—was awarded land in Arkansas for his service in the War of 1812. Born in Kentucky in 1797, he had been a private in the Twentieth Regiment of the United States Infantry. The land grant, Bounty Land Warrant #21796, was issued in July 1819. Between 1840 and 1847, Charles extended his property to more than two hundred acres. He was one of the first settlers along Osage Creek.

Much of the area had long been a favored hunting ground of the

Osage Indians. The Osage, originally from the Ohio Valley, were characterized as a "reckless and warlike tribe," so much so that, following the Louisiana Purchase of more than 500 million acres of land from France, the United States government moved quickly to push the Osage westward into it. With an 1808 treaty, the tribe ceded much of the land to white settlers like Charles Sneed. In the spirit of either tribute or triumph, the town originally named Fairview became Osage.

As the newer settlers staked their claims and cleared the forests for planting, they bore witness to one of America's deepest shames. Throughout the 1830s, a tragic procession of an estimated thirty thousand Native Americans passed from their ancestral homes along the Atlantic Seaboard and the Mississippi Valley through parts of Arkansas to assigned reservations designated by the federal Indian Removal Act. Their routes were known as the Trail of Tears; some ran through the northwestern corner of the state and across the Sneed homesteads.

The ghastly procession had largely ceased by the time Charles Sneed's final ownership entries for additional tracts were completed in the Carroll County records. He was also listed as sheriff of Carroll County from 1835 to 1842, and was the area's first postmaster. Charles's last will and testament, filed and witnessed in 1860, contained a prosperous man's detailed bequests of land and goods to his wife, Jane Sneed, three sons, and seven daughters. To Jane: "I bequeath her all my household and kitchen furniture . . . and also my negro man slave named Jack and my woman slave Phillis, and her infant child to have and to hold for her own use during her natural life hereby giving and granting to her full and absolute power to sell either or both of said slaves, if both or either of them, in her opinion shall become refractory or disagreeable to govern." The Sneed sons and daughters received household goods, livestock, and slaves chosen specifically for each heir from the household roster. Listed as rightful inheritances of chattel were Louisa, Dallas, Hannah, Luce, McDugan, Ellen, Steph, Zac, Dick, and Ann. Isabella Sneed, Jennie's grandmother and Helen's great-grandmother, received "a negro girl slave named Ann about 8 or 9 years old, and two good horses or mares, two good cows and calves and one good bed and bedding."

Charles Sneed had finalized his bequests just in time. The ensuing war years brought dreadful privations and violence to that corner of northwestern Arkansas. Jayhawkers—rogue antislavery groups that rose up in Kansas just before the Civil War—made occasional incursions and raids on slaveholding households in northwestern Arkansas. So did bushwhackers who were simply outlaws and renegade opportunists. These horseback pirates of shifting loyalties pillaged and murdered at will.

Within the state, loyalties were either sharply divided or dangerously blurred. The war did hit the area hard, and the violence that surrounded Helen's ancestors was anything but a clear-cut standoff between North and South. Marauders posed as partisans from both sides as they raided and robbed local families, depending on their victims' loyalties. By 1865, most of Berryville lay in ruins. Farms and private homes had been plundered by both armies and gangs of freelance outlaws prowling for food, livestock, fodder, and supplies. Charles Sneed's pretty homestead was ill-used during the hostilities, and so was he. In February 1865, the patriarch, then sixty-eight, was kidnapped by a Union soldier; some accounts claim his abductor was a bushwhacker. He was forced to ride over a mountain in frigid weather. The assailant made off with Sneed's horse and left him there to die. Tattered, starved, and weakened by his desperate scramble off the mountain, Charles Sneed made it back to his depleted homestead, where he died soon afterward. The cause given was exposure.

Just a quarter mile from Cleo Sisco's old home, on what is now Route 412, the keen eye will make out a weathered wooden sign that reads SNEED. The grass is waist-high in some places, obscuring the smaller, mossy gravestones that tilt around Charles Sneed's rather imposing monument, an orb-topped obelisk. The only sign of recent visitors: a few plastic Confederate flags driven into the ground snapped in a sudden breeze.

Much of what Helen understood about her people was colored by her mother's melancholy worldview. Even the story of Cleo's own courtship was more about regret than romance. Though she wasn't batting away the suitors like her younger sister Gladys, Cleo did catch the eye of another local schoolteacher, named Ira Marvin Gurley, who taught in both Carroll and Boone Counties and was briefly principal of Green Forest High School. In a replica of a one-room school in the Carroll County Historical Museum, above the rows of authentic desks and well-used primers, the walls are hung with framed class pictures from area schools, pre-Depression. In one photo, Ira Gurley, a short, hale-looking young man with a robust shock of curly hair, smiles beside his pupils.

Ira was born in 1891 to John Gurley and his wife, Cedella Lipps Gurley, in Alpena. John had come from Georgia; his wife's people were from North Carolina and Tennessee. Ira had three sisters and three brothers. Four of his siblings moved far from home, two to Texas and two to California. Ira had an urge to go as well, but he was slower and more moderate about his exit plan. Ira was a charmer who put on the full courtship press with Jennie, Alfred, and the rest of their brood. He hunted and fished with the boys and teased Cleo's sisters, who adored him as well. Ira had plans. In addition to teaching, he was attending law school. Someday he might have a thriving legal practice, or even run for political office. Ira Gurley could be good for the whole Sisco family. He presented himself as a sturdy, willing proposition for jacking up the clan's dismal prospects, and he seemed crazy about their petite, intelligent daughter.

No one paid much mind when Cleo began mooning over another boy she had met during her time at high school in Green Forest. William Leigh Bryan, known as Leigh, was no squirrel-gun-toting man's man. He loved books and was not athletic. His family was even poorer than the Siscos. Cleo was smitten, but he just did not stack up as a suitable prospect for her family, especially once Ira had duly acquired his law degree from Cumberland University in Lebanon, Tennessee, in January 1916.

This Ira accomplished with prodigious effort and considerable investment of his schoolteacher's wages. The university's bulletin from 1916 lists law degree requirements of two five-month junior and senior terms, costing about $150 each for room, board, textbook rental, and sundry fees. Needy students might compete for a cash prize by writing and delivering the finest, fieriest temperance lecture. Miss Sisco was indifferent to Ira's enterprise, so deep was her other attraction. It is unknown whether Leigh Bryan returned Cleo's affections. Cleo had begun to exhibit what would be a lifelong penchant for one-sided attachments, poor social acuity, and unrealistic expectations; it would lead to some bizarre family odysseys and awkward misunderstandings.

Cleo didn't love Ira, but he was steadfastly enamored of her and pressed his suit. The Siscos made their preference plain, and soon Cleo and Ira were engaged; they married in January 1917 and settled down in Green Forest. Their first home was a shabby little house as Cleo described it, with a yard full of weeds that Ira seemed content to ignore. He had bigger things on his mind, ambitions that would someday take them to finer places—maybe even to the state capital of Little Rock, 150 miles to the southeast.

Eloine Mary Gurley's birth, on November 18, 1917, came exactly ten months after the marriage, and it nearly killed her mother. Cleo was so small that it was an extremely difficult delivery, far beyond the limited skills of the country doctor called in to attend her. Her injuries were horrific and poorly treated; her recovery was long and incomplete. She nursed Mary, as they came to call her, in great pain and anxiety throughout the bleak Ozark winter. It must have been desperately lonely; often the route between Green Forest and Osage was impassable in winter, though Cleo would have found small comfort, if any, in her childhood home. Her mother, Jennie, was still having babies of her own. Worse, Cleo would tell her daughters later, she still did not love Mary's father—never did, never would—and would always pine for Leigh Bryan.

Married life had also delivered a jolt to Cleo's assumption that she would resume teaching when she was able. Helen was horrified to find out later in life that her beloved daddy had been "a devout male chauvinist, the kind they had in those days." Cleo had another name for him: "caveman Gurley." Ira was vehemently against women's suffrage and would loudly deplore the 1920 passage of the Nineteenth Amendment, which gave women the right to vote. Moreover, he would not allow any wife of his to work outside his home. After Mary's birth, he insisted that Cleo give up teaching, though they were very poor and her salary would have helped. No more could she take pride in the independence and satisfactions of her profession. Cleo's lot as a homemaker was settled.

In the fall of 1918, Ira began to fulfill his promise: he stood for a seat in the Arkansas House of Representatives, in the general election. He was a dark-horse Democrat, very young for the job at twenty-seven, and inexperienced in politics. He was hardly an imposing figure at five foot six and stocky. But with his ready grin and easy manner, he was the sort of man other men warmed to. Ira could tell a yarn or a joke, hunt and play cards with constituents while chewing over local issues. He had backers in Carroll County, some willing to buy paid endorsements in the Berryville paper, the *North Arkansas Star*: "Ira M. Gurley, Democratic nominee for the legislature, has made a clean, gentlemanly race of this office. He is a graduate of the law department of Cumberland University, one of the finest and most successful educational institutions in the south. He is worthy of support in every way and will make the county a credible representative."

Like many adoring children, Helen grew up with a somewhat inflated and incomplete understanding of her father's career. Records from the Arkansas State Legislature, along with election results and editorials in the Carroll County newspapers, offer a more accurate assessment of Ira's political moxie. On November 5, 1918, he won a seat in the state House of Representatives in a squeaker, 1,187 votes to the 1,023 cast for John Wells, an older Republican who would not soon forget the humiliation. The vote was unusually close for a heavily Democratic state.

Legislative sessions are short in Arkansas; during Ira's two-year term, the representatives met only from January through March, every other year. So Ira sensibly left his wife and child in Green Forest when the House was in session. By the time the next election neared, in the fall of 1920, the vanquished Mr. Wells, running for Ira's seat again, had some arrows in his quiver. He excoriated Ira's record in the hometown paper:

> Page 503 he voted to abolish Fish and Game Commission
> Page 733 he voted for 8 percent interest bill
> Page 506 he voted to abolish Actuarial Bureau
> Page 572 he voted against dog tax

And on it went. In a paid notice directly below Wells's charges, Ira invited his opponent to a gentlemanly debate: "Will you attack my record to my face as you do in my absence and let me defend myself?"

In the end, it was not campaign skirmishes but some disgruntled constituents that mounted the biggest challenge. With a political newbie's best intentions, Ira threw his energies behind a road project that many Carroll County voters had clamored for. Archival records of the session suggest that this was most likely Act 151, one of three bills he voted for that term, described as an "Act creating Carroll County Highway District No. 3 and for other purposes." Governor Charles Hillman Brough signed it on March 1, 1919.

Getting his constituents what he *thought* they wanted seems to have done Ira in. Wells prevailed by forty-two of the nearly twenty-four hundred votes cast. The November 1920 election results ran in the same edition of the *Star* as notices of livestock auctions, ads for Purina Pig Chow ("puts the gain on"), and a paid "invitation" announcing the formation of a local chapter of the five-year-old Knights of the Ku Klux Klan. The paper also had a sympathetic paid notice from a supporter deploring Ira's defeat and insinuating that he was turned out of office by a passel of "not-in-my-backyard" locals living smack-dab in the way of progress: "In the matter of the bill for the good road south from Berryville to Madison county line nearly the entire population signed a petition asking for this bill to be passed and for passing it it seems the people along this road became dissatisfied and voted against him for re-election."

It closed on a philosophical note: "Mr. Gurley is a young man and will learn that the path of duty often leads in curious ways."

Young Mr. Gurley wisely retreated to the relative security of clerk's positions in the House, as well as in the state's Fish and Game Commission, the very body he had once voted to abolish. Its offices were also quartered in the shining white capitol building set atop a hill in central Little Rock.

It is unknown whether Ira Gurley was in Little Rock or Green Forest when his wife felt the dreaded onset of labor on February 18, 1922, and wondered, quite reasonably, whether she and her second child would survive. Though the doctor attending Helen Marie Gurley's arrival was more skilled than the first, the result was just as bloody and perilous. So often did Cleo recount to her girls the tales of their harrowing births that Helen was still confessing her guilt, at age seventy-eight, at not being more sympathetic to her mother's ordeal:

> Cleo also told me a hundred times—two hundred?—through the years that her body was torn up giving birth to both Mary and me. Country doctors didn't know from Caesarians then, just "let her rip"; she still had pain. Did I ever bring up the subject of her residual pain . . . ? No. I knew my father, Ira, had taken her to the Mayo Clinic in Rochester, Minnesota, for repair work because Mary and I went along, surgery not real successful. For me that seemed to take care of the subject.

It is not a great leap to assume that the gory tales, constantly rehashed and with the specter of near death, did not make the idea of childbirth appealing to Helen or Mary.

Despite their excruciating entry into the world, Cleo did love her daughters; she would cook, sew, and fear for them, hover over their homework, comfort them, keep them in long underwear until April, spoil them beyond measure, and drive them witless with her own disappointments and depression. Through the crises yet to come, enduring it all together in the cramped intimacy of a series of small, ugly, and all-too-intimate homes, Helen acknowledged the inescapable tug of the mother knot. Whether it constituted a noose or a lifeline—she would always seem of two minds about it—there were a couple of evident truths:

"She didn't ruin my life, she was the making of it."

Love and bad luck would bind them to an ineluctable destiny.

"We were close as stitches."

Daddy's Girl

I'm just a little girl from Little Rock
I lived on the wrong side of the tracks.
—from the score of *Gentlemen Prefer Blondes*

IT WAS TIME TO LEAVE THE MOUNTAINS. By 1923, Ira was more secure in his employment with a succession of clerkships in the state house. As had been hoped, he was doing well enough to tender a little financial support to both the Gurley and the Sisco households. Helen was barely a year old when Ira packed up his young family and moved them to a new suburb of Little Rock. Though parts of the area are now called Hillcrest, it was first christened Pulaski Heights and advertised in the *Arkansas Gazette* by its developer in 1904 with this come-on: "Why live in the slums of the city or in the miasma of the flats when you can own a home on the Heights for half the cost?"

There were other promises: "negro cabins and shanties will be unknown" in the Heights, though black domestic servants would be allowed to live in their employers' homes. In addition, covenants were attached to each building lot, prohibiting their sale to anyone "other than those wholly of the white race." Henry Franklin Auten, a Michigan industrialist, conceived and organized the Pulaski Heights Land Company with an initial purchase of eight hundred hilly, heavily wooded acres northwest of the city's center. He lobbied for and obtained an extension of Little Rock's streetcar franchise into Pulaski Heights. By the time the Gurleys arrived, the development had indeed become a modern "streetcar suburb" with electric cars that could drop a man of business right downtown.

When Ira settled his family into the small clapboard cottage at 404 North Spruce Street, civilization had arrived in the Heights in the form of a few churches, a waterworks, and a diverse mix of housing options that made the area a livable suburb for a wide economic range of residents. Bankers, attorneys, and executives commanded elegant Craftsman and Colonial Revival homes that rose over the smaller cottages of railroad workers, tradesmen, and low-level civil servants. The modern conveniences—indoor plumbing, reliable electricity, and, before long, a telephone—must have thrilled even gloomy Cleo. Restaurants, movies, and department stores were just a short six-cent ride away.

The whole family could hop the 8 Pulaski Heights streetcar to Franke's Cafeteria downtown. Pronounced "Frankie's," the company began as a doughnut shop and bakery; Franke's fleet of door-to-door bakery trucks were known around town as "wife savers." Once the sprawling cafeteria opened on West Capitol Avenue downtown, much of churchgoing Little Rock ended up there after services for Sunday dinner. A man could treat his family well there: full, button-bursting dinners were fifty cents. Franke's basic fare was southern, sweet, and carb-loaded: sliced roast beef, breaded fried okra, candied sweet potatoes, egg custard pie, and the house specialty, a thick slab of syrupy "Karo Nut" pecan pie.

Nine reasonably good years followed the Gurleys' move. Though their domestic life was still tinged with undertones of sadness and regret on Cleo's part, the girls had two loving parents who cared for them well and dispensed affection in reserved but genuine ways. How the couple treated each other is a subject Helen's memoirs and interviews do not address, save to suggest that her mother did not seem a sexual sort of woman, and that Helen thought Ira tried to please his wife. The family road trip to the Mayo Clinic in Minnesota to address Cleo's ongoing gynecological woes suggests a decade-long struggle with the childbirth injuries and an understandable reluctance to risk having another baby.

Cleo kept close to home, brooding and reading a lot. Mary contracted a bad case of German measles, which permanently affected her eyesight; she began wearing thick glasses. Already she was showing signs of a deep melancholy and anger. She was beset by what Helen called her "goblins," which sometimes took the form of fierce tantrums. Soon they would harden into a habitual, sullen rebelliousness. "Some terrible need must have been in her," said Helen, and it "tore my heart."

But, overall, Helen's recollections of their early years in Little Rock describe two lively little girls simply mad for Daddy. "My father was a very affectionate man and he accepted all the love I had to pour out," Helen wrote in a 1975 Father's Day essay for *Good Housekeeping.* "I don't remember even once being pushed away or told 'don't bother me.' He really enjoyed being with me and my sister and we had marvelous times together."

Ira took the girls on trips to the Arkansas State Fair every fall in North Little Rock and indulged them in the full range of treats: cotton candy, soda pop, ice cream, greasy burgers, and Ferris wheel rides. On Sundays, he took them out to Adams Field, the rough-and-tumble precursor to today's Bill and Hillary Clinton National Airport, to watch the single-engine planes take off and touch down. One day, thanks to some pull from a state-house crony, Ira got himself a short trip into the blue; Helen and Mary, thrilled, watched him don goggles and a helmet, climb in with the pilot, and disappear into the clouds.

Cleo always stayed home. She had no friends that Helen could recall; few adults came to the house except the occasional relative and Ira's card-playing buddies, who settled in once a month to smoke, gossip, and sip coffee or lemonade; Prohibition was still in effect. Cleo was a talented seamstress, a deft copier of the latest fashions in adult and children's clothing. She had begun sewing for other women to supplement Ira's pay. She also saw to it that her daughters were beautifully dressed, despite their tight budget. In Helen's view, Cleo "poured all her frustration and sorrow into making little dresses for Mary and me." To her everlasting guilt and shame, Helen, like so many children who ascribe the greatest value to the store-bought and the brand name, did not like to admit that the exquisite little frocks were homemade. She stayed mum as her friends' mothers exclaimed over the tiny, even stitches in the smocking, the crisp puffed sleeves, the ruffles, ribbon trim, and meticulous hand-rolled hems.

One of Cleo's clients made a deep impression on little Helen. A long, chauffeured Pierce-Arrow would glide to the curb outside the Gurley home, and out stepped the wealthy Mrs. Bruce. Helen was four when the tall redheaded woman in furs first swept in, bringing with her the scent of glamour and an armload of lavender silk. It was to be made into an exotic leisure-class garment she called a morning coat—probably an "at-home" dressing gown. Mrs. Gurley's younger daughter made such a clamorous sort of fuss that Mrs. Bruce brought some silk remnants for her when she came for the next fitting; there was enough to make Helen a dress. In hindsight, the editor in chief who would later shamelessly, even gleefully wheedle free designer frocks, makeup, transcontinental flights, and discount hotel rooms seemed proud of her pre-kindergarten talent for snaring swag: "You can't tell me I didn't know what I was doing."

Helen's protracted fascination with the wealthy began in public school, where the children of bank presidents and railroad brake-men shared cloakrooms and confidences. She was not sure where her obsession came from and never blamed it on anyone but herself; Cleo and Ira did not discuss or have undue interest in wealthy people and never voiced any material aspirations beyond survival and comfort. But the rich people around town seemed enchanting to this small girl with hungry eyes—especially on the evening when Mrs. Bruce drove up with her teenage daughter, Edwina, in tow.

Edwina's birthday was coming up, and Mrs. Bruce had set Cleo to work on a sumptuous negligee as a gift. For days, Cleo had been submerged in whispery lengths of brown slub silk—a crisp and luxurious fabric given texture by the raised "slubs" in its weave. Mrs. Bruce, a playful, bon vivant sort, insisted that Edwina be blindfolded for the fitting, like a princess awaiting her dreamboat suitor. Once this was accomplished, Cleo slipped the shimmering garment over Edwina's shoulders to make her adjustments. As her mother pinned and tucked, Helen gawked at the beguiling apparition in their parlor. Once again, she piped right up with her admiration and longing. Mrs. Bruce was again generous with her remnants, and Helen got a darling brown silk dress to wear to first grade.

Despite Cleo's glum sequestration, things were looking up for the family. Ira moved steadily through a succession of positions at the capitol as clerk in the Fish and Game Commission, clerk in the House of Representatives in 1925, then as chief clerk of that body by 1928. The new Pulaski Heights Elementary School, a two-story brick building still in use today, was finished in time for Mary and Helen to enroll. If you drive the route from the Gurley home on North Spruce along Lee Avenue to the school, it is easy to understand Helen's complaints about the wear and tear on little legs. The hills are many and steep, but everyone walked to school, in all weather.

By the time Mary and Helen were school age, Cleo had begun her steady warnings that pretty girls got the best in life. They'd better learn to use their brains and wits. "She thought I was not pretty," Helen believed. Cleo never said it outright. She just made it clear that everything good happens to pretty girls, "and I [Helen] was not one of the golden girls." Though Cleo's hints were oblique, the damage was lasting. "I'll never recover as long as I live," Helen declared. The effects of Cleo's joyless upbringing in the shadow of her comely sister Gladys's radiant glow, Helen concluded, "ruined her life and it ruined mine."

When they were children, neither Helen nor Mary paid too much heed to Cleo's dour pronouncements. Then, one day, on the playground, Helen saw the stark truth of her mother's forebodings. She was six years old when the incident took place, but the dénouement was so wounding that she revisited it many times throughout her adult life. At age fifty, she retold it to a friend as though the pain of that day was still fresh.

Helen, who was in the first grade, was playing on the swings with a wealthy child named Ann Mahaffey. Ann was a perfect doll, an "exquisite little candy box Dutch girl." She was blond, of course. The girls were facing each other on adjoining swings, pumping higher and higher, hair flying. Suddenly Ann lost her balance and fell off—mercifully, at the lowest point of the swing's arc. Helen made herself slide off, too, also low to the ground. It was a calculated risk: the schoolyard was unpaved and pocked with potholes and rocks.

Having relived the incident over so many years, Helen had a theory as to her probable motive: perhaps she had been hoping for a bit of attention and fussing-over if she took a spill as well. Seconds after the girls hit the ground, an older boy who was a "pager"—a playground monitor from the third grade—came running over. He sponged little Ann with tenderness and vigor. Helen hovered nearby, calling to the oblivious savior about *her* knees, *her* poor skinned elbows.

Little Helen was left to tend her own scrapes, which probably didn't smart as much as her feelings did. She had some sweet recompense later that afternoon, when she heard that Ann's eager rescuer had subsequently been called to the principal's office. Apparently, he had done a bit too much heavy sponging. Helen laughed when she told the story, but the memory of the snub had lodged deeply. Lesson learned: Yes, there always *would* be a beautiful girl who only had to stand there and reel in the men. Almost always, she would be blond.

Boys could be just dumb, period. Helen would never blame the objects of their clumsy affections. Girlfriends were too important to her. Elizabeth Jessup, who lived about six blocks away, on North Ash Street, would remain one of her closest friends for the rest of their lives. Elizabeth was petite, blond, and beautiful, and Helen never held it against her; if anything, she was outright worshipful. Elizabeth was popular, always at the center of a cluster of girls, but never did she ignore or slight Helen. Neither could recall how they came to call each other Sassafras (Elizabeth) and Kitten (Helen), but they did so—playfully and fondly—for more than seventy years.

From grade school on, Helen and Elizabeth would do plenty of their giggling together in junior and senior church choirs. Despite the proliferation of churches back in the hills and hollers, Ira's was not a God-fearing house. Cleo and Ira were not religious at all and did not attend church, but they saw to it that Mary and Helen were both baptized and, later, duly shipped off to Sunday school at Pulaski Heights Methodist Church because it was expected of the young ladies and gentlemen in Little Rock. They were back at church in the evening for a program called Christian Endeavor.

The sisters loved winter Sundays, when there was no Endeavor and those family nights at home meant cocoa and toasted cheese sandwiches. The Sunday fare was a welcome respite from weekday suppers. Cleo, Helen judged, "was a lousy cook," given to serving up gray canned peas and boiling or pan-frying the bejesus out of anything that had once resembled fresh food. "Our darling mother, what did *she* know about nutrition?" Helen said. "Cleo grew up in a farm family where lard was a staple in all baked goods, where turnip greens were cooked six or seven hours and flavored with bacon grease."

In October 1929, when the gathering Depression hit full-force, it did not flatten the Sisco and Gurley clans. Up north, in Osage and Green Forest, people were too poor, isolated, and self-reliant to feel much difference. Much of the state's population was still reeling from the devastating Mississippi Flood of 1927, one of the worst in American history. Arkansas, second in loss of life, saw thirty-six of its seventy-five counties underwater, some by as much as thirty feet. There was still great residual misery from this natural disaster when the market crash of October 29, 1929, Black Tuesday, caused Cleo and Ira to sit their girls down that same day and reassure them: Ira had managed to get all of their money out of the venerable, family-owned Worthen Bank.

Even as the Depression deepened, some small indulgences were still possible. A door-to-door salesman badgered and shamed Ira and Cleo into a pricey set of the *World Book Encyclopedia* for those bright little minds. On Christmas Day 1930, Helen was in raptures over a handsome child-sized desk, a rolltop, with lots of cubbyholes for her important papers. Reminiscing about it to an editor at *House Beautiful*—Helen contributed to a story on people's most memorable gifts—she claimed some Hollywood provenance for her Christmas surprise: "The desk was absolutely perfect—a miniature of the one that was immortalized in *The Front Page* and I kept all my papers in there." She was a furious scribbler, notebook filler, and list maker, even then.

When the budget allowed, there were other excursions downtown. Sometimes it was to Gus Blass Department Store, the biggest and most established retail anchor of the shopping district. The Gurleys could not afford the upscale merchandise. But at the candy counter there, featuring locally made Schneider confections, Helen satisfied a sweet tooth that she would struggle to suppress for most of her adult life. "Calorie" was a little-known word in those days, when she stood on tiptoe to greedily consider the counter's delights. Fifty years later, Helen wrote her thanks for and remembrances of a favorite treat to Mr. Schneider in rather Proustian raptures. The confection she still dreamed of was "chocolate on the outside, a fine-grade honey comb crunch on the inside . . . the word praline keeps coming to mind . . ."

The whole family trooped to the new Arkansas Theatre when it opened downtown. They saw Sam Goldwyn's screen version of Flo Ziegfeld's comic revue *Whoopee*, starring Eddie Cantor; Helen learned the title song and loved to belt it out.

Helen coveted a new doll that every girl wanted. With great joy and evident pride, she became the owner of a Patsy doll. Patsy was designed by Herr Bernard Lipfert, a German immigrant who became an intuitive and hugely successful totem-maker for American girlhood. So appealing were his creations that Lipfert was dubbed "an industry monopoly" by a *Fortune* magazine article on the big business of American dolls. Of all of them, Patsy remained Lipfert's favorite. She became an improbable hit nationwide.

Patsy did not cry "Mama," and she certainly did not have the standard porcelain beauty of most dolls of that era. She was thirteen and a half inches tall and remarkable in her very plainness. Patsy was marketed as the doll "that looks like a real girl," "a loveable imp," and "The Personality Doll." This was a playmate that Helen could surely take to heart. Like Helen, Patsy had reddish-brown hair and brown eyes; she was sturdy enough to stand upright on her own two feet just fine, thank you. But, unlike Helen's busy yap, Patsy's rosebud mouth was sculpted shut.

Patsy was sold by one of the oldest American doll manufacturers, the Effanbee Company. She debuted in 1928 at the pretty steep price of $2.95. Yet Patsy sold well right through the Depression. Given her popularity, Patsy was a status symbol of sorts, a rosy-cheeked leveler between the poorer denizens of Pulaski Heights and the girls whose families belonged to the Little Rock Country Club. Patsy's arrival in the Gurley home also engendered an upbeat, pleasurable bond between Cleo and Helen. The family budget did not support the Effanbee-made wardrobe, at 89 cents per dress, much less the deluxe "Patsy Trousseau Suit Case." At a whopping $12.75, that was all too dear for Ira's $1,800-a-year clerk's salary at the Fish and Game Commission, roughly $35 a week before taxes. He earned the same as the department stenographers, which was far less than the rigorous positions of fish culturist ($3,000) and game breeder ($2,400).

So Cleo set to work on faithful reproductions of Patsy's clothes, but she could not resist embellishing them. Her delicately embroidered, pleated, and painstakingly hemmed facsimiles far outshone the mass-produced "originals." She also managed to scare up some sort of small suitcase for Patsy's growing wardrobe. Helen could be seen trekking with it through the neighborhood, headed for a long and satisfying afternoon of play with friends and their Patsys.

In September 1931, Helen packed Patsy's things for the big move to the Gurleys' final home in Little Rock, 415 North Monroe Street. The family had only to shuttle their belongings through the small Spruce Street backyard, across the alleyway, and into the yard opposite. After years of renting, Ira and Cleo had become homeowners. They bought from neighbors who seem to have been in financial distress; a warranty deed in the Pulaski Circuit/County Clerk's archives shows that Ira and Cleo paid J. S. Bailey and his wife, Leelah, a token ten dollars to take over their $3,250 mortgage from the Worthen Bank. The new house was also a small clapboard cottage, but with a larger front porch bordered by solid brick pillars. To the family's surprise and delight, the formerly balky radio played loud and clear at the new address.

In the summer of 1932, Ira had begun to contemplate another run for an office within the capitol, the Arkansas secretary of state;

candidates were elected by legislators. By then, Ira was a familiar figure in the capitol's halls and chambers; he was likable, competent, and, to his mind, quite electable. Evidence of his twelve-year career still hangs in the third-floor corridor of the Arkansas State Capitol building, in two official portraits surrounded by those of his legislative and administrative fellows. In the 1919 photo taken for his only elective term, in the Forty-Second General Assembly, he wears a jaunty, oversized bow tie and an expansive, mighty-glad-to-be-here grin.

On June 17, 1932, a Friday, Ira stood around the corner from where those portraits now hang, on the third floor, waiting for the elevator. The capitol elevators were equipped with open, cage-style cars then, and Ira could see who was within as the car ascended. Theories differed on exactly what happened next—whether Ira had just been careless, or he had been showing off, jumping into the car as it had begun to move. Some said there was a pretty young woman already inside.

Citing eyewitness accounts, the *North Arkansas Star* described the accident:

> Mr. Gurley was awaiting the elevator on the third floor of the building when the operator, Albert Sanders, opened the door. Miss Emma Hill, employed in the state comptroller's office, said that as she left the car, Mr. Gurley stepped aside to permit her to alight. Almost at the same instant, Sanders started the car, pulling the door shut simultaneously. Mr. Gurley stepped onto the floor of the car as it started up.
>
> He was caught between the elevator and the door opening, his head and feet inside the car, his back and hips outside.
>
> Sanders lowered the car to the basement where the ambulance crew took charge of the victim a few minutes after the accident. The operator then was permitted to go home. He was on the verge of nervous collapse.

Ira died on the way to the hospital. His neck was broken, and his chest was crushed. Ben Sain, another capitol employee, who lived across the street from the Gurleys, went straight home to break the news to Cleo. Fifty-year-old Albert Sanders was not the regular elevator attendant, but a relief operator. During the investigation of the accident, Sanders told Secretary of State Ed F. McDonald that he did not see Ira until it was too late. It was not clear why the operator took the car with its half-protruding passenger three floors down before he was extricated and laid—"squashed," as Helen would later tell Bill Clinton—on the cool marble floor.

Mary was fourteen. Helen was ten. Her memories of that day and the weekend to follow suggest a child processing the loss and its attendant ritual under severe shock; the unresolved grief—what Helen called her "daddy issues"—would propel her toward therapy a decade later. She recalled crowds of visitors to the Gurley home that Friday night, the phone ringing nonstop. More than grief, she experienced a sort of pride at first. Ira *must* have been a great man, because now he was famous, with so many people making a huge sort of fuss. The following morning, Helen was whisked off to a friend's home with her Patsy. When she returned that evening, her father looked like a fine, important man indeed. Ira was laid out in his best dark suit, in a coffin lined with gray velvet. Their home even smelled special: the plain parlor was transformed by banks of floral arrangements. Ira's photo and an account of the accident had made the front page of the *Arkansas Democrat* the afternoon he died; the story was in the *Arkansas Gazette* the following morning. Helen hadn't cried at all until she leaned in to kiss her father. Always a severe judge of her own behavior, she later concluded that those tears were not born of genuine grief, but produced to fit the drama of the moment. Mary put her arms around her little sister and drew her away from the coffin.

The following day, the body was driven north to Green Forest; Cleo, Helen, and Mary followed in a car crammed with flowers. Helen was still bewitched by the pageantry of it all, by the crowds of people converging on the Sisco and Gurley homes and at Glenwood Cemetery, on the northern edge of Green Forest. After the interment, as people began to walk away from the grave site, Helen gave way, racked with deep sobs. She finally realized: they were really leaving him there, all alone. Her mother and two aunts herded her gently to the car. Once, twice, three times, she broke away and ran, sobbing, back to the grave. When

Helen bolted a fourth time, she was swept up firmly and put into the car. They drove straight to Osage, where her grandparents Alfred and Jennie would keep her and Mary for a week, leaving Cleo to her grief.

Cleo's extravagant mourning mystified her daughters. She seemed so inconsolable that Helen later wondered if it wasn't guilt rather than true grief. She hadn't really loved Ira, had she? She had made that clear, even to his daughters. Surely, abject fear had much to do with Cleo's agitated state. She was a widow at thirty-eight in a downward-spiraling economy. Terrified for her future with two children, Cleo would soon take the wheel of the family's small gray 1930 Chevy and venture around Little Rock and beyond on some baffling, inchoate quests.

The first came just weeks after Ira's death. It is hard to imagine why Cleo took her ten-year-old daughter along to interview the elevator operator involved in her father's fatal accident. An autopsy and investigation had already cleared Albert Sanders of error or wrongdoing; the death was ruled accidental. Cleo did leave Helen sitting in the car when she went into Sanders's home to speak with him. But on her mother's return, the bewildered little girl got a detailed report.

The man had no new information for the widow; he had suffered no confessional breakdowns about its being his fault. Pressed about Ira's behavior—Cleo *needed* a reason for her plight—Mr. Sanders was non-committal. He couldn't say what caused Ira to jump into the ascending car. But, yes, there was an attractive young woman inside at the time. Afterward, Cleo would often refer to Ira's death—"witheringly," as Helen put it—as her father's "decision." This had to be confusing and troubling. Why would Daddy *decide* to leave them, and in such a horrible way?

Mary simply refused to go on Cleo's grim errands, to the elevator operator's home and then to a long, droning night session at the capitol that would determine the family's compensation for Ira's death on the job. It was again Helen who sat with a visibly agitated Cleo in the visitors' balcony, not far from where Ira had taken his fatal hop. No records of a session specifically devoted to the Gurley death compensation could be found in the state archives. Helen remembered the amount as about fifty thousand dollars, but according to Dr. David Ware, historian of the state capitol, that sum would have been exorbitant, and hardly plausible, given the Depression and the fact that it would probably have represented far more than Ira would have earned in his entire career there, had he lived.

Once the modest insurance and settlement money arrived, Cleo could be seen out and about more often, piloting the girls to dance lessons, choir rehearsal, or just on an aimless Sunday drive. At last, Cleo could venture forth on her own whim, all over town. She told Helen that the car took the place of Daisy, her stalwart little horse, and that she always felt a need to have ready transportation. Helen theorized that the Chevy conferred a sense of independence that Cleo had been missing as Ira's wife.

It was also becoming clear that Cleo was possessed by an unpredictable flight instinct that would land the trio in some very odd places. Though she did not tell her daughters, Cleo was formulating some plans—long-range, often harebrained schemes that required a certain mobility. She would bide her time to execute them until the right moment. Meanwhile, there were two girls at home who very much needed their mother.

3

Fear Itself

So, first of all, let me assert my firm belief that the only thing we have
to fear is fear itself—nameless, unreasoning, unjustified terror which
paralyzes needed efforts to convert retreat into advance.
—Franklin Delano Roosevelt, speaking of the Depression

HOW CLEO SPOILED HER FATHERLESS GIRLS. They could scarcely believe the freedom and the treats. In the first months after Ira's death,
Cleo's spartan kitchen became a sweet sanctuary; most days, Mary and
Helen mixed up a batch of fudge and consumed the whole panful as
soon as it cooled. Though each batch took two full cups of sugar and
half a cup of milk, Cleo did not limit or scold them. That first strange
summer, it also rained dimes. Cleo dispensed enough to send the girls
to the movies for daylong double bills that also included serials—
Tarzan, *Mandrake the Magician*. They went four and five times a week,
as often as the bills changed, and no matter what was playing.

As it happened, the Gurley girls' movie bingeing came at a time
when screen standards had become unusually lax. The motion picture
business experienced a worrisome attendance slump during the Depression; New York City movie houses reported their worst attendance
on record in the first quarter of 1932, and the empty rows were spreading nationwide. In an effort to stem the exodus, producers rolled in an
era of "S and S"—sex and sin. Its flashy hood ornament: Jean Harlow,

a screen siren morphed from an average ingénue into a captivating vixen by Max Factor, the Russian immigrant who transformed Hollywood makeup.

Tasked by the studio to make Harlow stand out from the crop of contract players, Factor bleached her blond hair into a lighter shade he famously coined as "platinum." For contrast, he heavied up the eye makeup and the dark, thickly painted lips. Factor adored his creation and the woman who inhabited it; as vamp ascendant, Harlow played trashy floozies with cheerful élan until she died of kidney failure at twenty-six. The lure of her artfully painted look was replicated by the likes of Bette "Jezebel" Davis, Ida Lupino, and Paulette Goddard.

In an effort to curb the industry's wanton drift, the Motion Picture Code had been established in 1930 by Will Hays, the president of the Motion Picture Producers and Distributors of America. But it would not be systematically enforced, with its "Purity Seal"—often to prudish and religious excess—until four years later. Thus, with Cleo's blanket permission, Helen and Mary were privy to some hot stuff: sexier starlets, untrammeled screen whoopee, gory lions-and-Christians epics, and the bodice-ripping beguilements of swashbuckling rogues. They became, in Helen's words, "total little movie freaks."

Perhaps their mother thought they would miss Ira less, sitting day after day in the dark, cocooned in make-believe; possibly, she needed the time to herself. But when the girls were at home, she was completely attentive to their needs. Cleo listened closely to her daughters' recitations of their days outside the home and helped with homework and church projects. Striving to be the good daughter and model student, Helen rarely got into trouble. The one time she was disciplined in school, it was all about boys. When they were in the fifth grade, both Helen and Elizabeth Jessup concocted a secret rating system of the dreamboats in their class and recorded their sentiments in a small notebook. Helen had left it in her coat pocket in the cloakroom, but a classmate ratted them out to the teacher. A mortified Helen was made to fetch the offending object and await her fate before the entire class. She took the fall alone, red-faced. She was instructed to confess to her mother *that very day* and then destroy the notebook. Like the incident with the pretty girl and the swings, it was a searing humiliation that Helen would churn up and recount many times in her adult life. She kept to Miss Baker's required penance when she got home that afternoon. Upon hearing the sobbed mea culpa, Cleo merely held her girl and promised it would soon be forgotten.

In her long hours alone at home, Cleo sewed constantly, almost obsessively. Before everything went so dark, six-year-old Helen had accompanied her mother on the train to Denver when Cleo took summer courses at Teachers College in Greeley, Colorado. She may have convinced Ira to let her upgrade her certification and teach again. But she hadn't the teaching credentials for a big-city school and as the Depression tightened its vise, there were no jobs, anyway.

Cleo dressed her daughters with a fierce and somewhat manic energy. She may have felt a sense of pride as Helen and Mary left for school in custom-tailored dresses and skirts. But there was no praise at home, and rarely even a thank-you from fussy little Helen, who still craved store-bought fashions. The ungrateful child confessed years later, "I was such a little prick." She was willful, even then. As a grown woman, subject to rare but intense flashes of anger, she would send small objects airborne—ashtrays, radios, full plates of food— sometimes in the most public arenas. As a child, vexing poor Cleo, Helen recalled, she went way over the line just once. The eruption was over, of all things, a clothing fad she referred to as a "scandal suit," which was a combination of blouse and shorts with an overskirt; no nice girls wore just shorts. Helen's friend Betty Tabb had a smashing version in a lively print—couldn't she have one, too? When Cleo picked Helen up after school shortly thereafter, a surprise awaited her in the backseat. It was fabric for her own scandal suit, a few yards of white cotton piqué.

Helen began to yowl; she had wanted a splashy print, too. She fussed all the way home and detonated once inside the house. Facing her mother, Helen ripped the dress she had worn to school—one of the frocks that Cleo had spent hours making—straight down the front and tossed it aside. Cleo spanked her darling, but good.

Fear was getting the better of Cleo; she was constantly lamenting the family's declining net worth, yet she continued to spend down Ira's settlement on treats for the girls. But she was hatching a plan, a bold endeavor that might set things right in her life once and for all and leave the paralyzing anxiety and regret behind them. She might even have a chance at happiness. She kept her scheme to herself; once she had decided on her first, exploratory phase, she presented it to the girls in the guise of a very special treat. Helen was ecstatic when Cleo announced that they were going to the Chicago World's Fair, due to open in May 1933; right away, Mary made it clear that she had no intention of going with them. As a teenager, she may have had keener radar than her little sister when it came to detecting adult guile. Using their dwindling funds for a distant and costly vacation was simply not like Cleo. When did she ever accompany Ira and the girls to a fair, even in Little Rock?

Helen and Cleo boarded the Missouri-Pacific or "Mo-Pac" train north from Little Rock's Union Station in the evening and alit the following afternoon in a glimmering midwestern Oz. The four-hundred-acre fairgrounds were right on Lake Michigan; there was an Enchanted Isle for children and a freaky, sideshow-like attraction, Ripley's Believe It or Not! Odditorium, boasting a man who pulled a small wagon with his eyelashes and a woman who appeared to swallow her own nose. The bright lakeside sky flew past above the Gurleys' heads as they rode open-top buses specially built by General Motors; a giant Morton's box poured salt from one billboard, and a river of Pabst beer flowed from another. Goodyear blimps floated lazily above Belgian villages and "real" underground diamond mines that exhibited live Kaffir and Zulu laborers drilling, in one of the exposition's more racist attractions. Cleo was indulgent, letting Helen ride the wondrous "electric stairway"—what we now call an escalator—up and down, over and over. They goggled at the exotic marine life in the Shedd Aquarium.

Helen wore her white scandal suit. Mother and daughter, ostensibly bound for sheer pleasure yet powered by Cleo's hidden agenda, wandered together through an exposition that would attract a paid attendance of more than 39 million, an astonishing figure for the height of the Depression, when a quarter of the nation's workforce was idle.

General admission cost fifty cents. With its motto, "A Century of Progress," the fair reflected American and global trends that may not have seemed obvious or relevant to the crowds gaping at robotic, life-sized dinosaurs in the Sinclair Oil Pavilion and chomping Belgian waffles on faux-cobbled streets.

Six years before the coming world war, Germany and Italy mounted extravagant martial and technical exhibits that were potent indicators of their darker ambitions. Thousands of Chicagoans lined the shore as the Italian aviator General Italo Balbo roared in off Lake Michigan, heading a formation of twenty-four powerful new planes. Graf Zeppelin, the iconic 775-foot-long German airship, flew over the city in a careful pattern that made only one of its silvered linen flanks visible to the crowds—the better not to display the twenty-foot swastikas of Hitler's National Socialist Party painted on the port-side tail fins.

U.S. domestic affairs were the fair directors' most pressing concerns. Keenly tuned in to the growing possibilities of American consumerism, they insisted that exhibitors display practical applications of new technology, things that impressionable fairgoers might step up and buy someday. By far the most attentive to that call to consumerism were the car men of Detroit. While poor white Okies were still fleeing the Dust Bowl in rattletrap Model Ts, automobile makers built massive chrome-and-glass shrines devoted to the future glories of the internal-combustion engine. Helen's recollections of her two trips to the fair do not mention automobile exhibits, but, given their popularity and Cleo's mad love of cars, it's doubtful they passed up some of the fair's most spectacular pavilions.

Taking note of the fact that more than 150,000 people a year toured Ford's assembly lines in Michigan, General Motors built its own factory right in the fairgrounds; it quickly became the most popular industrial exhibit at the fair. As crowds looked down from a balcony at two assembly lines, GM built twenty-five Chevrolet Master Sixes per day and gave away one $580 car each week to a fortunate fairgoer. A mechanized talking Indian, Chief Pontiac, narrated the story of steel. For the car companies and for American business in general, it was a bold venture during the Depression; industrial exhibitors spent more than $32 million to sell their visions.

Women's interests did not benefit much from such open-palmed investments. The Depression-era sea change in women's issues is documented in Cheryl R. Ganz's penetrating study, *The 1933 Chicago World's Fair*. Revisiting the fair along with the Gurleys affords a bird's-eye view of American sexual politics in flux while Cleo was raising her girls.

The "first wave" of American feminism that had resulted in the 1920 passage of the Nineteenth Amendment had crested; thereafter, women's issues lost traction in a trough of economic retreat and backlash. The regressions for women's concerns in this fair dedicated to "Progress" were appalling. The closest thing to a celebration of female achievement was a tepid curtsy to the American hausfrau's concerns: General Electric's Talking Kitchen. Its vision of progress for the fairer sex was sweet indeed: technicians demonstrated that the 143 steps once necessary to make a cake could be streamlined to 24 in a truly modernized kitchen. Women were tossed a few more random crumbs. There was a quilt exhibit, and the stately maternal presence of the popular painting *Whistler's Mother*, on loan from the Louvre. First Lady Eleanor Roosevelt did speak at the fair on "Women's Day" that November. Her topic was also fighting fear—fear of losing one's job, of being evicted, of being hungry and alone.

Far from the First Lady's righteous podium, on the fair's crowded and decidedly lowbrow midway, a perfectly scandalous woman held millions in thrall. Raised poor in the Ozarks, brazen and unapologetic in her sexuality, and gifted with a canny head for business, *that woman* was credited with saving the fair financially. Her success, her outrageous public statements and financial savvy, made for an early, cruder model of the mighty global enterprise that resulted in Helen Gurley Brown's rescue of the badly listing Hearst Corporation three decades later. Sex was at the center of this World's Fair triumph; commerce and erotic "art" waltzed gaily beneath a steady rain of cash.

That woman called herself Sally Rand. She was saucy, sly, and headline-grabbing, and she was the talk of the fair and beyond. So it is not surprising that Cleo steered her eleven-year-old daughter to the fair's midway and its Streets of Paris venue. The long lines outside were about 70 percent male. But women were curious as well and queued up to view the show described by some outraged citizenry as "a cess-pool of iniquity, a condition of depravity and total disregard of purity."

The Gurleys wedged themselves into the packed theater, which generated so much cash the fair accountants were forced to set up a separate banking facility with eight overworked auditors just to monitor the Streets of Paris daily receipts. The midway also sold alcohol for the first time in fourteen thirsty years. In March 1933, just two months before the fair's opening, President Roosevelt had signed the Cullen-Harrison Act into law, allowing the public sale of beer and wine. Between admissions, food, and drink, the "Streets" were pulling in an astonishing hundred thousand dollars a day.

As the lights went down, the music welled up. It was not the squealing brass of carnies and cooch dancers, but classy selections—Debussy and Chopin. Out from the wings came a beautiful blonde, gliding across the boards effortlessly as her strong, shapely arms deployed twin fans of ostrich feathers, each four feet wide. As graceful as Terpsichore, smiling directly at the rows of spellbound gawkers, Rand manipulated the fans to rising cries.

Was she indeed naked beneath the feathers? Dancing toward a large, backlit scrim, she dropped the fans, and all was revealed behind the thin gauze—the perfect upturned breasts, the muscular curve of haunch. There were gasps and screams as she retreated behind the fans and traversed the stage once more, whirling like a top with the fans held across the front and back of her torso. As the feathers flashed on a fast, deft pivot, there it was! Just a glimpse of breast and thigh—then back behind the scrim, fans down, in a bold chest-forward victory pose for an audience driven to a frenzy of tumescence, throaty roars, and shrieks.

Little Helen may have been confused by the hoopla, but she was impressed. Later, from their hotel, she wrote to her sister in Osage: "Mary, you ought to see this woman with fans . . . She switches them all around from her front to her back so you can't see anything but the audience makes a big commotion."

Sex, "tastefully" presented, did indeed save the Chicago World's Fair from insolvency, despite some predictable and fairly empty huffing. The "fan dancer" Rand got arrested four times in a single day at the fair for dancing naked or nearly so behind those huge, artfully deployed fans. The arrests were mere gestures on the part of law enforcement; everyone adored Sally, and fair organizers had a deep respect for Mademoiselle's attractive bottom line.

Just who was this pearly-skinned Valkyrie who led the charge? Born Harriet Helen Beck, she fled her mountain home in Elkton, Missouri, as a teenager. As Sally Rand, she had landed at the Chicago fair by way of a Kansas City chorus line, the Ringling Brothers Circus, vaudeville, and a modest Hollywood career that dimmed with the advent of talkies; it seemed that the comely Miss Rand had an incorrigible lisp. Rebooted as an exotic dancer artiste, Rand campaigned for and won a spot on the Chicago fair's midway with a Lady Godiva stunt. Astride a white horse, she crashed a fancy-dress pre-opening party for Chicago's elite wearing little more than an anklet of posies and a cascading blond wig.

Once installed in her own exhibition on the midway, Rand alternated between wearing a court-ordered pubic "fig leaf," a sheer body stocking, and just the special body makeup concocted by her Hollywood friend and ally, the peripatetic Max Factor. He painted her naked body with artfully Deco jagged stripes, and got arrested along with her at one Chicago raid. Rand's populist stance was catnip to the Depression-weary crowds looking for an affordable thrill. In her study of the fair, Cheryl Ganz concluded, "Rand became the fair's enduring icon for optimism and hope, a true Horatio Alger, rags-to-riches figure."

Helen was far too young to be impressed by anything other than the sheer spectacle and the mad excitement of Rand's audience. Overall, the Chicago World's Fair was all about escape. It touted boundless, blue-sky optimism, miraculous new products, and a progressive, somewhat more permissive future. All of it was good news for that key aspect of the American economy that had been on life support—consumer spending. FDR was so bullish on long-term effects of the fair's economic boosterism that he urged exposition officials to hold it open for another season, in 1934. They agreed.

Once they arrived home, Helen burbled to her sister and friends about the wonders she had seen, the exotic things they had eaten and ridden upon. It was just *dreamy*. She would not learn until a year later that the Chicago excursion was also a dry run for Cleo, a sly bit of recon involving train routes, city transport, and geographical distances for the secret itinerary she had in mind. Saying nothing about her plans, Cleo bided her time. The family settled back into the more somnolent pace of their own city. Summers in Little Rock, Helen observed, "were still as a postcard." It was so hot, even the streetcars seemed to roll in slow motion. When it was bearable, there were neighborhood games of Kick the Can, Run Sheep Run. Cleo had a terror of her girls participating in athletics, especially swimming in local dipping spots such as White City. As the girls cooled off, Cleo paced on dry land; she did not breathe easy until they were toweling themselves dry.

Helen and her girlfriends were hardly boy-crazy, but they were interested. Very interested. Helen talked about her sexual awakenings in a frank 1996 interview with David Allyn, for his book *Make Love Not War: The Sexual Revolution, an Unfettered History.* "We played naughty games with a couple of the neighbor boys, nothing serious. We played Post Office, that was just kissing. At age ten in Little Rock, and even at fourteen, kissing is serious—you know, you feel *vernal* feelings. You feel—what's the word? Not all the way to sexual, but you feel *stirrings*. And to play Post Office at age ten and fourteen is pretty far gone."

She remembered that game as a simple and very safe transaction. "You sent somebody a letter, and then when he got the letter you went some place in another room in the house and you kissed. Well, we were so innocent we didn't even kiss, we just sent each other letters and special deliveries. It was so sweet."

Often, in summers past, the Gurleys had retreated to the cooler and somewhat less humid hills, staying with Cleo's parents in Osage. They did so again for part of that summer of 1933. Helen, by then very much the city girl, found herself appalled by some of her relatives' plain and uninhibited country ways. As she explained, "I *never* liked the looks of the life that was programmed for me—ordinary, hillbilly and poor— and I repudiated it from the time I was seven years old, though I didn't have many means of repudiation. I didn't like my little-girl cousin who peed in the creek in front of a lot of other people. I didn't like all my cousins saying 'ain't' and 'cain't' and 'she give five dollars for that hat.' They were, and are, dear, lovely people who lead honorable lives in the Ozark Mountains, but I wanted something else."

That summer's visit to the hills had other somewhat disconcerting aspects. Helen told Allyn, "My uncle, who was about four years older than I, tried to have sex with me. They lived up in the mountains at my grandmother's house, and that was a hot and heavy summer."

Her teenage uncle shadowed her, panting and insistent as a randy coonhound. She wasn't sure what was going on. Finally, he lured her to the attic. "I was 11, he was 15. Nothing like a country boy at age 15 who is horny. And yet, I too felt—what would you call them? Feelings, crav- ings, longings. We once even tried it, but I was, of course, hermetically sealed. I was a tiny little person, virginal as I could possibly be, never been touched before, and he couldn't begin to get even close to me, and his heart wasn't really in it. He knew that that was naughty."

Helen waited awhile before she told her mother what had happened. Cleo took it calmly. "He was her beloved younger brother," Helen ex- plained. "She wasn't cross or cruel, she just said, 'Well that just won't do. He shouldn't have been doing those things.' I guess as I think about it she was fairly reasonable about the whole thing, considering that she herself I don't think cared much for sex. My father, I think, was much more sensual than she."

At the time, Cleo was applying the bellows to some embers banked in her own heart, but she kept any longings for male companionship well hidden. At thirty-nine, she had been a married woman for fifteen years and widowed for a year. Neither daughter had a clue about her ulterior motives in 1934, when Cleo proposed a second trip to the fair in Chicago.

4

Roads to Nowhere

"The excursion is the same when you go looking for your sorrow as
when you go looking for your joy."
—Eudora Welty, "The Wide Net"

ONCE AGAIN, MARY WAS having none of Cleo's sudden travel plans, and
stayed with relatives when her mother and sister headed back to the
World's Fair in 1934. As the train neared the Windy City, Cleo insisted
they bypass Chicago and get off in Cleveland, Ohio. Her explanation:
It was raining in Chicago. Why not wait for good weather so they could
best enjoy the fair? Cleo had *always* wanted to visit Cleveland! They
would seize the day. Taking advantage of Depression pricing, mother
and daughter checked into the grand, thousand-room Hotel Cleveland
downtown.

An exhausted and overexcited twelve-year-old Helen fell asleep,
and awoke in the strange room alone and frightened. She found a note
from Cleo saying she'd be back soon. When her mother returned, her
explanation was terse but truthful: she had gotten in touch with an old
friend, and they went for a walk. The following afternoon, Helen was
deposited alone in a movie house while Cleo had a second appointment to catch up some more. So vivid was Helen's recall of that unnerv-
ing afternoon that she remembered the movie that was playing: *Bulldog*

Drummond Strikes Back, a detective mystery/comedy starring Ronald Colman and the ingénue Loretta Young. Helen's absorption in the film dissolved with an ugly distraction. The man seated beside her unfastened his trousers and exposed himself. She moved to another seat. The man followed. When the lights finally went up and Cleo arrived to retrieve her daughter, a shaken Helen told her what had happened. They left for Chicago and the more benign transports of the fair the next day.

Not long afterward, Helen and Mary learned that Cleo had been with her lost love, Leigh Bryan, the man she should have married. Cleo heard he had moved to the Cleveland area to try his luck, and was said to be getting by as an ice cream vendor. Over the two exploratory trips north to the fair, the resourceful Cleo had tracked him to his Cleveland neighborhood and made contact. Beyond that, the girls heard nothing further of their mother's old sweetheart. They concluded that things hadn't gone too well in Cleveland.

One thing was becoming distressingly apparent to the Gurley sisters: Cleo harbored some assumptions about human relationships that were so off-base, so glaringly detached from reality, that it seemed she had been raised in a cave. As her anxious brain spun possibilities for sources of financial support, she could not or dared not give them voice. Out of pride or shyness, Cleo never asked outright for anything. Yet she seemed convinced that others would know what she was thinking and step up with exactly the right sort of help. A few times, she sent her younger daughter to make the pitch, though she never adequately prepared Helen for the missions.

Helen was confused and miserably uncomfortable when Cleo dropped her off alone to visit an elderly man up north in Green Forest. He had been fond of Ira, hunted with him, and possessed a valuable gun collection. Cleo's assumption, communicated to no one until afterward, was that surely the old gent would want to gift poor Ira's daddyless little girl with one of his guns. They could sell it for cash. As Helen later concluded, Cleo simply expected people to anticipate her needs. No commemorative weapon was handed to the child. Both parties ended the visit on a note of baffled embarrassment.

Mercifully, there was never a hidden agenda in the Gurleys' regular excursions to the Oaklawn Park Race Track in nearby Hot Springs, Arkansas. A day with the ponies was pure pleasure—for Cleo, most of all. Still a devotee of equine speed and beauty, she adored the whole spectacle. Cleo and Elizabeth's mother, Aleta Jessup, took turns chaperoning Helen, Elizabeth, and Mary to the track on Sundays in February and March. Every racing season, Cleo ran up new outfits for herself and the girls. Each had a glorious four dollars to wager, and they never lost it all. This was because the girls hedged their bets and simply put a dollar down on a favorite horse just to show. Helen, a girl who would learn the arts and merits of compromise, contented herself with minor expectations at the track. Her reasoning: winning *something* is better than just plain losing. This was a modest precursor to her adult business motto: never ask for something you don't think you can get.

Cleo's race day buoyancy always deflated once they left the track. More than ever, Helen and Mary preferred their friends' homes to their own. The Jessup house was a lively spot, even though Elizabeth had a busy working mother and was often cared for by her stricter grandmother. The Jessups had experienced their own Depression reversals. Elizabeth's father worked at a bank; his salary was cut by a third, then by another third. But at least his bank didn't close. Still, Helen noted, unlike her own home, "there wasn't any sadness there." Aleta Jessup treated Helen like a second daughter. Surely, she took a close look and recognized a very needy little girl. Nearly sixty years later, Helen wrote to Aleta to reminisce and thank her for the respite: "Let's just say things were never very happy at my house . . . When I came to your house there was *always* laughter and fun and certainly *music*, not to mention wonderful things to eat!"

There was a good deal of joyful noise at 523 North Ash Street. When Mrs. Jessup was at home, she was often surrounded by Elizabeth's friends, girls and boys, who gathered around her piano to belt out popular tunes: "These Foolish Things," "Got a Date with an Angel," "Blue Moon," "Goody Goody." Aleta Jessup enjoyed young people and music; she was unconventional and fun-loving enough to hold a real, grownup dinner party for a dozen boys and girls, Helen among them, that ended in a girls-only sleepover. She conducted the junior and senior choirs at the Winfield Methodist Church, where she also played the five-tiered "wedding cake" organ. At the home sing-alongs, she assigned everyone a solo, regardless of skill. No one liked the songfests better than Helen, who judged her own voice a "get-by alto."

Helen had followed Elizabeth and her mother to the Methodist choir. Up in the church loft, things were getting flirty between the girls and boys. Helen found that rehearsals and performances "had a sexual tinge" as twenty girls and boys spent hours together sharing hymnals and sidelong glances. As everyone approached puberty, getting close had its complications in the warmer months. Helen and her girlfriends found personal hygiene a challenge; as there were no deodorants, talcum powder flew several times a day, "like dusting an apple strudel endlessly."

Something was happening to Helen's best friend, a transformation that perhaps boys noticed first. The girls were in junior high, dressing in a locker room after a swim, and Helen was stunned by the sight of Elizabeth, Aphrodite-like, leaning down to snug her breasts into . . . a brassiere! She had acquired *booo*-soms, as Helen would call them the rest of her life. Helen's memory of the moment is rhapsodic: how perfect those new breasts were, how *unexpected* and breathtakingly beautiful. Suddenly the girls were different, in a hushed but profound way. Helen did not recall being envious of Elizabeth's new developments but simply, pleasantly aghast.

Despite this developmental gulf, coming of age together was a sweet and comforting partnership. Their chatter was kind, never competitive. The two girls grew to "loving boys in the yeasty, sensuous, long simmering summers of Little Rock." Even when they were too old for dollhouses, they would sit on the floor of Elizabeth's bedroom, indolently moving the dolls about in an innocent ménage à trois, the dolls representing Helen, Elizabeth, and Freed Matthews, a boy they both adored. It was nothing naughty; the dolls only had flirty conversations. It may not have been clear on those dreamy afternoons, but Helen would conclude later, "We were surely as much in love with each other as we were with Freed Matthews."

To their astonishment and horror, Freed became one of the first lo-cal victims of the rising polio scourge; he died swiftly. Little was known of that increasingly dreaded disease poliomyelitis except that it liked to claim its victims in the warmer months; given their mild climate, the southern states would see outbreaks year-round beginning in the 1930s. Theories on transmission ran the gamut, from mosquitoes to houseflies to swimming pools. Cleo added another unknown evil to her heavy rucksack of fears.

Freed was gently, briefly mourned. Life went on, and other boys caught their fancy. Girls still spoke about their crushes in rosy abstrac-tions and ideals; the grubby, furtive side of nascent sexuality seemed to be the province of boys with moist palms and a secret semaphore of urges and dares, especially when they were in packs.

Helen had a brush with their feral groping one Halloween. "I was out in the neighborhood during trick-or-treat, and a couple of boys made a pass at me. What *was* that? They had their hands on my back-side or something. And I was such a good Mommy's girl, it took me weeks to get up the courage to tell her what had happened. She [Cleo] was never punitive about it. I told her that these boys had been sort of fresh, and she was glad that I told her about it, and she didn't even say that they were bad, naughty, terrible boys. She just said, 'Well, you don't want that to happen.'"

Between the priapic young uncle, the movie theater creep, and neighborhood booty-grabbers, sex had not yielded very romantic or uplifting transports for Helen. Cleo's calm if cautionary reactions had probably helped put boys' impulsive behavior in some reasonable per-spective. Whatever she told Helen after the scary incident in the Cleve-land theater, Helen did not, in her telling of the story, seem permanently traumatized. She traced her curiosity about sexual matters as far back as age eight, when she and her Spruce Street neighbor Betty Engstron sat on the living room floor and peered closely at their own genitals. Helen also thought back to the times she and Mary would pore over the medical-equipment section in the Sears Roebuck catalog, wondering about trusses, bedpans, enema equipment, getting "mildly titillated . . . just tiny twigs of sexuality getting started." This was a young girl who would pay close attention to her own stirrings. She was, by her own admission, always *interested*.

From an early age, she was also committed to improving her chances for attracting a dreamboat. Helen and Elizabeth delighted in the standard pubescent beauty excursions. They hopped the streetcar to the Woolworth's downtown and circled the cosmetic counters, heads bent in protracted deliberations over which type and shade of lipstick to buy. Tangee was their brand of choice; it was cheap, chastely tinted, and sold everywhere. Between World Wars I and II, it was the most popular brand in America.

Unknowingly, the girls, their schoolmates, and their mothers were boosting one of the few industries to come through the Depression more robust than before. Cosmetics, and lipstick in particular, given its low cost, were hardly salves for the nation's huge problems. But the gay, vivid swivel tubes of molded beeswax, deer tallow, castor oil, and the vermilion hues of crushed beetle carapaces proved an inexpensive if momentary balm. A survey of buying habits in the 1930s revealed that Depression households were as likely to buy a tube of lipstick as they were to purchase a jar of mustard to enliven meager fare.

Seventy years later, Leonard Lauder, chairman of the Estée Lauder Companies, would tout an economic measure he called the "leading lipstick indicator." As *The New York Times* reported, "After the terrorist attacks of 2001 deflated the economy, Mr. Lauder noticed that his company was selling more lipstick than usual. He hypothesized that lipstick purchases are a way to gauge the economy. When it's shaky, he said, sales increase as women boost their mood with inexpensive lipstick purchases instead of $500 slingbacks."

Lipstick, with its phallic shape and glistening oral enticements, became both acceptable and politicized in future gender wars—as it was in skirmishes past. In 1912, the feminists Elizabeth Cady Stanton, Charlotte Perkins Gilman, and others led a suffragette rally in New York City with lips boldly painted as a gesture of emancipation. Tangee's 1934 advertisements claimed both allure and propriety for females of all ages: "Don't risk that painted look. It's coarsening and men don't like it." That hardly mattered to two girls at the Tangee display in the

Little Rock five-and-dime. They were thrilled to have permission to buy a specially formulated "one shade fits all" lipstick just right for teens entering the cosmetic market.

By junior high school, the girls were made to understand the basic rules of feminine comportment: Never overstate your availability. Look and act like a lady and marry well. Cleo wanted that for her daughters. But she also communicated a slightly subversive message drawn from her own disappointments. "Having babies isn't all there is," she told them, adding that, of course, she loved them both. She encouraged her girls to use their brains, but her ambitions for them were limited. Helen was never pushed hard toward anything; she felt that her mother's hopes for her never exceeded what she thought Helen could do. Cleo was hedging her bets again. Helen's theory: her aspirations for her daughters were limited by her own fears.

Cleo, a poor cook, reluctant wife, maimed by childbirth, and a virtual shut-in, was hardly able to school her girls in the finer domestic and social requisites of southern womanhood. Helen was encouraged to spend as much time as possible with girls from wealthier families, possibly to educate herself in the social niceties so utterly foreign to her mother. The homemaking education offered by the public schools was of little help. Helen recalled: "In my home-economics class in Pulaski Heights Junior High School in Little Rock in 1935, where we cooked baby meals, blancmange, a delicious, sugar-packed little vanilla pudding, was accorded all the gravity of meat loaf and string beans."

The lack of information on proper nutrition was on a par with the sketchy sort of sexual information she received. "I couldn't have had a more repressed sexual education than in Little Rock, Arkansas," Helen declared. "A, it was Southern. B, it was in the 1930s. And you were thought to be a very bad girl—a trashy girl, tacky, unacceptable—if you should have sex before you were married. But the real concern was that you would get pregnant. There was no birth control. And to be pregnant and not married—there was no abortion, either. Therefore you would have had to go to another city and spend the rest of your life in a nunnery or kill yourself."

In Cleo's vast panoply of anxieties, the premarital seduction of her daughters loomed large, perhaps disproportionately so, considering their worsening financial problems. She fretted aloud about the potential consequences of premarital sex, but did not offer any opinion on the act itself. Sex education per se was just not on the table.

"[Cleo] wasn't a zealot," Helen said. "She wasn't of the Catholic persuasion, nothing like that, but she wanted her daughters to be raised as nice Little Rock Southern, honorable, respectable young women and get married. And I'm sure she told me you have sexual relations *after* you're married. But we didn't really discuss it—it wasn't a topic of conversation in my house."

Instead, there was more of Cleo's oblique vocal apprehension, particularly when it came to the older Miss Gurley. Mary had emerged as the feisty, headstrong sister with a temper that no one wanted to cross. Given her volatility, Cleo did not dare push back when her elder daughter refused to go on those impulsive road trips. The little sister got an earful of her mother's growing misgivings. "She was terrified that my sister would be seduced or somehow get involved with a boy and get pregnant. She was *terrified* of that. I heard a lot about that: 'Mary's running with a fast crowd; oh, if we could only get her away from them.' And my sister was *not* popular. Was that because she was running with a fast crowd? And the nice girls had dropped her? Or had the nice girls dropped her and *then* she started running with a fast crowd? It [Cleo's] was a lot of concern about popularity and the correct people to be with. How did I escape? How did I escape from this?"

Sometimes the three Gurley women just got in the car, windows down, to air out the anxieties and unspent anger that suffused their small house. They were happiest on the move, with Cleo at the wheel. Dowdy as it was, the '30 Chevy had served them well. But in 1935, car-crazy Cleo was ready for an upward sort of six-cylinder mobility.

That year, Pontiac laid out its most aggressive campaign ever, to capture the "lower cost" market with its new line. A surviving promotional film made for the company's sales force boasts that the combined media buys—newspapers, magazines, billboards, radio—would create "seven billion, five hundred sixty million selling impressions" throughout America "day after day, week after week," for a full year.

Cleo was snared, besotted, and, given their finances, half-mad with desire. With Mary in high school and Helen in junior high, she bought her first brand-new car. The Pontiac sedan cost a breathtaking seven hundred dollars. Cleo let it be known that it was the happiest day of her life. She piloted her beloved off North Monroe Street and into the narrow, rutted dirt driveway beside the house, where it dazzled. The humpback chassis was fronted by a vertical chrome grille, topped by a Deco hood ornament, a likeness of Chief Pontiac himself. The girls thought the car stunning, and it smelled like heaven; Helen and Mary sat inside for hours, just inhaling. Helen, who would anthropomorphize every subsequent automobile in her life, christened their new chariot "Gloria Hibiscus."

Hallelujah! With gas prices averaging nineteen cents per gallon, the Gurley women could cruise Little Rock and beyond in comfort, style, and the heady assembly-line perfume of enhanced status. Helen loved seeing the gleaming sedan pull up to fetch her from after-school activities. Yet, though the car may have been a source of pride and pleasure, Cleo, as ever, had another, quieter agenda. She had bought her family a reliable getaway car. Cleo was contemplating another mad dash. Money was getting tighter; job prospects were still nonexistent. Suddenly, with no prior discussion, she announced a road trip. This was not a lark; it was to be permanent. She decided to move them all nearly three hundred miles away, to Tulsa, Oklahoma, where they knew no one.

Her logic for choosing that distant and unknown city was as half-formed as ever. The details emerged haltingly and made little sense to her daughters. Cleo knew that the older brother of Ola Stephenson, with whom she had shared a dorm room during that one semester of college back in 1914, lived in Tulsa. She had heard that Ola's brother headed a law firm. Perhaps he would help them out financially, or give Cleo a job. The attorney in question had not been contacted or petitioned in any way when Cleo hired movers and started packing the family up. Mary, seventeen and done with high school, was not having any of it; she took refuge with her grandmother in Osage. Once again, Helen was alone with tiny, hell-bent Cleo. Wedged into the tightly packed Pontiac, she sobbed bitterly at the loss of Mary, her dearest girlfriends, dance lessons, Aleta Jessup's musicales, and life at Little Rock High.

They followed the moving van northwest to Tulsa. Exhausted and confronted with the rashness of her flight, the widow Gurley was beside herself as soon as they arrived, presumably at a rental she had arranged sight unseen. What were they doing in that strange place, *all alone*? What had she been thinking? Cleo strode around distractedly outside the car, Helen recalled, "like Ophelia strewing petals." The moving men surveyed the pathetic scenario, conferred, and persuaded Cleo to head back with them that very day—at full freight, doubling the cost of her impulsive flight. The home goods went straight to Little Rock; Cleo and Helen reached Osage in the dead of night to fetch Mary. Back home, as the girls reveled in their reprieve, Cleo just wilted. A little sadburger, Helen called her—terrified, poor, and utterly without prospects.

After the Oklahoma debacle, which came on the heels of the car purchase, there was even less money. The strain of maintaining a certain genteel appearance was increasing. Cleo made it clear: falling again into poverty amid people they knew, sinking back to a grubby, subsistence sort of life such as they had had back in Green Forest, was simply insupportable. If they were destined to be wretchedly poor again, let it be someplace far away, where no one knew the depths of their fall. Cleo had resolved to avoid that humiliation at all costs. But this time she had to make a clean, clever break, and make it irrevocable. The deception needed to be seamless.

She was ready in the summer of 1936. Once again, there was the announcement of a road trip presented as a treat. They would drive to Dallas, visit the State Fair of Texas, and see Ira's brother James Gurley, also in Texas then, as well as one of Ira's married sisters and her family. The cousins would all have a fine time and get to know one another better. After Texas, they would head straight west to Los Angeles, where

Ira's brother John lived and worked sporadically as a mechanic. They would have a nice visit and see the Pacific Coast. Some part of that itinerary must have interested Mary, and she agreed to go along.

They did everything that Cleo promised. When the girls expected it was time to head for home and the start of Helen's school term, Cleo fessed up: she had sold their heavily mortgaged house and furniture back in Little Rock. There was nothing left to go home to. They would be setting up housekeeping in Los Angeles, where Helen could finish high school. Surely, Ira's brother John would help them.

Mary hopped a bus back to Little Rock as soon as she could.

PART TWO

Los Angeles

Good times were the core conviction of the place.
—Joan Didion, *Where I Was From*, on early California

5

What Fresh Hell

My shrink says that, given the set of problems I had growing up and
as a young woman, it's quite astonishing I'm not locked away in a
mossy little cell somewhere.
—HGB, *Having It All*

UPON REACHING LITTLE ROCK, Mary Gurley moved in with some girlfriends and took business courses. Cleo hadn't argued; Mary was
eighteen by then, and strong-willed. But her plan to make a stand in
Little Rock soured quickly. She was unable to find any sort of job there.
One of her roommates wrote to Cleo in Los Angeles and suggested that
she talk her daughter into returning to live with the family, and soon.
At a dead end, without income and having clearly worn out her welcome, Mary reluctantly went west to rejoin her family.

The Gurleys were getting by in a small rental not far from the family
of Ira's brother John and his wife, Nita, who lived on Fifty-Ninth Street.
True to her pattern of unreasonable and unfulfilled hopes, Cleo had
not received any financial support from that hard-pressed branch of
the Gurley clan. But there was the comfort of some family nearby and
occasional adult companionship. They knew no one else in that bright,
sprawling city. Since Ira's death, Cleo had shot out in all directions in
the hope of a lifeline: Tulsa, Texas, Chicago. Finally, in California, the
earthly edge of possibilities, she had better make it work.

On a Sunday afternoon in April 1937, Helen was out in the yard playing catch with her younger cousins Bob and Virginia when a deeply shaken Cleo arrived bearing terrible news. The "grippe" or cold that Mary had been suffering with turned out to be the dreaded and still-mysterious poliomyelitis. She was paralyzed from the waist down and in all likelihood would never walk again. Her arms were affected to a lesser degree.

Cleo's nameless terrors had metastasized into something horribly real. With no support base, and scant understanding of the brutal disease, Cleo was frantic to save her girl. Though Mary's suffering was by far the worst, the diagnosis was devastating to all three Gurleys, financially, emotionally, and socially. There would be many more hasty moves, but no more of Cleo's blind and inchoate flights; all future relocations, some of them cross-country, were planned according to the exigencies of Mary's care and its impact on the family finances.

While Mary struggled through the terrifying and acute onset phase of the disease in the hospital, her mother and sister moved to a rented bungalow situated on—of all places—South Hope Street. Cleo chose it for its proximity to Mary's best chance for any kind of relief, the Orthopaedic Institute for Children (OIC), which was just across the street. The hospital was founded in 1911 by Dr. Charles LeRoy Lowman, a man Helen credited as being of tremendous help and support to the traumatized family. Lowman was one of the few pediatric orthopedic specialists between New Orleans and San Francisco; by the 1930s, he knew more than nearly any practitioner on the West Coast about birth defects such as spina bifida, clubfoot, and spinal curvatures, as well as the diagnosis and effects of infantile polio. Though the paralytic disease had been seen and documented since the late eighteenth century, the first recorded incidence on American soil was in Rutland, Vermont, in 1894, an outbreak that struck 132 people. The twentieth century saw a great rise in the number of cases. Mary was infected in the escalating series of small local outbreaks that would reach a crescendo in the worst U.S. polio epidemic, in 1952.

In the baffling and desperate polio wars, Dr. Lowman was a hands-on gladiator. He threw everything at the deadly paralysis, using all the resources he could cobble together; he even turned an OIC fishpond into a children's hydrotherapy facility. He developed a new surgical technique, "fascia transplants" of muscle tissue, that allowed some polio victims to walk again. The hospital started the Orthopaedic Foundation to help parents afford their children's care. It is still active today, also specializing in children's hemophilia treatment. But in the late 1930s, given the lifelong expenses they were facing, the foundation was only of modest help to the Gurleys.

Not long after the diagnosis, desperate to cheer her sister, Helen sat down and wrote to five movie stars and to President Roosevelt, whose own struggles with a paralysis diagnosed as polio had led him to buy a run-down spa/resort in Warm Springs, Georgia, in 1926 and convert its twelve hundred acres with inns, cottages, and pools into therapeutic facilities. He ran it as a nonprofit open to all people immobilized by polio. Helen was sure this man would be empathetic. Having written her brief request and included Mary's hospital address, she signed off: "Thank you with all my heart, Mr. President."

None of the movie stars responded. The family was thunderstruck when an official-looking letter finally did arrive for Mary. The president had found a moment to dash off a handwritten letter, expressing his sympathy and his hopes for a complete recovery. The framed FDR letter moved with Mary for decades and, after her death, ended up on the Browns' apartment wall in Manhattan.

Having spent an apparently forgettable sophomore year at Belmont High in the Westlake section—Helen never mentioned it in any of her memoirs—she transferred to the public school closest to home and hospital, John H. Francis Polytechnic High School on Washington Boulevard and Flower Street. She enrolled as a junior in the fall of 1937. After school and in the evenings, she was often across the street, at her sister's bedside. During the months when Mary was in the hospital, Helen and Cleo fell into intimate rituals of utter frustration and despair. "Sometimes she [Cleo] would lie on the bed with her face to the wall, weeping, and I would lie down beside her, wedging myself up against her back, spoon fashion, and try to find out what was the matter. Sometimes she just cried from general loneliness. Whatever set her off,

I learned about depression early and well and I can always slip into it as comfortably as a kimono."

When family dolor threatened to suffocate them in the bleak house on South Hope Street, they tried the mobile therapy that had always buoyed them in Little Rock. Mother and daughter climbed into Gloria Hibiscus and drove around and around the City of Angels aimlessly. But these were hardly joyrides. Oh, sic transit Gloria! The beloved Pontiac, chariot for the brightest of aspirations when Cleo first wheeled it into their Little Rock driveway, became a grim utilitarian buggy and a mobile wailing wall. Wrote Helen: "We would drive around Los Angeles streets . . . and just cry up a storm . . . about the acne, about my sister, Mary, being in a wheelchair. About our not having a daddy, about money problems and life's general sadness."

There seemed to be little hope of improvement for either Mary's condition or Helen's aggressive acne. The remedies were completely counter to today's recommended treatments with topical medication and oral antibiotics. Twice a week, a discount doctor lanced Helen's cysts and pustules, perpetuating a moonscape of new eruptions and dark, hard scabs. Helen recalled being sent out into the world with a face that "looked as though it had been smeared with strawberry jam." Her tormented skin was also subjected to X-ray beams, an ill-advised and unregulated procedure that, she was told, made her skin thin and fragile in later life. Helen's assessment of the therapies available to both sisters was sadly correct: "At that time the medical profession didn't know any more about acne than they did about polio, and mine was virulent."

Particularly for a girl preoccupied with the notion of being "not pretty enough," the relentless disfigurement—and it was that—proved life-changing. At fifteen, with the acne's full onslaught, Helen was no longer the gregarious girl who had danced, teased her friends, and performed on any stage available back in Little Rock. At "Poly," they were already calling the Arkansas import "the Bashful Babe," though not unkindly.

Poly, the second-oldest high school in the city, then served about fifteen hundred students. Besides a standard curriculum in math,

English, history, and the sciences, the school offered technical training in everything from electrical engineering to auto repair and hairdressing. In her first months there, Helen found herself at sea for reasons besides her appearance. She realized that she had a southern accent. Also, to her dismay, there were no identifiable rich kids to glom on to, as there had been in Little Rock; the scions of wealthy Angelenos were cosseted in private schools.

"I got used to going to school with the very poor, the Japanese, the chinese [sic] and negros [sic]," Helen wrote. Poly absorbed the displaced children of several waves of immigration to the West Coast: Asians from the Pacific Rim, the children of destitute Oklahoma and Arkansas farmers who had fled the Dust Bowl shortly before the Gurleys rode west, as well as the growing Latino population from Mexico. It sure didn't look like the peach-cheeked junior class in Little Rock. Despite her introduction to this rainbow array of classmates, Helen declared herself most astounded by the presence of "the negroes." She had grown up amid almost complete segregation. African Americans descended from the slaves owned by Helen's great-great-grandfather Sneed and others in Carroll County had fled the area generations before she was born; in a 2012 survey, her birthplace of Green Forest had just a .04-percent population of African Americans—or fewer than a dozen people. When Helen was growing up in Little Rock, her schools, church, and neighborhood were entirely white.

Given Helen's upbringing, it was understandable that the mere presence of black students in her classes at Poly was cause for astonishment: "Would you believe, white students mingled with black . . . shocking! One year out of Little Rock, where a black man looking directly in the eyes of a white woman on the street could land in jail, where occasional lynchings still took place on Saturday night, I could have had a problem."

She credited her ready acceptance of this new social reality to her belief that prejudice of any kind, Ira's sexism notwithstanding, "had never been on the menu" in the Gurley home. This declaration might well have been genuine, though the language and the stereotyping were regrettable when she described her adjustment to Poly: "The dusky ones and I, after they got used to how funny I sounded, got along fine. Black boys were fabulous dancers, and the Amazonian black girls, towering over me on the basketball court, forgave my getting a ball—finally—into the hoop, but the hoop belonged to the other team." One of Helen's early Poly friends was a Japanese American named Setsuko Matsunaga, known as Suki. Back in Arkansas, some of Helen's friends were flabbergasted by the company she now kept.

The Bashful Babe was not enjoying her new invisibility. It wouldn't do, but the prospects for improvement seemed dim. Night after night, she pondered a version of the same question: "So, what does a sixteen-year-old with an invalid sister, depressed Mommy, terminal acne, and the financial pinchies do to cheer herself up?"

There was no booze or drugs, not in those days—nor was she ever interested in chemical escapes. Helen worked up her own Dale Carnegie–esque plan: just suck it up and get *on* with things. She could not accept a life on the sidelines, especially when home life was so dreary and sad. "I willed myself to become more outgoing, even extroverted, divert attention from the skin that was either forming pustules or scabbing up from excision." It was hard, very hard. Helen confessed that during those two high school years she was the most extroverted she would ever be, before or afterward. She undertook the charade, she explained, "Because I had to not go down the drain."

As she would for the rest of her life, Helen Gurley put it *out* there. Her plan was multifold—excellent grades, volunteerism, good rapport with teachers (she would be voted number-two apple polisher in her class). Recalling her best Poly teachers for an educational publication in Harrison, Arkansas, Helen admitted that her favorite academic heroine was a known and unapologetic bad girl. Her beloved Mademoiselle Davis was a French teacher and . . . *ooh là là!*

"Charlotte was sophisticated, fine-boned, brunette, alluring and a GOOD French teacher. She was also having an affair with the man who printed the school newspaper—married, I think—and he adored her.

She was so unlike a staid, prissy, proper USUAL public-schoolteacher in those days . . . She was always *interesting*."

Her second favorite was Ethel McGhee, an "ancient" forty-seven-year-old who took a special interest in Helen and had the kindness and patience to coach her for a public-speaking contest. There was no lectern Helen Gurley didn't aspire to, and she invented other ways to put herself forward, writing quick skits that she could perform at variety shows that drew most of Poly's student body. She admitted that many of her stage offerings were downright inane, even a tad desperate. But that didn't stop her. The school newspaper, *The Poly Optimist*, reported: "A clever monolog was given by Helen Gurley, who enacted campaign speeches of various types of students running for office."

She joined a clutch of Poly's fifty clubs and ran for school office—any office—if it seemed attainable. She reported as a busy "campus crier" for the yearbook staff and was elected president of the California Scholarship Federation, for which she moderated programs and organized events. Yearbooks and issues of *The Poly Optimist* were full of the unsinkable Miss Gurley, who also chaired a committee to choose "suitable" movies to be shown with the school's new projector. Along with a Disney short (*Silly Symphony*), they settled on the reliable rectitude of a Gary Cooper vehicle, *The Plainsman*. Over time, she was winning friends and admirers. "Orchids to Helen Gurley for her true Poly spirit," cheered the school paper. She had even earned nicknames: "Good Time Gurley." "Guppie." And, because she kept company with a certain Robert C. Brown, "Mrs. Brown."

By the time she celebrated her Sweet Sixteen birthday on February 18, 1938, Helen sounded pleased and upbeat in her letters back to Little Rock. On that day, she wrote to "Tabby," Betty Tabb, asking how she had felt to turn Sweet Sixteen. Helen confessed that she didn't feel any different, though she had the real sense she was growing up. She didn't want to, not just yet. She did relish the dating part of it. Helen held to the Little Rock term "beaux" for the boys who asked her out. "I wasn't a belle," she said, "but I wasn't a blip." Bob Brown was a nice, regular guy—a fellow member of her church choir—who would remain her ardent admirer, sending her a blizzard of letters and gifts during his war service in the South Pacific. Others were merely fun and companionable. Helen's penchant for creating a sort of male stable—guys for all occasions—began at Poly and would coalesce into a network of epic proportions by her mid-twenties, as a working girl. She explained: "My theory from high school on is that until you can collect a prince, you create a court from who's there, no matter how disparate the courtiers."

Helen maintained that there was nothing hot and heavy going on in high school. "I was sweet and nice and cute, I guess; I always had boyfriends. And at age sixteen I was on a date, somebody kissed me for the first time, a real kiss, not a kiss under the mistletoe, but a *real* kiss, and I almost certainly had an orgasm—that's all it took. So I must be highly sexed. It's always been easy for me to have that happen." There was some touching, yes. "In terms of petting, but that is with fingers. No genital kissing, that was *hundreds* of years later. But stimulation with fingers and kissing, yes. I didn't have a bosom, so that didn't really enter into the situation."

She did not give off signals that she was a "fast" girl. In fact, Bob Brown and his friends thought her so respectable and chaste that they did not invite her to their unchaperoned and untrammeled parties. She was still a proper southern girl, she explained. "A Little Rock–brought-up girl didn't go all the way *ever*."

Two of her favorite high school gallants were especially fun, good-looking, and never grabby. "I would now say they were homosexual," Helen said, "but, at the time the 'condition' didn't exist and surely wasn't talked about." Close friendships with gay men were a constant in Helen's life from the mid-1940s on. Joey and Lester, the two high school beaux in question, were probably just as pleased as Helen with the practicality and comfort of their nonromances. They simply had a ball. They went joyriding around L.A. and got a bit frisky from time to time: snatching a branch of blooms from the manicured parterre of a Bel-Air mansion was about as wicked as things got. They "baked" themselves at the beach, they picnicked.

How they danced. Everything seemed more dynamic and intense

in Los Angeles, even Helen's favorite pastime. She reported to Betty Tabb that the new dances were more intricate and wild than anything she'd seen back east, enough to leave her breathless and dizzy. But the steps were awfully cute. The "steps" probably included the Lindy Hop and swing dancing. The jitterbug would zap Los Angeles dance halls by 1939, four years after the bandleader Cab Calloway had a hit with "Call of the Jitterbug." As ever, black Americans mastered the hottest dances before their trickle down to the Brylcreemed and white-buck-shod ballroom set. Helen watched the joint-popping athleticism at Poly dances, enthralled.

In so many ways, for a car-crazy girl from a landlocked southern state, Southern California was a dream. Their home, with its wheelchair parked out front and the necessary clutter of braces and compresses, may have been more dreary than the Gurleys' house back east, but there were more varied and accessible means of escape. Cleo had discovered the racing scene at the gorgeous and nationally renowned Santa Anita Park, a sumptuous track built four years earlier at the foot of the San Gabriel Mountains. The best horses ran there; during the time the Gurleys were race regulars, runty, heroic Seabiscuit won the Santa Anita Handicap in the final start of his career. To the sisters' delight, the Hollywood thoroughbreds also turned out. The movie mogul Hal Roach was one of the track's owners, Bing Crosby and Al Jolson were stockholders, and fealty was expected from the studio A-lists. Come they did: Clark Gable, Lana Turner, Jane Russell, Betty Grable. A day at the races was heady catnip to inflame the girls' movie madness.

As the calendar turned to 1939, Helen sat down to write out her New Year's resolutions. The ten-point list included some December 31 standards: don't drink very much, listen to Mother and Mary, get exercise and a tan, buy good clothes. She vowed to concentrate on one person while talking to him or her, never to talk maliciously or gossip, and to keep more personal things to herself. The teenager who would become global champion of the average-girl "mouseburger" placed this near the top of the list: "Look out for the underdog."

"RELAX" floats commandingly at the center of the page, scrawled in large letters. And then, number ten, a final vow that might draw gales of laughter from those who knew her in later life: "Not be cheap."

The year 1939 was eventful for Helen. She would be voted third most popular girl in her class and elected valedictorian, and would begin some hard planning toward her goal of the college education her mother had been denied. Helen was more than ready to field those "What next?" questions from the yearbook committee. She had already run a five-day information program with visiting college representatives, an early version of the college fair.

Miss Gurley was going places. The faculty recognized her leadership by electing her to the elite Ephebian Society, "the highest honor to be won by students of the Los Angeles city schools." Helen was among nine Poly students to make the cut that year, along with her good friends Setsuko Matsunaga, Florence Stanley—and the dreamy Hal Holker, president of the student body, varsity letterman in track, aspiring to become an architect—a package that, in Helen's opinion, added up to a "Wow."

A profile of Helen in the *Optimist* celebrating her election to the Ephebians reported: "Guppie likes having her back scratched and frosted cokes, and dislikes being called 'Good Time' . . . Her ambition is to become a successful businesswoman."

In her breathless campaign to excel, Guppie sometimes spread her talents a bit thin. Heeding the sweet and transcript-plumping blandishments of Calliope, muse of poetry, she published verse in school pamphlets that suggested her artistic limits. From "Thoughts at Eventide":

> Sometimes at eventide I find
> That thoughts of nature throng my mind

Senior Prom was on St. Patrick's Day of 1939; the theme was all shamrocks and leprechauns. Helen hustled with her chores on the refreshment committee, all but ignoring the elephant in the crepe-papered, green-and-white gym: by that afternoon, Good Time Gurley still did not have a date. Up stepped the "Wow" himself, Hal Holker, lathered from his last-minute preparations on the orchestra committee and prom chairmanship. It was Kismet for the two overcommitted seniors; he asked Helen to be his date, and she accepted without hesitation. Helen emphasized that he did explain his eleventh-hour invitation: "It wasn't because he considered me a wallflower and probably not booked but, on the chance I wasn't, thought I'd be perfect."

How so? Holker was sure that this capable girl would require little maintenance during the dance: "Gurley could take care of herself . . . good dancer . . . lots of friends . . . wouldn't have to worry about her while doing stuff you have to do as a prom chairman."

Thus that first date was almost a business arrangement, but their relationship did blossom into romance, according to the Wow himself. Still living in California at ninety-three, Hal Holker had a strong recollection of that Gurley girl when reached through his daughter, Janet Kessler. Though a serious hearing loss left him unable to do an interview on the phone, he was pleased to answer questions relayed through Kessler. He certainly had kept track of the famous Mrs. Gurley Brown over the years, had even read some of her infamous writings. Of her presence on campus he said, "She was fun to be with and always had a wisecrack." Gurley was never loud, though, never pushy. "She was behind the scenes, but her voice was known throughout the school because of the newspaper." Yes, he was smitten after their prom date; yes, they kissed on that first date, and he did indeed take her out again the following week.

Shortly after Helen's Senior Prom, on March 23, 1939, another long-in-the-bud romance was finally consummated. Cleo Sisco Gurley and William Leigh Bryan stood before a Methodist minister, in the presence of a witness named Ardath Davies. After five years of what Helen and Mary supposed to be a final silence between the two after their clandestine meetings in Cleveland, Cleo and her long-lost love were married somewhere in Los Angeles, possibly at the county clerk's office. It is unclear whether her daughters stood with them, nor did Helen provide any indication of when Bryan came west from Cleveland, or when and how Cleo told her girls. Helen wrote little of the household's newest member and minced no words describing her lack of esteem for her stepfather. She declared him a decent sort but "embarrassing and ineffectual." Bryan cooked, which was a mercy, considering his new wife's barely edible efforts. But Helen could find little else positive to say.

Whatever Helen's assessment, Bryan was man enough to walk into a house with three very stressed and needy women, relentless medical bills, and one very sadburger bankbook. He rode in on a white steed of sorts—one that creaked and dripped once it was tethered outside the house. Helen was deeply ashamed of the new vehicle that had assumed a place beside Mary's wheelchair out front: a Good Humor pushcart. The love of Cleo's life, the bookish, sensitive boy with an ear for poetry, was pushing a cart through her adopted city, hawking ice cream bars.

Bryan's was a strict and exacting servitude. Jobs were still scarce, but Good Humor ice cream treats, a diversion as inexpensive and pleasurable as tubes of lipstick, also enjoyed a boom during the Depression. The expanding company drove its workforce with very long workweeks, strict dress code in GH whites, and only commission pay for street vendors; most of their wares sold for a nickel a bar. Bryan's contributions to the household economy were modest at best; another of Cleo's expectations for better times melted away.

As graduation approached, Helen continued the romance with Hal Holker, which made her happy and proud. Overall, her dogged race seemed won: in two years, the Bashful Babe had won the Big Man on Campus, been voted class valedictorian, gathered a circle of good girlfriends, and had every intention of going to college. The acne had even begun to subside a bit. On Thursday evening, June 22, 1939, friends and family crowded into the auditorium for Poly's commencement. Its theme was "The Genius of America." Suki Matsunaga offered a piano étude; Helen, having popped up and down for various honors during the proceedings, delivered her valedictory speech, titled "This Is My Own, My Native Land."

That summer, she and Hal Holker continued to date. He brought her home to meet his parents. Her assessment: "Some of the best smooching of my life was in those sweet summer months." Mr. Holker said, somewhat cryptically, "I thought we were girlfriend and boyfriend, but she thought we were a couple."

He was headed to Alaska to work as a commercial fisherman in hopes of earning college tuition; he had been accepted to Princeton, but in the end couldn't even afford the cross-country transportation costs. He began studying architecture at nearby USC, entered into a long and happy marriage, and eventually, with multiple degrees in urban planning and land management, built a distinguished national career in city housing, urban renewal, and planning.

Helen had settled on her next move, mainly decided by fiscal considerations. She would start at Woodbury Business College in Los Angeles in the fall, in the hopes that she would still make it to a four-year college somehow. Given the uncertainty of the family finances, the next two years saw a disjointed sort of education, traceable through matriculation records and rather vague references by Helen to the endless bus rides that took her between institutions and summer visits to Osage.

In midsummer of 1939, Cleo took the girls east, leaving her husband to ply his trade in the scorching L.A. summer. Mary and Cleo were heading for President Roosevelt's therapeutic center in Warm Springs, Georgia. Helen visited friends and relatives back home in Arkansas, then headed home and enrolled at Woodbury Business College on September 9, 1939. In January, she withdrew from secretarial school to attend the spring semester at Texas State College for Women in Denton, just north of Dallas. She enjoyed her tenure there, but, like her mother, she was forced to withdraw after a single semester for lack of funds. After yet another summer visit to Osage, Helen had decided to re-enroll at Woodbury; she could live at home and work at a school-arranged job to help with tuition.

Helen boarded a Trailways bus in Harrison, Arkansas, for the long haul back to Los Angeles, rolling west toward her shaky future quite alone. She would be living with other girls until she and her mother, sister, and stepfather settled into their next ramshackle home. The plan was simple yet daunting: she would attend secretarial school and work, both to help with tuition, as planned, and to begin contributing to the support of the struggling household. Cleo had forced herself to take a miserable and anxiety-provoking job pinning small tags onto garments in the basement of Sears Roebuck for fifty cents an hour. She was so frightened of the workplace and strangers that just getting her prepared for work and out the door and onto the Western Avenue bus each day was a family effort. But since her new husband was a disappointment as a wage earner and Mary's medical bills kept mounting, she had to keep the job.

Helen never invited friends or beaux to visit the crowded, unhappy little house. She never imagined that the family's next move would isolate them further—worse, that the next cheap rental would come with some highly undesirable co-tenants.

Sinking In

Nobody likes a poor girl. She is just a drag.
—HGB, *Sex and the Single Girl*

MOST AMERICAN RAGS-TO-RICHES NARRATIVES have a well-known poverty signifier, invoked again and again in histories and interviews: Abe Lincoln's log cabin, Sam Walton's family milk cow, Oprah Winfrey's potato-sack dresses. For Helen Gurley Brown, it was a plague of gophers.

She cited the rodents often when spooling her Single Girl origin myth—and they were only one aspect of her housing issues. From the end of 1939 through the mid-forties, her family landed in their worst rental yet, a small, rickety house on West Fifty-Ninth Street, south of Slauson Avenue. It was at the heart of the unfashionable east side of Los Angeles, in a stark and charmless neighborhood hemmed by the Santa Fe and commuter-line railroad tracks. Settling into this outliers' limbo, the family was startled by a thunderous and frequent roar. "The Super Chief or something went by twice a night," Helen wrote. "Talk about suspended conversations!"

The Super Chief was the glamour liner of the Santa Fe railroad, running between Chicago and Los Angeles. In later iterations, its engine was painted with a flashy feathered war bonnet. The train was often studded with celebrities commuting from Hollywood to the midwestern hub and points east. Schedules and Santa Fe route maps through Los Angeles from that time suggest that Helen's notion of being tormented by the elegant Chief might have been a bit fanciful; most likely, it was quotidian freight and commuter trains that rattled the windows. As they whooshed on down the line and quiet was restored, the scourge from below became audible. The tunneling gophers were most active beneath the bedroom shared by Helen and Mary.

Helen remembered their sorties as relentless: "You could hear the little bastards scratching away. Scratch, scratch, scratch. We never knew what night they might make it on through." When the varmints started pushing up the floorboards, something had to be done. "We once put a hose down a gopher hole, let it run several hours—talk about big spenders on *our* budget—actually flushed up a gopher! Poor drowned little thing, we didn't try to revive him. Maybe there's a secret cruel streak in all of us but this gopher was eating our carnations and trying to sleep in our bedroom."

Of course, it wasn't just one gopher; some of the five species populating Southern California can breed up to three times a year. And if you were raised beneath the dark, rolling cloud of Cleo Sisco Bryan's well-earned misgivings, the persistent clawing from below could also be heard as the harbinger of more imminent disaster: the very ground beneath their feet might dissolve, disgorging pestilence and more misfortune. There was no question of moving; they couldn't afford a better place, even though all oars were in the water and pulling hard.

Leigh Bryan was working the night shift, selling ice cream. Cleo, "shy to the point of verbal paralysis," still went shuddering to her job at Sears; sometime later on, her sewing experience got her a slightly better job in the pattern department of the May Company department store. Mary was working at home for C. E. Hooper, a radio ratings system. She telephoned listeners to find out which programs they were tuning in to. Overhearing her sister's daily supplications, Helen judged this numbing and demeaning work: "For forty cents an hour she sludged her way through hundreds of numbers copied from the telephone book, put up with hang-ups, no-comprendes, and couldn't-remembers, conscientiously recording data."

Perhaps the crucible of Mary's illness had softened some of the anger and rebelliousness that had so worried Cleo in her older daughter. The three women may have wept together over their collective woes, but Mary was not given to dwelling on the life sentence of her own misfortune. It had helped a good deal that their next-door neighbor at the house on South Hope Street was also a wheelchair-bound polio victim. She and her construction-worker husband had, Helen noted, "somehow got beyond the sads and depression that go with invalidism." The couple had been a huge help to an overwhelmed Cleo, taking Mary on outings and reminding her of all the things she could still do. Even when the Gurleys moved away from these supportive friends, Mary's quiet acceptance and cheerfulness amazed Helen, who correctly suspected that her sister's lifelong darkness had understandably deepened. "While my sister didn't ever cry or complain *ever*, God knows what demons occupied her."

Sometimes Helen pitched in to help Mary with the calls, but her own schedule was tight, between morning shorthand and typing classes at Woodbury and her afternoon job at the radio station KHJ in Hollywood, arranged for her by the school. To help toward her tuition, she was to work as general dogsbody for an announcer named Mr. Wilson, whose early-morning show, *Rise and Shine*, announced listeners' birthdays and anniversaries from information they sent in. Eighteen-year-old Helen made six dollars a week. There were some unfortunate moments when the pay seemed commensurate with her performance. By the time she got to work after classes, her employer had long since gone home, but if she had made some blunders in preparing his script, the atmosphere was sulfurous when Helen skipped in from the streetcar that brought her from school.

"Some afternoons when I got to KHJ, somebody there in the morning would report Mr. Wilson having gone mangoes, shrieking to be heard all the way to Cahuenga Avenue that his idiot secretary had screwed up again." It seemed that, thanks to Helen's errors in typing up listeners' requests onto index cards, sad little Deborah Jean over in

Gardena had not found her birthday gift under her sister's bed; Mr. Wilson had mistakenly hinted that it would be near her daddy's toolbox. Twin brother and sister were being congratulated on their fourth wedding anniversary.

Helen bore down and managed a bit more focus. A few months later, she was hauling in seven dollars a week, having increased her skill set with some advertising duties. She was tasked with placing two Alka-Seltzer tablets into an envelope to be dropped in a glass of water for live advertising spots re-creating the brand's soothing effervescence. This simple effect was derailed by the eager interventions of little Helen, who only wanted to help. She "tested" some tablets in a glass of water, wiped off the loudest and fizziest, and put them into the envelope; by airtime, the soggy discs were duds: Plop, plop. No fizz. It certainly was worse when a sponsor went mangoes.

Despite the poor pay, Helen felt the job did have its perks: "The place was loaded with men. I've never *seen* so many men in one company with so few corresponding females to louse things up." Radio men could be very naughty boys—especially the announcers. The layout of the station facilities provided for a separation of powers; the executives were in a main building, and the announcers, secretaries, music clerks, and engineers were all out back, in a separate stucco bunker that also held the studio. A certain frat-house mind-set back there led to an office game called Scuttle.

It was the sort of behavior that could induce a coronary in any present-day HR manager. The game had a Cro-Magnon simplicity. Helen described it thus: "All announcers and engineers who weren't busy . . . would select a secretary or file girl, chase her up and down the halls, through the music library and back to the announcing booths, catch her and take her panties off." Imagine such a hunt: laughing, shouting men, a frieze of exposed flanks and pubic hair, of screaming, red-faced women. Helen described the proceedings with jaw-dropping nonchalance. After all, girls could get their panties back right away—if they wanted them.

Her only distress regarding this predatory and abusive office sport? Helen was never chosen as Scuttle prey. She might have taken the exclusion quite personally, as was her wont, but she realized that it was not because the men found her too ordinary-looking to "pants"; they simply wanted to stay out of jail. Helen's acne had gone into near-complete abeyance, she had acquired some slightly detectable contours, and had begun a stringent lifelong habit of charting her bust, waist, and hip measurements. While attending Woodbury, she was five foot three, 103 pounds, and stacked like a garden rake at 28" x 18" x 28". Helen had noticed a group of the men eyeing her from the corner in deep conference. She heard them murmuring, "I don't know . . . seventeen, eighteen?"

Just before the job ended, upon Helen's graduation from Woodbury in early December 1941 with a bachelor's degree in secretarial science, she had edged up to a salary of twenty dollars a week. She could manage 130 words a minute as a stenographer, but her typing skills did not compare favorably. Helen would leave her mark at the station in a few memorable keystrokes when she sent her first teletype to all of KHJ's affiliates. The programming message was simple: "2:30 to 3:00 all stations fill." This meant the affiliate stations could choose their own programming for that half hour. Helen typed the first part correctly, then slid her fingers off the keys partway through the last word. When she put them back—a bit west of where they should have been—she typed the last word, "fill," and the teletype went out this way: ALL STATIONS FUKK.

There were a few choice return teletypes:

From Bakersfield: KEEN IDEA. NEED HELP WITH YOUNGER GIRLS.

From San Francisco: AFRA ACTRESSES DEMANDING MORE THAN SCALE.

For a working girl's first office experience, KHJ was special indeed. Pitiful pay, unbridled sexual harassment, and *ever* so much fun.

Helen continued to expand her constellation of beaux. But in the wider dating pool beyond Poly's fairly civil corridors, she found herself subject to some bruising, humiliating slights. She would revisit and rehash the worst of them for the rest of her life. Even when her progression of therapists urged her, over a few decades, to let it all go, Helen held fast to the hurts. In that respect, she was surely Cleo's daughter; the snubs and unkindness that other girls might have gotten past, Helen kept reliving, in the way that a tongue seeks a sore tooth. Should an episode be excruciatingly public, it was guaranteed a long and toxic half-life in her heart and in her memoirs. One such incident unfolded right on the Sunset Strip.

Woodbury Business College allowed sororities with all the trappings—rush, initiation, formal dances. In an eleventh-hour scenario much like her prom experience, Helen found herself still dateless for a party to follow a sisters-only Eta Upsilon Gamma dinner she had just attended. She stood outside a restaurant called Bittersweets on Sunset Boulevard, in the company of sorority sisters she likened to "the Rita Hayworths and Betty Grables of their time." They were knockouts, all. Every one of them had a swoon-worthy escort for the dance. Helen was about to call her mother to come pick her up when hope flickered. The sisters marched a pair of their superfluous males toward Helen for a look-see. They paraded past, gave her the once-over, and just walked away. So much for sisterhood. Left alone on the steps as the elite scrum moved off to the party, Helen awaited the mercifully dark and private sanctuary of Cleo's Pontiac. When she finally pulled up, Helen could be assured of sympathy—with a curdling soupçon of "Didn't I *tell* you?"

Beyond her damning-with-faint-praise mantra ("You are beautiful *enough*"), Cleo had a habit of nitpicking at exactly the wrong moment. Helen often left for a date beneath a buzzing cloud of insecurities. Before any social outing, Cleo worried aloud about her daughter's presentation, the suitability of her outfit, the *competition*. Could she maybe fix her hair a bit higher and neater? Wouldn't that yellow chiffon be more flattering? You *know* how people are . . .

It took Helen years to shake off the negativity. "In my own life later," she wrote, "looking at pictures of myself during those warning-from-mom years, I gleaned that I actually looked perfectly okay and didn't need to be so looks-worried but her assessment sunk in and never really left town." The proof is indeed in the photos. Candid backyard shots of Helen at twenty, shared by Hal Holker's family, show a well-turned-out girl in a flowered dress with a fuzzy angora chub tossed over her shoulders. Her hair is glossy and carefully done. Lounging in a lawn chair or leaning against a car, she looks directly at the camera; her smile is natural. She looks like fun. Holker's sister wrote to him: "Helen Gurley stopped by the other night. She is really one of the most attractive girls I've ever met. And very sweet."

So what *was* the problem?

In a word, Cleo. Helen's mother always insisted that she was just trying to soften the inevitable disappointments. Cleo's basic self-improvement message was a dour version of the one Helen would banner with big-sisterly cheer in her own bestsellers and in her magazine: *Honey, do the best with what you have.*

After the Sunset Boulevard humiliation, Helen's resolve to avoid such wounds became something of an obsession. Once again, she realized that it was all up to her. Just as she had worked to overcome her Bashful Babe mien in high school, Helen charted a plan for securing a certain womanly dignity, along with sufficient dates. Her new strategy was the opposite of trying to stand out, as she had in school. Referring to the sorority incident, she reasoned, "There were hideous turn downs like that, which convinced me that I had to be there and make an impression and *sink in* to somebody. I couldn't just do it by walking around the room."

She understood the fierce tyrannies of conventional beauty. For Helen, there would be no fateful glances across a crowded ballroom, no smoldering *coups de foudre*. This wasn't the movies. But she did live in Movieland, with an endless conga line of sable-lashed studio wannabes checking hats, slinging hash, and clinging to the frayed cuffs of low-level "talent scouts." Those girls would always be first off the shelf, and, from what she had seen, they were fairly disposable. Helen Gurley did not want to disappear.

Sinking in would become her signature skill, a flexible double whammy of psychological and sexual seduction. It would be built upon the timeless art of how to induce a certain . . . frenzy. On how to tantalize and become habit-forming. Eventually, sinking in to a man and a market would secure Helen's marriage and her fortune. Sinking in—generally through an orchestrated and dogged campaign of self-improvement—would become the mouseburger game plan that launched a global empire of *Cosmo*. But at twenty, Helen simply hoped it would afford a skinny poor girl some degree of insulation. It hurt her so, the quick and careless judging.

She did not approach the project with any sense of drudgery or dread. Sex was dandy. Helen had thoroughly enjoyed testing the powers of temptation while holding on to her virtue in high school, "jumping out of cars" when the action got too heated. She wasn't sure why, but she was aroused, easily and deeply, by the struggle itself. "I wouldn't take anything for the sexy hours when you struggled your brains out with boy or man, passionate, steamy struggling . . . foreplay that didn't actually lead to play . . . Since I could be brought to orgasm by kissing, why ask for anything more, and whoever he was put up with it. What the poor creature did when he got home was his affair."

Vive la lutte! And too bad about anyone's forlorn and unrequited arousal. She would get to matters of sexual reciprocity and mutual gratification soon enough. Helen's frank embrace of her own pleasure was bold and unusual in an era of largely dutiful and reactive female sexual response. She realized early on that hers was a healthy libido that would not be denied.

As she was about to finish up at Woodbury, she decided that she was at last ready to cross the great divide. She chose a very sweet young man who was crazy about her, to the point of declaring a private holiday, "Helen's Day," with a cascade of presents: Chanel N°5 cologne, an ankle bracelet engraved "R to H," a baby-blue cashmere sweater. He was employed at a shipbuilding plant and soon would be off to war as a second lieutenant in the air force. His devotion, according to Helen, was most gallant: "[He] had been my beau for two years, putting up graciously with Never Getting There (I didn't know what a penis looked like, had never seen one, was easily brought to orgasm by somebody not doing a great deal—let's don't elaborate.)"

It finally happened when they had come back from a swim and were taking showers in his apartment, after a Sunday at the beach. She described "the deflowering" this way: "The first time I had intercourse I was a virgin, everything was sealed over, I think I bled a little bit, I'm not sure about that, but I did have an orgasm, and this darling man went to the biggest jewelry store in Los Angeles and bought me earrings, so he was *darling*."

Helen loved being so adored, but she was not in love with her darling, a nice Jewish boy named Bob Platt. "He was off his rocker about me," Helen said, but he never did get to proposing. She assumed that it was because he wouldn't marry outside his faith. This was fine with her; she preferred to inhabit the immediate, comfortable, and libidinous moment. She said of their time together, "As far as I remember, I always had an orgasm . . . It was just, pleasant. It was nice to have a beau who adored me, though I wasn't terribly proud of him." She did not want to get married; mother and daughter had some of the worst arguments of their lives over Helen's intransigence on the matter. Cleo was horrified that her daughter was flatly uninterested in getting this young man to the altar.

When Helen and Bob Platt made love, they were never reckless. The terrible fear of pregnancy, Cleo's ultimate doomsday scenario, had also sunk in. Asked to describe her birth control methods at the outset of her adult sex life, and for a decade and a half afterward, Helen fairly shouted at her interviewer: "Condoms! *Condoms!*"

Bob was considerate in that sense and many others. "We were good playmates," Helen said. Once he was inducted into the air force, she did go to see him during basic training, and saw him once on leave; during his service, he flew what Helen believed to be a hundred missions. But they "drifted" after the war, which was fine with Helen.

Family exigencies, rather than romance, ruled Helen's criteria for marriage-worthy men. She rejected suitors with the chill, clinical appraisal that some boys had applied to her looks. The difference: Helen's gold standard was earning potential. She couldn't marry the boy who boxed groceries, or an assistant soundman at the radio station. Marrying simply for love was not an option. There were too many mouths to feed and doctors to pay. For Helen, it had to be a package deal, not unlike the agreement Ira Gurley had made: Marry me, help support my family. There was one major flaw in the plan: "I had hoped to marry somebody wealthy and solve all of my family's and my problems. Alas, I didn't have the credentials—looks, family background, emotional stability. (I *did* have the youth . . . we all get *that*.)"

She made light of this harsh reality in a snippet of poetry:

> Oh well he's got that je ne sais quoi
> While I, my dear, am from Arkansas

A few years into Cleo's second marriage, an unspeakable development rendered any notion of her happiness firmly, permanently out of the question. Leigh Bryan was diagnosed with incurable stomach cancer. He would spend the next few years in a slow and agonizing slide toward death. Watching Mary suffer had nearly undone Cleo, but it had seemed they were through the worst of it. Bryan's diagnosis was a knockout blow. The doctors had made it clear: there was no hope of saving Bryan, or even keeping him comfortable past a certain point. In terms of available treatment, cancer was not much ahead of polio. Helen wrote: "Those visits to him in the Los Angeles County Hospital with Cleo were as pain-filled as anything you would ever want to know. She loved him, and she deserved a little happiness."

Crueler still was the fact that Leigh and Cleo's tragedy was playing out beneath the shadow of another world war, with its attendant anxieties and scarcities. For a naturally fearful person undergoing one of the worst crises of her life, the stress level was breathtaking. Even trips to the hospital for treatment or to visit during Bryan's stays would have to be carefully planned with the advent of gas rationing.

All citizens of Los Angeles had a right to the jitters. Following the attack on Pearl Harbor on December 7, 1941, the Japanese threat to the American West Coast seemed all too plausible. "Tojo" had submarines, planes, and terrifying audacity, as the Hawaii attack illustrated. City officials scrambled toward preparedness. Los Angeles's first trial blackout was held while the Pearl Harbor wreckage was still smoldering. Santa Monica Bay was soon ringed with antiaircraft guns mounted from Malibu to the Palos Verde Peninsula.

The Los Angeles County Hospital, a sprawling institution originally built for the care of the city's destitute, was gearing up for increasing war casualties as Cleo ferried her husband there for treatment. Given her overwhelming concern with his worsening illness, Cleo might barely have noticed the sudden disappearance of her favorite escape—the ponies. That same year, 1942, war had driven the Thoroughbreds away from Santa Anita. The track's newly installed magnetic starting gate was dismantled, and work crews hammered in different sorts of fencing as the racetrack was converted into an assembly center for Americans of Japanese descent headed to internment camps. More than nineteen thousand men, women, and children were housed in hastily constructed barracks in parking lots and in the stables, which still reeked of manure. They were allowed to bring only what they could carry. Each arriving inmate received a cot, a blanket, and a straw tick to sleep on. It's likely that the families of some of Helen's Polytechnic classmates were among the detainees.

For a woman who wrote everything down, Helen made surprisingly little mention of the war in any of her writings. Her reminiscences give far more attention to the Depression, which, in her telling of it, clearly had the greater impact on her life, since it coincided with her father's death. There are glancing mentions of World War II privations—gas rationing, foods craved. Elizabeth Jessup did write to her of their Little Rock friends killed in fighting and basic training. Helen was mainly focused on her next job, the second of what would become a string of nineteen secretarial posts. Having forsworn trying to get close to L.A.'s reclusive rich while she was in high school, Helen had a new plan to cozy up to glamour and privilege as a career girl. She'd work in showbiz!

They were paying secretaries twenty-five dollars a week at the Music Corporation of America (MCA), by then a formidable Hollywood talent agency. Helen assumed that she would be working directly with show business people, the ones who seemed to have all of the golden things she was "ragingly longing" for: "Love, beauty, glamour, adulation." She would be happy with mere proximity to the glow and the dough.

A male acquaintance had helped her get a job in the band department of MCA; it was a solid part of the business in those radio days of big bands. He told her, "You're gonna flip out over the décor!" He spoke of a chandelier from the palace at Versailles, magnificent antique furniture—much of it, he suspected, bought on the cheap in war-torn Europe. The place had carpets thick enough to hide a kitten. There were newly working girls like Helen, platoons of girls, serving as stenographers and in the typing pool. Her friend warned her: The joint ran on girl power, sure, but you never saw them. Mr. Stein preferred them out of sight.

MCA's founder, Jules Stein, was a former eye surgeon who had played violin and saxophone in bands to help finance medical school. He was so successful in arranging dates for bands, including that of the popular Guy Lombardo, that he founded a booking-and-talent agency in 1924. By the time Stein moved his offices to Hollywood in the mid-1930s, he had an impressive roster of clients, and a set of swinish rules and prohibitions for the women who kept the place running. When Helen arrived at MCA's bright white two-story Georgian headquarters in Beverly Hills, it was estimated that Stein's shop represented half of the movie industry's biggest stars, including Bette Davis, Greta Garbo, Eddie Cantor, Frank Sinatra, Ingrid Bergman, and Jack Benny.

"I was scared shitless," Helen admitted. She knew less about the booking business than she had known about radio. Getting her first glimpse of her new workplace, she declared it exquisite. All was as promised, the lavish reception hall and the fifty-thousand-dollar French chandelier. The new employee was led directly to the secretarial pool, where the women were squeezed into a small, airless, glassed-in room that Helen likened to a fish tank. "It had everything but a rock castle and snails," she sniped. When supervisors did come by, they never greeted any of the women by name, and barely looked at them. If the men wanted anything, "they just rapped on the glass of our pool," Helen wrote, "like when it's time to feed the guppies."

Once in a while, Helen was allowed into the office of her boss, Mr. Barnett, to take dictation. But for the most part, the men preferred the more antiseptic transaction of speaking into a Dictaphone; the blue wax cylinders that recorded their utterings were delivered to the typing pool and the finished letters picked up.

To her deep disappointment, Helen never even saw the stars. Word of their arrival would crackle through the building: Ronnie Reagan in tennis whites! Errol Flynn! Esther Williams! Alas, office girls could traverse the building only on a back staircase that was nowhere near the reception areas. No secretaries were allowed on the top, executive floor. Ever. This institutional shunning of the secretarial staff inspired a few risky revolutionary acts. Helen was among the foolhardy few who crept into Stein's posh screening room to eat their lunches and nap on his buttery leather couches. "It was really chauvinist pig time around there," Helen said. Of her own boss, Mr. Barnett, she said, "He didn't treat me like a human being." Soon Helen joined the discreet parade of disgusted women clattering down the purdah staircase and out of the building. Job number two, *finito*.

At least there was big and happy news from Little Rock. Elizabeth Jessup had married her high school sweetheart, and Helen began addressing her letters "Mrs. Roy Bilheimer." A long letter to the happy couple in January 1943 begins with an effusive psalm of thanks. Helen had just opened the Bilheimers' holiday package. From its size and heft, she expected some bath powder and cologne, but inside was something far more precious: four cans of tuna fish, all but impossible to find because of rationing.

The one food sure to tempt Helen Gurley Brown from childhood throughout her skim-milk-and-diet-Jell-O adult years: tuna fish. She was so mad for the stuff it turned her into a guilt-ridden hoarder. She opened the first precious can while Mary was still asleep, having waited until Cleo left for work. "I had tuna fish cereal, tuna fish eggs, and tuna fish toast," she told the Bilheimers, confessing that she hid the remains of the can for another binge.

Helen regaled the newlyweds with tales of her odd but pleasant Christmas Day in Los Angeles. She had gone to an open house at the home of a Hollywood writer. The house was perched on a mountainside; inside, a fire roared. The company was lofty and a little loony. One of the guests claimed that he was the only man on earth able to speak seagull and that he had "translated all the works of Henry Wadsworth Longfellow into sea-gull. Nothing the matter with him!"

Helen was on her way in that tectonically unstable, mobile city that seemed to thrive on flux. Two secretarial jobs down, she mercifully had no idea how many more bad ones were in store for her. At least, in most of her subsequent positions, she would indulge deeply, freely, in one of the great pleasures and torments of her single life: men. For the longest time, she would pursue the unattainable "Him," tarrying with the married, the uninterested, or the downright psychotic. Helen would play a long game, alternately glorious, fulfilling, wretched, and demeaning. She would stay single way past thirty, which grimly tolled "spinster." She would enter relationships that engendered years of psychotherapy. Yet she had no doubts whatsoever: mastering that romantic/professional tango would save her life. It just *had* to.

7

Not Pretty Enough

Now the hidden assets of an *attractive* girl can be as fascinating as
the dark side of the moon. Plumbing the depths of a raving beauty
may be like plumbing the depths of Saran Wrap.
—HGB, *Sex and the Single Girl*

LIKE SO MANY PATRIOTIC AMERICAN WOMEN, Helen Gurley went
to war in an olive-drab rucksack. Photos of wives, girlfriends, sisters,
cousins, especially taken for the purpose, were carried from home to
eternity as the sweet, portable talismans of lives and loves left behind.
Helen said that the professional portrait she had taken of herself
in 1944 went to "multiple boyfriends in the Army, Navy, and Marine
Corps."

The hand-tinting of the portrait is clumsy and slightly garish, but
her look was very much of the moment. The brown hair was swept and
rolled into a lustrous, high pompadour. The eyebrows were carefully
penciled, the lips flaming red. She wore a string of demure pearls.
Beneath the fuzzy yellow-green sweater rose a pair of high and perky
breasts of such exacting circumference and symmetry as to suggest
a bit of legerdemain.

"Padded," she would later confess. Helen would never acquire the
natural means to jut, jiggle, or jounce. But in terms of genre poses, the
portrait was clearly influenced by the forties bloom of "sweater girls,"

such as Lana Turner and Jane Russell, who achieved fierce warhead effects with their Perma-Lift "bullet bras" thrusting vigorously against soft, straining angora. Ads for the mighty sling contraptions promised "the lift that never lets you down."

One of the men who shipped out with Helen's portrait was her high-school beau Bob Brown. An active-duty snapshot of Brown shows him lying on his bunk in a South Pacific Quonset hut, with a stogie in his mouth and Helen's framed portrait on a shelf behind him. Their letters back and forth have a playful, no-strings-attached tone, at least on Helen's part. Bob was not a keeper, but he was a heck of a nice guy. It was the least she could do.

On the home front, Helen's war efforts mixed pleasure and duty. After the MCA flameout, she was briefly the secretary for the Abbott and Costello radio show, which was often broadcast from nearby military bases. "I learned how it felt to be very, very popular!" she chirped; ". . . sometimes singer Connie Haines and I would be the only girls on the entire base for a day." On her own time, she danced at USO canteens at bases in the Los Angeles area, with servicemen on leave or about to ship out. More taxing, as the fighting went on, were her Wednesday evening trips to dance with patients at Sawtelle Veterans Hospital, a large medical facility built on federal land west of what is now the 405 freeway. Many were suffering from what was then called "shell shock." Helen remembered it as an unsettling sort of volunteer work; the young men were so terribly damaged that sometimes she had to force herself to go.

By the late spring of 1944, there was some encouraging war news: The British Royal Air Force and the U.S. Eighth Air Force were pounding Germany with round-the-clock bombing runs. To the particular relief of West Coast residents, Japan's last aircraft-carrier forces were defeated in the Pacific; a single battle with U.S. carrier forces destroyed 220 Japanese warplanes. On D-Day, June 6, Allied troops landed on Omaha Beach in the Normandy Invasion.

On June 28, as more war casualties continued to flood into County Hospital, a long, quiet struggle there was over. Leigh Bryan died, at age forty-eight. Cleo was fifty-one. For her, there would be no other. "Cleo slept with a total of two men in her life," Helen observed, "both of whom she married first." She was deeply sorry for her mother, but otherwise not much affected by her stepfather's passing. Helen was of troubled mind about so many other things. Since she was ten years old, their household had absorbed so much sorrow and uncertainty. She was surprised to find herself still struggling with what she termed daddy issues, with her shaky self-esteem, and with the growing pressure of supporting the family. As a young adult with an uncertain future, she had no trusted elder whom she could ask for advice. Though Cleo was supportive, her greatest expertise seemed to be in deploying fear and doubt; she still knew very little of the wider world that Helen had paddled off to. Cleo had hauled her family to land's end in California in one of her panics and found that she hated it; Los Angeles was too big, too fast, and way too far from home. Her menial job cowed and further depressed her, and Mary's care was a constant strain. Worst of all, Cleo had had so little time with the man she had waited for so long before she became his caregiver, too.

Helen badly needed attention as well; she wanted wisdom, reassurance, a more sophisticated ear. Something within was beginning to frighten her. She made a decision fairly unusual for the times, certainly unheard of in her family. "In 1944, I went to a therapist—at 22," she wrote. "Since that time, I have never been without one."

That lifetime commitment is remarkable, given her initial experience, with a psychotherapist in Pasadena. In their first session, having heard a cursory rundown of Helen's love life, he asked, nastily, whether her mother "put out" as well. At first Helen was confused. "I didn't even know what that meant," she said. She thought that maybe "put out" meant lying down on command and being taken against one's will. Then it was explained. "Translation: he didn't approve of my single-girl sex life and wondered if I had possibly learned it from Mom." Finding the good doctor downright sadistic, she discontinued treatment and kept looking for Dr. Right: "I think I went through psychiatrists like I went through jobs."

There were three recurrent leitmotifs throughout her lifelong therapy: men, work, and not being "pretty enough." She noted some doctors' impatience with her stubborn inability to move on past her old hurts and slights, and her preoccupation with beauty. But Helen was a brave and eager analytic subject who invited challenge; she had no interest in the sort of therapy that merely validated one's basic personality, foibles and all. She cried a lot in sessions. But she really did hope to change. Whenever she was sounding like a broken record—and wasting her own money at it!—she expected to be called out for it.

"I was always attracted to psychiatry," she said, ". . . but it was so expensive; it was twenty-five dollars an hour, which was half of my weekly salary—even in the forties it was twenty-five dollars an hour." With some therapists, she cut deals for discounts. Yet she wanted top-drawer talent. She researched area therapists and decided that she would go with, as she put it, "the famous-est and the best-est." At the time, that was Dr. David H. Fink, author of one of the earliest self-help books. Published by Simon & Schuster in 1943, *Release from Nervous Tension* was a huge bestseller in a stressed and war-weary nation. Despite Fink's stature, Helen was able to talk him into an affordable rate—there was something about that Gurley girl. Fink would preside over the breathless recitations of her first big affair and the frustrating liaisons that followed.

It never cost anything to talk to her girlfriends, and they were plentiful, loyal, and terrific at helping her lighten up. Like so many other places around the nation at that time, Los Angeles was very much a city of women, many more of them working now than before the men left to soldier. They were more visible, more mobile, and seen around town enjoying one another's company. Helen kept up with friends she met on various jobs and with her sorority sisters, working girls all. They occasionally held sewing nights to repair and restyle their work wardrobes; thanks to Cleo, Helen was a fair hand with a needle and thread. Hems rolled up and down; buttons and trims changed, beneath laughter and a cocktail or two.

One longtime friend from that era was Yvonne Rich, who said they met at an Eta Upsilon Gamma alumna function. It was held in a restaurant on the west side; Miss Helen Gurley, class of '41, was front and center when Rich walked in. "The first time I ever saw her, she was sitting at the bar with her legs crossed and wearing those black fishnet stockings," said Rich. "Just making herself look as come hither–ish as possible." As the restaurant filled, Rich was not the only one to think, "*Who's that girl?*"

Like her beloved tuna sandwiches, fishnet stockings would become an HGB signifier; she wore the vampy hose to her ninetieth birthday party. In the mid-1940s, only known bad girls—strippers, hookers, burlesque queens—dared snap them to their garters. When crossed and dangled from a bar stool, those legs encased in spidery webbing had a certain "hey, sailor" semaphore. Helen must have loved the look, to have flouted propriety so boldly; perhaps they added a bit of contour to her very thin gams.

"Well, that was just . . . Helen," Rich said. They hit it off immediately, and remained friends for more than forty years. Rich said that she was never one to judge what she calls "Helen's sex thing." Certainly, they both enjoyed men. Rich said that Helen was the maid of honor at her first wedding (there were four of them), as well as a witness in "one of my divorces." When she spoke about their long friendship, Rich was ninety-five and living in her sprawling, memorabilia-crammed home of many years in Altadena, California. Helen and David Brown had been frequent visitors there, as she was to their home in Pacific Palisades. Rich still has stacks of correspondence from Helen and misses her old friend. "All four of my husbands are dead," Rich said, "and my latest boyfriend says he's worried." She is at work on her own memoir, which will surely feature some adventures with Helen. Rich said she had to admit it: even when it was happening, she could not keep track of all of Helen's jobs and boyfriends.

The persistent allure of showbiz drew Helen back to MCA for a second tour of duty. This time she had a better boss—or so it seemed. She was secretary to Mickey Rockford, head of the radio division. MCA was expanding so quickly that management had begun to let a few guppies out of the typing pool. "I was one of the girls who got to sit outside my boss's office," Helen said, "because he had the hots for me." Rockford was short, stubby, and far from a matinee idol. He liked having Helen outside his office, called her in often, and made his infatuation clear. Helen enjoyed her new vantage point for its improved view of the agency's male "possibles." One agent, Herman Citron, used the same term when discussing that new Miss Gurley with another agent. "Possibles" had an earthier connotation when used by MCA males. He wondered whether she would go out with him.

Helen's description of Citron is that of a sharpie on the make: "He looked a little bit like Eddie Cantor . . . but not bad . . . kind of ugly, but very sexy. Very sexy." The 10-percenters of the day affected a "say, check me out" sort of sartorial flash: "They had white on white shirts and white on white ties," Helen recalled, ". . . sort of a slicked up *Guys and Dolls* thing." While wrangling talent back east in the crowded paddocks of Broadway songwriters, gag men, and hoofers, Citron had surely played the part of an operator straight out of Central Casting, chorus girls and all. He told Helen he'd left a girl in New York who was in the line at the Copacabana; she thought that was *really* showbiz.

On the hunt for profitable clients, Citron was feared by lesser dealmakers, who called him the Iceman. Mel Shavelson, a radio and film writer who was then a client of Citron's, put it this way: "Herman was a quiet-spoken man. So, I understand, was Attila the Hun. Citron's reputation in a cutthroat business passed belief. He represented a large percentage of Hollywood's top stars, and his handshake could be deposited in the Bank of America and draw interest."

Helen and the Iceman began an affair, in spite of strict company policies against fraternization. Too embarrassed to have him pick her up at the gopher palace on their first date, she met him in Beverly Hills. She lied and said she was going to the movies—could he pick her up there? He pulled up to the Beverly Theater in "his slick little car" and drove her to Villa Nova, a hot spot on the Sunset Strip. They drank, talked, had dinner, and went back to a bachelor apartment she gushed over with the adjectives of the time: Jazzy. Nifty.

All in all, Citron looked to be the Ultimate Possible. He had a lavish lifestyle and movie star clients, and no man she'd ever been with was better in bed. She said that she had an orgasm every time—she thought this was the norm for people very attracted to each other. The sex was so spectacular, she said, that memories of it had never faded. "Wow!" she said. "I wish I could feel it again." Straightaway, she realized that the kapow factor was mutual. Citron was fourteen years older than Helen, but he didn't know what hit him with this skinny little creature.

It was the first time she truly observed and understood that "sex is power," a new personal mantra that became a bolder iteration of the genteel art of "sinking in." Helen had come to realize that sex was a surprising and thrilling equalizer between the sheets. She was only sorry that she had been unaware of its fullest potential during their affair. Citron was so sexually smitten, and remembered the interlude so fondly, that he would call Helen, generally on Fridays, for years beyond her marriage, just to hear the sound of her voice.

While they were together, Helen was still unaware of her full potential as temptress, and more bedazzled than he. She would often slink out to the MCA parking lot for a rendezvous. Like so many of her escapades, the practice ended up in one of her books, with only the names changed: "Veronica used to date one of the salesmen in this 'hands off your co-workers' atmosphere. She finished work before he did and would wait in his car, lying down to avoid the Gestapo eyes of the management or its informants (like her girlfriends!). Every time Ronnie opened his car door, he would suffer a momentary spasm of horror thinking he'd found a dead woman in the front seat!"

Citron did take her out on the town. They went to glamorous restaurants, places to see and be seen, yet he never introduced her to anyone. It took a while, but she came to understand: "I was so gauche. So totally gauche!" The night Citron did dare to take her to an industry event, a movie premiere, she chose a slinky black cocktail dress and a giant, broad-brimmed hat she thought was the height of glamour—just like Paulette Goddard!

To wear such a big and attention-getting chapeau to a movie theater was plainly idiotic; Citron was annoyed, and she was mortified. It was the first of many times during her single years in California when Helen was undone by her rather sweet if clueless "gaucherie." She used the word often in explaining her failure to land the big fish. Nearly always, she blamed herself. Time and again, she lamented, "I blew it!" Still, with Citron, the sexual attraction continued to exert its pull. She felt she had him, all right. Helen was stunned when he made it clear that he was not in it for the long haul. He told her that, as a devout Jew, he felt she just could not fit into his family. She understood that he was right about that, but found herself brokenhearted.

There was no time for a slow glide to a gentle end. Helen's boss, Mickey Rockford, got wind of the affair, and in a towering fit of jealousy—Helen had let Mickey kiss her a few times—he fired her. Apart from his vindictive rage, canning hot little Miss Gurley was simply the better business decision. Stenos were occupational chump change; fierce, insatiable agents like the Iceman could make it rain commissions.

Helen endured a few more forgettable jobs, including a short stint at the William Morris Agency. Stubbornly, she was still aiming for a suitor in show business. She said that she "fooled around quite a bit" with the actor Walter Pidgeon, very much her elder, whom she later described as "one of the biggest swordsmen in Hollywood." She found him very sweet, and most valuable for buying groceries. She gadded about with a few band boys from her days at *The Abbott and Costello Show.* Then there was a man clinging to the edges of showbiz who seemed to want to marry her. Helen had a perfect horror of it. Marvin the Gag Writer, as she referred to him, was part of a stable of funny-men kept on staff by Eddie Cantor in rooms at the Hollywood Roosevelt Hotel. Helen was the secretary—yet another dead-end job. The four joke writers worked in a seedy bullpen stale with cigarettes, male funk, and overripe gags. They bellowed their zingers across the room to try out on their Girl Friday:

"Gurley! Come over here! Guy sez to his mother in law . . ."

Gurley got it all down, 130 yuks a minute. Short, fat Marvin was a laugh riot even outside the office. He had a habit of turning to Helen in the crowded hotel elevator, thumbing a wad of bills, and asking, "How much you say it was, Myrtle, fifteen or twenty?" It always set the captive audience howling; not so Marvin's red-faced foil. Marvin could be a damned troll, but when it was just the two of them, he made Helen laugh, too. Soon he was also churning out buckets of comedic corn for Bob Hope. For years after they worked together, Marvin called Helen to try out his bits.

Hey, kiddo . . . Guy sees a rabbi out on the golf course . . .

The Keptive

A secretary offers the only kind of polygamy we recognize in this
country, the chance to have a second wife while you have your first
and not go to jail . . . Turning your secretary into a girlfriend has one
big advantage. You know where she is all the time.
—HGB, *Lessons in Love*, on LP, 1963

DURING THE PERIOD that Helen referred to as jobs "three through
seventeen," Yvonne Rich met a good number of the men who streamed
through her friend's life. She generally cannot remember their names,
but one of them she recalls more vividly than most: "She had a real
good-looking boyfriend, very handsome. This one was an attorney." In
Helenspeak, he was a Wow.

His name was Paul Ziffren. He was from Chicago, the protégé of
a well-known political fixer there, a city alderman named Jacob Arvey.
Ziffren had been a junior partner in Arvey's law firm. When he relocated
to Los Angeles with a tight web of connections from his mentor, Ziffren
soon found himself in need of a new secretary; the one he had made it
plain that she loathed legal work. Helen's boss at yet another showbiz
job, a publicity firm, brokered a trade; Miss Gurley admitted that she
"didn't get on well in publicity." She went to work at Ziffren's firm, Loeb
and Loeb. "I hated legal work, *too* when I found out about it," Helen
said, "but a girl has to *eat*."

She landed in the right spot for that. On her first day of work, her new Jewish boss, already a very connected guy in his adopted city, gifted her with a precious slab of *trafe*: ten pounds of bacon. Though most rationing had ended, it was still almost impossible to get except on the black market. He also gave her a Max Factor makeup kit in a leather case. Paul Ziffren was *darling*.

In short order, he and Helen began a brief affair. Ziffren was indeed handsome, affable, generous, and married. Helen harbored no illusions that he would divorce his wife for her. She continued to work with him after their fling. Possessed of a certain Henry Higgins–like pedagogy, Ziffren sought to help his Eliza Doolittle, the miss from Arkansas. Helen's gaffes and malapropisms could indeed be charming, but Ziffren knew that, without intervention, some of her lapses in education and taste were bound to handicap her. He seemed to have empathy for the pressures of her family obligations. At that point in her life, Helen wrote, "I was frequently a *metastasized* case of the sads . . . I was so wantonly depressed—and *careless*—that I even told men about my sadness and problems at home . . . It didn't depress the men usually, just removed them from my side!" Ziffren, noticing an especially deep wilt one day, took her to lunch and declared he was henceforth going to call her Atlas, "because you are obviously carrying the weight of the world on your shoulders."

Much later, when Ziffren was terminally ill, Helen wrote to thank him for the pains he had taken in civilizing her on the job: "Having not gone to college and landing in the secretarial pool at MCA not too long after highschool [*sic*], I knew *nothing*. Would you believe—it's true!— you turned me on to Shakespeare and Emerson. You thought Ralph Waldo's essay on self-reliance might do a little something for me but mostly you were mad about his words."

Ziffren read her a favorite passage from that classic essay: "In every work of genius we recognize our own rejected thoughts: they come back to us with a certain alienated majesty." He read her Antony's speech following Caesar's death and pointed out its duplicities. If he deemed it necessary, he told her some unpleasant but true facts of life. When Helen begged him to introduce her to a wealthy Loeb client "so that I could marry for money," Ziffren gently lowered the boom regarding her prospects. She just wasn't pretty enough. "You weren't all that blunt about it," she assured him in her letter, "but you explained these men could have about anybody they fancied and they often fancied actresses or glamour-girls." It stung, but she took it as wise counsel—sort of: "It probably set me on the road to achieving though I would definitely have played it the other way if you had been more encouraging!" In her farewell letter, Helen appended a final accolade to the dying man: "You were very good in bed . . . strong and ardent and caring."

There is no doubt that Ziffren presented as a kind and gallant friend, but there was a whiff of sulfur beneath his savoir faire and fine tailoring. Either Helen did not detect it, or she chose to overlook it. Since she admittedly paid as little attention as possible to his legal work, she might not have known that her boss had an ugly penchant for enriching himself through the misfortunes of others. At about the time he hired Helen, Ziffren was busy on a special investment scheme. In *The Last Mogul*, his biography of the MCA titan Lew Wasserman, Dennis McDougal provided a thumbnail portrait of a man on the make as Ziffren became a Hollywood, then a political player: "When Ziffren first came to L.A. during World War II, he demonstrated just how well Arvey [the Chicago alderman] had taught him the lessons of political exploitation, by organizing a consortium of investors who bought property vacated by Japanese-Americans during wartime internment. Ziffren worked closely with attorney David Bazelon, yet another Arvey protégé, who had been appointed by the Truman administration to oversee 'alien' land sales."

It may have been smoother and cleaner than the Nazi confiscation of the property of interned and murdered Jews, but the sanctioned thievery was just as bold and unapologetic. When Japanese Americans were eventually released from internment camps, they returned to the Los Angeles area to find new stores, restaurants, and movie theaters— with new owners—where their homes, farms, and businesses had been. After this efficient scouring, President Truman rewarded Bazelon with a federal judgeship.

Ziffren made money, very quietly. He had a few other questionable activities on the down-low. By the time he was California's Democratic

National Committeeman, in the early 1950s, Ziffren would also be known to the LAPD as an elegant, pinstriped procurer. According to a police report, he was "observed delivering two known call girls to a Tahoe gambler in the bar of the Beverly Hills Hotel." Police found Ziffren's name in many of the call girls' "trick books."

Helen's fling with Ziffren was the first of a few liaisons with men possessed of healthy bank accounts and dubious moral fiber. Her dalliance with Ziffren hadn't been too important to either of them, she concluded. Of the affair's end: "Who knows who left whom?" Helen wrote. "I was *finding* myself."

Watching Helen flit from job to job, therapist to therapist, man to man, Cleo made a difficult decision. Helen was still allotting a good portion of every paycheck toward household support. Given her family obligations, she could not yet afford a place of her own in perhaps a slightly better neighborhood. Besides, Cleo was more than ready to quit California; living there had only enveloped her in further anxiety and grief. In 1946, Cleo decided to move back to her parents' home in Osage with Mary. She told Helen that the cost of living there was much lower, and perhaps some of the brothers and sisters Cleo had carried on her hip would help out with Mary's care. Helen saw it as an acknowledgment of her need for independence: "Cleo's separating me from them was a courageous, unselfish act . . . she could easily have sacrificed me to be a handy, unpaid bound-by-blood helper forever."

Even after her family went east, Helen sent them support checks, if slightly smaller. She closed the door on the rodent-plagued house on Fifty-Ninth Street and moved into a small studio apartment on the top floor of a Spanish-style white stucco house at 144 South Elm Drive. This was workaday Beverly Hills, with neat two-story homes, many divided into rental apartments, and the occasional scraggly palm, just a few blocks from the glistening "Wilshire Corridor." It was the first of a string of bachelor-girl apartments. After a short stint on Elm, Helen moved in with her friend Barbara nearby on South Canon Drive. They entertained other young Angelenos there under the gimlet eye of their landlady, Mrs. Tuttle.

It is just as well that Mary and Cleo were tucked back in the Ozarks, though Helen wrote to them daily, without fail. Helen's romantic life was about to take a darker, troublesome turn toward patently transactional sex. About to take her fifteenth job in six years—she had sorely vexed her employment agency, but they placed her yet again—Helen went to work for a movie mogul wannabe, a wealthy dilettante who was, she later concluded, "a psychopath."

It was clearly a piercing and regrettable life experience. She wrote about the man many times, in carefully shaded versions and guises. Helen's public retellings were generally breezy and comedic, with the eager Miss Gurley depicted as somewhere between the fifties TV ditz My Little Margie and Irma la Douce. Throughout her writing career, Helen's published confessions and Single Girl vignettes were wrought with the illusory skills of a fan dancer—Sally Rand caliber—giving us versions of herself and her lovers. Their pseudonyms and their peccadilloes flicker and morph with each telling. So it was with this man.

Helen cloaked his identity in "The Perils of Little Helen," the job history appended to *Sex and the Office*, calling him "Mr. Wilson." In other books detailing his unsavory traits, she also used pseudonyms. But close textual comparisons, alongside some of Helen's unpublished fiction and her recorded conversations with Lyn Tornabene, make it possible to sync the salient details. Helen walked into the arrangement with this man thinking it might solve all her money problems. It is clear that at the affair's outset, she didn't anticipate the psychic and emotional cost to herself. The experience led her to call herself a "keptive," bought and paid for, and forbidden to live a life of her own.

She had been looking for a sugar daddy; her new boss seemed to fit the bill. Helen said that his real name was Mason Miller; she claimed that he was a member of the Morgan banking family. No search of that family's genealogy turned up anyone by that name; perhaps, given the revolting aspects of his personality, Helen considered it prudent to mask his identity. Whatever his pedigree, his demeanor was that of an East Coast snob torn from the pages of a Henry James novel, all Brahmin affectations, bespoke suits, and, beneath, a cruel and withered soul. Miller had an estate in Gatsby country, on Long Island. He and his wife took frequent trips to Europe, returning with antiques, Parisian fashions, and fine wines.

Miller arrived from New York with a healthy fortune and built his own motion picture studio from the ground up, though he knew nothing of the business. He was a womanizer, a dabbler, and a drunk. While Helen worked there as the only secretary, all but one of the studio's nine new soundstages, still smelling of sawdust and paint, stood empty. Miller did make money in California real estate, Helen said. He had a knack for that. A little piece of land he owned in Bel-Air would be a catalyst for the affair's undoing. She understood from the outset that Miller would never leave his wife. He was too fond of their socialite life. Instead, he would keep his sexy little secretary in the style in which wealthy men kept their "girls." The boss let it be known that his previous mistress had done very well for herself: Real estate! Securities! Cash!

At the outset of her relationship with Miller, Helen carried her few misgivings straight to Dr. Fink. To her surprise and relief, her therapist delivered no stern lecture on becoming a kept woman. He reasoned that being kept nicely was an improvement over what she had been doing, and it sounded as if the man liked her better than the others had.

"Pretty hip advice for 1947," Helen concluded later. She thought it was probably sage counsel as well: if she was going to keep getting mixed up with men of means, it might as well be with someone who seemed to like her and would not be exploitative. Money was still tight; Helen's tax return for the previous year, 1946, lists three different employers, including the William Morris Agency; her declared dependents are Cleo and Mary, and her total income was just under $2,700. She surely would be relieved to stop paying rent.

In her book *I'm Wild Again*, Helen described the speedy start of the affair: "Interview Monday, sex Thursday. Our first carnal encounter took place in his office on a cushy Moroccan leather couch." She didn't have to keep her eyes closed. She described him as "not that bad. Not a beauty but not a mongoose. About 5'10", WASP-ish features, a bit pinched, not that old . . . I could handle it." At forty-three, Miller was nearly bald. He had a limp from an auto accident, and his signature scent seemed to be stale if expensive Scotch. There was no fuss about birth control, because he was infertile; he and his wife adopted children. Better yet, there had been some alluring talk during the job interview, with the sort of sweet nothings Helen had been longing to hear: "words like *stock portfolio, bonds, investments, real estate* were floated about and I would have my secretarial salary to live on."

Having started her at thirty-five dollars a week, Miller would soon be paying Helen eighty-five, "when every other secretary in town was making forty." Given the lack of studio business, Helen had little to do but read every Pearl S. Buck novel in the Melrose Library and munch Planters peanuts by the can. The office pace was desultory at best. The boss was nearly always hungover, to the extent that "the rustle of carbon paper was too much before noon." When Helen was called in to take a letter, she made the most of it. "I would sit curled up like a little cupcake across from him with my pristine shorthand book."

It took less than a week for boss and secretary to agree on an arrangement, and Helen began the hunt for a love nest. A few stark motel and office couplings had convinced Miller that it was worth a modest investment. His chauffeur took Helen all over town and looked at apartments with her. She found a modest flat on South Curson Street, in the Wilshire–La Brea area. The apartment had no kitchen, but she wasn't there to cook. It was carpeted and scantily furnished; their lovers' bower was a Murphy bed tugged down from the wall. She was allowed to purchase a few pieces of furniture. Miller also urged her to add some tonier accents to her wardrobe. Perhaps some cashmere? Helen shopped for outfits befitting her new status, driven from store to store by the chauffeur.

In the office, they gossiped and talked for much of the day; for some reason, Miller had an almost anthropological fascination with Helen's Ozark roots. He would press her for details, and, eager to please, she laid out the rudiments, the "hillbilly" aunts and uncles, the lack of electricity, the outhouses—replete with examples of the local accent. He couldn't get enough detail on her "déclassé" tribe. Miller could bring out the worst in his new mistress, owing to her eagerness to please. For years, Helen had flirted with the hillbilly shtick, caricaturing her relatives to the men she dared not let pick her up at home. It was a hurtful habit, Mary had warned her. Nonetheless, when Miller pressed for more details of collards, fatback, and privation, Helen served them right up during the office cocktail hour, which began promptly at five—Haig & Haig Pinch Scotch in paper cups. Sometimes Helen opted for a more ladylike shot of Harvey's Bristol Cream sherry. At six, she would wend her way home, "crocked," to await Mason's pleasure.

Occasionally, the boss's wife would waft into the office to deposit a hamper of caviar and other jewel-like *amuse-gueules* from Jurgensen's, a gourmet emporium in Pasadena. She was a beauty, a former repertory actress. She wore Balenciaga and Mainbocher. Helen knew that she was hopelessly outclassed. Yvonne Rich recalled that Helen's "at homes" featured "a drink made from bourbon and vanilla ice cream and served in great quantities." Not long into those Sunday brunches chez Gurley, said Rich, "we'd be down on the floor, reading the funny papers. Upside down."

Helen learned quickly that her rich, well-positioned new lover was the least tolerant and compassionate of men. He told her about the many people he had "ruined" back in New York. He loathed commies, Catholics, Roosevelt, and noise of any sort before lunchtime. But he harbored a special, obsessive hatred for Jews. He railed, he roared, he spewed gobbets of cabalistic misinformation torn from the standard "Jews and world finance" conspiracy lit. Rather stupidly, Miller hadn't realized that he had built his movie studio deep in enemy territory. He did not know that his own studio's only tenants, the Justman brothers, were Jewish. Helen had been savvy enough not to mention her serial affairs with Jewish men. Still, she was faced with a singular dilemma: the pay was too good for her to quit, but she couldn't very well feign hatred of Jews if she had no idea who *was* Jewish.

As best she could, she made light of the ugly situation: "In Little Rock, where I grew up, religious discrimination didn't exist or none that I knew about. Maybe Jew-denigrating was buried deep down under Main Street . . . we were pretty busy with Apartheid." She did ask Miller: Just what had Jews done wrong, aside from *being* Jewish, to make him so angry? "We never got it sorted out," she said, since everything that the man offered as a solid reason sounded so silly. Though she was more perplexed than outraged by his anti-Semitism, Helen did submit to cultural instruction. These lessons were absurd, hateful, and patently insane: Miller took her to Hollywood power restaurants so that he could point out what he took to be Jewish hair and facial features among the lunchtime deal-makers. Stranger still, even her half-Jewish former roommate, Barbara, offered to help gin up a Jewish identi-kit of typical traits so that Helen wouldn't continue to irk her employer by keeping the wrong company.

Many years later, this repellent racial profiling exercise was something Helen thought might work in her musical, in a lighter version. "I think that would make a wonderful song for us, Lyn," she said to Tornabene. "It would be 'How Do You Tell a Jew?'" Tornabene is Jewish, and had written an affectionate and popular humor book for Random House, *What's a Jewish Girl?* She explained to Helen that Miller's viciousness was just too dark and ugly to put on the stage, even as burlesque.

Little by little, aspects of Helen's consorting with the enemy leaked out to her boss. Miller spewed imprecations upon hearing of her previous employment in that nest of Hebraic vermin, MCA. He thundered condemnation of Cleo's gross negligence; how could she have failed to educate her daughter about this peril within? Upon finding out that Barbara and Helen's other dear friend Berna were Jewish, that she had even more Jewish friends, he bellowed, "My God! My God! . . . I just never dreamed the agency would send me a . . . a . . . a . . . Jew lover!" After that outburst, they ultimately reconciled, but Helen observed that "he was never quite himself again." He forbade her to see any of the offending girlfriends and Helen acquiesced. The isolation was suffocating.

Though all of her accounts of the affair make it clear that she felt the man was "a nutcase," it would take decades for Helen to address the morality of staying in the relationship and participating in Miller's offensive Jew-hunting safaris amid the power lunchers in Hollywood.

She devoted a paragraph to the dilemma in *I'm Wild Again*: "Was I abandoning principle with my attempted Jew discernment, forsaking not only friends but ethics? I was being fearfully tacky, yes, but I didn't then or even now feel too bad about my pursuit. I wasn't trying to learn who they were so that I could hate anybody *ever* . . . This was just me trying for a little enlightenment for a Special Situation, *temporary* eschewal of a particular group until the arrival of Financial Security."

How did Helen "blow it" this time? Again, it was a matter of Miss Maladroit's youth and ineptitude. Subtlety, patience, and impeccable timing have enriched many an experienced courtesan. But in her mid-twenties, Helen had no such qualities. She told Tornabene about the Sunday that Miller picked her up in his immense Cadillac and drove her to a hilltop in Bel-Air; he parked on a prime lot that he owned, just across the street from Ginger Rogers's house. They made love in the car, a fetish of his. "He actually said the lot could be mine and he would build me a little house." About a month later, Helen called him on it, baldly. She reminded him that he had not yet transferred that lot on top of Bel-Air to her, the one he had said she could have. He was not pleased to be accused, however sweetly, of breaching his promise.

She was sure that had she played it correctly, she could have had the Bel-Air lot with a darling love shack built on it—and more. Miller told her that "Marcella," his previous secretary/mistress in a New York bank, had wound up with more than $100,000 in cash and goodies. "And this man was not a liar," Helen said, convinced of Marcella's bonanza. "But I blew it." Asking directly for the property deed was *not* proper mistress etiquette. But how could she know the current acceptable practices of that ancient art? "I was totally inept," Helen wailed of the hilltop confrontation. "It was just the absolute frontal attack. The man was appalled by such gaucherie."

Not surprisingly, Miller's movie business went belly-up within months. He had to sell it off to a savings and loan company at a huge personal loss. Soon after selling the business, Miller moved Helen to a larger, two-bedroom apartment with the promise that she could send for Cleo and Mary. Committing yet another mistress taboo, she had begun to hector him about being so much alone. She knew it was silly, but she had become wildly jealous. His wife kept their calendar full. Given their many social engagements, Helen was relegated to after-work quickies and Miller's visits on Sunday afternoons.

By then it was not making love, she wrote later, but "two people copulating." To her surprise, the preternaturally orgasmic Helen had to fake it, time and again. Her body refused to cooperate. "Maybe I wasn't conscience-dead," she ventured. The little bird was expected to stay in her cage, always available, yet always alone. When Miller left her in the flat at 6:30 on weekdays to meet his wife for their evening plans, Helen passed the long hours reading or writing letters to Mary and Cleo. She binged on dinners that did not require a kitchen. This included bear claw pastries and a potent comfort food that prefigured the classic sour cream and onion soup–mix California dip of the fifties. "I would squash up a batch of Philadelphia cream cheese, mash up several cloves of garlic, wolf the globby treat down with a massive bag of potato chips, gargle Listerine before work the next day." By the time Helen would come to edit *Cosmo*, such empty-calorie therapy would be pitiable, unthinkable. But her emotional/editorial street cred would be unassailable. Pussycats, she'd been there. She *understood*.

One Sunday when Miller failed to show up, she was plunged into despair. "I really thought I was going to die," she recalled. "I had blown all my close friends, I had no boyfriends obviously, I belonged to him." Her humiliating mission as a kept seductress had failed; there would be no windfall to make life more tolerable for herself, Cleo, and Mary. She spent all of Sunday downtown at the movies, as she had in those days after Ira died.

Tucked amid Helen's unpublished writings—some typed, some in a stack of legal pads handwritten from edge to edge in her loopy script—there is material that suggests that this "keptive" relationship Helen joked about in her bestsellers had in fact been deeply troubling to her. The small trove includes some frank erotica, short stories, and love poems such as "I Love My Bruises." The prose, if sometimes florid, is creditable for its detail and consistency of voice; the tone is always *pauvre tristesse*, a woman used and unfulfilled. Taken together, the short pieces evoke a melancholy seraglio of female souls thinking aloud, whispering those subjugated woman blues. There is a roughly deflowered virgin, bleak couplings with uncaring and abusive male lovers, a sad miscarriage. There is, most clearly, a barely fictionalized version of Helen's front seat tryst in the Bel-Air hills with Mason Miller. The dialogue is convincing if unsavory, the sex act brutish, the mistress achingly forlorn.

Even as Helen prepared to make light of the sorry keptive chapter in her Broadway play, she reminded Tornabene that she was in treatment with a psychiatrist at the time. It's difficult to imagine what Dr. Fink might have made of the fanatical anti-Semitism; possibly Helen could not bear to tell him. She was not unaware of the deep sadness she had brought upon herself. She felt as though she were in solitary confinement in the keptive apartment. More than ever, she needed her girlfriends to confide in, but their comforts were forbidden her. She recalled it as one of the worst periods of her life. As ever, she blamed herself in the end.

"I very carefully picked my predators."

The affair with Miller mercifully, quietly faded out. He was going to Europe for at least three months, he told her. Los Angeles was just not his best business milieu. Perhaps they would resume if and when he returned. But in the meantime, it would be a good idea for Helen to look for another job. "I don't remember gulping in pain at the notice," she wrote. "Applied for unemployment insurance the minute he left, first time ever and the last, not working was not my style."

Helen came away from the Miller affair with few material gains: a couple of cute sweater sets, some dresses, a bit of cheap furniture, and a seven-year-old, wood-sided eight-cylinder forest-green Buick station wagon with a hundred thousand miles on it. The wagon had been a utility vehicle on the Millers' Long Island estate. The roof leaked badly and its new owner weathered downpours with an umbrella over the driver's seat. She christened the heap Appletrees, the name of Miller's estate. Helen had caught Cleo's car lust and even a clunker gave her a new mobility and a sense of pride. She painted the name on its side.

Before her first unemployment check arrived, Helen got job number seventeen at the Sam Jaffe literary agency, which sold properties to the movies. She promptly sent for Mary, Cleo, and their three cats. She splurged and brought them west in style on the Super Chief. "Alas, none of the felines or people were real happy in their new home," Helen said. Two of the cats expired in short order. To Helen's astonishment, there was much wailing at their demise. Cleo was heard to grumble, "Such fine healthy cats when we brought them here." After six unhappy months, she and Mary decamped for Arkansas, with plans to find companions for the surviving feline, Minnie. Until it was torn down for sheer decrepitude, the Sisco house in Osage would be known for spilling as many felines into the tiny hamlet as the family had once produced squalling babies.

Alone again, Helen lost the literary agency job. Out of work and without Miller to pay the rent, she had to move to a smaller, more affordable apartment. Imbued with a new resolve—this mistress thing was too iffy and she would take care of herself, thank you—Helen stuffed her belongings into a few bags and hauled them to the next stark little flat. Feathering her nest would have to wait until she was settled in. There was the matter of job number eighteen.

Dear Mr. B . . .

It was exciting to work for an important man.
—HGB, *Sex and the Office*

ON A SATURDAY MORNING just after her twenty-sixth birthday, in February 1948, Helen presented herself, without much enthusiasm, at another address provided by her employment agency. Downtown, *again*? She had finally installed herself in a decent, affordable flat on Bonnie Brae Street, also downtown, but she longed for the hills and a tonier address. She judged the heat-baked and bourgeois flatlands "possibly one of the most un-chic areas this side of the Ganges." Having no hill or ocean vistas and no hot spots save the La Brea tar pits, downtown seemed a concrete and stucco hive for worker bees. Worse, a secretarial spot in an ad agency did not sound at all sexy.

Helen's spirits drooped further when she was ushered into the darkened lair of Don Belding, the chairman of the board of Foote, Cone & Belding. The brown suede drapes were drawn shut against the bright day. One small light shone on the desk. Belding's secretary was leaving—his second helpmate lost to matrimony—and he needed to replace her. Once the reluctant applicant adjusted to the dark, her eye was drawn to a painting hanging behind the great man. It depicted two caveman types with spiked clubs doing battle in a misty glen; each had a stump gushing blood in place of an arm. The crimson blood spattered throughout the painting was the only bright spot in the room. The artwork's title: *The Ad Game*.

Could there be a more vicious work arena than show business? The man in the chair did have a rather forbidding mien. "Mr. Belding himself looked like Lionel Barrymore," she observed, ". . . balding, lean, lion-like and quite handsome, despite having only one good eye." The drapes were drawn because of his vision problem, he explained. This was the result of the first trauma in Belding's benighted military career during World War I. His eye was badly injured during artillery training in Virginia; shipped too soon to France, he was treated improperly there and much too late. The muscles were torn badly enough to afford no control of the eye's motion or dilation, rendering it permanently useless. Then Belding was gassed, landing him back home in a veterans' hospital with a case of pulmonary tuberculosis the doctors deemed fatal. Don Belding had strongly disagreed.

A few minutes into the interview, and despite her initial ambivalence about the job, Helen suddenly found herself "numb with fright." There was a certain hawk-like fierceness to the man, cordial as he was. Trying to address his good eye unnerved her; in the deep gloom, she could not tell which eye was looking at her. As she peered around the office during an awkward silence, she was further discomfited by the bizarre dissonance of Belding's office décor.

Clearly he was a Man of Consequence; there were personally autographed photos of Harry Truman, Herbert Hoover, Dwight Eisenhower, and the future German chancellor Konrad Adenauer. In jarring proximity was a chorus line of ad posters, all with daftly smiling women engaged in waxing linoleum, crafting sandwiches, and rinsing out their dainties using products hawked by the agency. There were strange curios as well. Belding kept a trio of stuffed and mounted birds, iridescent, long-tailed quetzals sacred to the Mayan and Aztec peoples. The quetzals, native to Central American rain forests, were accompanied by a display of pre-Columbian art and Guatemalan costumes arrayed under glass. A very large American flag stood in a corner. Sizing up the workplace she would occupy for nearly a decade, Helen decided that it looked like the Field Museum, the Chicago natural history collection she and Cleo had visited on their trip to the World's Fair.

Don Belding was an odd bird in the trade. He hadn't put in the standard migratory years of most admen, and had spent his entire career on the West Coast. He had a hardscrabble beginning as a miner's son in the small backwater of Grants Pass, Oregon. After the Great War, he had learned his metier from the ground up, steered toward advertising by a veterans' job training program. He began with an unpaid internship, then a mailroom job at the San Francisco branch of Lord & Thomas, the ad agency that was eventually absorbed in the founding of his own partnership firm, Foote, Cone & Belding (FC&B), in 1942.

FC&B did a good deal of wartime work, mostly public service announcements regarding conservation; the agency presided over the creation and introduction of that forest safety icon, Smokey Bear. But the advertising industry had begun retooling itself toward more consumer accounts after the war years when Miss Gurley fortuitously if grudgingly walked into it. The late forties and early fifties saw a comprehensive sea change as the new medium of television began to supplement, and sometimes surpass, the standard print and radio campaigns. For FC&B and Helen it would prove a golden decade, with lucrative auto, tobacco, and cosmetics contracts and a base of staid but reliable accounts: Sunkist citrus fruits, Johnson Wax, Kotex, Dial soap, Purex. The Hollywood arm of the agency built a roster of top-drawer celebrities, among them Bob Hope and Jack Benny, who were eager to host new TV programs sponsored by FC&B clients.

Once that paralyzing fright overtook her, Helen could claim little recollection of her interview with Belding save that it was halting, uncomfortable, and lasted less than ten minutes. He did make a point of telling her that he was often out of town, "probably to cheer me up," she figured. On Monday morning, she got the call that the job was hers, at $75 a week. Her rent was $72.50 a month, so it would work nicely, allowing a substantial stipend—at least a week's salary per month—for her mother and sister.

She could not know it, but broke, itinerant, and unfocused Helen was about to find solid ground on several levels. Surprising even herself, Helen had checked her reflexive flirtatiousness at Belding's imposing door. She explained the change in behavior this way: "After I met him he was the father in my life and he was a very strong man. It never occurred to me to sleep with him, 'cause he was Daddy." There is no question that apart from the long-lost Ira Gurley and her future husband, no man would be as important to the long march toward Becoming HGB. Belding opened the path to serious skills, a genuine career, and the sort of professional satisfactions Helen would later wish on *Cosmo* readers, even more than toe-curling orgasms. In an undated letter to Belding wishing him a happy birthday, Helen told him: "There isn't any question that you've influenced my life for the good more than any person I've ever known."

Belding and his second wife, Alice, did all but adopt his eager if unfinished new secretary. Helen gratefully noted that they "took her off the streets" on formerly desolate holidays and assured her a place at their table every Christmas and Thanksgiving. The Beldings were the openhanded, sophisticated, and well-situated family that Helen had long dreamed of. Writing to Alice Belding, Helen declared that her time at FC&B was the happiest in her single working life. "It was like finding a haven," she told her, "after so many years of bumping around."

The work threw her at first. Belding's affianced secretary had stayed on to give Helen two weeks of very detailed instructions. "She was a whirlwind, tweedy, fantastic with figures, lovey-dovey with stock quotations . . . a really dreadful girl," Helen complained of the efficient Miss Cunningham. Once she left, bedlam ensued as Helen struggled on multiple phone lines to connect clients, wife, ex-wife, and respective sets of children at the boss's command.

"Get Sargie on the phone!"

She quickly learned that this meant phoning Belding's houseman to put Mr. B's beloved German shepherd, Sarge, on the line for some sweet nothings from Daddy.

"Didja get some gophers today, Sargie?"

Worst of all for a girl's beauty sleep, Belding was "a nut about punctuality." Commuting by car in Los Angeles was murderous even then, and Appletrees was anything but reliable; the Buick's doors were held shut with ropes and its composite roof worn so thin as to appear translucent. Daily, Helen boarded a fat red Pacific Palisades bus while the moon was still up, popping out hair curlers and daubing on makeup as it jounced through still-sleepy downtown. It was challenging, but all rather scrumptious.

"I was living just an adorable career-girl life," she said, "and I was not kept at all."

She was happy to pay the price for such gleeful independence. Helen rarely knew what to expect on any given day; she became an inventive scrambler as the eccentricities of some FC&B clients caused her to make some odd requests around town. She pleaded with the Santa Fe railroad purser for special Super Chief accommodations. She needed to book an extra connectable sleeper berth just for the feet of one Philip Liebmann, president of Liebmann Breweries, the producer of Rheingold beer. The railroad was unsympathetic, the client resolute.

"I am a tall man, Miss Gurley," Liebmann said. "Do you honestly want me to sleep with my knees under my chin all the way to Chicago?" The same gentleman objected to the number of diners—thirteen—at a business meal Helen had arranged at the Brown Derby. The deeply superstitious Mr. Liebmann refused to sit down until a restaurant cashier, coaxed by Miss Gurley, agreed to be the fourteenth in the party.

Professional paranoia was common in such a competitive business, but no FC&B client was as furtive as Howard Hughes. When Belding was unavailable to personally receive Hughes's communiqués, Helen escorted messengers from Hughes's various businesses (RKO Pictures, Hughes Aircraft) into the boss's office. Once the door was shut, seals were produced and warmed globs of wax were pressed to secure tamper-proof envelopes, to be opened by Belding only. To Helen's great disappointment, she never witnessed Hughes's late-night visits to the office, when, office scuttlebutt had it, he obsessed over the visibility of Jane Russell's impressive cleavage in print ads for the RKO film *The Outlaw*. Hughes's favorite new actress was pictured reclining on a hay bale, scantily clad and alternately posed sucking on a bit of straw or dangling a big revolver toward her crotch. Up and down, by millimeters, FC&B art directors moved the top of Russell's blouse at Hughes's direction, trying to outflank the decency patrols.

Watching her boss meld business with his political activities afforded Helen a window into national and global power-brokering that would have floored the young politico Ira Gurley. Belding's idea of celebrity was a five-star general; Omar Bradley, U.S. Army field commander of operations in North Africa and Europe during World War II, was a friend and idol. Helen soon learned the significance of the huge freestanding American flag in the office. Belding was a civic and political dynamo fueled by such conservative Republican zeal that within a year of Helen's arrival, he would, with the financier E. F. Hutton and Kenneth Wells, another adman, cofound the Freedoms Foundation, a nonprofit patriotic organization headquartered near the national park at Valley Forge, Pennsylvania. The foundation's summary of basic freedoms, "The American Credo," was hammered out with the help of General Dwight D. Eisenhower, who was by then president of Columbia University. Eisenhower would also become a Belding friend and ally. Ever the adman, Belding saw the organization as "an effective device of continuously selling the American system to its people."

The Freedoms Foundation was not without its critics, who suspected another, more right-wing agenda beneath the apple pie patriotism. Don Belding was hell on commies at home and abroad. He worked with RKO executives to make the eighteen-minute film *Letter to a Rebel*, a paean to American capitalism. The plot: a college kid questioning the American Way gets schooled in the virtues of honest capitalism by his newspaper editor dad. Thirty million people saw it in movie theaters as a short feature in its first year of release.

As gatekeeper of Belding's tenebrous inner sanctum, Helen also had an intimate view of the growing postwar camaraderie among business, the military, and politics. Tycoon types were whisked off on what were called "orientation trips," often in the company of military brass. These civilian moguls from ad agencies, soft drink companies, and steel mills were given tours of impressive military installations. They were taken out on battleships, wined and dined in the officers' mess. Belding often returned from such outings exhilarated and pumped with patriotic zeal. "They were kind of indoctrinated," Helen observed.

Belding was also the vice president for operations of the Citizens Food Committee; President Truman tapped the businessman Charles Luckman to lead the committee's effort in food conservation at home and to ease severe postwar food shortages in Europe. Shortly after Helen went to work for Belding, she watched him cobroker a deal to speed U.S. grain to war-ravaged France before Soviet wheat could win hearts and baguettes. She was impressed and pleased to have a bird's-eye view. Handling the confidential memos and telegrams about world affairs certainly beat typing up the tripe churned out by two-bit gag writers.

In her unseen, Zelig-like presence, Helen was a rather privileged witness to deep national changes afoot, during and after the Eisenhower years. For one thing, advertising would gain a solid foothold in the electoral process. As he began his presidential campaign, Eisenhower worried his Republican advisors with his utter lack of telegenic charm. It was still a black-and-white world on TV, and Ike was popping up on the monitors a solid, dull gray; the only spark was his shiny bald pate, aflare in the harsh studio lights. His speeches bordered on soporific. Why not put a professional sales team on the case?

As Helen first began learning the basics of commercial persuasion at FC&B, a reluctant Ike made the first political TV spots ever, designed by the adman Rosser Reeves of the Ted Bates agency. Reeves, known as "the prince of hard sell," had previously hawked soap, toothpaste, and deodorant. He saw little difference in selling a pol, though he did convince the candidate to loosen up a bit and powder his gleaming dome. As the filming ended, Eisenhower was heard to mutter, "To think that an old soldier should come to this." A poem in *The New Yorker* lampooned this newfangled selling of the candidate: "Feeling sluggish, feeling sick, take a dose of Ike and Dick." Ike's rival Adlai Stevenson deplored "selling the presidency like cereal."

Wrestling, albeit briefly, with her Democratic upbringing, Helen switched parties to please her boss. "It was that or go underground," she reasoned. She didn't mind being Republican for a while. What did it hurt? "Other girls have embraced Zen Buddhism, the International Kite Flyers Society and World Federalists without any harm to their psyche or integrity."

Helen worked hard and never took the standard coffee breaks, but there was a great perk—relaxation and hospitality in the boss's country lodgings. Belding, soon a respectful "Mr. B" to Helen, was also somewhat of a gentleman farmer. Pauma Vista, his hilly, seventy-acre ranch beneath Palomar Mountain in San Diego County, cultivated avocados, oranges, lemons, and grapefruits, which Helen frequently brought home from weekends there. The pretty place also succored Helen during the relentless romantic tempests of the next decade. She grew comfortable in the Beldings' welcoming town and country homes and found herself at ease amid their often powerful guests.

The effects of this immersion were apparent and pleasing, especially to Helen. Those vexing gaucheries shrank in number and severity and her life skills broadened. She would learn how to take accurate dictation in a moving limo, pacify millionaire clients' bizarre (nonsexual) peccadilloés, and plan a funeral for six hundred attendees. Dispatched to meet Belding in Santa Barbara as he came ashore after the yacht races, she would be swept off in the limo by his driver, along with the boss's correspondence. Being so essential and cosseted tickled her: "I found it very romantic slipping along in the night under a fur lap robe like Marie Walewska being spirited out of Poland by Napoleon."

Helen dressed and spoke better; by sheer perseverance and some elocution lessons, the Arkansas accent had finally been hog-tied and slaughtered. Alice Belding's domestic arrangements conferred some basics missing from Cleo's slapdash ménage. Before long, Helen could distinguish a fish fork from a salad fork, a Beaujolais from a Chablis. She also knew a stock from a bond, and managed her own finances better with Mr. B's advice. Under the couple's protection and tutelage, Helen would finally feel safe. "They really cared about me," she said.

Helen relied heavily on another kind of ad hoc family, one that she had always found loyal, supportive, and loving. "Girlfriends are very important," she said—and wrote—many times. In 1949, Helen hired a new secretary for her department and welcomed her to the cubicle adjoining her own outside Don Belding's office. Charlotte Kelly was nineteen, Helen twenty-seven. They would remain the closest of confidantes for the rest of their lives. Charlotte, fun-loving and emotionally operatic, became "Carlotta" to Helen. Kelly was a pretty dark-haired woman with a "why the hell not?" worldview, an utter incapability of managing money, and a perfectly dreadful backstory.

Both women had been raised by single mothers who struggled with family tragedies and Depression-era privations, but Kelly's family history was even darker than Helen's. Growing up, she had been told that her maternal grandparents, James and Rena Ferrara, had died in a mining accident in Tonopah, Nevada, a raw, tumultuous silver town crowded with many Italian immigrants like themselves. After their deaths, Charlotte's mother, Anne Marie, their only child, was raised by relatives in Seattle. Working as a soda jerk there, Anne met and married Charles Kelly, the hard-drinking son of an oil baron; they moved to Los Angeles, where he soon abandoned Anne and their little girl, Charlotte.

Mother and daughter were very close; Anne Ferrara Kelly was a very beautiful woman who struggled to support herself and her daughter while also coping with breast cancer. Helen spent a good deal of time in their home; she admired Anne Kelly's cheer and humor in the face of adversity, something that Cleo had never managed.

The true story of the Ferraras' deaths was Wild West gothic. Anne Kelly waited until her daughter was older and her cancer recurrent and advanced to tell Charlotte the truth. There were newspaper accounts—"Murder & Suicide at Dawn"—in *The Tonopah Daily Bonanza*. On the morning of January 17, 1916, a drunken miner named Aldo Vambonie shot James and Rena Ferrara, point-blank, in their bed. James died instantly. Rena, with a bullet in her brain, survived for three days. The murderer, a jealous lover, shot himself soon after. The paper called it "the act of a drink-crazed man for the love of a woman." Snuggled in the bed beside her bleeding mother was little Anne Marie, Charlotte's mother. The child was catatonic for a year.

The two secretaries bore their pasts and made their own lives, relying heavily upon each other for support, secret sharing, and as much fun as they could manage. But on the job, Helen was known for her unwavering sobriety. Speaking of those times in a speech many years later, Kelly said, "Helen was tiny . . . frugal . . . driven . . . vulnerable to her own insecurity . . . She was also smart, talented, quietly tough, and a genius at creating opportunity." Helen didn't party with the rest of the FC&B staff at the Los Angeles Advertising Club, all-too-conveniently housed in the same building as FC&B. "I mean, it was our branch office," Kelly said. "Many of us drank and made fools of ourselves there, but never Helen . . . She was always upstairs writing copy, entering contests, or planning to visit her invalid sister via Greyhound bus."

Kelly's fiscal imprudence left her perpetually broke; relief always came from the toe of an old boot in the back reaches of Helen's closet; she squirreled away nickels, dimes, and dollar bills. Helen was saving for something; her friend had no idea what.

Despite her loftier position as executive assistant to the chairman, Helen maintained generally good relations with the other secretaries. But a small breach in the office sisterhood did lead to yet another stinging and public embarrassment for her. Just as her dateless humiliation at the sorority function had galvanized Helen toward her "sinking in" mode of snaring a man, this small event, negligible to everyone else, helped Helen score a coup that would propel her out of the secretarial rank and file forever.

Once again, it involved a slight. Helen had long made clear her dislike of engagement, wedding, and baby showers and their requisite gift buying. The giggly rituals seemed needlessly expensive and tedious and, to Helen, somewhat exclusionary. She already understood that she was not the kind of woman whom men were rushing to the altar. Yet in postwar America, women her age were marrying in a fever; many of them seemed to expect some celebration of the fact.

Having somehow offended the hostess of an upcoming shower, Helen found herself the only woman at FC&B not invited. On the night it was to be held, she stewed as everyone else covered their typewriters and carried their prettily wrapped gifts out into the bright evening. It was humiliating, galling. "I felt like the blackballed freshman of the year," she groused.

What to do for the long night alone to keep her mind off this exclusion? In her desk, there was a clipped-out questionnaire for entering *Glamour* magazine's "Ten Girls with Taste" contest. In those days, in small display type below its logo, *Glamour* tagged itself, "For the girl with a job." Helen loved the magazine, from its unusual attention to the very existence of single working women, to the cute accessories— hats, gloves, bags—that could convey a professional edge without sizable investment. How dreamy it might be, then, to be declared a Girl with Taste by her favorite publication. Yvonne Rich, then a legal secretary, had been a winner the previous year and wound up with a trip to Europe and a new wardrobe. At the time, "envy had practically unhinged me," Helen admitted, a fact Rich laughingly confirmed.

Helen would win that contest, too. She'd show them all. While her coworkers were enjoying cocktails and cooing over silk teddies, she stayed at the office for three hours, hammering out her entry. It was a yearly contest for *Glamour*. There were eight pages of questions geared to finding ten young women "of average income" who demonstrated good taste in every area of living.

Doubtless Helen did not write about the free TWA travel poster over her stove depicting a smoking-hot matador that she found "really goose-bumpy." Certainly, for the hospitality questions, she did not disclose her recipe for Chloroform Cocktails: coffee, gin or vodka, rich vanilla ice cream, and nutmeg—sometimes served with "canned sausages, piping hot." Despite the Beldings' tutelage, in some areas, she admitted, "I had the taste of an aardvark."

To her astonishment, she was chosen a semifinalist for the 1951 crop of tastemakers; she was one of seventeen women flown to New York for the final round of judging. The trip was exciting but she didn't make the cut; she was sure that having one of the Los Angeles–based judges tell her that a man Helen had been dating was a two-timing skunk had thrown her off her game a bit. But the worst part was going home and telling Yvonne that she was a loser. How it stung! Helen skipped entering the contest in 1952 but vowed to try again—and again—if she had to.

In the meantime, she continued to pay close attention to her favorite magazine's style directives. Photos of Helen at the time—cute, fairly chic, with a sleek cap of hair—bear witness to the way she put herself together in those days, favoring dresses accessorized with inexpensive but au courant little purses and hats. Lack of funds had kept her out of beauty parlors for ten years. At a time when many women around her were going blond, she kept her own hair color because it was a pretty brown. She studied *Glamour* for tips on working-girl chic, and declared it her style "bible."

Beyond wanting to win the *Glamour* contest—the prizes included a new wardrobe and a fabulous vacation—Helen's ambitions were modest. Her job had grown so absorbing that for the first few years, she never thought beyond being Mr. B's secretary. The closest she had come to "creative" input was conducting the maddening search for identical little girl twins to star in the "which twin has the Tonette?" home permanent ads. She knew from his itinerary that Belding was always on the hunt for good copywriters, but it was his habit to cast his net far beyond the home office; never would it extend to female secretaries, anywhere.

Some seeds of change were planted during a headhunting mission that took Belding to the burled and smoke-filled advertising warrens of Madison Avenue in Manhattan. He told the story himself in a written narrative included in his archived papers. His wife, Alice, accompanied him on that trip and when he came back to the hotel complaining of the weak candidates, he found her reading a stack of Helen's "while you were away" memos and telegrams. When her boss was on the road, Helen often spent the better part of her day writing and rewriting her "Dear Mr. B" missives, condensing incoming correspondence and messages and adding her own pithy commentary. Her dispatches were crackling with energy and intelligence; they flew after Belding wherever he went, often via Western Union, dropping reminders and sharp-eyed observations. Helen considered this a survival skill: "I was always able to write," she said. "The men I worked for depended on me to say exactly what they wanted to say. Memos, business letters, all sorts of correspondence. That's what kept me employed."

Alice Belding handed him one of Helen's letters that night in New York. "Read this," she said. "Don't you think she's creative? Why don't you give her a chance? You never give the women a chance in the better jobs. I think she's a better writer than some of the copywriters you've got."

Back home in California, Belding pondered, but did nothing. His wife continued to nudge. "Alice, get off the case, she's a secretary," he pleaded, until finally, he ordered the account supervisor to give Helen an assignment for a "safe" client, in a distant radio market, one that could withstand a novice attempt or two. Helen was excited, but she wasn't sure how to begin. One morning, while Yvonne Rich was in the kitchen with her baby girl, Deborah, in the high chair, she got a call from Helen. She was phoning from work, rather agitated, and got straight to the point: "What can I say about an orange?"

Helen had been assigned to help on the Sunkist account. She was desperate for a new angle on this commonplace and dimly orb. What a funny coincidence, Rich told her. "Deborah's sitting here in the high chair and she's chewing on an orange."

"The peel as well?"

"Yes, there's a lot of good in the orange peel."

"Oh, *thank* you for that!" Helen rang off quickly and plunged into research on the chemical makeup of peel and pith. *Riboflavin!*—aka vitamin B_2. She wrote it up with nutritional hosannas for the Sunkist campaign. The radio ad ran in the hinterlands of Albany and Schenectady, New York. Belding allowed Helen to work on the Sunkist account every holiday season—a prime time for citrus sales—over the next few years. But he was still too hidebound to consider a female full-time copywriter. At least the Sunkist account kept her in the game.

Hungry little Deborah got no credit for the save. In fact, Rich recalled that Helen—who had been her maid of honor—rarely even asked after the child.

"She had no use for babies at all," Rich recalled. "No interest."

The baby boom had begun on a postwar tsunami of optimism: the GI Bill was setting returning vets up with college tuition and loans for that dream cottage for two—or three. Helen's vocal antipathy toward procreation seemed almost unnatural to some of her friends. She expressed no longings of her own as her Los Angeles and Little Rock girlfriends began gestating and knitting booties. Helen was touched when Elizabeth Bilheimer named her newborn daughter after her and asked that she be the baby's godmother. Yet even pushing thirty, then considered the outer limits for a first pregnancy, Helen felt no great urge.

There was a certain low-level curiosity. She began a quiet and generally pleasurable experiment. Every now and again, she "borrowed" a little girl, the daughter of friends. The family came for dinner on Saturday nights, then left their daughter for a fun sleepover digging into Helen's closets and trying on costume jewelry. On Sundays, Helen had her "child day," taking her little surrogate to the movies, the zoo, or shopping. She did this every six months or so, until she no longer felt the desire to test the waters. Though she would stay close to the girl as she grew up, Helen concluded that she did not need or want children.

She could barely manage the most basic of pets, as Charlotte Kelly remembered it. "Helen's L.A. lifestyle could not support the four-legged kind. Her solution? Three goldfish. Their names: Foote, Cone, and Belding." Once finances permitted, Helen did accept a small, yowling ball of fur into her solitary life. A coworker gave her a male Siamese kitten. It was the first of a long line of Siamese Helen would take to heart and hearth. Indulging the same extravagance with which she named automobiles, Helen called her first kitten Semditch Paramder Mongkut—the full title of Anna's Siamese potentate in one of her most beloved musicals, *The King and I*. Helen shortened it to Spam.

She fell hard for the feisty little cat. He seemed unusually vocal and restless, even for a Siamese. Helen hoped that neutering him would quiet things down. When it seemed to be the right time for the procedure, the vet had some interesting news: there was nothing to alter. Spam suffered from cryptorchidism; his testicles remained undescended firmly inside his body, yet he still had the hormonal urge to mate, poor frustrated darling. The condition is more prevalent in purebred animals and is now corrected with surgery then unavailable to the unfortunate Spam. As a result, the handsome but perpetually horny cat grew into "a living spitfire." He howled a lot. Helen found there was little she could do to comfort her companion save to tell him over the racket, "Sex isn't everything."

Outside the FC&B office, Helen also enjoyed the camaraderie and laugh-filled gripe sessions of a ladies' lunch bunch. "Helen and I had a mutual friend, Margaret Thalken," said Yvonne Rich, who spent half a century working in Los Angeles law firms while raising her daughters. "The three of us all worked downtown. We would meet in a restaurant on Spring Street and have lunch. We always noticed what each other was wearing. I said, 'Helen, that's a beautiful red suit you have on.' Helen was small and she said, 'I got it in the children's department at the Broadway'" (a Los Angeles department store).

Buying dresses and coordinates in the children's and preteen departments was just one of Helen's inventive economies; she was an early fan of Anne Klein Junior Sophisticates. Personal grooming was a snap to manage on the cheap; she washed her hair with the powdered sweater detergent Woolite and dry-shampooed with corn meal. When she wrote to the Woolite company to praise its silky-soft effects, she was rewarded with a case of the stuff, sent gratis.

Rich said that the friends talked about men over salads and tuna sandwiches, but never in intimate ways. Some girls went all the way and some girls didn't; Helen had other friends with whom she could compare notes on foreplay techniques and postcoital etiquette. "We knew what she did but that was her business; we didn't discuss that at lunch," said Rich. "The rest of us were not doing the same thing and we just accepted that was Helen's way. There was always someone paying the bills. She often said that the man in your life should be paying for accommodations, dinner, booze."

Unmarried sex was never a taboo in Helen's mind. "Even in 1947, I knew it was okay to sleep with men and not be married to them," she said, having been reassured on that front by her first helpful therapist,

Dr. Fink. She knew that she was far from the only one having taken the plunge and did not see herself as special or unusual in that way. She enjoyed sex and saw no reason that it should be forbidden to those with a naked ring finger. It was no big deal. "I've never been a revolutionary," she said; "I was just reporting what was true for me, true for my girlfriends." Women who indulged, including Charlotte Kelly, did compare notes. There was even a low-level competitiveness on bedding the same man. "We talked a lot," Helen said. "Everybody knew who was having sex with who, and whether they enjoyed it, and I had two girlfriends who were pregnant with the same man."

They relished their liberties, but they were conscious of some potentially painful consequences. Some men did cling to the double standard, eager to leap into bed, but ultimately judging such a free-spirited woman unsuitable for marriage. Friends with serious troubles of the heart found a compassionate ear with Helen. Over dinner she would often find herself cheering up "the walking wounded." They were all so vulnerable, these young women, she recalled. She was, too; how *many* times had she let herself be hurt in the past?

Along with her professional advances, the FC&B years also bracketed the period when Helen would become both a master of sex and a prisoner of love. Heartbreak, and its attendant depressions, cycled through those years. The feeling of being cheated on or rejected, the collapse of marriage dreams, those there-goes-my-future "sads" fostered a torment Helen knew too well. There were so many clear exit ramps for men and still so few rickety stepladders up and out for the women they left behind.

The only downside of unmarried sex that seriously concerned Helen was the repercussion that Cleo had so feared for her daughters. Helen always insisted that she had never been pregnant in her life, though there had been some "scares." She saw girlfriends through abortions, frightening, excruciating affairs that generally involved a harrowing and expensive trip to a back room in Mexico. "Abortions in those days? Very serious matter," Helen recalled. "I think they cost five hundred dollars." For a working girl making anywhere from thirty-five to seventy-five dollars a week, the burden was staggering.

So astonishing was the ignorance and so great the terror that when one of Helen's roommates became pregnant she denied the possibility for some time, ignoring the pleas of Helen and their third roommate to see a doctor when she got "sicker and sicker and fatter and fatter." When she saw the doctor, she still would not admit to intercourse because she and her lover hadn't "gone to bed" to do it. The lack of sex education was flabbergasting to Helen. "Then she starting doing things to try to unload this baby. Of course, nothing did any good. She was young and healthy." The boyfriend came up with money for a Mexican abortion. They were married shortly afterward, then had two children.

There were very few happy endings like that, Helen observed. Some women would come to recover at Helen's apartment after their abortions; a girlfriend should be pampered and monitored as she recovered and cheered up as best her hostess could manage. Helen observed that the risk, pain, and fright of the procedure itself nearly always gave way to a tremendous sadness afterward, despite the relief of having it over with. If you were caring for a young woman who was so "wounded," as Helen put it, it was best to listen and not advise too much. Nearly always the man involved vaporized, though sometimes he paid for the procedure. But from what Helen had seen, he would never, ever be there to buoy the woman up in the aftermath of the abortion.

This was her mission, and she took it seriously. As the sad-eyed ladies reclined on her sofa, Helen refused to utter that unhelpful cliché "You'll be better off without him." She understood that they absolutely did not want to hear that—not right then as they bled and grieved but often still hoped the relationship would survive. She would tell them this: "You've got to go on with your life. This is so *horrible*, you don't want any more of this, you can't take any more of this . . ."

Through it all, her boss was an amused witness and sometimes father confessor for the many affairs. If Helen needed a few days in Mexico to recover from her latest romantic upheaval, Mr. B would generally give her the time off. Belding himself, wittingly or not, was the conduit for Miss Gurley's sexual dalliance with members of an impressive military delegation bivouacked at the Beverly Hills Hotel.

"I'm going to give you to the boys tomorrow," the boss told Helen after General Omar Bradley had arrived in Los Angeles with three military aides, two from the army and one navy man. The war hero was in town to deliver a speech on Armed Forces Day, May 19, 1951, at the Los Angeles Memorial Coliseum, a venue that seated more than a hundred thousand. Belding had a hand in planning the general's itinerary, giving a lavish party for Bradley and his entourage and offering any other services he might need. "It'll be fun for you to go out there and pal around," Mr. B told Helen. Her boss kindly made his car and driver and his secretary available to the general for the duration of his stay in Los Angeles. During that call to duty, there was a good deal of covert action that Helen never alluded to in her books.

The event at the Los Angeles Coliseum was to be, Helen understood, "a pretty goddamned big speech," and the military aides huddled with Bradley at his bungalow to hone the text. Miss Gurley mostly sat poolside with the brass, sipping cold drinks and chatting. Bradley had been much in the news as a top advisor to the Truman administration on whether, in the wake of Hiroshima, the United States should pursue development of "the Super," or hydrogen bomb. As the head of Truman's Joint Chiefs of Staff, Bradley had told the president that "it would be intolerable" to let the Russians perfect that nuclear trump card first. Truman respected Bradley tremendously; going ahead with the "H bomb," if only as a deterrent, was one of the commander in chief's first momentous decisions in office. The green light had come in January 1950, securing Bradley's status as a Cold War hero.

"It was pretty heady stuff," Helen said of kibitzing with these much-decorated guardians of freedom. But there was some serious business to attend to for Mr. B's secretary. With only an hour and a half before Bradley was set to stand and deliver, Helen sat down to type his just-completed speech on a strange bit of equipment that had been delivered to the bungalow. She had never used an electric typewriter. Panicked, she could not make that strange, perplexing beast do her bidding. It hummed; it threw its own carriage back with shocking force and stuttered at the merest touch . . . *kkkkkkkkk*. There were so many strike-overs, the speech looked as if it had been redacted by a government censor. Helen slumped over the machine, defeated. In a soothing chorus, the general's men murmured: "Don't worry your pretty head about it."

A hotel typist competent on the newfangled machine got the job done in a trice. For the light chores during the remainder of their visit, Helen borrowed a manual typewriter for some correspondence work. In the evenings, when Bradley retired for the night in the bungalow, his two army aides slipped out surreptitiously on alternate evenings to entertain Miss Gurley. She swore that neither knew about the other's dalliance. Army people were *very* heterosexual, she declared—at least the ones she knew. Both men were married and able to effect military-quality secrecy around their trysts. Somehow, Bradley's naval officer aide seemed immune to Miss Gurley's charms.

Helen's relationships with these military men opened yet another portal. She learned that even if men didn't buy you "prezzies," they certainly could take you places and open your eyes to things you might not dream of. An alliance with a powerful man could afford one world travel, a keener perspective, sophistication, and the considerable excitements of being present at the edges of . . . well, history.

Of those two aides to Bradley, the one Helen came to care deeply for was Chester "Ted" Clifton, Jr. Just the month before he arrived in Los Angeles, Clifton, along with Paul Nitze, director of policy for Truman's State Department, had drafted the letter relieving General Douglas MacArthur of his command, at Truman's request. Omar Bradley signed it. Clifton was soon promoted to major general and went on to serve with the army's European command in Paris. He later became senior military aide and communications officer for Presidents John F. Kennedy and Lyndon B. Johnson; Clifton was in the Dallas motorcade the day JFK was assassinated. The general remained as military aide to Johnson until 1965.

Clifton had been such glorious fun, and the perks were grand on the gold-braided arm of government expense accounts. For years, once Helen began traveling for business, Clifton would meet her anywhere: New York, Rome, Washington, Paris, Kansas City—even Little Rock if Helen happened to be making a visit home to Cleo and Mary. She had far less of a relationship with Willis Matthews, the second Bradley aide

("I didn't like him much"), but she agreed to meet him in Little Rock on another occasion and teased him unto madness at first; he chased her clear around the hotel. Having thoroughly enjoyed their fox hunt, she surrendered, explaining that it felt fabulous for a man to "have the hots," to be so out of his mind for you that even the H bomb could not distract him mid-mission. In recalling those military lovers, Helen said that she learned *very* early to be *very* good in bed. She had also learned to talk dirty. Herman Citron, the MCA agent, had coached her. She wondered whether other girls did that. They ought to try it, really.

Here was the silly little secret, a hard-won fact that finally conferred a certain confidence and satisfaction upon the girl who always considered herself "not pretty enough." Certainly, men love beautiful women. But when the lights went out, Miss Universe might just as well be the poor, sooty little match girl if she couldn't make him shout hallelujah. Helen's proof? Many of her men, like the generals, kept on coming back. She was discreet with all of her married lovers but never was she apologetic about the joys of those liaisons. Even as a long-married woman she would declare, somewhat wistfully, "I don't think there's anything like mistress or unmarried sex."

Nonetheless, the little girl who had withstood so many ugly jolts in a household of breathtaking insecurities had seen enough to make a crucial distinction between her two great loves: men and work. Sex and romance were too damned unpredictable. A girl couldn't depend on anything. She could be sweet and adorable and sexy, yet still something would happen to ruin it all.

The workplace, despite its ups and downs, was a far safer bet.

"Business I could rely on. It never went away and left you. It was not capricious. It did not go out with another girl. If you did good, it would do good by you."

10

How Ever Did She Do It?

> She is a *feeling* being. She is completely aware of her own longings—
> to be needed, to be reassured that she is attractive and desirable, to
> belong intimately somewhere to someone. She is all Woman. And
> probably her greatest—and most uncomfortable—womanly virtue is
> her lack of pretense about it.
>
> —from a job evaluation of the copywriter Helen Gurley, done for
>   Foote, Cone & Belding

ON A FROSTY EVENING IN JANUARY 1953, the hotel guest Miss Helen
Gurley, wearing only a silky petticoat beneath her heavy topcoat, left
the Waldorf Astoria in Manhattan and walked as far as Penn Station, a
bit over fifteen blocks away. Her heels clicked a rapid staccato; it was
too cold for a languid sashay. Years earlier, she had seen Betty Grable
do something just as impetuous in a movie. Helen thought it would be
fun. She was stunned to find that New York in January is not the back
lot of 20th Century Fox in July. As numbness and good sense set in,
she scurried back to the hotel for some beauty sleep "in order to look
ravishing the next day" for long hours before a panel of *Glamour* magazine judges. She had entered the contest for the second time, and again,
she was flown to New York as a finalist.

Three months later, the discernment and sophistication of the
executive secretary Helen Marie Gurley was trumpeted in newspapers
from Los Angeles to New York, Little Rock to Honolulu. On her second
try, Helen was chosen to be one of "Ten Girls with Taste." There had

been nearly thirty-nine thousand entries, the largest field ever, according to the story in the *Arkansas Gazette*. The paper also reported that Miss Gurley, daughter of Mrs. W. L. Bryan of Osage, "wins a two week trip to San Francisco and Hawaii as guest of Glamour and a complete vacation wardrobe to be selected especially for her trip and presented by the Joseph Magnin store in San Francisco."

How ever did she do it? How, among nearly forty thousand aspirants from sea to sea, plenty of them from top-drawer colleges and proper, gingham-curtained Colonial homes and golfing, bridge-playing parents, did Helen Marie Gurley pull it off?

Hers was a very savvy and determined campaign. Helen might indeed have wowed the judges in person. Some of them may have met her when she was a finalist on her first try. The photograph submitted with Helen's application was no amateur snap. She scored a coup in having her portrait made by the celebrity photographer John Engstead in a pose worthy of his usual subjects: Bette Davis, Joan Crawford, Marilyn Monroe. Engstead was a talented conjurer of womanly glam; he shot for *Vogue*, *Life*, and *Mademoiselle*, and he knew how to sell a Look. He posed the contestant Gurley seated, in semi-profile, with one elegantly gloved hand raised toward her flowered hat and the other caressing Spam, nestled regally on her lap. She declared it "the photograph that helped me win."

Helen's account of filling out the *Glamour* contest questionnaire shows an early talent for scanning, parsing, and reconfiguring popular culture signifiers in a way that beamed straight to a target audience—in this case, the tastemaker doyennes of women's magazines. As she answered the questions, the girl who had long struggled to "pass" as not poor and not *too* terribly gauche took very close notice of the turn of a collar, as well as the style and syntax favored by aspirational magazine copy.

What is a typical outfit you wear to work? (She made one up from studying fashion pages.) How would you entertain four people for dinner? (Since she had never done so, she conjured a sumptuous spread by poring over the food sections of *Ladies' Home Journal*.) What is your philosophy of life? (She cobbled herself an ethos from having listened to many five-minute *This I Believe* radio broadcasts; Edward R. Murrow hosted that hugely popular motivational series in the early fifties.)

Perhaps the clincher was the high note of compassion chiming above the food and fashion burble in her winning entry. *Glamour* cited this passage: "Helen believes that good taste 'starts with that most basic commodity—one's own self—and extends outward to speech, clothes and possessions. It reaches its supreme station . . . in kindness to another human being.'"

Helen Gurley could sling it.

That August, Mr. Cyril Magnin pinned a corsage on Helen at the San Francisco airport before she was whisked off to his department store to be fitted for her vacation togs. Then it was off to Hawaii. Helen took in blazing Waikiki sunsets on the veranda of the rosy pink Royal Hawaiian Hotel. She posed for bathing beauty photo ops with Diamond Head in the background and island-hopped to Maui. There was also some activity unplanned by the good women at *Glamour*. General Bradley's third aide, the navy man who had somehow resisted Miss Gurley's charms, was then stationed in Hawaii. They managed a little reunion.

After a week's R&R, Helen sailed back to Los Angeles, tanned and triumphant, aboard the *Lurline*, the venerable and luxurious Pacific liner that had ferried Amelia Earhart and her small plane across the ocean toward their fateful flight. Helen savored every minute, but as ever, she did not, would not forget the snub that set it all in motion. "It was all quite princessy," she allowed, "but it started with loneliness, a Remington with a new ribbon and lots of hours to kill."

Shortly after she returned from Hawaii, Helen learned that Mary Campbell, the personnel director at *Glamour*'s parent company, Condé Nast, had phoned Don Belding and strongly suggested he give Miss Gurley a try at copywriting; her contest entry was impressive with its essay on the values of women's professional organizations. Like Miss Campbell, women achievers recognized something in Helen Gurley, a steely aspirational drive belied by the soft voice and habitual "little me" dissembling.

Don Belding was finally convinced. When notice of the promotion to copywriter went to the company personnel office, Helen was called in and questioned closely. Did she want to leave a nice, secure secretarial post for something she might just fail at? As if Helen, on her umpteenth secretarial job, could not find another. Yes, she told the man, she really, really wanted to try. Helen got her own office with her name on the door. Her first big account was to be Catalina swimsuits. Helen installed Charlotte Kelly as Belding's new secretary. Unencumbered by any "daddy" feelings about her new boss, Kelly embarked on an affair with him. Her only reservation, she confided to Helen, was that the much older Mr. B might be called to Glory during their exertions.

Once Helen moved out of the twin cubicle and into her own office, she got herself to another therapist, immediately. "I was utterly terrified," she wrote. "Though I could afford just one half-hour session a week, a patient, adorable psychiatrist used to prop me up and spoonfeed me my ego ration every Saturday morning until I'd begun to score a few points in my new job."

At thirty-one, Helen had come to know her own frailties. During her twenties and thirties and on into the years of her greatest successes, she suffered from colitis and sudden outbreaks of hives after physical activity, ailments long thought to be aggravated by stress. She found that Pyribenzamine, a first-generation antihistamine prescribed for the hives, also made her drowsy enough to help with the frequent insomnia that resulted from nighttime anxieties. She would use it for forty years, until it was no longer manufactured. More than two decades after the onset of these maladies, Helen self-diagnosed her digestive torments: "I did get the colitis, which I have to this day, from worrying about money."

She also recognized her cyclical lapses into almost paralyzing bouts of hypochondria. After all, she had seen the ravages of polio and cancer at very close hand. "Every year I go through this psychosomatic fit which seems to involve X-Rays," she complained in her early thirties. She confessed to having convinced herself that she had "tuberculosis, acute appendicitis or a big fat tumor." In sultry weather, once thought to be an incubator, she imagined "a touch of polio." Despite the costs, ranging from ten to fifty-five dollars a visit, she took herself off to specialists and always received a clean bill of health. She called it her expensive relief. Even Don Belding had learned to recognize the onsets of her maladies, real and imagined, and kindly bundled her straight to a doctor with his driver, William.

Through it all, talking things out was her remedy of first choice. She understood that the root cause for most of these afflictions was her susceptibility to paralyzing anxiety. Having been raised during the Depression in a family home suffused with fear, she lived with this undermining surety: *Something can always happen to ruin everything.* Fear would trail her like a slinking pariah dog, just lying in wait to tear into her success, her solvency, her hopes for a truly loving man. For the ensuing half century, psychotherapy was the flaming torch that kept the beast at bay.

She also realized that there was much to congratulate herself for. Though she would also work on the rather dowdy Stauffer System weight loss campaigns—and win awards for her copy—the Catalina account had it all: glamour, celebrity, travel, and prestige. It got Helen out of the office a good deal, to the client's offices and on photo shoots. Humphrey Bogart allowed Helen's creative team to photograph their clothes on his yacht, the *Santana*—owing, Helen was sure, to the machinations of Mrs. Bogart, Lauren Bacall, who cast a keen eye toward the freebies for the entire family. Bogie was genial and obliging, donning a Catalina sport shirt for the ad.

Helen was game. She clambered on slippery rocks with Dixie cups of bourbon to warm model mermaids as they flopped their tails and shivered in the dawn mists of Malibu. She hauled supplies, spare swimsuits, and props along the mile trail in from the Pacific Coast Highway. The conditions were far more hospitable when shooting at the sumptuous Neptune Pool in William Randolph Hearst's boundless pleasure dome, San Simeon; there was even a surprise meeting with Hearst himself as he and his family arrived to stay in the lordly "bungalow" on the estate.

Helen was apprehensive when Catalina suggested she get some re-tail immersion. That meant barnstorming fifty department stores na-tionwide with the company's Trade Relations Service team as Catalina rolled out its newest line. The swimsuit selling period was a tight two months; close vigilance over the hits and poor performers was essen-tial. Helen knew it would be a brutal grind, hitting a store or two a day for a month, talking to buyers, sales clerks, and customers from nine to nine. Having soldiered through it, she wrote up the value of her so-journ in the retail trenches for a trade magazine, *Western Advertising*, in an article titled "Four Weeks Behind the Counter." She sold suits herself in thirty stores. Some days, it was murder: "The Alamo looked pretty good after I'd squeezed a size 16 into several size twelves (she insisted)."

Less exhausting but deeply annoying was Helen's stewardship of the long-stemmed Hillevi Rombin, a Swedish beauty crowned Miss Universe for 1955. The Miss Universe franchise had begun three years earlier as a local "bathing beauty" contest sponsored by Catalina in Long Beach. After winning her title, Rombin was sent on a department store tour to model the company's suits. Chaperoning a natural beauty like Miss Rombin through the backwaters of Milwaukee and Duluth was hardly an ego-boosting exercise for Helen. "When there were men in the same room I felt like I'd become part of the furniture," she crabbed. When unencumbered by Norse goddesses or tweedy product managers, Helen would often meet lovers in far-flung cities. Let *their* expense accounts foot the bill for the Chateaubriand if she could bank her FC&B meal per diem; out of habit, she also hoarded hotel soaps, stole towels, and deftly padded expenses wherever she could.

It was sometime during this period in the early to mid-1950s that Helen took a deep breath and ventured where no twentieth-century Gurley had ever gone. She quietly borrowed five hundred dollars from Alice Belding and took herself to Europe, alone and clueless, for the first time. She was tentative and frightened when she set foot in London, but she managed not to commit too many tourist faux pas on the Continent. There was an impractically high heel caught in some cobblestones, a mortifying pratfall, no harm done. Why, it was plain, perfectly reasonable frugality that made her fall out of a bidet and onto the WC floor like a wet flounder in her cheap lodgings at London's Green Park Hotel ("$4 a night with crepe paper curtains"). Helen discovered that the strange porcelain fixture had the same hot water one had to pay a maid a shilling (then fifty cents) to fill a whole bathtub with down the hall. Those tubs were "large enough to wash a Nash Rambler," and it cost a tidy sum to fill one. Why *not* try to fold herself into that warm, frothing source for free? Even after the unfortunate flop, Helen washed her hair in the bidet; she couldn't get her head under the sink tap. But oh, such nice linen sheets everywhere . . . no extra charge.

It is possible to travel along with that game American girl in Paris— and in Madrid, Venice, Florence, Rome, Nice, Monte Carlo, Positano, and a few more breathtaking perches along the Amalfi Coast. Pages from a stenographer's notebook, doubtless pinched from the supply closet at FC&B, chart Helen's bold and often harrowing solo adventure; she also wrote of the trip in some of her books. Her commentary veers between Lucille Ball and Colette. In between the scrawled calculations for currency exchange and ferry departures, the journey spools out. Here, in her own breathless style, an interpretive re-creation of Helen Marie Gurley's very first Continental tour:

Paris. Stunning. But so lonely.

A little sad.

Exactement, tristesse! *It would all be better with a lover. Still, she is undone by the beauty, knocked out by the art, maddened anew by Gallic plumbing.*

But here he is! Helen has arranged the briefest rendezvous with General Ted Clifton in Paris; he is on NATO business, or something like that. He has swept her from the low-rent Normandie hotel to the sumptuous Plaza Athénée. Cinderella creeps back to her thrifty garret at dawn. Dinner at the Tour D'Argent. Bliss . . . but then a whole day to kill alone; he is a busy man. They take in a high-class strip show; such tight, heavenly bodies on these French girls . . .

The military caravan moves on.

Alone again. And in the streets, the eyes have it. Men's eyes are on her everywhere. She can hardly write fast enough; there are scrawled exclamations that conjure the raw male hunger of Tennessee Williams's Suddenly, Last Summer—*that moment when Elizabeth Taylor emerges from the sea all but naked in a wet white swimsuit:* The men! The men! So many hungry eyes. A horde of locusts, *Helen thinks.*

Why is it a nice girl can actually like the wrong kind of attention? Why?

She feels their bold stares, marvels at the brazen stalking from glove store to kiosk to café. Then, a train south to Monte Carlo, where she is sweetly touched by Lady Luck in a casino, winning a quick five hundred dollars. She can pay Alice Belding back, pronto.

Florence! What a knockout. The Duomo. The men.

She gives herself a hard talking-to:

You are after what, *Helen Marie?*

Romance? Fortune? Both?

Here are more men, murmuring to her in blunt, task-specific English. Goddamn them all for their rote, class-conscious pick-up lines:

'Scusi. Are you a college woman from Smith or Wellesley? Do you study here?

Goddamn them! They can tell she is not like those other girls on their Continental tour, of course they can. They know bloody well she isn't studying Renaissance painting at Barnard.

When she dares, she looks hard at them, too. She knows what they are after, but for heaven's sake—at home, no one would even look. But every man in Florence seems . . . interested. She does not miss the bland and dismissive American male faces. Basta!

These men as lovers?

They ply a well-honed art of seduction, as though a woman is a piece of clay to be patted and smoothed. Is she in some sort of swoon? Let's be fair; it is a heady thing for a woman, not a ravishing beauty, to be so relentlessly pursued.

Still, a girl feels conned. Used, yes. Of course. How they lie, bold and guiltless as six-year-olds caught stealing candy. Sure he's "never done this before with anyone." He only wants to do it to you, cara mia. *Oh please.*

Please do.

When it's over? No sentiment, no promises. You will be missed no more than the sweet pastry consumed three days ago.

There she sits in her budget rooms with their worn chenille spreads and million-dollar views, a small thin face in the window, taking her own measure with the keener sextant of the solitary voyager. Perhaps she has never felt freer. On October 13, there will be a morning flight to New York. She is thinking of her return and the all too familiar vistas.

American men do not have mouths like succulent grapes.

They are clumsier.

She still does not understand bidets.

Arrivederci!

Alice Belding got her five hundred dollars back; work reassumed its place as the main adventure for forty-nine weeks a year. The performance evaluation of Helen that FC&B commissioned from a Colorado research firm limned a dogged perfectionism, obsessive attention to detail, and the willingness to undertake grunt work among her virtues. It is clear that she spoke her mind to the interviewer(s), who noted: "She is just as charming and responsive as we thought. She loves everything about her job situation. However, she feels she could handle more assignments and would like to earn more money, for the family drain on her finances is quite severe. Moreover, it is very important for her to feel she is accomplishing something—going somewhere—that her life is not at a dead end."

Call it frankness, oversharing, or the product of so much therapeutic introspection; Helen would retain the habit of "going deep," in workplace and public discussions, sometimes with startling non sequiturs that pulled the conversation toward highly personal matters. So it was with this interview. It is also apparent that she volunteered her thoughts on office fraternization. Helen was never able or willing to separate sexual longing from the workplace, declaring years later that with the exception of her years at *Cosmo*, "I have never worked *anywhere*—and I've worked a lot of anywheres—without being sexually involved with *somebody* in the office."

As a copywriter, the evaluator concluded, Helen understood exactly how to reach her chiefly female audience for swimsuits and weight loss programs: "With a subjective, feminine, intuitive sensitivity; most certainly not with rational, objective, or even very communicable logic."

Translation: Well done, little lady—however you pull it off.

Helen was hot professionally, winning awards for her campaigns, including three "Lulu" statuettes, awarded for the best copywriting by advertising women on the West Coast. Some of her most valuable endorsements were from clients who responded to the way Helen presented her copy. Often in pitch meetings, clients requested, "Get Gurley to read it!"

Feeling somewhat established in her new career, Helen decided that it was time to transform her poky little dwelling. She had a bit of mad money put aside from the *Glamour* contest, and she had exercised another of her wily fiscal ploys to add to the nest egg. In her earlier dating days, she would pay off a cabbie and hop out once the taxi drove out of sight of the date who gave her carfare. Helen would then catch a bus home and pocket the difference. This time, she had pulled off that old switcheroo on a grander scale by exchanging her first-class ticket for one in coach when flying to New York for the *Glamour* judging.

Having the enchanting career-girl apartment, a stage setting for seduction and socializing, would be a longed-for and affirming accomplishment. She simply had no idea how to pull it off. So how exactly might one so untutored furnish what her magazine would later call a "Man Trap"? She was able to tap the talents of two useful men in her "stable," in this case a gay couple she called Mark and Schuyler. She was entranced by how they had transformed their odd, twenty-by-fifty-foot apartment—$62.50 a month—in a "rabbit hutchy" old building in Beverly Hills into what she described as "a corner of Versailles."

The gentlemen pruned and purged; they banished a hideous faded davenport to the care of a more desperate friend. So, too, went the red and chartreuse flowered chairs. Those irredeemably tacky gewgaws?

Gone, sweetie, to the land of things that should not even be *given* away. The fate of the sizzling toreador poster is unknown. A color scheme emerged: moss green, hot pink, and white; that saucy palette would be reproduced endlessly in *Cosmo*'s home décor features. "Over the year, a few dollars and a few deeds at a time, the boys stole, cajoled, borrowed, coaxed, begged, painted and polished my apartment into something pretty terrific," she concluded. To her astonishment, she found herself house-proud in mad, midcentury Los Angeles. "People talked about that apartment," she crowed. "It brought me great pleasure."

Once the lair was completed and the stage set, the action chez Gurley was nonstop. There were Sunday brunches. The Chloroform Cocktails flowed freely; on occasion, Helen called them London Fogs, which sounded a tad more upscale. Bold imbibing was encouraged ("Piffle to the guest who drinks Puritanical highballs even at brunch"). Canned sausages were served, along with canned cling peaches heated and goosed with orange peel, cinnamon, and a maraschino cherry. Having few culinary referents, Helen looked to Irma S. Rombauer's classic, *The Joy of Cooking*. Sometimes she surrendered to the heavily sauced and syruped postwar fare served up by the test kitchens of women's magazines, which were then cozying up with burgeoning American food conglomerates. Entrees and desserts were built with white bread, American cheese, instant pudding mix, and canned cream of mushroom soup. Along with this chemical banquet there was Sunday revelry as well; sometimes Helen gave dancing lessons. She deemed her early to mid-thirties "my really popular era."

Her romantic flings effervesced, cooled, and sometimes collided. Some of the most rewarding affairs conferred experiential rather than material gain and drew Helen far from her comfort zone. In most cases, it was a good thing. But she must have been insane, she reasoned later, to have sat steadying the controls of a rickety little plane on the ground while its private pilot, Freddy, a smitten Swiss import at FC&B, tried to restart it by twirling the propeller. They flew often on weekends. Whenever they found themselves aloft and lost, Freddy bounced the little plane down on remote airstrips. Helen hopped out and ran to get directions; if Freddy turned the engine off it might not restart. As they flew slowly and ever so low, she watched the desert scud by below—they practically skimmed the cactus tops—as they putt-putted toward Vegas for a weekend.

Freddy was on his way to becoming very rich, but he was not marriage material. He had a wife back in Zurich. Helen didn't care; she was having too much fun. The fearless and handsome young Swiss opened her eyes to places she thought she knew by then, including Los Angeles and New York. He availed himself of the cities' offerings in huge gulps and insisted she partake. On a trip to Manhattan, he took Helen to the Statue of Liberty and to the classic Broadway plays *South Pacific* and *A Streetcar Named Desire*. Dear Freddy even escorted her to the three Bs of the city's fashion-forward: Bendel's, Bergdorf's, and Bonwit Teller. Out west, he propelled her toward natural wonders, among them the Grand Canyon and the staggeringly lush wildflower bloom in the desert at Palm Springs. Looking back, Helen admired his capacity for wonder. Freddy certainly showed his committed career woman what it might be like to fully embrace one's joie de vivre.

"I never really got it," she confessed. "I was too busy working. Always have been."

And yet . . .

Other men also gifted her with indelible moments of joy, not all of them horizontal. On her own in the Eternal City, Helen had stood in piazzas awhirl with beautiful young Romans on motorbikes; she longed to experience the Vespa transports of *la dolce vita*. She told a young man in a glove shop that she would just *adore* a ride on his machine. He set Helen and her shopping bags on the back of his scooter and they rode all day through the fabled Seven Hills, the marketplaces. With her arms wound tightly around this "darling Italian boy," she found herself at the Colosseum at twilight as a light drizzle glazed that cruel architectural wonder. She declared that day, in all its gorgeous, reckless whimsy, one of the best of her life—and she did *not* sleep with the man.

When it came to male conquests, Helen was feeling what she called "the power." By her early thirties, she felt that she had reached the peak of her sexual prowess. She reminisced in *Having It All*: "I remember splendid years of slipping out of the Beverly Hills Hotel at dawn to pick up Appletrees, my fourteen-year-old Buick station wagon (parked on a side street because she really wasn't up to being seen at the Beverly Hills Hotel porte-cochere), feeling as alive as an eel from having been at it all night with a New York friend I had a long liaison with, and another time leaving a lover at the Plaza Athénée in Paris to taxi across town in rumpled red chiffon to my eight-dollar-a-night room at the Normandie, loved senseless . . ."

Clifton, Freddy . . . Affairs sometimes "overlapped," she noted in a whopping understatement. Sometimes she and Charlotte had a tag team going; Clifton also had a fling with the vivacious Miss Kelly. As it happened, there was an artistic rendering of Helen's surging sexual wattage that survived those days. She had a brief affair with an art director at FC&B, a sweet, talented man who seemed quite ardent. He was distressed, at first, to arrive at her apartment one day and find two other men already visiting. Then he got over it and began working on a comic tribute to Miss Gurley's puissance as the siren of Bonnie Brae Street. The artwork, Lyn Tornabene recalled, was framed and hung in the bathroom of the Browns' Park Avenue apartment. It was a rendering of Helen's apartment building, with men hanging from the rafters, men falling out windows. The stairway was clogged with men; the street outside was beset by a traffic jam of suitors. Two women stood outside the building, taking in the mayhem. The caption had one saying to the other, "I think her name is Helen Gurley."

As is often the plotline of bodice-ripping romance novels, a blackguard had her heart all along. He tossed, dribbled, and drop-kicked it mercilessly over eight tumultuous years. Helen wrote about him in a number of her memoirs and in several guises; he appears in *Sex and the Single Girl* as two different offenders. She may have monetized some of the heartache in print, but none of the published works capture the raw pain, the wrenching scenes, and the deep psychological torments that emerge in her conversations with Lyn Tornabene.

The villain is nearly always referred to as Don Juan; only once did Helen tell Tornabene his full name. In other writings she called him "Bill," "W.G.," or "Willie." He was in the advertising business, the creative director at a smaller agency. Given the many coy discrepancies and disguises over the years, he will appear herein as DJ.

He was "a real sex man," Helen declared. He was also a Wow. She likened him to a Greek god, lordly at six feet plus, with a sensual Dionysian countenance beneath black, curly hair. He was two years older than Helen; she was twenty-nine when they met. She said that he was very, very good in bed. At first she was so besotted that she didn't see the signs that he was a serial heartbreaker. But the man was sick. *Sick, sick, sick.*

By Helen's description, DJ could have been a two-button, single-vent, white-shirted prototype for the advertising executive Don Draper, the dark, driven swordsman in the TV series *Mad Men*. Both wreaked serial, unrepentant, idiosyncratic hell on women. It took a while, but Helen came to realize that it pleasured DJ greatly to have her know that there were other women, many, in his life, to constantly "stick the shiv in," as she put it.

"He was very romantic, the most romantic man you could possibly ever hope for in your whole life. I wanted to marry him, he would come back to me after a hiatus with the flowers, a Brooks Brothers shirt, the pen that says, 'I have grey hair, brown eyes and a black heart.' It was this wonderful sterling silver pen that he would have made. It was so cute. And rotten to the core. He would come back and he would say, 'Okay, we're going to be together, if everything goes well, we'll get married.' Idiot! I fell for it about three different times. He'd come back, we'd be in trouble, we'd break up again."

She began to see how carefully he planned his tortures. A cuter, much younger lover showed up banging on his apartment door while Helen was in his bed; gee, he'd thought that girl was still in Europe. He left letters from his other women where she could find them. Helen, a scant AA cup, did *not* need to know, from snooping into one steamy missive, that he had named a New York girlfriend's generous breasts "Liebchen" and "Schatzi." He bought gifts for his harem in multiples— Brooks Brothers oxford cloth shirts, pens from the popular silversmith Allan Adler—monogrammed for each. One Christmas, Helen saw stacks of these gifts in his apartment, marked for different women. DJ did not deny his philandering but calmly explained the gifts to other women as necessary expiations. Of course she was the One.

Psychopath. Sadist. Egotist. Pretentious ass. She knew him to be all of those things. And yet there she was, hopeful and compliant. If he went out, she prowled his apartment with the intensity of a hungry badger, sniffing and pawing for signs of betrayal. Helen judged herself "a purebred masochist," tormenting herself by snooping in DJ's fat, loose-leaf address book for entries penned with different-color inks—new girls were generally in blue or green. Fittingly, Helen's entries were jotted down in mournful purple.

To everyone else, and often to Helen, DJ was charming and funny. He was an openhanded spender: champagne by the case, mad weekends in Mexico and Hawaii. His exes stayed in his life, to the consternation of those still "in play." He acted the gallant, seeing women through their divorces, even squiring one of Helen's friends to a Mexican abortion. He gave the women financial advice, asked about their mothers . . . their pets! Many of his conquests had been very wealthy, a fact he often mentioned to Helen, making her feel like "a nothingburger." DJ extolled his ex-wife, her beauty, her Cordon Bleu cooking, her perfect ease as a hostess. Most cruelly, he belittled the thing that gave Helen the most self-esteem, her so-called career. Beginning way back with her Sunkist orange debut, he was patronizing, sometimes mocking about her ad copy, as though she were a little girl playing at a big man's game. They were the lowest of blows, and, coming from a successful pro, the jabs went deep.

Charlotte Kelly took Helen's sobbing phone calls, tended her on "healing" weekends at the Beldings' ranch, and tried to be supportive when she kept going back to her demon lover. "It was painful to watch and share," Kelly wrote. "I finally spoke. 'Helen, if you do not put some distance between yourself and this man, you're going to flip out.' She agreed and retreated to Mexico for 10 days. The problem was, she took him with her."

Though Helen's published accounts of his psychological abuse were leavened with self-deprecating humor, she confessed some serious anger issues. Her scenes with DJ became operatic and more frequent. When a blond model walked by their table at the Santa Ynez Inn and greeted DJ, Helen poured a pitcher of water over his head in a spasm of jealousy. Objects began to fly and shatter; she threw a pitcher of icy gimlets, she hurled shoes, papers, books, but never an ashtray—she didn't want to *hurt* him! Finding a letter in his glove compartment, she screamed at him, "You're seeing your wife again!" She took his car, parked it at the edge of the ocean, and refused to tell him where it was for three days. She sobbed, shrieked, and pleaded, sometimes for hours, to the point where only chugging a quart of milk could ease the hiccuping frenzy. DJ reveled in it; the more intense her agitation, the greater turn-on it was for him. His voice became calmer and sexier as he tried to soothe her.

Silly girl . . .

She came to realize that her unseemly meltdowns were DJ's "Academy Awards." Duly rewarded, he performed the role of cad with increasing élan. As Helen saw it, she was a prisoner of sex. "Whatever the emotional problems, I feel still that sex is such a dynamic incredible happening that your brains go bye-bye if you're mad about this person. You can't be sensible, you can't say, 'Well, I'll just sleep with him but I'll go have somebody else who's nice. I'll marry somebody else and I'll keep this person as a playmate.' You can't do that. If you're sexually zonked, that's it. That's *it*."

Zonked she remained. She left DJ many times over those eight years, sometimes for six months at a time. She found pleasure, if not solace, in other men's arms. She had plenty of other beaux, "from Holly Golightly's super rats to soft, marshmallowy fellows that mothers would approve of." The dalliance with the military men was during one such hiatus from DJ. So, too, was one of her more lighthearted and most public affairs. It was encouraged by none other than Don Belding, who thought it good for business. Helen called it an office romance. The prizefighter Jack Dempsey, a likable palooka, was endorsing Bulldog Beer, the product of an FC&B client, Acme Brewing Company.

The sportswriter Damon Runyon dubbed Dempsey the "Manassa Mauler" for the small Mormon town in Colorado he hailed from, as well as for the ferocity he displayed in the ring. Dempsey had an eighth-grade education and had been a cowboy and a miner before he made a phenomenal living with his fists. In 1926, Dempsey's championship match with the challenger Gene Tunney took up two-thirds of *The New York Times*' front page, as well as most of pages two through seven in the main section. The bout, which Dempsey lost by unanimous decision, paid him an unheard of $850,000—worth about $11.3 million today. Helen was four at the time of that heavyweight title match; meeting him long after those glory days, she declared him a "super stud," still strong and rather voluble in the clinch. When close to the Moment, he was given to shouting, "Straighten me out, darling!" Said Helen, "Presumably, I did."

Such a couple, bearlike Dempsey, sixty-two, and tiny Helen, thirty-one, prompted some good-natured ribbing. Perhaps they needed an interpreter to speak to each other, wags suggested. The fact was, Helen later noted, both she and Dempsey shared a tunnel-your-way-up background, and they got along just fine. Helen and her prizefighter were together for nearly a year. Dempsey squired her to Chasen's, that clubby Beverly Boulevard canteen where the clientele—Sinatra! Bogie! Hitchcock!—was as hot as its famous chili. At the Mocambo club, Helen was elated to show off her best moves on the sizzling-est dance floor in town. She adored being at the center of it all—showbiz, at last! Flash-bulbs haloed the Champ when he was out on the town; on Dempsey's mighty arm, Helen was popping up in the gossip columns, though most often as "unidentified brunette."

In time, the affair petered out. Helen complained of the meager leavings: a silk lounging outfit worth a couple of hundred dollars, bought in Las Vegas. Dempsey still had a healthy income from his eponymous restaurant in Manhattan as well as the Bulldog endorsement, but alas, it was not reflected in his gift giving. He had two ex-wives and three daughters to support. It had never occurred to her to ask Dempsey for money, she said. He was thoughtful in his way, always sending flowers. She was offended, though hardly heartbroken, when Dempsey suddenly decamped for New York to deal with a labor dispute at his restaurant and got himself engaged, briefly, to a rich widow. The Champ sent Helen a cheesecake.

11

The Cures

I believe psychiatry helps most dramatically in taking the joy out of
punishing yourself.
—HGB, *Helen Gurley Brown's Outrageous Opinions*

THE MEETING SPACE OF THE GROUP psychotherapy practice was a large
room atop a rambling old house in the Griffith Park section of Los
Angeles. Upon entering, Helen noted the unusual décor. The room was
fitted out with the expected hodgepodge of chairs and an array of most
peculiar therapeutic aids: a punching bag, pillows and ropes, bean
bags, boxing gloves, and an adult-sized portable potty. Even compared
with happenings in the edgier quarters of late-fifties Los Angeles,
where bongos sounded above the surf from the Venice Beach beats and
Elvis blew minds in the Pan-Pacific Auditorium, this scene was way,
way out.

But Helen was desperate. She could not pull free of DJ, who pursued her relentlessly and reeled her back in with a smug possessiveness.
When the pain became too excruciating, when she feared seriously for
her health and sanity, she would turn to another man to help break her
addiction. He practiced the wildest, most demanding psychotherapy
she had ever known. The Los Angeles therapist Charles Cooke was
known as Charlie to his patients. A decade before the bloom of Esalen,

est, and other California-based, crawl-on-the-carpet paths to full self-hood, Cooke developed a most unconventional and sometimes excru-ciating group therapy practice.

Helen's gynecologist had recommended that she see Cooke. Besides participating in his group, Helen also had private sessions with Cooke twice weekly, some involving hypnosis. At its most intense, her therapy totaled four hours per week. She was frantic to free herself from DJ as well as from the less tangible demons that had beset her for so long.

She suspected that she *still* had some daddy issues. She was also prone to spasms of the depression that hobbled her mother. Despite her very busy social life, she was too often met by a curdling despair when she returned to her empty apartment from a date or a night with the girls. She found that, like her abusive lover, the darkness came upon her with a perverse beckoning: "Depression is waiting for you with your robe and slippers and a highball in its hand. 'Hello, Dear, I made myself at home,' Depression says. 'Sure, I'm still here. Did you think I had anyplace *better* to go?'"

She could lightly mock the problem, but its persistence frightened her deeply. There was also the constant, undermining murmur of that "not pretty enough" cant. This she recognized as a key neurosis, her most stubborn "N." "It's such a dull, ordinary, run-of-the-mill neurosis I hate to mention it and only do so because it's *mine* . . . ," she con-fessed. "I think I am not pretty. I mean I *know* I am not pretty. On big N days I think I am not even passable. On those days or nights I really suffer."

Thus Helen arrived at Charlie Cooke's practice with a substantial to-do list. Assessing her experience there years later, she said that much of the work involving her family and upbringing had been done in the private sessions: "I sort of expiated the pain of losing my father. I was hypnotized a lot, and got out the pain and the grief."

Helen, by then a practiced spiller, had little difficulty in adjusting to speaking in a group setting, though her manners would prove some-what lacking. Cooke kept the group that Helen joined to a mixed dozen of men and women; the cast changed slightly during her time there. The walls and furnishings bore witness to their exertions; over the months, Helen watched the space get trashed to splinters as group members wrestled with their issues and, sometimes, with one another. The cardinal rule: no one should get hurt. Cooke's methods were shocking at the time; they included nudity, hypnosis, and intense role-playing. But by Helen's reckoning, his results were liberating and life-affirming for her. "He [Cooke] said, 'You must not go back to that man who's pursuing you,'—who'd been after me and hurt me so often. But he was the best of all the therapists when it came to sex. He said sex isn't dirty. Sex is fabulous, and you enjoy it, and enjoy your enjoying it. It's the most wonderful thing two people can do."

On this last point, Cooke was publicly emphatic. Drawing on his therapeutic experience, he authored two books on his practice and fields of interest, *The Hypnotism Handbook* and *Sex Can Be an Art!* In his introduction to *Sex Can Be an Art!*, Cooke called for a reassessment of the very purpose of sex; he believed that as contraception technology continued to improve, society's outdated mores constrained modern lovers. For the first time in our culture, Cooke contended, the two functions of sex could be separated; ecstasy need not be chained to procreation. "The sex urge is as strong in each one of us as it was in our parents or great-great-great grandparents," he wrote. "The Urge is to copulate, not to make babies!"

Helen certainly found nothing to argue with in Cooke's call for a new set of values that recognized sexual joy as fulfillment in itself, rather than a grunting genetic imperative: "We must acknowledge the pleasure *value* of sex," Cooke went on. "We must make shared joy MORAL."

This was hardly canon in the buttoned-up Eisenhower years, though other therapists and sex researchers had begun to question hidebound and conservative sexual mores on a more national stage. In 1958, as Helen was so immersed in Charlie Cooke's private revolution, the Columbia-based psychoanalyst Albert Ellis published his classic and controversial manifesto, *Sex Without Guilt*. Helen became an early and keen reader of his work. Ellis also worked with Alfred Kinsey, whose 1948 study of white American males, *Sexual Behavior in the Human Male*, churned up great controversy and sales.

Kinsey's report was shocking at the time; it found that 37 percent of the male respondents had had homosexual experiences to the point of orgasm. Half of them had had sex outside their marriage and more than two-thirds had paid prostitutes for sex. Reactions were predictably polarized. The general public was intrigued: despite the report's size and cost—it was 804 pages with a steep price of $6.50—it sold 200,000 copies. The guardians of taste were more tentative: though its reporters duly covered the furor around Kinsey's research, *The New York Times* primly and resolutely refused to accept advertising for the hardcover edition.

And what were women really up to behind closed doors? International and American press had flocked to Kinsey's headquarters at the University of Illinois in Bloomington in anticipation of "K Day," the August 20 release of his 1953 study, *Sexual Behavior in the Human Female* (later known as "the Kinsey Report"). It trumpeted the truth that Helen already experienced: In a sample of just under six thousand white American women, half reported having had premarital sex. Twenty-five percent said that they had engaged in extramarital affairs.

Kinsey's metrics and sample size were not unassailable, but the general truth was incontrovertible: single women were having sex and enjoying it. Kinsey's unsettling news got his portrait—graced with a flower and a honeybee—on the cover of *Time* magazine. Scantily clad women on the September 1953 cover of then-staid *Cosmopolitan* magazine pointed toward its cover line about the study. Coverage was widespread, in *Reader's Digest, Life, Newsweek, U.S. News & World Report*—and *Modern Bride*.

Despite the attention, or perhaps because of it, the conservative backlash undid Kinsey. He was tarred as a Communist by conservative Republicans and his funding from the Rockefeller Foundation was cut off. The attacks left him a broken man whose contributions were not reevaluated until after his death, which came just three years after he published his report on women. Mid-fifties popular culture did show signs of resistance to old-guard repressives. Fundamentalist fogies may have been tossing Elvis records into bonfires, but the kids were buying them faster than they burned; runaway sales revealed that Grace

Metalious's sex-in-the-suburbs novel *Peyton Place*, so tame by current standards, was going home in millions of plain brown wrappers.

Upstairs in Charlie Cooke's hang-up lab, solid citizens, male and female, were enduring highly unorthodox exercises to shake off their repression. Because of Cooke's background as a marriage counselor, many of his referrals included singles and couples with sexual and intimacy issues. Even within the confidential circle of the group, Helen found it could be a rough go. She wept a good deal. Some sessions sent her climbing into Charlie Cooke's lap for solace. Never, she insisted, was there sexual activity of any sort in his sessions, with him or between group members. Cooke was the daddy figure. Often he found himself mediating squabbles between other members and the outspoken Miss Gurley. Helen was a blabbermouth by nature, she admitted, and she did tend to go on about things. She also wanted to get her money's worth. Occasionally, she was confronted by other group members with issues far more traumatic than her romantic disappointments. After a while, a few of them were losing patience with that Gurley girl, a stubbornly pragmatic multitasker who sometimes tended to personal grooming or light chores as others poured out their deepest anguish. Helen described the consequences of that frustration: "I would always bring along a little something to do while various members droned on about their problems! One night I did my nails and was getting ready to put up hems when a fellow member broke his hand pounding on the floor because he was irritated with me."

Even then, she could be that vexing a woman, at times hardly conscious of her effect on others. Another evening, Helen's rambling recitation about yet another string of romantic conquests set off a bomb in the room. Suddenly, one of the women piped up. She just had to go ahead and say it:

Helen Gurley was nothing but a *slut*!

Spoken with venom, it had the effect of a gut-punch. Though Helen "went to pieces" under the assault—weeping, she sheltered in Charlie Cooke's lap—she was also somewhat bewildered. What *was* a slut? Displaying a cultural myopia worthy of Cleo, she truly did not know. Maybe it was something out of a trashy southern novel, she thought at first. She looked up the word as soon as she got home and could not find a definition listed. She knew that it must be something horrible, so she asked friends. They explained: a slut was a woman with "round heels," as the old expression for prostitute conveyed, someone easily pushed over backward into bed. Helen was stunned.

Slut-shaming is an ancient yet ever-vital blood sport; now haters may sling tweets and mortifying Instagrams instead of real stones, but the brutish motivation is no more civilized for its high-tech delivery system. More than a century and a half after the embroidered badge of shame flamed on Hester Prynne's chest in Nathaniel Hawthorne's *The Scarlet Letter*, the practice has been so entrenched and enhanced, its barbs now so expertly aimed and massively deployed via social media, that the effects of online slut-shaming became the subject of a TED talk delivered in early 2015 by Monica Lewinsky, the ex-lover of the former president Bill Clinton. She received a standing ovation.

In the late fifties, even for the sexually liberated Helen Gurley, slut-shaming had a traumatic effect in that first startling moment. "*Slut!*"— the English word itself is shaped to be spat more than spoken, rather like *puta*, the Spanish word for whore. From Helen's stung recollection on first hearing the term hurled at her, it is apparent that she honestly viewed herself not as a "sleep-around girl," but as someone who just had "a lot of trouble with men."

Here is how she described herself in those days: Not the memorable sort of girl who wowed anyone at a party. Not at all good at social chitchat. Not the kind of girl men took home to Mother. She said it herself: Helen Gurley was somebody one took to bed—if she agreed to it. Sure, she knew what she was doing, but she did not feel that she was a bad person for it. Most assuredly, she would not describe herself as . . . that *word*.

There were no equivalent derogatory expressions for males. Men were and are players, ladies' men, womanizers. "Prick"—a word Helen came to use freely and with relish—would not enter wide usage for decades. By contrast, Don Juan, the name of a legendary cad first created by Tirso de Molina in the seventeenth century, has rarely been perceived as a coarse term. Helen's choice of Don Juan to describe her tormentor almost civilized him. That bad-boy male archetype has intrigued intellectual lights from Camus (the essay on "Don Juanism" in *The Myth of Sisyphus*) to Mozart (the opera *Don Giovanni*) to that deft chronicler of refined sexual warfare, Jane Austen. Upon seeing a pantomime titled *Don Juan, or the Libertine Destroyed* in 1813, Austen confessed in a letter to her sister, Cassandra, "I must say that I have seen nobody on the stage who has been a more interesting Character than that compound of Cruelty and Lust."

Thus the centuries-old divide: The bad boy could fascinate even as he spiraled to his comeuppance. The bad girl more often invited shaming and disgust. The disapproval and anger Helen heard that night in therapy would come roaring back at her again and again after the publication of *Sex and the Single Girl*; it would menace her fiercely at some live appearances. She would learn to withstand it, even surf the swells of such public opprobrium on prime time if the kerfuffle sold books. Through it all, Helen would remain as unapologetic as she was in Charlie Cooke's house of pain.

Overall, she voiced only one complaint about her therapist's perspective on sexual activity. "He almost took the fun out of it," she said. "Because you couldn't fantasize anymore, sex was not naughty, you didn't need to have fantasies with your beaux, you didn't need to use naughty words, because sex was as clean as the driven snow. I don't think people should be separated from their fantasies. But he was a wonderful influence."

There was another aspect of her therapy that Helen seemed to have found more problematic to work through. Before Cooke wrote about men's and women's physical insecurities and the manifestations of bodily shame in *Sex Can Be an Art!*, he was exploring the subject with his group patients in a most excruciating exercise. Those who dared would strip naked, one at a time, and talk about their bodies in terms of perceived assets, deficiencies, and insecurities. Others were invited to comment. No one was forced or pressured to participate. Helen made herself do it. Having undressed completely, she faced a dozen pairs of eyes trained on all the areas that shamed her, took a breath, and dove into a recitation of her most personal complaints. She found it mortifying.

Cooke may not have freed Helen of all her physical insecurities, but after about a year of his treatment, she walked away from DJ for good. She was greatly relieved and continued group sessions and phone consultations with Cooke awhile to stave off any relapse. She was also in need of another sort of rehabilitation. Helen's physical health had suffered, too, during her long, humiliating tango with DJ. The increased stressors of climbing the ladder in advertising took a toll as well. Just as foreshadowed in the bloody artwork on Don Belding's wall, the ad game had proved to be a brutal business.

Burnouts were common in the trade and Helen was putting in punishing hours. There were seven other copywriters on staff, all male. Night after night she watched them leave at 5:00 or 6:00 p.m. for their patio suppers in Pasadena and Altadena. Some of them shot her resentful glares as she continued to tap away. One of those copywriters complained to their boss that it simply wasn't fair. He and the other men had to go home to their families! Gurley was taking advantage of them because she wasn't married and didn't have to go home. In fact, Gurley had to work later and work harder to keep her place among them. She was, after all, just a girl copywriter—pale, thin, and very, very tired.

For nearly a year, friends had urged her to see a certain Los Angeles nutritionist, a former housewife turned health guru whom Helen described as holding court "sort of like Gandhi" with hopeful petitioners lined up outside her storefront for consultations. Gladys Lindberg had taught herself about good nutrition in an effort to restore her own family to the rosy-cheeked robustness she knew as a child in South Dakota. She and her husband, Walter, opened their first health food store in Los Angeles in 1949. Gladys Lindberg's clientele built rapidly, from the rank and file to the famous: the actresses Doris Day, Merle Oberon, and Gloria Swanson, and the entire Occidental College track team. After store hours, a limo would deliver "the Queen of Gospel," Mahalia Jackson, a woman who surely needed her strength. By then,

Jackson was regularly sounding her sanctified clarion at civil rights events at the behest of Ralph Abernathy and Martin Luther King, Jr.

Helen had called Mrs. Lindberg, who refused to treat her over the phone. Annoyed, she resisted visiting the shop until she felt "lower than a worm." Helen hit this nadir after two hard, humbling weeks in Long Beach as the unhappy Boswell to vacuous and very young beauty contestants preparing for a telecast. It was Miss Universe time. Again. The Catalina-sponsored contest had become a tiara'd colossus with serious network legs. During pageant season, Helen found herself hovering on the perimeter of photo shoots and makeup sessions, collecting personal information about the contestants to feed a slavering press corps, "pressing for news of dating at Keokuk High or water-skiing in Helsinki." It was humiliating and exhausting.

She bore up as long as she had to, but once sets were struck and the runway dismantled, a shaky and exhausted Helen headed north in "Catharine Howard," the well-used '49 Chevy she had bought after putting the failing Appletrees out to pasture. She pulled up outside the Lindberg shop on Crenshaw Boulevard in southwest Los Angeles. There was no missing its garish neon sign; one had to get people's attention to talk about health food in those days.

Helen took her place in line, and when she finally reached the presence of the wise woman, she launched into a typical overshare about her torments in Long Beach: "I explained to a cast of about thirty that I was suffering from an acute case of jealousy as well as symptoms of disappearance." The busy and sensible Mrs. Lindberg bade the young woman quit talking and stick out her tongue. When told that it was purplish, with a deep groove down the center, Helen began to cry copiously, though she had no idea what malady her livid tongue foretold. Lindberg's diagnosis was hardly surprising: fatigue, compounded by vitamin deficiencies and years of lousy food.

It was the beginning of a long and restorative relationship. Helen walked out that day with sacks of whole grains, soy pancake mix, and a full supply of "Varsity Packs"—the vitamins and minerals that Lindberg fed to the athletes who sought her help. Also included: the makings for Lindberg's Serenity Cocktail, a blended elixir that became a daily staple. It consisted of fresh pineapple, soybean oil, raw milk, brewer's yeast, and iron-rich dried liver powder. Helen whirred up a pint of Serenity in a blender each morning and carried it to work in a thermos, downing half in midmorning and the other half to ward off a mid-afternoon slump.

Like many of Lindberg's followers, Helen enjoyed much-improved health, fairly quickly. Given more energy, she began to exercise. In short order, she was a devotee of yoga and trail walks; she hiked amid coyotes and skirted gopher holes along the winding trails of Will Rogers State Park. Half a century before the primacy of kale, kombucha, and the proliferation of "yoga rooms" in major airports, Helen Gurley's wellness quest placed her firmly in the category of kook. She did not care; in fact, she proselytized, touting the transformative potency of powdered liver with the whispery zeal of a street-corner pusher. Friends acknowledged the restoration of her health and forgave the whole grain and organ meat sermons. Oh, that's just *Helen*.

She was thirty-six, and though she was pleased to find herself more robust and finally free of her demon lover, Helen continued to wrestle with another bothersome "N," her long-standing money neurosis. That anxiety had finally eased up a bit, given Helen's cheap rent, the modest two dollars in gas she fed the Chevy weekly, and the comfort of some real savings. Thanks to scrimping in the secretarial days and her ten-thousand-dollar copywriter salary, Helen's bankbook from the Security First National Bank showed a reassuring eight-thousand-dollar balance. The old boot in her closet was stuffed with bills and change as well.

Thinking that she might feel safe in replacing her ten-year-old car, she went looking at used Thunderbirds. A T-bird would be *darling*. She took along a man she was dating who worked at the William Morris Agency. They walked together through the used car lot, admiring ragtops, the signature "porthole" windows, and spoked chrome wheels. Suddenly, displaying the reckless auto lust that had propelled Cleo toward her pricey Pontiac, Helen went plumb crazy. She fell hard for a handsome, "cloud grey" 190SL Mercedes sports car, technically "used," with just two thousand miles on it. The car smelled like success and handled as sweetly as a responsive lover. As if in a trance, Helen handed over the keys to the Chevy and five thousand dollars in cash and christened her new steed "Bismarck."

Charlotte Kelly had visited the Beldings at their ranch with Helen the weekend before she would actually take possession of the car. The Mercedes, Charlotte finally realized, was the thing Helen had been saving for for so long, stuffing cash into that old boot. "Upon congratulating Helen on the purchase of the car, she burst into tears and cried the whole way, three hours sopping wet." The splurge had made Helen utterly sick and unable to sleep. Was she a crazy girl? She cried all the way to and from Tijuana when she and Bismarck ferried Charlotte and their friend Angela to the bullfights. It had been a mistake, some horrible lapse in judgment. She would just have to learn to live with it—and take it easy on the curves. She wasn't used to the kind of power the smooth German "performance" engine delivered.

Just as she settled into her relationship with Bismarck, an intense professional courtship surprised and unnerved her. In the tenth summer of her tenure at FC&B, a rival agency, Kenyon & Eckhardt (K&E), began pursuing the talented Miss Gurley. After fierce competition, the company had just won the sought-after $4 million Max Factor cosmetics account over many rivals, including FC&B. The cosmetics client had seen Helen perform during the agency "bake off." Max Factor made it clear; Gurley would seal the deal, so K&E was aggressive about getting her on their team. "They needed to staff up girl writers in a hurry," Helen explained; "I was a logical acquisition." She turned K&E down a couple of times; they kept coming back with more money.

In an undated recollection—it appears to have been part of a speech—Don Belding recounted the circumstances of Helen's departure. He noted that she had been doing very well for FC&B, particularly with the Catalina and Stauffer accounts. "We were paying her $10,000 I believe, and they made her an offer of $20,000 and Helen was all upset. She came and talked to me and I said, 'We can't pay you that, but if they're so anxious to get you, why don't you say you'll come for $25,000 . . .'"

Belding had leveled with Helen; he and his partners were in no position to match the offer. The agency was reeling over a catastrophic campaign for Ford Motor Company's epic $350 million bomb, the 1957 Edsel. Helen realized that she could not say no. But leaving home was terrifying, as Charlotte Kelly described it. "She couldn't say yes without me coming down to her office and literally holding her hand while she called to accept the position." As Helen packed up the office with her name on the door and prepared to leave, Mr. B wished her well— they would remain close friends until his death in 1969.

Helen hadn't wished to seem pushy and accepted the offer at twenty thousand dollars, despite the grisly tales she had heard about Max Factor's volatile ad manager. She soon learned how the notorious Mr. Gross had earned his reputation when she arrived for a meeting at the Max Factor offices one day with a delegation from K&E. Spring lipstick and makeup shades were to be discussed. Instead of the usual opening pleasantries, Gross announced: "I've got a new gun."

Veterans of such announcements steeled themselves; Helen nearly fainted when Gross leveled a Smith & Wesson sidearm at the K&E account executive's head and fired. The report was thunderous in a conference room. Gross shot blanks, or, with a specially rigged shotgun, he sometimes sent a trio of fuzzy snakes animated by coiled springs toward the creative team. Gross's very expensive new copywriter, Gurley, learned how to shriek bloody murder whenever he reached into his arsenal; he seemed most pleased by visible demonstrations of terror. It took Helen a few more blasts to understand: the louder she screamed and carried on, the better Gross seemed to like her. Helen Gurley had become—as far as she knew—the highest-paid woman in West Coast advertising. If feigning terror meant job security at that salary level, she'd scream the place down, then get down to business: "Okay, let's name a lipstick!"

Helen applied her adjectival wizardry to every pot, potion, and tube of female enhancers the company brewed up. She preserved some of her old copy and lists of makeup and lipstick names. Let us imagine ourselves seated at Mr. Gross's conference table and "get Gurley to read" her list of possibilities in a breathy aria of innuendo and alliteration:

"Silkidacious . . . Kiss Kiss . . . Sylph . . . SSShhhhh! . . . Mam'Zelle . . .
Arctic Rose . . . Bahama Skies . . . I Like Men! . . . If You Can't Be Good,
Just a Little Wicked . . . Love in the Morning . . . Madness a la Mode . . .
Oh You Kid! . . . Pyro Pink . . . Rubies by Firelight . . . Timid Tempt-
ress . . . Virtue 'n' Vice . . . With My Eyes Open . . . Who's That Girl? . . .
Red, Your Move . . ."

And finally . . . "Yes, Darling."

In Helen's new position, the beauty business revealed itself to be
paranoid, pitiless, sexist, and very ugly indeed. As a client, Max Factor
proved a nightmare of mistrust and indecision on all levels. The over-
thinking was maddening. "One Sunday," Helen wrote, "we had a three
hour meeting to decide whether the headline should be 'Eight Obstacles to Beauty' or 'The Eight Obstacles to Beauty.'" Worse, she found that
her new agency was no less frustrating than the client. She worked until
midnight and on holidays and Sundays. Management churned through
scores of supervisory hires with varying styles and peccadilloes one
needed to adjust to; Helen "went through" nine creative directors and
four office managers during her four-year tenure at K&E.

As a courted and prized hire, she was shocked and dispirited to find
herself summarily tossed into a Positively Pink ghetto with two other
women copywriters, Mary Louise Lau and Marilyn Hart, who were
also brought aboard to work on the Max Factor account. The women
liked each other a good deal, but the agency insisted they all work on
the same assignments, with the expectation that the dear ladies would
simply claw it out. They were given one another's copy to work over,
leaving them "locked in a death grip," as Helen put it, with no autonomy or authorship.

The office the women shared had once been part of a dental suite.
The fixtures remained—sinks, basins, lavatories, and outlets for Bun-
sen burners; the practice had also made false teeth. It was painted livid
green, dark and airless. "The whole effect was rather mossy," Helen
declared, ". . . and you can't tell me it didn't affect our cosmetics copy."
Despite the salary, Helen was miserable; her copy was regularly and
completely eviscerated. Whatever persuasive professional voice she had
developed to get herself to this place was stifled and devalued. For a

time she was slightly encouraged by being assigned to write an "adver-torial" Max Factor beauty column for *Seventeen* magazine; she then watched seven men rewrite it before they took it away entirely.

Helen had consulted with one other man besides Belding about taking the new job. She had just started dating the movie executive David Brown in June 1958 when she asked for his opinion of the K&E offer; she believed him to be the shrewdest of businessmen. He had told her to take the money and skedaddle over there. Unhappy as she had become at K&E, she wouldn't think of tossing that advice in her new lover's face. More than a year before they were formally introduced, Helen Gurley had decided to seek the ultimate cure for her long-unsettled life and marry this man a friend had told her about. It was time. Finally there was a candidate who—at last—met all of her requisites for a lively and secure retreat from the singles arena.

As she told a friend, "David came to me presold."

The Marriage Plot

Helen wants to marry and the three traits she's seeking in a man are intelligence (he must be smarter than I), affection (to the point of nausea) and stability (he must be grown up).
—Miss Helen Gurley's thoughts in a *Los Angeles Mirror* article, 1959

HELEN WAS WILLING TO PLAY THE LONG GAME. It was a plan, impressive in its dogged forbearance, that began this way: In mid-1957, Helen was taking some exercise with her friend and hiking companion Ruth Schandorf, who told her of a newly divorced male friend of hers. David Brown was then a well-regarded story editor at 20th Century Fox studios. It was an important job title in those days, second to "head of production" in a studio's creative department. Schandorf thought that, given time to let off steam with a few starlets and a candy box of other assorted nymphets, David just might be a "possible" for Helen. He was no matinee idol, but Schandorf assured Helen: "You'll never be bored."

Helen had seen David Brown once at a party, still with his wife, and thought him "dishy." Might she get an introduction? Soon?

Schandorf agreed to watch closely and signal when the moment was right, warning that it might take a year or so. She had known David since his arrival in Los Angeles and had lunched often with his most recent wife, whose abrupt departure had left the man in tatters and in therapy. Schandorf laid out the full dossier for Helen: Dear David had no trouble getting women, but he was a two-time loser in matrimony. Married for seventeen of his forty-two years (eleven to the first wife, six to the second), he clearly wasn't averse to the institution. Yet both wives had walked out on him, the first a lively dancer with a roving eye, the second a stunner with screen test looks and a Vassar degree. This left the mogul-in-the-making "alimony poor" in a pretty but neglected Spanish-style manse in Pacific Palisades. He was making eighty thousand dollars a year securing literary properties for the studio. "I thought he was John Paul Getty," Helen recalled. But she wasn't after the money at that point, she said. "I wanted security."

Schandorf promised that when she felt David might be ready for an adult relationship, she would arrange something casual, but *intime*. Perhaps a small dinner party. Helen was game; meanwhile, she enjoyed herself with a sweet younger man from William Morris, among others.

It would hardly be Kismet, then, the coming together of David and Helen Gurley Brown. Helen Gurley was obliged to perform her own version of the Labors of Hercules to "sink in" to the psyche and libido of her mustachioed, pipe-smoking catch.

She admitted to being in a bit of a hurry by then; at thirty-six, her hair was already turning "salt and pepper," though the rest of her was in fine working order. But she was done with being "the girl." She had been the girl for long enough, and for too many.

Describing his dating mind-set at the time, the die-hard New Yorker David Brown made the odds of a bicoastal matchup seem slim indeed: "California's a wasteland with regard to intelligent females," he declared. "Helen was different. She was just old enough to be wise and just my type, but I was on a kick of dating only geisha and peasant types. I had only just shed a working wife, and for awhile I wanted girls who had absolutely no rights." Watching them navigate their courtship year—he drifting languidly, she paddling madly—is to appreciate the sheer unlikelihood of it all.

Ruth Schandorf's dossier on David mainly concerned his romantic history. Helen, universally described as a nonpareil listener, would have no difficulty coaxing the details of David's Runyonesque beginnings from him. As his three late-life memoirs would reveal, he had as few qualms about sharing his intimate history as Helen did.

He was born into a rapidly changing New York City; its first sky-scraper, the sixty-story Woolworth Building, was only three years old when Lillian Brown delivered her first child in that city on July 28, 1916. That month, as young French, British, and German soldiers began dying in droves in the protracted Battle of the Somme, America drifted closer to the Great War. Yet there was still optimism at home, with a booming economy, more and higher steel beams thrusting into the Manhattan skyline, and, nationwide, a rather Yankee Doodle outlook toward the quotidian pleasures of American life. But early on, there was little to suggest good fortune for this child of a doomed marriage and a coldly abandoning father. It was viewed as a mixed and thus ques-tionable union then: Lillian Brown was Jewish; her husband, Edward F. Brown, was raised in Southampton, a dyed-in-the-seersucker WASP, according to his son. He was a man of various mundane trades and master of none, save philandering. At that, his son owned freely, Edward Brown was indefatigable and wildly creative.

Early into his marriage, he began an affair with a renowned violin-ist named Nathalie Boshko. Much later in his life, David would learn from Boshko that she first knew of his existence on an evening she followed her lover home on the streetcar; she had become suspicious because Edward Brown would never reveal to her where he lived. She alit from the streetcar, keeping well behind him, and found herself in then-prosperous Sheepshead Bay. Crouched behind hedges outside the small house Brown had entered, the musician watched in horror as he kissed Lillian and dandled baby David. It was not far to the ocean; Boshko considered drowning herself in the Atlantic. Instead she rode back home and composed her ultimatum: divorce the woman in Sheepshead Bay and marry me—immediately—or we're through. So it went; Edward Brown disappeared from his son's life for the next seven-teen years. He managed his new wife's concert tours; they had a son and a daughter. He did not tell the children about his first wife and son, even after his second family returned to New York and he took a job doing public relations for the milk industry. He made no effort to see or contact his firstborn.

David was raised by his mother, who had gotten remarried, to a wealthy man much her senior, Isadore Freundlich. For a time, life was, in Cole Porter terms, swell-egant. The couple sailed to Europe every summer; the little boy in short pants waved from a Hudson River pier beneath a bright shower of confetti. David was six in 1922 when the family moved to Woodmere, Long Island, seeking the well-pruned gentility of "the country life." Five years later, an awestruck David watched Charles Lindbergh sail over the trees and into history from the dirt runway of nearby Roosevelt Field. In the area, those living close to the airfield learned not to paint their homes white as the burgeoning aviation age sent billowing dust clouds from its unpaved runways. David was a boy of lively curiosity and enthusiasms; he read science fiction and tinkered with a crystal radio set. On May 19, 1928, he stood in the middle of Pine Street peering through smoked lenses at a total eclipse of the sun that dropped a surreal, Magritte-like darkness over the well-kept homes.

David became fast pals with another Woodmere boy, Ernest Lehman, who was destined to become a successful screenwriter (*West Side Story, The Sound of Music, The King and I, North by Northwest, Who's Afraid of Virginia Woolf?*). The boys spent hours tuning in to distant voices on ham radios, an enthusiasm David maintained throughout adulthood. Suburban life was cushy and carefree until the 1929 crash decimated the net worth of David's stepfather. With their home on Pine Street about to be sold for delinquent taxes, the family hastily downsized to an apartment back in Manhattan. Though she had never received alimony or child support, Lillian Freundlich was resolute that her only child should attend college, despite the family's reduced circumstances. A meeting was arranged with David's long-absent father, who agreed to send him through Stanford University.

The summer before he left for California, David's father thoughtfully arranged a job for him in the morgue at Bellevue Hospital. The experience left him with a lifelong terror of doctors and all things medical. At seventeen, David helped saw open human skulls for brain extraction. He injected lab mice with the pneumonia virus, sliced and diced them, and tried to make the best of it. "There was no air conditioning in 1933," he wrote. "The general sultriness and presence of death around us made us feel very horny. I remember a nurse named Jo who was refreshingly uninhibited . . . My little lab was across the way from a ward for insane women. Hideous-looking former prostitutes beckoned me with obscene gestures."

Doubtless he was relieved to inhale the sea air as he boarded a steamship west in August. The incoming freshman Brown sailed off to college via the Panama Canal, chosen by Edward as the cheapest way to ship his boy to school. The bargain-rate voyage took three languorous weeks. David studied psychology and took a few gut courses. There were only three students in his "Business of Theater" course. Another, "Psychic Phenomena," was given at the bequest of the university founder Leland Stanford's wife, who was a devotee of spiritualism. Course work included coed séances with "a certain amount of manmade levitation under the table." After graduation in 1936, David headed straight for New York and journalism school at Columbia University. He had his master's degree a year later and set out to make his way as a writer.

By the spring of 1937, while "Bashful Babe" Gurley was still coping with acne and a southern accent in her Los Angeles high school, twenty-one-year-old David Brown was shacked up with "a commie girl" in Manhattan's Greenwich Village. Over breakfast, they argued about the Spanish Civil War. He thought it the best of times.

Young David liked to stay out late and sleep in, so he got a job that let him prowl Broadway as a second-string drama critic and night editor for the fashion trade paper *Women's Wear Daily*. The Depression was still spreading miseries, but he described it as "a palmy time" for him, bunking in a serviceable flat with three other young men and Anna, the card-carrying Communist. In his first memoir, *Let Me Entertain You*, he outlined the simple and liberating math of his carefree youth: a salary of twenty-five dollars a week, eleven dollars in rent. As to the rest: "The remaining fourteen dollars easily saw me through an active social and sexual life. Who cared if banks failed in Yonkers?" Sounding much like a certain single girl, he added, "It was exciting to be in New York and get out of strange beds before going to work."

In the beginning, David Brown had nearly as many writing gigs as Helen Gurley had secretarial jobs. For a time, as writing partners, he and Ernest Lehman even wrote horoscopes; their chief literary client was the Peerless Weighing and Vending Company of Long Island City. In 1941, while writing a Broadway section for *Pic*, a pictorial magazine positioned as a blue-collar version of *Collier's* and *The Saturday Evening Post*, David married a lithe, twenty-year-old ballerina named Liberty "Tibby" LeGacy. He waxed rhapsodic in recalling her charms: "achingly beautiful, fragile as a lily with long blonde hair and lean, exquisitely shaped legs that never ended. Her breasts were small and perfect and her green eyes could render a man helpless."

They had a son, Bruce LeGacy Brown, a robust nine-pounder born at the Lying-In Hospital in Manhattan, on October 4, 1942. That year, David left *Pic* to become nonfiction editor of *Liberty*, a popular general-interest weekly given to pulpy covers and meaty prose. Life was still palmy in the Brown household despite the nation's entry into World War II. David assumed that acting as an air raid warden in a designated shelter near Park Avenue was sufficient military service, but in 1943 he was drafted. He was aiming for a post as an intelligence officer until he made an unfortunate blunder while marching his squadron around at Officer Candidate School; he dismissed them in front of the wrong barracks. "Does not know where his men are quartered," was the damning citation that washed him out of OCS.

By the summer of 1945, he was released from tedious stateside service in the army after the liberal Washington columnist Drew Pearson wrote about the thousands of men still idling at American bases "picking up cigarette butts" at taxpayers' expense. As stipulated in the GI Bill of Rights, *Liberty* had to give its returning soldier a job; since the nonfiction slot had been filled, David became fiction editor and, eventually, editor in chief at twenty-nine. His pride in being elevated at such a young age was quickly punctured when he learned that *Liberty*'s newest owner had bought it as a needed tax loss. It was destined for the chopping block. And his marriage to the green-eyed Tibby "was on the critical list." In 1949, David was hired as managing editor of *Cosmopolitan* magazine with the personal approval of the owner, William Randolph Hearst.

The outsized newspaper and magazine tycoon had bought the tame general-interest magazine for a song in 1905 and turned it into a sensationalist cudgel to further his own agendas. *Cosmopolitan* was first published in 1886 with the expansive motto "The World Is My Country and All Mankind Are My Countrymen." Within a year of Hearst's taking ownership in 1905, a splenetic President Theodore Roosevelt lambasted one of Hearst's lieutenants at the *New York Journal* in the wake of *Cosmopolitan*'s scandalous multipart congressional exposé, "The Treason of the Senate," which aimed particularly at the Roosevelt crony Senator Chauncey Depew. It was classic and gleeful muckraking; the alleged calumny sold like crazy.

The magazine's many iterations are keenly mapped in James Landers's history *The Improbable First Century of* Cosmopolitan *Magazine*. *Cosmopolitan*'s drift toward the literary during the Jazz Age, Landers wrote, "established it as the premier popular fiction magazine in the nation." The magazine published Theodore Dreiser, Edna Ferber, Ring Lardner, Sinclair Lewis, Booth Tarkington, Damon Runyon, P. G. Wodehouse, Adela Rogers St. Johns, and W. Somerset Maugham.

Cosmopolitan had made a good deal of money for its owner. But by the time David Brown arrived, Hearst's flagship publication was listing badly. Though they were still publishing literary fiction and nonfiction, the market for it was much reduced. Television had begun to compete with magazines for the nation's leisure hours and for advertising dollars. David's mentor at the magazine was the man who hired him. The urbane and fastidious Herbert Mayes was a trusted and energetic editor who oversaw *Cosmopolitan* in addition to being editor in chief of *Good Housekeeping*. It was Mayes who schooled David in the sly art of writing cover lines. "Mayes's blurbs had a twist on them," Brown recalled. "They resembled a curve ball at a baseball game: They twisted outward, sometimes inward but they always contained a surprise. He readily dispensed superlatives like 'Best Christmas Ever' or 'a story that will change your life.'" Using Mayes's rules, David Brown wrote cover lines for the 1949–51 editions, a skill he would become known for during Helen's tenure at the magazine.

When David was at *Cosmopolitan*, a sophisticated, Paris-returned young Wellesley grad named Judy Tarcher, later the bestselling novelist Judith Krantz, was the shoe editor at *Good Housekeeping* and wrote fashion copy as well. She often gave parties attended by work and fashion friends and her high school friend Barbara Walters. At Hearst, Judy was friendly with a *Good Housekeeping* coworker named Wayne Clark. "Wayne was gorgeous," Krantz recalled. "She was a natural beauty and she was just voluptuous, tall, beautiful brown hair. She was a copyeditor."

Employee fraternization was forbidden under Mr. Hearst's directives. Judy Tarcher was shocked, then, to find that Wayne had been keeping a secret. "I gave a big party at my parents' house one night. I invited Wayne and she showed up with David, who was in many respects my boss, and I managed to keep my cool and say hello to him—not say, 'Oh my God, what are you two doing together?'"

David was newly divorced from Tibby. The court had granted her custody of Bruce, and her famous lawyer, Louis Nizer, wrested a fairly ruinous alimony from David, who promptly married Wayne. She, too, was recently divorced. Possibly Hearst executives were too preoccupied to enforce the company fraternization policy; *Cosmopolitan* was still sinking fast. As personnel changes were made and David was passed over for the job of editor in chief, he had the good sense to leave New York and its fickle magazine world.

David's name came up when the 20th Century Fox mogul Darryl F. Zanuck instructed his New York vice president to find the best editor in town to come west and acquire literary properties to be made into movies. Wanting to put the vast prairies between himself and Tibby, David, along with his new wife and his nine-year-old son, Bruce, walked a red carpet to board the 20th Century Limited for Chicago, where they caught the Super Chief to Los Angeles. Despite the custody decree, Bruce's upbringing was fairly bicoastal. Sometimes it was just better for him to be with his father. But overall, the cross-country disruptions must have been bewildering to the boy. It was said that Bruce took a shine to his pretty new stepmother.

Embracing Los Angeles was problematic at first, since David Brown did not drive. Wayne ferried him from their home in the Hollywood Hills to Santa Monica Boulevard, where he caught a streetcar to the studio, then a company tram to his office. Since this was an unseemly entrance for an executive, he made a note to learn to drive. As soon as he had his license, he picked up Robert Evans, handsome roué, film producer, and dear friend, who gasped a few minutes into the ride, "You drive the way I fuck!" (Both men survived for another half century of friendship.)

The newly mobile David moved his family to a bigger and more expensive rent-toward-purchase house on Radcliffe Avenue in Pacific Palisades that had a commanding view of the ocean. He thought that Wayne wanted it. He worried that such a lively, cultured woman might be unhappy as a hausfrau. While living in the West Village, Wayne had socialized with the likes of Mary McCarthy, James Agee, and the painter Jackson Pollock. David encouraged her to continue working; she took a job he had arranged for her at a friend's press agency. "It worked out well for Wayne but not for our marriage," David concluded. He lost his second wife to Robert Healy, the head of Interpublic, Inc., arguably the world's largest ad agency then; the dominant McCann Erickson was merely one of its subsidiaries. The wealthy and powerful Healy walked into the PR office one day and fell hard for the captivating Mrs. Brown.

Judy Tarcher spoke to a stunned and devastated David just after the wrecking ball hit. "He got home one day and there was no Wayne," said Krantz. "He couldn't imagine why she left, she didn't warn him. She took all her clothes and was gone. He said, 'She had everything she wanted. She had a house on the Pacific Palisades.' And I thought, no, that's not what she wanted! I don't think he ever got over Wayne—my opinion. I think when he married Helen he was still in love with Wayne."

Wayne Brown quickly married Robert Healy. She had decamped with most of her belongings, save for the painting an artist friend had given her, a work so baffling and loathsome to David that he had just nailed the canvas straight to the wall in a room he rarely entered. Wayne did come back briefly to carefully pry the spattered abomination off the wall, roll it up, and take it away. It was a Jackson Pollock that, according to David, was later hung with a bit more care in the San Francisco Museum of Modern Art.

David was still paying alimony to Tibby and trying to make good on debts that Wayne had incurred with her impeccable taste. She graciously offered to return his mother's diamond ring—perhaps for his next wife?—and gave him the pawn ticket with which to retrieve it. David had hired a housekeeper to shore up the domestic arrangements and to help shepherd Bruce, who also spent some time back east with his mother. David loved the boy deeply but he could see that at sixteen, Bruce was becoming sullen, secretive, and the bane of private school headmasters. A large collie named Duncan served as comic relief.

13

Let the Games Begin

"I wish I was a woman of about thirty-six dressed in black satin with a string of pearls."

—Daphne du Maurier, *Rebecca*

FINALLY, IT WAS TIME. Ruth Schandorf had judged David Brown receptive to a setup and told him, "I have someone perfect for you. She's a little neurotic and she's no Jayne Mansfield, but . . ."

In June 1958, Helen had invested in a light blue "shift" dress for Schandorf's dinner party; she felt chic in this new, waistless style that skimmed her slim frame. On arrival, she was relieved to find the dress most appropriate for the elegant little gathering. She was careful that none of the old gaucheries would mar her first impression and barely spoke as David held forth at table. After brandies, he walked her to her Mercedes, parked at the curb. She let it slip, canny girl: Yes, the Benz sure was a beauty. She had paid for the car herself just three weeks before. In *cash*.

Knowing David's history with profligate wives, this was the first cupid's arrow Helen let fly. She had a hunch that for this man, her independence and solvency might be a potent aphrodisiac. Schandorf's comprehensive briefing had made Helen confident in her opening gambit. "I've never doubted I eventually persuaded him to marry me," she maintained, "because he had never known a girl who paid all cash for a pair of *stockings*, let alone a sports car."

Game on.

He did not call for a week and a half. Then he invited her to dinner. They went to Jack's, a popular joint at the beach. Helen dressed to thrill; she purrrred across the table and deployed the soon-legendary HGB Eye Lock, a fixed gaze so mesmerizing, so laser-like in its "there's nobody in this room but you" intensity, that any male felt trembly yet grateful to be in its crosshairs. After dinner, Helen summoned the Power; she could not keep her hands off the man, was "all over him like a tent." She did not go to bed with him but allowed that "I went pretty far." He liked it. She could tell.

Another ten days passed. Helen had fretted herself into a tense knot of uncertainty when David finally invited her to dinner at his home. He still lived in what Helen called a crumbling mansion in Pacific Palisades, sixty-six stoplights away from her apartment, just murder with a stick shift. Post-Wayne, the Brown ménage included a bossy British housekeeper, the aforementioned sloppy and spoiled dog, and the increasingly troubled Bruce, who had watched his father chase skirts like a man possessed over the last year and a half. Bruce harbored few positive thoughts about acquiring a second stepmother.

From the dinner party onward, the blueprint for Becoming HGB was unfurled with steely resolve. Helen had completed Phase One by demonstrating her solvency and self-sufficiency and making clear her intention to keep on with her career, no matter what. Yet she sensed a vexing inertia on David's part. For the longest time, he would not even give her his home phone number and Helen was forced to contact him through "Mr. Brady," the maddeningly discreet and inscrutable gatekeeper at David's answering service. Helen turned it up a notch or three; the sex was frequently and fabulously administered. This Helen believed: hooking a man on your personal brand of sex, then threatening to withdraw it, you can finally get what you want—provided you've laid the groundwork well and properly. She exulted in her sexual prowess and boasted about it into her eighties. Never, in all of her books, articles, and correspondence—or to friends—did she describe David Brown as a captivating lover; she always cast herself as the aggressor/temptress. She observed that some people can really *cook*, and some just make scrambled eggs.

A few years before she began her relationship with David, Helen considered a change in birth control methods. After a decade and a half, she was weary of condoms and longed to try a diaphragm, which she understood to be far less disruptive, since the spring-loaded latex devices could be inserted some time before intercourse and left in for hours afterward. Diaphragms also freed a man from any bother at all. Plenty of women were using them by then. Yet Helen found that making the switch was still problematic for a single woman. The first doctor she went to asked an odd question: "Are you engaged to be married?"

"No."

His tone was peremptory. "Well, we're not doling out diaphragms to single women."

Helen left his office humiliated and outraged. Eventually, she found a gynecologist with a more liberal outlook who was willing to fit her for the device. She preferred being responsible for her own reproductive safety; it was the smart woman's solution, and given the man's comparative freedom with a diaphragm, it seemed ever so gracious. From then on, serious Possibles such as David Brown would be spared the fumbling and the responsibility; the magic could just . . . happen.

Despite Helen's determined and steamy crusade, the courtship lurched along. David was still dating others. Among them was the newest publishing It Girl, Rona Jaffe. In 1958, Jaffe was in the news for her sexually frank and bestselling novel *The Best of Everything*, about the lives of five women in the secretarial pool of a New York paperback publisher. The Radcliffe graduate had spent four years as a file clerk at Fawcett Books, where she gathered much of her material. The film version of *The Best of Everything* came out just after the book, in 1959. It was a synergy of production and promotion that David Brown found most attractive. He had watched the whole process very closely. *The Best* was the pet project of the producer Jerry Wald, his coworker at Fox. Like David, Wald was always scouting literary properties. He had been visiting the publisher Simon & Schuster in New York when he told an editor there, "I'm looking for a modern-day *Kitty Foyle.* A book about working girls in New York."

Kitty Foyle, a novel by Christopher Morley, had brought Ginger Rogers an Oscar for Best Actress in the 1940 RKO film version. She played the title role of Kitty, a Philadelphia department store saleswoman. Wald was looking for someone who might write him a better, updated working-girl property that might be as profitable. *Kitty* had been a huge hit; it even inspired a line of Kitty Foyle dresses. Wald found his property in a chance encounter. The editor he met with in New York knew Rona Jaffe; she was a close college friend of his assistant. The editor knew that she had been toiling in the paperback mill and had plenty of stories. He told Wald, "Rona's going to write a hell of a novel someday." The subject was broached with her, briefly. Jaffe had thought it all preposterous but out of curiosity, she got *Kitty Foyle* out of the library. "I thought it was dumb," she wrote later. "I said to myself: He [Morley] doesn't know anything about women. I know about women. And I work in an office."

She let the matter drop until she was in Hollywood on vacation with the same college friend and Wald invited them to lunch. "I wanted to say something interesting to him," Jaffe recalled, "so I casually remarked, 'I'm going to write that working-girl book.' He replied that he was going to produce it." The novel-to-be was placed at Simon & Schuster in the care of the editor Robert Gottlieb. Jaffe supplemented her own observations by interviewing fifty working women. She heard things that were not often mentioned in polite and mixed company: "Back then, people didn't talk about . . . going out with married men. They didn't talk about abortion. They didn't talk about sexual harassment, which had no name in those days. But after interviewing these women, I realized that all these issues were part of their lives, too."

Gottlieb told his twenty-five-year-old author to "look back in horror and write." He spoke to Jaffe regularly as she spooled out her story; meanwhile, a few doors down from David Brown at Fox, the producer Wald was cranking up a huge publicity campaign for the book that

Jaffe hadn't yet written. "It was a surreal and nerve-wracking time," she said.

Jaffe delivered in five months. She took the purposely ironic title from a *New York Times* help-wanted ad that began: YOU DESERVE THE BEST OF EVERYTHING. While the book was in production, signs were encouraging; the lathered team of typists assigned to produce the final version of the 775-page manuscript as quickly as possible were captivated by what they were reading; some of them called Jaffe to find out what was in the chapters other women were typing. When the book came out and long lines formed at in-store signings, the young author got requests to inscribe copies to "all the girls on the forty-ninth floor."

Jaffe's ensemble cast of working women looking for love was built on a reliable template that had previously supported Clare Booth Luce's play and film *The Women* (1936), Edna Ferber's theatrical boardinghouse in *Stage Door* (1937), and beyond. Just before her death in 2005, Jaffe called her first novel "*Sex and the City* without the vibrators."

Wald brought Jaffe to Hollywood to consult several times during the film's production, and it was then that she met David Brown. His regard for her outlasted their brief period of dating. He had long admired a certain flock of literary rara avis—iconoclastic and uppity women writers. As an editor at *Cosmopolitan*, he was in thrall to the legendary Adela Rogers St. Johns, whose exploits as "the World's Greatest Girl Reporter" were as vivid as her prose. She had covered the Lindbergh kidnapping trial for Hearst and made "special friends" with both Clark Gable and that busy gentleman Jack Dempsey. Long before Barbara Walters was eliciting on-camera waterworks in celebrity interviews, St. Johns was known as a popular "sob sister" for her revealing Hollywood profiles. In his work with her at *Cosmopolitan*, David observed her to be "quite a swinger before she got religion."

Thus when Rona Jaffe emerged as another sort of sly, brainy observer of What Women Want, David Brown, bachelor literary scout, remained deeply interested on both professional and personal fronts. Given his admitted prejudice against California girls, it didn't hurt that Jaffe was also a die-hard, Brooklyn-born New Yorker.

David infuriated Helen by suggesting that she take a nap one afternoon so that he could watch Jaffe on TV undisturbed. Helen was getting
a bit testy about the competition, real and imagined. She complained
that her inamorato also had a highly irritating tic; over and over, as
certain female virtues occurred to him, he limned a vision of his ideal
wife, the one who would finally be right for him—someday. Helen did
not recognize this woman in herself: She was a career girl who made at
least a hundred thousand dollars but would give it up if asked to. Could
she cook! Escoffier quality. She would be very good with people and a
fabulous hostess. Beautiful? Of course, along the classic lines of . . .
hmmm . . . the actress Gene Tierney. Not that he wanted to actually
marry again, of course not. But *should* she appear . . .

Every description of this clearly unattainable dream wife made
Helen want to scream: *What about me? I'm right here!*

Helen had come to terms with the realization that she never really
was "wife material." She didn't believe for a second that she could perform that role in the traditional manner. In no way could she see herself as one of the inanely content creatures polishing breakfronts and
smiling from those ad posters in Don Belding's office. She had always
been "mistress material," she conceded, but perhaps she might come
up with her best version of a wife. She knew she was doomed to failure
as a hostess and sparkler on the Hollywood party circuit. Dating David,
she had found herself intimidated by such women.

But David wasn't looking for a Bel-Air hostess type. He was not a
red carpet kind of guy. He preferred cozy evenings with his old friend
Irving Berlin and Berlin's wife, Ellin, to big industry functions. Overall, Helen understood that she was at her best advantage when she
and David were alone together. She coddled him—went full-out geisha—
and she cooked madly in her well-appointed Man Trap. Whether it
was ten-minute broiled lamb chops or a labor-intensive chicken dish
laboriously basted in honey and butter, David wolfed it all contentedly. His favorite Scotch and brandy were laid in, his cigars and pipe
graciously permitted. In his home, Helen tried to make friends with
Bruce, who was upsetting his father deeply with school discipline issues. Helen coaxed him to the dinner table and tried to engage him in

conversation. He seemed uninterested in knowing her, but he did like her car.

Eyes rolled in group therapy once more as the gabby Miss Gurley unburdened herself about the difficulties of reeling in her intended. After all, she and David had been dating for six months, sleeping together though not living together. Helen insisted that she had "forsaken all others." Sort of.

She indulged in just a soupçon of what she called "latent revenge sex" with an heir to one of the world's most fabled fortunes. For months, she had been doing a slow simmer at being the one forced to propose, and with no definitive results. Her disappointment and resentment boiled over after a silly little incident. During an evening at David's home, she had watched, slack-jawed, as his housekeeper, Mrs. Neale— a portly know-it-all sketched with Dickensian savagery in Helen's descriptions—cooed over fabric swatches that "we" might redecorate the house with. Helen was mildly amused to know that Mrs. Neale had been married three times and that one of her husbands had expired in bed on their wedding night. But this possessive and presumptuous majordomo was a constant irritation, especially with her slavering devotion to the black-and-white collie Duncan, whom she called "Baby" (she being "Mother"). With exaggerated politesse, Mrs. Neale also demonstrated a patent dislike for this pushy interloper with the unladylike sports car.

Something snapped in Helen when Mother held up a salmon-colored swatch of brocade fabric she had in mind for some sofas and declared that Baby liked it best; he had told her so. As soon as Mrs. Neale, rigged out in her standard white uniform, bobby socks, and oxfords, tacked triumphantly back into her kitchen, Helen erupted: Shouldn't *she* be helping fix the place? Wasn't she going to be living there someday? He'd love her help, David countered. But no, he was not ready to marry. Helen tore home and dialed the Beldings to invite herself to another ranch getaway.

The Beldings were used to her sudden romantic tempests and said yes, of course. So great was Helen's agitation that she nearly totaled the Mercedes and herself on the drive south. Chastened and shaking,

Helen pulled through the familiar gates of Pauma Vista. She settled in with some unusual reading that she had brought along, books on Arabian oilfields and petroleum dynasties. She was so angry with David that she had said yes to a date with a Getty scion. Jean Ronald Getty, known as Ron, was the uncontested black sheep of that roiling billionaire clan. Ages before she had begun seeing David, Helen had begged friends who knew him to introduce her to this potential Main Chance. Finally, he was to be in town and at liberty. Helen agreed to go on the blind date right after the weekend at the ranch.

The petroleum prince was about her age and unattached. Getty was handsome enough but not at all charming; he seemed animated by an alarmingly entitled sort of lust. After lunch with the couple who introduced them, he fairly tore Helen's clothes off on their first date. She resented "being peeled like a banana." She was not even sure how he landed in her bed; she fled outside the apartment to rebutton herself between rounds of wrestling the boor. No. Just . . . *No!* This Getty was profoundly "full of shit," Helen declared, and closed the door on him, with dispatch.

There was another reconciliation with David; mini-breakups were getting to be a habit. Helen took the next bold step: proximity, at huge sacrifice. Her name had finally come up for an apartment in the sought-after Park La Brea apartment complex; Helen had been on the list for three years, but turned down the prized eighty-nine-dollar two-bedroom, furnished-and-with-a-patio apartment when it was offered. Instead, she moved to a white modern cube in Brentwood, just fifteen minutes from David's home. She felt sure that if she stayed downtown, an hour's drive from her intended, she would lose him.

As it was, every now and again David "misplaced" her, seemingly forgetting that they were an item, or that they even had a date. One night she was driving home after group therapy, waiting at a light on Santa Monica Boulevard, when her worst nightmare whooshed by: it was David's big white Chrysler 300, coming from Linden Drive. There was a blonde "smashed up against him" in the front seat and she was *all over him.*

Helen did not take his calls for the next day and night. When she finally did pick up the phone, she used all her strength not to shriek and instead negotiated a limpid rapprochement. (David insisted the blonde was his business manager.) Helen told herself that he was really an okay guy, "just frisking around." She was still determined to marry him and she had to be honest with herself. She was not deeply, romantically in love, either; she was hardly as obsessed as she had been with DJ. Yet she was taken with David, even told herself that she adored him. At thirty-seven, it was time. Helen held on.

Then she started to push again. The ring, please.

One dreadful night he pushed back. They had been to the theater. Afterward, David seemed uncharacteristically distracted and ruffled. He threw up his hands. What was he going to do? He just couldn't, absolutely could not marry again. Helen told him—calmly this time—that she understood, but that it was over. He was not to call her again. She went home and cried. And cried. The following morning at 8:00 a.m., she laced up her sneakers and lit out for her fortress of solitude, Will Rogers State Park. Up, up, and around she marched, past the beloved humorist's old polo fields, so teary and bereft as to be almost oblivious to the wildflowers along the winding paths, the soothing canopy of eucalyptus trees, the dusty wake of equestrian trail riders, the glories of the vista at Inspiration Point. By the time Helen trudged back to the parking lot she was fairly wrung out. There stood David beside his big Chrysler. He knew exactly where to find his distraught health nut.

"Come on home," he said, "we'll work it out."

During that summer of 1959, their marriage plans were on and off at least five times by Helen's reckoning. Cleo, out for a visit, dared ask the question aloud: "Helen do you think maybe David really doesn't want to get married?"

He finally agreed to set a date: September 25, 1959. Even if he hadn't forbidden her to tell anyone, Helen would have stayed mum. She was dying to trumpet the news, but dared not. "I didn't want to get the train that far and have it derail with some extravaganza. What if he got cold feet and didn't show up? No, we did it David's way, just a judge and his secretary as witness."

As a stealth bride, she had indulged herself in one splurge. Denied the customary trappings—invitations in crisp calligraphy, bridesmaids, reception, and even a stupid old wedding shower—Helen ordered her wedding dress from Jack Hanson, the former Los Angeles Angels short-stop turned women's clothes designer who declared himself a "beauty freak" and tooled the Hollywood hills in a 1934 Rolls-Royce. Hanson could afford it. Sold under the Jax label, his well-cut slacks sheathed the hips of Jackie Kennedy, Audrey Hepburn, Elizabeth Taylor, and Marilyn Monroe. Hanson had become such a habit to certain slinky, shiny ones, the deeply devoted "Jax Pack," that Miss Nancy Sinatra, Jr., was heard to declare, "The most important men in America are my father, Hugh Hefner and Jack Hanson."

Helen had long been a Jax fanatic. She went to work countless times in a sturdy but stylish plaid Jax dress and invested the breathtaking sum of eighty dollars in a slinky black frock that she wore to death. (How fabulous when she found that David *adored* slinky black!) For the wedding, Hanson came up with a surprisingly demure affair with a high neck and long sleeves, accessorized by a chic, barely there hat and a small bouquet of orchids. This nuptial rig spoke quietly but firmly: "Dearly beloved, I mean business."

It was a small group that assembled at Beverly Hills City Hall on the afternoon of September 25, 1959: the happy couple; Ruth Schandorf; David's secretary, Pamela Hedley, as witness; and, stuffed into a suit far too small for him, the glum and reticent Bruce Brown. David had quietly left work early that day, telling his boss, Buddy Adler, "I'm taking off for a couple of hours, see you Monday."

Charlotte Kelly joined the wedding party for a short celebration afterward. David had reserved the Swan Suite at the Hotel Bel-Air for the weekend. On their wedding night, they were taken to dinner by Ernest Lehman and his wife, Jackie; the couple had been "at or near" all of David's weddings. They convened at Perino's, a cherished grotto-to-the-stars on Wilshire, where Bette Davis kept a booth and Sinatra spilled martinis into the Steinway. The foursome went on to the Largo strip club on Sunset to catch the spectacular and athletic Candy Barr. Helen judged her "a damn fine stripper."

After their weekend at the Bel-Air, the bride completed her transition to the ocean-side aerie as Helen Gurley Brown. She loaded the Mercedes herself with some essentials. The things she carried: a pair of six-pound dumbbells; an exercise slant board; a prodigious supply of soy lecithin, powdered calcium, and yeast-liver concentrate for those Serenity Cocktails; an electric contraption said to stave off wrinkles; "and enough high-powered vitamins to generate life in a statue."

Congratulatory wires to the happy couple had greeted their return to 515 Radcliffe Avenue. One of them was from the housekeeper and the collie. It read primly, "Much happiness for the future." It was signed "Baby Duncan and Mother."

14 🕊

Whiskey Sours with Carl Sandburg

Unlike Madame Bovary you don't chase the glittering life, you lay a trap for it.
—HGB, *Sex and the Single Girl*

HELEN SURVEYED HER NEW DOMAIN, having quickly swept it clean of the hot blond accountant and the disapproving Mrs. Neale. The ocean sunsets were a thrill, if one gazed at their splendor above the neglected landscaping. The house, a rambling stucco affair built in 1928, was in disrepair but it had good bones. Furniture and rugs were worn and tatty. There were a couple of rooms that no one entered. A small study referred to as "Wayne's writing room" had been sealed off. Helen likened it to the grieving Maxim de Winter's preservation of his lost Rebecca's ghostly rooms at Manderley. The library was David's pride; he told Helen that it held more than two thousand books. But David had ceded his capacious hexagonal den with its fireplace, ocean view, and separate bath and entrance to Bruce.

One afternoon when Helen was home alone, putting things to rights, a strange young woman turned up at the front door looking for David. She was vacuum-packed into a pair of black toreador pants and a purple T-shirt and her hair was a greasy, unkempt catfight of blond and black. She looked to be in her late twenties and seemed rather "off" to Helen, who did not let the stranger inside when she asked to come in.

Was she the new Mrs. Brown?

As Helen answered, the woman peered past her at the white couches that had come from her apartment.

Redecorating? The way she asked implied a familiarity with the home. Uneasily but politely, Helen showed her the gate. That evening, on hearing of the visit, David seemed upset. The interloper must have been Nadine, his longtime stalker. Helen was dumbfounded; though the bedevilment had been going on for nearly two years, David had never mentioned it, possibly to avoid scaring her. He had given the aspiring actress—weren't they all?—a ride home from a party once. He felt that there was something odd about her right away; she had so un-nerved him that he drove her straight to her run-down little boarding-house, no hanky-panky, no thanks.

Nadine began turning up at the house; David would send her away in a cab. He swore that there was never any relationship, that he had been to the Beverly Hills police chief and his own lawyer to try to deal with Nadine's escalated harassment, which often took the form of twenty to forty calls a day to his office and answering service. The police thought her a persistent but mild sort of stalker, assuring Mr. Brown that they'd seen scarier huntresses. For Helen, it was an uncomfortably close look into what she called Hollywoodlandia, the dark and fevered twilight zone populated by bitter hearts. There were more frightening incidents. Helen came home from work to find her white couches and coffee table splattered and still dripping with rivers of black ink. Lovell Addison, the Browns' new cook/housekeeper, was gibbering with fright at the mess and intrusion; she had seen no one, heard nothing. Bruce was questioned and genuinely seemed surprised at the break-in.

Nadine. How the hell had she gotten in?

So began a domestic life that found Helen feeling alternately trium-phant and storm tossed. David seemed inured to the Nadine disrup-tions, but the changes in Bruce had reduced his father to a hand-wringing insomniac who stared at the ceiling many nights. He often sat quietly with the collie, puzzled and despondent over what he saw as a new recalcitrance in his son. He didn't know what to do, having grown up without fathering himself. Bruce was no longer wearing the brown regimental uniform of the military academy that Helen had first seen him in, since the headmaster of the Harvard School for Boys had requested he not return after the term's end. David had subsequently enrolled him in the Rexford School.

Despite the difficulties at home, the Browns settled into a satisfying social life with David's studio friends, the Lehmans, and some of Helen's girlfriends, especially Charlotte Kelly. She was a frequent visitor to the Brown aerie, sharing conquests and confidences from her very active single life. Helen still adored the dish. Yvonne Rich, then on her second marriage, visited the Browns at home and had them to dinner. "Eating was an interesting subject with Helen," Rich said. "When she would come to dinner at my house in Alameda, you always had to sit her in a certain place where she could see herself in a mirror. Helen also liked to eat with her fingers. If she had a salad she'd pick up each little piece of lettuce and put it in her mouth."

At home, with the help of her "bride's cookbook," she turned out some extravaganzas for David and Bruce: lamb glazed with lime marinade, Chantilly potatoes, avocado stuffed with orange ice. David wolfed it all down with gusto, earning the lifelong nickname "Basker" from his beloved. It was a reference to the Sherlock Holmes tale *The Hound of the Baskervilles*. Helen labored long but ate very little, weighing and measuring herself constantly. She hit the floor each morning with her version of the Royal Canadian Mountie calisthenics and a few saucy stretches from the fitness pioneer Bonnie Prudden's "Sexercise" regime. Helen had a dread of David's "firing" her as a wife. The man was surrounded by starlets and Jax Pack sylphs. At dinner parties, Helen was beginning to develop the anorectic's seething resentment of a fine meal laid out for her enjoyment. "A plague on hostesses and their self-centered little souls," she crabbed in a diatribe that was only partly facetious. "They never understand we don't eat their exquisite food not because we have no taste or taste buds or are trying to make them miserable (they've cooked, they've slaved) but because we are trying—desperately—not to gain weight."

She was relieved to have her debut evening as Hollywood hostess take place *not* at home, and with absolutely no food involved. Best yet, it was glamorous; David was holding a private screening of a new film at the studio and suggested she invite some of her work colleagues as well. It was the first mix of their work worlds; Helen asked K&E's West Coast creative director and his wife, and several friends from her days at Foote, Cone & Belding. After the movie there was a gathering at the home of a wealthy Max Factor executive to toast the newlyweds.

Over the reassuring pop of Dom Pérignon corks, Helen looked around the room and told herself: *You're a wife! Not a guttersnipe with her nose against the window—no more! A wife!*

The couple rode home happy with each other and with the way the evening went. As they walked through the front door into the two-story entryway, shards of glass glistened all over the floor. Two large stained glass windows were broken. Smashed eggs slid down the walls and squelched underfoot. God*damn* it, what now?

Bruce was found in his room studying, insisting he'd been there all night. Nope, heard nothing.

Helen was indeed a wife, for better and for worse.

It was a busy time for David. By the beginning of 1960, some of his story acquisitions were panning out well and in production. He had put Ernest Lehman to work adapting John O'Hara's novel *From the Terrace*, and the studio had cast the golden newlyweds Paul Newman and Joanne Woodward in the leading roles. With tympanic pomp, Fox had announced production of its biblical epic *The Greatest Story Ever Told*, to be directed by George Stevens. David flew to Chicago with Stevens to call on the nation's beloved poet, historian, and three-time Pulitzer winner Carl Sandburg, in hopes of cajoling him into writing some of Christ's dialogue for the film.

Putting words into the mouth of the Son of God was a dicey business, far too sensitive to trust to some West Hollywood wiseacre. Stevens felt that only Sandburg could write dialogue "as majestic as that contained in the King James version of the New Testament." The two movie men had to rent a Chicago theater so that Sandburg could watch some of Stevens's films, among them *Giant, Shane,* and *I Remember Mama.* Sandburg agreed to help. Stevens, who would spend five agonizing years on the film, wept on hearing the good news; he and David repaired to a few Chicago bars and got happily drunk.

When the time came to run the Lord's lines, the studio flew the octogenarian poet west and put him up at the Hotel Bel-Air. David invited him to a home-cooked dinner. Bruce was excited and promised to be home for supper. Helen panicked at the thought of a literary lion at her table. She had heard that Sandburg was fond of whiskey sours. She called a bartender at the Brown Derby, who shared a fail-safe formula of sugar, crushed ice, half a lemon, and bourbon—exactly one ounce of the brown stuff.

Helen had become a near-teetotaler by then; she felt she should be in control at all times—and besides, the empty calories! She brewed a batch of sours with exactly an ounce of spirits per serving and found it delicious. David fetched Sandburg from his hotel and settled him in to enjoy the Pacific sunset. Helen was relieved when the "cutie pie" poet gallantly commended her on the mixology. Of course it would be ever so nice if he might keep the bourbon by his side to freshen up the delicious basic mix from time to time.

He made liberal use of the decanter. Over dinner he was charming, rosy with bonhomie and bourbon. Facing his three varyingly depressive hosts, Sandburg, a man of Whitmanesque enthusiasms, wondered aloud: How is it, when one awakes to the sight of tender green leaves outside a window and the lilt of birdsong—well, how can one *not* be happy? The man must be a kook, albeit an adorable one, Helen figured. At evening's end, Sandburg departed toting a good portion of their classical music records on loan to play in his hotel suite. Helen wondered if the lofty sounds might be inspiration for scripting the syntax of Jesus— in this case, the Swedish actor Max von Sydow. Displaying the insecurity and caprice typical of the industry, the studio used some of Sandburg's work, but without screen credit. The film, which portrayed Jesus as the ultimate misunderstood outsider, was a colossal failure.

In the Brown home, another wave of intrusions had begun that could not be blamed on Nadine. There were armies in the night, bivouacked in Bruce's quarters. Helen did not dare snoop in her stepson's rooms, but there was always a trail of alien belongings scattered here and there, the detritus of more "friends," many of whom slipped into the house in the wee hours. She found a hypodermic needle in a bathroom; Bruce claimed that it belonged to an unnamed acquaintance. Helen frequently came home from work to find her housekeeper up in arms. Lovell's kitchen was under constant siege at lunchtime by a parade of unfamiliar young men who seemed unusually voracious, even for teens. Some were older and hairier than typical high school kids; David thought they were "beats," a hairy counterculture tribe getting bemused coverage in the Los Angeles papers and *Life* magazine for their libertarian views and unabashed drug use.

The cook tried to keep up with their crazy thirst—what *were* they doing in there? Lovell was ordering twelve quarts of milk every other day, an extravagance that made Helen wild. Mounds of sandwich makings disappeared in a trice; ziggurats of dirty dishes rose and teetered in the sink. To Helen, her husband appeared grief-stricken, baffled at the transformation of his bright, loving boy. The couple consulted a few child psychiatrists for advice. Certainly, Helen's arrival was part of the issue, all the experts concurred. But Bruce was never around to take or return his mother's calls, either. Tibby wrote him letters that Helen believed went unanswered. Helen and Duncan the dog did their best to console David. Then in June 1960, the collie developed sudden intestinal troubles and died. David sobbed for hours and mourned for days. On July 12, he called Helen at her office, in tears again. "We've lost Buddy."

His friend and boss Buddy Adler had died of lung cancer at fifty-one. David was an honorary pallbearer; the interment at the storied Forest Lawn cemetery was excruciating but for the grin-inducing engraving on Adler's tombstone: "From Here to Eternity." Genuinely mourning his friend, David was stunned and disgusted by the jockeying by other studio execs to get into the "right" limos in the funeral procession. Industry speculation on Adler's replacement as head of production at Fox was rampant before the first spadeful of dirt hit the coffin lid. Some of the handicappers favored David Brown for the job; the trades called him a dark horse for the slot. Congratulatory phone calls had begun, albeit premature. The choice rested with the studio head, Spyros Skouras, a Greek shipping magnate who had made his second fortune in owning movie theater chains, and had produced classics for Fox, among them *The Hustler, Gentlemen Prefer Blondes, The Seven Year Itch*, and Helen's beloved *The King and I*. Skouras was immensely rich, and, during his tenure as president, things had been on the upswing for David's career. The two had always talked frankly.

On the day after Skouras's decision, David returned home deflated and depressed; he had been passed over for a barely literate, older, and sickly Brit. At a meeting, David challenged Skouras about his choice; the Greek turned on him, red-faced and furious. Shortly afterward, David was relegated to the role of producer with four minor projects, and forced to endure the humiliation of a thousand slights, studio style. Overnight, his calls and memos were ignored. Helen watched in horror as he was stripped of all those glorious perks: The expense accounts! The parking spot! The car! He was only thankful he still had a job.

Helen grieved with him. Fuck Hollywood! Look what it did to her darling. David was plunged into the first depression she had seen, having lost his plummy perch as literary arbiter. The dog was dead, the stepson likely using drugs and disliking her intensely. Her own career was drifting badly, with little to engage her. She was finding it harder and harder to shift through her new commute of fifty-nine signal lights and descend to her days at Kenyon & Eckhardt. The work that had once distinguished her was still being spindled and mutilated. One humdrum day, Helen was summoned to the West Coast manager's office from her moldy perch in the old dental lab. She nearly doubled over from the shock when he made an abrupt pronouncement: her salary was to be cut by a third, effective immediately. As soon as she was able to speak, her reaction was rather girlie; she couldn't help it: Didn't they *like* her anymore?

Oh, they liked her just fine. But they had decided—never mind those months of mad wooing and Max Factor's imperative to "get Gurley" at all costs—that Mrs. Brown just made too much money. It didn't sit well with management. If she didn't want to work for less pay, and that was understandable, they'd allow her to leave.

Allow her? Was that what this was about—they wanted her out?

Oh heavens no. They were happy with her and her work was just fine. She just made too darn much money. The West Coast office had to cut expenses. And, "We know your husband can support you and all that." Blurting that she would think it over, she hustled out of the man's office, drove home, and laid her burden down. David was as stunned as she was, and furious. They didn't need the money. He told her that she shouldn't even show up there the following day or ever again. But Helen needed to work; she simply had to. It was the way she defined herself and her place in the world. There weren't any comparable slots for women anywhere else in town; she was at the top of the heap and out on a ledge. Helen went back, took the cut, and worked as hard as she ever did. She could never dog it. What if they fired her?

To help herself bear the mad injustice of it all, she stole. She started in the mailroom, filching three- and four-cent stamps and, occasionally, some airmail stamps. It proved a lukewarm teaspoonful of revenge, and she quit the mailroom capers after filching about four bucks' worth of postage. Helen then upped her larceny to swiping steno notebooks, three hundred file folders, a quart of typewriter cleaner, and reams of onionskin paper and carbons. She would find a use for that flimsy pink stock soon, banging away on a used typewriter she'd bought from FC&B. David had been after her to write something besides ad copy. The man passed book ideas around to other women like chocolates. Maybe he had one for her.

15 🪶

For All the Single Ladies . . .

In those days, the only people who made love were these: in the colleges, stringy-haired, lonely daughters of left-wing urban parents; in
the high schools, pretty girls who got pregnant and got married; in
the adult world, women who, in typing, teaching, theater, publishing, art, were stymied in their jobs.
—Renata Adler, *Pitch Dark*

I guess it was a pippy-poo little book and yet it had great sincerity
to it.
—HGB on *Sex and the Single Girl*

FIVE MONTHS INTO THE MARRIAGE, while Helen was in Arkansas for a
visit with Cleo, David was searching for something in a storage room
at home and came upon a sheaf of Helen's old letters and carbons; when
she typed personal letters, she often kept a copy. Some of the letters
in the packet were on Foote, Cone & Belding stationery. They were
between Helen and a certain Chicagoan, Bill Peters, who worked at
J. Walter Thompson, a large public relations firm. They were both in
the business of deft and gentle coercion. It was apparent they had met
on an airplane in May 1949 and struck up a hot little correspondence.
David settled in with the packet of letters and read on.

The single secretary jouncing along on the early-morning bus to
FC&B came to life for him, as did her cultural leanings at twenty-
seven; it seemed that Helen was a keen S. J. Perelman fan but she was

not especially enjoying Norman Mailer's *The Naked and the Dead*. She swooned over her LP recording of *South Pacific*, played it until it was worn to "a handful of dust." Since Peters—eager boy!—also wrote to Helen during her visits to Osage, her return letters from there helped David picture his wife as she might have been that very moment. Helen's home place was the dark side of the moon to him. He had asked her— what the heck *did* she do in Arkansas? Now he knew: she slipped back in time, custom, and memory, floated in cool, lazy creeks as she pondered her home state's "unprogressiveness," ate fried chicken, and hand-pumped Cleo's wheezy Hammond organ long enough to play the score of *Kiss Me, Kate* and "Onward Christian Soldiers." Poorly.

As for Peters: he sketched himself as a restless husband and father of two, trapped, at twenty-eight, in a corporate job unworthy of his intellect. He was reading Dreiser and *The Saturday Review of Literature* (he was a would-be novelist) yet building the little postwar dream house in a Chicago suburb. The foundation concrete was poured, the sewer hookup done, and through it all, he claimed to dream of that free bird, Miss Gurley. The billets-doux comprise a midcentury minuet of coquetry and longing. There is no overt sexual talk from Helen. Yet soon Peters is mad for her, confessing the aphrodisiac effect of her tart, witty dispatches. She *excites* him. The ardor fizzled on a brief West Coast meeting. In her letters, Helen had hinted gently, then sternly ("you're married") that it wasn't meant to be. Read between their lines and it's evident that the chemistry is all wrong; Helen's ardent correspondent is just too darn pleased with his sewer hookup in Squaresville, a "patio" type after all.

David refolded the letters and returned them to their place. He was indifferent to the unfulfilled romance; he never cared to hear about his wife's past dalliances, but he was struck by her art of persuasion. Helen had utterly bewitched an intelligent stranger with words. Though Mr. and Mrs. Brown had clashed in a couple of rousing arguments on advertising—David was loudly contemptuous of its venal deceptions— he realized for the first time that Helen could actually write. It wasn't art, but she could engage. The voice was welcoming, conversational, mercilessly self-deprecating, and often funny as hell. When she returned from her trip to Osage, he told her, "You have a delightful writing style. I'd like to think of something for you to write."

No one had complimented Helen's prose in a long time. The almost total dismissal of her copywriting stung. She complained that her assignments were growing scarcer. Her workdays at K&E had become so stultifying that she was taking afternoon naps on a small strip of red carpet she rolled out on the floor. She asked David: Did he have a little book idea for her that she could peck at on those tedious afternoons?

If only he'd known she was really interested in trying to write a book. He had a corker, one that would have suited her perfectly. It was a guidebook of sorts for single women, something along the lines of "how to have a successful affair." He had listed the key elements in a snare-the-guy campaign: the right clothes, food, and sex tips, of course. There was a slight problem, though; he had just given the idea and outline to someone else.

"My God, that's my book, that's my book!" She insisted that David get the idea back. He did, quickly. Helen rolled a page of that purloined K&E onionskin into her typewriter carriage and set right to it. Almost immediately, she hit a wall. Except for the constant churn of letters to family and friends, her prose had chiefly been composed in terse copy blocks and thirty-second TV spots. For days, then weeks, she sat there stumped, rattling off what she called "dibs and dabs" and trashing every attempt.

David was gentle but unsparing in his critique. First the tone was too self-conscious, then too pretentious. After each attempt he urged her, "Sit down and try again." She did. Again and again. It was not pleasurable. Whatever was she *doing*? But what else was there? Her salary had been slashed, her copy mangled, and her professional self-esteem was on life support. She didn't imagine any sane woman would stick with the vexing little project. "They would have said, 'To hell with it! To hell with it! To *hell* with it!'"

Such was the bumpy start of a collaboration that would eventually seem as natural as breathing. Helen had begun showing David her ad copy for Max Factor while they were still dating. But the Browns' working relationship as pop/cult co-conspirators was never as male-dominant or one-sided as the standard Svengali and protégé model. Helen was no pliant ingénue. Instead, the two would click with the unerring force of a pair of magnets drawn to each other's opposite poles: literary versus instinctive, promoter versus executor, canny versus candid. The New Yorker and the Californian were right and left of coast, brain, and loyalties.

Sometimes they would disagree, loudly. Helen came to realize that she and her husband had different views of what her book should be. His notion was sassy and cutie-pie; Helen found it "a bit on the gamey side." It came down to this: David wanted to titillate and amuse. Helen wanted to help. She surely could have used the counsel of a wise veteran while navigating the bachelorette shoals. She reset her course: "I got into something more personal and poignant." Her focus sharpened when she looked at a sheaf of notes she had been jotting down, some of them written while she was under the hair dryer; she abhorred "dead" time— why waste even a *moment*? She realized that she had been drawn to a subject no one was talking about in a meaningful way: women without men. She was still fuming over the recent media and cocktail party debates set off by an article of that title in the July 5, 1960, issue of *Look* magazine.

"Women Without Men," by Eleanor Harris, did get people buzzing. But Helen found the chatter wrongheaded and maddening. She was especially appalled by the picture Harris painted of a parched and barren single life; she seemed to believe there was little a woman could do to escape the default miseries of not having a husband. Harris's tone, alternately pitying and scolding, was downright traitorous to her sex. The more Helen read of it, the angrier she got.

By the time Harris's article appeared, hundreds of thousands of the 21.3 million single women in America had moved to cities in hopes of finding better lives for themselves. Harris contended that though they left home in search of husbands, they found "only work," a dismissal that raised Helen's professional hackles. And a lack of male attentions was hardly Helen's experience in Los Angeles, or that of the New York working girls interviewed by Rona Jaffe. Harris was still passing judgment on Girls Who Did: "Many unattached women of 'nice' background are as much drawn to sexual relations with men as married women or perhaps more so; relentlessly, they go about most of their lives trying to find sexual fulfillment." But since most of these randy hunt-resses of "nice" pedigree didn't do it without a ring—at least in Harris's view—this proved problematic. Harris reported that a third of the un-married women in America were somehow "getting along" without steady male companionship.

Helen fumed. *Getting along?* Whose side was this journalist on? With feminism in woeful postwar eclipse, with many wartime work-ing women having ceded their jobs to returning military men, Harris's ideal for women—a secure, married life as wife, mother, and helpmate—was maddeningly retro. It amounted to de facto surrender.

It got worse. In concluding her dispatch from the dispiriting, camphor- and cabbage-scented boardinghouses and bedsits of spinster-dom, Harris appended a couple of paragraphs devoted to an eccentric coven of single women actually enjoying a "man-free life." She concluded with an admonishment to their desperate sisters: "It would do no harm if our frantic hordes of unwed women would think over those [man-free women's] statements. Perhaps several million of them would stop their headlong hunt and finally settle down for a well-earned rest."

Harris stopped just short of suggesting kitten adoption and a hot water bottle between the sheets.

Helen's typed volleys came quickly, and con brio: "There is a tidal wave of misinformation these days about how many more marriage-able women there are than men (that part is true enough) and how tough is the plight of the single woman—spinster, widow, divorcee."

Then she delivered a backhanded swat to the annoying machinations of mothers, pushy aunts, and smug marrieds: "I think a single woman's biggest problem is coping with the people who are trying to marry her off!" Helen knew that it was hardly an either/or situation. Why didn't people understand that being single didn't have to be "man-free"? That an unmarried woman could want something better than merely "get-ting by"?

Helen did think of herself as a *nice* girl, always; she believed just as strongly that unmarried sex was "a wonderful, delicious, exquisite thing." Considering Harris's caricature of "frantic hordes," knowing so well the disappointments and dreams of that misunderstood population, Helen said, "I just felt something in my gut."

She'd go ahead and do it—make a reasoned case for the contrarian view. She refused to see singledom as merely a sentence to be served. The unmarried needn't be default ascetics. Instead, she wrote, "The single years are very precious years because that's when you have the time and personal freedom for adventure." She plumped up her point with a quote from Tennessee Williams's play *Camino Real*: "Make voyages. Attempt them. That's all there is."

How much better when those daring transits involve men, good sex, great female friends, fulfilling jobs, travel. What a dull time it would have been for Helen without her frisky pair of generals, the luminous transits over the Mojave Desert with her dauntless pilot, Freddy, her divine spin through the glories of Rome with her Vespa boy, the sizzling afternoons with a clutch of girlfriends held rapt by the blood, dust, and drama of Mexican bullfights. If anything, she berated herself for being too boring with those frugal weekend projects, making curtains—even pajamas. Gawd, who makes *pajamas*? Looking back, she said, "It's one of the regrets of my life that I didn't screw all that and learn French."

Helen kept typing; she set the lynchpin of her immodest proposal right on page thirteen of the manuscript: "This then is not a study on how to get married but how to stay single—in superlative style."

She worked on the book all day on Saturdays and part of Sundays, leaving time for the Will Rogers walks with David. On weekday afternoons in the office, she put aside the charts of lipstick shades and stacked storyboards. She clacked along on her manual machine, looser of wrists and lighter of spirit. The title of her first sample chapter, aimed squarely at all that dull and uninformed spinster-pity, was a lapel-grabber: "WOMEN ALONE? OH COME NOW!"

Helen cast off any ill-fitting writerly language, stuck with the confessional and the colloquial, and began to tell her own story. She might have been talking to her reader over a tuna salad plate at Woolworth's lunch counter: *Listen, kiddo* . . .

> I am not beautiful or even pretty. I once had the world's worst case of acne. I am not bosomy or brilliant. I grew up in a small town. I didn't go to college. My family was, and is, desperately poor and I have always helped support them. I'm an introvert and I am sometimes mean and cranky . . .
>
> But I don't think it's a miracle that I married my husband. I think I deserved him! For seventeen years I worked hard to become the kind of woman who might interest him.

She told the truth as she saw it: Any girl willing to work at it could do as she did. No one need be defeatist about being single. She summoned the anger that had been aroused by the *Look* article and the rest of the depressing media cant: "Frankly, the magazines and their marriage statistics give me a royal pain. There is a more important truth that magazines never deal with, that single women are too brainwashed to figure out, that married women know but won't admit, that married men and single men endorse in a body, and that is that the single woman, far from being a creature to be pitied and patronized, is emerging as the new glamour girl of our times."

So to hell with it! To hell with the pity parties, the dismal surveys, and the finger-wagging pundits. It was Mrs. Brown's sincere desire to gently deprogram the brainwashed single women, those "frantic hordes," and set them on a sensible path to fulfillment in love and work. No one else had made the effort, at least not in such a direct, concerted way.

What we now call the self-help book genre was hardly new; Dale Carnegie's 1936 bestseller, *How to Win Friends and Influence People*, has burgeoned into a personal training empire still winning fat contracts with corporate HR departments nationwide. The twin sisters Pauline Phillips, writing as Abigail Van Buren (Dear Abby), and Eppie Lederer (under the pen name Ann Landers) dispensed a folksier

pastiche of syndicated advice and etiquette from the mid-fifties onward. But that middlebrow school of self-improvement relied on conservative canon: chaste, Calvinist, and dull as dirt. This was not for a
scrabbler such as Helen, who complained that "most of the advice givers were still pretty puritanical—Abigail van Buren, Joyce Brothers,
churches, teachers. Unless a girl could afford to go to a psychiatrist,
which I had done, there wasn't really anybody terribly hip who would
be responsive to questions she would dare not ask anyone else." She
would position herself as a different sort of girls' guide: "I was the
sophisticated older sister in whom they could confide."

As she wrote, she heard the sentences as a private conversation—
just us girls. Having been there, she could anticipate those Questions
Never Asked and provide some meticulous and slightly lubricious
operating instructions. The book Helen had outlined was a practicum
and was never intended as an overtly feminist tract. Systemic change
was not at all on her radar; instead she addressed herself to bettering
the small, quotidian lives toiling within the status quo—those, herself
included, she would come to call "mouseburgers." Sexism was not even
in her vocabulary, though it had dogged and demeaned her relentlessly.
Let someone else tackle the social and intellectual aspects of the problem; she was a realist, not a revolutionary. Anger may have fueled some
of her own advances, but she believed less in getting revenge than in
getting busy. Fear was ever at hand; she was forthright about her own
failures of nerve along the way, and acknowledged it as both a shackle
and an animator.

An invigorated Helen kept at it; David kept fine-tuning. What she
came up with reads like a crazy quilt of truth and dare, justice and compromise, good sense and downright inanity. There would be much to
admire and plenty to wince at; some of her idiosyncratic man-hunting
tips bordered on parody: "Some girls keep a chinning bar across the
door of their offices. Men love to use it when they swing through
the door and it's good for you, too. You can get one with green stamps.
Two books."

Her petite economies ran from the savvy to the *euuwww*: "Give the
man who showers at your apartment a luscious, toga-size terry bath

sheet. Sometimes you can buy seconds at a sale." "Negotiate with doctor's offices about bills . . . Wear your oldest clothes and emphasize your modest circumstances." "Try to like kidneys, hearts, liver, brains . . ."

She offered no overnight transformations and confessed that many times she had "worked like a rat" in the office and in bed with a man just to get by. Her own journey had been a creep, not a leap, and she counseled the sensibly incremental approach: "I know that everybody is always tugging at you to shuck off your slob suit, to be as dynamic as Ethel Merman, as well-adjusted as Lassie, to learn Portuguese, cook with seaweed, embrace Yoga, know Shakespeare. At the very least you must sandpaper your calloused heels and organize your closets."

Helen's Way was a working girl's iteration of Kobayashi Issa's classic haiku:

> Oh snail
> Climb Mount Fuji,
> But slowly, slowly.

Even if your prince wasn't waiting at the top, the journey could and should transform, she insisted. The tone was never shrill or salacious; Helen addressed her reader calmly, as though she were suggesting a new form of pressed face powder: "Perhaps you will reconsider the idea that sex without marriage is dirty."

The corollaries to that audacious principle were simple yet incendiary for the times. Mrs. Brown's growing manuscript declared that it was okay—even imperative—to enjoy sex outside marriage. That equal rights for women should extend to the bedroom. That meaningful work outside the home was essential to a woman's security and self-esteem. Regardless of Helen's intent at the time, the book's combination of cheerleading and how-to's did indeed presage the self-help boom and an unapologetic, self-affirming "second wave" feminism that would rise up in the ensuing decade.

About the pippy-poo aspects: Helen had a way of slipping off the moral high ground and into the inane and undermining. A good part of the problem lay in the breezy way she framed things: "I needn't remind you: career girls are sexy. A man likes to sleep with a brainy girl. She's a challenge. If he makes good with her, he figures he must be good himself."

Of course there were shortcuts and temptations toward itty-bitty venial sins: You work *hard*, for little pay and scant appreciation. Pilfer from petty cash if you can. Whenever possible, men should pay for everything. The manuscript went deep Lorelei with examples from her own scuffling days: Diamonds (or even a bus fare paid for by a beau) can be a girl's best friend when she's wondering how to make next week's rent. A man should always replace the liquor he drank chez *toi*. Take it from a child of the Depression: M-O-N-E-Y rules, and you'd be a fool, darling, not to accept cash and "prezzies" from a man you've been, um, entertaining.

Helen did not talk down to her reader but looked her straight in the eye; she was addressing her own, still-struggling underclass. Her message was beamed to working single women with limited options and means, those who were still thrashing in the steno pool, who slept fitfully in a metal crown of bobby pins when the salon was too dear. The text is larded with reminders of Helen's unlovely journey upward, even in her apartment advice: "Creep up on decorating as you would any new skill. Remember how long it took to learn shorthand?"

In its way, Helen's little book was as much a class struggle as a feminist imperative. In her manifesto, the Single Girl, long the outlier in two-by-two *Leave It to Beaver*–land, was swept past those tedious tract ranch kitchens and told she deserved the best table in the house—at Sardi's, the Polo Lounge . . . and in the boardroom. It carried a stern caveat: nobody's going to hand it to you, sister. Hers was not a plan for sissies: "There is a catch to achieving single bliss. You have to work like a son of a bitch."

Helen neatened up her opening salvo and showed it to David.

"I think you've got it. This is nice. Now go!"

Rather than being peeved that she had veered from his original vision for the book, he seemed excited by its headstrong new direction. His enthusiasm was galvanizing for both of them, Helen said. "There apparently aren't many men who encourage their wives to take on some professional adventure. But David was like a child with twelve pounds of Swiss chocolates. He was just blooming and blossoming throughout the entire writing of *Sex and the Single Girl*."

Perhaps he sensed a hit, or at the very least, a balm for his wife's misery on the job. And how she had needed his encouragement. "I never would have been me now except for David because I had a built-in, sleep-in editor." More confident, she tore through the rest of her introductory chapter and followed it with a second called "The Men in Your Life," a compendium of types and hunting grounds. Then she drafted a comprehensive outline, from aphrodisiacs to zits.

There was one knotty contradiction to dispense with before she could go on; Helen had to address the fact that she was now writing from the Other Side, married and thrilled to be so. She had grabbed the brass ring after all, but she tempered her triumph with this flat declaration: "I think marriage is insurance for the worst years of your life. During your best years you don't need a husband. You do need a man of course every step of the way, and they are often cheaper emotionally and a lot more fun by the dozen."

Having secured her own insurance, she had no serious regrets about leaving her single years behind. Even though she had "crossed over," she claimed good authority as an advisor: "I was single 37 years. Who better than me?"

16

We Have Liftoff!

We stand today on the edge of a New Frontier—the frontier of the
1960s, the frontier of unknown opportunities and perils, the frontier of unfilled hopes and unfilled threats.
—Senator John F. Kennedy, accepting the Democratic nomination
   for president, 1960

You can fail in your brazenry. It's no disgrace.
—HGB, *Sex and the Single Girl*

WHILE SHE WAS WRITING the beauty advice sections of her manuscript,
gently scolding her single girls to get it together on lip-shaping ("What's
the matter you aren't using a lipstick brush? Got the shakes? The stub-
borns?"), Helen made some bold aesthetic adjustments of her own.
Though David had remarked upon her "salt and pepper" hair when
they first met and seemed to find it attractive, she began a meaningful
relationship with Miss Clairol's "chestnut brown" shade, subduing the
hints of gray with suitable brunette camouflage. She also indulged in
the first of many plastic surgeries to come.

Helen decided to have her nose "revised," as she put it. She chose
Dr. Michael M. Gurdin, who also worked on Marilyn Monroe's chin—a
fact only revealed a half century after the star's death, when the late
Dr. Gurdin's surgical records were found in storage by his partner, Dr.
Norman Leaf. Monroe had come incognito to their posh clinic, where
her file was under "Marilyn Miller," from her marriage to the playwright

Arthur Miller. Celebrity cosmetic surgery was still extremely hush-hush. Helen got the recommendation from her friend and officemate Marilyn Hart, whose nose job she judged to be "sensational." Gurdin's staff, quite experienced with high-maintenance women, had their hands full trying to prep the new patient for her procedure.

Mrs. Brown, please!

Helen's face had turned red and puffy even before the gleaming scalpel was in the surgeon's hand. Dr. Gurdin was perplexed, then annoyed, when his new patient sobbed so piteously, so ceaselessly as he attempted his pre-operative procedures that he could not administer the local anesthetic necessary. If she did not quiet down, he warned, he would send her back to her room in his clinic. Helen quit sniveling but the pattern would persist; even though her many ensuing cosmetic surgeries were by choice, she tended to carry on during pre-op like a Parisian *duchesse* facing the guillotine.

Once the good doctor got busy, he effected a subtle resculpting. Profile and frontal photos of Helen and Cleo together show that Helen had the broader and rounded tip of the Sisco nose thinned around the nostrils; a small bump on the bridge was planed straight and narrow, ending in a WASPish point. She was thrilled with her modest emendation. As an early joiner of the growing trend for surgical enhancement, she was eager to trumpet its physical and psychological effects. She tucked her experience right into the end of her book-in-progress, in a section called "Kisses and Makeup."

"Plastic surgery is admittedly expensive, not covered by Blue Cross, horribly uncomfortable for a few days—but oh my foes and oh my friends—the results! The lovely cataclysmic results are the kind you can't get any other way." She explained that her new nose was like her first one but smaller; some friends who hadn't seen her for a while didn't notice. "They just tell me I look pretty, or rested, or something. Yes, plastic surgery is very, very 'natural!' . . . I'm just a cheerleader."

Helen had purchased her new nose during a time when plastic surgery was on the upswing. In the mid- to late 1940s, surgical innovations necessitated by horrific war wounds had introduced the developing specialty to the public in "miracle" stories about the restoration of badly wounded veterans. The press attention to reconstructive plastic surgery went a long way toward establishing the skill and advances in the surgical specialty. In 1946, a series of articles was published over three weeks in *The American Weekly*, a Hearst newspaper supplement that ran nationwide. The series umbrella title was "Farewell to Ugliness." The articles drew a direct line from wartime surgical reconstruction to shoring up common "turkey neck" and other mortifications of the flesh: "The matron with too many crows feet around the eyes will have new hope and faith because of plastic surgery on wounded veterans."

For the surgical profession, there was an economic imperative. With peace came a sharp decline in patients. The doctors' plan to expand the specialty is traced in Elizabeth Haiken's study *Venus Envy: A History of Cosmetic Surgery.* "In the years after World War II," Haiken wrote, "plastic surgeons led what would become a widespread trend toward marketing medical techniques and technologies to particular groups. The first problem they targeted was aging, and the first audience they targeted was female—specifically middle-aged, middle-class women." Helen was squarely in the crosshairs of their campaign. She decided that her cheekbones would be next.

What magazine trend pieces had been calling "the democratization of beauty"—more affordable potions and procedures for the middle class—was in keeping with a general uptick in national morale and expectations. Helen was pecking away at her outlier treatise as America stood at an optimistic threshold. The war had been over for a decade and a half; prosperity was holding. Seeds for technological advances sown in the fifties had surfaced and were vining upward.

Americans even saw themselves differently. After generations of black-and-white pictorial, the nation began to dig itself in full, "living color," most gloriously in Uncle Walt's Fantasyland. With shrewd foresight, Disney had shot its films and TV shows in color. They ran in black-and-white until the wider adoption of color broadcast technology; in 1960, American families began gathering before the box religiously on Sunday evenings, enthralled by Disney's *Wonderful World of Color* on NBC.

On the sexual frontier, there was better living through chemistry;

the expansion of sexual freedom that the birth control activist Margaret Sanger, Alfred Kinsey, Albert Ellis, and Charlie Cooke had envisioned was finally at hand. The first oral birth control drug, commonly referred to as the Pill, was approved for general contraceptive use. Over the previous three years, half a million women had already begun using Searle's Enovid 10 mg for menstrual disorders. Diaphragm use plummeted in favor of the more effective and easy-to-use pharmaceuticals. Being a habitual early adopter, from health food to yoga to psychotherapy, Helen would switch to the Pill in 1963.

As the next election cycle churned forward and a telegenic young John Fitzgerald Kennedy—a Catholic!—began his campaign for the White House with his "New Frontier" acceptance speech, Helen saw her dear friends the Beldings dive into a frenzy of political activism on behalf of the opposition. Don Belding's unpublished notes detail his growing friendship with and support of Richard Nixon. He huddled with the Republican candidate and provided him with a nineteen-point plan for campaign speechwriting. He received a warm thank-you and Nixon's promise, never realized, of a place on the six-man "behind the scenes" team to draft the new Republican administration's platform.

Quietly, Helen had changed parties and become a Democrat again. Having married a liberal New Yorker, the old-time southern Democrat found her return to the fold made good sense and better domestic harmony—at least at the time. Maintaining her distance from the Beldings' Republican fiestas was prudent for Mrs. Brown, though not because of any political disagreements. There were some dicey overlaps in her old friends' social circles. When the Beldings gave a party for the Nixons, Don Belding ushered the guests of honor into his hotel suite. "There they met our other guests," Belding wrote. "Three of Omar Bradley's aides and their wives, Clifton, McDuff and Matthews." Since Helen had executed some hot field maneuvers with both Clifton and Matthews, the sight of her chatting over canapés with those good army wives might have rendered the military men paler than the blanched asparagus tips.

———

As David Brown settled into his new role as producer and Helen juggled her double shift between the book and her job, there were more crises to grapple with at home. Toward the middle of what should have been his senior year of high school, Bruce Brown was asked not to return to Rexford after the Christmas break. He was said to be disruptive, combative, and disrespectful to faculty and fellow students. Against David's will, Bruce was determined to take night courses and get a day job. It turned out he did neither, and kept to the company of his hairy, freeloading posse. David considered cutting off his allowance and throwing him out of the house, but couldn't bear to take such an extreme step. Just how Bruce obtained his high school diploma or its equivalency remains a mystery, but by the late spring of 1961, the news was joyfully received on Radcliffe Avenue: Bruce was college bound. He was headed three thousand miles away, to New York University in downtown Manhattan, in the heart of David's beloved Greenwich Village. The achievement seemed no less remarkable than the astronaut Alan B. Shepard's first suborbital space flight that May. The three Browns got by under the same roof as best they could until the fall, when Bruce enrolled as a freshman at NYU. A welcome serenity bathed Lovell's kitchen and the Brown marriage; it was Tibby LeGacy Brown's turn to oversee her son in the big city as best she could.

David took Helen's proposal—two chapters and a detailed outline—and set to selling it, working his publishing connections on both coasts. Both he and Helen talked it up at a party in Los Angeles with his friend Oscar Dystel, then president of the paperback publisher Bantam Books, who seemed interested. Dystel, a graduate of both Harvard Business School and the promotional department of *Esquire* magazine, is credited with saving and revitalizing Bantam when the entire paperback industry had all but imploded.

To the Browns, approaching a paperback publisher was simply a matter of "take my book, please." Said Helen, "David and I both felt that whoever published my manuscript would make us very grateful, so it really didn't occur to us to go to a hardcover publisher first." Dystel was visiting the West Coast when the couple approached him about Helen's book-to-be; he enlisted his colleague Marc Jaffe to help pitch the proposal at Bantam in New York. After a couple of months they gave the Browns the bad news. These single women of Helen's were not miserable enough; they couldn't sell happy talk about a woman alone. Who'd believe it? If Helen wanted to recast it on a less triumphant note, they would take another look. Perhaps she could tone it down, so that her single girls struggled and suffered more. Dystel and Jaffe simply didn't know what to do with all of these "racy" girls having fun in bed.

Such a rewrite was as joyless as tap-dancing in galoshes, but Helen had a go at it and submitted a new, subdued draft and outline. A short while later, Dystel met the Browns for dinner at the Hotel Bel-Air. He lowered the boom during the entree. They just couldn't use it, period. Helen fought back tears. She summoned everything she had to act like a proper wife and do nothing untoward at a business dinner. She told herself over and over—*don't cry don't cry don't cry*. At home, she sobbed all night. The following morning, a perturbed and sleep-deprived David called Dystel. Wasn't there *something* they could do with it? She'd worked so hard . . . Dystel had one idea. "There's this crazy guy in New York . . . he does really crazy things."

Bernard "Berney" Geis was a canny, puckish publishing type, the son of a Chicago cigar maker. He had worked in the industry for twenty-five years, rising as high as editor in chief of Grosset & Dunlap, before he took his more radical, often unseemly notions of how to publish and started his own company in 1959. The cramped East Fifty-Sixth Street headquarters of Bernard Geis Associates featured a fire-house pole between its two floors. Women employees in skirts were urged to deliver manuscripts and mail by sliding down the pole. Groucho Marx was a Geis investor, author, office pet, and provocateur. One day, Groucho gave cigars to all the women in the office and induced them to light up; the outré spectacle of all those maidens sucking on fat stogies had long been a fantasy of his.

Geis maintained a small list and roster of writers that made a big noise in middle America, including the TV host Art Linkletter, Abigail Van Buren (Dear Abby), and the former president Harry S. Truman. Groucho's first mock-memoir, *Groucho and Me*, was a solid bestseller. Linkletter's first book for Geis, a tie-in to his *Kids Say the Darndest Things* program, took off like a Roman candle after he held it up on TV. From that moment on, Geis's shining path was the Tao of the Tie-In.

The upstart Geis business model was pinioned, sliced, and diced in the writer Dick Schaap's article "How to Succeed in Publishing Without Really Publishing," in *The New York Times Book Review*. Schaap outlined the operating system: Geis published a list of just ten or twelve books a year, with huge print orders, massive promotional efforts, and distribution by other publishers to further cut the overhead. Most of Geis's books were distributed through a contract he had negotiated with Random House. This gave his staff the opportunity to talk their product up at the giant publisher's sales conferences. The *Times*' disdain for this literary Barnum was displayed in the cartoon accompanying Schaap's piece: A clownishly costumed author is shot skyward by a circus cannon with nearly naked dancing girls prancing atop its barrel emblazoned "Bernard Geis Associates." A brass band heralds the send-off.

Geis's track record, albeit short, was nonpareil. In its eleven-year existence, Bernard Geis Associates landed a quarter of its books, seventeen of them, on the *New York Times* bestseller lists. Geis cared less—far less—for a hardcover original than for its subsidiary rights (movie deals, paperback, magazine excerpts) and related merchandising. The actual hardcover book was almost incidental, since Geis had his eye on the lucrative back end. His brash publishing apostasy—*sub rights über alles*—had its risks, but when it all lined up, the payoff was huge. Concluded Schaap: "He is a home-run swinger in a league of bunters."

A week and a half after David shipped the proposal, the Browns had an offer from Geis to publish the book, which David had titled *Sex for the Single Girl*. Helen didn't like it but acquiesced. "It sounded just like another Kinsey Report to me," she said. But Geis wanted it! A check for a six-thousand-dollar advance was enclosed with his letter. The deal was structured with modest sales in mind; Helen's earnings would be capped at fifteen thousand dollars a year. The payouts would continue regularly over the years at that set fee until all royalties had been paid. Stringing out earnings is great for tax reporting, Geis told all his authors. It also let him hang on to royalty payments longer to keep necessary cash on hand. Though the Browns eventually hired a literary agent, Lucy Kroll, David negotiated all deals. Through him, Helen made her wishes known, down to the last sub-clause, and executed the documents.

Once the contract was signed, Helen stowed the intrusive phone in the refrigerator and went back to writing in a state she described as "euphoric." Finishing the manuscript took a year; despite David's entreaties to hang up the damnable ad game, she insisted on keeping the job at K&E. David edited every chapter, sometimes heavily. She pushed back a bit, explaining that "when he crossed out or rewrote whole passages, I realized it wasn't working and I'd start over because David's and my styles are totally different. He's formal and stately. I'm less proper and much more casual and conversational. He's a better writer, but I'm a more popular writer."

They went back and forth a good deal over the chapter on having affairs, the original nut of the project. Helen redid it three times. She asked and then answered those questions rarely posed in polite company: "Why Does She Do It? Who With?" "Should a Man Think You Are a Virgin?" "Can You Sleep with Two Men at Once?"

Lesbians got a cursory but courteous acknowledgment: "I'm sure your problems are many. I don't know about your pleasures. At any rate, it's your business and I think it's a shame you have to be so surreptitious about your choice of a way of life." Male homosexuals, whom she counted as some of her closest friends, got fond if stereotyped consideration. First she had a few tips on identifying guys who wouldn't be shopping for that solitaire diamond ring: "If he has a male roommate and he's over *forty*, there's little doubt about his sex. He's a girl."

Kept as dear pets, confidants, and style consultants, she valued them highly: "They make wonderful friends—loyal, sympathetic and entertaining. They will sit by your bed when you have a strep throat . . . will give you sound advice about men . . . and give the best parties of anyone I know. They are frequently devastatingly attractive—and a girl can't surround herself with too many attractive men."

Unflinching, Helen marched straight into the danger zone: the Married Man. Mrs. Brown waved a silky red negligee in the faces of American wives when she suggested to her single readers that other women's husbands may simply need good sexual love instead of stultifying domesticity: "Babies, rump roasts, wall-to-wall monogrammed towels, that's all that *really* matters! Not to him! He's *had* all that. And his needs may be as tearing and searing as *your* needs, just different."

Helen was having no part in the nationwide stampede toward *la vie domestique* that engendered the baby boom. *Fortune* magazine, citing the economic good times that encouraged all that seismic coupling, characterized the era as "optimistic philoprogenitive." Helen didn't give a damn about the leading economic indicators, asking bluntly, "What's your hurry?" As to choosing a mate, she counseled taking the time to find out who *you* are first: "I could never bring myself to get married just to get married . . . how much saner and sweeter to marry when you have both gelled."

It was easier for Helen to prescribe time and patience, since she was uninterested in children. The serious gap in her counsel, one that would run throughout all of her subsequent books and her magazine, lies in her disregard and, in many instances, her outright disdain for the messy and complicating requisites of breeders. At the time her book was published, she was certainly bucking the boomer-producing tide.

The "ticking biological clock"—another menacing media trope—had yet to be invoked, but there was still a strong cultural imperative in place. Women in Helen's age group at the time had begun childbearing at an average age of twenty-one; more than 70 percent of first births were to women under twenty-five. Thirty-seven percent of women in Helen's generation had four or more children. The number skewed sharply downward in women born in 1960; they were most likely (35 percent) to have just two children.

"I guess if you've gotta foal, you've gotta foal," Helen typed, with bemused resignation. But even future broodmares would agree that the first mandate for all single readers was to find and lasso the right stud. In her discussion of marriage choices, Helen pleaded for the insistence on suitability and self-worth that had so sadly eluded Cleo: "I beg you not to settle."

When the manuscript was sent to New York, Geis's skeleton staff set to work getting it in shape for production. Letters between Helen and Geis show that he kept a close watch on his first-time author, urging speed and a bit more confidence. He was sure she could turn out a "smasherino," and gently suggested the adoption of a certain professionalism: Would she kindly proofread what she sent?

A comparison of Helen's original manuscript with the published book shows remarkably few differences. Apart from these few blue-pencil tussles, the prose was amazingly intact, especially for a first-time author. The most important change was a tiny adjustment in the title. Random House, which was none too thrilled about distributing this smutty bombshell under its contract with Geis, would not allow the use of *Sex for the Single Girl* because sex was still understood to be out of bounds for unmarried women; it would be unseemly for a reputable firm to suggest it was *for* such a thing. Geis stepped in and changed "for" to "and." The title was cleared for liftoff on the Spring 1962 list.

As radio, TV, and in-store bookings were being set up, Berney Geis brainstormed with his most formidable consigliere, a petite blond Brandeis graduate named Letty Cottin. (Soon afterward, Letty Cottin Pogrebin.) Here was a tireless and inventive publicist who could dream up stunts and write pitch letters to melt the flintiest assignment editor. Wrote Schaap, "Letty Pogrebin is an impish, energetic young lady who is utterly devoted to submerging her own literary tastes and hustling any book that bears the Geis imprint. She even reads all of the books, which is a measure of her great loyalty."

In promoting Geis books, Pogrebin cleared fences like a border collie acing agility trials. Faced with balky reviewers, media-shy authors, and bookstore bannings, she could pivot her campaigns on a dime. In any city an author visited, she engineered a tiered set of bookings, from radio and TV to bookstore appearances. Little dissuaded or delayed her; she threaded through Manhattan traffic congestion on a motor scooter. No one, save Geis himself, would be more influential in terms of launching Mrs. Brown's 267-page subversion.

Pogrebin would go on to become one of the feminist founders of *Ms.* magazine; a decade after directing the campaign for *Sex and the Single Girl*, Pogrebin, by then married with twin daughters and a son, would also write her own guide, *How to Make It in a Man's World*. Her frustrations with sexism in the "gentlemanly" business of publishing had landed her on Geis's team. She had been secretary to the editor in chief of a large publishing house. "But when I applied for a raise I was told that no woman in the company was making more than eighty dollars a week and never would. That was the personnel director's line. She was a woman." She quit. Berney Geis saw something in the ambitious and energetic young woman who applied for a job; he offered her a hundred dollars a week. Within a year, Letty Pogrebin would be vice president of Geis Associates.

Months before the publication date of *Sex and the Single Girl*, Geis flew Pogrebin out to California to coach their new author—to toughen her, really—for the noisy and personal assaults that he dearly hoped would come, broadcast by as many kilowatts as possible. If things went well on her publicity tour, Helen was in for a multi-city round of slut-shaming sure to bolster sales. Shrillness would sink her; so would tears. Helen was a copious crier; she'd have to dam the waterworks for the duration. She would have to absorb some coruscating offensives, and kill softly, with charm.

In her sessions with Helen, Pogrebin channeled the gamut of interrogators: the ornery macho radio jock; the sweet-as-sorghum lady chat show host who would pretend to be an ally, then take out the hatpin. Pogrebin started pitching hardballs at her author, with the occasional tricky slider. "You know, 'Mrs. Brown, I am concerned that you are corrupting the minds of young women and young girls . . .'" Helen held up with aplomb. "She got kind of polished at it," said Pogrebin. "And she always had that sort of whispery half smile. She could pull that off."

Finally, Pogrebin was satisfied that her author had absorbed her cautions and coaching; the diminutive Mrs. Brown seemed possessed of a samurai resolve beneath the soft voice and liquid brown eyes. As their sessions drew to an end, Pogrebin was surprised when Helen turned the tables and began coaching her publicist on another subject entirely. "It was about nutrition and skin. She said I'd have to eat this kind of green or wheat germ and I have to do this and that with my skin. I remember her telling me about her skin person. It was almost like a quid pro quo, a 'thank you for coming over and training me and now here are *my* tips.'"

Helen only wanted to help.

17

Roadshow

I understand that if I do not feel that this book can show me how to enjoy single life while being in a better position to win a man, I may return it in 7 days for return of purchase price.
—publisher's guarantee for *Sex and the Single Girl*

AS PUBLICATION DREW NEAR, Helen had been fretting about the lure of her look. How might she best present herself in the all-important book jacket and publicity photo? Hot? Chic? Author-ish?

The conservative book design deliberately belied its racy contents; it was bound in light gray cloth and wrapped demurely in a type-only blue cover. The black-and-white headshot needed for the back cover would precede and follow Helen everywhere on tour, from bookstore windows to press releases. Everyone at Geis Associates was weighing in; they tried at least four portraitists. Helen had some test shots done by none other than John Engstead, the Hollywood celebrity shooter who had made the portrait for her *Glamour* contest entry a decade earlier; maybe he could work his mojo again. The women in Geis's office loved his va-va-voom shots but the boss was on the fence. Geis complained to Helen that the Engstead proofs he saw "made you look like a $500 call girl." Another shooter's prints suggested to Geis "a Marseilles waterfront Apache dancer."

Yes, he agreed with Helen that her hair should be "more yummier."

But he was resolutely anti-glitz in some shots he had seen: "Let's avoid the evening gown and the Shah of Iran's jewelry." He was looking for something in between siren and sensible; he needed to book his author in New York *and* Kenosha. He urged her to keep trying with Engstead and others, and damn the cost. Geis suggested one Peter Samergian, whose shot did grace the final version of the cover.

Helen is wearing a prim solid-color dress with contrasting edging. Her hair is in a neat sixties "flip" with bangs, and there is a pencil angled discreetly at her elbow for the auteur accent. Smiling ever so faintly, she looks strikingly like *The Honeymooners'* wisewoman Alice Kramden (as played by Audrey Meadows), the prime-time embodiment of plain girl power able to quell three hundred blustering pounds of Ralph with a single raised eyebrow.

To loose Helen Gurley Brown upon the unsuspecting nation, Berney Geis kept to his winning strategy of promotional spending: big, loud, and front-loaded. He gave Pogrebin a thirty-thousand-dollar budget to start with—as much as two years' worth of royalties for their author—to be spent between the pub date, in late May, and early July. Geis allotted up to fifty thousand dollars for a full campaign, depending on the book. In a time when print ads sold books briskly, many with the use of clip-out order coupons, Geis spent lavishly on space in major city newspapers, in *Esquire*, *Redbook*, and even the lefty alt-weekly in Manhattan *The Village Voice*. The initial half-page print ad began with a little teaser quote from the author:

"Theoretically, a 'nice' single woman has no sex life. What nonsense!"

Helen's beloved "bible," *Glamour*, would not take the ad; presumably her book was deemed inappropriate for any Girl with Taste. *The New York Times Magazine* did not find it fit to print. Nine magazines turned down Pogrebin's pitch for excerpting on grounds of taste and probity. The Geis expert team shaped a basic two-column ad that would ballyhoo the book's content and celebrity endorsements. Albert Ellis, author of *Sex Without Guilt*, conferred his professional gravitas in a box at the top of the ad: ". . . The discussion of the single girl and her premarital affairs is unusual for its honesty and realism—and remarkable for having been written by a woman." (Helen would return the favor in 1964 by suing Ellis for title infringement when he published *Sex and the Single Man*.) The remaining endorsements made for a crazy salad of American womanhood: the actress Joan Crawford; the fitness advocate and Post Grape Nuts spokeswoman (and Geis author) Bonnie Prudden; and America's most lovable tart of gold, the stripper Gypsy Rose Lee.

The selling of subsidiary rights began before the book was on press; as is usual for such campaigns, personal connections were deeply mined. Saul David, a friend of the Browns and a former editor at Bantam, bought the movie rights to the book for Warner Bros. for $200,000. They were such good friends that Helen had shown Saul the first chapter of her work-in-progress right before he went to work for Warner Bros., when he was still in publishing; he told her then that he could "unload it" for her, no problem.

A *Life* magazine story pointed out the most shocking aspect of the studio purchase: "$40,000 a word: That is what the title of Sex and the Single Girl gets its author Helen Brown." It was true; Saul David was just buying the snappy title, since there was no plot, fictional or otherwise, to Helen's rambling little guidebook. The studio head, Jack Warner, said to be apoplectic about the price, spluttered to one of his executives, "My God, we bought a bunch of recipes, and how to fix up the apartment!" Sniped *Variety* in its chewy argot, "Helen Gurley Brown's 'Sex' tome didn't have enuf yam to spin a film, confirms producer Bill Orr."

A screenplay would have to be invented out of whole cloth, much as one had been knit for the movie version of the playwright Jean Kerr's suburban mom memoir *Please Don't Eat the Daisies*. In the Hollywood parlance of that time, it was advisable to buy such a "presold" title property that carried with it a "pretested" audience, presumably buyers of the original book. Even now, a catchy or evocative title—think *Snakes on a Plane*—can almost set its own price, plot be damned. In today's dollars, the rights fee paid by Warner Bros. for *Sex and the Single Girl* computes to a bit over $1.5 million, or a tidy $375,000 per title word. David had wisely negotiated a deal that freed Helen from any screenwriting responsibilities. The fee, *Life* reported, was "the highest sum

Hollywood ever paid for a nonfiction book—or more accurately a nonfiction non-book." Even before Helen began her promotional duties, it looked as though Geis had knocked another one out of the park.

Despite all the good news, Helen had been wrestling with a deep anxiety that she did not confide to her publishers. She waited until April, when finished books were expected any day, to send the galleys to both her mother and her father-in-law, Edward Brown. Cleo's first blast was devastating. In a fairly hysterical return letter, she warned her daughter that the little abomination would draw huge headlines— but then "so do murder and rape!" She begged Helen to withdraw it and railed against the influence of her married life in Hollywood, that sun-drenched Gomorrah "highly contaminated with carnal lust." She sniped that Helen had better find herself a safe place—perhaps in the Browns' "one hundred acres of virgin forest near San Francisco," an investment Helen had boasted of in the book. Cleo also advised airing the manuscript often lest the vile thing spontaneously burst into flames.

Helen cried bitterly. It wasn't fair. Instead of being proud that her daughter would be a published author, Cleo had expressed only bafflement and despair. Cleo simply couldn't understand: Helen had it all, a good husband, a respectable career—why spoil it all like this? She also took some things very personally; did Helen have to mention that her mother was a terrible cook? ("Mother's steaks resembled the hide of an armadillo.") Helen was stunned and angry at first. Then she realized what seemed to distress her mother most, though Cleo did not speak to it directly. Somehow, and it seemed incredible given their years living together so closely in that city of carnal lust, Cleo appeared to have convinced herself that Helen had been an *intact* single girl—a virgin!

It was delusional, of course, some sort of protective denial. But Helen had to acknowledge that the publicity surrounding her as sexual buccaneer would be excruciating for Cleo, especially at home in Osage. There had been no loud and notorious female in Carroll County since 1909, when the temperance leader Carry Nation bought a cabin and sheep farm in Alpena Pass for a quiet end to her hatchet-wielding days smashing barrels of demon rum. Cleo, who was back in that area teaching school, might want to sink into oblivion herself once the church ladies and her fellow faculty members got wind of her daughter's cavalier tips on poaching husbands during lunch hour. How *could* Helen toss it off so casually as this: "It seems to me the solution is not to rule out married men but to keep them as pets."

Helen was less forgiving of her father-in-law's reaction. The man who had so coldly abandoned his baby boy David, that pompous, incorrigible skirt chaser, pronounced her book utterly distasteful and suggested that if his daughter-in-law must publish, she should do it under a pseudonym to spare the proud family name. Edward Brown, milk industry flack and self-styled Park Avenue grandee, admonished his son: How could he allow his wife to write something like that? Henceforth, Helen had a private pet name for her father-in-law: *Pretentious Bastard!*

In Berney Geis's hive, activity had ratcheted up for the launch. The letters Pogrebin sent Helen outlining their "gets" and hopes for bookings routinely ran four or five pages, single spaced. At the end of April, Pogrebin informed her author that they had just struck gold. *The American Weekly*, a tabloid-ish Hearst magazine supplement tucked into Sunday newspapers, had taken the unprecedented step of devoting an entire issue to an excerpt of *Sex and the Single Girl*. In the mid-fifties, circulation had hit 10 million, but incursions of television and Hearst's refusal to place it in newspapers not its own would soon scuttle the randy old rag. Helen caught its last hurrah.

Pogrebin had reason to exult. In 1962, securing that fat national insert was the equivalent of having Oprah Winfrey holler up the book on the Times Square Jumbotron—with a live national uplink. The four-color insert, billed as a "full condensation" of Helen's book, would reach an estimated 3.5 million homes. Better still, newspaper subscribers tended to keep those magazine inserts in the home for about a week, widening the window of exposure and "pass-on" readership. Pogrebin explained the value of such a coup to Helen with a recent example: When *The American Weekly* ran a small article on a book about the utterly unsexy Trachtenberg system of "speed" mathematics, it became a bestseller overnight. "At a time like this," she told Helen, "all I can say is Mazel Tov."

A bit of fishing on eBay reeled in a brittle but intact example of this priceless promotional grail; it is stamped with the logo of the *Seattle Post-Intelligencer*, one of nine big-city papers it ran in. By today's shrunken newspaper standards, it is extravagantly large, ten by thirteen inches, with the full fifteen pages of editorial devoted to the book. The front cover is a stunner of early-sixties kitsch—bright blue, with a cartooned single gal surrounded by male arms bearing gifts: perfume, candy, champagne, an engagement ring. A yellow banner across the front reads "The Wonders of Being Single." Open the magazine and there it is again as the inside headline: "Women Alone? Oh, Come Now!"

Well *hell* yes! After years of magazine gloom and doom on her prospects for happiness, what interested single woman wouldn't pluck that bright blue and promising object from the stack of Sunday funnies and classifieds, nudge the tabby aside, and settle in with it on her sleek midcentury davenport? What secretarial pool wouldn't have a copy or two in the break room, coffee-stained and tattered by multiple readers? The clip-out coupon to buy a copy of the book was on the last page so that its use would not bite into the editorial.

Team Helen did not rest after that triumph. No connection was too small to exploit. When Pogrebin wrote to the Jax boutique in Los Angeles that the book contained a couple of shout-outs to Helen's adored designer, *Sex and the Single Girl* popped up in its windows to intrigue all the willowy dream girls wafting in from the canyons for their fanny-cupping Jax slacks. She contacted the Concord resort and Grossinger's in New York's Catskill Mountains; those hotels often ran weekends geared to Jewish singles. Pogrebin had a *yiddische* fixer in those hills. "I sent Helen up there with a man named Joel who used to be the go-to guy to get into that scene," she said. "Grossinger's had hundreds of people over one weekend." Geis pushed Helen to ask a huge favor of the actress Joan Crawford, who seemed to have a liking for his author: get her to do some radio spots. Helen visited Crawford, who readily agreed. Ever the movie freak, Helen filched a few squares of the star's monogrammed toilet paper on the way out.

There was some thought that a little stone-throwing at this scarlet woman author might bump up sales. Helen and Pogrebin put their heads together on ways to awaken a bit of righteous outrage; getting banned in a few places could be boffo. Helen thought hard about who might condemn the thing in a way that guaranteed a few inches of newspaper coverage. The Vatican? The DAR? The Girl Scouts? As it happened, the very Catholic nation of Spain was beginning its yearlong (and ultimately successful) process to have the book banned; Ireland would follow. Germany would move energetically, if futilely, to ban Helen's first and second books on grounds of being "youth endangering." Alas, churning up such official opprobrium proved a fruitless angle on this side of the Atlantic.

On May 23, pub day, a telegram was delivered to Helen's Manhattan hotel, predicting a long and lusty life for Mrs. Brown's literary baby, with kisses from all the gang at Geis. Helen hit the road. She was an instant crowd-pleaser at the podium and at the book signing table. She was poised and prepared. She was also frankly, wryly *Helen*. Pogrebin saw right away that women responded well to her. "She was fantastic. You couldn't wish for more because she had that wonderful combination of being ladylike plus a concerted sexiness. A studied sexiness. It didn't come naturally to her. She was wearing short skirts and I thought to myself, 'This is the last woman who should be wearing short skirts,' because she had such skinny legs."

Perfection was not what women wanted to see. Helen delivered the common touch despite her best efforts toward flawlessness. Her slipups were small and humanizing: a nylon stocking cobwebbed behind one bony knee; an earring dangled askew; her lipstick needed blotting. She was anything but cool and prepackaged. As the long lines began to form at book signings, Helen looked up and put the Eye Lock on each paying customer, answered every question, dispensed advice in a concerned murmur.

He still won't marry you? Try this . . .

"I think women sensed this was not somebody to be jealous of, the way you might if Angelina Jolie is giving you advice," said Pogrebin. "I think that's what made her so successful. She understood that, sadly, in our culture, most women are raised feeling not pretty enough. She tuned into that at a very deep level."

The insert in *The American Weekly* ran on June 2, right in the sweet spot; the author was on the road and on radio and television and the books were in the stores, though rarely for long. *Sex and the Single Girl* began moving immediately. In New York City, hundreds of thousands of young women making their way to work saw a snappy banner for the book running above the logo of the *New York Post* for a few days' worth of excerpts. The city had more than 1,500 newsstands back then, conveniently anchored to subway stops, drugstores, bars, and cafeterias for maximum traffic. Pogrebin, who had negotiated the excerpts, could scarcely believe the placement. "It said 'Sex and the Single Girl' on every newsstand in New York. There were pictures of it. And after the *Post* took it, I was able to sell syndication rights. I do remember that it took a lot of heavy lifting to get the *Times* to run the ad."

In just three weeks after *Sex and the Single Girl* went on sale, more than forty-five thousand copies were sold. Geis was going back to press for the third time. Helen's road-warrior tenacity would lead to sales of more than two million copies in the United States and twenty-eight foreign editions of *Sex and the Single Girl* in fourteen languages. By July, *The New York Times* had relented and was accepting ads for the book, which was number eight on its own nonfiction bestseller list. Helen hit number nine in *Publishers Weekly*, number three in the *San Francisco Chronicle*. Sales numbers jumped wherever she went.

In Geis's office and in the Brown home, the letters were piled hip deep. Pogrebin told Helen, "Your fan mail is fascinating." It included agony letters, thank-yous, testimonials, pleas for advice. They heard from secretaries and file clerks, saleswomen, divorcées, stranded and struggling single moms. Women alone were reaching out to their new "champion," as the promo lit billed her. David and Helen sat and read the letters together. They were nearly all about men. Many of them are preserved in Helen's archives. Paging through the handwritten histories, the stories of transformation and triumphs achieved by using Mrs. Brown's advice, it is clear that though Helen's prime audience was fellow rank-and-file "mouseburgers," her famous term for plain Jane female strivers, her messaging reached beyond city limits and the stratifications of class. The "silly little book" was calling *all* girls. Joan

Ganz Cooney, who would go on to found Children's Television Work-shop and co-create *Sesame Street*, said that she read the book when it was published, at the outset of her own career in Manhattan: "The thing I remember from it, which I practiced, was when you're single, don't hesitate to have lunch with married men, because you should be engaging with men. And I did. She was right about it. Sometimes they wanted to go farther than that lunch and one could control that. It was an easy 'no.' Her idea was to have fun and have men in your life and I took it quite seriously and it made a difference. I made some great friends of men."

It almost didn't matter that some of the reviews of *Sex and the Single Girl* were mocking and unkind, especially since the author charmingly dissembled at most appearances about her "little" offering. She never claimed it was *Anna Karenina*. The vicious slam in her hometown paper, the *Los Angeles Times*, did sting. The critic Robert L. Kirsch found it "as tasteless a book as I have read." He accused her of hating and manipu-lating men. Then he opened up with both barrels on Mrs. Brown's bona fides: "She rushes breathlessly from punchy paragraph to compressed exposure, a creature of the advertising age, endorsing the phoniness and the hard/soft subliminal sell, which substitutes for individuality, candor, sincerity. What she describes as sex is not sex at all but a kind of utility. Perhaps futility would be a better word."

Mr. Kirsch may have thought he did his best to dismiss the tawdry spectacle. Doubtless he went mangoes, as Helen might say, at the reac-tion of his own newspaper to this sly, calculating creature of the ad age. In December 1962, the Los Angeles Times Mirror syndicate contracted with Helen for as many of those punchy paragraphs as she could fit into a thrice-weekly syndicated column to be called "Woman Alone," which would be carried by up to seventy-five papers nationwide. She reasoned that it was also a sensible way to handle her huge volume of mail, targeting columns to subjects most inquired about. (Number one was men, of course.) She was already signed up for more books for Geis, and the movie rights payments were coming in. The newspaper column would be an awful lot of work, she confided to Pogrebin, but that bully pulpit was just too delicious to turn down. Helen's five-year contract with the Times Mirror Company in January 1963 stipulated that she would get half of the syndication's gross revenue, with a guaranteed minimum of $165 a week; should it bomb, either party could terminate the agreement.

Cleo had calmed down, somewhat. A month after her initial blast of disapproval, she sent Helen what at first seemed to be a conciliatory letter, allowing that she was sure the book would be an inspiration to career girls. She said that she was proud of her daughter and her talent for writing. But despite her attempts to make peace for one paragraph, the old anger boiled up mid-page. Cleo admitted that she was still smarting from being portrayed as a nitwit in the book, a "doddering old bore who sprang from share-cropper stock." She had a suggestion: Why not write the next book about certain women, too young and unformed to know better, who married the wrong men? Women who stayed for the children. She named other unhappy wives in Little Rock who had suffered her own cruel fate. The squall fills the page and ends, cramped at the bottom, "Mother." Having gotten that out of her system, Cleo found it in herself to praise Helen in the weeks to come. She actually said it: Helen looked beautiful on *The Tonight Show*, and so at ease. She sure hoped that they paid her well. Henceforth, the letters were again signed with love.

As Helen continued her triumphant march, David Brown was preoccupied with a metastatic studio disaster that had been spreading insidiously since 1958, when he and Helen first met. Movie attendance had been down during that period; Fox films had been tanking badly. The studio head, Spyros Skouras, had sent David, still his trusted scout at that point, a memo: "Dave, we need a big picture . . . Find me a big subject." David dove into a history of all the studio's productions and found that the Queen of the Nile hadn't barged across the silver screen since the silent-era star Theda Bara had played her in 1917.

Skouras green-lighted the new Cleopatra movie, and by late 1962, it was bringing down the studio. The reiteration of *Cleopatra* starred Elizabeth Taylor in the title role and Richard Burton as her Roman lover Marc Antony. It would end up costing $44 million (about $344 million today). Such spending was an astonishment back then; the epic *Ben Hur*, chariot races and all, had cost only $12 million and delivered eleven Oscars. *Cleopatra* went through two directors and two casts, and was shot in four countries over two and a half years of wretched excess. Speaking of the pricey sets built overseas, David Brown observed, "Only the Romans left more ruins in Europe."

The production churned up enough boldface scandal to all but melt the frantic tabloid presses. Lust! Betrayal! Brutality! And that was just off-set. The incendiary affair of Burton and Taylor, both married to others at the time, was a drama so public, operatic, and volatile that its lurching progress, featuring drunken fights, a Seconal overdose, and vengeful spouses, got about as much ink as the astronaut John Glenn's little stunt of orbiting the earth in February 1962. A Vatican newsletter felt obliged to pillory Taylor for her "erotic vagrancy."

Such a divine, louche way of putting it; Helen would have killed for a papal condemnation. At home, she listened with a movie fan's absorption and a wife's concern to the latest studio confidentials. David was astounded by the epic overspending and tabloid spectacle that had taken over his little notion for a picture. Even Richard Burton professed himself amazed by the public obsession with his on-set dalliance, the paparazzi dangling from cliffs over the Mediterranean, the thundering papacy. He confessed to a friend, "It's like fucking Khrushchev! I've had affairs before—how did I know the woman was so fucking famous!"

Cleopatra would not reach the box office until 1963; to float the bloated thing into theaters required a drastic jettison of baggage at Fox in the fall of 1962. Skouras was out as studio head and Darryl F. Zanuck was in. To save the company, Zanuck sold Fox's most precious asset, the 260-acre studio lot south of Beverly Hills, for $43 million, a giveaway so desperate it's been described as "a transaction that would come to resemble Peter Minuit's $24 deal for Manhattan." The property became the site of the massive development Century City. Though he had nothing to do with *Cleopatra* beyond suggesting it, David owned his part in the debacle: "When I gaze upon that gargantuan complex of hotels, office buildings, and shopping centers known as Century City . . . I think of how I may somehow have been responsible for starting it all."

Zanuck closed down all productions except *Cleopatra*; he fired nearly everyone, and began to rebuild. David Brown was told to pack up and leave in November. It was the greatest calamity to date for the Browns. Helen took it personally. She was deeply affronted on behalf of her husband, a loyal company man. Why, she spluttered, her darling had never even filled his boaty gas-guzzler from the pump on the back lot! Not once! She carried on for a while in operatic gusts of indignation and hand-wringing, then settled into their new reality: David was unemployed!

It was no small consolation that David could occupy himself with counting Helen's royalties and seeking a better payout structure. Given the size and pace of funds rolling in, sticking to Geis's boilerplate fifteen-thousand-dollar yearly cap on royalty disbursement meant Helen's earnings would take fifteen years or more to pay out. There was already a quarter-million dollars in the publisher's coffers when David asked to revisit the arrangement. Helen had to pay considerable tax on the first installment of the movie rights deal; where would they find such funds? After a good deal of back and forth, it was agreed; more payments could be loosed as advances against yet more books. David pointed out that in speaking for his wife, he hoped that Geis understood: Helen still wished to be in contact with him personally on "creative" matters.

Helen had been working up a few ideas for her next Geis nonfiction book. She was thinking lesbians. Geis did have a certain knee-jerk male enthusiasm for the subject. He acknowledged three questions that so many men really want answered about women loving women: How did they get that way? Why? And what *really* goes on between them?

In a long and thoughtfully laid out letter, Geis outlined all of the tedious journalistic things Helen would have to do to make it fly. Securing medical and scientific acceptance of the same-sex "phenomenon" would require the endorsement of medical professionals; she would have to interview many doctors. And frankly, Geis pointed out, a book full of medical citations and factual limitations was not the sort of book Helen wanted to write, was it? Nor did he want to publish such a thing. Helen should be free to express her own singular voice.

Deftly, Geis had steered his author to a more salable alternative with a sequel-like title: "Sex and the Office." She set to work right away, after taking time for a short stint in a Los Angeles recording studio. Gene Norman, a Los Angeles producer who began by recording jazz greats such as Lionel Hampton, Art Tatum, and Dizzy Gillespie, thought it would be a great idea to have Helen speak some of her womanly wisdom on vinyl. Norman's label, Crescendo, also recorded spoken-word discs with the comedian Mort Sahl and the plummy-toned Orson Welles. The Browns were intrigued. But to their consternation, they found that the Warner Bros. movie deal included recording rights to the book material. Helen cobbled up a slightly different assortment of her tangy aperçus and called it *Lessons in Love*.

The packaging took a page from the Geis playbook with an "adults only" warning stamped beside a shot of Helen's *Sex and the Single Girl* jacket photo and another caution: "Not to be played on the air." Side A is "How to Love a Girl," directed toward men. Women get their tips on Side B, "How to Love a Man." A choice cut: "How to Talk to a Man In Bed." After a strange ramble about a half-dressed girl wielding a potted plant to avoid getting raped, Helen got down to the sweet talk in the event that you should actually *want* to be in bed with a man: "As for naughty words and four-letter words, most men love you to say them and if you don't know any, they'll tell you some you can use."

Overall, the LP is a trifling, disjointed ramble, campy enough to draw delighted shrieks from bridesmaids at any of today's retro-themed, margarita-fueled bachelorette parties. It sold ten thousand copies and earned only enough royalties for a couple of Jax ensembles. Though they toyed with notions for more albums, Helen and David wisely let her recording aspirations slip quietly away.

Despite David's baffled disapproval, Helen was still hauling herself to the office. By November 1962, the stalwart trio of women copywriters at K&E had been mistreated unto diaspora. The first to leave, the most creative in Helen's opinion, was fired outright. She went straight to another agency with responsibilities for $3 million in accounts. The second grew so frustrated she moved to a large agency in another city and was made copy chief. Helen, sure of her immediate future as an author, newspaper columnist, and record-setting seller of screen rights, having outlasted several irksome regimes at K&E, packed up her storyboards, her cosmetic samples, and her nap-friendly rug and closed the door on her nineteenth job.

18

Meet the Press

It's hard to stop me, because mine is such a good example of somebody quite ordinary *wanting* to write, *trying* to write, having no particular talent and then "getting there."
—HGB, *The Writer's Rules*

IN EARLY FEBRUARY 1963, David Brown wrote to his college boy in
New York with some good news: it wasn't to be made public yet, but he
had a new job. He was headed back to publishing, as a vice president in
editorial for New American Library, a literary paperback house. Bruce
could expect Helen and David to be living in New York by April. And
what a happy reunion it would be. The rest of the letter congratulated
Bruce on the lovely young woman he had recently introduced to his
visiting father as the love of his life. David told Bruce, by then an avid
reader of philosophy and political science, that love is "the greatest moving force in our civilization." Love or the lack of it, he amended.

David also wrote to his son's new girlfriend, Kathy Ames, with
a warm welcome that suggested a father's immense relief; his long-
troubled son had found someone to love and care for him. Just a thought:
maybe Kathy could even get Bruce to cut his hair. David added a P.S. to
his future daughter-in-law: "I hope you like my Helen . . ."

Bruce had been living in an apartment at 177 Waverly Place in
Greenwich Village with a classmate, a prelaw major named Marc

Haefele. After a career in book publishing and newspapers, Haefele is now based in the Los Angeles area as a print journalist and radio commentator on NPR stations. Recalling the roommates' friendship and its abrupt dissolution, Haefele said that he spoke to Helen only on the one occasion she phoned the apartment looking for Bruce. "There was no love lost between those two," he said.

His friendship with Bruce Brown began with all the promise of a heady, parent-free collegiate life in early-sixties Greenwich Village, then a banquet of soulful and seditious arts. Both young men had college draft deferments; the Vietnam War had yet to make its campus incursions through draft "lotteries." David Brown forwarded Bruce's draft card to New York with the reassurance that his son's young life would not be disrupted.

Haefele has pleasurable memories of their movable Village feast: Bob Dylan was playing at Gerde's and the proscenium-busting plays of Bertolt Brecht were wrinkling foreheads in a half-dozen Off-Broadway productions. There was pizza at Emilio's and drinking at the White Horse Tavern with classmates and neighbors. "One night we went to the 5 Spot Café to see Thelonious Monk," Haefele said. "But instead a young pianist and vocalist named Aretha Franklin showed up. We'd sit up late, listening to Orson Welles reading Whitman on WBAI." For young men studying history, literature, philosophy, and politics, life downtown was grubbily idyllic, at least at first. They were close, companionable roommates. They talked books and music and conducted genial arguments enlivened by weed and bargain booze.

"We both used a fair amount of marijuana, he more than I," said Haefele. "Occasionally I'd encounter him at home in a stoned condition, but I assumed it was marijuana use. I never saw any syringes. But one night he stole and downed an entire prescription of mine for Demerol, maybe eight or ten pills—enough to have killed the normal person. It was then I realized he was into harder stuff."

Adding to his suspicions, there was a perplexing remark by his roommate's mother, Liberty LeGacy, as Tibby was back to calling herself. She appeared at the apartment about once a month, trim and chic in jeans and a bandana shirt tied around the midriff, to help tidy the shambles only college boys could perpetrate. One day she asked Haefele how he was doing with his diabetes.

"I told her I wasn't a diabetic," he said. "I think that maybe Bruce told her that I was, in order to explain a neglected syringe she might have come across in our place."

David Brown had occasionally come to visit on Waverly Place when he was in town; he was an urbane, tweedy presence, stepping around the drifts of reading lists and pizza boxes and gamely sipping their rotgut Scotch. They discussed writers and films; he regaled the roommates with tales of his encounters with the likes of Alfred Hitchcock. To Haefele, he seemed proud and deeply fond of his scholar son. Bruce finally seemed to be thriving in classes and in the churning bohemian bazaar that his father had wallowed in so happily back in the thirties with his "commie girl."

There was no doubt that Bruce Brown was a brilliant student. "Some of his teachers thought he was a genius," Haefele said. "He had a quick grasp of dense modern philosophy. He whizzed through Sartre and Husserl, was fascinated by Wittgenstein and Heidegger, and quickly absorbed phenomenological ontology and existentialism. He wrangled toe to toe with some formidable professors like Sidney Hook and William Barrett."

Hook was a pragmatic social democrat known for his vigorous condemnation of Marxism and Stalin as well as his opposition to Senator Joe McCarthy's red-hunting, which he damned as "a heavy liability to American democracy." Barrett, a pioneering American interpreter of existentialism, was also a literary critic and associate editor of the *Partisan Review*. His friends included Mary McCarthy, Hannah Arendt, and, closest to him, the poet Delmore Schwartz. Bruce Brown seemed able to hold his own with, and even challenge, these exceptional teachers. At home, he would recap the dizzying play-by-play of his ontological derring-do in charged NYU seminar rooms. "In our first year, we enjoyed sharing each other's learning," said Haefele, "but he drew way ahead of me. And he became quite arrogant."

Their friendship curdled at about the time Bruce had loudly and wholeheartedly embraced dialectical materialism, the fundament of

Marxism. He grew erratic and hostile and sometimes growled that he would kill Haefele, though he was never physically menacing. Finally, Bruce just disappeared one day, having removed his belongings while his roommate was out. A few days later in that stinging-cold February, the landlord came by and conducted Haefele to the street for nonpayment of rent. He learned that the money he had been giving Bruce monthly was never paid to the landlord, nor had Bruce seen fit to pay rent at all for some time. Haefele surmised he had lost his rent money and his lodgings to Bruce's growing drug habit. He still cannot be sure. There might be a less nefarious explanation: "Suppose he stole that rent money simply because he was a total asshole?"

Out on the icy street with his possessions, Haefele called Tibby LeGacy, who took him in, helped him find another place, and reimbursed him what she could. She was kind, apologetic, and concerned. Here the trail of Bruce Brown ends for a while. He did finish at NYU and go on to Washington University in St. Louis for graduate school, studying history. Kathy went with him and got an undergraduate degree there. But except for the rare and incidental mention, Helen stopped writing about her stepson or speaking of him to anyone. Few of the Browns' friends in New York, old and new, would ever know that David Brown had a son.

The third Mrs. Brown scored another media coup on March 3, 1963, when a *Life* magazine article trumpeting her multimedia triumphs hit the stands. Though the Browns' maid was mentioned, there was no reference at all to the third member of the family. The writer, Shana Alexander, was patently underwhelmed by the sensational Mrs. Brown. Alexander, the first woman staff writer and columnist at *Life*, was just three years younger than Helen. She was a native New Yorker and Vassar graduate; she would go on to a career in broadcast news as the liberal voice in "Point/Counterpoint" on CBS's *60 Minutes*, a combative segment gleefully satirized on *Saturday Night Live* with Jane Curtin as Alexander.

One wouldn't expect the embedded textual hostility, given the lavish opening photo arranged by *Life* and its headline, "Singular Girl's Success." Helen, seated in a flowered shift and white stilettos, looks up at the camera from the midst of a circle of smiling men in suits who help manage her "$500,000 enterprise" (the equivalent of $3.8 million today). She is posed as a comely, broadly smiling conglomerate. Labels identify each man's specific fealties to the lady: Contracts, Publishing, Record, Syndication, Husband, Movie, Book Sales, Publicity. They hold up their products. Smiling down at his wife, David Brown is displaying what looks to be their marriage certificate.

It's immediately apparent that the reporter has little patience for this literary lightweight and her wee book with the gargantuan payday. Alexander described the bestseller this way: "There are only bits and pieces of Helen's personal story, fragmented like walnuts and thinly spread through a gummy chocolate fudge of grooming hints, advice to the lovelorn, jokes, snippets of psychological insight, decorating suggestions, exercise regimens, stock market tips and recipes. There is even some bold talk about sex but no orgies."

Asked about the personal thrills of her multiplatform success, Helen committed the sin of hubris rarely framed attractively in print: "'It's me, me, me! That's what's so heady about it,' she crows."

Within days of the *Life* story, Helen was back on the newsstands in a media platform generally accorded to the likes of Albert Schweitzer, Jawaharlal Nehru, and the historian Arnold Toynbee, all of whom sat, with dignity and seriousness, for the lengthy interrogations required. Helen Gurley Brown was the first woman asked to do "The *Playboy* Interview"; it appeared in the April 1963 issue. She was preceded in February by Frank Sinatra, and by the British philosopher and social critic Bertrand Russell in March. The issue after Helen's brought Alex Haley's incendiary sessions with Malcolm X. This was what Helen would call "heady stuff." Of eighty *Playboy* Interviews throughout the sixties, only four others were with women: the novelist Ayn Rand, Princess Grace Kelly, the atheist Madalyn Murray O'Hair, and the sex researcher Virginia Johnson (jointly with William Masters).

Though they appeared to be on the same team in terms of sexual liberation, *Playboy*'s interviewer, Richard Warren Lewis, did not lob softballs; he went straight to topics that Helen's own publisher had declared verboten: abortion and birth control. Helen did not mince words about her frustrations with Geis's prohibitions. She had plenty to say on women's reproductive rights and clearly relished the forum. Of American abortion laws, she said, "The whole thing needs to be overhauled. It's a shame that girls have to go to Mexico or Europe to be operated on. It's outrageous that girls can't be aborted here." She also harked back to the needless fear and horror she had seen her friends endure, along with the threat of infection from back-room procedures: "If a girl would be able to go to a hospital now, there would be practically no danger to her . . . The only problem with an abortion is finding someone who can perform it. And also, it's hideously expensive, like dope. I understand the going rate in Los Angeles right now is $500, and it has to be cash, right then. Well, kids don't have that kind of money. Career girls don't either."

When the conversation turned from larger issues to the personal, *Playboy*'s Lewis zeroed in on Helen's writing. He read her excerpts from some of the most vicious criticisms of *Sex and the Single Girl*. Asked whether phrases like "pippy-poo" and "teeny weeny" constitute good writing, Helen seemed unperturbed: "Those phrases seem to have annoyed people, especially the word 'pippy-poo'—they just climb walls. I can't blame it on my advertising background. I write letters that way. Let's just say I've made a thing out of writing very girlishly . . . I don't think these words offended anybody but men." As the interrogation came to a close, Helen was tasked with explaining her success. After conceding that it was a fluke and somewhat "ridiculous," she made a case for having simply told the truth as she saw it:

"Why do we have to pretend that we love people that we hate and that marriage isn't a horrible bore much of the time? The reason my book is successful is that there's none of this crappiness about it . . . Anytime one can say of your book: 'Yes, this is really how it is,' you're apt to have a hit on your hands, if it isn't too grisly. You can have verisimilitude and be commercially successful."

In a subsequent issue, *Playboy* ran reader mail about Helen's interview; she said it was the most scurrilous attack she had ever experienced.

She was stunned and hurt; she complained that readers called her a slut, a prostitute, and a lesbian. So much for the "honor" of being one of the rare females interviewed.

Helen's encounters with the mainstream press were hardly as friendly and gratifying as the radio shows and bookstore appearances that had drawn her an enthusiastic constituency following the publication of *Sex and the Single Girl* a year earlier. For Helen, it was a somewhat puzzling disconnect. She asked Letty Pogrebin for a sampling of the hate mail coming into Geis's office, along with any bad press. Pogrebin obliged; the press clips included a lashing in *Cosmopolitan*, in an issue on "Women and Immorality." A low-grade backlash against Helen's girlie-girl mien had begun, and female interviewers, seemingly the only reporters assigned to such a "women's story," were to lead the charge.

Generally they were graduates of Seven Sisters colleges, women who had worked hard to gain a foothold in a very male field. Some were already concussing their excellent brains on newsroom glass ceilings. Helen's flirty public persona might have been irritating, but there was a palpable slighting of her professional bona fides. Few articles from that time even mention Helen's stellar advertising career; Shana Alexander briefly referenced the secretarial jobs but omitted the admirable climb to copywriter, the awards, the "highest paid ad woman" distinction.

While Helen may have been personally stung by some of the dismissive press, David had a more practical reaction: let's move on. Just after Helen had finished her book tour for *Sex and the Single Girl*, he had begun working with her to expand her brand to other media. A year earlier, the FCC chairman Newton Minow had famously declared American television a "vast wasteland." The weekly network lineup certainly was a vastly male preserve: *The Jack Benny Program, The Red Skelton Hour, Ben Casey, Perry Mason, Rawhide, Route 66, Have Gun— Will Travel,* and *Bonanza*.

The Browns batted around ideas for TV projects that might be salable. Helen's proposals for a half-dozen series ranged from sitcom to public service, from the prescient to the ludicrous. While some of the treatments are amateurish and clumsy, she was once again ahead of her time in proposing the types of shows that would one day, with the right talent, prove huge hits. The Browns' brainstorming produced these trial balloons:

The Single Girl Sandra: Sandra Sloan is a woman copywriter in the advertising business, a career woman in her late twenties "who isn't panting to get married" yet wants a rich, full life surrounded by great women friends and platoons of men. In its rejection letter, ABC declared that the public was not at all interested in advertising and in any case, series based on female leads had been "uniformly unsuccessful" in the history of television. That simply wasn't true. There were popular female stars, though safe types such as Molly Goldberg's *yiddische* mama and madcap hausfraus in the Lucille Ball mode were preferred by network schedulers. Working-girl comedy had some traction in the late 1940s and early '50s, with Gale Storm as a cruise director in *Oh! Susanna* and Eve Arden as a high school English teacher in *Our Miss Brooks*.

Helen tried again with *That Tully Girl*, another sitcom centered on an office temp who spread havoc in every new job. A third workplace sitcom, about life in a company called PyroDynamics, which installed tech equipment, revolved around a bumbling president named Dinwiddie Crump who hadn't the foggiest idea how to run a company (think Ricky Gervais, then Steve Carell, in *The Office*).

Striking out with office themes, she tried the domestic arts: *Cook's on the Fire* laid out the scenario for a TV cooking game show, innovative but far tamer than the two dozen culinary competitions flambéing the egos of aspiring chefs on cable channels today. *Normal Like Me* was Helen's title for a series based on some hellzapoppin' group therapy. She drew on her experience with Charlie Cooke and his feisty dozen, right down to the punching bag in his therapy room. A decade later, hitching the same premise to a proven and brilliantly deadpan comic star proved a solid hit with *The Bob Newhart Show*, which was centered on the group practice of a Chicago therapist.

Helen intended to star in another program herself, as the "immoderator" in *Frankly Female*, which would pit her against a male cohost in debating women's issues and complaints. The suggested subjects ranged from the vapidity of women's magazines to abortion rights. In her sketch of the proposed show, Helen briefly mentioned that very hot topic with an example ripped from the news: In 1962, Sherry Finkbine, an Arizona actress who hosted a local version of the kiddie show *Romper Room*, made headlines for seeking an abortion after ingesting some pills that she did not know contained Thalidomide, known to cause severe birth defects. She was pregnant with her fifth child and her doctor recommended a "therapeutic abortion." Having been assured anonymity, Finkbine spoke to a newspaper in order to alert other women to the dangers of the drug. When her identity was revealed, she received death threats, lost her job, and endured public shaming as well as legal threats before flying to Sweden to have the procedure. The surgeon informed her that the fetus had one arm and no legs and could not have survived.

The Finkbine case was pivotal in the growing call for abortion rights; after covering the story, *The New York Times* published an editorial calling for reform of the archaic abortion standards. It might have made for absorbing and controversial television, but it's hard to envision any program director green-lighting a show by a woman given to pushing such flammable envelopes.

Nothing sold. With much the same wisdom that single-girl Helen had declared herself "America's guest" rather than inept hostess, she abandoned the notion of becoming a network show runner and settled back into guest spots as the infamous and provocative Helen Gurley Brown. After all, she had another book to sell.

PART THREE

New York

Give me such shows—give me the streets of Manhattan!
—Walt Whitman, "Give Me the Splendid, Silent Sun"

19

She'll Take Manhattan

New York, I soon recognized, loves women, whereas Los Angeles loves girls.
—HGB, *I'm Wild Again*

IN THE EARLY SPRING OF 1963, the Browns closed the door on 515 Radcliffe Avenue. With some difficulty, they wrangled their two Siamese cats, Samantha and Gregory, and set off to spend the rest of their lives as New Yorkers. Toting the yowling cats in a carrier, David and Helen tucked themselves into a first-class compartment on a swift eastbound train, the *City of Los Angeles*. Their pared-down possessions would follow in a van, and not too quickly, they hoped. They still did not have a place to live. In Chicago, the menagerie changed trains for the *Broadway Limited*. It was a pleasant, cushy journey, as David described it, save for the nervous Samantha's penchant for peeing on him in the upper berth.

Upon arriving in Manhattan, they checked into the Dorset Hotel, left the maids to deal with the disoriented felines, and went in search of an apartment. It didn't take them long to decide; home was to be on the "Gold Coast," 505 Park Avenue at East Sixty-Fifth Street, in an apartment costing a shocking $550 a month. At first, David noticed that his wife seemed disoriented. "Helen became—may I say?—catatonic and was afraid to leave the apartment in a scary new city far from her bright, sunny, friendly Southern California. There were bad patches, and Gregory and Samantha, in their catlike way, responded to them all. Sometimes nervous, sometimes hissing, they were aware."

It helped tremendously that Charlotte Kelly was already a New Yorker, albeit of recent vintage. She gave the Browns a welcome cocktail party; it was also somewhat of a thank-you for helping her build a new and lively career. Back in Los Angeles, David Brown had helped her get her job as executive secretary to the producer David O. Selznick, who was trying to mount a theatrical production of *Gone With the Wind* that he hoped to open on Broadway. Selznick was moving all his operations to Manhattan for six months, and Kelly went along, having little idea what she had signed on for.

The secretarial work was copious and exacting; Kelly's new boss was a perfectionist known as "David O. Semicolon." His personal life was as tumultuous as his prose was orderly. Kelly regaled the Browns with the ongoing adventures of life in the great man's ménage, which included Selznick's wife, the actress Jennifer Jones, their six-year-old daughter, her full-time nanny, and Kelly as secretary and general factotum, in a capacious suite at the St. Regis hotel. Said Kelly, "We settled in like a ship of fools."

She took dictation at warp speed, ran to FAO Schwarz for lavish toys, and acted as liaison between the hotel and Selznick's studio, which sent a weekly expense check for ten thousand dollars. Helen loved getting her friend's dishy dispatches on life with "DOS," especially because the hotel suite was teeming with exotic visitors: Lauren Bacall, the Duke of Windsor, Leonard Bernstein, Salvador Dalí, and Truman Capote, along with the Selznicks' grown children from previous marriages and a Japanese pyrotechnics team claiming to have invented a technique to safely create a raging fire onstage. Selznick was determined to re-create the realistic burning of Atlanta as the ultimate theatrical experience, without singeing eyebrows in the orchestra seats.

Soon into the Manhattan stay, Selznick contracted a case of infectious hepatitis and the suite was turned into a hospital ward with a quarantine section. His recovery was slow and the Broadway production fizzled. The Selznicks retreated to Hollywood. Kelly stayed in New York. Selznick had some parting advice. Having watched Kelly flail through frequent romantic and financial crises and knowing her charged family history, he advised her to go into therapy: "You are the most self-destructive young woman I have ever known and if that remains unexplored and unresolved, your assets will not serve you—for they will never reach fruition. And that would be a shame."

For years, Helen and Charlotte had discussed how their missing fathers may have affected their relationships with men, their strained upbringings, the mutual worry that as grateful if shaky escapees, they might just lose it all, anytime. Finally, with Helen's urging as well, Kelly did begin therapy. She settled in as an editorial assistant at *Ladies' Home Journal* and soon rose to a public relations position there. She had found a $140 a month apartment in a stately Stanford White building in the East Eighties. Helen and David were just a short walk away on Park Avenue, and they were a stabilizing anchor. The two women were thrilled to be together again.

The Browns' New York work lives had gotten under way as soon as they arrived. David began his new job at New American Library and Helen's first "Woman Alone" column appeared in about fifty newspapers nationwide. Given her work on the second book and the newspaper endeavor, there were weeks when Helen did not leave the apartment but once or twice. She had spread herself very thin and some of the "Woman Alone" columns read as though they were quickly dashed off, retreads such as "27 Ways to Spend Saturday Night," "Delectable After Forty," and a zippy paean to Gladys Lindberg's "High Powered Meat Loaf." She also tackled subjects ranging from good nutrition on a low budget to dating advice for single mothers, the benefits of therapy ("To Shrink or Not to Shrink"), dealing with chronic blues ("Flight from Depression City"), and a series of columns, "Women Alone—Second 'Round," devoted to widows and divorcées.

One column read as a book review of sorts. An original typescript slated for June 28, 1963, is titled "Envy Anyone?" It is a rousing hurrah for a fascinating and heartening book that Helen had come across, *The Feminine Mystique*. (Helen misspelled the author Betty Friedan's name throughout as "Frieden.") That landmark feminist platform had been published eight months after *Sex and the Single Girl*, in February 1963. It landed smack in the heartland, excerpted in both *McCall's* and *Ladies' Home Journal*, which conferred a combined readership of 36 million, most of them housewives. *The Feminine Mystique* hit the *New York Times* bestseller list in early May and stayed there for six weeks. Helen's column about it never ran in newspapers; presumably it was spiked because the book had been out so long before Helen discovered it. Her unedited typescript explains why she found the book "wonderful."

"With an impressive body of research, Mrs. Frieden presents a spine-chilling account of the nameless frustration felt by many women who are supposed to be the most fortunate in the world—spoiled American wives."

Mrs. Friedan had minced no words, declaring that American women were trapped in the "comfortable concentration camp" of suburbia. Helen cheered the skewering of some apple pandowdy shibboleths: "Mrs. Frieden also blames the mystique [on] women's magazines who fill reader's heads with recipes for Quiche Lorraine, but never a thought about the common market." It is doubtful that Helen herself spent much time pondering international trade agreements, save for their effect on perfume duties at foreign airports. The larger point taken: it was time to get homemakers' heads out of the oven.

The Brown and Friedan readerships were complementary segments of American womanhood, taking in mostly working class singles and securely if not happily married middle class wives. Helen clearly felt a resonance in Friedan's scholarly wake-up call. With its opening evocation of the "strange stirring" among married American women, of the silent question so often asked ("Is this all?"), the audacious unveiling of "the problem that has no name," Friedan's book seemed to validate all of Helen's diatribes on the stultifying life of the American wife.

Friedan could speak as one of them, though she had more advantages than many. She was married to Carl Friedan, an advertising executive; they had three children and lived in an eleven-room house in

Grand View-on-Hudson, New York. Born Bettye Naomi Goldstein a year before Helen in 1921 in Peoria, Illinois, Friedan was a formidable researcher, thinker, and writer. As an undergraduate at Smith College, she campaigned for unionizing the college housekeepers. As a graduate student at Berkeley she studied psychology with Erik Erikson. She had an early career as a labor journalist. As a married woman with three young children, she also had household help three to four days a week; it afforded her that precious commodity lost to so many homemakers: time to think. To research her book, she was able to conduct all those interviews with her former Smith classmates, to sink herself into Freud and Margaret Mead, Alfred Kinsey and Bruno Bettelheim, whose research and scholarship helped support Friedan's subversive conclusions.

The two noisy outliers took vastly different paths after their best-sellers. Helen would carve her niche well outside the complacent circle of the "Seven Sisters" women's magazines. Friedan got divorced and made a new, activist life on the barricades. Three years after writing *The Feminine Mystique*, Friedan became the inaugural president of the National Organization for Women, and along with Gloria Steinem and Bella Abzug helped found the National Women's Political Caucus.

Helen wrote cute, but took the enormous step of starting the conversation on women's sexual needs and rights. Friedan wrote canon; *The Feminine Mystique* has enjoyed lasting sales—more than 3 million since its initial publication, with a new edition for its fiftieth anniversary in 2013. It will command gender studies attention in perpetuity. The book has also been assailed periodically by contemporary critics challenging everything from its primary sourcing to its exclusion of working class and nonwhite women. Such are the cycles of reverence and revisionism accorded a true revolutionary.

It would serve little purpose to venture into that well-trampled thicket here, or to parse the vast and obvious differences between Friedan's and Brown's high-impact books. Of more interest will be the women's interactions once Helen acquires the subversive propagandist tool they both derided in their first books: a women's magazine of her own.

———

Not long after the Browns had settled in on Park Avenue, Helen began a close friendship with another female iconoclast, a fabulous creature unlike anyone she had ever met. It happened by accident. Helen was headed home, hurrying against the spring chill, when a red light stranded her on the manicured, tulip-trimmed traffic island that bisects Park Avenue. She nearly bumped into a statuesque, impeccably made-up woman and her shorter, balding husband. Having just moved to the city, Helen did not recognize the face of the attractive but dreadfully untalented actress who had settled for being the pitchwoman for Schiffli Lace embroidery supplies in ubiquitous metropolitan-area TV ads. From beneath a tower of raven hair, the stranger stared closely at the smaller woman.

"You're Helen Gurley Brown!"

"Yes."

"I'm Jacqueline Susann." She introduced her husband, the producer Irving Mansfield. Within a minute or two, the women discovered their connections. Both were Geis authors; Susann's paean to her French poodle, *Every Night, Josephine!*, was about to be published and become a surprise hit. Letty Pogrebin and Berney Geis, still flush with the success of Helen's book tour, had worked up a similarly punishing itinerary for Susann.

As she was getting ready to tour for *Josephine*, Susann was already pecking at some attempted fiction that would become, with editorial shoveling and grammatical whippings that rivaled the labors in the Stygian stables, *Valley of the Dolls*. If Helen wrote in "snippets and smatterings," Susann was given to mere sentence fragments and participles that did not so much dangle as screech and drown. No matter—Susann, too, "wrote what she knew," which was Hollywood backstage and backstabbing. That she had failed as an actress and daily popped the pills or "dolls" to assuage her own deep pains and sadness lent the book that certain salable "verisimilitude" Helen had touted to *Playboy*. Like Helen, Jackie had been "that girl" to too many unappreciative men in Los Angeles.

The trio stood comparing notes as the lights changed and changed again and traffic roared by. It was the beginning of a close couples' friendship between the producers and their infamous wives. Berney Geis was glad for the camaraderie of his authors; Helen was a perfect example to invoke. She was hands-down his hardest-working author, she loved money and would do nearly anything to maximize her profile and her sales. Jackie Susann was also very, very interested in money. Once she got out on the road and found herself booked at a radio station in some no-name town with wattage that barely reached the state highway, she'd bawl at Geis on the phone: "Did Helen Gurley Brown do that?"

Assured that she had indeed, Susann would soldier on. Once Helen was out on her *Sex and the Office* tour, they would sometimes do all-night radio shows together; their outrageous, dynamic tag team would become much beloved by night jocks like Long John Nebel. Together, the "sex lady" Helen and the unabashedly profane Jackie made riveting radio. Just a coupla great dames, dishing in the dark.

Helen was thrilled to have such a knockout gal pal. She told Susann's biographer Barbara Seaman, "I loved the way she looked because it was always showbizzy. It was sequins, it was chiffon, it was high heels and ankle straps and lots of jewelry and the beautiful dark hair. I adored her." Susann could pull off a leopard-skin pillbox hat, a sable coat, a diamond ring the size of a cocktail olive. Never mind that the spiteful literati-gnome Truman Capote would famously liken Susann to "a truck driver in drag." Susann subscribed to the PR agent's bromide that any publicity is good; her husband agreed.

Like David Brown, Irving Mansfield was canny and tireless in promoting his wife. Soon, the Mansfields would become regular visitors at the Browns' apartment. Susann did not cook or even suffer to have a kitchen, preferring hotel life. The refrigerator in the Mansfields' Central Park South suite in the Navarro Hotel contained only champagne, a jar of capers, and dog food.

By the spring of 1964, after almost a year's work, Helen was nearly done writing *Sex and the Office*. This time, the editorial exchanges between Helen and Geis were bumpy, some bordering on cranky; there would be many more discrepancies between her draft manuscripts and the final product. As they hashed out their considerable differences, there was some soothing news: *Sex and the Office* was a financial success before it was fully written. True to his sub rights imperative, Geis had already sold paperback rights to Pocket Books for $125,000, based only on a scant twenty-page outline.

Sex and the Office was not the book Helen had envisioned, chiefly for its omissions. What emerged from her disputes with Geis was a flash-fried hash of a book, oddly disjointed and teeming with repurposed characters and tales from *Sex and the Single Girl*. There was some solid advice on strategizing, professional conduct, jousting with office bullies, and negotiating salary issues. Finally, if briefly, Helen addressed the needs of the working mother. But the end product was once again stripped of the issues that mattered so much to its author, birth control and abortion. She had complained to *Playboy* that the excisions of those subjects from her first book had to do with money: "He [Geis] thought it might hurt sales . . . and if I went so far as to tell a girl how not to have a baby we might be thrown out of the Author's League or something. It was a commercial decision." It was also a legal imperative; even Letty Pogrebin agreed. Contraception was still a crime in some states and abortion was still outlawed nationwide. Helen and her publisher might be seen as condoning criminal behavior.

Geis also insisted that Helen move the section on strategies for women wanting to advance in their workplaces from the front to the back of the book; he contended that only a minority of Helen's readers—about 10 percent—had such aspirations. It might be off-putting, even threatening, to display all that naked aspiration in a chapter called "The Keys to the Men's Room" up front. Geis did approve Helen's spicy "reportage" in a chapter titled "Three Little Bedtime Stories." Helen claimed to have sat down with three women and taped their recollections of office-related sex. All three "interviewees" tell their tales in the singular, flimsily disguised voice of Helen Gurley Brown.

The kinky vignettes are gratuitous and rather *Fifty Shades of Grey*. The first is simply a boff-a-thon between a married TV producer and a single freelancer who sometimes works with him. ("Eight times for the weekend, if you want to know the box score.") The second recycles another triste secretarial "keptive." The third is a misbegotten whopper: Lyle, the "cuckoo-nut." The employers of the narrator, Miss Lanebrawn, have hired an efficiency expert named Lyle. (While at FC&B, Helen did have an affair with a nerdy "motivational researcher" who wore turquoise socks and, she claimed, wanted to marry her.) He tricks her into an affair, claiming she has been promised to him sexually by her employers as payment. Soon he makes her ride in his car topless. Then the recitation purples like an ugly contusion: she gives him silk scarves; he binds her, facedown, with a pillow in her mouth, whacks her across the rump with a riding crop, then makes love to her. She finds the après-flogging sex thrilling. Afterward, Miss Lanebrawn admires her trophies: "I used to look at them, fascinated. They were exotic. Women like bruises, I think, maybe even non-cuckoo women . . . Maybe bruises make women feel feminine and helpless."

Reader, she marries the creep.

Besides affording a flash of Helen's fantasies in the slightly dark, rough trade scenarios that play out in the book and in her unpublished writings, there is nothing in these vignettes to help or inspire the average single woman in an office setting. Even as cautionary tales, they are just . . . cuckoo.

Some of the most credible aspects of *Sex and the Office* are presented as an afterthought. Geis decided to include an appendix about all nineteen of Helen's jobs, presented as book "research." Since the economics of including them in the 309-page book as part of the main text were unworkable, Geis scrunched them into tiny agate type, with his own introduction, and titled it "The Perils of Little Helen." Despite the pseudonyms employed for bosses, companies, and lovers, "The Perils" is a reasonably accurate curriculum vitae for anyone trying to trace Helen's workplace persecutions and ascensions. But when it was published, it was as a long, forgettable footnote in micro-type.

Sometime during that busy summer of 1964, Cleo arrived in New York for a visit. Thirty years after their trips to the Chicago World's Fair, mother and daughter made plans to visit the New York World's Fair, just the two of them.

This time, the exposition was rising up from a body of water somewhat less majestic than Lake Michigan—the sulfurous marshlands of Flushing Meadows. The attractions were built on a notorious dump site. A fierce tempest was brewing as mother and daughter bounced along in the backseat of a yellow cab through the unknown borough of Queens. They still couldn't see that twelve-story U.S. Steel "Unisphere" globe pictured in all the papers. Where in heaven's name were they? Helen, still new to the city and ever leery of being taken for a ride, was hectoring the driver. Cleo took his side. She told him, "Don't pay any attention to her, she doesn't know anything." She went on to warn him that her daughter had a rather bad temper. Helen was struck by a sudden blaze of anger. Later she said it was just reflex, but yes, she *did* it— Helen reached over and hit her mother. It was a good solid swat.

Resentment had been simmering for two years, since Helen had read Cleo's letter begging her not to publish *Sex and the Single Girl*. At forty-two, Helen had heard more than enough about her foibles from the broody termagant in the flat little hat. She remained unrepentant about having raised her hand to her. Later, when working on her Broadway musical project, Helen would tell Lyn Tornabene that she'd be just fine with actually staging the backseat smackdown to make a point: Cleo could be *such* a royal pain.

How dutifully, and sometimes desperately, Helen had tried to do right by Cleo and Mary. It was a bifurcation of affection and energy that only deepened as her own happiness and success grew. For forty years, she would keep to a faithful routine: almost daily letters to Mary and Cleo, two phone calls a week, on Wednesdays and Sundays, and at least two trips a year to visit them. Since her marriage, Helen had never wavered in her financial and emotional support for her mother and sister, with her husband's full approval.

Having insisted on the right to monitor household finances soon after the wedding, Helen made sure that she had a hand in all domestic money decisions, though David would remain the point man on all of her business negotiations. A draft of a will made in 1964 indicated that

David Brown left all of his property to his wife, except for a $15,000 bequest to Bruce, who would inherit any remains of the estate following his stepmother's death. Should Bruce predecease Helen, the remaining estate was to be divided between David's alma maters, Stanford and Columbia Universities, upon Helen's death. At the time the draft was made, the Browns' net worth was stated to be about $250,000, part of it a $150,000 life insurance policy. A notation indicated that Mrs. Brown also wished to provide for her mother and sister, Mrs. Bryan and Mrs. Alford.

Mary Gurley had married. To Helen's amazement and initial relief, her sad, lonely sister became the wife of one George Alford, whom she met while having consultations on her legs at a veteran's rehabilitation facility in Okmulgee, Oklahoma. Veterans of World War II and Korea were having successes with new treatments there, but given the total paralysis of Mary's legs, it was found that she hadn't the strength to ever relearn to walk with crutches and braces. It meant the end of hope, but she had fallen in love. At last, Mary might have someone to love, support, and care for her, finally giving her a certain independence. When the couple met, Alford was seeking relief at the rehab facility for debilitating pain. An elevator accident had maimed Mary's new husband. This one occurred in a grain elevator. Alford's shoulder was crushed and nerves were badly damaged. His pain was unremitting. The couple settled in Shawnee, Oklahoma, not far from the capital, Oklahoma City, and its hospitals.

It soon became clear that man and wife carried deeper troubles to their marriage. The sheer difficulty of Mary's life had worn her down; she was an alcoholic and she chain-smoked, which was very bad for her polio-damaged lungs. To her sister's evident horror, Mary had also become obese. Soon, there were escalating troubles with Mary's husband. Complicating his own alcohol dependency, George Alford's ceaseless pain had left him addicted to prescription drugs.

So began a fresh round of family agonies and ministrations. There was little Cleo could do in Osage; it would fall to Helen to try to sort it all out. She dreaded the "phone calls from hell," and struggled with the tangle of anger and grim empathy that besets an addict's loved ones.

Of the ordeal with Mary's husband, Helen wrote, "For as long as he lived, I was involved with his pain . . . I schlepped him many places trying to find doctors or treatments that would help. George belonged to my sister, was usually good and helpful with her, so he went with the territory for me." Helen and David paid for his treatment and transportation at facilities from Salt Lake City to Manhattan's NYU Hospital.

After a few lapses, Mary did get sober with the help of AA; and she grew close to friends at the Methodist church where the meetings were held, did AA support work, and got involved with stray cat rescue. Helen didn't mind attending AA meetings with Mary when she visited. But even as a cat lover, she was sorely taxed when she bedded down on the Alfords' living room couch; six to eight cats prowled and climbed over her at any given time; candles and room deodorants did little to dispel *l'eau du chat* and the added pungency of two rescue mutts. Eventually, Helen would switch to the relative comforts of the Shawnee Holiday Inn.

The trips to Oklahoma were not all pain and drudgery. Helen remembered some of them as "deep-dish soul visits" with her sister, sitting by Mary's bed as they recalled their childhood, listening to music (mostly Mary's country favorites), watching the Westminster Dog Show on TV, and chowing down on the tamale pie and baked apples served by Mary's housekeeper. The ties that bind soothed both women in those moments, at least temporarily.

At summer's end, with the nettlesome Cleo back in Osage and the Alfords reasonably stabilized, Helen arrayed her wardrobe and packed up for her *Sex and the Office* tour. Taxing as it was, the road trip might be a welcome escape. She gladly stepped back into Helen Time, alone, focused, and unflappable. Or so she thought.

20

"How Dare You, Helen Gurley Brown?"

I just want to say that this Sex for the Secretary creature—whatever her name is—certainly isn't contributing to the morals in this country. It's pathetic. Statistics show.

—caller on a radio show during HGB's *Sex and the Office* publicity tour

"WE ARE GETTING OVEREXPOSURE SIGNALS ON HGB."

As Letty Pogrebin began lining up the publicity campaign for *Sex and the Office*, there were glimmerings of resistance. She alerted the Browns. She had heard it from *The Les Crane Show*, *The Tonight Show*, and others: Helen had just been on the air too much and was not of interest to their audiences at the moment. Even Pogrebin's PR wizardry had been neutralized. Admitting defeat, she told Helen and David that "no amount of suggesting, controversy proposals or cajoling can change their minds it seems." It was time for Helen to take some lumps, a fate not unusual for the sophomore outings of first-time authors with "surprise" bestsellers.

Pogrebin was able to book Helen on a fairly new talk show in Cleveland. It seemed tame enough; its host had done a stint on *Hi, Ladies*, a Chicago daytime klatch given to such segments as "Cleaning with Ammonia." Helen understood from her first book tour that the Midwest could be a touchy and censorious marketplace for a disruptive female, however charming. She had come to recognize the acrid tang of sanctimony emitted by both sexes; the first whiff would put her on her guard.

On September 21, 1964, she sensed a vague tension almost as soon as she took her chair onstage in the bare-bones thirty-eight-by-one-hundred-foot studio of *The Mike Douglas Show* at station KYW. The audience of about seventy people, mostly women, sat wedged in a set of bleachers. In hindsight, Helen thought it must have been a setup, a live ambush. There was something fishy, despite the welcoming smile of her host.

Douglas was a bland and affable sort, a former band singer/piano player who was somehow drawing big ratings for the show's delighted parent company, Westinghouse. On the production staff was the future Fox News mastermind and CEO Roger Ailes, who would famously meet Richard Nixon in the program's greenroom in 1968 and become his media guru for the presidential campaign. Ailes had begun on the Douglas show as a sixty-eight-dollar-a-week prop boy but had advanced to producer by the time Helen arrived on her book tour. He had been schooled in entertainment value by his boss, another very young producer and show runner from Chicago, Forrest "Woody" Fraser, who was just twenty-three when he conceived and sold the Douglas show to Westinghouse.

Ailes's biographer Gabriel Sherman wrote about the early schooling of the Fox power broker: "From Fraser he [Ailes] learned that great TV had more to do with drama—conflict, surprise, spontaneity—than with expensive sets . . . Fraser said, 'The most important ingredient for a daily show was to keep it fresh, and one way was to keep people off balance, not knowing what would happen, sitting on the edge of their seats.'" Fraser and Ailes would throw in mystery guests and surprise gags. "The occasional ambushes notwithstanding," Sherman concluded, "it was a safe place."

For the most part, that was true. But Woody Fraser had the brashness of youth and the desire to put his new show on the map. He was willing to tweak the daytime talk show formula and unafraid to make the big "asks" at KYW. So far he had been suitably rewarded: he got John

Lennon and Yoko Ono to act as cohosts for a week, gave Malcolm X one of his first TV forums, and coaxed a nervous young Barbra Streisand through one of her early TV appearances. The eclectic mix and the show's ratings, impressive for a small midwestern production, helped the Douglas show become the first syndicated daytime program in television.

Now eighty and "working harder now than I did then," Fraser called from his car, stuck in the rush hour honk of a Los Angeles traffic jam; he was on his way home from Universal Studios, one of a few places he still has programming. He also runs a few shows on Fox TV in New York. "Talk to me," he began, "so I won't be bored to death out here."

He would like to get one thing straight from the jump: Helen brought the whole thing on herself. Fraser said that he got a phone call from this Helen Gurley Brown woman pitching *Sex and the Office*. Hard. "We had never done a book before. She said that it was a breakthrough book, she was very candid about this, saying books would sell." Fraser was undecided but Helen was persistent. "She called me back two or three weeks later. She talked me into it. I thought she was going to be this hot New York chick. She was extremely smart and knew how to sell. She was a woman with vision, you know what I mean?" He questioned his instincts when she finally arrived. "She walked into the studio and I thought, 'Holy shit, we've got nothing here.' She was very plain, no makeup, didn't have much of a shape. The minute she opened her mouth, I said, okay, this is a sharp, sharp woman. All I wanted to do at twenty-three was do the best show I could. And right away, she was money in the bank."

He assigned Ailes to produce her book segment, briefing Douglas and settling their guest into a rudimentary greenroom. Fraser sat down to compose some provocative suggestions for the audience Q and A session. Helen had agreed to take questions from the audience, but she had no idea that Fraser would rile them up ahead of time. Her instincts were correct; it was a setup of sorts.

"I would make sure that the [audience] questions were not just 'How do you do your hair?' No. It was 'Would you have sex with someone in your office, maybe a married person?' They were incendiary questions, let's put it that way."

Fraser then stirred the pot further; his questions were read to the audience as cues for writing their own. "I did all the audience warm-up. I would ask, 'Is this book based on real examples of people cheating in the office? Why are you advocating sex in the office? Aren't you ashamed of yourself to do a book like this, why did you write that book?'"

Duly roused by Fraser's intro, the audience members scribbled questions before the show; Fraser went over them and selected eight. The chosen interrogators could hold their written questions at their sides but were instructed not to read them. Fraser wanted fresh, impassioned delivery; it made for better TV.

Recalling that day, Helen said that she had felt uneasy from the start. The studio audience gave off a restive sort of buzz. She would come to believe that the audience had been purposely packed with angry housewives come to confront the Scarlet Woman. She remembered it with a shudder: "There were dozens of them and one of me. It was rough." Once the Q and A segment began, they flew at her like furies, shouting over her answers, flinging accusations. Fraser said that the studio's phones trilled instantly, and madly. "We had like fourteen lines in the office. When I had Malcolm X on, the phones went nuts. When I had Helen Gurley Brown on, same thing, people yelling 'Take her off the air, she's a sex queen!' People didn't swear then like they do now, they were more thoughtful, like 'I'm surprised Mike Douglas would condone this kind of woman.'"

In the studio, the unexpected and collective anger may have blown back Helen's hair, but it did not ruffle her composure. Fraser and Ailes stood watching, amazed at the woman's moxie. "You could never put her in a corner, she would always fight her way out. And she wasn't afraid to be very clear about the message in what she wrote, which is 'This is the way life is. Your guy is going to cheat on you and sex rules the world. And it rules the world if you're single or married.'"

There it was again, Helen's impolitic, hot-button truth: single women were having and enjoying sex, with whomever they chose. Get used to it.

Most of the Douglas audience had never read the book, Helen was sure. What could they have been so riled up about? "God, were they angry," she said. "They were furious." This had never happened anywhere else. The insults were varied and colorful but the general tenor was outrage: *How dare you?*

When the cameras' red lights blinked off, Helen bolted to the waiting car and away from the flying squad of heartland harpies. They did not threaten her physically, but all those faces contorted with anger, the sheer *noise* of them was unbearable. She cried. When she called David to tell him how frightened she had been, how she might want to stop putting herself out there like that, he was sympathetic but firm. Helen simply had to stay out there and do the shows. She would always have to do the shows. He explained: "We are pimp and prostitute, without any question."

He meant it in the nicest way; she understood and accepted his characterization. David and Berney Geis had sent her out there for whatever form of love or lashings the public might bestow; she knew the risks. Helen had walked into it with a sincere heart and a straightforward mission: *sell it.* The Brown family enterprise was up and running, though it had yet to hum with peak precision and profit margin. The collaborative process was direct and efficient: David dreamed up an idea; Helen wrote it, labored over its refinement, and performed it superbly. Then they took it to the bank.

Of course it was up to the front woman to take the heat. The women in Cleveland weren't the majority, they were just loud and upset and possibly reacting to some unfortunate misunderstanding. After all, there had been plenty of admiring, grateful women along the way as well, those who told Helen their own stories at book signings, grasped her hands and thanked her many times over. At KYW, Woody Fraser was delighted with the outcome and would have her back on the show several times. "In Cleveland she was fabulous. We got along great. I didn't realize till this day that I scared the shit out of her."

Gamely, Helen went on with her tour. In her papers at Smith there is a note to Roger Ailes, thanking him for "putting me on the map in Cleveland." Ailes sent Helen Christmas cards for some years; she wrote him gushing notes from time to time during his ascent to political and media power broker for the conservative right. A decade after that first Douglas show, Fraser would book Helen as a regular member of his on-air "family" on the program he created for ABC, *Good Morning America*. Helen seemed to bear both men only goodwill for the Shaming in Cleveland. They all shared a like-mindedness on the subject of compelling TV: keep 'em watching, no matter what.

Said Fraser, "*Fabulous* woman."

Just how good was she out there? How potent a pitchwoman?

As you settle in beneath a pair of headphones in the archives at the Paley Center for Media in Manhattan to summon the aural HGB of so very many radio outings, it is helpful to close your eyes and listen to that voice speaking in the dark. Often, in big cities and at lesser stations of questionable wattage, Helen did late or all-night radio shows—whatever it took. Her voice is well suited to the dark, whispery in tone, pleasant and young-sounding, with a musky minor note of boudoir. No matter the insult hurled her way by a ratings-driven host, her reply is devoid of anger or hurt; she is a nice, reasonable woman who never raises her voice and offers a polite parry for every megawatt affront.

Listen in as she braves the Los Angeles lair of Joe Pyne, a crusty primogenitor of the Limbaugh/Beck/O'Reilly yawp-radio cabal. Pyne was a tough, crabbed, chain-smoking right-winger who zinged his guests and callers with a quiverful of signature insults: "Go gargle with razor blades!"

In Helen Brown, he booked a pigeon and got a smiling lynx. At her first cue, Helen leaned in to the mike: "This is Helen Gurley Brown, and I think the office is the sexiest place on earth!"

"This is Joe Pyne, and I don't know what I'm doing here."

Oh yes he does. Hear him thunder after his guest burbles about the glories of lunchtime trysts with a married boss: "You've got a chapter here, 'The Matinee,' where you actually instruct a young girl how to have an affair during the lunch hour with a married man in the office. You even give her recipes. How dare you, Helen Gurley Brown? You terrible woman. You have instructed this girl almost as someone conducting a symphony. She starts out making sure all the preparations are right so the action begins as soon as he walks in the door."

Pyne reads a recipe title for a hot lunch: "Fishy Fodder for a Lover."

Consider them, both grinning across the studio desk in their glass recording booth, a pair of savvy cage wrestlers who both know exactly what they must do in between swap meet announcements and thirty-second spots for psoriasis cures. Keep them. Make them stay, hanging curious in the dark. Pyne presses:

"I never met anyone before who not only is in favor of sin but writes a book on instructions for it!"

Imagine, too, David Brown, lifelong radio buff, wreathed in pipe smoke and listening in from his Park Avenue perch with a smile of deep satisfaction as his agile darling bats it back, sweetly: "Joe, sometimes I think there was no Santy Claus in your life."

Pyne tries another tack; with all this talk of husband poaching, would she rather go back to her predatory single days?

"No, I'm delighted to be married. I've been married five years. I married a dreamboat and I'm very happy with him. However, I don't wish I'd met him any earlier. I met him when I was thirty-six, married him when I was thirty-seven, and I did enjoy all those single years. I must say I kind of identify more with single girls than I do with wives, that's true."

"Thank you, Helen Gurley Brown, you terrible woman. This is Joe Pyne."

One reporter, as slim and bird-boned as her quarry, had been peering at Helen day and night through the studio glass as the hiss and yowl of crackpot America was piped out beyond the sound booth. On assignment for *The Saturday Evening Post*, thirty-one-year-old Joan Didion was spending a few days hitting California bookstores and radio stations with Mrs. Brown on that *Sex and the Office* tour, a punishing marathon of more than three hundred radio and TV shows—mostly radio, given Pogrebin's difficulty in booking TV spots. Helen made stops at friendly forums such as *Girl Talk* and Long John Nebel's surreal midnight-to-5:00-a.m. radio shows, as well as the irascible Pyne's smoky lair.

It is delicious to picture these two tiny and angular women taking each other's measure in greenrooms and hotel coffee shops along the tour. These were Californians of diametrically opposed trajectories and miens, the commercial and the intellectual, the "Arkie" arriviste and the native daughter. Didion went to school with Arkie and Okie migrants resettled in the Sacramento Valley. She did not care for them much. She was of undiluted, barrel-aged West Coast stock; some of her maternal ancestors wagon-trained across the plains in the company of the doomed Donner party before they had the luck or good sense to drop off at the Humboldt Sink in Nevada and veer north to Oregon.

Didion was younger than her interview subject by twelve years. The cultural distinction between them was as wide as the Mojave. And over their careers, the women would amass their very different cadres of fan girls. Yet they shared some striking similarities. Both of them were painfully thin, prone to depression, and known to be epic public criers. They sobbed anywhere from the strain of it all, Didion in subways and Laundromats, Helen in TV studios, restaurants, in the middle of Park Avenue. From an early age, Cleo Gurley had burdened her girl with the anxiety of not being "pretty enough," and Eduene Didion informed Joan that she was destined for the often crippling fragility of the women in her family. Both writers had childhoods that, owing to Cleo's misfortunes and Frank Didion's military service, found both families struggling to get by in too many cheap, temporary homes.

There was one crucial nexus shared by Joan Didion and Helen Gurley Brown: both were restless women of strong ambition who changed their fortunes dramatically with winning entries in contests run by Condé Nast monthlies. Didion had been a *Mademoiselle* guest editor, or "GE," flown to New York City to work on the magazine's "College Issue." That collegiate summer idyll was made famous by the poet Sylvia Plath's nightmarish rendition of the experience in her novel, *The Bell Jar*. At the end of her GE service, Plath threw her clothes off the roof of the Barbizon Hotel and went home in a borrowed peasant blouse. She made her first suicide attempt while the special 1953 guest editor issue of *Mademoiselle* was still on the stands.

Successful survivors include the writers Joyce Carol Oates, Meg Wolitzer, Mona Simpson, Francine du Plessix Gray, Gael Greene, Diane Johnson, and Ann Beattie, the fashion designer Betsey Johnson, and the actress Ali MacGraw. Being a GE conferred a public and prestigious conduit; smart, gifted women surfaced and shone. Wolitzer, who was in the final "class" of GEs in 1979, put it this way: "To me, Mademoiselle was to Vogue what Skipper was to Barbie: her younger, crisply put-together sister who read Mary McCarthy and attended a Seven Sisters college instead of lolling around the Dream House all day."

Didion had won her *Mademoiselle* spot by submitting a draft of a short story; as a rising college senior she flew to New York in May 1955 for her summer turn as GE. Precocious talent that she was, Didion was then welcomed into a second Condé Nast sisterhood. The "Prix de Paris" contest at *Vogue* was for college seniors; it was the same contest that the Vassar/Sorbonne undergrad Jacqueline Bouvier had won earlier. First prize was a job, post-graduation, in either the magazine's New York or Paris office. Didion's winning essay for the "Prix de Paris" contest secured her a job at *Vogue* in New York, where she began as—yes—a promotional copywriter, churning out thirty-line spurts of enthusiastic prose, "the kind that was sent to stores as advertising support."

One of her first encounters at *Vogue* was with the personnel director, Mary Campbell, the same compassionate soul who had phoned out to the West Coast and urged Don Belding to promote Miss Gurley. Campbell had begun her career as personal secretary to Condé Nast himself; by 1955, she had shepherded and encouraged hundreds of bright young women. Encountering pale, lost-looking Didion in the corridors, Campbell would ask her, "Have you called your mother?" If the answer was "not lately," she was marched into Campbell's office to dial Eduene.

The young women who won early contests at *Glamour* were flown to New York for final judging at Condé Nast headquarters, but not for on-site editorial internships. Most were already working women, like

Helen. Who could get the time off? An article and photo in the magazine, a week's vacation in Hawaii or Europe, some free fashions from advertisers, and a bit of cash would do nicely. *Glamour* did add a "Top Ten College Girls" contest, changed to "College Women" as the women's movement gained strength; its 1972 winners included Kate White, who would be the third editor in chief of *Cosmo* and, later, a bestselling novelist. While *Mademoiselle* and *Vogue* guest editorships were golden portals for "serious" writers, the two *Glamour* magazine winners who went on to create global empires—Helen Gurley and Martha Kostyra (Stewart), winner in 1961's "Top Ten College Girls"—were cited for their taste and style. Their shared aesthetic: aspirational practicality. Art or commerce, poems or essays, a glossy magazine or enamelware casseroles sold at Macy's—all their achievements spoke to the ambitions, aesthetics, and exigencies of these young women's lives. Despite the many justifiable criticisms of women's magazines of those times, a talented minority of the Condé Nast chosen had achieved transits beyond their dreams.

By the time Helen had begun working on *Sex and the Single Girl*, Didion had earned a spot on the *Vogue* masthead as features editor and was soon publishing essays and short stories in the magazine as well. She also believed in hedging her bets, taking a University of California correspondence course in shopping-center theory in case this writing thing didn't pan out. When Didion took the magazine assignment to shadow the famous Mrs. Brown toward the end of a punishing twenty-eight-city tour, Helen had sold more than two million copies of her two books combined. And so it was that in late 1964, their populist and cerebral proclivities had landed them in the same studios and greenrooms, headed toward a certain stark inevitability: pinioned by Didion's unblinking raptor gaze, Helen Gurley Brown was deftly plucked and shredded.

The article, "Bosses Make Lousy Lovers," was a sharper, more skillful takedown than Shana Alexander's snarky *Life* piece. As such, it's an early example of Didion's edgy, crystalline takes on banal and middlebrow America, this one refracted through the bent vibes and voodoo incantations of talk radio. Didion first skewered Helen's late-night radio audience, which took in "the twilight world of the lonely, the subliterate . . . the culturally deprived people whose last contact with the printed and bound word was 'Calories Don't Count.'" She drove the shiv further: "Her market seems to be composed of people who ordinarily set eyes upon a book only when Johnny Carson holds one up."

At a Los Angeles station, Didion sat listening to Helen from midnight to 5:00 a.m. and wrote up the conversational segues on air as near hallucinatory, with radio callers' secondary dialogue winding around and beneath the main "sexy office" topic:

Say, does anyone know if rattlesnakes can swim?

On air, Helen yattered through the aural labyrinth, dauntless. Facing Didion as an interviewer, she was enthusiastic and unguarded. She burbled brand-name affirmations of her success with the pure glee of a parvenu: she was being accorded the best hotels, the finest champagne, real caviar, star treatment. She addressed her critics: "They can't put me off by hinting I write to make money," she says. "I love money. And I'm promotable. Some people aren't . . . I've never turned down a show, never lost my temper. I do them all, and I'm always Charming's Mother."

As the caravan moved on, interviewers and makeup men kept telling Mrs. Brown that she looked tired. Her days and nights were nonstop; the damnable Santa Ana winds were blowing, too, with their own sly subliminals that whispered of madness and migraines. Didion noted Helen's responses to her hosts' concern: "'I should rest,'" she would say doubtfully. "'I should get something done to my face.'"

When she hopped off Helen's road show, Didion paged through Helen's two-book oeuvre and concluded, "To read, after listening to the Night Owls and their soulmates, what the author alternately calls her 'silly little girlish books,' her 'little pippypoo books,' and her 'very sincere little books,' is a curious experience. It is then that you realize that the voices in the night respond not to the books but to some idea of the books, not to Mrs. Brown's written word but to the calculating provocative voice she has transmitted on more than 300 radio and television shows this past year."

Didion heard it loud and clear above the schizo static of call-in

America: Helen's was the voice of the ad woman ascendant, child of the Radio Age, Boswell to beauty queens, conjurer of the thirty-second mascara spot. All those years, beginning on those grueling early media tours, Helen was not selling sex itself, but the very idea of it, the possibilities, the promise. In that fairly timorous time in America, the seduction was aimed between the ears, not at the crotch. And yes, oh my yes, Helen could still sling it, freer and more focused than ever now that the message and the royalties were her own. She was her own best client, and, as such, she was that much more effective because she believed in what she was selling. She truly did.

Helen was also a nice woman who desperately wanted to be liked; to get her bit across, she'd damned well conduct herself like Charming's Mother. The trouble with the increasingly skeptical reportage like Didion's was that, unlike evanescent radio insults, the print stuff hung around. It left an acrid aftertaste. One's friends saw it in New York and Los Angeles. How deeply did Helen feel Didion's cuts? We shall see some dark indications further on. But at the time, she may have been too busy plotting her next move to stop and lick her wounds.

As the promotional tour wound down and *Sex and the Office* was posting disappointing sales figures, a worried David wrote to Geis, "While Helen doesn't show it or say it (and acts as though she has just written Gone With the Wind) I know her morale is low. Like the rest of us, she is depressed by the failure of SATO to become airborne . . . My course for the future is to get Helen back to work on something promising."

Helen was already on it. She seriously considered a return to the ad game, which had become a far livelier high-stakes casino, especially on Madison Avenue. Helen approached the best and brightest, a legendary ad woman and child of the Depression from rural Ohio whose ascent had been the talk of the business for nearly a decade as she rose through the giant agency McCann Erickson. Along her way, Mary Wells had already heard of the West Coast copywriter Helen Gurley, who had won some awards and gotten a bit of good buzz in the industry.

Now in her mid-eighties, Mary Wells Lawrence (in 1967 she married the airline executive Harding Lawrence) is savoring the rewards of one of the most spectacular careers in advertising. Referring to her own revolutions, she says that she "let loose the bear" when she started her agency in 1965. By 1969, she was the highest-paid executive in all of advertising. Her firm, Wells Rich Greene, set the ad game on its blue serge derriere. Who else dared paint Braniff planes in swirling Pucci prints and dress stewardesses in swirly frocks commissioned from the maestro himself? That one signature campaign turned commercial airline travel into the wild painted zoo of kiwis, koalas, eagles, and kangaroos tethered to today's airport gates.

Lawrence's revolution in advertising was supple and diverting—no more bashing the consumer with static and unimaginative close-ups of Product. "I began to theatricalize what I sold," she explained. She ran her agency "as if it were a motion-picture company with a lot of productions happening at one time." A few greatest hits were "Plop, plop, fizz, fizz," for Alka-Seltzer; "I [heart] NY," for the city's tourist bureau; and "Flick your Bic." Online "meme maker" apps still trade on the recurring iterations of Alka-Seltzer's dyspeptic "I can't believe I ate the whole thing" koan, which has been famously recycled by the likes of the cartoon dunderhead Homer Simpson and Jack Nicholson in *The Shining*.

Lawrence sold her company for $160 million in 1990. After some blissful years in the couple's Italian villa, she was widowed in 2002. Now her feet barely touch the ground; she relishes the cruising life with a rotating cast of friends and grandchildren aboard her 156-foot yacht, *Strangelove*. When she left the twelve-person crew in its Mediterranean winter port for her customary March stopover in Manhattan, Lawrence found time to recall her strange little encounter with Helen Gurley Brown. She thinks it was probably in late 1964. She can't quite recall, except that it was before she started her own company the following year. That would put it at the end of or just after Helen's *Sex and the Office* book tour.

But first, said Lawrence, a word about those *Mad Men* days. Never mind the horny hijinks you've seen on cable TV, or in Helen's books. Yes, Lawrence herself did end up marrying a client. But she would have it known that there was very little sex in the office, at least in her shop. "I worked very hard. Advertising at the time was very hard because it was changing from doing something that was boring and easy to doing something very creative. We were having to sell it and resell it. It was an enormous challenge. That's one of the things about *Mad Men* that amuses me—nobody at Wells Rich Greene was making love in the back room. We weren't interested in other people. We were in love with ourselves."

This brought her to the very talented Mrs. Brown, who turned out to have some very definite ideas of her own worth as a copywriter. At the time they met, Lawrence was a major player at Jack Tinker & Partners, an odd duck spinoff agency, more of a think tank of imperceptible wizardry. They were working in rather unusual headquarters, a duplex suite at the Dorset Hotel. Applicants churned through all the time looking for copywriting work. Throughout her career, Wells interviewed hundreds and hundreds of hopefuls, she says. But she remembered Helen Gurley Brown quite clearly.

"I was looking for a really terrific top-flight writer. I'd heard that she was very good. I was running Tinker by then. She [Helen] called and made an appointment. When she came in, she was charming and bright and we talked for quite a long time. I did offer her a job. She accepted. She was talking about her ability to be a great copywriter for me, about the kind of writing that she imagined she'd be doing, what she would love to do. And in the middle of that she suddenly just stopped dead and said to me, 'Nope.'"

Lawrence stared at her, puzzled. Helen seemed to be shaking her head slightly, working out some inner debate.

"She looked at me very strangely and said, 'You know, I take that back. I'm not going to work for you. I won't work for you. You are younger than me. I realize in talking to you that my big mistake is that I should be running something myself. I should be doing what you're doing.'

"She said that she realized that I was already running my life, I was already the boss, I was already a star. She kept using the word 'star.' She said, 'I realize talking to you that I have to be the star. I have to run something of my own, I can't work for you, I can't work for anybody. I have to get my own thing.'"

Hitching her wagon to a supernova like Mary Wells in the mid-1960s could well have been a spectacular ride, if Helen could cut it. It was an uncharacteristic flare of ego and ambition that let her walk away from a slot that other copywriters of the day would have sold a kidney for. Wells started her own agency shortly after her encounter with Helen, in 1965. By the end of its first year, Wells Rich Greene had more than a hundred employees and $39 million in billings.

Lawrence said that she never did any business with *Cosmopolitan* once Helen had found her place in the firmament; she had made a conscious decision not to go after women's accounts. Like Helen, she had worked for Max Factor and found it madly stultifying. "I did not want to build a boutique agency or a fashion or a cosmetic agency. I didn't want a small, feminine agency. I wanted an agency that competed with McCann Erickson and with all the big boys. I wanted major accounts, I wanted cars and airlines. I wanted Proctor and Gamble."

She never read Helen's magazine but had periodic, cordial encounters with her, sometimes in the offices of the dermatologist and cosmetic surgeon Dr. Norman Orentreich. Helen was always charming. "Those early days of her rise, she was very much a star," Lawrence said. "People were entranced by her, people were amused by her. They were entertained by her. They liked what she was doing."

Of that flashy, ad-friendly star vehicle Helen finally rode to glory, Lawrence said, "I think she was brilliant in terms of branding. I think everybody thinks she was brilliant. It took guts to blatantly talk about women and sex the way she did. In those days it was very unusual. I think she had innate courage."

From time to time, Helen did think of the advertising titan whose offer she refused. She, too, thought about the strength it took to be a woman at the top of that brutal game, wondering aloud to a friend: Did Mary Wells ever feel like a vulnerable girl? Could she still be hurt? Did she ever cry?

21 🦢

In Which *Cosmopolitan*
Gets a Makeover

In those days, *Cosmopolitan* was a failing horror. I had an editor in
chief who kept asking if Moby Dick was the man or the whale.
—Lyn Tornabene, former editor at the magazine

IN THE WINTER OF 1964, Helen sat in the small dining area of the
Browns' apartment and cobbled together the beginnings of her life's
greatest triumph. On the table: a pot of glue, scissors, and a stack of old
women's magazines. It is likely that the cats were the only witnesses to
the moment of creation. Painstakingly, and none too skillfully, Helen
drew a shaky logo that read *Femme*, the proposed name of the new
magazine she and David wanted to launch for that vastly underserved
market, single women. It just might become that longed-for star vehicle for the restless Mrs. Brown.

Helen's mock-up cover for *Femme* featured a large close-up photo
of a woman in a bikini that looks like it was clipped from an ad for diet
aids; her execution might land a solid "C" in a middle school art class.
The subhead, pasted on in typewriter script, reads "For the woman on
her own." There were two cover blurbs, also typed and pasted on: "U.S.
Presidents Who Liked Girls" and "Where the Men Are."

Yet again, this cut-and-paste project had begun as David's idea.
One day at home, as they marveled at the mail that was still coming

in, he told Helen, "You really ought to have a magazine for these girls." Helen had struggled mightily to answer the torrent of letters. So many of them touched her. How could she not send a few lines of encouragement and thanks? David went on: These single women writing to Helen were "loving, warm, sexy and terrific," just as she was. But most of the women's magazines were talking to married women about God, motherhood, and home. What a bore, and what an opportunity gone begging. David's solution was so very logical: "You ought to have a book for good citizen swingers like you were."

Helen knew exactly what he meant by the term and would use it herself. "Good citizen swingers" were really very decent, well-meaning single women who simply wanted all the other aspects of a good life available to married women and men: a good, independent work life, equal and decent wages, supportive friends, male and female, and as much good sex and romance as might befit their needs.

The Browns had discussed the idea sitting in their apartment with Charlotte Kelly. It made sense for Helen and David to ask for their bachelorette friend's help on the magazine idea. She worked at *Ladies' Home Journal*, exactly the sort of staid, marriage-centric women's book that Helen disdained, and had plenty of ideas on what *not* to do. As a younger single woman with a romantic past in the same spirit, if not with a comparable number of conquests, as Helen, Kelly was also the perfect sounding board and potential reader. David Brown summed up their discussion that night: "We decided it would have to appeal to single girls, somewhat alienated young married women who were tired of PTA meetings and women's service magazines, and others addicted to Helen's frank, feminist views."

David had left his publishing job and returned to 20th Century Fox as a vice president, still hunting screen properties and working chiefly from New York. He didn't have a lot of extra time, but he was eager to settle his wife into something that would keep her challenged and further the family enterprise. He understood that Helen unemployed would be Helen unhinged. A magazine seemed just the thing, given his own editorial expertise. The Browns and Kelly, each with a pad, began listing article ideas with a descriptive sentence for each. Helen scribbled pages of them just by recycling the beauty ideas that had been rejected by Max Factor. Many subjects of interest in her own life landed in her article list: "The World of Falsies," "How to Have More Fun at the Racetrack," "How to Seduce a Man," "Cat People."

Serious topics got monthly columns; women's health issues—everything from frigidity to "colonic difficulties" and thinning hair—would be addressed in "Doctor, Can I?" Written by a qualified psychoanalyst, "The Analyst's Corner" would "probe the psyche of the woman on her own." David wrote up a preamble pitch about *Femme* as an ad vehicle. They added what Helen called a few more "philosophic thoughts":

> *Femme is for women who like men.* "Women have stronger sexual desires as they grow older."
> *Femme is for women who like themselves.* "They want to progress financially, physically, emotionally."
> *Femme is optimistic, affirmative, upbeat.*
> *Femme is bold.* "Because women really are bold . . . Femme cannot pretend that women are not the equals of men—mentally, physically and emotionally. Femme sees no reason to dwell on this subject, however—the equality of women—but only to acknowledge it by the selection of editorial material."

Helen's magazine would not rock the boat; it aimed to just steer its own quietly feminist course, laden with plenty of tips for career advancement, makeup, lingerie, and well-equipped man-hunting. She typed it all up; Berney Geis had it photocopied at his office. "It was all loving hands at home," Helen said of the final product.

As they pondered how and to whom they might try to sell their next venture, the Browns enjoyed a very merry holiday season. The risqué ads for the film version of *Sex and the Single Girl* had been everywhere for weeks, picturing Natalie Wood as "Helen"—sexuality researcher and bestselling author—crisscrossed at groin level atop her romantic costar, the tabloid reporter Tony Curtis. The copy: "Is it true what they say about Sex and the Single Girl? Yes!"

While Warner executives fretted over ominous rumblings from the ratings overlords at the Production Code Administration (PCA), the studio's unit publicists had been feeding salty tidbits to the trades. A press release to *The Hollywood Reporter* crowed, "A new slanguage has developed on the set of a new WB picture. That overworked expression 'sensational' has evolved into 'sexsational.'" Security guards on Stage 6, where the movie was filming, answered the phone "Stage Sex."

Helen's positively dreamiest prezzie came on Christmas Day 1964, when the film opened. There were huge lines of ticket buyers, overwhelmingly women, outside two theaters premiering the film, the Rivoli and the Trans-Lux 52nd Street. Helen's fan base was out in force. The *New York Times* reviewer A. H. Weiler described pandemonium outside and within the theaters. The high-pitched sound of female anticipation clearly took him aback. Weiler didn't love the movie and he didn't hate it; he seemed surprised, along with much of Hollywood, that Warner Bros. had indeed cobbled a movie from that five-word title and inflated it with star power: besides Tony Curtis and Natalie Wood, they cast Henry Fonda, Lauren Bacall, Mel Ferrer, and the always-droll character actor Edward Everett Horton. The novelist Joseph Heller, newly famous for *Catch-22*, was one of the screenwriters. Except for the sharper-than-usual rom-com writing and the savvy performances of Fonda and Bacall, the movie was a pretty standard confection along the lines of Doris Day vehicles like *Pillow Talk* and *Send Me No Flowers*, madcap finale and all. In terms of plot and character, the film version worked a reverse twist on the book; despite having written a sexy bestseller, Natalie Wood's Helen was a virgin, and a prissy one at that. The movie was an utter cop-out. As *The Atlantic* would later put it, "The alley-cat cultural force that was *Sex and the Single Girl* got de-clawed."

None of it mattered. *Sex and the Single Girl* was a solid hit, if not of the magnitude of other 1964 releases: *Mary Poppins*, *Goldfinger*, Elvis's *Viva Las Vegas*, and the Beatles' *A Hard Day's Night*. Asked about the reversal of her heroine's sexual behavior from adventurer to prudish good girl, Helen insisted she had no problem with the discrepancy, adding, "I thought the movie was absolutely *adorable!*"

The movie was still opening in more theaters nationwide in January 1965 when David Brown began pitching the *Femme* idea. Helen's home-made cover rendering went with him, affixed to the more professional twenty-page presentation. "It was a dear little prospectus," Helen judged. Making the rounds alone, David presented his case for targeting a hith-erto untapped readership. In meetings at Dell Magazines and at Fawcett Publications, he read aloud the Browns' optimistic numbers: more than 13 million unmarried American women, plus 1.7 million divor-cées, 1.4 million women legally separated, 2.6 million with "absent" hus-bands, and 8.3 million widows, totaling more than 27 million potential readers. A long list of possible advertisers followed, taking in every-thing from cosmetics to cars, diet foods, and beverages, airlines, resorts, candy . . . and brokerage houses. Cover stock and the suggested sixty editorial pages (plus ads) would be on paper equivalent in weight to that of *Playboy*. Suggested cover price: sixty cents.

The proposal contained bios for both Browns. David was listed as "originator" of the concepts behind *Sex and the Single Girl* and *Sex and the Office*, and as "overseer" of their production and writing. His stated intent was to create and sell "exploitable properties" based on those titles. *Femme* would be geared to make its initial profits on circulation, but the Browns expected it to become a highly profitable advertising vehi-cle. The *Femme* proposal was the first boldly articulated statement of the Browns' wider ambitions for the "woman alone" market; the family enterprise was refining its message and intent on expanding its reach.

Everyone turned it down flat, save for David's former colleagues at Hearst. In January 1965, Berney Geis first took the proposal to his friend and former *Esquire* colleague Richard "Dick" Deems, then pres-ident of the Hearst Corporation. Deems was frank in his distaste for the Browns' title. He told Geis that the company was in no financial position to start a new magazine, but would consider "superimposing" their new format on Hearst's limping bunny *Cosmopolitan*. Still unsure, Deems sent the proposal back to Helen, with a request to suggest writers for all those articles and approximate pay scales. Between them, the Browns knew enough writers; David's magazine experience allowed them to come up with reasonable fees that wouldn't seem extravagant to the financially challenged Hearst. Helen and David both went to brace Deems in his posh lair in the Waldorf Towers, though David reported that during the negotiations, "Helen was cowering in a corner somewhere. She had never edited a magazine. I don't think I had ever seen her read one."

David knew all too well what his wife would be facing, having watched and assisted at *Cosmopolitan*'s precipitous slide. By the mid-fifties, the once-proud book was moribund; its ad pages were down to seventy-nine per month, numbers so dismal they were last posted in the early Depression years. It had fared even worse under the recent stewardship of Richard Berlin, a tough, some said ruthless, manager who took the helm of the much devalued Hearst Corporation in 1943.

Herbert Mayes, David's friend and mentor at *Cosmopolitan*, had been at Hearst since 1927 and watched Berlin's swift ascension. In the 1930s, Mayes wrote, "the dynasty was in receivership due to Hearst's extravagance." Enter Berlin, who "swept the Hearst landscape of obstacles, becoming the single dominating figure in the hierarchy." By narrowly avoiding a bankruptcy and getting the company back up on its shaky legs, Berlin became a trusted lieutenant of the octogenarian William Randolph Hearst. But Berlin disliked *Cosmopolitan* as much as the old man seemed to cherish this relic from his glory days. Hearst had been dead for more than a decade when the Browns made their proposal, yet it seemed that Berlin was still unable to drive a stake through the frail but beating heart of *Cosmopolitan*.

He certainly had tried. Earlier, Berlin had implemented a Draconian new regime for this hemorrhaging liability: he eliminated promotions, discounts for subscription renewals, and radio and newspaper ads, and retained just a tiny, dispirited staff. An average of 140,000 copies per month were going unsold on the newsstands. By then, the magazine had gone from literary/general interest to a "sort of" women's magazine.

Even some of *Cosmopolitan*'s former marquee writers had sought to disassociate themselves. Lyn Tornabene, an editor then, remembers a rainy night, sometime in the mid- to late fifties, when she was working late in the *Cosmopolitan* offices, alone. The security guard walked in and said there was an anxious-seeming man who appeared very eager to see an editor there, any editor. Tornabene agreed to see the man and froze when he appeared before her desk, tall and stern-looking. It was J. D. Salinger. He said that he had heard that there was to be a special fiction issue of the magazine. He explained his visit: "I absolutely do not want any of my stories reprinted in this magazine. Can you make sure that doesn't happen?"

After hearing her promise several times that she would relay his message to the editor in chief, Salinger thanked her and left. His history with the magazine had been turbulent since 1948, when some unnamed editorial lunkhead had disregarded Salinger's own short story title "Scratchy Needle on a Phonograph Record" and ran it as "Blue Melody" without consulting him.

"I'm pretty sure they went ahead and tried to run both of Salinger's stories," said Tornabene. "It was that kind of place then. We were under a dozen of us on the staff of failing *Cosmo*. We started to assign and write freelance pieces under pseudonyms and pay each other. I was 'Nina Borghese' and my friend Harriet [LaBarre] was 'EMD Watson,' for 'Elementary, My Dear.' They found out at Hearst what we were doing. I got called down to Richard Deems's office. He said we were very bad people and we had to go back to making thirty-eight dollars a week or whatever it was, so I quit. They didn't even know I was there for twelve years at Hearst." The staff felt even less cherished when Hearst moved the magazine out of its main offices to temporary space above a car dealership in the nearby General Motors Building in the summer of 1964.

So it transpired: Helen's longed-for star vehicle was handed over, broken-down and unloved as it was, not unlike her giveaway old station wagon Appletrees. At eight hundred thousand, the magazine's circulation was at its lowest in half a century; the ad page sales were comparable to the publication's beginning numbers in the late 1800s.

Along with their agent, Lucy Kroll, David negotiated the new editor in chief's contract. Helen was presented with a two-year deal that paid thirty-five thousand dollars for year one. It had a bonus structure that provided an additional five thousand dollars for incremental circulation jumps after she took the reins. Bernard Geis was required to sign a release stating that he would make no claims on Helen's work or ideas for the magazine. As a sop, and perhaps in genuine gratitude for his help, Helen agreed to pay Geis 20 percent of each bonus she received for the duration of that first contract.

Berlin and Deems had more stipulations: Helen would have to create her new version, from cover shoots to salaries and paper clips, on the old and barely adequate budget of about thirty thousand dollars an issue; she had to pledge that she would not publish sex-related articles that were smutty or graphic. She would report to two Hearst executives, Dick Deems and a money and marketing man, Frank Dupuy, Jr. They would prove the "good cops" to Berlin's censorious and disapproving overlord. Berlin had vigorously opposed Helen's appointment on the grounds that Hearst, which had become a highly cautious and conservative publisher by then, might alienate its public and advertisers with a nationally known loose woman at its helm.

It was understood within the company that Helen Gurley Brown would have to be closely monitored. There were no female editors topping the masthead at any Hearst publications. Women did not edit magazines for women anywhere in the mid-1960s, save for Beatrice Gould, who coedited *Ladies' Home Journal* with her husband, Bruce; and Eileen Tighe at *Woman's Day*. Herbert Mayes recalled the building-wide consternation when Helen's appointment was announced. The murmurs ran along these lines: "Helen Gurley Brown, that ad agency copywriter—the Hearst morons think *she* can save *Cosmopolitan*? Well, we can say goodbye to good old *Cosmo*."

For Berlin, it was actually a safe and canny bet; if Helen failed, she'd take the heat and he could finally close the troublesome book, with a very small investment in her salary and minimal start-up costs—some fripperies for her office décor, a new hire or two. If by some miracle the daffy little upstart turned it around, he would be the hero who gave her a chance to save the founder's favorite.

Helen was due to take over the magazine on the ides of March 1965. The night before she was to present herself to her staff, she and David went to dinner with their friend the author Irving Wallace, known as a "blue-collar writer" who churned out sexy if clumsily written adventure yarns, most of which reaped fat movie sales. The men were walking up Park Avenue trying to comfort Helen, who was weeping copiously. They calmed her somewhat and daubed at her tears, but once the Browns got home, the night grew long and darker still. She was nearly catatonic with fear. She had no clue how she might begin. Once the long-dreaded day had dawned, Helen shivered herself into a soft blue wool jersey shift dress with a ruffle at the neck and hem; she was aiming for demure and none too threatening. David accompanied his quaking wife in a taxicab; they rode around and around until she felt she could go into the building. Helen asked David what she should do first.

"Ask the managing editor to lunch," he told her. He or she should know all. At the very least, the ME could tell Helen which articles had been assigned and which were in-house; it would be a decent opening gambit that implied some knowledge of a magazine's works. Helen could get busy inspecting the inventory she had inherited. This raised her spirits until she was told, upon reaching the office, that the managing editor already had a lunch date and would not even consider breaking it to accommodate her new boss, and, by the way, there were no article lists; they just kept things "in their heads." Someone brought Helen a sandwich. By day's end, she had made sure to meet and greet everyone; she shook their hands, looked them in the eye, and promised only this: she didn't expect to fire any office staff.

Helen's behavior after her first day at work has become part of the HGB creation myth, told and retold in slightly shifting versions. The truth: yes, David did indeed find her curled in a fetal position beneath his desk in the middle of the night. She had no idea how long she had been there when he coaxed her back to bed. He reminded his wife, as he had so many times before at K&E and as she struggled with her books: "This job is not the end of the world."

Two days later, the managing editor—she who had been too arch to lunch—quit. Helen immediately replaced her with the only man in the place. George Walsh wasn't a perfect fit, as Helen later wrote, but he seemed the best at close hand: "He was a big political maven, staunch Catholic (I was still considered something of a scarlet woman), family man, not *too* beastly hard a worker—not *just* what I needed, but then I had David." Walsh was eventually replaced as managing editor by Guy Flatley, who served Helen for many years as a fiercely loyal lieutenant and confidant.

As the true chaos of the place was slowly revealed, Helen despaired. Any story that the staff could remember assigning, Helen did not like; little of the ephemeral "inventory" was appropriate for her vision of the magazine, so she canceled nearly everything. There were heaps of unused manuscripts all over the office. She tottered home with a sack full and began to read, finding most of them unusable. Helen went back into the office with a sheaf of culls as well as article ideas from their prospectus. To set about assigning them, she began to see the few *Cosmopolitan* writers who seemed simpatico to what she had in mind. One of the first was Lyn Tornabene, who was freelancing by then. She had written some celebrity profiles that Helen liked very much; she was also the dauntless, feet-on-the-ground sort of journalist Helen could appreciate. One could ship her to Cape Canaveral for a first-rate dispatch on the real lives of astronauts' wives or send her to lunch with Marlon Brando; she never disappointed.

"I go in for our meeting," said Tornabene, "and I'm ushered into the office which now looks like a Hallmark greeting card. One of Helen's things was that it's intimidating to most people to be talked to across a desk. So she curls up on the sofa, which was beautifully upholstered, in one corner, and gestures for me to sit next to her. The first thing she said to me after the greeting was 'These aren't my cheekbones.'" Tornabene laughed. "I loved it. She said [Dr. Norman] Orentreich did them. Then she said, 'This isn't my hair, this is a Kenneth fall.' That was my how-do-you-do. I think I was quite quiet. After all, what was there to say?"

Helen did have one more bit of unsolicited personal information to share: before her marriage, she had made love with 178 men. Agog, Tornabene could not begin to calculate how that was feasible. Though the number has stuck with her all these years, she never has worked out the math or determined the seriousness of Helen's astounding boast. Once she recovered her equilibrium, the rest of the meeting went well. Tornabene agreed to continue doing celebrity profiles for *Cosmopolitan*; they settled on the queenly sum of about one thousand dollars per feature.

Like many incoming bosses, Helen found that she had to do some housekeeping and sweep away any regular *Cosmo* writers unable or unwilling to execute her vision. She also needed to gauge the compatibility of those staying on. In her autobiography *Natural Blonde*, the columnist Liz Smith, then *Cosmo*'s entertainment editor, recalled the trembling soul that was ushered to her desk and introduced: "She had a self-deprecating Arkansas charm and a kind of sweet, dithering Billie Burke manner. She seemed so helpless I thought I'd save her the trouble of firing me and resign. But soon she asked me into her corner office, transformed with scarves over pink lights, pillows, candles, kitty cat knickknacks and needlepoint."

Helen sought and got reassurance that Smith would continue as entertainment editor, a job she inherited when Lyn Tornabene had quit. Smith would keep writing her features, mainly profiles of movie stars, but she did not want to continue doing movie reviews. Instead she put forward her protégé Rex Reed. Helen was perplexed. "Why would you recommend a person to take one of your jobs?"

"I thought he was a far better writer and critic than I was," said Smith, "and I told Helen that."

On a long, wintry afternoon in his apartment at Manhattan's storied residential fortress the Dakota, surrounded by framed photos of himself with half of Hollywood, Reed rewound back to his days as a fresh and naive arrival from the Lone Star State. After lean freelance times writing press releases for turkeys like *The Three Stooges and Snow White* ("my God, it was a *skating* picture") and scrounging by on sixty dollars a week as a press agent's assistant, the twenty-five-year-old Reed lobbed a Hail Mary pass toward the editors of *Cosmopolitan*. He wrote a review of *Lilith*, starring Jean Seberg, Peter Fonda, and Warren Beatty, and sent it in to Liz Smith, who took it to the editor in chief who preceded Helen, Robert Atherton. The *Lilith* review ran in the magazine; they hired Reed immediately as their movie reviewer; he also wrote features.

"*Cosmo* was my first paid job in New York City," Reed said. "Liz and I became very good friends. I used to go to her apartment and she would make her Texas chicken fried steak dinners. Nobody in New York had eaten anything like this. Everybody came to Liz's, she was in there beating the steaks into submission with a Coke bottle, making chicken fried gravy, and of course that's what I grew up on. She lived at Thirty-Eight East Thirty-Eighth Street in a wonderful house with a spiral staircase and a sunken living room, a great apartment. But nothing worked. In the middle of her parties, she would blow fuses and everybody sat in the dark."

The apartment had a cozy fireplace and a real decorator's touch; the fashion designer Chuck Howard, then doing sketches for Bill Blass and working with the very young Donna Karan, had conferred his sharp eye and chic/casual touches. Smith's ad hoc dinners fed a shifting mix of Texas expats and writerly locals, most with an edgy and liberal outlook. Theirs was a spirited, Holly Golightly sort of crowd; the Texan Tommy Thompson, the *Life* staff writer who first discovered Lee Harvey Oswald's home and wife after the JFK assassination, was a regular. Both Gloria Steinem and Gloria Vanderbilt dropped in, as did the director Robert Benton, the writers Gael Greene, Mary Ann Madden, Nora Ephron, and Ephron's then-husband, Dan Greenburg. The majority of Smith's guests had more ambition than money; they shared a penchant for bourbon, high-spirited arguments, and a free meal.

Helen and David Brown, often invited after her debut at *Cosmo*, seemed "a bit like hicks" to Smith in these roiling gatherings; somewhat agog, the Browns took in the loud, progressive pastiche. They seemed to love the celebrity drop-ins and arguments and general carryings-on, but as Smith remembers it, Helen hung back, "more ladylike" than the rest, and watched with great interest. They weren't *her* people, but they were *somebodies* or about to be somebodies that it behooved her to keep track of.

Soon after Smith told Rex Reed of the change at *Cosmo*, he was asked to come in and meet with Mrs. Brown. Helen's red datebook for March 25, 1965, had Reed penciled in at 10:30. Lauren Bacall was due at 11:30, so she would have to be efficient.

Reed claims that he still cannot fathom the precise meaning of pippy-poo, could not parse its implications even as it fatally damned his copy that day, breathily delivered from beneath fluttery false eyelashes and a wig. After a while he realized that the little woman sitting atop her desk, legs crossed, was giving him the gate.

"I've read your reviews and they're very disturbing," Helen told him, "because you have opinions. And I don't want to upset my girls."

Helen had been fine with Liz Smith's movie reviews, which were rarely as caustic or critical as those of Reed in full cry. He wondered what sort of magazine the new boss had in mind. "Who are your girls?" he asked.

"They're girls who have never heard of [director] Mike Nichols. That's much too esoteric for my girls. They've never seen a movie with writing [subtitles] on the bottom of the screen, they don't go to movies in black and white and they only want to know about a movie they can go to on a Saturday night date at the drive in. They write to me about their menstrual problems."

What? Reed was confused indeed. "How do you know such a girl exists?"

"Because, dear, I *was* that girl."

Helen was quick to assure him that his firing was nothing personal. "Don't feel bad, there are a lot of other writers I'm having to discontinue or not hire. I can't use their work, they're too upsetting."

Reed recalled her reeling off the names of some other untouchables, many from the stable of writers favored by the editor Clay Felker, who made journalistic waves with his 1964 supplement to the *New York Herald Tribune*; the insert soon became *New York* magazine, which in turn would incubate and debut *Ms.* magazine in its pages. Felker was an early champion of the "New Journalism"; his go-to writers included

Tom Wolfe, Gloria Steinem, Jimmy Breslin, Dick Schaap, and Elizabeth Crow. They were probably not for the new *Cosmo*. And Helen made it clear to Reed: there would be absolutely "*no* Joan Didion."

Reed thought of his idol then, the writer who had so inspired him to have a bit of sport with conventional journalistic formats. He asked Helen, "Not even Gay Talese?"

"No, I won't be able to use her, either."

Helen was not editing for dumb bunnies and rubes; later, the reader research would bear her out: they were well educated and employed, with decent incomes. But no matter what, she was not buying the same sort of literary navel-gazing that had nearly killed *Cosmo*. Helen gave Reed one last chance. She called him at home with a socko, must-have idea. It involved a showbiz hypnotist with clouds of platinum hair named Pat Collins, known as "the Hip Hypnotist." Collins, a skilled practitioner, performed at her night spot, Pat Collins' Celebrity Club on the Sunset Strip; she was frequently on TV mesmerizing the likes of Lloyd Bridges and Lucille Ball. Her latest proposed stunt was something Helen wanted covered by a reporter; she felt strongly that it must be written by a male witness to the big event.

"Pat Collins was going to have a baby under hypnosis," said Reed, "and Helen wanted me to interview her in childbirth." He pleaded something burning on the stove and rang off, saying he'd call Helen back. "That's the last I spoke to her. What a thing to ask a man! My days there were over."

Rex Reed took himself off to *Esquire* and the New York newspapers; in 1973, "Do You Sleep in the Nude?," his profile of a melancholic Ava Gardner, would appear in Tom Wolfe's anthology of the New Journalism along with nonfiction by Norman Mailer, Truman Capote, John Gregory Dunne, Hunter S. Thompson, and Terry Southern. And Joan Didion. Helen held firm to her criteria for writers as she assigned the first round of articles. "Fancy" writers were just too self-absorbed for her girls. "You must converse with your reader," she explained. "Write the way you would talk. A person shouldn't have a dictionary in their lap when reading a magazine! I could not let that go on."

This standard was firmly in place when Helen Gurley Brown's first issue of the new *Cosmopolitan* hit the stands in July 1965. She set the tone in her chatty editor's letter, which she called "Step into My Parlor."

"Hello, I'm *Cosmopolitan*'s new editor . . . The stories and articles in this issue were picked for one reason only. I thought they'd interest you, knowing that you're a grown-up girl, interested in whatever can give you a richer, more exciting, fun-filled, friend-filled, man-loved kind of life!"

Her inaugural main feature: "Oh, What a Lovely Pill!" In touting the benefits of birth control pills, the reporter did not mention that unmarried women were still unable to get prescriptions for them in many states due to chauvinistic old statutes and the stubborn cultural persistence of the no-sex-before-marriage canon. Until a month before Helen published the article, contraception was still a crime in Connecticut. Long outdated and intrusive Comstock Laws passed in 1873 and dubbed "bedroom patrol" statutes still forbade the use of contraceptive medications and devices, for anyone.

On June 7, 1965, in the landmark Supreme Court decision *Griswold v. Connecticut*, the justices found for the plaintiff, Estelle Griswold, who brought the case on behalf of the Planned Parenthood League of Connecticut and its birth control clinic in New Haven. Justice William O. Douglas wrote the opinion for the 7–2 majority; it declared the Connecticut law unconstitutional on right-to-privacy grounds. The decision specified that only citizens in marital relationships were finally granted the right to birth control.

Unfortunately, full access to that "lovely pill" would not arrive for all women, most particularly those unmarried and sexually active *Cosmo* girls, until a second Supreme Court case, *Eisenstadt v. Baird* in 1972, which granted the right to contraceptive freedom to unmarried people as well. Men had been walking on the moon for three years before single women were allowed prescriptions for the Pill nationwide.

Helen's new *Cosmo* did not address this pesky little problem, one that might well upset and even outrage her girls. Fact-checking would never be the magazine's strong suit. The "Lovely Pill" article offered only the good news about that "honey of a hormone," estrogen, contained in the pills. It was a miracle drug, said to confer fabulous side benefits beyond birth control. Better sexual responsiveness! Smoother skin! Thick, glossy hair! A later-onset menopause!

It might be said that at forty-three, *Cosmo*'s new editor was showing her private concerns in her very first issue. Soon she would be a fervent devotee of the form of estrogen used for the drug Premarin, taking far more than her doctors' recommended dosages as an early convert to what came to be called hormone replacement therapy. As Helen began her reign as HGB, the new *Cosmo* readers still had glossy hair and smooth skin. They relied on the "lovely pill" for its primary benefit. Much like Helen and her dear Carlotta in fifties Los Angeles, *Cosmo* girls simply didn't want to get knocked up.

22

Weekdays in the Park with David

> "A man must feel he runs things, but as long as you control yourself, you control him."
> —Jacqueline Susann, *Valley of the Dolls*

AS THE LEFTOVER ARTICLES WERE USED UP, Helen began to stamp her imprimatur on *Cosmo* editorial. Over the next three decades, she would order up, edit, and publish countless responses to that famous rhetorical question posed by Freud to his favored patient and muse, the brilliant and tormented heiress Marie Bonaparte:

"*Was will das Weib?*"

"What does Woman want?"

After his own thirty years of study, Freud confessed himself baffled by the vast and mysterious "female continent." Helen, who had been plumbing her own complex desires in and out of therapy for almost as long, felt it was her mandate to toss out as many appealing answers to the Big Question as she could: Her readers wanted good men, a great job, better posture! Cheaper car insurance! Help with problem perspiration! They wanted to better understand *themselves*; as she had planned in the *Femme* prospectus, she also hired a psychotherapist to write what would become one of the magazine's evergreens, a monthly column, "The Analyst's Couch."

Dr. William Appleton, a Boston psychotherapist, wrote that column for nine years. Yes, his editor Bobbie Ashley sent him real reader letters; he collected some of the funnier ones over the years. But Helen was not looking for sensational or sexy topics; Appleton said: "I think Helen's idea was to keep the lonely girl company. It was about women understanding their own psyches, about being fearful and getting through the night. It was mostly about hurt feelings, more interpersonal stuff than the techniques of sexual acrobatics."

Helen's expanding fan base responded almost instantly; the letters poured in. As she steadied her course over the first year, Hearst executives were astonished by her numbers. In her first three years, circulation went from 782,000 to 1.05 million and kept rising. Ad pages more than doubled. *Cosmo* was finally, emphatically, out of the red. Handwritten hosannas from Dick Deems arrived scrawled on the weekly memorandums of newsstand sales estimates: "In the merry month of May—just wonderful!" "The word is FANTASTIC!" "This must be the best June report in the entire industry!"

The whole industry took note: for seven years straight, Mrs. Brown's *Cosmopolitan* would enjoy an unprecedented "sell-through" rate. More than 90 percent of the issues that went out to vendors for single-copy sales flew off the racks. The sales appeal lay in Helen's editorial mix, the monthly recipe of service, celebrity, fiction, and emotional/psychological pieces, later known as "emo" articles. She delivered a variety pack of interests far more diverse than those in conventional women's magazines. "There's always the basics," she said. "Office politics, men and women in love and wrong relationships, ambition, personal fulfillment, health." But she went far beyond those categories.

Hers was a "Questions in the Night" form of editing; she took note of the crazy things that troubled her in the wee hours, the sorts of queries that we now compulsively type into search engines at 2:00 a.m., unwilling or unable to ask anyone else. It took in everything from bad boyfriends to going Dutch treat (never!), stubborn armpit stains, masturbation, and the gorgeous (rich) bitch who covets your boyfriend. Some article titles offered the same guilty pleasures that now churn massive traffic to list-heavy websites. Seeing the title "What's the Oldest

Thing in Your Refrigerator? Celebrities Confess Their Leftovers," who wouldn't be tempted to peek inside?

Given her efforts to please most of her readers all of the time, some of the juxtapositions in *Cosmo*'s table of contents could be breathtaking. The January 1966 list featured the psychotherapist Albert Ellis on "New Kooky (but Workable) Cures for Frigidity," just above "Religious Retreats for World Weary Girls" and "Six Tricks to Fake Discotheque Dancing." *Love, Pray, Boogaloo.*

Helen's nonfiction and service articles covered the waterfront and then some:

"Have You Heard About the New Catholicism?"
"Women and Snakes"
"Give Your Husband an Alcohol Rub"
"How to Read a Painting"
"The Poor Girls' Guide to America's Rich Young Men"
"Foiling Flashers"
"How to Talk Jazz"
"How to Give Your Cat a Pill"
"A Day in the Life of a Nuclear Power Plant"

Over the first several months, Helen leaned heavily on her live-in magazine maven. David Brown had promised that at least in the beginning, he would read and choose all fiction to be run, which short stories and novels to buy, and which to condense. He also wrote *Cosmo*'s cover lines for more than thirty years. A brief sampling:

"The Bugaboo of Male Impotence"
"I Was a Nude Model (and this is what happened)"
"Things I'll Never Do with a Man Again"
"The Astonishingly Frank Diary of an Unfaithful Wife"
"How to Make a Small Bosom Amount to Something"
"Why I Wear False Eyelashes to Bed"
"65 Depressed Celebrities Tell How They Fight the Gloom"

"What the Pill Is Doing to Husbands"
"Living Together Is a Rotten Idea"

When she felt herself to be the shakiest of rookies, Helen would call David at some point, nearly every day—she had a dedicated phone line installed in her office—and ask him to pick her up in a taxi. Their "nooners" were all business. Said David, "We'd ride around Central Park in a taxi while I went over page proofs, cover blurbs, captions, article ideas, and read manuscripts hurriedly." It was undoubtedly the only time in her long Manhattan life that the fiercely frugal Helen Gurley Brown took taxicabs with abandon. Fear allowed for such an extravagance—and she didn't dare expense the fares.

The Browns also conferred at their dining room table. She would read a snippet from an article, he'd blurt out a cover line, and they would tweak it to perfection. Running gobs of fiction that readers could settle in with was a part of Helen's master plan to deliver value; up through the 1980s, her issues would average thirty-four to forty-two pages of fiction and poetry (much of the latter erotic).

Guided in large part by David's input, Helen's fiction choices ranged from mysteries and thrillers to bodice-rippers and well-crafted, somewhat feminist short stories. David Brown had an eye for the literate as well as the potential blockbuster; the affable, high/low cultural dynamic that characterized the Browns' marriage was clearly visible in *Cosmo*'s contents page, month after month. In Helen's second issue, August 1965, she ran a story, "August Is a Wicked Month," by the fiery young Irish "It Girl" of letters, Edna O'Brien, who would go on to write nonfiction for Helen as well. In the same issue, Helen used a little nonfiction bagatelle that Jacqueline Susann had pulled out of a drawer somewhere called "Zelda Was a Peach."

Helen wanted to get in on the ground floor with Susann. She had some insider's tips about her friend and fellow Geis author. The Browns and the Mansfields kept close company, and all four of them had a penchant for mutual, remunerative log-rolling. They all knew that Geis was planning a typically socko launch for Susann's first novel, *Valley of the*

Dolls, which had finally coalesced as the tale of three Hollywood agony sisters and their struggles with men, the movie biz, depression, and "dolls," slang for prescription barbiturates. Letty Pogrebin had an unusually strong feeling when she got her hands on a newly minted copy of *Dolls*. "I just knew that it was going to sell and sell and sell," she said.

While Susann's aggrieved and exhausted editor, Don Preston, was still wrestling her ungovernable prose to the mat, Geis had used smoke, mirrors, and flat-out lies to gin up a paperback deal with none other than David Brown's friend at Bantam, Oscar Dystel. This (and bigger lies about Susann's literary chops) gave Geis leverage when talking it up with the movie guys. In that "all loving hands at home" spirit that Helen had invoked, the movie rights to *Valley of the Dolls* were snapped up early by David Brown. Fox optioned the book for $80,000, with a series of escalator clauses that would bring the Mansfields up to $200,000 in up-front fees—the equivalent of about $1.4 million today.

Letty Pogrebin began her mightiest campaign; thanks to the paperback sale, her *Dolls* publicity budget was the fattest yet, at $50,000 for this first-time novelist. She began to tease book reviewers and editors with a few campy gimmicks. One mailing held notices that looked like a doctor's prescription pad, with the scrawled message, "Take 3 yellow 'dolls' before bedtime for a broken love affair; take 2 red dolls and a shot of scotch for a shattered career; take Valley of the Dolls in heavy doses for the truth about the glamour set on the pill kick."

To get through the 250 promotional appearances in 11 cities—in just 10 days—Susann did pop amphetamines, so as not to "droop on TV." And she did not. Like Helen, this former TV pitchwoman was an indefatigable doyenne of hype and this was her Moment. Within the year, the hardcover would hit number one on the *New York Times* bestseller list and stay there for 22 weeks. When the Fox movie came out in 1967 it was enthusiastically panned, very well attended, and destined for many half-lives as a trashy cult classic. Helen completed the two-family cross-promotion with a feature story in *Cosmo*; after all, this was a movie her girls flocked to. The article was about the lead actresses

Sharon Tate, Patty Duke, and Barbara Parkins and was titled "The Girls Who Play Jennifer, Neely and Anne." She got Rex Reed to write it.

In the year of *Dolls*'s release, David Brown's studio grossed more than $44 million in domestic ticket sales in return for its $200,000 option and $5 million filming budget. The Mansfields had solidified the foundation for a burgeoning empire; by the 1970s, *Dolls* would be registered by the *Guinness Book of World Records* as the bestselling novel of all time, surpassing *Peyton Place* with 17 million copies sold to date. And Susann kept writing.

To Helen's advantage, *Cosmo* was assured of a direct line to All Things Jackie; she had items for her editor's column, book excerpts, and an enviable "girlfriend" presence in the magazine. The bestselling fascinator wrote and contributed to articles such as "The Camille Complex," about getting over a cold. ("Take two aspirins and a glass of milk with a jigger of Scotch.")

Helen and Jackie made a fabulous pair of media molls, one petite and whispery, the other tall, loud, throaty, and gleefully foul-mouthed. Both adored the designs of Emilio Pucci, the Florentine purveyor of clingy, wildly patterned frocks, the sort that announced, "Here she is!" Jackie ordered Pucci drapes for the Mansfields' hotel suite; her closet was crammed with thirty Puccis dresses. Helen indulged in about half as many and wore them for forty years. By the late 1960s, the output of Helen Gurley Brown and Jacqueline Susann flared across American pop culture on newsstands, bestseller lists, radio waves, and TV talk shows. It was a bright, binary constellation: two brazen dames, two canny producer/husbands, two bestsellers, two hit movies, and a vast marketing universe as yet unexplored.

Helen did suffer one brief and public stumble, a largely forgotten foray into daytime television: In December 1967, she sat in a Manhattan television studio in a hot pink dress, waiting for her eyelash glue to set and fielding questions from a *New York Times* reporter about her latest venture in expanding the national dialogue—well, at least in eighteen King Features Syndicate cities—on intimate subjects, mostly s-e-x. For a very short time, she was the interviewer/host on a half-hour show named after her anthology of syndicated columns, *Outrageous Opinions*. It was a one-on-one interview format. She would be coaxing famous people to talk about sex. Helen reasoned that she could be a compassionate but provocative interviewer thanks to her own years of analysis: "It teaches you to be casual and informal. I mean, it makes it seem all right to air your dirty linen in public, and to talk about bouts with drinking or cancer—or your little mongoloid brother. You used to keep him locked in the attic."

Despite such a gauzy and bizarre summary of her modus operandi, Helen did lure some big names to her hot seat: Otto Preminger, Cleveland Amory, Barbara Walters, David Susskind, Woody Allen, the comic Jackie Mason, the actress Joanna Pettet. Helen was confident that she could get them to loosen up and dish. Pettet did reveal a glancing lesbian encounter; Woody confessed a compulsion to kiss mailmen ("Probably the uniform and the leather pouch get me"). The show had its moments, thanks to Mrs. Brown's breathy directness as an interviewer.

She marched into the studio to cross-examine Norman Mailer, who seemed confused at first. He was told they'd be discussing "ideas." In her soft little voice Helen braced the literary lion: "Norman, why are you so violent?"

"I'm not violent."

"Does it have something to do with proving your manhood?"

"You're the first lady analyst I've ever seen in pink."

They thrashed their way through a prickly thicket; yes, Mailer surmised, every man worries at some point whether he's homosexual. And it was just nobody's business why he had stabbed his second wife, Adele, at that party.

As a host, Helen was still Charming's Mother. She didn't see the upside of being a tough interviewer: "Nobody likes you when you're a bitch, nobody wants to go to bed with you or take you to Bermuda." Alas, charm was not enough for the daytime audience of housewives, never a robust constituency for HGB. There was a history of mutual enmity; materializing between the detergent and diaper rash commercials to prod guests on their sexual peccadilloes, Helen Gurley Brown was still *that woman*. When the show was quickly canceled, Helen had to accept what she had suspected all along: she really was most effective as America's guest.

The Browns and the Mansfields grew closer. Yet no one but Susann's husband and doctors knew of her very private sufferings that included an autistic son, Guy Mansfield, living in an institution, and Susann's recurrent breast cancer, serious pill dependencies, heavy cigarette habit, and deep smoker's cough. Nonetheless, she was determined to celebrate her ascent to "N.Y. Times Bestseller!!" with her dream team. Don Preston, Susann's editor at Geis, recalled the evening when he and his wife were invited to the lavish celebration that the Mansfields threw for themselves and the Browns at '21': "Jackie stage managed that dinner, and they must have worked on it a week . . . I think [the wine] was a Chateau Lafitte. Caviar and vodka was standing in front of us when we sat down, and I drank Helen's vodka because she didn't want it. She tried to send it back, but I wouldn't let her."

There would be no mad abandon for HGB; she was thrilled for her friend, but there was always an issue to get out. *I have work to do.* It was a mantra she would invoke before cossetting herself away even in the most glamorous and exclusive playgrounds that success had admitted her to—at friends' Hamptons estates, on exotic movie locations, even at Wyntoon, the "Bavarian Village" retreat in rural Northern California that William Randolph Hearst plundered and imperiled his publishing companies to build. Helen wrote to friends that she and David had slept in the bed of Hearst's mistress Marion Davies; the tycoon had retreated to Wyntoon with Davies and their dachshunds shortly after Pearl Harbor. Each morning when Helen rolled out of that historic bower, she hit the floor for an hour and a half's exercise, then went at the manuscripts she had packed with her hiking clothes. She would never let her work go. Back in New York, she put in seventy to eighty hours a week at the office; staffers who had been out to dinner and walked home past the office building looked for her office light, always the last one glowing.

Helen believed in delivering a big bang for sixty cents per issue; in short order, her magazines were mammoth. The small, dense type ran nearly to the edges of the pages, so close to the cut that one could barely read the page numbers. The issues grew thicker, the ads plentiful. The dense bound volumes of late sixties, seventies, and eighties *Cosmopolitans* require effort to pry and keep open; piled high on a library cart, they seem to possess the atomic weight of lead. It was a magazine that a reader could spend a lot of time with. Hearst was sanguine about losing some of that valued "pass-on" readership beloved by advertisers, so long as more and more women bought their own copies and hung on to them. *Cosmo* readers were exceptionally loyal; between 92 and 96 percent of sales were single-copy purchases rather than subscription, more than double the industry average, month after month.

Helen's night terrors had subsided somewhat as the circulation grew. Life as a real editor in chief was dizzying, but it was becoming rather divine. Blasé New Yorkers began to recognize Helen in the street. Advertisers were jostling for placement up front and in the editorial well; young women were still writing for advice in the thousands.

How exactly did she do *that*—and so quickly?

Though Helen's editorial message and mix had their multifaceted appeal, her numbers were also buoyed by a demographic tsunami that she could not take credit for. The baby boom, that massive postwar urge to breed that Helen had so disdained, had produced many more daughters of working age. The first wave was hitting the workforce in the 1960s. By the early 1970s, there were half again more working American women between the ages of twenty and thirty-four—15.1 million—than there had been at the end of the 1950s (9.6 million). This increase delivered a new and relatively solvent readership, with spenders even more attractive to advertisers than the daddy-dependent teens, college students, and housewives who bought *Glamour, Mademoiselle,* or *Ladies' Home Journal.* Running the only magazine specifically geared to that independent, employed woman, Helen saw her circulation jumps keep a brisk pace with the surging female workforce.

Work and sex, the twin linchpins of *Sex and the Single Girl*, were coalescing in a robust new constituency—the "singles scene," part of what magazine trend stories were calling the sexual revolution. Far fewer young strivers were still living with their parents, or were financially dependent upon them. They were free to make decisions as to how and where they chose to live, and with whom. It was not their mothers' stay-at-home-until-marriage sort of young adulthood. As Helen was assigning more articles on birth control and cohabitation, the term "sexual revolution" began popping up elsewhere in the media. Jacqueline Susann saw it; her *Dolls* heroine Anne Welles fled Papa's house in "Lawrenceville" for a secretarial job in Manhattan:

"She had escaped. Escaped from marriage to some solid Lawrenceville boy, from the solid, orderly life of Lawrenceville. The same orderly life her mother had lived. And her mother's mother. In the same orderly kind of a house. A house that a good New England family had lived in generation after generation, its inhabitants smothered with orderly, unused emotion, emotions stifled beneath the creaky iron armor called 'manners.' "

The runaway popularity of *Cosmo* and *Dolls* was concomitant with the loosening of hidebound, male-dominated sexual etiquette. Women were beginning to listen more closely to their own desires, and act upon them. There was even new science about women's sexual lives in the laboratory discoveries of Dr. William Masters and Virginia Johnson, researchers who probed the uncharted physiology of human mating. The *New York Times* reviewer, a physician and Planned Parenthood administrator, admitted his own prudery in writing (favorably) about their book, *Human Sexual Response*: ". . . somehow I find the thought disconcerting that at bejeweled dinner parties across this nation . . . gentlemen on miladies' right will ask, 'Did you know that old Sigmund Freud was wrong? Masters found that clitoral and vaginal orgasm are essentially the same?' The reply will be, 'I found that interesting, but even more fascinating the fact that the size of the male phallus bears no demonstrable relationship to the degree of sexual satisfaction.' "

The doctor noted the shift from the old Freudian vaginal orgasm–only paradigm: clitoral exploration got twenty-two pages, vaginal forty-two. He warned that no one should buy the book for their porn collection; the prose was ponderously academic and chilly; sexual partners and masturbators were wired like lab rats. But the findings were heralded by the "new woman," who, like Helen two decades before, found the conventions of married life in suburbia—sexual and otherwise—little more than Colonial-style coffins. Like Anne fleeing Lawrenceville, they packed their bags and shopped for vibrators, discreetly wrapped.

Their migrations were unprecedented and liberating. In *Re-Making Love*, an insightful post-analysis of the sexual revolution subtitled *The Feminization of Sex*, the authors contended, "The birth control pill . . . contributed to women's sexual revolution but by no means *caused* it. The causes of the sexual revolution were more sociological than technological: Without a concentration of young, single women in the cities, there would have been no sexual revolution."

During the 1960s, there was an 80 percent rise in single households. Most of the change was happening in urban areas, where young men and women flocked for employment opportunities. *Cosmo* was reaching them back in Lawrenceville, and in the cities. In 1969, two-thirds of *Cosmo*'s readership lived in the cities or suburbs; by 1983, the figure would jump to seven out of eight. The book/TV series/movie colossus *Sex and the City* was still three decades away from Helen's debut *Cosmo*. But the stage was being set in countless sixties fern bars.

It all made for a fruitful and seemingly limitless synergy of message and demographic, and Helen was running far ahead of the pack. Yet at Hearst, she was still on a short leash. As she watched her numbers come in, Helen asked for a bonus structure keyed to circulation increases and without a cap. Richard Berlin, the cost-slasher in chief, refused to entertain the idea. Despite the incredible and growing circulation numbers, the huge increase in ad pages and revenue, Helen's "bonus" was limited to a thin dime per copy sold over the previous year's circulation. Millions more were pouring into Hearst coffers by the early seventies and her salary hovered around sixty thousand dollars.

As often as she dared, Helen asked for a decent editor in chief's travel budget and was repeatedly rebuffed. Instead, she traded shameless editorial mentions, often in her "Step into My Parlor" column, for free flights and accommodations to spread the *Cosmo* gospel. Of TWA's New York–to–London night flight, she gushed, "It is simply a floating pleasure palace! If they're not filet-mignoning you, they're white and red wining you, and there's the movie and the stereo. (David accused me of waking him up out of a sound sleep so I wouldn't even miss even the hot-towel course.)"

Hearst also sought more control over Helen's public image. She was proud of her frequent television appearances and growing visibility, yet her extracurricular efforts were frowned upon in the executive suite. In a letter stiff with censure and condescension, Dick Deems suggested that since she would be receiving vast sums of money in her next contract—richly deserved, of course—perhaps she should take care in accepting outside assignments that might "decelerate your progress on the magazine." To hell with daytime TV gabfests, then; the Hearst men wanted more growth and revenue, faster.

Helen would also receive a demoralizing note from Richard Berlin. Though he had congratulated Helen on her stunning sell-through numbers, Berlin expressed regrets that the woman who saved *Cosmo* and shored up the entire company's sagging bottom line would not be welcome at Hearst's fiftieth-anniversary party in the summer of 1969. He explained that "it's strictly a stag affair." By way of consolation, Berlin made a lordly offer to reserve a conference room in order to instruct her in the august history of the privately held company. The message was clear: though Helen's triumph had indeed made Berlin a hero, though her new office was certainly an improvement on the fusty dentist's suite at her last ad agency, the glass ceiling at Hearst had the primal fixity of a polar ice cap.

23 🌿

Recipe for Success

It is better to get hollandaise all over your negligee sleeves than to wear something appropriate to cook in when you are entertaining a man.

—HGB, *Helen Gurley Brown's Single Girl's Cookbook*

HELEN DID NOT LET UP, not for a second, though she ran on a strict 1,200 to 1,500 calories per twelve- or fourteen-hour workday. Her optimal regime "when I'm being good" looked like this:

Breakfast: one-quarter of an envelope of Carnation Instant Breakfast mixed with Gladys Lindberg's yeast-liver powder, stirred into 6 ounces of hot skim milk.

Lunch: exactly 4 ounces of cottage cheese, half an apple or pear, and a 3-ounce daub of tuna salad made in large weekly batches by the Browns' housekeeper.

Snack, 5:00 p.m.: same as lunch.

Dinner: 4 to 8 ounces of "some kind of meat," with vegetable.

She passed most evenings in bed surrounded with manuscripts and the two cats. If Helen had a productive evening, she rewarded herself with an 11:00 p.m. dollop of tuna. She also worked weekends, to David's glum disapproval. Despite the new mayor John Lindsay's insistence that New York was a "fun city," Helen wasn't succumbing to its blandishments. They still went to Liz Smith's parties and to weekends in the Hamptons, where Smith shared a house with the food, style, and entertaining guru and host extraordinaire Lee Bailey. David Brown owned a home and a sizable tract of property in the Hamptons, but they rented it out; Helen, still wary of the "patio life," could not see herself as a weekend hostess. In town, the Browns often saw Herbert and Grace Mayes and their daughters, Vicki and Alex; David and Herb Mayes had lunch together every Saturday. Helen was working, of course.

She rarely strayed from the reams of "emo" copy to immerse herself in national and world news. Thus the *Cosmo* girl was a fairly oblivious creature as events of the late sixties deepened national fault lines; the article mix remained fairly insular and upbeat, despite the onset of assassinations, civil rights protests, and the agonies of Vietnam. In 1966, Helen did run a brief article about that conflict ("Vietnam: What's It All About?"), a sort of crib sheet for the girl who wished to sound informed. She preferred personal "news" stories; a year and a half before Robert F. Kennedy's murder in June 1968, she assigned a perky profile, "The Incredible Go Go Go Superlife of Ethel Kennedy."

As cities, including New York, began to burn in the wake of Martin Luther King's April 1968 assassination, Helen kept to small, personal, and very occasional articles on race relations. Readers of color scarcely registered. The same could be said of most women's magazines of the time. *Cosmo* wasn't a magazine that championed diversity beyond its occasional African American cover models and a few generally clumsy pieces involving race. Despite its earnestness, one unfortunate first-person article in *Cosmo*, "What It Means to Be a Negro Girl," got carpet-bombed by white and African American reader mail alike ("I personally do not know one Negro woman who fits the vapid creature presented by your article"). There was a similar but more nuanced reaction to a thoughtful piece by the director Sidney Lumet's wife, Gail, on their interracial marriage. Race and sex was still such a freighted issue that another article, "The Black Man Turns Me On," drew both rage and huzzahs in the reader mail column.

Let the great world spin; Helen kept her head down, and the copy flowing. Weekdays, she generally ate spartan lunches at her desk at the office. When necessary, she took writers to lunch, but never anything too *too* extravagant: Longchamps, Gallagher's steak house, Toots Shor's, Patsy's, La Grenouille. Entries in her thick red office diaries often break down expensed meals to the penny. Lunch with the fashion designer John Weitz was an investment of $10.59; nibbles with an editor from *Women's Wear Daily* in the Pool Room at the Four Seasons was *madness—*$19.74!!! Peter Rogers, an advertising executive best known for the iconic "What Becomes a Legend Most?" Blackglama fur and Vidal Sassoon hair product campaigns, says he adored HGB and their lunches à deux. "I had lunch with Helen about once at month at an Italian place near her office. One of us would pay every other time. The best thing was that she would get out her change purse and start taking out nickels and dimes. It was hysterical. All her friends were extravagant people. That change purse killed me. And yes, she did eat her salad with her fingers."

No one appears in the HGB diary lunch slots more frequently than Liz Smith, by then a good friend and consigliere, and "Char" Kelly. They often convened, one-on-one, in Helen's favorite booth in the bar area of the Russian Tea Room at 150 West Fifty-Seventh Street. The restaurant was presided over by Faith Stewart-Gordon. She inherited the Tea Room from her husband, Sidney Kaye, who had owned it since 1955. Stewart-Gordon ran the restaurant after Kaye's death in 1967.

The "Tea Room," or RTR, had long been a favorite midtown refuge for show business types as well as Hearst employees, who used it as a convenient canteen just up Fifth-Seventh Street from the offices; Judith Krantz still rhapsodizes over the ninety-cent entrees, glasses of strong tea, and mammoth sandwiches from her *Good Housekeeping* days. When Helen and David Brown came for business lunches, Stewart-Gordon noticed a pattern. "They'd be there on the same day. David was always with his movie people; Helen was with her friends or colleagues. If it was a one-on-one, whether with Liz Smith or Geraldine Stutz [president of Henri Bendel], Helen liked to sit in the last bar booth. She really came to talk to the person she was with. She certainly didn't come to display herself. David would be sitting on the other side of the room in a booth with [the agent] Sam Cohn." She recalled that Helen often came in with her boss, Dick Deems. "He treated her like a combination of a daughter and a girlfriend. He would always make sure that she knew that he was the boss. He was very condescending."

To stay at her "ideal" 105 pounds, Helen did not actually eat, said Stewart-Gordon. "At the Tea Room, she'd have some sort of little salad, nothing memorable; she never would eat blinis and caviar or chicken Kiev. That would have been anathema. She did like food, she did care, she just showed this tremendous willpower. She had this thing in her head that she was fat, I guess." Sometimes, said Lyn Tornabene, Helen feasted with her eyes. "At the Tea Room she'd order Perrier with a straw and sit and stare, leaning on an elbow, at what I was eating. I like food. I like blinis. She would say, 'Is that as good as it looks?' I'd ask, 'Helen, darling, you want a bite?' Always it was, 'Oh no, that's all right.'"

Helen knew that she needed food features on her editorial menu; it brought advertisers, and some *Cosmo* girls actually enjoyed eating. One day, when she was sorting through the piles of books and galleys the previous tenant of her office had left behind, she came upon a small, literate, and witty confection published in 1963, the year after *Sex and the Single Girl*. *The Seducer's Cookbook* was written by Mimi Sheraton, who would go on to become a respected food writer and *New York Times* restaurant critic. Its come-on: "Helping men to get the answer that they want (yes), to give women a reason for saying it, and to keep America from becoming, sexually, a have-not nation." Seduction by food was an ancient art, Sheraton insisted, larding her thesis with testimonials from Plato, Shakespeare, Casanova, Balzac, and the Marquis de Sade, who insisted that "a good dinner is cause for a physical voluptuousness."

Sheraton's seductive menu plans were egalitarian and unisex, posing "20 situations into which men may lure women, and vice versa." The recipes are fairly classic—caviar omelets, baked oysters casino, squab en cocotte—but the book's sexual content is decidedly outré for 1963. Women and men, married and unmarried, leap from table to bed and back again with Moll Flanders gusto. Helen called Sheraton; a sexy food writer was exactly what she needed. She was extravagant in her praise, raving over Sheraton's genius in "discovering" the food/sex connection and suggesting a series of excerpts from chapters such as "What to Do with Leftovers (how to end an affair)" and "After Bed, What? (a light snack for an encore)." But Helen needed some alterations for her girls. "This book was mostly written for men seducing women," Sheraton said. "And Helen said, 'I want to turn it around and make it women seducing men,' because the magazine was primarily for women. She felt I should have done the book from the other angle. She said that men didn't buy books."

Soon, Sheraton was the kitchen temptress in *Cosmo*'s "The Seductive Cook." A dozen excerpts were revised and ran as a series. Afterward, Sheraton found that Helen was hungry for more. "She asked me if I could do a hamburger diet, so I did. I suggested a piece about how to get over a broken love affair, called 'Is He Really So Special?' Then I did one on what kind of man makes the best lover, by profession."

Sheraton said that Helen was an agreeable if exacting editor. But she didn't seem to be a serious *eater*. She did not get the sense that Helen liked food at all. "I think she was afraid of food. She's the kind of woman who would order four asparagus and say 'I'm so full I can't have dinner.'"

Success did usher in a ruthless and long-term pattern of self-abnegation for Helen. The sensible diet and exercise habits of her Los Angeles years, the Gladys Lindberg supplements and Pacific hikes, had hardened into a regime of almost maniacal daily imperatives. Helen did a tough hour and a half of floor exercises without fail, usually in the morning, but sometimes in her office at lunchtime. Her idea of a mad treat: diet Jell-O, every day, mixed with less water than recommended on the box to make it more gooey. Perhaps a few almonds. Helen was certainly a woman of appetites, but she was most comfortable with the sort of indulgence that burned calories rather than ingested them.

Besides, David liked her skinny. He said so himself: "I agree that skinny women can't look too thin. Skinny women look younger but skinny men look mummified."

At home, the couple fell into a fairly traditional arrangement of care and feeding. Helen did everything. In the morning, she gulped her murky potions and cooked David breakfast: eggs, mushrooms, toast. Every day, she made him get on the bathroom scale. To his relief, Helen could not monitor his business lunches. At home, they rarely dined together. Helen "cooked" for David, generally frozen entrees, simple chops, or chicken, supplemented by dishes left by the Browns' housekeeper. Full-time domestic help was out of the question, Helen declared, and no way would she hire a cook. They ate your food and had too much time to sit around doing nothing. The Browns relied on a part-time housekeeper, Anna Freimanis, who served them for thirty-seven years, still sewing on buttons and putting up hems at ninety.

None of her abstemious tendencies stopped Helen from producing a cookbook to fulfill her three-book contract with Berney Geis. This was a woman who made salads dressed with mineral oil, the cheap emollient that most cooks use to maintain wooden cutting boards. She wisely farmed the recipe development and testing out to a pro and merely seasoned the copy with her commentary. *Helen Gurley Brown's Single Girl's Cookbook* was chiefly the work of Margot Reiman, author of two previous cookbooks and a frequent contributor to *Cosmo*. Besides some rudimentary HGB encouragements ("Most butchers are darlings") there is little to feast on save some tangy chapter titles: "Food to Take to Bed," "Come Fry with Me," and "What a Friend We Have in Cheeses." The book was fried by critics, but given Helen's growing brand, it sold nearly 150,000 copies and had foreign sales in ten countries. Berney Geis negotiated a modest paperback sale.

As a new editor, Helen felt fortunate to make contact with all of the potential contributors at Liz Smith's chicken fried salons. She wasted no time in using some of them, even the edgy New Journalism sorts whom she had sworn off when she fired Rex Reed. In a roundup article titled "Six Current (but perennial) Fascinators," the subhead promised "a covey of fabulous (but dovelike) female writers flutter their wings over the men of their choice." Edna O'Brien chose Richard Burton. Rona Jaffe celebrated Marcello Mastroianni. Here is Gloria Steinem on the actor Peter O'Toole: "Next to a Cary Grant or a Rock Hudson, O'Toole looks slightly tubercular. But . . . he makes the conventionally good looking seem like underwear ads in Sears Roebuck. And about as interesting."

Nora Ephron was game for nearly anything. She said that Helen provided her first crack at magazine journalism. She explained in a 2001 interview with the Los Angeles writer Margy Rochlin: "I remember very clearly when *Sex and the Single Girl* was published. That was in '62 and I was working as a mail girl at *Newsweek*. I remember reading it [the excerpt] in the *New York Post*. It was about two years later that she took over *Cosmopolitan*. She gave me my first freelance assignment, 'How they chose the chorus line at the Copacabana nightclub.' I was grateful, I'll tell you that. It was in a period where I was trying to get magazine assignments and all they ever wanted to know was 'what magazine articles have you written?' And Helen didn't have any of that, she just called me cold and said, "I've been reading your stuff [in the *New York Post*, where Ephron was a reporter]. Would you like to do this?"

Following the Copa story, which was "not fun," Ephron went on to write a wallflower's lament in "Men, Men, Everywhere But" and a scrumptious dressing down of the bossy fashion bible titled "*Women's Wear Daily* Unclothed." In that piece, Ephron gave Helen her best early work; it was a gleeful dissection that also dared to take on "the Ladies," the women with classic-eight apartments on Park Avenue who spent fifteen to seventy thousand dollars yearly to maintain their 10021 zip code chic. It was a tribe that Helen was just getting to know: "Mrs. Charles Revson of lipsticks . . . Charlotte Ford Niarcos of automobiles . . . Mrs. Winthrop Rockefeller of Arkansas . . . Gloria Vanderbilt Cooper." And why did the Ladies desperately need their fresh copy of *WWD* served with the jewel-like *fraises des bois* and black coffee set down by the maid? Besides the surety of knowing whom and what to put on one's back, Ephron wrote, "There is one more reason that The Ladies read *Women's Wear Daily*; it serves as their Surrogate Bitch. Delightful, delicious, delectable, and delirious the newspaper *is*, but it is also as bitchy as can be."

Within the year, *WWD* would have its tasty revenge, thanks to a nameless viper in *Cosmo's booo-som*. "Some little bitch," Helen lamented, leaked her memo to women staffers wanting to know "what pleases you in terms of having your breasts caressed." Her questions on the subject were classic HGB; it was Helen's wish that a strong article cataloging those desires could "help a lot of men make a lot of girls more happy." She intended to use the response to instruct men in precisely how to cherish *booo-soms*. The leaked memo induced delirium in the *WWD* editors, who published and burlesqued it. How the Ladies tittered over their consommé at La Côte Basque. Dick Deems and Richard Berlin were mortified and spiked the piece. Helen declared she'd fire the traitorous bitch if she knew who she was. And of her bosses: "The use of anatomical words bugs them . . . But I plan to lie low for a while and come back with my boosom article later. I read it tenderly, like a little love letter, every so often."

Ephron also had the guts to submit herself to a *Cosmo* beauty makeover, "before" pictures and all, surrendering herself to Lupe, a single-named hairdresser with solid gold scissors, a trim Pierre Cardin suit, and a peppery Latin imperiousness. The next aesthetician asked dourly, "Is this your regular makeup? You're certainly not pretty-pretty." Ephron was pleased enough with the *WWD* and makeover articles to include them in her first anthology, *Wallflower at the Orgy*.

During the same period, Helen bought a piece by Tom Wolfe, collected in his book *The Pump House Gang*. Wolfe embedded himself in the privileged circle of London's hip young things in "Life of a Teenage London Society Girl." Helen, whose basic instruction to all writers was "write the way you speak," ran several thousand words that made for as hyper-oxygenated and kandy-kolored a prose pile as Wolfe ever hove onto a page. It is fairly hallucinogenic with Brit teen talk, and Wolfe displayed an italic habit as heavy as Helen's. One of his shorter, tamer sentences might have been written by a certain single girl, alone in

Europe for the first time, circa 1952: "Italian men! They are so quaint. In Rome, *wicked* Rome, they have this quaint old notion about *seduction* and if they sleep with a young, tender, blond, English society girl, their little chicken chests puff out and they have accomplished a *seduction*."

The stylish writers were creeping in after all. Helen remained resolute: no Joan Didion, no way. Not that Didion was concerned, or even interested. But Gail Sheehy, she of the multi-book *Passages* juggernaut, turned into an early favorite for Helen, reporting on everything from putting one's husband through school ("She Works While He Studies") to "What Your Sleep Habits Reveal." Sheehy also did some single-girl travelogues for the magazine. Ski bunny trips and Caribbean windjammer cruise dispatches had lush adjectival passages that hinted at the erotic possibilities: "My partner suddenly pulls me over a stone wall and we drop into the sand . . . it is very quiet now as he draws me close, water lapping at our necks as though in a jar. All senses are sustained, joined to the great natural forces of water, air and wind . . ." The idyll ends with a chaste "late day tour of the island straddling a stick shift."

Gael Greene did not trifle with innuendo. She was an unapologetic sexual adventuress—she had once scored with Elvis! Here was a writer heaven-sent for the new *Cosmo*. Greene, another former *Mademoiselle* guest editor, had been a regular *Cosmo* contributor before Helen's arrival, and one of the writers Helen had very much wanted to keep. She had done her own ribald "little book," an unsuccessful knockoff called *Sex and the College Girl*. Reporting mostly from the erogenous zone for *Cosmo* ("How Sexually Generous Should You Be?"), Greene was also developing the lusty gourmand persona that ripened, like triple-crème brie, into the "Insatiable Critic" in the dining-out pages of *New York* magazine. Her memoir of that time, *Insatiable*, is a steaming lagniappe of sex, foie gras, and cinema studs. Greene settled into an agreeable, natural collaboration with her new editor. In short order, she became *Cosmo*'s resident sexologist. She was married, if just for a short while longer, to the *New York Times* culture editor Don Forst. But Greene braved a bit of participatory journalism for *Cosmo*; she slept with Clint Eastwood when dispatched to interview him on the sweaty desert set of *Two Mules for Sister Sara*. He was one tough hombre with a tender touch, and Greene was not shy in re-creating the cataclysmic attractions in her memoir: "I remember the sweet smell of soap and the sun smells of his skin, the feel of his beard, how lean he was, how tall, the long muscles wrapping his bones . . ." When they met in a hotel for a second assignation, she reported, "my knees buckled from the impact of his Clint Eastwoodness."

Greene's rationale at the time: what happens on the road does not get packed and taken home. She explained in *Insatiable*, "It never occurred to me that what we had might have gone on beyond the Beverly Wilshire. It was wonderful sex in an era of wonderful possibilities. I still believed I was having sex on the run to be a better wife to my husband."

Myrna Blyth was a married young mother, a fiction writer, and a nonfiction reporter when she began writing for Helen in the late sixties. Now senior vice president and editorial director of AARP Media, and formerly the longtime editor of *Ladies' Home Journal*, she is also the author of *Spin Sisters: How the Women of the Media Sell Unhappiness— and Liberalism—to the Women of America*, a conservative excoriation of the "female media elite."

Blyth's short story called "The Wife-Eater," a mordant marriage dissection, appeared in the early HGB *Cosmo*, along with her nonfiction articles. Blyth respected Helen's editing skills, but found her a cold fish. "I liked Helen, she was admirable. But she didn't have a normal human conversation. She was interested in fodder." She says she sensed Helen's tone deafness to the lives of real women during a phone call when her toddler son was laughing in the background. Helen assumed he was fussing and crying; she simply had no idea what a happy child might sound like.

Given the fact that two-thirds of *Cosmo* readers at the time were married and likely to have foaled, Blyth found it an unforgivable blind spot. As time went by, reader demographics did skew more toward singles, to five out of every nine by the early eighties. But there were plenty of divorced and married women who Blyth felt were underserved by

Helen's determined myopia. "She was always trying to find ways that you might get respect—for being skillfully sexy, or very interesting, or beautiful. She didn't understand that women also get respect simply because they're mothers. I would say she had a total lack of understanding of the real lives of millions of women. Yes, younger women are more focused on sexuality and looks. Fine. But because of the circumstances of her own life, she didn't understand that you usually mature out of that. Or she had no interest in it."

Regardless of Helen's alleged blind spots, Blyth respected her engaging and inclusive olio. Some of the banner names of Helen's early issues, besides Ephron and Wolfe: Françoise Sagan, Nadine Gordimer, Jane Howard, Iris Murdoch, Isaac Bashevis Singer, Ross Macdonald, George Plimpton, Kenneth Tynan, Norman Mailer, Yukio Mishima, Joyce Carol Oates, Gail Godwin. In her February 1966 special issue on men ("3 dozen articles!"), Helen dispatched the renowned Italian journalist Oriana Fallaci on an assignment that she would have killed for herself, a rare interview with the legendary Spanish matador El Cordobés. Helen's sigh is almost audible as she writes, "Oriana spent several weeks at El Cordobés ranch to get the story."

"When you look at the *Cosmo* that Helen edited," said Blyth, "it looks like *The Atlantic* compared to the *Cosmo* of today."

24

Big Sister and the Youthquake

Wanted: Keeno, diggo, coolo, chico . . . Bark it to me, baby, swing out, snap those fingers, gravy. Freak into my arms with loving broom-feathers and we will definitely be in "the horn." Be my Valentine, Marko S., Alexandria, Va.
—classified ad in Hearst's *Eye* magazine, 1968

IT WOULD BE INACCURATE to say that Helen kept her vow of no staff dismissals; some people left rather than deal with the pressures exerted by an untried editor with a hardwired doomsday mentality and a pair of Hearst minders breathing down her neck. To feed and fatten the loose-leaf notebook containing article ideas, an object that would become a talisman of Helen's editorial control, editors were expected to churn up scores of ideas, weekly. "You had to come up with ideas or you were out . . . A couple of people had nervous collapses from the stress," said the editor Harriet LaBarre.

Though she was happy to have the writing assignments, Lyn Tornabene dreaded the low, whispery calls that came after she had turned her stories in. There was always the preamble of breezy flattery, followed by a cold front. On the phone, Helen's voice sounded "like Jackie at the White House," said Tornabene, but the hushed tones often belied a stern mission. "I was really having trouble with Helen at first. I'd send in any article and a call would come. 'Lyn, darling. Oh, you shouldn't work so hard for me, I don't deserve to have you working for me, no, you're too *good*. But I *hate* your lede. You have to do the first thousand words over because they're *terrible.'*"

Writers dealt with it in their own ways. When Liz Smith's movie reviews were worked over with a pickax and a pot of treacle, her form of therapy was to write an excoriating letter to Helen that she never sent, begging to resign as movie critic rather than suffer the editorial mauling. A short excerpt: "My name cannot go on the reviews this month as they have been rewritten. They are trite, banal and devoid of any punch. We did not always put out a magazine that was so homogenized and simplistic . . . and every interesting word like 'ersatz' or 'pellucid' expunged." Finding even her critic's opinions completely reversed by an unknown hand, Smith asked, "Who is it that has the guts to just keep doing this to me month after month?" It was professionally embarrassing; Smith did quit writing reviews and stuck with features.

It was apparent from the outset of her tenure: Helen was a complicated woman to deal with. Often, the aggrieved or merely indifferent parties, male and female, were disarmed by a certain snake charmer's je ne sais quoi. For months, at the beginning of Tornabene's association with the new *Cosmo*, her husband, Frank, also a journalist, had listened with empathy to his wife's complaints about Helen's editing. He had been prepared to loathe the petite gorgon on sight when they finally met at an office Christmas party. Tornabene says the application of the HGB whammy that night was a wonder to behold: the Eye Lock, the light caress, the resulting deer-in-the-headlights stupor. "Later, we're waiting for the elevator and my husband says, 'Don't you *ever* say anything mean about that adorable woman.'"

Helen continued her conquest of the Tornabene males. It was Thanksgiving, circa 1967. As happened so often, the Browns had no holiday plans with friends or relatives. Still counting herself as America's guest, Helen called Tornabene at home in Greenwich, where she was hosting "both families, a lot of strays, and four dogs." The Browns had just dined alone in a restaurant in nearby Bedford, New York. Might they drop by?

"They come in a huge limo," said Tornabene. "Helen spots my

father-in-law, who is a very handsome, elegant man—an exiled northern Italian, very tall. She goes over and sits on the arm of the sofa, then realizes she's looking down on Dad. She wouldn't sit higher than a man, ever. Like Anna and the King of Siam. She slithered to the floor. And they bonded. A sponge would have done fine to pick him up off the sofa. Meanwhile, in the kitchen, is my mother-in-law, Marie, a very round, Calabrese Italian lady and she is calling for my husband, Frank. She's yelling, 'PUTANA! PUTANA! Get her away from your father!' Poor Dad, he never recovered."

Tornabene admits to having been in a sort of thrall herself; wherever she went, despite all of the famous men and women she interviewed, she had the same experience as Liz Smith with other people's curiosity. Never mind the movie stars; America really wanted to know: What was Helen Gurley Brown *really* like? "I adored her," said Tornabene. "She was like no other thing on earth, Helen Gurley Brown. I never could predict her, I never anticipated an answer to a question."

Mrs. Brown had begun to intrigue a wide spectrum of New Yorkers. The composer Irving Berlin was crazy about her, as was Walter Cronkite. Even the *New York Times* columnist Russell Baker wrote her admiring notes. And soon, Helen had a new blue-blood friend whom she met at Liz Smith's soirees. She had taken an immediate liking to the straight-talking heiress, artist, and socialite, Gloria Vanderbilt DiCicco Stokowski Lumet Cooper, still best known by her family name throughout those four marriages. She already had a connection to *Cosmopolitan*. "I had written for the magazine when Bob Atherton was running *Cosmopolitan*," said Vanderbilt. "I had written a couple of short stories. When Helen came in, I started doing book reviews. I felt total confidence in her take and her point of view. She was very focused on how she wanted the magazine to be. I never had any problems with her at all as far as editing went."

Vanderbilt became *Cosmo*'s regular book reviewer, and would also contribute her design and fashion flair to *Cosmo*'s generally outdated and uninspired decorating features. Both Vanderbilt and the respected music writer Nat Hentoff enjoyed considerable leeway in reviewing books and records. A typical Vanderbilt mix: a literate biography of

Marie Antoinette, a memoir by the lefty columnist Jack Newfield about his years with the late Bobby Kennedy, and a posthumous collection of poems and essays of the folksinger/writer Richard Fariña, who was married to Joan Baez's sister; Fariña died in a motorcycle crash two days after his first book, a novel, was published. For her new editor in chief, Vanderbilt included a thumping great reference book on Broadway musicals.

Helen and Gloria, the Arkie and the heiress, were both in Los Angeles in the late thirties and early forties, but, said Vanderbilt, "we never spoke of those years. It wouldn't do, you know." They were contemporaries; Helen was the elder by two years. But discussing their L.A. experiences would not be *gentille*; the gulf was too wide and the comparisons too stark. Helen had to accept Vanderbilt's silence on those years. There was plenty more to discuss; they discovered that they both enjoyed men, very, very much. Vanderbilt had married her final husband, the author Wyatt Cooper (father of the CNN anchor Anderson Cooper), just before she and Helen met; she had also been linked romantically with Marlon Brando, Frank Sinatra, Roald Dahl, and Howard Hughes. Both women were plain, direct talkers with no inhibitions about discussing men, romance, sex, and, when they got around to it, which juicy novels to review next in the magazine. Like Helen, Vanderbilt adored dancing. Peter Rogers took both women for a whirl with David Brown one uproarious night at the Waldorf; even David, a reluctant dancer, hit the floor a bit. "We danced all night there," said Rogers, who became one of Helen's most adored partners. "Helen could do anything, she was a wonderful dancer. She loved to boogie. If I do say so, we both were pretty good." Nights out with Helen and Gloria were mad fun, he said, because of the women's great élan and their friendship. "Gloria was crazy about Helen," he said. "They were together quite a bit, to the end. Helen's friends stayed with her and she stayed with them."

As her own star rose, Helen had the pleasure of watching some close women friends go on to madly successful careers. Vanderbilt was already a wealthy and successful woman when they met, but she would become a national brand when she jumped in on the designer jeans

craze early, along with Calvin Klein. Jackie Susann's was an astonishing trip, and she and Helen were together all the way. Another break-
out success came to Judith Krantz, the former fashion assistant at *Good
Housekeeping* who would become fabulously wealthy as a novelist of
the rich, bitchy, and infamous.

Judy Tarcher had first been a good friend of David Brown since
their early days at Hearst and they had stayed in touch, partly through
their mutual friendship with Herb and Grace Mayes and their daughter
Alex. She met her husband, Steve Krantz, in 1953 at a Fourth of July
party given by her high school friend Barbara Walters. Steve Krantz
was a TV and film producer; he would become known for his bawdy
animation feature *Fritz the Cat* and for TV miniseries of his wife's bestselling novels *Scruples*, *Princess Daisy*, and *I'll Take Manhattan*. Like
the Browns, they were a family franchise; Krantz's novels were copy-
righted under the name "Steve Krantz Productions."

Given all the professional and personal overlap, the Browns and the
Krantzes became friends, sometimes traveling in Europe together and
sojourning at the Krantz apartment in Paris. Judith Krantz, now a
robust eighty-eight, spoke of their long association from her home in
California, where she had just finished her daily session on Pilates
equipment custom-upholstered with pink leather. She said that she lost
no time in expressing her interest in Helen's *Cosmo* reinvention. "I proposed myself to Helen," she said. She was fed up with the gingham'd
confines of *Good Housekeeping* and *Ladies' Home Journal*, and she had
a crazy little article idea. "I had heard a word—funky. And I thought
funky was a great word and that *Cosmo* should have a little piece on
it—just a short one. I wrote a note to Helen suggesting this. And Helen
wrote back and said, 'I don't think funky is going to last.'"

At Helen's suggestion, they had lunch. "And then I started working
for her for the next nine years." Krantz recalled the early days of the
loose-leaf binder. "They gave me assignments from the book. The minute I found one I liked, I grabbed it. It was wonderful, because I had
always worked for men who wanted me to bring in a dozen assignment
ideas a month, and that was hard." It helped that she knew Helen's
articles editor. "Bobby Ashley was a very good friend," said Krantz.

"But Helen personally edited my work. She would call up and say, 'Look on page four. The third paragraph down. And the fourth line down from the top. There's a word there that I think you should substitute another word for. That's not a good word.' And we'd talk about what was a good substitute. She was the most definitive and best informed editor I've ever had."

Krantz says she welcomed such micromanagement of her copy, at least at first. In her experience, male editors of women's magazines simply did not engage with women writers. "I'd always worked for male editors, and they'd say things like, 'Well, run it through the typewriter again,' which doesn't help at all. Helen knew exactly what she wanted, either in or out, and she would tell me. We would go through the whole piece that way, and when it was finished, it was exactly the way it was printed. There was never another editor like that. Never. No word went into *Cosmopolitan* that Helen didn't approve of."

Krantz had the feeling that *Cosmo* had almost *become* Helen. "The magazine was her holy grail. It was her sense of what was right."

Hearst executives felt that Helen needed another seasoned pro at her side and began a search. They hired Jeanette Sarkisian Wagner, a well-credentialed journalist then at *The Saturday Evening Post*. From the beginning of her tenure at *Cosmo*, Wagner noticed a substantial and growing gap between the real magazine and the public perception of it. "People make a mistake when they think of *Cosmo* as a sex magazine. *Cosmo* was not a sex magazine. *Cosmo* was the big sister telling the baby sister how not to screw up. In her own life, Helen had no role models."

Wagner, now retired from an executive position at Estée Lauder, wore a few hats at *Cosmo*. In addition to assigning and editing for the regular magazine, she helped Helen recycle and monetize the immense body of editorial content into a series of hardcover and paperback anthologies, among them *Cosmopolitan's Hangup Handbook, Cosmopolitan's Love Book, Cosmopolitan's Living Together (Married or Not) Handbook,* and a collection of short stories, *The Wings of Love.* One of Wagner's hires for that enterprise was a talented writer named Veronica Geng, who went on to a career as a humor writer for *The New Yorker* before her early death from brain cancer. Geng wrote sharp, droll essays for *Cosmo* and assisted Wagner in packaging the themed book anthologies. "She was brilliant," said Wagner. "I just loved her."

Wagner would also help create the magazine's first international editions, often traveling the world with her husband, Paul, and the Browns to help launch them. All along the way, though she liked Helen, Wagner was often frustrated by her boss's limited and sometimes myopic worldview. She found it very difficult to divert Helen from her obsession with money and financial security, both for herself and for her readers. "Everything was colored by her lifelong worry about money. No matter how much money she made, she never got over that. Clearly she made a great deal more money than I did as an editor. If she liked a dress I was wearing she'd say: 'That's a great dress, what did it cost?' I would tell her and she'd say: 'Oh, I couldn't afford that.' And of course she could have."

It follows, Wagner said, that "there was no wasted space in *Cosmopolitan*." Wagner watched Helen incentivize her staff to fill every inch. One could pack thrifty and transformative tips into three lines at the end of an editorial column. ("Flies or bees bothering you? Spray them with hairspray and they will take a quick dive.") There were regular, required meetings to come up with ideas for fillers. The editor with the most ideas per meeting got a bottle of champagne. Wagner found Helen to be a good and fair boss. "I never looked at it as 'she-who-must-be-obeyed,' I never did. I recognized and honored her for paying meticulous attention to what her vision was. And that it was genuine. She really cared about that baby sister, she really wanted to help. That was not *my* baby sister but I understood it and I respected her. Her commitment to her audience was genuine and one thousand percent. In every way."

Without warning, in 1968, Hearst expressed its confidence in Helen by handing her another magazine to supervise, a new publication with a planned readership utterly alien to her: hippies! The growing "youth culture" was opening up a tantalizing new market. To her horror, Helen was suddenly tasked with becoming Groovy Big Sis, developing a new magazine for a younger readership she knew absolutely nothing about. Hearst decided that it should cash in on flower power and other lucrative by-products of the late-sixties "Youthquake" by launching its own unisex counterculture magazine, titled *Eye*. "It was to be patterned after a French magazine which was about the teenage kids and was making a fortune," said Wagner, who believes the project was doomed by two very serious errors in judgment. "One: Hearst Corporation is to the right of Attila the Hun, and these kids they hired for the magazine were all the way on the left. Two, they made Helen the consulting editor."

HGB would never refuse a summons from the executive suite, but she had a perfect dread of this assignment. At forty-five, she was on the wrong side of the "don't trust anyone over thirty" divide and it made her deeply uneasy. What did she know of teenage boys and girls and lava lamps and Bob Dylan? What did she care? Helen would be paid an additional twelve thousand dollars a year to oversee *Eye*; she was so dubious about its future that she inserted a clause that stipulated she be paid each year in full, even if Hearst's new magazine flopped aborning. In the search for an editor in chief for this misbegotten and mistrusted product, Helen remembered a young writer named Susan Edmiston, who had done a madly popular teen column that ran in the *New York Post*, alternating weekdays with Helen's "Woman Alone" column. After Helen's syndication deal ended for lack of readership, Edmiston's column was still drawing heavy ad placement for the growing bazaar of teen-related products falling into the new marketing category of "hip consumerism."

"She called me up and asked me if I was interested," said Edmiston. "I sat down and wrote down a hundred ideas for such a magazine. Then she asked me to get a dummy done." Edmiston called her friend Nora Ephron, who suggested someone to help her produce a viable, young-looking magazine dummy. "The first thing they did was to hire Judith Parker," said Edmiston. "Judy was a brilliant and very strong art director, so she and Helen were butting heads right from the beginning. We had a piece on a young model. There were beautiful, typical model photos and then there was a shot of the way she looked in the morning with no makeup. So Judy of course wanted to use the no makeup, unglamorous photo as a full page and use the model photos as little ones on the bottom of the page. I recently looked back at that issue to see who had won." Edmiston laughed. "Helen."

Before long, it was full-out war between Parker and Helen, who tried to enlist Edmiston on her side. She refused to join the fray. "I'm not a combative person. I was working very hard and had a lot of wonderful contacts from my years on the *Post*, through my friendship with Nora, so I had access to these writers. It's impressive who was writing." Contributing editors included Ephron and Lillian Roxon, the godmother of rock writers who could command the rare access for "101 Hours with John Lennon and Paul McCartney" during their magical mystery tour of Manhattan. Tom Wolfe, Nik Cohn, even Bruce Springsteen's manager-to-be Jon Landau wrote for *Eye*. There were articles on Esalen, Dylan, John Lennon, Jean-Luc Godard. But there were echoes of HGB in some of the story assignments: "Five Self-Made Rich Kids Tell How They Did It." "Mother Jealous of Your Freer Sex Life?"

The counterculture staff parried with stories like "Miss America Is a Bummer" and "Sorcerer of Rock: Jim Morrison Raps." Helen's input centered on subjects she knew best: fashion, makeup, dating. She disliked the visuals intensely. "A lot of the photography was by Judy's boyfriend [the British rock-shooter Michael Soldan]," said Edmiston. "It was very psychedelic-influenced and this was great for the magazine, except that they [Hearst] didn't understand it or the market."

Eye's youthful fashion looked like so much nasty burlap to Helen. She told Edmiston, "Don't make the models look poor." On the rare occasion that Helen and her editorial team visited the loft space that housed *Eye*, she found it distasteful and disorienting. "They would come down in a limousine," said Edmiston. "The office was on LaGuardia Place, in a former art gallery. Some people described it as a seedy part of town. It wasn't, it was just the Village." The writer Sheila Weller, then a staffer in *Eye*'s fashion department, described the vibe in *The New York Times*: "It was a magical place, all the more so as few people remember it . . . The art department girls were cocky and beatific, as if cutting and pasting bits of swirling psychedelic typeface was a completely uninteresting part of their personal cosmic order." There had never been good chemistry, said Jeanette Wagner. "Helen didn't like those kids. She thought they were screwing up their lives, and they weren't working hard enough, they had money, their parents had money." The clash between Helen and Judy Parker reached a hopeless impasse in the late spring of 1968. Edmiston received a phone call on a Friday morning. "I was told they were firing Judy and the rest of the art department, and they were coming to change the locks. They were afraid Judy would steal artwork or God knows what." Parker and her staff had left before the Hearst operatives arrived. "I just felt these people were thugs," said Edmiston, "because of what they did with the firing and the lock changing."

Judy Parker and Michael Soldan decamped to Long Island and boarded their small sailboat on the Long Island Sound with another photographer. "A big storm came up and that was it, they couldn't deal with it," said Edmiston. All three were presumed drowned; their bodies were not recovered. According to a footnoted roundup of sixties tragedies in Sheila Weller's book *Girls Like Us*, Parker and Soldan "took acid after their boss, Helen Gurley Brown of *Cosmopolitan*, scolded them for their hallucinogenic colors; then got in their boat in Long Island Sound in a storm and drowned." Edmiston is not sure about the scenario. "Acid? I think everybody was saying that, but how would they know?" Still, it may have been the case. "The notion that they might take drugs after this firing is reasonable." A new art director was hired; Edmiston heard that people were being interviewed for her editor in chief job, and she quit. She went on to work as articles editor of *Redbook*, and cofounded *Savvy* magazine. She is now a writer, living in Northern California.

Jeannette Wagner was sent downtown to try to get *Eye* on a better track, but hip and Hearst were a hopelessly poor fit. The monthly folded after fifteen issues, in May 1969. Soon afterward, Wagner got a phone call from the Hearst executive suite. "They said, 'Okay, we now want to start this international edition [of *Cosmo*], so I became the editor in chief of the international edition. And then we did a book club."

Repackaging content was something Helen could wholly embrace. The *Cosmo* engine was humming with more foreign editions, plus paperback and hardcover anthologies of past articles. "We also did a merchandising division," said Wagner. "We did the *Cosmo* Girl's crochet-it-yourself bikini." She laughed. "We sold thousands of them."

25

A March Forward, a Few Steps Back

The feminists attacked me . . . Kate Millett came into the office and
I was backed up against the radiator but it wasn't very hot.
—HGB

MARY ALFORD'S HOME COMPANION, Teresa Rowton, wrote to Helen about a funny little thing she'd noticed. She had heard a strange noise coming from Mary's bedroom and peeked in. Mary was running over sheets of bubble wrap with her wheelchair. She seemed to be enjoying herself; Rowton stood just watching for a while. There was always plenty of the plastic wrap around, since Helen sent frequent packages full of free cosmetic samples, magazines, and other giveaways that came to the office. Decades before the wrap's manufacturer, Sealed Air, began marketing its "Bubble Wrap 100866453 Anti-Stress Box" as a modern calmative sold on Amazon, Mary had discovered the satisfying if small release in popping the honeycombed sheets of packing.

Life just wasn't getting any better in the crowded little home in Shawnee; George was in ever-escalating agony, floating in a distant haze of alcohol and pills. Desperate, Helen tried to find him an acupuncturist. The ancient medical art was still illegal in the United States, but David's buddy the producer Robert Evans had connections. A grateful Helen said that Evans "got his friend, Los Angeles lawyer

Sidney Korshak, to fix me up." They flew Alford to California for treatment; it didn't help. Helen tried neurosurgeons and, later on, contacted the televangelist Oral Roberts, whom she had met on *The Merv Griffin Show*. Helen generally distrusted religion, but she was looking for a miracle. Roberts prayed with the Alfords. He also proffered an excerpt of his wife's book, *His Darling Wife, Evelyn*, to Helen. When his pious spouse gasped, "*Cosmopolitan?*" Roberts cited the magazine's huge readership. "Besides," he added, "I like Helen Gurley Brown." Roberts was pleased to accept a ten-thousand-dollar donation from Hearst for his eponymous university.

Mary had become so obese that it was difficult for anyone to get her from the wheelchair into a car. She needed to get to the Methodist church for its fellowship and for A A meetings. Helen got Hearst to donate a van with a handicap lift to the church. It wasn't enough. It was still difficult to get the manpower necessary to drive and use the van, as much as Mary might have benefited from it. Cleo, suffering from some age-related maladies, moved in with the couple and their ménage of animals and caregivers.

Nature's implacable cruelty had inflicted another bad joke on Mary; it was discovered that her backyard grew a self-sustaining crop of "lucky" four-leaf clovers. They just kept coming up. Mary's housekeepers would find, press, and dry them and send them to Helen, who passed them along to acquaintances in need of luck or encouragement. She swore by their efficacy and tucked them into notes to those facing lumpectomies, biopsies, love and job troubles, public humiliations, and prosecution. Well, it just *might* help.

For the New York branch of the family, the outset of the 1970s was exceeding expectations. David, working at Fox in tandem with Darryl F. Zanuck's son Richard, had delivered a hit movie destined to become a classic so revered that it is number fifty on the American Film Institute's list of the "100 Greatest Movies of All Time." Zanuck had been the one to act quickly and invest four hundred thousand dollars in *Butch Cassidy and the Sundance Kid*, teaming Robert Redford, Paul Newman, and the director George Roy Hill. Helen glammed up for the red carpet at the Dorothy Chandler Pavilion; *Butch Cassidy* won four

Oscars in early 1970; it lost Best Picture to *Midnight Cowboy*. Domestic box office for *Cassidy* in 1969 was just over $100 million.

Helen was fighting trim; her measurements, faithfully taken bimonthly, "without straining tape measure any," then typed onto *Cosmopolitan* memo paper, had held steady—no more than half an inch difference up or down over the last year: 33″ (bust), 24½″ (waist), 37″ (hips). Success hadn't plumped up anything but her sales figures, which kept rising.

David's son and daughter-in-law were back in New York after studying at Washington University in St. Louis. So cheered was Helen to have Bruce married off that she had shown up at their 1965 wedding in a blindingly pink dress and matching turban. Bruce Brown was a regular contributor to *Liberation*, a pacifist magazine, and was said to be working on a book. He was also doing some freelance programming, mostly on drug-related topics, for WBAI, a progressive station in Manhattan at 99.5 FM that was listener-supported. Helen and David were fond of his wife, Kathy; she began work as a copy editor at *Liberation*, then became copy chief at *Cosmo* and would go on to a top editorial position at *Mademoiselle*. The couple was not as independent as Helen might have preferred. David recalled a conflict that left him uneasy.

"I felt tensions building up to a dangerous level of anxiety . . . My son was in the hospital for a knee operation with the prospect of piling up medical costs. My wife, Helen, jealous perhaps or perhaps correctly, had said, 'Why do you subsidize this boy of twenty-eight? What Indian sign has he got on you?' It all came to me. Helen was the one who had the Indian sign on me. She could make me feel like a wrongdoer."

The tension eased when it became clear that only a short hospital stay was necessary.

Everything was lovely, really, until the chill day in early 1970 when Helen encountered Kate Millett and a stone-faced group of radical feminists in the *Cosmo* reception area. They meant business; Millett said that she was disgusted by the magazine's "reactionary politics."

Helen doubtless saw her as a somewhat wild-eyed weirdo. But before year's end, Millett's doctoral thesis at Columbia University, *Sexual Politics*, would be bound in sturdy cloth, raised aloft at rallies, and embraced on the bestseller list. Her portrait, painted by Alice Neel, would be on the cover of *Time* magazine. It was that kind of year for the women's movement; fast-moving, deeply factional, and boldly, fervently fractious.

Helen was annoyed—she had *work* to do—but she kept her cool. In her quiet voice she explained that *Cosmo* considered itself a feminist magazine; she had met with a feminist group, Women in Media, earlier and was agreeable to printing more feminist articles—but on her terms. Shortly after the protest, Helen was invited, and strongly encouraged, to participate in a consciousness-raising session, explained to her as a confidential circle in which women honestly examined their own "hangups." The women had no idea what they had unleashed. Mrs. Brown, who had so long ago stood naked and confessed her insecurities to a dozen other people in Charlie Cooke's hang-up laboratory, had little trouble getting into the groove. She wrote about it in her editor's column: "Twelve of us—I almost said girls, but they say I must stop that and refer to us as women—sat about and related our hang-ups. Frankly, I was only to my eighth hang-up when I had to relinquish the floor to the next hang-upee." At least she didn't bring along a manuscript to edit while the others shared. She closed her column by recommending consciousness-raising sessions to her women readers. Who knew—it just might *help*.

During that office invasion, Helen got off easy, merely backed up against a radiator for a mostly well-mannered discussion. There was little civility at the sit-in at *Ladies' Home Journal* that March. After a hundred demonstrators burst through the doors at 9:00 a.m., it became an eleven-hour siege. The publisher and editor in chief was forty-two-year-old John Mack Carter; the women who occupied his well-appointed office were from the National Organization for Women (NOW), the Redstockings, and the New York Radical Feminists. The writer Susan Brownmiller, one of the group's leaders, told reporters that they targeted *LHJ* "because it is one of the most demeaning magazines toward women," and because it reached so many of them—6.9 million. The protesters demanded Carter's replacement by a woman, along with day care for the forty-seven women on his staff and an end to "exploitative" advertising. Carter, while shaken, held the line, telling a reporter that "though they may have a point, they can't have my job." The demonstration got a bit physical; a couple of women tried to push Carter off his desk, where he was seated. They helped themselves to a box of cigars and puffed away on them.

The following month, Helen did run a surprisingly forthright article reprinted from *The Village Voice*. It was by one of its staff reporters, a mother-to-be and an essayist and critic later called a "feminist oracle." In 1970, Vivian Gornick was pregnant and distressed by the deepening hostilities between men and women at her dinners with friends. The article was titled "The Women's Liberation Movement!" The subhead was a bit pushy for *Cosmo*: "The next great movement in history may be yours. Are you speeding or impeding its arrival?" Gornick opened with the litany of complaints and misperceptions about the movement she had heard among her own friends:

From a husband at a dinner party: "What is all that crap about . . . They're mostly a bunch of dykes, anyway."

From a "college-educated housewife, fat and neurotic," a shrug: "I'm sorry, I just don't *feel* oppressed."

Gornick found herself feeling unaccountably depressed. Sizing up the historic intransigencies of the inequalities, she pulled no punches: "Because no one has ever had any intention of turning over any serious work to us, both we and the blacks lost the ball game before we even got up to play. In order to live you have to have nerve, and we were stripped of our nerve before we began. Black is ugly and female is inferior; these are the primary lessons of our existence." It was raw and radical for a Hearst magazine. But Gornick's grim polemics were wrapped in approachable personal anecdote and soul-searching. For a policy piece, it's a good read with an upbeat conclusion about the important work of feminists: "They are gathering fire, and I do believe the next great moment in history will be theirs. God knows, for my unborn daughter, I hope so."

———————

In late summer, Helen decided to try a bit of activism herself; it would be the first organized event for social justice that she had ever participated in. On August 26, 1970, an estimated ten thousand women marched down Fifth Avenue in Manhattan to a rally at Bryant Park, behind the New York Public Library at Forty-Second Street. Its organizers called it the Women's Strike for Equality. The action was in support of abortion rights, day care for working women, and equality in education and employment. NOW urged passage of the Equal Rights Amendment (ERA), which had first been introduced into Congress in 1923 and finally seemed to be getting a bit of traction.

Helen was passionate enough about women's reproductive rights to slip on some sensible shoes and get out there. Her first abortion-related article, "I Didn't Have the Baby, I Had an Abortion," had run three years earlier. The pseudonymous first-person account was lengthy, graphic, sad, and rueful. It did not present abortion as casual or inconsequential, but as a deeply considered and painful choice; Helen ran both pro and con reader mail in a subsequent issue.

She must have approved of the 5:00 p.m. timing of the march step-off, set so that working women could attend. By the time it began, one of the demonstration's key organizers had navigated a very long and trying day. Early that morning, Betty Friedan had been twenty minutes late for her first radio interview. Her excuse was amusing enough to the predominantly male editors of *The New York Times* that they featured the item above the fold in its front-page coverage of the march, set off in a highlighted box. Its derisive headline: "Leading Feminist Puts Hairdo Before Strike." Friedan had an emergency appointment at Vidal Sassoon's salon to get her shoulder-length gray hair curled and styled. The *Times* reported her explanation: "'I don't want people to think that Women's Lib girls don't care about how they look,'" she said as she paid the cashier ten dollars. "'We should try to be as pretty as we can. It's good for our self-image and it's good for politics.'"

Helen would have agreed with that statement; beauty on the barricades never hurt. But it had become clear that Helen and Friedan were miles apart on many other things. Friedan had lambasted *Cosmo* as "quite obscene and horrible," adding, "It embraces the idea that women are nothing but a sex object." Never mind that in Helen's first year as editor, she had run a huge Friedan report, "Working Women 1965," and that later, in 1978, when Helen called her asking, "Is the women's movement over?" Friedan would oblige with a lengthy *Cosmo* article exploring the question. Perhaps she considered her articles placed in the frilly enemy camp as Trojan horses of sorts.

Despite the two women's freighted interactions, the rhetoric on the day of the march was nothing Helen could argue with. At the rally, Friedan, who drew the loudest cheers of any speaker, declared, "This is not a bedroom war, this is a political movement. Man is not the enemy, man is a fellow-victim." Well, that was good to hear. The potential for scaring men away was long one of Helen's chief if misguided reservations about the women's movement.

It was by no means a homogenous march; radicals and moderates, downtown lesbians and straight suburban moms, lactating hippie wives, the Socialist Workers Party's Emma Goldman brigade, and a spirited contingent of original suffragettes were all herded into one designated lane of Fifth Avenue in rush hour traffic. Horns blared; women chanted. Helen strode along with Friedan, Gloria Steinem, Kate Millett, Eleanor Holmes Norton, and Bella Abzug, past cheering women and girls and the inevitable hecklers calling the marchers "bra-less traitors." One male counter-demonstrator wore a bra as he taunted marchers as they passed by St. Patrick's Cathedral. Marchers carried signs that read "Repent, Male Chauvinists, Your World Is At an End," and "Liberté, Egalité, Sororité."

The march was tied to the fiftieth anniversary of the ratification of the Nineteenth Amendment on August 26, 1920. Politicians were realizing that this was a movement to be reckoned with; the brain trust of the newly founded NOW had done some vigorous lobbying. Though it was merely a ceremonial gesture, Mayor John V. Lindsay, Governor Nelson Rockefeller, and President Richard Nixon had issued proclamations endorsing the significance of "Women's Strike for Equality Day." Rallies were held in Boston, San Francisco, Miami, Seattle, Los Angeles, and other major cities that day. The New York rally went on until dark. One of the speakers was New York City's commissioner of consumer affairs, Bess Myerson. She had begun her public life as Miss America of 1945.

When she left the office to join the march, Helen's desk had a pile of upbeat editorial matters awaiting her attentions. Production was in high gear for the October issue, featuring the deep, laced-trimmed frontage of Raquel Welch on its cover; it was no coincidence that Welch was the marquee star in a Brown/Zanuck project at Fox, *Myra Breckinridge*, in release as the issue went to press. Some of the upcoming cover lines might have gotten Helen drummed out of the line of the march that day: "The Slightly Kept Girl," and "Why (Sob) Didn't He Call and How (Aha!) to Make Him." Most surprising was a bold cover line in the bottom right corner: "'Play It As It Lays,' from the Smashing New Novel by Joan Didion."

How could that be? Five years after her vivisection by Didion, Helen had bought the first excerpt from her second novel, published that same August. Generally, Helen waited to buy the far cheaper second serial. Just what might have brought her around—and at a higher price? It could have been Didion's growing reputation as a hot young writer and cool, brainy antidote to the California surfer girl trope. The now-iconic "Stingray" publicity photos showed Didion in a clingy long dress, wispy, smoking, and leaning against her beloved Corvette. "I've never read such rave reviews for a novel," Helen gushed in her editor's column. "The New York Times recently compared her to Nathanael West." Helen also credited serious lobbying for the excerpt by her book editor, Junius Adams.

It was, after all, a Hollywood-based story, which would appeal to Helen's readers. Besides the movie industry bitchiness and a broken marriage, there is stark treatment of back room abortion, albeit in an upscale home. Didion would write repeatedly and unstintingly of abortion in three of her five novels. Over her lifetime, Helen's most enthusiastic and committed activism would always be for abortion rights. But in the end, it was probably the good manager who listened to her book editor and snapped up the first serial of a novel that went on to win the National Book Award. For *Cosmo*, Helen could put some personal feelings aside.

At about that time, Helen agreed to sit for another memorable magazine profile. Her interviewer was a writer whom she knew and liked. Nora Ephron's *Esquire* article was titled "If You're a Little Mouseburger, Come with Me. I Was a Mouseburger and I Will Help You," and it stands as the smartest comic/simpatico distillation of HGB's maddening complexities to date. It was a good match. The two women shared a penchant for light, self-deprecatory writing about their own feminine insecurities. Ephron's essays did not spare her own bodily anxieties, from "A Few Words About Breasts" in 1972 to her 2006 anthology *I Feel Bad About My Neck*, which also included a meditation on that freighted female appendage, "I Hate My Purse."

Ephron was a seasoned journalist by then, but she was not prepared for HGB's insistent candor. Helen gave Ephron the name and phone number of a married ad executive she had an affair with during her single years. Ephron interviewed the man, who was still married and was perplexed that Helen would identify him. She judged it too awkward to use in the article.

"I can't believe you gave me his name," Ephron told Helen later.

"Oh. Well. Yes."

Unbidden, Helen also announced to a startled Ephron that she was very good in bed and she liked sex, very much. Ephron served it all up with both glee and deadpan reserve; she had the canny and humane instinct to merely quote Helen at length, and meticulously. By her Helenisms, ye shall know her.

It was not a puff piece, by any means. To illustrate the more aggravating of HGB tics, Ephron tapped into her own editorial outrages at *Cosmo*, citing a cruel and unusual rewrite. In an innocuous article on how to start a conversation with a stranger, Helen's blue pencil had violated a fine, defenseless Ephron sentence by inserting a bizarre non sequitur about not being afraid to take a bath while menstruating. Her editor Harriet LaBarre had the onerous task of reading the change to Ephron over the phone. Helen was insistent and the writer was apoplectic—at least at first. Ephron wrote: "I hung up, convinced that I had seen straight into the soul of Helen Gurley Brown. Straight to the foolishness, the tastelessness her critics often so accuse her of. But I was wrong. She isn't that way at all. She's just worried that somewhere out there is a girl who hasn't taken a bath during her period since puberty . . . And don't you see? *She is only trying to help.*"

It continued to be an eventful year in *Cosmo* editorial; in the November 1970 issue, the word "penis" appeared in the magazine for the first time. In her editor's column, Helen cautioned readers that the article containing that startling reference, an excerpt of Kate Millett's scholarly *Sexual Politics*, "isn't easy reading but it's well worth it." Helen chose a section on Freud, "who managed to denigrate women pretty badly and who felt women never recovered from their early shock (and jealousy) over not having a penis!"

The column jumped to another wacky HGB non sequitur; she was positively *purring* over a new addition to the *Cosmo* family. The magazine's new mascot and logo was a cartooned kitty cat named Lovey. Helen hoped that the puss would become as recognizable as *The New Yorker*'s monocled Eustace Tilly or the Playboy bunny. Lovey was that issue's cover girl; her image was printed on a T-shirt that allowed zero cleavage on the model wearing it. Lovey was bright pink, sporting a perky red bow; she would pounce into *Cosmo* merchandising on T-shirts and tote bags.

Lovey was the last good thing that happened; December brought the Browns' year crashing to a dismal end. Their misfortune played out in excruciating, public, and bicoastal slo-mo. David Brown and Richard Zanuck were summarily, viciously fired from Fox by Zanuck's father, Darryl. David called their stage-managed dismissal the Ritual of Severance. On the afternoon of December 29, the two men made their way through a gauntlet of tipped-off reporters in the New York lobby of the old Art Deco Fox Building in the neighborhood known as Hell's Kitchen. "No time was wasted," David wrote. "We were asked to resign forthwith from the board and from our positions as president and executive vice-president. Like criminals, we were allowed one phone call—to our lawyer. He said get it over with—resign."

A final ceremony of humiliation, studio-style, awaited the Fox pariahs at Fox headquarters in Los Angeles. As their stunned secretaries looked on, Brown and Zanuck were stripped of their credit cards; they watched as their names were removed from their parking spots; security guards they had known for years were instructed never to admit them again without appointments. It was not lost to the trade papers that Papa Zanuck, a man with the appetites and charisma of Caligula, was putting his own son's manhood in a very public vise.

And why? It seemed Butch Cassidy himself couldn't have rescued the partners from their most recent capers gone bad. The disgraced pair had been responsible for an expensive series of lurid disasters: *Portnoy's Complaint* (the rights were bought but the film was never made at Fox), the bizarre and X-rated *Beyond the Valley of the Dolls*, and the disastrous adaptation of Gore Vidal's transgender novel *Myra Breckinridge*. Fox still had a cash-flow problem; the studio had never fully recovered from the *Cleopatra* debacle. Worse, the modest profit on *Dolls* was offset when the Mansfields sued Fox for making an unlawful sequel and tarnishing Jacqueline Susann's literary reputation.

The industry humiliation was bad enough. But David's private reaction was a deep depression. "Failure is always at your heels," he wrote of the plunge. "There is no way to avoid it. It's terrifying. It unsettles you. It disorients you. It puts you into deep depression. It's a form of death. Whenever I have a failure, I go into mourning."

Suddenly, the Browns' life together went dark, though to those encountering the couple in the Manhattan caravan of dinners, galas, and screenings, David Brown seemed just fine. But at home, the gloom was unbearable. Helen described the onset: "My darling's depressions, usually short-lived, thank God, are cataclysmic. They roll through the apartment like bolts of soggy gray flannel, enveloping everything in sight including the furniture, certainly including *me* . . . Finally when his pain has caused me such pain I can't stand it any longer (smoothing his brow, supper on a tray, rubbing his feet get you nowhere), I tell him I'm ready to jump."

He countered: Couldn't he even tell her bad news? "What am I supposed to do . . . pretend to be happy, wear a vacant smile so that *you* won't be inconvenienced?"

As the Browns reeled into 1971, David and Richard Zanuck began drawing up plans to become independent production partners. Helen was preparing for some modest promotional duties. She had reissued her eight-year-old seminal work and retitled it *Sex and the New Single Girl*. Published by Geis, it was another HGB rehash, replete with anachronisms and barely updated save for her newest beauty regimes. The book came and went like a cat in the night.

Another American author, quite beloved by then, made it known that she was most unhappy about her glancing appearance in Helen's magazine. In July 1971, *Cosmo* felt obliged to run her letter of complaint; the writer felt herself misrepresented in an article about the publishing business written by Stephen Birmingham. It referred to her first and only novel as "a dog-eared manuscript turned down by virtually every publishing house in New York." The complainant countered, "The fact is that I received a contract from Tay Hohoff, senior editor at Lippincott on the basis of a first draft of an unfinished manuscript that had been submitted to only one publisher. As for Miss Hohoff's guiding the writing 'paragraph by painful paragraph,' she *did* give me invaluable encouragement and support. But the truth is that I wrote the novel by myself. By hand. In Monroeville, Alabama."

It was signed by Harper Lee. Her cavils about *Cosmo*'s misinformation regarding *To Kill a Mockingbird* hit on a serious deficiency. Despite its humming commercial enterprise, Helen's six-year-old remake of the magazine still hadn't anything resembling a dedicated fact-checking department and Helen saw no need to have one. It was a liability and a journalistic failing that would cost her dearly later on.

It was common practice then to run wholly made-up articles. "I Was a Sleep Around Girl" was authored by William Manville, then married to the writer Nancy Friday, another *Cosmo* contributor and the author of *My Mother/My Self*, the book that enabled many therapists to consider buying second homes. Manville, a novelist, had told Liz Smith he needed to make some quick money. "I told him to think of sensational things, sexy stories," Smith recalled. "True or not, Helen will never know. And she'll love them. I think one was about nuns climbing over a convent wall." Smith had to fess up about fabricating her article on the Park Avenue call girl "Nicky." It was so realistic and well-read that the director Alan Pakula offered to hire Smith to advise Jane Fonda for her role as a prostitute in *Klute*. She had to tell the director, "I lost my moral compass when I did that, so I am no expert on call girls." They had a roaring laugh over it at lunch.

Judy Krantz called Helen with an idea she swore she could research in accurate and vivid detail. Krantz declared that damn it, she had had enough of reading about the rolling cascades of orgasms that women were *supposed* to be having. Bestsellers such as Dr. David Rubin's *Any Woman Can* and *The Sensuous Woman*, by "J," featured women with climax capability in the two and even three digits! Oh please—another thing to make normal women feel inadequate? Despite the headlines, the percentage of "multi-orgasmic" women was actually minuscule, Krantz contended. Who *are* these women? And who's counting? It was time someone reassured *Cosmo* readers that there was nothing sub-par about one big fabulous O at a time. Krantz proposed the article and its memorable title: "The Myth of the Multiple Orgasm." Helen loved it.

Krantz made cogent cases for doubting some of the reports on multi-orgasmic women; few of the bestselling sexologists gave actual percentages for such fortunate creatures. And though she praised Masters and Johnson's *The Human Sexual Response* as "the first important breakthrough in understanding women's sexuality," Krantz wanted to see numbers, please, and in real bedrooms. "Some women . . . (again, we are not told how many) 'may enjoy' multiple orgasms—but consider, please, that these took place in a *laboratory* where women were *masturbating* . . . not when making love with an actual partner."

She had her own laboratory, and it was one very active petri dish. Steve and Judy Krantz had moved to Los Angeles, he for the production work and she in a new role as Helen's West Coast correspondent. Once Helen okayed the article, Krantz began working the denizens of luxury spas and industry parties to get her story. Much of her later success as a novelist rested with her big eyes and ears; she was and is a peerless and very amusing observer of the idiosyncratic mores and louche lifestyles of the bitchin' famous. Krantz didn't doubt that certain L.A. women would dish on orgasm experiences as readily as they swapped personal trainers and colonic practitioners. "I introduced myself as West Coast editor of *Cosmo*, wanting to do an interview on orgasm. Any party that I went to, I brought it up. I was able to get a lot of people. And I came up with eight percent of the women I interviewed had had multiple orgasms."

She didn't claim scientific accuracy; she was just fulfilling the *Cosmo* mandate: help normal women be okay with a single satiating O. Still, the A-list anthropologist in her was amazed at some of the "oral histories."

"One of them needed two hours of foreplay before she could have her first orgasm. She'd been married five times. The husband who told me about her divorced her soon after. Very tired husband. She said that once she had one orgasm, she just would have more and more. She said her head and her toes would touch the mattress and the rest of her was up in the air having an orgasm. If she hadn't had an orgasm with her husband the night before, she would go to work and pick out the man she would have lunch with, then afterwards they would go to bed. She couldn't take two days in a row without orgasming. Very strange girl. Oh, I kept a straight face, I didn't laugh. I would just be amazed. And the more you're amazed the more they tell you."

Krantz's article was well received, cheered by the mono-orgasmic majority; it became rather legendary. At least a decade later, having been introduced at a party to the then-editor of *Vanity Fair*, Tina Brown, she was tickled by Brown's reaction. "She said, 'Oh my God, you're Judy Krantz? You're the one who totally changed the way we could write in magazines.' I said, 'I am?' She said, 'Yes! Ever since "The Myth of the Multiple Orgasm," we can write much more frankly in magazines. Did you know how important that was?'"

Krantz confessed that she hadn't a clue. "I just thought it was a wonderful title."

26

Cosmo Goes to Harvard

My favorite magazine says one should buy lots of cosmetics, learn how to make small talk, and cultivate a sophisticated aloofness with sexual overtones. I love that magazine . . . I enjoy fellatio and I'm not ashamed to admit it. I guess you'd have to say I'm that *Cosmopolitan* girl.

—from *The Harvard Lampoon's Cosmopolitan* parody issue, 1972

THE TONIGHT SHOW FLICKERED ONSCREEN in the delft-tiled castle that is headquarters to *The Harvard Lampoon*, the undergraduate humor magazine that has been published at the university since 1876. The *Lampoon* members Eric Rayman, Jim Downey, and Sandy Frazier were idly watching TV in the top-floor Ibis Room and brainstorming about which magazine they might parody next. That night in March 1972, the assembled *Lampoon* staffers were having difficulty choosing a victim.

Playboy? No, too soon after the *Lampoon*'s 1966 send-up; it was a winner. The staff crowed: "It sold faster than Nixon's ambassadorial appointments." Hef himself sent a telegram professing his delight.

Life? Nope, the magazine had done that a few times, starting back in 1911. Its most recent *Life* parody, featuring the earth as a broken egg on its cover, lost money. Rayman, the Lampoon president and a Harvard junior, figured that it was because it didn't have sex on the cover. A successful 1968 *Time* parody with a naked woman at a newsstand and the cover line "Does Sex Sell Magazines?" had done just fine.

Rayman's crew needed a hit that would sell very well on newsstands nationally. In 1972 the *Lampoon*'s meager endowment was again in need of a serious cash infusion. Rayman had taken the helm at a challenging moment in the magazine's history, just as the university was navigating the post-sixties churn of sexual politics. Gender skirmishes were erupting on campuses nationwide as "coeds" chafed at the very term. A Boston-based collective of feminist writers had just published *Our Bodies, Ourselves*, a frank, empowering guide to the female body by and for women; some men were studying it as a user's manual. At Harvard, Brahmin paternalism was giving little quarter. A hotly debated "non-merger merger" agreement in 1971 gave Harvard control of day-to-day operations at its sister school, Radcliffe; this included moving some female undergraduates into Harvard houses for the first time. Could women be full-fledged Harvard students? Could they be funny enough for the *Lampoon*?

"Women started trying out for the *Lampoon* my freshman year and sophomore year," said Rayman. "The *Lampoon* opened its candidacy to women but didn't elect any; it was very controversial, you can imagine, fights, blackballs, everything." Then, in the fall of 1971, the freshman Patricia Marx became the first woman elected, followed by the senior Elizabeth Stern and two more women the following May. Marx said she had no feminist imperative in applying.

"When I got to Harvard, I thought, well, I'd sign up for this. I had no idea that there was a problem—that they didn't take women. I knew that I was the first girl because there were newspaper stories about it, but it didn't seem like a political thing to do." Marx did notice some changes on campus, notably on her diploma. "I applied to Radcliffe and got a Harvard degree." She was hearing ramped-up rhetoric from some of her women friends. "The student ratio was three to one [male to female] then. I remember a friend of mine saying, 'We've got to fight to change the ratio, because all those boys *look* at us.' And I said, 'But that's why I came here.' I thought it was great that there were more boys than girls."

On the staff in 1972 were some future perpetrators of an edgier new humor, a comic sensibility that would claw past all boundaries of taste and mix old-school pratfalls with a penchant for being fiendishly, gleefully politically incorrect. Jim Downey wound up as head writer for *Saturday Night Live* in its glory days of Coneheads, "Weekend Update," John Belushi's Samurai deli man, and Eddie Murphy's ghetto take on "Mr. Rogers." Patty Marx would become an *SNL* writer, a novelist, a *New Yorker* contributor, and the 2015 winner of a Guggenheim Foundation grant to perpetrate more spare, elegant absurdities. Ian "Sandy" Frazier has long been a nonfiction writer and humorist at *The New Yorker*.

Rayman, now a well-respected Manhattan publishing attorney, could throw a comic punch line with the best of them; he was also the Guy in Charge, able to negotiate with printers and distributors on the business side and keep the merry pranksters on task. Sometimes. Despite its talents, the group was making little progress choosing its victim that night until inspiration beamed down obligingly from the TV set. The *Tonight Show* guest Helen Gurley Brown, smug as a tabby with a mouthful of canary feathers, announced that *Cosmopolitan*'s April 1972 issue would have an exciting new feature: a nude male centerfold. Why *shouldn't* women have equal ogling rights? *Cosmo* would be the first magazine ever to make it happen.

In the Ibis Room, an epiphany: "And we'll be the second!"

So it was decreed in the comedy castle. In doing her coquettish promo from the *Tonight Show* couch, Helen had pitched the Harvard team a fat home run; they could have sport with its cover *and* the male centerfold. The new *Cosmopolitan* was a coltish seven years old, but its cover girls had already been stamped with the saucy imprimatur of its Image Maker in chief and her trusted co-conspirator the photographer Francesco Scavullo. Thus far, theirs was a successful cover formula: models wore mysterious Giaconda a-go-go smiles above *booo-soms* artfully cupped and cantilevered in the latest peekaboo Qiana frock. It was time to lob a few eggs into that décolleté.

Helen seemed pleased at the news when Rayman phoned her. *Harvard* was calling! In fact, the *Lampoon* was a bit late to the *Cosmo* media roast. The newsmagazines had weighed in; *Time* accused Helen of creating a simpering idiot in the *Cosmo* girl, a creature in need of italics and underlined instructions just to paint her nails. Tongue firmly in cheek, *Newsweek* had branded Helen "the working girl's Simone de Beauvoir." In 1968, a *New Yorker* cartoon showed a tawdry urban street with SEX writ large over doorways, in windows, on trucks and water towers. The caption has a matronly passerby remarking to her male companion, "I suppose we have Helen Gurley Brown to thank for this." Even the conservative moral arbiter William F. Buckley felt compelled to burlesque HGB's wanton ethos and girlie syntax with a 1970 cover story in the *National Review*; his essay was titled "You Are the More Cupcakeable for Being a *Cosmopolitan* Girl."

Buckley held his patrician nose and did a deep read of Helen's "Step into My Parlor" editor's columns, "which are pure HGB," he noted. He read articles as well. One of the most luscious pieces caught his fancy. He limned *Cosmo*'s helpful how-tos this way: "Are you, sir, a breast fetishist? I mean, *madam*, is your *lover* a breast fetishist? Don't despair. Don't go away. Hear what *Jill* did. *Cosmo* reveals that on her wedding night '*she came to bed with a dollop of Hershey's milk-chocolate syrup tipping each breast. Honest! Stan is still a fetishist. But his fetish is his wife. And they keep a can of Hershey's by the bed. Does that hurt anyone?*'"

Buckley had taken the cover line for his essay from one of Helen's own high-fructose sentences: "*You've got to make yourself more cupcakeable all the time so that you're a better cupcake to be gobbled up.*"

Could it be that prose of this caliber was almost . . . unburlesqueable? Posing seductively in the crosshairs of culture and gender wars, *Cosmo* and its italic-dependent editor had become easy and rather delectable targets.

Patty Marx was not a *Cosmo* reader. "Before I went up to Cambridge for the summer to work on the parody, I was in Philadelphia at my parents' and I had to get copies of the magazine so I could study them. I remember being so embarrassed to go into the drugstore to get *Cosmo*. My mother did it for me. It was like buying rubbers or something. I just thought it was a dirty magazine."

Helen didn't seem intimidated by the brainy college kids and their pranks. As a rule, the *Lampoon* never sought permission from its magazine targets, but tried for a certain cordiality. Rayman's call was a courtesy. Helen's sole stipulation, she told him, was that she be shown the cover beforehand. This was strictly a business requisite. It would not do to have *Cosmo* and its doppelgänger on the newsstands together with covers too similar in color and image. Mrs. Brown could take a joke, but she was not prepared to lose a single newsstand sale to an impostor.

At the time, much of Helen's attention was focused on her greatest gamble yet, that male centerfold. She had first floated the idea in 1968 and Hearst executives reluctantly funded a naked photo shoot of the actor James Coburn. In a priceless memo to Dick Deems slugged "Cosmopolitan Nude Man," Helen reported on the resulting photos with evident horror; the otherwise scrumptious Mr. Coburn seemed to have slid into some mystical Eastern phase. The two shots approved by Mr. and Mrs. Coburn exuded a whiff of visual patchouli, with "almost a hippie look." Helen suggested they eat their losses and wait for Mr. Right.

Deems scrawled back, "How about Dick Nixon?"

Burt Reynolds became the anointed one. Helen met the actor in late January 1972 when she appeared on *The Tonight Show* and he was guest-hosting. Helen and Reynolds hit it off on the air and backstage; inspired by a certain yumminess of wit and physique, she made her indecent proposal during a commercial break. Reynolds figures that he may have had a few cocktails in the greenroom that night. "Helen didn't have to talk me into it," he confessed in his 2015 memoir, *But Enough About Me*. "I said yes before we came back on the air."

Reynolds went to Helen's office the following day to finalize the details. His friends and his agent advised against such frivolity; he was in a "serious" picture due out that summer, *Deliverance*. Reynolds went ahead anyhow. He stopped for two quarts of vodka on the way to Scavullo's studio, ambled around in a robe for ages, then finally dropped his wrap and took his place atop that centerfold cliché, a bearskin rug.

As promised, the centerfold appeared in *Cosmo*'s April 1972 issue. Scavullo posed a grinning, hirsute Reynolds with one hand over his package and a rakish cigarillo dangling from his lips. The issue was a sellout: 1.55 million copies. The morning of the on-sale date, Reynolds awoke to a keening noise outside his home. When he left the house, his car was surrounded. Everywhere he went, he was mobbed by women waving the centerfold. His mailbox could not contain the wild torrents of lust and longing. Most of the mail was "positive and polite," though there were also "some of the filthiest letters I've ever seen," along with Polaroids of nude and willing women and one mash letter with a tuft of pubic hair encased in waxed paper. Perhaps his agent had been right.

In the *Lampoon* castle, there was jubilation over the Reynolds sellout as the staff pored over stacks of *Cosmo* back issues provided by the Hearst Corporation. Clearly they had picked a winner. When they had a cover mock-up readied, Rayman and Downey boarded a bus to New York and were ushered into Helen's office for their audience. She was welcoming and cordial, wrapped in clingy black behind her rococo gilt desk. When Rayman showed her the cover, there was silence. And then:

"*Ooooh.*" Her brightly outlined mouth made a small circle. For a moment, Helen was quiet again, considering the vision before her.

The cover girl was a smirking skank, half-clad in the sort of ragged-hemmed, *Clan of the Cave Bear schmatte* that only Tina Turner can carry off with élan. One breast was nearly popping out. A leering jester, the *Lampoon*'s mascot, peered from behind her shoulder. Helen's voice was calm and gentle as she explained to the long-haired parodists: "You can go with that if you want, but that's *not* a *Cosmopolitan* girl. Nobody wants to sleep with a girl who looks like that. She's so . . . *bedraggled* looking."

Rayman and Downey exchanged panicky looks as Helen continued: "A *Cosmopolitan* girl always has a little smile, a twinkle in her eyes, something . . . there's a little *spark* to her. That's not a *Cosmopolitan* girl."

The Harvard men had been schooled by a master marketer. By the summer of 1972, the real *Cosmo* cover girl was no joke. In the months following the centerfold issue, Helen's circulation figures reached

1.6 million copies a month, double the numbers she had begun with. Ad pages had soared to 112 pages a month; the monthly ad revenue difference before and after HGB: $57,000 in 1965 and $434,000 in 1972.

That day in Helen's office, Rayman and Downey couldn't know the might of *Cosmo*'s rising numbers, but they recognized their error quickly enough. It wouldn't do to make Helen's curvaceous hood ornament unrecognizable and it surely wouldn't sell their parody. She was right; they needed a subtler joke than just turning their model into a troll. They thanked Helen and left.

"We got on the bus," Rayman said, "we went back to Cambridge, sat around with the staff, and came up with a very simple cover. It would be a shot of a beautiful model with just a hint of smile. We shot it with the same one-bounce flash off the photographer's reflector to look just like a Scavullo cover." They allowed themselves just one comic twist: the model's eyes were crossed.

The *Lampoon* staff had rented the Victorian home of the innovative Harvard anthropologist Irven DeVore for the summer. It was comic Kismet; the vibes in the old, weird house were most hospitable to *Lampoon* apery. Since it was often used for "simian seminars," the rooms were filled with specimens, baboon skins and skulls. "We would dress up in skins," Marx said. "We never slept. It was a party."

While the children were having their fun, doing an interview with the first Talking Barbie and mocking the cheesy improve-your-bustline ads, Helen had more misgivings about that first cover girl they showed her. In August she wrote to Rayman: "She looks gloomy . . . I don't think anybody is going to be attracted to that bosom!" She also complained of an undue emphasis on sex in the cover lines they had shown her: "The two I object to most are 10 WAYS TO DECORATE YOUR UTERINE WALL and TURN YOUR PERIOD INTO A DASH. I'm enclosing our September issue of COSMO so you can see how few of our *own* cover lines are sexy."

Helen was correct about that; her issues from that year never had more than one or two sex-related cover lines, and at that stage they were quite tame—none of your icky "Untamed Va-jay-jays: Guess What Sexy Style Is Back" and the online doozy "Men Are Having Their

Nutsacks Ironed Because YOLO" dreamed up by some of Helen's more recent successors. Even in her first years at the helm, the public perception of *Cosmo*'s sex mania didn't fit the facts. In the years from 1965 to 1972, sex was the subject of just 78 of 1,503 nonfiction articles, a shockingly modest 5.2 percent.

The misperception was largely a result of Helen's ceaseless media fan dance, vamping on TV. And the centerfold stunt didn't help. For those who didn't actually read her magazine, the gambit landed *Cosmo* squarely in the "naughty book" category with *Playboy*. Helen had no one to blame—or congratulate—but herself.

That same August, Helen decided to reward Burt Reynolds's good sportsmanship with a full profile in the magazine. In July, Reynolds got his first serious critical raves for his role in the southern gothic odyssey *Deliverance*. He was a star! Helen had a *teensy* bit to do with that, she said. Reynolds was filming *White Lightning*, an ex-con/car crash/moonshiner genre smashup. He was on location in Little Rock, of all places. Helen dispatched Gael Greene.

Before she left for Arkansas, Greene decided that she would absolutely not fall into the sack with her subject, as she had with Clint Eastwood. She intended to give Reynolds, then thirty-six, a stern bit of career advice. "I thought he was foolish to do the centerfold. He complained all the time that people didn't take him seriously. Then he distributed photos of himself wearing a football jersey and obviously naked below. So I had that opinion of him when I went out to interview him."

She flew to meet Reynolds on the movie set and found him in the hotel bar. "He was dark, heavy-browed, his sulky lips involved with a vodka and tonic . . ."

Uh-oh.

"We tried to talk in the bar and there were too many interruptions," Greene said. "We decided we would go to his room and order dinner. Jumpsuits were hot then and I had this really sexy satin fringy jumpsuit. I decided to wear it because I had vowed to myself that I would *not* have sex with Burt Reynolds. I did not want to be one of just a thousand women that year. I wore the jumpsuit because I knew there was no way you could gracefully get out of it."

Once they were in his room, lust trumped grace; fringe parted obligingly.

He never spoke to Greene again.

"He hated the article," she said. "He didn't like when I said that he should stop sending out naked pictures of himself. He didn't like being criticized." Greene spilled her writer's remorse to her therapist, who was not at all sympathetic.

"Gael, why did you do that? It was so stupid. You didn't *have* to."

"Well, I'm a journalist."

"You consider *Cosmopolitan* to be journalism?"

"She was right," Greene concluded, "I really regretted it."

Back in Cambridge, after some spirited debate on the right poster boy—there was support for Ralph Nader, Dick Cavett, and Wilt Chamberlain—the staff realized there was only one choice: the nation's globe-trotting secretary of state and most eligible bachelor, Henry Kissinger. They would pose him on a fuzzy faux-panda rug. (Kissinger, also a former Harvard professor, had recently been in China conducting talks with Premier Zhou En-Lai.) They created a composite photo that set Dr. K's head atop the slightly zaftig body of a fifty-year-old Boston cab driver. "It sold over a million copies, the biggest *Lampoon* sale ever," said Rayman. "We even went back to press and the *Lampoon* made a ton of money. It got national attention. Henry Kissinger was in Vietnam when it came out and there were news stories about Kissinger autographing copies of it for the GIs."

Now *everyone* was in on the joke and it was all in good fun—wasn't it? Helen had pulled it off again, landing just off-center of national affairs, in the nightly news and the print media buzz, and all but swatting off eager advertisers. The tremendous profits helped the *Lampoon* bolster its anemic endowment. A much-relieved Rayman realized that their original cover would have been disastrous. Four decades later, he remains convinced: Helen Gurley Brown had staved off potential disaster for the smarty-pants college magazine, just as she had rescued

Cosmo for Hearst. Her rules were simple and unassailable: build a brand, baby it, and never, ever mess with its most recognized signifiers.

In the Hearst Building, executives were thrilled with the sellout and circulation bump following the centerfold gambit, but Helen realized that she had to carefully manage her sizzling new feature. There would be a few more: the athlete/actor Jim Brown and dimply John Davidson would follow in 1973; Arnold Schwarzenegger in 1977; and finally, in 1982, the *Baywatch* beach Adonis David Hasselhoff, with a pair of obliging shar-pei puppies snuggling on his crotch.

All these years later, Burt Reynolds remains rather testy about his pioneering role as male sex object. He is convinced that it cost *Deliverance* the Best Picture Oscar, which went to *The Godfather* instead. He was deeply distressed when he tried to act in serious theater afterward: "I did *The Rainmaker* in Chicago and the audiences were rowdy: instead of applause there were hoots and catcalls." In his earlier memoir, *My Life*, Reynolds had been more direct about his discomfiture, with a plaint that might well have been composed in the Ibis Room:

"They cared more about my pubes than they did about the play."

27

Isn't She Lovely?

"Beauty" is a word that's gotten a bum deal. People think beautiful
is boring, but that's not true. To be beautiful is to be godlike.
—the photographer Francesco Scavullo

AS THE *LAMPOON* STAFF FOUND, Helen's cover girls were not so easy
to burlesque. Helen had worked doggedly to create those over-the-top
embodiments of her "sex is power" maxim, beauties with the bold,
direct gaze that drilled the passerby and challenged, "take me"—to the
register, please. Today, some women trade vintage *Cosmo* covers online
like baseball cards.

Helen's models ranged from unknowns to supermodels: Gia Carangi,
Christie Brinkley, Paulina Porizkova, Kim Alexis, Patti Hansen, Cindy
Crawford, Claudia Schiffer, Kathy Ireland, Beverly Johnson, Rene Russo,
Janice Dickinson, Margaux Hemingway, Brooke Shields. But it didn't
matter who she was; once a model entered Francesco Scavullo's chilly
studio in the basement of his town house on East Sixty-Third Street,
her transformation into Helen's ideal became a process like no other.
It usually required up to four hours in makeup and hair work for a
half-hour shoot. Editorial work was still dismally low-paying in the
mid-seventies—perhaps $150 for a cover. But nailing a *Cosmo* cover be-
came the hot booking that could plump a model's portfolio overnight.

At Helen's insistence, cover shoots were minimalist, intimate, and budget-friendly. There was no sign of Mrs. Brown, no hovering fashion editor or art director, just Scavullo and his team: Sean Byrnes, the photographer's assistant and life partner; the makeup genius Way Bandy; the studio manager, Bob Cass; and one of a select roster of hairdressers that included Suga and Harry King. Cass, now sublimely happy as a charter boat captain in the Caribbean, has plenty of wild, storm-tossed recollections from his years as Scavullo's right hand and enabler. Weathering the photographer's emotional problems, treated over the years with lithium, shock therapy, and hospitalizations, could be exhausting. There were many nervous collapses.

But never with Helen. Unlike some imperious editors Cass had seen joust with the maestro, this was no drama queen. As Helen set to sculpting and tinting her big beautiful doll, she consulted closely with Scavullo, whom she paid $1,500 for each cover shot.

Cass said the *Cosmo* sessions almost always went smoothly; rarely was there a reshoot. The reason was simple: "Helen Gurley Brown let him do what he wanted." That extended to what her models were wearing. Cover outfits were chosen by Sean Byrnes, who had no fashion background. Helen had made it clear in a 1967 staff memo on cover requisites that *Cosmopolitan* was not, and never would be, a fashion book. Since she didn't get the fashion ads, she could totally ignore the designer sun kings whose ad pages kept the editors of fashion magazines hyperventilating on seasonal trend alert.

Her most important dictate was this: "About one cover in three should have bosom showing. Decolletage dresses are not in fashion so I know it's a challenge."

Booo-soms über alles, on schedule, and on demand. And hair? The bigger the better. It might be said that the *Cosmo* Girl's evolution toward extreme hair was compensatory; Helen's own hair drove her crazy. It was thin, dry, and receding; she "mainlined Minoxidil," the second-market heart drug that was found to grow hair. For two decades, Helen also relied heavily on the wizardry of Nick Piazza, who went straight to beauty school when he returned from his tour in Vietnam as a marine and landed in the renowned salon of Kenneth (Battelle), known as the world's first single-named celebrity hairdresser. Piazza worked with Jacqueline Onassis, Lena Horne, Eartha Kitt, Eunice Shriver. Helen was hooked on his deft cuts and superb custom falls and wigs. She had several at any given time. Piazza recalled that Helen had even submitted herself to a tattooist's needle: "Because she had a receding hairline, she had little dots tattooed in to sort of simulate some fullness in the hairline." It helped for a while. "Yeah, but they turned orange," Piazza said. Helen rolled with it. Unlike so many women he has helped, she fully understood her beauty shortcomings and was realistic about how much could be done. "Helen wasn't upset with any of that. That was just life."

But how she enjoyed her cover excesses. Her models had dream hair, glossy, copious, tousled, just-out-of-bed hair. No one would do it bigger and fuller than the British hairdresser Harry King. He did eighty-five *Cosmo* covers with Scavullo.

"I started that chopped, natural, fucked-up look," King said. "They all wanted it." This is how he made the glorious mess: "I spritzed it with this stuff and then I got my brush, picked up huge chunks, teased it at the root and brushed it through the ends. The whole process took me fifteen minutes, max. Once we got on the set, I would create shapes with my hands." Sometimes the tousle got more *sauvage* with help from studio fans. "And when the photographer would change a roll of film, I would go in and completely give a new hairstyle, in minutes. The photographers loved that because I didn't take hours. Helen Gurley Brown loved the hair."

Though she would never have all the enviable assets herself, HGB had built her avatar; Bob Cass says that her creation came to life courtesy of a bank of lights Scavullo called his light cannon. "Most photographers would bounce light into an umbrella, which really just had a very commercial look. His light was funneled into and through an umbrella to diffuse the light." This gave the *Cosmo* Girl the arresting gaze that Helen so adored.

And for the models? Beverly Johnson would like to explain how her first *Cosmopolitan* cover made her a woman. No lie. Listen.

"I really want to do *Cosmo.*"

The model agency duenna Eileen Ford looked at little Beverly Johnson, waving a copy of that vulgar thing at her. Ford dispatched her girls to *Vogue* and *Bazaar* and to the runways. *Cosmo*? It was a creature of the magazine industry's clawing underclass. Out of the question, dear. It was déclassé, unladylike. Don't ask again.

Johnson, a skinny, brainy African American girl from Buffalo, New York, politely but resolutely got up in Mrs. Ford's business. "Why not?"

Nearly forty years after this impertinence, Johnson sat in a Manhattan hotel suite, serene and stunning at sixty-three, in town for some work during Fashion Week, pleased to talk about how her first *Cosmo* cover transformed her—in the business, and in her own head.

"I saw a Naomi Sims *Cosmo* cover—she was the top black model at the time and I was on her heels. It was so beautiful and so classy and I was saying, 'Look, everybody's doing it and I want to do it!'" Johnson had some standing at Ford, even at her young age; *Vogue* had already put her on its cover, in a chaste cornflower-blue crewneck, the sort of treatment that Mrs. Ford approved of for her upstate ingénue. Johnson tumbled into the business like Alice down the rabbit hole. Her mother had brought her A student to the *Glamour* offices to take a typing test. She did poorly but soon landed on the magazine's cover.

"I knew nothing about the business, I just kind of fell in. I was this little five-foot-nine, one hundred and three pounds, flat-chested high-fashion model and I got this *Vogue* cover and I did the Halston show." Never mind the couture treatment; little Beverly longed to grow up and get real. "I wanted to see every aspect of the fashion world and *Cosmo* was a part of that. And, so, I began to beg. 'I really want to do *Cosmo*, I really *really* want to do *Cosmo.*'"

Then Johnson saw Helen Gurley Brown at a cocktail party and made a beeline for her. "Unfortunately I wasn't dressed like a *Cosmo* Girl because I had on a gingham yellow shirt and I wore this bow tie and I had on a silk suit with a skirt. I cozied right up to her. She was just so friendly. I said, 'I really want to be on the cover of *Cosmo*.'

"I don't know, I just don't know. Well, let me talk with you but I don't know if you really fit, you know, the *Cosmo* Girl look."

Johnson went home downcast, kicking herself for the gingham and man-tailored getup. But the call came. She found out later that Sean Byrnes had lobbied hard for her. He insisted: Scavullo's team could make Miss Beverly Johnson into a sizzle-lean *Cosmo* Girl. With her face finally camera-ready after three hours beneath Way Bandy's brushes and a fixative dusting of baby powder, Johnson braced herself. "So now the hard test was the taping of the boobs—and I was like, my God there's nothing there." She stood naked to the waist as Bandy nudged and taped what real flesh he had to work with. "I had a handful. You know, like thirty-two double A."

Bandy stood back and surveyed the flatlands. "Okay, we'll have to draw you some breasts."

He worked with the precision of a Dutch master, shading, blurring. "What he did with my face, he did for my chest. And I'm thinking, 'Oh my God, it's not going to work.' And sure enough, it looks like I have breasts. And now, I have the dress on, looking like I have breasts. I am this *woman*."

Bandy was yelling: "Oh my God, you're Sophia Loren!"

They draped his trompe l'oeil frontage in Elsa Peretti diamonds by the yard. Johnson shivered in Scavullo's lair. "Ice cold: that's just the way he likes to shoot. All the assistants are scurrying around, trying not to look. So I'm saying, 'Oh my God, they're looking at me in a different way.' I looked in the mirror and I was like, 'Wow, who is that woman?' That is the day that I *became* a woman."

They were waiting for her. Scavullo had descended to the studio. "I remember walking out and I just thought I looked like the sexiest woman in the world. I mean, I really *felt* that. I remember Sean standing behind Francesco with these huge lights on me, on . . . everything."

"*I need quiet now!!! Beverly—lie down!*" Down she went on the white painted floor. Scavullo preferred to shoot from above the models. Cass handed him a loaded camera, and they were off. Scavullo talked his talk—the low purr and sigh between flashes, *Ohhhh, Beverly! Unbeliev-able.* Her cover, February 1976, was Valentine red.

"It changed my life. I started seeing myself as this real sexual being. As a model, looking like that, you really didn't get a lot of action [from men]. In real life, you don't look normal. On most magazine shoots, we're objectified, flat and two-dimensional. There's no curves. With Helen's magazine, we were women. We were women who were proud to be women."

As a very pretty baby girl, Brooke grew up before the lenses of the best. "Scavullo was Uncle Frankie to me," said Shields, who was a *Cosmo* cover girl thirteen times, from 1981 to 1996. "I met him when I was eleven months old." Shields debuted in *Cosmo* in February 1981, the same year as her infamous "What comes between me and my Calvins?" jeans ad. At fifteen, she was *Cosmo*'s youngest cover model. That day at Uncle Frankie's, they gave her wispy bangs for the first time, beneath huge, wild hair; Sean Byrnes tucked her torso into a taut leatherette bandeau. It was odd, but okay. "I was never known for the body. I was known from the neck up. I was the face. It was funny, it felt older, because it was *Cosmo* and it was going to be a full-length shot. In most of my covers I'd be wearing jeans and topsiders beneath that white board. This was decked out, buffed up, and above the board."

As one of the most photographed women in the last half century, Shields has only positive memories of those shoots. "I was always comfortable with it. It wasn't like you were doing *Playboy.*" Helen's covers did not push her toward anything she hadn't been dreaming of. Every time she went to work in Scavullo's studio, she looked up at her ideal. All the men in the studio adored the model Gia Carangi. Her image covered the walls. "I'd stare at the picture of Gia, the one in the sand where she's sort of nude. I thought she was the *most* beautiful. I'd go, 'Ohhh, when I grow up.'"

Shields developed almost a family relationship with Helen, who got along well with the notoriously difficult Teri Shields, Brooke's mother and manager. "My mom was from Newark and poor and here was Helen, this self-made woman, outspoken when nobody was, and put together and fabulous." She found Helen's stream of affirmations nourishing. The little notes on pussycat stationery would flutter in after a shoot or a promotional event. "I started writing her notes, too, and sending her things. I just became sort of like an adopted niece or something. Anything she wanted me to appear at or show up at or speak at, I would just say yes."

As a mother of two, Shields has not been in studios that much of late, but when she does step into today's lavish photographic events in industrial lofts, with mountains of achingly curated catering and a sprawling cast of hair and makeup teams, editors, clients, she appreciates the efficiencies of Helen's operation and its family feel. "It was easy and great. That little makeup room, and that little bathroom with the picture of Barbra Streisand in boxing gloves over the toilet. It was very much like being at home. You'd go upstairs for lunch with Uncle Frankie and hang out afterwards." Most often, though, she couldn't stay and play. "I was in school. I had homework to do."

28 🐚

High Tide

Start the shark!
—Steven Spielberg, on the set of *Jaws*, 1974

ONE AFTERNOON IN MID-MAY 1973, as David's father, Edward F. Brown, lay intubated and near death in a veterans' hospital, kept alive very much against his wishes, David sat in the Carlyle hotel dining room with a fine Meursault, a filet of freshly caught salmon, and the remaining members of the Brown family, deciding when to end the patriarch's life support. With any luck or divine mercy, the comatose roué was replaying his life's bold adventures beneath crepey eyelids—perhaps the night his brother Al brought "fifty beautiful, copper-colored girls" from the chorus line at the Cotton Club to the Brown apartment while his wife was off in the Hamptons with the children.

David's stepmother, Nathalie, was at the table that day, as were his half brother, Edward, and half sister, Natasha. They agreed on a time. It was a cool discussion, even for the widow-to-be. Edward had always insisted on a WASP standard of veiled emotion, even though he cheated on Nathalie constantly. She never openly challenged Edward's gross infidelities. "I didn't want to spoil his pleasure in deceiving me," she told her stepson. Edward, eighty-seven, died alone; per his instructions, there was no service and no one accompanied the plain pine box to a veterans' cemetery on Long Island. David had never loved him, but he admired the old man's sangfroid at facing the final curtain. As it happened, Edward Brown died as his son's fortunes were about to turn in a spectacular way. Something huge was lurking, unseen as yet, but there was a tug on the line.

Within days of his father's burial, David would make his deal of a lifetime. It was for a literary property rooted in true events that occurred just before his own birth in late July 1916. During the last two weeks of Lillian Brown's pregnancy, the city broiled in a fierce heat wave that drew millions to the New York and New Jersey shores, until a series of fatal shark attacks began. Headlines screamed the horrors: "Shark Kills Bather off Jersey Beach; Women Are Panic-Stricken as Mutilated Body of Hotel Employee Is Brought Ashore"; "Armed Posses Comb Coast to Snuff Out Man-Eating Sharks."

What became known as the "Jersey Shore Attacks" splashed and chomped into legend during the first two weeks of July; within sight of crowded beaches, four people were killed and one injured, by either bull or great white sharks. Panicked seaside towns sent out bravado flotillas of shark hunters to slay the voracious monsters. The attacks were largely forgotten for more than half a century, until Brown and Zanuck cast their wide, efficient net for more movie properties.

In the wake of their banishment from Fox, the partners had been operating on both coasts at manic speed; sometimes they worked out of their cars or from hotel rooms, with two sets of secretaries to field calls. As industry veterans, they had the advantage of direct access to agents, publishers, attorneys, and ready conduits to studio cash, mostly at Universal. They were pinning high hopes for some operating capital on an upcoming Christmas 1973 release. *The Sting* was a caper film reuniting Robert Redford and Paul Newman, directed again by George Roy Hill. The partners were scouting new directorial talent as well. They had let themselves be persuaded by a young director named Steven Spielberg to let him cowrite and direct a prison break/car chase movie.

It was based on a true-crime story of a young mother and her incarcerated husband trying to keep custody of their son, starring the ingénue Goldie Hawn. Filmed in Texas, *The Sugarland Express* would be Spielberg's first big-screen film as a director. He had also directed *Duel*, a TV movie that starred Dennis Weaver as the motorist being chased down an empty road by a mysterious stalker in a tanker truck.

Brown/Zanuck continued to ply their contacts for more low-investment, high-yield film properties. Said one industry veteran, "David would cultivate sources the way cops cultivate an informant." Enter Lyn Tornabene, who had become Helen's go-to writer for any *Cosmo* features related to David's films. Tornabene had been dispatched to the set of *The Sugarland Express* to write a piece on Goldie Hawn. Through her presence on the film sets and her friendship with the Browns, she knew that David was always on the hunt. Tornabene had a good friend named Norman Darer, then president of the CBS Consumer Publishing Division, who saw a lot of available new properties. He was in charge of looking over literary submissions for possible paperback buys; since he was basically a numbers guy, he occasionally asked Tornabene to read a manuscript for story and marketability and share her opinion. He sent her a manuscript by Peter Benchley, a novel about a marauding great white shark that killed several humans near the beaches of an East Coast resort area. Benchley had received a $7,500 advance. "There was a question of paying three hundred thousand dollars for it," Tornabene said, "and Norman needed to know whether it was worth it."

Darer passed; it seemed expensive for a fish tale. "I thought there was something in it for a movie," said Tornabene, "and I gave it to Helen to show David." After all, there hadn't been a good, scary sea monster flick since Disney's 1954 version of the Jules Verne classic *20,000 Leagues Under the Sea*, with its giant squid, and, two years later, *Moby Dick*. Tornabene says that she was the one who put the new property straight into Helen's hands. Other versions of the great discovery would persist; for years, Helen made vague comments about a secretary pulling it from a slush pile in the *Cosmo* office. Tornabene has no idea why she did so.

But there it lay, in David's hands. As a marquee terror title, *Jaws* was certainly evocative and efficient. Having read the manuscript, the partners set about trying to buy it, and quickly. There was a sudden chop in the water around Benchley's novel. Bantam's Oscar Dystel offered a $575,000 paperback deal. At the time, Benchley was down to about six hundred dollars in walking-around money. Book clubs began committing, and *Jaws* was suddenly a hot property. Carl Gottlieb, who would cowrite the film script with Benchley, described the frenzy for the film rights: "There were agents working on both coasts and so were Zanuck and Brown. Dick was handling the negotiations in L.A., while David did the talking to the New York people. At one point, both principals were seated in different chic restaurants . . . Dick at the Bistro in Beverly Hills and David at the Palm in New York. They were both negotiating with different agents."

They nailed it down in late May, for a base price of $150,000, with another $25,000 to Benchley to write the screenplay. (Gottlieb would earn $10,000 for his screenwriting services and another $5,000 for acting a small part.) It was to be made by Universal, which had Steven Spielberg under contract. Spielberg, then twenty-six, balked at first, asking, "Who wants to be known as a shark-and-truck director?"

Around Thanksgiving of that year, Mary Alford wrote to Helen after doing some stargazing out her bedroom door. She was eagerly anticipating Comet Kohoutek; she had read of its discovery in March of that year in *Reader's Digest*. Mary was looking forward to the December nights, predicted by astronomers, when she might wheel herself out back and watch it streak, fiery and miraculous, across the southwest firmament. The sky was dark around suburban Shawnee; it would really be something to see. The whole idea of it—the bright, wild trajectory— intrigued her, Mary told her sister. "And its orbit will take it into the backyard of other solar systems. How about that?"

Even the *Peanuts* comic strip had Snoopy and Woodstock awaiting the comet. When the moment came, Kohoutek proved to be only modestly visible, and like so many of Mary Alford's promises—to stop drinking, to lose weight, to find another source of income beyond keeping the books for a small local company—the comet was declared a fizzle, unworthy of the hype that preceded it. As it streaked off toward another galaxy, Kohoutek faded into a clichéd pop/cult reference for any spectacular dud.

Brown and Zanuck had better results; *The Sting* took off spectacularly on Christmas weekend. The fish picture was going forward; Spielberg had finally signed on to *Jaws* and David set to work protecting his investment in the property. Within the film industry, Carl Gottlieb said, it was rumored that David had also gamed the bestseller system to protect his investment. The book needed to get on the *New York Times* list and stay there to keep interest high while the film was being made. "David had an inside track to which bookstores were tracked by the *Times* bestseller list; they were known as the recording bookstores, a bit like TV's Nielsen families. And they bought like a thousand copies in those stores." *Jaws* made the list, but David probably needn't have spent the money or the anxiety to maintain visibility for his investment. The hardcover edition would stay on the list for forty-four weeks. Helen did her part, making sure that an excerpt of *Jaws* appeared in *Cosmo*—with no mention that her husband owned the movie rights. Later, during production, there were five mentions of the movie in "Step into My Parlor." By then, Helen was delighted to reveal that her husband was coproducer.

In April 1974, as David was busy scouting possible locations and conferring with his director, Helen flew to Los Angeles to join Jackie Susann, Garson Kanin, and *The Exorcist*'s director, William Friedkin, on a panel sponsored by the Amazing Blue Ribbon 400, an arts-related charity begun in 1968 by Dorothy Chandler, a leader in Los Angeles cultural circles. The subject was to be "public taste," keyed to a landmark June 1973 Supreme Court decision, *Miller v. California*, that many people in the media and arts found alarming. The decision returned standards for determining obscenity to local authorities, effectively decentralizing screen censorship. Obscenity prosecutions would once again become the purview of local authorities. Jackie Susann was horrified: there went the Bible Belt as a market. She hated to think of going back to the bad old days: "Think of how many girls in the Ozarks went wrong without any books or movies at all. With only Uncle Clem to misguide them."

Susann was desperately, fatally ill, but she willed herself to fly west for the panel; she had promised and she felt strongly about the issue. When Helen saw her friend, she was stunned by her weight loss; Susann was down below a hundred pounds and it was a gauntness that not even Helen could envy. She observed that Susann "seemed very frail, but even at that point I thought it was the old respiratory problem. She was so fragile, but she got through the morning. She was practically carried off."

Having fought breast cancer for more than a decade, Jacqueline Susann died in New York on September 24. Her third and final novel, *Once Is Not Enough*, was still selling; she was the first author to have three novels in a row make the bestseller list. The Mansfields' lawsuit over *Beyond the Valley of the Dolls* was still in court; Irving Mansfield received the $2 million in damages after his wife's death. The suit was "just business" and had never caused a rift between the couples. Still, the Browns were stunned that their friends had kept so many of their agonies secret, even from them. David wrote, "As close as we were to the Mansfields, we had no idea Jackie was dying of cancer or that they had a retarded child in an institution. Behind the glitz, theirs was a sad life." The Browns last saw the Mansfields walking hand in hand down Park Avenue after a screening they attended together.

Once *Jaws* production began on Martha's Vineyard, Helen had to fly there if she wanted to see her husband. Given the production's ongoing crises, either Brown or Zanuck had to be on the set at all times. Disasters occurred with such scary frequency that Carl Gottlieb's book *The Jaws Log*, which documents the singular hell of making the movie, has sold nearly 2 million copies since its publication in 1975. To begin with, wrote Gottlieb: "Dick and David had innocently assumed that they could get a shark trainer somewhere, could get a great white shark to perform a few simple stunts on cue in long shots with a dummy in the water." Disabused of this notion—these were fifteen-foot, two-ton engines of single-minded predation, not Flipper— they embarked on the tortuous path to building three versions of a two-thousand-pound mechanical shark. One sank on its maiden voyage, prompting the crew to nickname the robotic killer "Flaws" and "the Great White Turd." The actor Roy Scheider was trapped in the cabin of a rapidly sinking production boat, the *Orca II*, and fought his way out just in time as cameras, tripods, scripts, and lights sank into the deep. Richard Dreyfuss fell into more sulks than Liz Taylor on a bad hair day.

Later, Peter Benchley would insist that the novel was not based on the shark attacks that occurred in New Jersey at the time of David Brown's birth. Yet in the movie, a shark expert played by Dreyfuss warns the mayor of a newly terrorized town in New England that "it happened before! The Jersey beach! . . . 1916! Five people chewed up on the surf!" Whatever its source of inspiration, the yarn was riveting on the big screen; Gottlieb saw its matchless fright factor even during postproduction. "There were moments when lab technicians would jump in surprise. They never get involved in story. But they were going, 'Whoa, look at that!'" The sound cutters, the Foley artists, even Gottlieb, who had been on set, jumped or shrieked at the first moment the shark leaped out of the water toward a kill. Sneak previews drew rising choruses of screams; ratings cards given to screening audiences were spectacular. Oscar Dystel and David Brown reveled in a career peak of mutually profitable synergy: the movie posters used the same titillating image as the bestselling paperback cover. An oblivious woman swims on the surface with the monster below, open-mouthed, nose and teeth pointed toward her belly.

Hollywood handicappers still argue whether *Jaws* was really the first summer blockbuster based on the industry's ever-shifting calculus of "first weekend" grosses and number of theater screens. Gottlieb said that the release was fewer than five hundred screens as opposed to a more typical two thousand now. But there was an undeniable new phenomenon: "When *Jaws* came out it was a great opening weekend. Then a great second week. Then a great summer. Then it developed legs and a pattern of return viewers, people who went back to see the film two, three, five times, paying each time. That was the breakthrough."

Worldwide grosses to date are at nearly half a billion dollars; Brown and Zanuck spent $7.5 million to make the movie. *Jaws* won three Oscars in 1975, for sound, editing, and score; it lost Best Picture to another blockbuster sequel, *The Godfather: Part II*. Three sequels (*Jaws 2*, *Jaws 3-D*, and *Jaws: The Revenge*) were made without Spielberg and diminished in quality each time. Never mind—it kept the franchise humming through 1987. The two indie producers and their wives were financially set for life. Helen Gurley Brown, Depression baby, would never be fully convinced. Despite the cascade of seemingly boundless riches, she admitted, "I always have, always *will* run scared."

Once it was clear that *Jaws* would continue to mint money, Brown and Zanuck decided to reward Bill Gilmore, the head of production, a solid, unflappable veteran who had endured the torments of Captain Ahab to get the movie done. "So when the millions were pouring in," said Gottlieb, "Zanuck and Brown, as a gesture of magnificent gratitude, gave Bill Gilmore a big-screen TV. Whereupon he quit. He knew what he had done, he knew what the picture was making."

Within the industry, the producers were known as world-class cheapskates; they maintained that the habit was key to their success. Lyn Tornabene took their parsimony a bit more personally as she watched the movie's momentum build. "I'm getting these phone calls about the bidding on *Jaws*, then finally the movie is being made, Helen's on Martha's Vineyard, I'm hearing all about the filming. When they got home, a long while later, Helen and David wanted to take Frank and me out to thank me for finding *Jaws*. They wanted to take us to their favorite place in Bedford. They brought along a gift box, about eleven by fourteen inches, and after dinner it was time to open my present."

She had speculated throughout the meal. The box was quite light; maybe pearls? An Hermès scarf? She opened her gift. "It was the first *Jaws* T-shirt, the one with the shark's head popping up. I took it home and shredded it."

Said Gottlieb, on hearing her story: "Of course, they got the shirt for free."

————

David Brown wanted an aerie where he and Helen could settle into their astounding success. He also wanted it to be a home for life. In 1976, Alice Mason, a prominent New York residential real estate broker, helped David find his castle in the Beresford, a classic luxury apartment building designed by the architect Emery Roth. It is on Central Park West at Eighty-First Street, and Helen was not at all keen on leaving Park Avenue. "It was supposed to be tacky over there," she said. With the success of the *Jaws* franchise and *The Sting*, which had collected seven Oscars, including Best Picture, with *Cosmo*'s numbers still climbing and Helen's salary inching toward eighty thousand dollars, including bonuses, it was time to leave the posh building where Helen had to beg the landlord for a workable stove.

Alice Mason was the sort of broker whom certain families retained to find them permanent and suitable residences, mostly along Manhattan's Gold Coast. She did not trade with arrivistes and flippers: "I had my own firm from 1958 to 2008, that's fifty years. Everyone I ever sold an apartment to never sold it. They died in it. They came to me, they found the best apartment they could afford." The Browns wanted that sort of permanence, and something rather commanding appealed to David. Penthouse 22D is the four-floor, towered crown jewel of the Beresford overlooking Central Park and the American Museum of Natural History, with its copper-domed Hayden Planetarium. The apartment's three separate terraces take in more panoramic views west to the Hudson River. There are several fireplaces, including one in the tower room. At the time, it was owned by the film director Mike Nichols. He was about to marry the TV newswoman Diane Sawyer, who was said to prefer the East Side. "It was a very dramatic apartment and I thought they'd really like it," said Mason. "I knew Mike also. I called him and made the appointment to show it. They wanted to buy it right away. I think the price was something like three hundred fifty thousand. Or maybe it was a million. Helen wasn't a free spender but David was and David wanted it. He made the decision."

He was certainly in a position to make an all-cash offer, pronto. Soon, *Forbes* magazine would report that, having earned more than $60 million pretax—the equivalent of close to a quarter billion today—the

Brown/Zanuck partnership was "one of the most successful independent production companies in the entertainment business." David invested his film earnings across bonds, oil and gas, cattle, and real estate
in such a smart and stable configuration that the magazine assessed his
net worth at $40 million, about $170 million in 2015 dollars. He was
pleased to take his well-earned place at the Beresford; over the decades, other famous tenants have included Isaac Stern, Rock Hudson,
the gambling czar Meyer Lansky, Diana Ross, Tony Randall, Laura
Nyro, Beverly Sills, Calvin Klein, Meryl Streep, Arturo Toscanini, Igor
Stravinsky, and Jerry Seinfeld.

The architectural critic Paul Goldberger, who has lived in the Beresford for the last nineteen years, recalled asking the Browns for a tour
of their apartment not long after they had moved in. They were happy
to have him see the place for an article he was researching on two of
his favorite prewar residential architects, Emery Roth and Rosario
Candela. He climbed the spiral stairs to the tower room, with its huge
windows and wood-burning fireplace. "It's the grandest room," said
Goldberger. "Nothing else had that height. Its location is so eccentric as
to crown this little mini chateau that is the apartment. It's almost like a
conservatory in a grand house. Roth's great gift was in making ample
spaces, big, beautiful, generously laid out family apartments. Those
three tower apartments were situations in which his normal practical
instinct was set aside to do something greater. The building has set-
backs as it gets higher toward the towers and you end up with space
that is not laid out as naturally and gracefully as anything below. The
choice was to allow a couple of apartments in which you assume that
the unusual and spectacular nature will be enough to make up for the
absence of an easy, flowing layout."

The property was glamorous but not at all suited to a family; it has
only two bedrooms, besides a couple of cramped staff rooms on the bottom level, where David would install his ham radio. The Browns were
healthy and their only domestic ménage was the two cats. So at the
time, rooms set between four sets of stairs without an internal elevator
did not pose a problem. Given her admitted décor impairment, Helen
turned to the *Ladies' Home Journal* decorator Nathan Mandelbaum to

redo the place. The real estate photos of the Browns' apartment up for sale in 2015 showed it to be unchanged since his ministrations in 1976, with a mood-ring-trapped-in-seventies-amber ambiance. One can easily envision Angie Dickinson as *Police Woman*'s Pepper Anderson lounging before the living room fire on the faux leopard carpet.

Mandelbaum gave them a red lacquered dining room with a striped, wraparound banquette, a living room with overstuffed sofas in many patterns, and scads of chinoiserie—screens, equestrian statues, armoires. The tower room, which Helen called the belfry, was packed with what she called "airport sculpture, the kind of thing tourists pick up last minute at the airport, but I like it." Later she would add oversized plush stuffed animals. The master bedroom, with its huge, curtained canopy, was a riot of pink print with accents of crimson; the carpet was bubblegum-pink shag. Taking in the breadth of it, with its countless patterns and enough sets of fancy china to set up a high-end skeet range, David declared the apartment "bizarre," yet homey. Helen found it "romantic."

The Browns were well settled into their final home when Helen sat down to bang out her November "Step into My Parlor." Exciting news: she and David had gone to their first state dinner at the White House! The German chancellor, Helmut Schmidt, and his wife were the guests of honor. Dinner was in massive white tents set up on the lawn; Helen was seated between the American ambassador to Germany and the former Redskins player Sonny Jurgensen—"both charming!" There was an after-dinner tour: "Blue Room, Green Room, Red Room. My dear, those rooms are goose-pimply! . . . Nancy Kissinger looked smashing in navy chiffon with scads of green eyeshadow."

The rest of the column carried the best news of all from the editor's perspective: "*Cosmo* is burgeoning . . . October carried the most advertising pages in our history (203), and, as we go to press, the August issue sold 319,000 copies *more* than August a year ago for a total of 2,515,000. Each month we sell almost all the copies we print—pretty big stuff in the magazine business." Thanking her readers for their support, she also gave a shout-out to the girls and boys of the so-so *Cosmo* volleyball team, who won thirteen games and lost ten.

The turn of the year brought another Oscar race; David Brown had no horse in it, but he and Zanuck had armfuls of statues from *The Sting* and *Jaws* and, with their triumphs, the sort of social standing that elevated David and his smart, saucy editor wife into what gossip columnists liked to call "*le tout* New York." The term took in a very rarefied sliver of that populous island, those *tout* enough to be invited to the literary agent Irving "Swifty" Lazar's exclusive Oscar-watching party at Tavern on the Green in Central Park. A *New York Times* reporter was eavesdropping on the crowd during cocktails: "Nora Ephron was talking about *Esquire*, Shana Alexander was talking about Patricia Hearst. Halston was talking about Elizabeth Taylor . . . next to Halston, Mrs. Helen Gurley Brown was talking to Mrs. Walter Cronkite." There were so many more: Diana Vreeland, Jimmy Breslin, Françoise de la Renta, David Brinkley, Eric Sevareid, Elia Kazan, Yul Brynner. When Swifty got up to pay tribute to the dozen former Oscar winners in attendance, Helen watched her beaming husband accept his tribute. Swifty also announced that it was his seventieth birthday; following the rousing applause, waiters burst through the doors with cutlets of veal cooked in cherries and rolled in hazelnuts. Thank heaven, there was pureed broccoli; Helen Gurley Brown could enjoy the bacchanal. Irwin Shaw dozed through the Oscar telecast. When Paddy Chayefsky won his Oscar for writing the screenplay for *Network*, the exhausted hostess, Mary Lazar, leaped up and did a little dance, doubtless grateful that it was over for another year, and the limos of *le tout* were beginning to converge outside to bear them away.

If it hadn't been a chilly March night, the Browns could have strolled home from the party along Central Park West. For Helen, their new address conferred the greatest perk of all: the M10 city bus stopped right out front of the Beresford; its final stop, generally a ten-minute ride, was Fifty-Seventh Street and Eighth Avenue, practically at the doorstep of the Hearst Building. Heaven! Every weekday, the doorman saw Helen out onto the avenue clutching her sacks of work, some cottage cheese, and the precious container of tuna salad. Dropping her fare into the change box was a reassuring sound: only fifty cents!

29 ᘓ

Victory Lap

My only previous exposure to Helen was on Johnny Carson. I
thought she was a complete ditz. I didn't think she was running the
magazine . . . there must be someone else and she was the poster girl.
When I went to work there, I had an enormous amount of respect
for her. She was fair, she was clear, she was focused.
—Bobbe Stultz, associate art director at *Cosmo*

MARY ALFORD WATCHED FROM her front door in terror and amazement as her sister executed a Cruella de Vil fishtail into the driveway,
piloting a huge Cadillac owned by the proprietress of the local Holiday
Inn. How'd she do *that*? Sheer desperation. Renting a car at the Oklahoma City airport wasn't an option, since Helen no longer had a valid
license, a fact she must have kept from the kind innkeeper. Helen played
the wheelchair card, the faithful, frequent, *and famous* customer card,
the whole royal flush to get her preferred room and to have the pool
kept open late for her so that she could dog-paddle away the stress.

The Caddie was an added blessing; there were no cabs in Shawnee
at the time, and Helen needed wheels. Things were falling apart in
the little house on Pesotum Street. By the late seventies, Cleo was failing; she suffered from atherosclerosis and had a couple of mild strokes.
Any housekeeper they could get to stay on the job had her hands full
with the needs of both women; George Alford, having become too de-
bilitated, had been moved to a nursing home. With great effort, Mary
brought him home for visits a few times a year.

When Cleo turned eighty-five in October 1978, Helen sent her a long, loving letter. It acknowledged her mother's trials: "I want to weep for your being burdened with child care as a little bitty girl yourself, then, having no place else to put your talent, pouring it into your own children." She recalled the sacrifices a self-centered little girl would not have thought twice about: "With your first paycheck from Sears Roebuck you bought me a little wolf jacket that was my greatest JOY!" The letter meandered, sweetly, through the years and stuck a perfect landing: "Cleo, you were a good mother. The best. If I'm something special in the world of working women now, it's because you put me there and David took up where you left off . . . Everything good you wanted for me I got."

She had written a very different letter to Mary. Helen had to acknowledge the torments Cleo was still inflicting on her sister once she had moved back in with her. In a letter that was partly an act of contrition, Helen chastised herself at first for expecting too much of her sister, given what she had had to bear; she realized that she had sometimes gone over the line with her holier-than-thou temperance lectures and torrents of books and articles on new diets to try. If it had taken food and alcohol to ease the aches, she understood that as well.

But . . . by God, *Cleo*. The amateur shrink in Helen was convinced; whatever stubbornness and resentments Mary had shown over the years had to be due in large part to so many years of "bearing up" under their mother. Hadn't Helen, able-bodied and on the cusp of great success, hauled off and belted Cleo herself? She wouldn't minimize her mother's burdens, her terrible grief and endless disappointments. Maybe she and Mary had been hard on their mother, but she had been plenty tough on them. It came down to this, she told Mary: Few things were worse to live with than Cleo's hostility toward people. Toward life itself. Never mind that it was all well founded from an early age. Hers was a curdled little soul, and her misery seeped into her girls like a slow and invisible toxin. They would just have to endure it and love her anyhow.

On October 27, 1980, four days after her eighty-seventh birthday, Cleo Bryan closed her eyes in the last of her crowded, substandard, and sorrow-filled homes and died, of atherosclerosis. Helen sobbed for nearly the entire flight west. Once she got to Shawnee, she and Mary hung on to each other across the arms of the wheelchair, just as they had during those bleak early days in Los Angeles, and cried. Now they were two. In her messy, terribly complicated grief, Helen did not care how much anything cost as she arranged for a coffin and transport to send her mother back to Osage, to rest with her people. There was a service in Shawnee at Mary's church. How did Helen get Mary to Osage? They must have used the church van; perhaps the Nelson Funeral Service in Berryville, the same family firm that buried Ira Gurley, had rounded up some strong and compassionate drivers.

At 2:00 p.m. on Halloween, there was a graveside service in the Sisco family cemetery. It was right below the house where Helen and Mary had spent all those childhood summers with their grandparents Alfred and Jennie Sisco, where Cleo had cared for those waves of squalling babies and escaped down the road on Daisy's broad back. Five of Cleo's nine siblings survived her. Aunt Gladys, whose luminous beauty had cast such long shadows of discontent around Cleo and her daughters, was already in a nursing home.

Helen knew it wasn't over when the first clods of earth thudded against the coffin. It didn't take a squadron of therapists for her to realize: she would wrestle with Cleo's disappointments for the rest of her life. But once she got back to New York, her grief, as with most of her family worries, remained private.

Joni Evans, an editor and executive at Simon & Schuster, had settled into one of her favorite editing spots, poolside at the Beverly Hills Hotel. She had authors to see in Los Angeles and she always brought books-in-progress to work on. She was peering closely at a manuscript by Helen Gurley Brown, another memoir/how to/advice book with the tentative title *Having It All*, due for publication in 1982. Helen wasn't crazy about the title, but it was to be a valedictory of sorts; the subtitle was a pithy synopsis of her triumphs: "*Love-Success-Sex-Money Even if You're Starting with Nothing . . .*"

Helen didn't know it yet, but she had begun her long and final victory lap. The *Cosmo* juggernaut was growing ever stronger, with more foreign editions and a surprising uptick in paid subscriptions at the rate of 25 percent a year during the eighties. *Cosmo* readers were *committed*. Newsstand sales were still flourishing at 2.62 million copies a month. The magazine's core constituency delivered another surprise: pass-along rates had soared to seven readers per issue. Women were sharing all that advice and current fiction at the bargain price of two bucks an issue; advertisers could be assured of more eyes per copy on their campaigns for spring lip colors and feminine hygiene sprays.

By the early eighties, Helen's name and image recognition—what media analysts were calling a Q-score—was strong enough for her new agent, Swifty Lazar, to have negotiated a tidy deal with Simon & Schuster's imprint Linden Press. Joni Evans estimated that the whole package could bring up to $2 million in hard- and softcover sales.

Evans had blue-penciled her way through the career chapter "How to Mouseburger Your Way to the Top," as well as those on diet and exercise. Her eyes widened as she paged through to a section Helen called "How to Go Down on a Man."

Waiter, more coffee please?

Helen began with the basics: "Flick your tongue around this nice penis head and move it on *down* the penis, putting more and more of it down your throat . . ." She was also reassuring: "Only a very *large* penis will gag you and you can always stop and come up for air." Evans was agog, yet appreciative of her author's craft. "She could do how-tos better than anyone. She took all these subjects seriously and gave them great respect. She was earnest in her approach to . . . blow jobs."

At this point, Helen felt that her girls could handle such plain talk. The language in the magazine had become more frank, without reader pushback. The word "orgasm" first appeared in a cover line in 1970, and "lesbian" the year after. By the mid-seventies, there were more references to "penis" rather than "male genitalia." The catchall of "oral sex" was specified as "fellatio" and "cunnilingus." Helen's loyalists were talking back in a very intimate way. In January 1980, *Cosmo* had invited readers to complete and send in a questionnaire about their sex lives.

Its seventy-nine questions covered premarital and extramarital relationships, types of sex acts, orgasm frequency; 106,000 women—Texas housewives, New Jersey schoolteachers, high school girls, ranging in age from fourteen to seventy—sat down and answered. In 1981, as Evans was working on Helen's manuscript, the survey was published as a book, *The Cosmo Report*. It showed that some things had indeed changed. Only 5 percent of women reported having their first sexual experience with their husbands; it had been 50 percent in the early fifties when Alfred Kinsey was asking. More than 20 percent of respondents had sex before they were fifteen, and 90 percent had by the time they were twenty-five. Helen's survey had made her case: even if women didn't have it *all* just yet, they were having *It* a good deal sooner and more often.

Camped at the edge of the sun-dappled pool deck, Joni Evans kept working; as she considered the quandary on "ball-sucking" (which one first? both at once?), she wondered what the sit-down edits with Helen would be like. She was coediting the book with the company's editor in chief, Michael Korda, who had also shepherded Jacqueline Susann's *Once Is Not Enough* and lived to tell about it. The edit sessions with Helen—one held in the Browns' frigid, unheated tower room—moved along reasonably until they reached a bizarre impasse.

They stalled out over a pubic hair. "It was her idea for a gift for your man on Valentine's Day," said Evans. "Take a single pubic hair of your own and encase it in some sort of Lucite frame, which could be worn around the neck, or as a bracelet. It was just appalling." Korda recoiled as well; the two sparred over which of them would tell Helen it had to go. "We were all chicken, even Swifty," said Evans. "I went to Liz [Smith]. I knew they were close friends." Smith agreed on the ickiness factor and caucused with Helen. "Whatever she did," said Evans, "she got it out. We were so grateful." Korda had almost as strong a reaction to Helen's signature appellation: "I hated the word 'mouseburger,' but I couldn't get her to drop that. I still think it's a stupid word."

Korda believes the book's success was dependent upon Helen's being Helen: "It was a combination of her being outrageous and her being transparently sincere. That worked. She went a long way with it, frankly. But that's the key to it. Her recommendations were outrageous but they were offered in a voice of total sincerity and a certain degree of naivete and charm. Naivete particularly. That's a difficult combination and I think it's very much a part of her character. It's not something you can fake."

When *Having It All* was published, Dick Deems was appalled by Helen's candor—the impropriety of the woman! Having seen the splashy *New York* magazine feature by Jesse Kornbluth timed to the book's release, a stormy Deems appeared in Helen's office and delivered a withering dressing-down: The word "penis" was in the article! Helen had let herself be photographed in skimpy PJ tops, exercising—in bed! (She looked terrific at sixty.) Helen sat there and took it, mortified and furious. Revenues were at an all-time high; advertisers were jostling for space. "Penis" was in *Cosmo* that very month—and in nearly every other women's magazine. How dare he? She shot Deems a long note the next day, answering his charges point by point, insisting she hadn't been any sexier than usual in the interview. She reminded the pompous ass: "I know what I am doing."

Neither party brought up the most shameful aspect of Kornbluth's article: it reported that Gloria Steinem had recently asked Helen in an interview about Hearst's failure to elect her to its board, despite her monumental contributions. Didn't that indicate that even very successful women were still denied ultimate power? Helen's answer, if there was one, was not quoted. Gloria was always *pushing*, though Helen knew she meant well. She and Steinem were doing a cable TV show when Kornbluth, researching his article, tagged along. He caught a tough/tender moment as Steinem braced Helen about her reflexive self-deprecation. It amounted to a mini therapy session. Steinem began: "On TV, you giggle and flirt with the host and tell stories about bedroom manners. You're a much more serious and complicated person than that."

"Oh, Gloria, you're trying so *hard* to make it seem as if I'm victimized."

"I'm just suggesting that we as women go on playing certain kinds of roles even when we have the power to change. And I would like other people to know you as I know you."

"Yes, I would like to be known as a serious person . . ."

"Just say it straight out, 'I am a serious person . . .'"

"I'm scared! I'm scared!"

"Just say what's inside your head and your heart."

"I care, I care."

"Well, that's it. 'I'm a serious person and I care' is a start."

The two women were not close, but Steinem was never as dismissive or combative as Friedan had been. Steinem had a tough upbringing with a difficult mother herself and was more keenly attuned than most to Helen's insecurities. In 1974, Steinem had called Helen just to reassure her that the women's movement meant her and her readers no harm; in her thank-you note, Helen was clearly touched. Steinem wrote for *Cosmo* and sat for a fairly intimate portrait, "The Glorious Triumph of Gloria Steinem," by writer Joan Barthel. Over the years, Helen peppered Steinem with congratulatory notes on TV appearances, on her late-life marriage. But Helen complained to Charlotte Veal that Steinem kept her distance: "Carlotta, she's never been friendly to me though I admire her wildly. She *is* smart . . . the *smartest*!"

Cosmo day-to-day was a sisterly, civilized, and nearly all-female workplace, according to interviews with a dozen former staffers. There were perks beyond the free cosmetics samples on the ladies' room shelf and the bizarre recycled freebies—press kits, workout headbands, cheesy promotional watches—that Helen distributed at Christmas from what was known, sub rosa, as "the regifting closet." Perhaps fancying herself as the Madame Récamier of Fifty-Seventh Street, Helen began holding Friday afternoon "salons" in her office. *Quel éclat!* when staffers walked in and found the boss sitting in the lap of New York's governor, George Pataki. Woody Allen stopped by, as did Rupert Murdoch, Ted Turner, Henry Kissinger, Steven Spielberg, Elizabeth Dole, and Walter Cronkite. "She would invite somebody she knew that she found fascinating," said the former associate art director Bobbe Stultz. "We also had Mike

Wallace, Liv Ullmann, Vernon Jordan. It wasn't just entertainment people who would talk about frivolous things. She would invite a certain level of staff—I just squeezed in. We would ask this person questions, and she would. It was fantastic."

Other employee benefits fell into the "be careful what you wish for" category. "A lot of the people on the staff got their apartments made over, and you really couldn't find a lot of people who wanted that," said Stultz. "A friend of mine, Judi Drogin, did. She had a small apartment in the Thirties. It was a wreck." Judi, now Drogin-Feldman, who was one of Helen's personal assistants, said that she gasped when she walked into her new digs just as on those TV home makeover shows. "It was pink," she said. "And I mean screaming, bubblegum pink, everywhere. But they did a great job with the built-ins and I was grateful." After the photo shoot, she repainted. It took many coats to diffuse that *Cosmo* glow. Drogin-Feldman, now a real estate agent, was one of the two assistants Helen had at all times. She also dropped to the floor in Helen's office and did ab crunches with her at lunchtime. "She asked me in the job interview whether I exercised. It wasn't a requisite, but I stayed in good shape working for Helen."

Cindy Spengler has vivid memories of the day Helen's confidence in her as advertising director of *Cosmopolitan* was put to its greatest test. Spengler had flown out to San Francisco with a presentation—a Hail Mary pass, really—designed to make a big save. She was nervous as she carried her materials into a conference room filled with ad agency executives, mostly male. At stake was nearly $20 million in billings for a lavish set of magazine spreads to roll out General Motors' new car, the Saturn. "We were originally on the media plan for Saturn," Spengler said, "and the client took us off because the magazine was too racy. A lot of pages were going to our competitors." Spengler's West Coast reps told her that the client particularly disliked *Cosmo*'s rather intimate "Irma Kurtz's Agony Column."

Spengler had scoured other women's magazines for sexy material in advice columns and relationship pieces. "I started out with showing headlines and cover blurbs and asked them to guess what magazine they were from because they all sounded like *Cosmo*, but they were from *Redbook, LHJ, Glamour, Mademoiselle.*"

Spengler pushed on. "I read aloud a letter wanting to know how to give fellatio. I'm glad I was young, because now I think it would be gross if I read that thing today."

She asked her listeners: "Which magazine do you think this is from?" *Cosmo*, of course, came the chorus. Then she held up the magazine that she had read it from. "I think it was *Glamour.* We got the business back. The revenues for *Cosmo* were huge."

Helen was an empathetic and activist mentor to this young ad woman who started out in the field and performed so spectacularly that Helen brought her home to New York. They traveled together to see West Coast advertisers. Helen was her boss, but she was also . . . Helen: "This was a woman who climbed stairs in hotels for exercise and got locked in the stairwell once. She took her clothes off down to her underwear while I was there and started doing her exercises. Helen didn't ever have to put on airs; she was who she was. She was confident in who she was and she never apologized for it either, being feminine."

She could also be tough. When a very upset Spengler found out that one of her male subordinates on the West Coast was making more money than she was, Helen sat down and banged out a sample letter to brace Hearst management with. Spengler wrote her own, with some of Helen's advice, and quickly got the adjustment made. The boss also advised her in love, and when things reached a dicey point with a boyfriend reluctant to wed, Helen counseled a tough stance ("Move out!"); unbeknownst to Cindy, the ad executive Peter Spengler sought counsel with Helen as well. HGB danced up a storm at their wedding.

As effective as Spengler and her team were, there was no greater sales force-of-nature than HGB, who had no qualms about cozying up to advertisers. Spengler went with her to the regular luncheons with representatives from agencies and their clients in a private room at '21'. "It was a long table and Helen sat right in the middle and had the most important people on either side. She always started out with a bit about her own story—'We're mountain people.' Beforehand, she knew of any sensitivity that was a concern of the people in the room. She remembered names and people very well."

Sometimes it got warm in the upstairs dining room. Spengler nearly choked on her salmon as she saw Helen slide off her ladylike Chanel jacket. She was wearing only a camisole beneath. "It was a pretty one," said Spengler. "But she seemed not to realize that it was actually underwear and not a business top." No one seemed to mind.

Helen valued, admired, and pressed her sales team; perhaps they reminded her of her own mad ad days. During a sales retreat in Bermuda, Seth Hoyt, a former ad guy about to become publisher of *Cosmopolitan*, tossed a silk-clad Mrs. Brown into the pool. She laughed and executed a leisurely paddle to the ladder.

30

Thin Ice

It's bad enough that people are dying of AIDS, but no one should die
of ignorance.
—Elizabeth Taylor

HELEN HAD CERTAINLY HEARD THE NEWS: by the mid-1980s, a growing scourge had invaded Francesco Scavullo's busy hive and devastated
his studio family. In August 1986, the makeup artist Way Bandy's *New
York Times* obituary stated, at his insistence, that AIDS was the cause of
his death. Too many people still refused to name the beast aloud. Bandy's
memorial was held on November 13 of that year; envelopes were passed
for contributions to AIDS research. Five days later, Scavullo's darling
and *Cosmo* cover girl Gia Carangi was gone as well; shared needles
from her heroin addiction led to her contracting HIV and an excruciating death from AIDS complications. Scavullo told friends, "We were
hysterical crying in the studio when we heard."

Carangi was one of the first American women known to die of AIDS.
Hers was a lonely, degrading end; having resorted to turning tricks for
drugs, she was found raped, in withdrawal, and suffering from exposure on a rain-soaked street. Such ugliness was not spoken of. There
were no obituaries of the famous model at the time, save a small mention in her hometown; no contingent from the traumatized fashion

world turned up at her funeral in Pennsylvania. Paralyzed by grief and depression, Scavullo sent a mass card. Angelina Jolie would portray Gia in a 1998 HBO movie; a pathetic scene shows the model, bloated from methadone treatment, wedged into a Fabrice gown and woozily trying to pose for her final *Cosmopolitan* cover; the actor playing Scavullo positions her carefully to conceal an ugly needle abscess on her hand.

The deaths saddened Helen, of course, but she didn't want to hear a damned thing more about this AIDS business. It wasn't a problem for her readers, she was sure. She was also adamant: she felt that all this business about sex killing people could set women's hard-won sexual freedom back years, and she refused to be a part of it. She had hectored Ronald Reagan about abortion rights, written to the Supreme Court justice Sandra Day O'Connor about protecting *Roe v. Wade*—she was still worried sick about some crazies overturning it. And here they were, all these AIDS crusaders, scaring the bejesus out of women about having sex again. It wasn't right.

Her thinking was woefully uninformed, and as a result, *Cosmo* lagged way behind in its coverage of the growing epidemic. Its earliest mention was two sentences in a 1983 health column as "another frightening new disease." A reader's "fear of AIDS" was treated with reassurance in "Irma Kurtz's Agony Column." A 1985 cover line asked, "Is There Gay Life After AIDS? The Devastating Changes in Male Homosexual Relationships."

In the pages of *Cosmo* it was still a "them" issue—homosexuals and druggies. On a personal level, Helen's refusal to engage or even become well-informed on the issue frustrated some of her close friends. Liz Smith was involved early in the American Foundation for AIDS Research (AMFAR). Hadn't Helen, who had just personally done a Liz Taylor interview, seen the star everywhere as a concerned AIDS activist and poster girl? What did it take to convince her? Smith recalled blurting at Helen one day, "Don't be one of those women—the ones who have fired their hairdressers and tried to ignore this thing."

Helen was not one of that panicky and heedlessly cruel tribe who suddenly shied away from even air kisses at the salon and the fashion showrooms, but she had little interest in the growing body of information on AIDS caseloads and transmission paths; she cared only about the inhibiting sexual realities the coverage seemed to be causing. It was a stubbornness that caused Judy Krantz to refuse Helen a blurb for a book of hers: "In the book it specifically said, if you're sitting next to an attractive man on the airplane, and he asks you to go to a hotel with him go and do it. I said, 'Helen, you don't seem to realize the danger of AIDS. How can I possibly give a blurb to a book that says go with a strange man whom you know nothing about and fuck him? I'm sorry but I just can't.'"

Alex Mayes Birnbaum recalled a trip to their country house in upstate New York with the Browns in the summer of 1986, during which her husband, the travel writer Stephen Birnbaum, had offered to help Helen bone up for a debate on modern sexuality she was to participate in at the University of Oxford that October. His wife noticed that as they worked together, a major disagreement was Helen's belief that "heterosexuals can't get AIDS, women can't get AIDS. The stupidity was staggering. We knew by then, the world knew, that women and heterosexuals could get it. She just wouldn't have it. David would be very silent during these discussions."

Helen wouldn't let it rest. In January 1988, she published a story suggested by her senior articles editor, Myra Appleton, who was friendly with the doctor who authored it. It ran during some of the darkest days of the AIDS epidemic with this upbeat title: "Reassuring News About AIDS: A doctor tells you why you may not be at risk." It was bunk at the outset. *Cosmopolitan*'s longtime laxity in fully vetting its medical articles came home to roost in a catastrophic way. In Dr. Robert E. Gould, Appleton chose a ringer to legitimize the specious headline. He was a clinical professor of psychiatry, not a researcher or practitioner with clinical AIDS expertise. Yet he made the controversial and erroneous case that if women's male lovers were not in the known risk group—engaging in homosexual or bisexual sex or sharing needles for IV drug use—there was very little chance that women would contract HIV through normal vaginal intercourse. The doctor's contentions also bore a nasty whiff of racism; he asserted that while it was known that some African women had contracted the disease from vaginal sex with men, it was because "many men in Africa take their women in a brutal way, so that some heterosexual activity regarded as normal by them would be closer to rape by our standards."

Even in other populations, Gould conceded, such "macho thrusting" and rape can cause vaginal lesions that let the blood-borne virus in. Gould's presentation was sloppy at best; he did not even distinguish between the terms "HIV" and "AIDS." He assured women that a "healthy vagina" was naturally protected from the disease. His scientific proof? If that *weren't* the case, the number of infected women would be exponentially higher. In terms of science, the whole "reassuring" package was the dog's breakfast.

Soon after the article hit the stands in late December, AIDS activists fairly hugged themselves; Helen had teed up a perfect platform to call attention to the dangers of misinformation on AIDS. Maxine Wolfe, a longtime activist on women's issues, was then a member of ACT UP (the AIDS Coalition to Unleash Power) and helped plan and implement a *Cosmo* protest. Because of her community work, Wolfe was knowledgeable about some of the earliest research and clinical work done on women and AIDS. She knew that women were getting AIDS from heterosexual intercourse. The ACT UP planners began by calling Dr. Gould to ask if they might meet with him to share their data and clinical experience on women and AIDS. He agreed, if reluctantly. "We also called Helen Gurley Brown and she would not even speak with us," said Wolfe. "When we went to speak to Gould we brought Denise Ribble. She was a nurse practitioner at the Community Health Project, and she had started the first group for women with HIV and AIDS. She had been running those groups for several years already."

Heterosexual transmission was happening; Ribble had seen women showing up in her groups horribly sick, shunned and terrified. Often, they were misdiagnosed by doctors unfamiliar with the disease. Though the women presented Gould with evidence of these female HIV cases, he was insulting and dismissive. Before they were shown the door, his visitors asked: Why was there no peer review of his alleged findings? What were his sources? Why didn't he disclose that he was a psychiatrist and not a practitioner of internal medicine? He refused to answer.

To the barricades! Wolfe cued up a grainy video showing the scene outside the building housing the *Cosmo* offices, which were not then in the main Hearst Building but nearby at 224 West Fifty-Seventh Street. January 15, 1988, was a frigid day; protesters were braced against the cold and the encroachments of a phalanx of hired security guards. Signs read "For Every Cosmo Lie, More Women Die." "The Cosmo Girl Can Get AIDS." "Don't Go to Bed with Cosmo." Wolfe doesn't think Helen was even in the building that day; she may have been tipped off by a "Page Six" item in the *New York Post* that had leaked word of a possible protest. As about 150 people convened outside the *Cosmo* building, it seemed clear that the private security force was prepared. "We couldn't get into the building because they had hired goons to block the doors." Picketing began; the police arrived. Trained in civil disobedience tactics, some protesters began taking badge numbers of officers, who began pushing them back. When one protester, Geri Wells, was placed inside a police van, others began chanting for her release and pushing at the van. They knew that Wells was the only one who couldn't afford to be arrested that day. "Geri's brother, who had HIV, was in the hospital," said Wolfe. "He needed a blood transfusion that afternoon and she was going down there to give blood."

Wells was released and there were no arrests as the frozen protesters eventually dispersed. *Cosmo* got the sort of publicity any media company would cringe at, yet Helen did little to defuse the situation. She went on ABC's *Nightline* with a stern Ted Koppel. "We have come so far in relieving women of fear and fright and guilt," she said, "and now along comes this thing to scare the daylights out of everybody forever. And since there isn't too much proof that AIDS is spread through heterosexual intercourse, I think our side should be presented, too."

Koppel pushed back: "When your readership, ten million mostly young women, read an article like that, and draw the conclusion that, therefore, maybe they don't need to urge their partners to use condoms, do you feel entirely comfortable with that?"

Helen said, "I feel quite comfortable with this."

In *Cosmo*, the contretemps got only a few lines in Helen's April editor's column; they were appended to an account of a trip to Washington for the National Abortion Rights Action League (NARAL) celebration of the fifteenth anniversary of the *Roe v. Wade* decision. Helen was a vigorous and longtime activist and fund-raiser for that group. Of the AIDS controversy she said only this: "Koppel is tough but fair. And brilliant!"

Helen had also received a personal letter from Surgeon General C. Everett Koop, who complained of a substantial amount of misinformation in the article, then listed its errors in numbered paragraphs. Among his points: the majority of the 1988 incidences of AIDS contracted in heterosexual intercourse occurred in females. Helen's chilly two-sentence response had all the concern of a form letter, but the surgeon general was persistent. Dr. Koop cited the *Cosmo* article during a Capitol Hill hearing. He told the lawmakers, "It is just not true that there is no danger from normal vaginal intercourse."

Helen never printed a correction or future in-depth articles that kept up with evolving AIDS information; she would even refuse the request of revered AIDS expert and activist Dr. Mathilde Krim to wear a red ribbon for the cause to the Academy Awards, telling her, "I have never been an active supporter in your cause." Instead, in April 1988, a headline asked, "What's Everybody Doing About Sex?" More solid *Cosmo* reporting on the big chill in the age of AIDS: the bar revenue at Pig Latin, a hot spot in the Hamptons, was down 40 percent as singles fretted about losing self-control. The worried barkeep had invented a new drink: " 'It's called Safe Sex on the Beach,' Steve says, 'made with peach schnapps, vodka, and orange juice, and garnished with a condom.' "

There was another, more personal disruption in the Browns' life two months later; David Brown and Richard Zanuck called it quits on their partnership after thirty years. The men were always close; Zanuck's two sons were the Browns' godsons. Helen and David were both very fond of the boys. Hollywood insiders laid blame at the feet of Zanuck's third wife, Lili Fini Zanuck. She was invited to join the company by David, but the triad formation was ultimately divisive; soon she was generating the most column inches in industry press. The official word was "amicable." Privately, Helen made no bones about blaming Lili Zanuck, but David was ever the gentleman. Explaining the split to the *Vanity Fair* writer Joanne Kaufman, he made it sound as though he just missed the "buddy picture" part of the long partnership, and his autonomy. "There was no breach of friendship," he said; "I was just feeling that I was no longer as powerful as I had been." He said he wanted to be like his wife: "Helen is the boss. Once a year she submits a budget to the Hearst Corporation. She doesn't have to go to *anyone.*" David named his new production company the Manhattan Project, because, he said, "the Manhattan Project produced the world's biggest bomb."

Amid the customary quips, David offered a bit of late-life introspection: "I am a very complicated older man who is knowing for the first time a degree of security and peace within himself owing to a great many mistakes. I've suffered many, many traumas, many bouts of joblessness, many bouts of being unloved. I'm not very secure socially. I'm always afraid of offending. I'm an incomplete person working against time. I guess you couldn't say I'm that *Cosmopolitan* man."

Of course, he would be there in the klieg lights, beaming, as he escorted his wife into what amounted to a coronation of sorts. In 1990, Hearst threw Helen a twenty-fifth anniversary celebration that spared no expense. Helen's fete was a black tie affair at the Rainbow Room; in the many photographs, her expression radiates utter joy.

Helen was bejeweled and pulled together perfectly, ever-so-Helen in a short pink dress with a skirt that looked like shredded coconut. Her hair was glossy and full, her light pink stockings intact; she kicked off the gold strappy heels to dance most of the night and have her photo taken with some of the guests: The former *Time* managing editor Henry Grunwald and his wife, Louise, were just back from a two-year residence in Vienna, where Ronald Reagan had appointed him U.S. ambassador. Merv Griffin and Zsa Zsa, Beverly Sills, Liz Smith, Barbara Walters. The prezzies were paramount: Helen's vintage (1960) typewriter had been replated and a plaque affixed. A sleek Mercedes 550

SEL—silver for the anniversary—was presented with a paid driver, courtesy of Hearst. Dick Deems closed his remarks this way: "I've concluded that Helen is like Salome of the seven veils and if one is able to see behind one or two of the veils there is still so much mystery hidden by the others. She's a paradox of perfection who understands the frailties besetting the human condition."

Within the year, David would have his glittering valedictory moment as well. In Oscar season of 1991, the Browns flew to Los Angeles and once again walked the red carpet outside the Dorothy Chandler Pavilion. That night David Brown and Richard Zanuck, partners no more, jointly received the Irving G. Thalberg Memorial Award for lifetime achievement in film, presented periodically to "creative producers, whose bodies of work reflect a consistently high quality of motion picture production." At age seventy-seven, David found himself amid the lions: Cecil B. DeMille, Walt Disney, Ingmar Bergman, Billy Wilder, Darryl F. Zanuck, as well as David's beloved Buddy Adler. David walked offstage carrying the nine-inch statuette that weighed nearly eleven pounds; his guardsman's mustache bristled above a wide smile. The future looked bright as well; Kit Golden, the young woman he had hired to help run the Manhattan Project, showed real talent and a good eye for properties.

A couple of months later, in May, a sadness overtook the *Cosmo* offices. Everyone's darling, a talented associate art director named Abelardo Menendez, had been hospitalized with AIDS and was desperately ill. In mid-May, Helen wrote to him at his West Village home:

> Abelardo dear:
>
> I miss you—dreadfully . . . you are a part of my life and always will be . . . I know you are battling very hard your particular illness and I still have faith that it can be bested. I'm sending some special newly-minted four-leaf clovers from my sister's house in Oklahoma, said to be very potent!
>
> All my love for ever and ever.

Abelardo Menendez died soon afterward.

The months passed uneventfully until late October, when Helen did it again—stuck her tiny Gucci sling-backed foot into her mouth at another national moment of excruciating sensitivities. *The Wall Street Journal* solicited comment from a few prominent women regarding the Senate hearings on whether the newly confirmed Supreme Court justice Clarence Thomas had sexually harassed Anita Hill when she worked with him on the Equal Employment Opportunity Commission.

It wasn't as bad as the AIDS debacle, but Helen's *WSJ* piece, "At Work, Sexual Electricity Sparks Creativity," lamented the dearth of men on her staff who might harass women staffers; then she resurrected the Scuttle thing—that cute steeplechase at the California radio station when men stripped the underpants off young women. Harmless fun, right? Helen ended her piece this way: "Many people have suggested articles on sexual harassment to *Cosmo*. Though a devout feminist, I have resisted. I have this possibly benighted idea that when a man finds you sexually attractive, he is paying you a compliment . . . when he doesn't, that's when you have to worry."

Devout feminist? Public opinion cried blasphemy. For Hearst, it was another PR train wreck. The letters to the *WSJ* editor were bristling with condemnation and disbelief. The media coverage was universally damning and the industry tom-toms were beginning to thrum.

Some of Helen's strongest bulwarks against superannuation had been her hires who did their best to keep the editorial age-appropriate and au courant and the magazine's bottom line tight and firm. HGB was no devil in Prada; she was not threatened by strong, savvy women; she sought them out and leaned on them. She welcomed her newly hired book editor, Betty Sargent, this way: "Okay, you've got the job. I just hope your brain is as beautiful as you are, dear." In her sixteen years at *Cosmo*, Sargent oversaw a big chunk of the most valued editorial real estate. "Helen hired me herself," said Sargent. "A quarter of the magazine came from my department every month, including nonfiction excerpts. We were doing a huge amount of fiction when I took over. We started out with one 25,000 word condensation, two

5,000 word short stories and then the rest of the nonfiction every month."

Sargent's first imperative from the boss: forget expensive serializations of big books. "Helen was so smart. We didn't need to be competitive. She realized that first serial didn't mean anything to middle America. You could pick up a second serial within a month for $500, maybe $2,500 for something big. She saved a fortune that way." Publishers were so eager to get their books into the magazine that Sargent needed more highly qualified young women to help to scout and edit: "I used to hire these brilliant girls from Harvard, Yale, Princeton, really the smartest women in town who went on to extraordinary careers."

Sargent's thrifty and timely editorial encouraged pass-along readership. Advertisers liked the page proximity. Perhaps Dick Deems was right after all; Helen should just stay behind her desk. She was not helping herself or the magazine with her latest press. And she was looking a bit like her readers' Auntie Mame. Helen was sixty-seven, twice as old as the upper age of her magazine's demographic. Was she still, as her fervent admirer Irving Berlin had written, "a girl who really knows her onions"?

31

A Sort of Crisis

It's not true that the rest of life is the best of life. You've outlived your
doctors and maybe a wife or two—even a child. You ache, you stag-
ger, you repeat yourself and even you can't remember what you said.
—David Brown, *Brown's Guide to the Good Life*

IN OCTOBER 1993, David Brown was on location in Canada, producing
Canadian Bacon, a comedy directed by the documentarian Michael
Moore. Its cast included Alan Alda, Rhea Perlman, and John Candy.
David Brown and Kit Golden were on their way toward a string of suc-
cesses over the next decade: *Chocolat*, *Angela's Ashes*, *Driving Miss
Daisy*, and *A Few Good Men*. But at the moment, David had chosen to
oversee mundane preproduction details on *Bacon* for a few weeks in
the chilly Canadian fall.

Filming had just begun when he got a call he had long been expecting from his executive assistant, Doris Wood, in New York. She was
deeply upset by the message she had to deliver. Close to his fiftieth birthday, which would have been October 4, Bruce LeGacy Brown had died
in Philadelphia. The cause of death, according to two of the people
closest to David Brown at the time, was AIDS, believed to have been
contracted from intravenous drug use.

Bruce was long divorced from Kathy, who had remarried. Acquaintances of Bruce had heard that he had been dealing drugs as well as

using them. Whatever his son had been up to during the years before his death, David had paid for treatment and caregivers during his illness. Checks were mailed from his production office by Doris Wood and sometimes by Kit Golden. Alex Birnbaum also knew of Bruce's diagnosis, and confirmed that his death was from AIDS related to intravenous drug use. How long had David and Helen known? There is only one potential clue, in Helen's book *The Late Show*. She wrote, "I weighed 105 for years, carefully maintained, but in the summer of 1989 I went from 105 to 95 in just ten days. A sort of crisis made me just not hungry . . . Then my hair fell out."

What worse crisis might there be than a death sentence for her husband's beloved son, stricken with a disease that, in those days of misinformation and fear, had caused Helen Gurley Brown to commit the most public and irresponsible blunder of her professional life? What a fathomless and isolating grief it must have been for David Brown. This was a man who had wept for days at the loss of his collie. Bruce's end had clearly been a death foretold for some time, and by then, his father had to know how agonizing it could be. The torments of an AIDS-related death were well documented; less than two months after Bruce Brown's death, the sheer hell of it would reach the big screen in Jonathan Demme's *Philadelphia*, with Tom Hanks as a dying lawyer and Antonio Banderas as his lover. Why was Bruce Brown in Philadelphia? Who was with him when he died? It is unknown whether David Brown saw his son between his diagnosis and death. Alex Birnbaum said she did not know, but that "they were long estranged."

For David, bearing the loss of his only child while on the set of a third-rate comedy production must have been ghastly. But it is just as conceivable that, as Bruce's condition worsened, exile in the north was his father's chosen, if bleak, way to distance himself from the inevitable. Just who saw to his son's remains and their final disposition is unknown. The film David had been working on was also ill-fated; John Candy did not live to see *Canadian Bacon*'s release and critical drubbing in 1994. He died of a presumed heart attack in March 1994 at age forty-three while shooting his next movie in Mexico. *Canadian Bacon* grossed just $178,104 in U.S. box office sales, hardly justifying its $11 million budget.

Helen did not speak of her stepson's death publicly or to any friends except perhaps Charlotte Kelly Veal, married by then to the Prudential insurance executive Speed Veal; the two couples were close. With the exception of Bruce Brown's college roommate Marc Haefele, who had been in touch with Bruce's former brother-in-law, no one interviewed about Bruce Brown, including some of his New York friends and associates at the radio station WBAI, knew the date or cause of his death; no one saw an obituary or heard of a memorial service. Even the record of Bruce Brown's death was difficult to access in the Social Security death registry. Someone had entered his name as merely B. Brown. Birth, marriage, and divorce records were not retrievable for Bruce LeGacy Brown in any online database; a search done by a broadcast news organization with more powerful engines than commercial genealogy sites also turned up nothing.

Besides a smart, scholarly book he published in 1973 on Marxism—reprinted in 2009—the only traces of Bruce Brown are the brief epitaphs in two of his father's books: "The birth of my first and only son, Bruce, nine pounds of beautiful baby born in Lying In Hospital—inconceivable that he would succumb to drugs decades later. My love for him never dies." (This was added to the 2003 paperback edition of David's 1990 memoir.) And this: "Not having children pains me now but pleased me in my carefree earlier years. My son, whom I lost (to drugs). He is a love I never replaced." David repeated one phrase that friends found somewhat puzzling: "My son was a victim of the war on drugs." This might hint at a conviction; the term "war on drugs" implied a renewed enforcement and conviction policy dating back to the Nixon years.

Michael Korda, who worked with both Helen and Jacqueline Susann, sees a parallel in the way the Browns and the Mansfields held their sadness close. "I did know that David had a son. I seem to remember hearing that he was a drug user. This [secrecy] is not an uncommon thing. Jackie Susann and Irving Mansfield, whom I knew much better than I knew Helen, had a son. In all the publicity and everything about her, you would never have known it. I guess I only know it because her publicist was a friend of mine."

In the aftermath of her son Carter's suicide in the summer of 1988, Gloria Vanderbilt spoke of it publicly and wrote a book, *A Mother's Story*, a decade later. But shared grief is not for everyone, Vanderbilt said. "There's a side to David and to Helen that was absolutely closed off to the world, which I think was probably sensible. One of the reasons they stayed together for such a long time so successfully is that they managed to invent for themselves, somehow, a private life."

32 🐚

The Politburo Must Fall

Someone asked me this week if the Hearst Corporation was looking
to ease Helen Gurley Brown out. This rumor surfaces over and over
when someone reaches seventy. In America they immediately hire a
guy to follow you around with a shovel in case you die and they need
to pat you in the face.
—Liz Smith, at a "roast" of HGB

IT FINALLY HAPPENED: some pretty young woman offered Helen a seat
on the M10 bus. She muttered something about getting off soon, thank
you, dear, and scuttled toward the crowded front; Helen was not getting off yet, but she'd hide amid the trench coats until her stop rather
than accept the seat and the truth: goddamn it, she was *old*. At seventy-
one, she finally made herself say it out loud, sort of, in her book of
advice aimed at women over fifty. Helen dedicated *The Late Show* to
Dr. Janet A. Kelly, the therapist that Faith Stewart-Gordon had found
for her when Helen just couldn't shake her depression over aging.
Dr. Kelly, who was a few years older than Helen, had let her weep for a
few sessions, silently handing over Kleenex. Helen wrote: "Shrink listened, said I reminded her of Scarlett O'Hara, stomping her feet and
shrieking, 'But Ashley loves *me*, he will *not* marry Melanie!'" She
snapped out of it and wrote a book about the wrinkles and the wrath as
yet another form of therapy. It made the bestseller list for a short time;
there were plenty of women who had faced down that "ma'am, would

you like a seat" moment. And yes they did want to know about vaginal lubricants, sex after seventy, and fighting the "sads."

The rest of the nineties were to be very trying for Helen, professionally and personally, fraught with anxiety and more loss, but never without some bracing gobs of fun. Take Moscow. How Helen had needed it then, embracing, amazing, rejuvenating *Moscow*! Really, it was too astonishing. The May 1994 launch of a brand-new edition of *Cosmo* there was uproarious, divine, insanely successful! Helen was mobbed, photographed, loved to *pieces*. The networks were there to cover the American incursion: BBC, ABC, CNN, NBC, CBS. And once again, the media attention was all positive.

Helen and David arrived at the launch party in a blaze of media heat lightning. She stood out in her flaming red suit. Many of the business-type guests wore black formal attire; some were accessorized with bling and bodyguards. And what a party. Helen had insisted upon dancing. Pity the scarlet-faced young Russian dragooned into partnering Mrs. Brown as she executed a wild form of elder boogaloo. Helen wrote to Liz Smith, "1,400 people turned out for our press conference—of course they haven't much to do in Moscow at night! They really seem ready for this magazine . . . Moscow is like a *boomtown*. I really never got so excited about a launch before . . ."

Since the Soviet Union flag had been lowered on Christmas Day 1991, things had been rather dreary. For the previous two decades, the only periodicals for Soviet women were drab if earnest stalwarts such as *Krestyanka* and *Rabonitsa*, which translated, respectively, as "Peasant Woman" and "Factory Worker Lady." But in May 1994, the pink joys of a new international edition of *Cosmo* bloomed in street and train station kiosks. Cindy Crawford was on the cover.

The audacious bit of media détente, with a business plan that would set the template for *Cosmo*'s global domination, had been the brainchild of George Green, the first president and CEO of the newly created Hearst Magazines International (HMI). In 1993, Green had gone to Moscow on a reconnaissance trip. Hearst had been trying, through its news division, to copublish a newspaper there with the once mighty Soviet paper *Izvestia*. It was disastrous. Corruption and virtually unchecked organized crime had tanked the project. Green noticed that at any meeting with Russian investors, everyone was seriously if discreetly armed.

Disheartened, Green went for a long walk around Moscow. He recalled, "I went into food stores, I went into beauty stores, I went into department stores. I wasn't sure what I'm looking for . . . Then I noticed that every single cosmetics brand in the world was there, but there was no way for any one of those cosmetic brands to distinguish itself . . . nowhere for them to advertise; there was no promotion. There were pamphlets put out by the Women's Workers' Party, but no magazines. And I said to myself, 'I've got a business.' "

With Helen's supervision on editorial and a pair of Russian coeditors, Green got *Cosmo* up and running in Moscow within the year. Despite some serious challenges, the first issue carried forty pages of ads and sold sixty thousand copies. Most of the articles were written by Russian women; the general tenor was upbeat, post-babushka, and, by Russian standards, cheerily disruptive. One article asked, "Are Husbands Necessary?" The text took issue with a rigid cultural given: any unmarried woman over thirty was an old maid. *Nyet*! Now these women were fun-loving, independent *singles*. In fact, the Russian *Cosmo* girl was in her twenties or thirties and urban (mainly in St. Petersburg and Moscow), had a job in one of the newer post-Communist businesses or with a foreign company, and made a comparatively high salary of two hundred dollars a month.

David, a devoted reader of *The Economist*, had turned up another astonishment about *Cosmo*'s new market that deeply interested Helen. An *Economist* article reported an odd situation in women's reproductive health. Due to the lack of available alternatives, abortion had been the commonest method of birth control; in 1989, 10 percent of Russian women of child-bearing age had had an abortion. By the time *Cosmo* arrived, that figure was halved with the increased availability of contraception methods, generally for those living close to Moscow. But better and more available contraception was still an issue that Helen might champion, albeit carefully.

The Russian circulation was minuscule by Helen's stateside standards, but it augured great things; Hearst made back its initial investment on the first issue. Russian *Cosmopolitan* would eventually become the bestselling women's magazine in Europe, publishing more than a million copies of each issue. Green was jubilant: "This was as good an investment as I will have ever made, or expect to make, for Hearst." He was wrong only in underestimating the functionality of his business model, which relied on local partnerships in future foreign editions; the returns would prove staggering.

The international ad/editorial partnerships had been strengthened by none other than the former *Cosmo* editor Jeanette Sarkisian Wagner. By then Wagner was an executive at Estée Lauder. Impressed with her ability to expand the *Cosmo* brand beyond U.S. borders, Leonard Lauder hired her to help do the same for his products. "He was looking for somebody who could take a basically U.S. concept and make it global without destroying the DNA of the original concept. And I had already done that for *Cosmo*." Of course, Wagner placed plenty of Lauder ads in all those new *Cosmo*s. Helen's baby colossus was still "all loving hands at home."

George Green had stumbled upon the hunger for American imports that seized many post-Communist republics. But with *Cosmo*, there was a deeper motivator than the global carbo-creep of McDonald's and KFC. The women's imperatives—"*I beg you not to settle*"—that Helen had begun tapping into in 1962 were awakening in former Communist bloc and underdeveloped nations worldwide, among the rich Saudi women wearing La Perla lingerie beneath their chadors, the Bollywood fangirls in Mumbai dreaming past arranged marriages to true love. This could be a wave as powerful as the booming, newly independent female workforce had been for the earlier *Cosmo*. Much of the appeal was commercial as well. A new class of wealthy consumers was emerging along the Pacific Rim, in central Asia, the newly democratic Soviet republics, the postcolonial African nations. Readers were hungry for the name-brand consumer goods advertised in Western-style magazines. Once again, *Cosmo* was in the catbird seat—and in the kiosks off Red Square.

Back in the office, Helen got on with business as usual. She had a growing sense that her tenure was nearing its end. But she did make time to
deal with the escalating problems of a dear friend in need. Charlotte
Veal's husband, Speed, had been diagnosed with Parkinson's disease and
it was progressing swiftly. He could no longer walk or feed himself and
was in and out of a veterans' hospital. The Browns had helped with
paying some dental bills, and David had wanted to contribute to more
caregivers at their apartment to give Charlotte a break. She wouldn't
allow it. The Veals' friend Robin LoGuidice said that Charlotte had
been arranging regular schedules of visitors and lunch dates to ease her
husband's isolation. "Helen came on a regular basis and sat by his
side. She wasn't an outwardly affectionate person, but she was so loyal.
Speed would joke, 'Yeah, Helen came by. She brought a lettuce leaf.'"

There was nothing Helen could do when a second big blow rocked
her friend's life. In her late fifties, as Speed was nearly incapacitated,
Veal was fired by Hearst after nine years. "She was running all of Hearst
magazines' PR," said LoGuidice. "She was traveling for the job. When
she came back they had cleaned out her office." Another, younger
woman had Veal's desk and title when she returned from her trip. Veal
was told to leave immediately; no settlement was offered. "They [Hearst]
weren't going to do anything for Carlotta. She had to get a lawyer. She
got a severance and a pension—not what she deserved, but she got it."

Charlotte Veal was well-known in the industry. The *Ms.* magazine
editors Gloria Steinem and Pat Carbine hired Charlotte almost at
once to work on special projects there. Speed Veal was worsening and
would not last much longer. Charlotte would need a full-time job to
support them both. Over nearly nine years, Speed's illness and care
had taken its toll on her in worry lines and weight gain. It took ten
months, but Charlotte managed to lose forty pounds. "The body was
in shape," she said, "but I had the wrinkles of a shar-pei puppy."
Who'd hire her?

Helen got her a face-lift, gratis. She swapped it, even-up, for an ar-
ticle on the surgeon's practice in *Cosmo*. She guaranteed, in a letter to
Dr. Helen Colen, that "your article, 'Change Your Face, Change Your
Life,' will run in the October 1994 issue of *Cosmopolitan* . . . As you

know, I am fervently pushing for the surgery date for my friend . . ." The results were glorious. What's a girlfriend for?

Not long afterward, Helen reconsidered her long avoidance of breast augmentation surgery. She had given up stuffing her bras, as she explained in *The Late Show*. "I quit that and just went with small and cute and fuck you, these are my tits, and I got used to going braless and weightless and it hasn't been bad." At seventy-three, two years after she wrote those words, she got herself a pair. David was not happy about it. He said he had always loved her small breasts. A few years earlier, he had lost it completely when he arrived home to find her swollen beyond recognition and in agony after a facial procedure and burst out, "Jesus, the things you do to yourself—the self-inflicted pain!" Helen kept a sexy can of her preferred emollient, Crisco, on her nightstand to rub into her surgical scars. She also swore that Proctor & Gamble's canned vegetable fat was miraculous at keeping away age spots on her hands.

Helen was displaying her new frontage rather boldly on October 3, 1995, her former staffer John Searles recalled. Now a successful novelist, he said it was his first day on the job as an assistant in the book department, and his first close proximity to the boss, whom he came to adore in nine years on her staff. Everyone had trooped into Helen's office to hear the announcement of a verdict in the O. J. Simpson murder trial. She had the only TV in the place, a small, cheap model. Helen barely looked up; she was sitting behind her desk, working. "She had this miniskirt on, this plunging top to show off her new breasts," said Searles, "bangle bracelets up her arms, her hair all teased, lipstick, makeup. Everyone's staring at the TV and Helen was just working away and not even listening." There were gasps and shrieks when the verdict was announced. Helen looked up briefly, saw the stunned faces around the room, and bent her head back to work, no comment, barely a flicker of acknowledgment.

Increasingly, there were signs that Helen was preoccupied and stressed; might they really take it all away from her soon? The anger and anxiety management techniques that she had long employed— chiefly bending flatware during tedious event dinners—had helped calm her for many years. Bored to the boiling point, Helen would hold a spoon beneath the ballroom's starched napery and let her skinny fingers bend the damned thing—fully in half, David reported. Beneath the table, she would hand it to him as a signal: *I've had it, we're out of here!* Over the years, Helen's leavings had puzzled a legion of hotel busboys.

One Friday night after a long workday, the Browns were taking Alex Birnbaum to dinner at the Tea Room. "We had barely sat down and Helen said, 'I want that special salmon.' It was salmon coulibiac, so I said, 'Are you sure? It has hollandaise sauce.' She gave me an odd look. The waiter came, put the dishes down, and Helen said, 'That's not what I ordered.'" Birnbaum had no warning and no time to duck. Helen upturned her dish and flung it. The slithery, heavily sauced fish hit Birnbaum full frontal, from neck to sternum.

"Bring me grilled," Helen ordered the flabbergasted waiter, who made haste back to the kitchen. The ladies' room attendants took Birnbaum off to be sponged down with soda water. Beneath their ministrations she wondered: What to do? What to say? When she got back to the table, not a word was said by either Brown. "It really stunned me."

More often those days, a sudden anger overtook Helen, and she threw a few public tantrums. She wrote about some of them, for expiation, exorcism, or comic relief. Most involved airplanes. She created a stir on a long flight when she attempted to use the first-class aisle as an exercise mat. "I can't eat this shit!" she declared, upending a full, untouched tray of airline food when the flight attendants ran out of what she had ordered. Her most shocking episode of air rage: "I recently screamed at a baby on an airplane—a *baby*!—who had been screaming at *me* or *something* from Oklahoma City to LaGuardia . . . two hours and forty minutes of straight screaming and my nerves had had it. You never saw such shocked parents—or fellow passengers." By way of explanation Helen wrote, "I find that airports and airplanes are big scream launchers." Who would argue? But a baby?

On that flight, Helen had been on her way back from another distressing trip to Shawnee. George Alford had died a few years earlier. But for her housekeeper/caregiver and rescue cats, Mary was alone and in woeful condition. After more than sixty years in a wheelchair, she had breathing difficulties stemming from the damage the polio had done to her lungs and years of smoking. She was nearly blind, suffering from macular degeneration; it was still a desperate juggling act with caregivers. Helen had left Oklahoma with an unpleasant foreboding and her nerves on edge.

Stress, family or otherwise, could not explain Helen's arrest at the San Antonio airport on November 17, 1995. It was a pleasure trip; the Browns were attending the marriage of the Hearst executive Frank Bennack's daughter. There was a police report of the incident, listed as a "Disturbance" on Airport Boulevard. Helen had gone off to find a cab while David collected the luggage. After a bit, the police located him by walkie-talkie. It crackled, "We have a demented woman here." It seemed that Helen had leaped out of the cab, without paying, when it was clear the driver had to circle back to fetch David. Oblivious to airport traffic loops, she had become convinced he was cheating her. Two police cars pulled up, lights flashing, to stop the skinny little woman stomping dangerously in the Arrivals lanes. "That's my wife," owned Mr. Brown, who found her fulminating: they could put her in jail *the rest of her life* but she *would not pay.* Things were smoothed over, another cab found. Helen fed it to Liz Smith, police report and all, and urged her to have fun with it in her column.

In the Hearst executive suite, quiet discussions about her replacement had been under way for some time. The media speculation and internal Hearst scuttlebutt had been rising; there was rumor of a quiet *Cosmo* redesign being done at an outside firm. If nothing else, the magazine needed a face-lift. Helen's office, quipped one staffer, "looked like the inside of *I Dream of Jeannie*'s bottle"; the magazine pages were fussy and dated as well. The search for a youth infusion had actually begun back in the late 1980s. The Hearst executive Gil Maurer had invited Bonnie Fuller, then the editor of a Canadian fashion magazine, *Flare*, to have breakfast in Montreal. He told her that he would like her to meet Helen Gurley Brown. "He arranged a trip to New York for me to meet her," said Fuller. "I guess he thought there might be an opportunity for me to work for her. She just was so friendly, and warm, and wanting to know everything about me, and asked me a ton of questions. And she asked me at the end of our meeting if I would send her some story ideas."

Fuller sent her a hundred *Cosmo*-centric ideas; Helen shot back a laudatory note and suggested they stay in touch. "From then on, I was 'the girl with the hundred ideas.'" In the interim, Fuller moved to New York with her family for another opportunity. "I had a job offer to take over this magazine called *YM*. It had been a tween magazine and they wanted it to be a full-on teen magazine, to take on *Seventeen*. So I ended up going there [in 1989]. From time to time I would send Helen an issue and a note, to keep in touch. Helen was very warm and gracious whenever I would see her. I never thought that *Cosmo* would ever be in my future. Never crossed my mind."

Fuller was next approached by the president of Hearst's magazine division, Claeys Bahrenburg, about a new magazine the company was launching, the U.S. version of the French fashion book *Marie Claire*. Fuller soon became its editor in chief. Then Gil Maurer was at her door again, this time about the top job at *Cosmo*. "I was very complimented," said Fuller, "but I was conflicted because I really liked Helen and I also loved what I did. I wanted to know about how they were going to transition. I respected Helen and this wasn't something that I'd sought out. So, part of me was really uncomfortable about it. But Frank [Bennack] and Gil were people that I trusted. They really talked to me for a long time."

A takeover plan was soon in motion; it remained to force the issue with Helen. Frank Bennack, the Browns' very good friend, broke the news. It was time to go, but he wasn't telling her to leave the building. Fuller would be "deputy" editor until the full takeover; Helen would get two more years at full salary and, after that, a new job: editor in chief of the international editions. She would still have a place to go every day, and world travel; David could go along. It all seemed reasonable enough. The announcement was made on January 17, 1996; Helen's final issue would be the following February, then Fuller would officially take the reins.

Helen had held it together after Bennack left her office; later that day, she was scheduled for a TV show. HGB had never been a no-show. She wrote, "Probably the best interview I ever did was an hour with Charlie Rose on PBS just after the announcement . . . Somehow I was calm and quiet and said everything exactly the way I wanted it to be said." Not that Helen was downplaying the devastation: "What did it feel like being told I wouldn't be editor-in-chief of *Cosmo* anymore? . . . Gruesome! They had to tell me it was over . . . I would never have got around to telling them . . . I knew, at seventy-four, I was getting way too far out on the ledge (to put it mildly) to continue to be guru of an eighteen-to-thirty-four-year-old reader."

Friends of the Browns noticed a serious disturbance in the field. Shortly after the announcement, David and Helen were dining with the *New York Times* theater critic Frank Rich and his wife, the *Times* writer Alex Witchel. "We went to Le Bernardin," said Witchel. "Helen was really angry, and hurt, and she was not quite herself. She was always pretty much put together. But I remember that night, her hair was sort of dented in a funny way, she was generally askew in the way that she looked, and she was very upset. I said, 'Look, write about it.'"

Helen told Witchel that she just might, but she never did. They might fire her altogether.

It was her birthday a month after the "firing," as Helen referred to it privately. She felt lousy. She told Liz Smith that she was still reeling from an article *The Wall Street Journal* ran, declaring that she had been axed and outlining the long-simmering plans by Hearst to get rid of her. It mentioned the AIDS and sexual harassment disasters and bristled with nasty blind quotes, some allegedly from within Hearst. Helen was mortified. The girlfriends bore her up with a birthday lunch at Mortimer's, the A-list East Side clubhouse. Greeting Helen in the restaurant's front window was a giant mock-up of a *Cosmo* cover, screaming "Götterdämmeruung at Hearst!" and "Sex for Septuagenarians" and "It Ain't Broke Don't Fix It." There was a fudge brownie cake; Helen ate some, to hell with it all.

David Brown may have suffered most in the aftermath. At home, Helen persisted in reliving the Moment, ad infinitum. Finally, David told her, gently, "Helen, if you'll cut a tape, I'll promise to listen to it every night right after Larry King."

The dual transitioning was cordial but hardly smooth; Helen was still in her own office planning a boffo final issue. Fuller was still editing *Marie Claire* for a few more months and dashing down to a basement room Hearst provided in its old, castle-like building on Fifty-Seventh Street to build out her new *Cosmo*. Cathie Black, who had just taken over as head of all Hearst magazines, consulted with Helen. "I would see her as regularly as I would any of the other editors; the difference was that I would spend an equal amount of time with what Bonnie was developing along with her longtime creative director, Donald Robinson."

Fuller had brought a team of about half a dozen to the cramped bunker, where she and Robinson focused on a redesign. Atoosa Rubenstein, who had started in 1993 as a *Cosmo* fashion assistant just out of college, says Fuller's lab became known as "the pod." What sort of new *Cosmo* Girl were they hatching down there? As one of the youngest on staff, Rubenstein hoped they would bring the poor girl up to date. "The eighties were so feminine and coquettish and that was so perfect for *Cosmo*. Helen was *maximal*. But in the nineties, sexy was a subtler thing. Calvin Klein was very big, and it was almost androgynous. You still had to be sexy, but define the new sexy. The height of 'cool' at that moment was not sexy at all. It was very androgynous."

Veteran staffers were wary of the pod people. "It was a really awkward time," Rubenstein recalled. "It wasn't as much, 'poor Helen.' Everyone was looking for a new job. In the same way that Helen's covers were not very au courant, a lot of her staffers were also not very modern. There was a lot of fear from those people because they knew the jig was up." Rubenstein, who always had a good relationship with Helen, would land on her feet as editor in chief of the short-lived tween version, *Cosmo Girl*. When she got the job, Helen gifted her with a crumpled tissue; inside was a beautiful diamond "eternity" ring, one of Helen's own.

Finally, it was time for the big reveal. Cathie Black was all for it. "We all believed that the magazine needed a refresh for a more modern woman who was used to a different look. Bonnie put together a dummy, which was presented to Frank Bennack. Frank was a little surprised at the look of it. But Bonnie was really amazing, she just kind of stood up and said, 'We are talking 1996 to '97, and this is what it should look like.' And from day one it was very successful."

It was gratifying that ASME, the American Society of Magazine Editors, elected Helen to its editors' hall of fame that year, and so thoughtful of Hearst to present her with a newer model Mercedes. But nothing made it better, or even okay. Faith Stewart-Gordon had asked her advice about selling the Russian Tea Room at about the same time and Helen had jumped all over her: "Don't sell, Faith. When you lose your base in New York, nobody will remember you for five minutes."

Things got worse. Speed Veal died in May 1996. Helen was one of his eulogizers. Charlotte was devastated and still trying to find a full-time job. Helen soldiered on, preparing her *Cosmo* funeral barge, heavy with ads; the last issue was an extravaganza of high points and tributes in February 1997. She allowed herself a bit of bragging in her final editor's letter: out of 11,343 magazines published, according to the Magazine Publishers Association, *Cosmopolitan* was number six at the newsstand. "We have 29 international editions, Argentina and India the latest. Russia, launched two years ago, is a *wow*!" David, that darling man, had helped with *380 sets* of cover blurbs. Helen made it clear that she was not retiring, but headed to a new global post. "I'll give it a shot!"

Seven months later in that annus horribilis, Helen found herself aboard a jet for Oklahoma City, making her final trip to Shawnee. Mary Gurley Alford had died on September 17, 1997, two months shy of turning eighty. After a service at her church, Mary was buried beside Cleo in Osage. In July 1998, Helen was diagnosed with breast cancer. Thirteen days later, she had a lumpectomy, followed by six weeks of radiation and follow-up treatment with the drug Tamoxifen. She wrote to her surgeon, Dr. Patrick Borgen at Sloan Kettering: "I will never be able to tell you how grateful I am that you saved my bosom." He removed a small area; the implants were intact. Privately, Helen wondered about the cause of her disease; publicly, she absolved herself: "I also don't dwell on the possibility of having given *myself* cancer with the heavy dosage of Premarin for 33 years. Occasionally a doctor suggested taking less but nobody slugged me."

At the time, Helen told no one of her cancer, save David, her assistant Susie Schreibman, and three close girlfriends. Her reasoning: "At the office I wanted to be continued to be perceived as a healthy rat, despite my age; management, who pays me (well), must always be encouraged to feel they are getting a bargain, don't want them concerned with my vital signs."

The magazine industry was stunned when Bonnie Fuller exited *Cosmo* after just a year and a half to become the editor of *Glamour*. When she recovered from her own shock, Helen wished her well; she had never harbored any enmity toward her replacement, and her parting gift was a suggestion that Fuller have occasional lunches with David, who enjoyed giving career advice to young, smart women.

Fuller's successor, Kate White, had a deep résumé: editor at *Mademoiselle*, editor in chief of *Child*, *McCall's*, *Working Woman*, and *Redbook*. She would run *Cosmo* for fourteen years. While Helen would occasionally shoot her a cautionary note ("Are you a crazy girl or something?"), she had approved of White from the day she met her in the late eighties, when White came to interview her as a journalist. Helen told her, "I could so see you as editor of *Cosmo* one day." When White was working at *Mademoiselle*, Helen called her in for a bit of brainstorming. Even then, White said, Helen knew that she needed a younger eye. "She said, 'Look, I've got to stay fresh, and the magazine has to go through a refreshing.' I did put some ideas together for her, and she asked me to do a critique." Helen skimmed through it when they met, then said again, "'Kate, you could be the editor of this magazine one day. I'm not going anyplace anytime soon. But you could start to shape things up a bit' . . . So I'd had those couple of kind of prophetically weird moments with her."

When White did take over, she was surprised to feel some anti-*Cosmo* attitudes that persisted in some younger women. The quartet of career women on *Sex and the City* had far out-brazened the *Cosmo* girl. Yet White was getting signals that some still found her magazine to be sexually incorrect: "I remember trying to get Lena Dunham to write a piece before her show even started. We got a curt no. Well, if that show

[HBO's *Girls*] isn't about pleasing men . . . What's wrong with pleasing a guy?"

White felt that *Cosmo* was a bold disrupter in letting men know exactly what women wanted and exactly how to administer it. "When I took over it, you were the agent provocateur. You were expecting to have a man address your needs. In fact, at that point we had three million male readers and the number one reason they said they read the magazine was to find out how to please the women in their lives. I love pleasing my husband. I want my husband to feel really pleased by me. What's so bad about that?"

Helen's stash of four-leaf clovers hadn't done her much good personally, but she was still dispensing them, with a dollop of compassion. Over the years, she kept a soft spot for those who had suffered public castigation, as she had. The sales of Erica Jong's ribald novel *Fear of Flying* were robust—it has sold 27 million since 1973. But the slut-shaming backlash, some from women critics, was brutal. Helen's personal and extravagant embrace in the pages of *Cosmo* over the ensuing years made for a soothing antidote. "She understood," said Jong. "I was very, very young. She was older and nurturing. I was very wounded. I was a 4.0 [literature] student at Barnard. And then I published *Fear of Flying* and people decided I was the Happy Hooker of the literary world." HGB offered some lessons in perspective for Jong: "I thought I was going to triumph by quoting James Joyce—she knew it was all a matter of tits. Not all of life is about intelligence and good taste. Now I realize you have to be fierce to change people's minds. So I'm less a snob now and more a realist. Above all, Helen Gurley Brown was that."

Helen also defended the writer Joyce Maynard when she was pilloried for publishing a book about her May-December romance with J. D. Salinger. When Woody Allen created a furor by marrying his partner Mia Farrow's adopted daughter Soon Yi Previn, Helen gave the happy couple a dinner party. She wrote to both Patricia Hearst, whom she had known since childhood, and the Studio 54 owner Steve Rubell when they were in prison. She even sent a lucky clover to the PR woman Lizzie Grubman after she ran her SUV into a crowd in the Hamptons.

In the electronic media, Helen would pop up in familiar and down-right weird settings; she was a special favorite of the host Alexander Heffner on the long-running PBS show *The Open Mind*. Utterly surreal was her 1996 partnership with the comic Dave Chappelle on a BBC oddment called *Where's Elvis This Week?*, a quasi quiz show hosted by a young, dark-haired, leather-jacketed Jon Stewart. Helen and Chappelle were "debating" a British comic and the very perplexed-looking cultural critic Christopher Hitchens, whose facial expressions were priceless as he tried to take in the singular Mrs. Brown.

The Browns had circled the globe a few times; they had ballooned in Europe with Malcolm Forbes, had cruised through Polynesia, and were mad for Japan. They took an Amazon tour where all the guests were issued machetes. But they still had a bucket list. They wanted to go to Angkor Wat and Bali; Helen had been saving air miles. She also engaged in some more intimate exploration. At seventy-six, a time when an arthritic shoulder and creaky hips were beginning to get in the way of a limber tango swoon, she decided to hit the floor and have a close look at the body part that had caused her such tumult and pleasure in life, that mighty but unseen Motivator, her vagina. She had just read Eve Ensler's *The Vagina Monologues*, the feminist book and theater piece that was being performed in more foreign countries than Helen's magazine was being sold in. *The New York Times* called the stage version a "consciousness-raising global blockbuster."

"This is the craziest book I ever read!" Helen said. Yet it intrigued her. It should have been a bestseller, she thought. Why didn't more women know about it? She told Charlotte Veal, "Spurred on by this book, I decided to look at the area they're talking about." Helen explained that she had instructions, gleaned from the book: "You lie down with a mirror and a pillow under your fanny." The rest took dexterity, one hand to hold the mirror, the other to part the draperies. "It's impossible to see anything," Helen grumped to her friend. "You can't get the area opened up with one hand. I'm not recommending this procedure to you—just reporting."

Her conclusion: "The vagina is a closed circuit."

33 ⁓

"What the Hell, We're Off to Korea!"

Find out what you can still do, and enjoy it.
—HGB's advice for those over eighty

THE WOMAN COULD STILL TANGO—IN HEELS. Unknown to anyone but David and Charlotte Veal, who flatly refused to join her, Helen left her penthouse on Thursday nights and got herself to a church on the Upper East Side that ran a ballroom program called "Danse Elegante." So it wasn't the Mocambo. So some of the men had as much rhythm as a Maytag washer that's slipped its belt. But once a gentleman held out his hand and the evening began, the music was ageless and so were they. In cold weather, Helen swept into the drafty church hall in her favorite full-length lynx coat; she loved to startle friends when she put her hand in a pocket and the coat suddenly growled, *rwoooowrrr*. Kit Golden's husband, Tom Mangan, had given Helen a souvenir key chain honoring Penn State's Nittany Lions; it roared on command. Helen adored it. Just as she had named her cars, she christened her furs. The lynx was Jezebel. One day she called Mangan in distress: "Jezebel has lost her voice." He showed up with new batteries.

David and Helen had made it to Angkor Wat in 2000; he was eighty-four. They were still flying around launching *Cosmo* editions—the number reached forty-three during Helen's international stint. As Helen put it to a friend, "What the hell, we're off to Korea!" Into the new millennium, the Browns boarded jets and cruise ships, bouncing between left and right coasts, for work and for pleasure. They loved getting paid to talk about their careers on "author cruises" and set sail from Southampton on the *QEII* with the mystery writers P. D. James and Dick Francis. At home, they sat on their terrace at the Beresford and never tired of the glorious sunsets over the Hudson River; the sound track was Berlin and Gershwin classics, playing on one of David's many radios. They both took more pills than they wanted to and kept their freezer full of Lean Cuisine.

There were still occasional hops to Los Angeles, for awards events and the like, and Helen enjoyed revisiting their old haunts. She was surprised, in June 2001, when the journalist Margy Rochlin got in touch and asked whether Helen would fancy taking a tour of the bachelorette pads she wrote about in *Sex and the Single Girl*. Helen was game; she confessed to Rochlin that the trip hadn't been too terrific so far; Jackie Collins had snubbed her at a party. Imagine—after all those excerpts? In a Jeep piloted by an intern from her publication, *LA Weekly*, Rochlin picked Helen up at the hotel. HGB appeared in a short black dress, patterned stockings, and a cluster of pink rollers barely contained in a black-and-white polka-dot scarf that she had tied beneath her chin.

Consider the astonishment of the Latino family finding the vision that was Helen at their door in South-Central L.A.—the former gopher palace. "Please let me in! I used to live here." They finally opened the barred door to the strange, insistent old lady. The stuffy back room Helen had shared with Mary was so very tiny. Rochlin learned that Cleo and Leigh Bryan had slept right in the front room. Helen went out to the backyard. Rochlin wrote: "Standing in calf-high weeds on the hard-packed dirt, she surveys the nearby train tracks. It occurs to me that this might be the ground zero of man-trap feminism." They did the full tour, though they were unable to locate the "keptive" apartment where Helen had waited for the crass anti-Semite. "He got what he came for, which was my little body," she told Rochlin. "But I didn't get the money, and I didn't get him."

When there was no answer to her knock at the Browns' "married house" in Pacific Palisades, Helen, in high heels, startled her companions by bolting down the steep slope to peer in the windows. "It's fun," Helen said of her blast through the past, "but kind of weird." HGB wilted visibly on the way back to her hotel. Rochlin asked if something was bothering her. "I'm distressed because I don't have another idea for a book . . . Maybe I've run out of material."

This seemed to be the case. Helen had written another iteration of her Book again, and quite recently. This time she called it *I'm Wild Again*. Jamie Brickhouse, then a publicist for St. Martin's Press, fell madly for his author, but he just couldn't get her on TV much. Even the belles of the Richmond Junior League disinvited her from their author luncheon after reading the "keptive" part in her book. Liz Smith obliged with a column item about HGB being blackballed in Richmond. But it was a tough sell all around, Brickhouse found. "She wasn't the editor of *Cosmo* anymore, so the media wasn't calling her. *I'm Wild* is really her batty musings, it's read-out-loud-on-the-beach fun. If she had done some kind of tell-all, it might have sold. But she'd never do that."

Brickhouse was right about that disinclination to go deep. For decades, Helen had been writing the ultimate tell-all. But unlike the dashed-off autobiographical pages she shipped to the Smith archives, it was never intended for public view, nor did she let David know of it. The truest recounting of her improbable life had been kept in a spot that, during Helen's working life, seemed inviolable to her: the Hearst Building. Somewhere, unless they have been secreted in a new place or destroyed, there are two sheaves of personal papers, enough to fill two oversized manila envelopes. Within them lies the real, no-filter HGB.

Why did she set it all down? Compulsion? Self-analysis? Helen was addicted to talking to herself with a number-two pencil long before this oversharing Age of Memoir; she was the Samuel Pepys of the third grade, stuffing her scribblings into the compartments of her tiny roll-top desk. She kept her very adult papers under lock and key at various places in the building, moving them when events—such as ceding her office to Bonnie Fuller—made it prudent. Each time, Helen notified Charlotte Veal of the new location, with a crisp, rewritten letter. Only Helen's trusted assistant knew the location of the papers and had the key to the cabinet or drawer. That person, no longer in Hearst's employ and bound by a confidentiality agreement with the corporation—though not by Helen's stipulation—had precise directions. Upon Helen's death, only Charlotte Kelly Veal was to take possession of the papers, ASAP. This is how Helen put it to her friend: "The minute you hear I have konked out, please come to my office and present this letter and ask them to give you the envelopes."

According to Charlotte Veal's friend, attorney, and executor Robin LoGuidice, "The papers are a record of her affairs that she never wanted David to see. She was having affairs, but she liked to keep this front up, that she was flirtatious but never was unfaithful to him. The only person she could trust was Charlotte." At Helen's request, and as a friend, LoGuidice had done some research about securing the papers; a second attorney had suggested that they might be safer in some sort of trust. Helen would not hear of it.

If it were anyone else, any woman who hadn't encouraged extramarital affairs in her books and to her friends, who hadn't bedded married men with zero guilt, who hadn't slept with more men before marriage than a score of women of her generation might in two lifetimes, who hadn't admitted that she really missed single and "mistress" sex, it might be a surprise. But it should not be. This was Helen Gurley Brown, who declared that "sex is power." After her marriage, and for decades, she indulged in occasional flings that may have been as essential to her as the cosmetic rejuvenations.

HGB's flirty ways were well-known. Over the years, she did things that had people wondering. When the wealthy financier Pete Peterson, cofounder of the Blackstone Group, was newly divorced in 1979, he was baffled by a letter he received from Helen, ostensibly asking to meet him—privately—for financial advice. "It sounded like she wanted much more than that," he said. "I had never seen anything like it." He kept the crazy thing, and showed it to his subsequent wife, Joan Ganz Cooney, whom he married in 1980. Not long afterward, the couple began to see the Browns socially. Every now and then, Cooney thought of that outré letter. "It wasn't 'Dear Pete, I need a financial advisor.' It was very provocative, and quite long. It was the first time I wondered if she ever had affairs. It was so provocative that it caused one to think—did she really write this?"

To those who knew about her divertissements, Helen made it clear: they posed no threat to her marriage to the man she loved and depended upon. On plenty of occasions, she had burst into tears imagining a hundred ways that David might leave her. Yet she was not that careful. She confided in some friends and occasionally requested their complicity. Early on, Helen pressed Lyn Tornabene to act as a beard for her and a well-known actor. After his death, Helen put information intimating the relationship into her papers at Smith College, along with material about General Clifton. Simone Levitt, the wife of the Levittown builder Bill Levitt, recalled a talk with Helen aboard their yacht in Monaco: "They had their little affairs and they each knew it and accepted it. I don't know with whom, but I know she let me believe that these affairs didn't bother her because it gave her the freedom to do the same. I would say they were a happy couple, absolutely."

David Brown heard rumors about his wife. He wrote about one unsettling incident: He was dancing with a woman, a friend of theirs, who whispered that Helen and her husband had had an affair. She proposed a lunch, he wrote, "so we could discuss what to do about it. As politely as I could I extricated myself from both the dance and the lunch date. Years later I casually mentioned the incident to my wife but never asked whether what I had heard was true. Perhaps I didn't want to know. There are secrets even a husband and wife should not share."

There may be a simple reason for David's silent forbearance—with the flying plate of salmon, the airliner tantrums, and the whispers of infidelity—in his musings on Helen's fierce attachment to him. He needed and loved her, very much. "I'm married—my third marriage—to Helen Gurley Brown, who seems in all respects save carnal desire to be the reincarnation of my mother. Stick a pin in me and she jumps. If someone appears to hurt me she cries out. If I'm overweight or overwrought, she hustles me to a doctor or shrink. She is in all ways as totally attuned to me as my mother was. Is she my mother? . . . Has she been ordered into my life by the power of a mother's will? How could I be so important in the cosmic order of things? I often wonder."

Among Charlotte Veal's other close friends, it was an open secret; Helen borrowed her apartment from time to time and her requisites could be damned annoying. Helen being Helen, she would even dicker over the amount of small "honorarium" she placed on Veal's mantel when she left. At one point she halved it; Helen's excuse for cheaping out: "David doesn't have a job right now." The two women could get into some operatic tiffs, but LoGuidice said that Helen's faith was well-placed. Helen put her thanks in her epic poem to "Carlotta."

> *When I wanted to borrow her flat she gave*
> *And my secrets will go with her to the grave!*

But not quite. Helen could be a pill and Veal grumbled to a few of her friends about being marooned when Helen used the apartment. Yet, true to her pledge, said LoGuidice, "Charlotte never told me names." It was a sisterly pinkie-swear that went back to 1949. "They had hard, hard lives," said LoGuidice. "And they came up by hook or by crook. Charlotte would tell me that when they were young, they would have competitions about who would sleep with whom. They were wild and reckless."

What Veal knew above all was that Helen needed and adored her husband; the flings posed no danger, in Helen's mind, to a union destined to last until death. In this sort of thinking, she seemed to subscribe to another, almost Continental double standard—the discreet affair that never threatened a solid and sophisticated marriage, and might even enhance it. Helen clarified her philosophy on affairs in her final book: "Why *are* we (not me) so horrified that people cheat? I guess I don't know. Carrying on as though somebody sleeping with somebody, not your legal mate, is just this side of bombing churches . . . seems a little extreme to me . . . Doesn't anybody *get* it . . . adultery is about sex. Sex is about it *feels* good . . . *very* good."

For years, until well into the 2000s, Helen also maintained a correspondence with her tormentor Don Juan. Their communication was mainly one-sided and often not personal at all; he forwarded random, multiple-mailing bloviations to many friends and acquaintances. Helen often sent DJ's letters to Veal with comments of the "can you believe him?" sort. Besides one long, very personal letter to DJ about their romantic history that Helen included in her 2004 volume of correspondence, *Dear Pussycat*, she also included a few of his letters—one crassly speaks to their romantic past—in her archives at Smith. He is still living, in his late nineties, and will not be named here. It is clear from the correspondence that Helen never fell back into his arms, and had not seen him for decades. A photograph tucked into one of his letters shows a silver-haired popinjay in a three-piece white suit. She had *David*, she said to Charlotte. Whatever had she seen in *that* one?

Two years after Helen's experiment with the mirror and pillow, Eve Ensler, the author of *The Vagina Monologues*, arrived at Helen's office for one of a half-dozen interviews they did for *The Good Body*, Ensler's book in progress on women's body images. She found Helen on the floor, doing sit-ups. Ensler looked closely at Helen's face. There was something different, but she wasn't sure what it was. Ensler had been traveling, and before she left, Helen had promised her: no more procedures on her face. The two women, so different in age, lifestyle, and feminist politics, enjoyed talking to each other. Their conversations ranged way beyond Ensler's requisites for her book project. They talked a good deal about Cleo Gurley, and her indelibly wounding remarks about Helen's plainness. Ensler peered more closely at Helen's face.

"Helen? Your promise?"

"I just couldn't do it."

Helen began talking, between sit-ups. She was exercising every time Ensler showed up; HGB was still loath to give up the battle with her cursed "tummy pooch." What she said to Ensler between ab compressions amounts to an extraordinary burst of self-awareness.

Eve dear. Come in pussycat . . . Don't mind me, I'm multi-tasking . . . Eighty years old, one hundred sit-ups twice a day; I'm down to ninety pounds. Another ten years I'll be down to nothing. But even then I won't feel beautiful. I accept this terrible condition. It's driven me to be disciplined and successful.

Through Cosmo I've been able to help women everywhere. Well, almost everywhere.

Through Cosmo, I've been able to help everyone but me. Ironic. Come closer, Eve. I don't bite. Let's have a treat!

(Opening edamame.) *Edamame, my new favorite treat. It's food that isn't food. Energy. That's the closest I ever come to cooking. I never did get the nurture gene.*

My mother never saw me. She saw acne. She took me to the doctor twice a week for five years. He opened, postuled [sic] and squeezed my face. He left it battered. He would keep an X-ray machine on my face, five minutes at a time. He burned the bottom layer off my face. After the appointments, we would drive around, my mother and I. She would cry, I would cry. "How can I be a happy person, Helen?" she would say. "Your sister is in a wheelchair with polio. Your father is dead. And you, Helen, have acne . . ."

(Doing sit-ups again.) *Don't get things fixed, Eve. Don't do it.* (Stops sit-ups.) *If you do, another thing always breaks down. I had my eyes done at forty. I thought that would do. But no. Tried it again when I was fifty-six. First full face-lift at sixty-three. Second at sixty-seven. Third at seventy-three. I'm desperate for another, but there's no skin left on my face. Yesterday they took some fat out of my backside and they shot it into my cheeks.*

So that was it. Fat injections. Ensler thought of the needles and the pain.

I think even you would approve, Eve. I am recycling. My shrink says I'm doing this for my mother, Cleo's gone almost twenty years. Can you imagine I'm doing this for her? I never had a daughter but, if I did, I would tell her she's beautiful and lovely every minute . . . Eve, I would have to practice this. One thing I never had to practice was sex. I took to it like a duck to water. It's been a good week. My husband and I had sex two days in a row. Not bad for eighty. He's feisty, always has been. The crazy thing is he's always thought I was beautiful, but of course that doesn't count, I mean he loves me.

In November 2004, when Ensler performed a version of that mono-logue as HGB onstage at the Booth Theatre in New York, Helen and David Brown were in the audience. They went backstage after the cur-tain. Helen made a beeline for Ensler.

"You got me!" she said.

She was smiling broadly; David said he loved it. By God, he still loved *her*, through all the craziness and countless cans of Crisco rubbed into so very many surgical scars. Ensler said, "Afterwards she wrote me a note that said I had honored her and told the truth." Maybe it would help somebody.

Ensler has had more than a decade to think about her conversations with Helen. She never expected to become so very fond of her. All along, Ensler got the feeling that a lot of Helen's image issues came down to . . . Cleo. "That woman!" said Ensler. "The stories just got me so angry, and so sad for Helen. She talked about her father, too, what a misogynist he was. But really, I think a lot of the scarring was as much from her mother withholding that approval as from the acne itself."

The dreaded things, the "old people" catastrophes, began deviling David, and at first Helen tried to make light of it. The first mishap, in 2005, was kind of funny. They were at home, unpacking from a trip to Paris. "He was trying not to drop a bottle of scotch somebody gave us," Helen wrote to Liz Smith, "a quart not a fifth and god forbid I would leave it in the hotel room . . . Well, instead of dropping the scotch he fell over and broke his hip!" There was nothing amusing about the second broken hip, the following year. His kidneys were not in great shape.

They muddled along, and every May, as she had for over a decade, Helen phoned a "young" man, now sixty-plus, David Patrick Colum-bia: "Pussycat, can we count on you for Thanksgiving?" Months ahead of time, it was reassuring to hear his "Yes, of course." At last, David and Helen had a family for the holiday. To make a fourth, it had always been Alice Mason or Charlotte Veal. Mr. Brown still commanded one of the best tables in the Pool Room at the Four Seasons, and treated his guests to a whole turkey, full trimmings. The restaurant's co-owner Julian

Niccolini said the staff always liked to see them coming. "They were very nice, normal people. Sweet. David would tip up to a hundred percent on a check." With Helen, it was the notes. "My God, the notes, it was too much. I still have some of them. Hundreds over the years!" They fluttered in after every business lunch, and yes, after every turkey.

Columbia says he never understood why they chose him, a Manhattan columnist who founded, edits, and writes the online A-list chronicle *New York Social Diary*. Though *The New York Times* has called him "Boswell to the Bluebloods," Columbia's pedigree was as modest as Helen's. He grew up in a small town in Massachusetts, the son of a factory worker. He recalls first meeting the Browns at a lunch with Alice Mason. Columbia began having lunches with David; the holiday meals became a standing date. For their last few Thanksgivings, Columbia walked or helped wheel Helen and David through the Pool Room. Often, he would walk Charlotte Veal home afterward and hear her tales of the wild old days with Helen.

Having survived gales of Category 5 air kisses, having observed and documented the ways of *le tout* Manhattan, Columbia found the Browns to be the real deal. They saw and enjoyed their own set of "nobodies," just as they relished the private life they maintained for themselves. "They were the most *couple* couple I've ever known, because they were always together," said Columbia. "They were a single act. Helen and David were not intellectuals at all. They had the common touch. They never lost that ordinariness. That's what made them so attractive to people. Helen was *ordinary*. That was her strength, her money in the bank—she never lost that."

34

The Long Goodbye

please don't die
I won't if you won't
we're going to take little baby naps—his and hers
little baby bear catnaps
—scrap of poetry by HGB

ON FEBRUARY 1, 2010, the morning of David Brown's last day on earth, Helen went to work. It was a Monday; her darling driver, Michael, would be waiting to take her to midtown. What else was there to do? She was not making David's breakfast anymore, or marching him to the bathroom scale. He could not walk; Helen herself could barely get around but she carried on the only way she knew how.

She had gone off to work five days a week for seventy-one years. By then, "work" meant being gently bundled into the silver Mercedes for the familiar ten-minute ride, whisked into an elevator, and wheeled to a room on the thirty-seventh floor of the gleaming Hearst Tower that had been fitted out as a cozy but nonfunctional replica of the office where she had been her most vibrant and commanding self. The frilly faux office was a comforting sanctuary in an increasingly alien world. Her assistant, Susie, helped her into the office, settled her in, and closed the door. Mainly, Helen napped. Once in a while she would be wheeled down to the gleaming new cafeteria and helped into a chair. It's a safe bet that she had tuna fish.

Occasionally, she would lunch with old friends and colleagues there. The editors Sally Richardson and Elizabeth Beier, who had published Helen's last two books at St. Martin's Press, were saddened by her apparent loss of memory, but pleased to see that she still had a few canny coping strategies. She fished for memory aids to remember who she was lunching with: "Have you two got business cards? I'm afraid I've misplaced all of mine." She looked quite different. By her lifelong standards, Helen Gurley Brown was plump; about thirty pounds over her steady 105, largely the result, Alex Birnbaum said, of the sweets Helen had long forbidden herself. David did tease her about it. The Browns' caregivers took to hiding the cookies.

Knowing that David was near the end, Birnbaum made regular visits to the Beresford. For the last six to nine months of David's life, he spent his days in his home office/library, where a hospital bed had been set up. "I would go over every Sunday and spend time," said Birnbaum. "By then he was on dialysis but his mind was absolutely clear. Helen's was not at that point. Whether David recognized it or not I don't know."

David Brown was ninety-three; his kidneys had all but failed. Home dialysis had been arranged. His production partner, Kit Golden, went to the Beresford on weekdays to talk of work when he was able, or just to visit and reminisce. She often brought her little daughter, Callie. By late January, it became apparent that the end was near. Golden witnessed what she felt to be a turning point. "I remember being there the day before he passed away, and he was doing this." She made a pointing and tugging motion with her hand. "Like he was trying to get the IV out. And I remember coming home and saying to [her husband] Tom, 'He's ready.'"

Helen had been sleeping on a sofa beside his hospital bed, but that night she fell asleep upstairs in the big canopy bed. Navigating the apartment's many stairs had become problematic. At 3:45 a.m., David's nurse called upstairs to Helen's caregiver; she knew the end was near and Helen made her way down to say goodbye.

When Alex Birnbaum telephoned *The New York Times* to announce the death, she did not tell the obituary writer, Bruce Weber, that David Brown had a son who predeceased him. "I wouldn't have said anything about it because David wouldn't have said anything. Also, I don't think Helen would have liked it." There was little point to raising questions about a subject so painful—not while Helen was alive. Weber said that even if she had given him the information, the paper had no firm policy on requiring the inclusion of predeceased offspring. Bruce Brown was buried a second time.

Birnbaum was in deep grief herself; she had known and adored David since she was eight years old. They shared a birthday and celebrated nearly every one together. She would continue her weekly visits to Helen for as long as she lived. On the morning of David's memorial service, Birnbaum went to the *Cosmo* offices at Hearst, where the new widow was receiving tender mercies from members of the editorial staff. "They were getting her all jacked up, the fashion department and everyone. They were so sweet in getting her together. Because by that time, she was not obese but she was about thirty pounds overweight."

Birnbaum said that Helen seemed dazed, but cognizant of the awful ritual she faced. David's service was held at Frank E. Campbell, the Funeral Chapel, the last stop for Manhattan's mighty and wealthiest. Kit Golden sat beside the widow, who would turn eighty-eight in two weeks. Steven Spielberg, who had flown in for the service, sat on her other side. "Helen was very quiet," Golden said.

The first person to speak was Richard Zanuck, who choked up when he recalled his last, one-sided conversation with David the week before; someone had held the phone to David's ear and the man Zanuck had spoken to every day for forty years whispered, "See you."

Zanuck recovered himself with a few David-isms:

Work yourself to death; it's the only way to live.
*For years I've been known as Helen Gurley Brown's husband and I've
    loved it.*

Liz Smith does not think that Helen had quite processed the enormity of her loss. "I spoke with Helen at the funeral. I don't think it much registered. I called her the next day to check on her and she said, 'Oh, Lizzie, did you know that my husband has died?'"

It was a traumatic break, and following David's death, she began a precipitous decline. After a while, life went on in the "workplace," with Helen shuttled between home tower and office tower, and various doctors' appointments. Given Hearst's well-managed cocoon, it is difficult to imagine how Scott Spears, interviewer with WMRN in Ohio, managed to get Helen on the line for a radio chat. Spears said that he just called the switchboard, got Helen's assistant, and it happened quickly and directly, without Hearst brass or PR types being involved. It was done by phone from her office.

Helen's voice, always so distinct on the air, had slipped into a quavering near-whisper. The pauses were long and awkward. Spears wanted to know how she had "gotten over" her husband's death. After a moment, Helen answered, "Well, I haven't coped too well as a matter of fact, because we were so . . . together. And every day of my working life we would go home together. And sit in the den and watch television and he would think, and do whatever he did, and I would work. We were just so . . . *close*. I can't stand it that he's gone."

How had she dealt with it?

"Well, I come to work every day."

There is no question that Helen's Hearst friends and minders saw to all of her needs with care and kindness. But there were some puzzling disconnects; Helen, the longtime cat lover, was presented with a puppy, which she refused to accept. Some visitors, old and close friends, were turned away in the lobby of the Beresford, per instructions given to caregivers. A list posted in the kitchen detailed who was admissible.

It was not possible to determine when the two girlfriends, Helen and her Carlotta, last looked upon each other's face and had a final giggle. Having suffered a bad fall and other health problems, Veal had not been able to attend David's memorial service. She managed to get herself to the Beresford to visit Helen but was turned away. For many years, she had the key to the Browns' penthouse; when they were away, she moved in and fed the cats. "She was told she could not come over without an appointment," said Robin LoGuidice. "And Helen had invited her over. Charlotte was absolutely devastated." The two friends kept trying; Helen had one willing caregiver who would dial Charlotte for her, but they began having difficulty communicating on the phone. Neither friend had planned for this awful contingency: Charlotte Veal was slipping into dementia as well and would be unable to carry out her custodial pledge for Helen's papers.

Helen didn't go out much beyond the office, but she did get up to Columbia University in early August 2012 to see Nicholas Lemann, then dean of the Columbia Graduate School of Journalism. She was in a wheelchair. With them was Helen's executor and then general counsel for Hearst, Eve Burton; she is also president of Helen's Pussycat Foundation, which is distributing all of the Browns' wealth—more than $170 million—to educational institutions and charities. Lemann was showing Helen the plans for the largest bequest thus far, $30 million for the Brown Institute for Media Innovation at Columbia. "Helen's idea was that, since David had gone to Stanford as an undergraduate and then to Columbia Journalism School, she wanted to put together a gift that would bring together his two alma maters," said Lemann. "We ended up with a partnership between us [Columbia] and Stanford Engineering School, particularly the computer science department. We created a dual degree program, between computer science and journalism at Columbia."

Helen seemed pleased with the architectural plans he showed her, Lemann said, though she was adamant that some existing bars come off windows on the building to house the new institute. But she was not a brick-and-mortar donor at heart; subsequent bequests have gone to "Magic Grants"—Lemann said that Helen insisted on the term—for tuition to students in need, plus $15 million to the New York Public Library to fund a literacy program in the Bronx and Manhattan and $7.5 million to a program for the Browns' neighbor across the street, the American Museum of Natural History; teenage girls interested in the sciences learn computer coding there. The girls in the tuition-free classes are Brown Scholars.

On August 8, a few days after her visit to Columbia, Helen went to her office for the last time. Alex Birnbaum got the call from a Hearst employee; Helen had died at New York–Presbyterian/Columbia hospital on August 13. This time it was a corporate representative phoning *The New York Times* to announce the death; no cause was given. The obituary writer, Margalit Fox, could not resist a parting shot right in the opening paragraph: "She was 90, though parts of her were considerably younger."

The Hearst send-off for Helen in October was a pink and leopard extravaganza held at Alice Tully Hall in Lincoln Center. It was fizzy, showbizzy, bedecked with long-stemmed former *Cosmo* models, a song from Matthew Broderick, a tribute from the then mayor, Michael Bloomberg, film clips of some iconic "Little Girl from Little Rock" moments in *Gentlemen Prefer Blondes*. Helen would have loved it. Her friends were there, and some of them spoke from the big stage. Their quieter elegies follow . . . a girls' "den night," as Helen would say.

35 🐦

The Women: Can We Talk?

A best girlfriend is like Mentholatum . . . inexpensive, nobody is trying to get it (her) away from you, soothing on nearly all occasions.
—HGB, *I'm Wild Again*

Helen's whole life is this monument to artifice, yet her friendship
is very real.
—Liz Smith

NO MATTER THEIR VINTAGE OR HERS, Helen always called them girlfriends. Some of them were just that; she was in third grade when she
first met one special playmate in Little Rock who stayed in her life for
the next seventy years. Many friends from Helen's New York period are
women of accomplishment and of privilege; there are also some stalwart "unknowns" among her most adored. Helen's girl group was an
ever-shifting configuration, not of loyalties but of availability, circumstances, datebooks, and PDAs—this was boldface, A-list *Manhattan*,
pussycat, where Park Avenue falls dark as the innermost courtyards of
a souk during the summer months, where in the autumn, shiny obsid-
ian Navigators and Mercedes migrate in knowing herds to the right
places on the right nights. More privately, Helen's women friends met
in pairs and trios over a cozy lunch; they picked at Dover sole and
Cobb salads at Le Cirque and Michael's and spooned the livid magenta
borscht at the Russian Tea Room. Of course, Helen didn't eat. Talk was
the essential nutrient.

Singly, the women recalled their relationships with Helen, and doing so, they laughed a good deal. A few got teary. They were unanimous on this: once she faded from them, life was a little less fun.

GLORIA VANDERBILT, ON LOVE, SEX, ANOREXIA, AND LOSS
"We always went to Michael's. That's where she always wanted to go. She'd order nothing." A laugh. "She just had no idea how thin she was. I think when you're anorexic you never think you're thin enough. You look in the mirror and what you see is not that person. I thought she was just painfully thin."

Almost always, it was just the two of them.

"I liked David, I respected him, and I was thrilled to see this wonderful couple because it's very rare to see that. But he didn't interest me. Helen was my friend. My focus was all on her and we always had so much to talk about that there wasn't room for anything else. She talked about men she'd been involved with. She was almost like Pamela Harriman, a great kind of courtesan who really knew how to make men feel great. I trusted her and she trusted me. We mostly talked about men and sex." Big laugh. "We never got into graphic discussions, nothing like in her books where she describes how to do a blow job and all that. Why go there when you know all about it anyway?" Understand: their talk was about the *thrall*, not the *mechanics*. There was another husky laugh from the woman who published an erotic novel called *Obsession* at age eighty-five.

"I just remember once, we were talking about—you know the Spanish word *encantado*? It means sort of charmed, as when someone is sexually involved with a person and you've really got a bond that's extremely intense and important. Nothing's going to come between you. She was the most wonderful friend to talk about that sort of passion. Also she was so supportive and a hundred percent trustworthy. Absolutely. I never ever felt that if I confided something that she was going to go around gossiping about it at all. Ever. The only confidence she shared was how much she loved David Brown. She didn't have to say it, one just knew it. They were the most wonderful team and they loved each other so much and they were both so supportive of each other. It was just divine."

Vanderbilt had noticed, though in a way she couldn't exactly define, that the Browns were not like a lot of other New York people. They were simpler, more direct. She was especially glad of that during the long, unthinkable ordeal following her older son Carter's suicide. Despite the heat of that July day, he had asked for the doors to stay open on his mother's penthouse balcony; suddenly he dashed out, dangled his feet over the railing, and, heedless of her pleading, went over into the air. In the aftermath, as she and her surviving son, Anderson Cooper, struggled for some ballast, most Manhattanites observed the prim protocols of death: calling hours, condolences by appointment. Not the Browns. Helen had insisted. They just had to go over. She was worried; she just had to see Gloria.

"It was after the funeral. Of course there were people coming all the time to see me. But a couple of weeks after, all that had kind of stopped. Nora, my housekeeper, came in to me and said, 'Mr. and Mrs. Brown are here.' It was wonderful to see them. It was surprising and sort of very small town. I've never, in New York, experienced somebody just *coming*. It was quite amazing. It meant a lot that they were there."

During their lunchtime confidences, Vanderbilt looked keenly at her friend, watched her push food around, saw the lifts, the "scrapings," as she described them, faint scarifications of her relentless surgical enhancements. "I think everybody is a person of contradictions, really. I think she loved beauty and she wanted to be as beautiful as she possibly could be. One way of doing that is through plastic surgery and she chose to go that way. I think that she did not have a clear image of herself, of how far she went, losing weight, having a lot of plastic work done. I don't think she looked in the mirror and saw it."

If the other women noticed the alarming tautness, the thinning, over time, of hair and skin, they never said a word. Nor would they suggest a more age-appropriate hemline, a lipstick a few tones down from the five-alarm reds. What would be the point? There was no stopping her. "I think she saw it [surgery] from the point of view that every time, she was getting closer to achieving beauty. Also, I think many people feel that having plastic surgery is a kind of rebirth. I think she felt that every time she had it, it was reinventing herself. It was *excelsior*, it was higher, it was better.

"I do think this 'not pretty enough' thing is the key, isn't it? I mean, we all get the image of ourselves growing up, if you have a mother and a father, that's who you get it from. That sticks, that's kind of like a stamp. If it had been said to her, 'You're pretty and you've also got brains, look out world,' everything might have been different."

Few women of Vanderbilt's acquaintance seem to understand the transformative power of sex as Helen did, how it could burn past the so-called "hot" years, and still smolder toward the grave: "I remember in one of her books, she was planning what she was going to wear in her coffin. It was a Pucci dress."

A long pause.

"I loved Helen dearly. And I really miss her."

BARBARA WALTERS, ON MAKING A CLEAN EXIT

Speaking on the eve of her own "retirement" from regular broadcasting at eighty-six in July 2015, Walters was, by her admission, a bit out of sorts. *Now what?* Helen was miserable after they took her magazine away; she always worried that people would quit calling. When Walters turned up for Helen's last birthday at the Beresford, her ninetieth, it was a thin crowd, mainly a few women from Hearst and Helen's much younger personal friend, Lois Cahall. In photographs from the party, there is a vast difference between the well-coifed, still-working Walters and Helen, who sat in an armchair, chubby, dolled up in a black dress and bolero jacket and, of course, fishnet stockings, badly torn in one knee. Blowing out the candles, she looked like a contented grandma— like Cleo, without the Sisco nose. "She talked very honestly about what it was like to get older," Walters said. "I think about her saying there was nothing good about aging except for taking a hot bath. So when I get into the hot bath I think, 'Helen, you're right.'"

At the height of their careers, their solo lunches were hard to manage, especially given Walters's schedule. "We would have lunch together twice a year and talk very intimately to each other, Helen in that teeny-weeny voice. She was very private but she was a very loving and generous friend. We discussed our siblings, our work."

She knew that over the years, there were endless crises with Helen's family, the frantic calls, the worries. Walters could relate. "I had a sister who was what we would call today developmentally challenged. And she had a sister who had a physical impairment. It's difficult when you're well and strong and you have a relative that isn't. Dealing with that was always a big part of Helen's life." Some things were walled off, even between friends. Walters didn't know about Helen's breast cancer until years later. Helen never mentioned Bruce Brown, even when he was alive. "I remember being surprised to learn that David had a child. She never discussed it. Nor did she want children—that we did discuss."

Over the decades, Walters was aware of the public dialogue on Helen, the potshots and feminist condemnations. She does not think it just to overlook her friend's role as disrupter of the sexual status quo, to have been brave enough to start the conversation. "What she did was make women feel that it wasn't a crime to be single and have sex. She also didn't think it was a crime to be with somebody else's husband, and that there were times when a married man was the kind of relationship you should have. She made women feel they could be sexual. This was an amazing contribution. It's what made the magazine so popular. She said enjoy your body, enjoy your sex life, enjoy the man in your life, enjoy somebody else's man. She was criticized by Gloria Steinem and the women's movement for being too feminine. I remember Gloria Steinem saying a woman needs a husband the way a fish needs a bicycle. To Helen it was wonderful to have a man. To women in the movement, it wasn't necessary to have a man, so Helen became not just silly, but detrimental."

Helen was very insistent that all her friends have men in their lives. She could be a bit much on that issue. "There were times that she wanted to fix me up with this one and that one, people that I thought were totally unsuitable. I'd say, 'Helen, he would not be interested in me.'" Helen also astonished Walters with her economies, some of which were . . . well, not flattering.

"It was funny that she was so cheap, even with her clothes. She would wear the same little outfits year after year, always very short. Many inches above the knees and we would joke with her about why she was so cheap. It was pathological, it was obsessive. We talked about this great need to hold on to money, this fear of losing it. But she was wonderfully generous about David. David loved women, and she loved the fact that he loved women. I don't mean that he cheated on her, but he loved being with women and Helen encouraged that. She used to encourage me to have lunch with David and I enjoyed that, he was a lovely man. I always thought that was generous and wise and showed the kind of relationship that they had."

Over the years, Helen sent Walters a blizzard of huzzahs, thank-yous, and "gee your hair looked great on *GMA*" notes. "It was remarkable. It was almost too much. She must have done these every day to I don't know how many people." Walters is one of the few people interviewed who did not keep at least some of her HGB missives. She does have one memento. "When she died, to my amazement, she left me a tea set. She must have had a will and gave something to every woman she knew."

Unlike her friend, Walters is not a saver, a hoarder of tokens and proofs. For one thing, she has lived on camera for more than half a century. For another, she's just not the kind to box things up so others can poke at them someday. "I have no archive. It takes a different kind of interest in yourself, I guess. I kept no notes, no letters, no diaries. And fortunately nobody's writing a book about me, so I don't have to worry about it."

SIMONE LEVITT, ON RESILIENCY AND OH, THE SEX

Simone Levitt knew some very hard times growing up in wartime Paris; Helen could not hear enough about exactly how she survived. Simone was a beautiful child in a hideous time; when the war came, her mother played poker and baccarat to keep them alive. Simone sold cigarette butts she found on the street. She was half Jewish, half Greek. "I was in jail. I was with the orphans. I almost went to Auschwitz. I was a survivor. At eleven, I was raped by a French policeman."

Hers is an astonishing story; Levitt had just returned to her one-bedroom rental on Fifth Avenue after giving a lecture about her life to passengers on the *Queen Mary 2*. Let us pick up in 1964, when she married one of the richest men in America. Bill Levitt built the postwar development Levittown in Long Island and sold seventeen thousand houses there. Simone's wedding present was the matchless 227-foot yacht *La Belle Simone*. The Levitts met the Browns at a Manhattan party, then invited them to cruise in the Mediterranean; they always moored longest in Monaco. Simone has been widowed since 1986; Bill had lost the fortune and died at eighty-four, unable to pay for his final hospital care. Simone Levitt and the Browns remained friends until their deaths. She says that in all that she has experienced, there was not a creature like Helen.

"I remember the first morning [on their first cruise together], she was typing away, working on the ship all morning. And when she finished typing she would come up and light up the whole ship. She was a fascinating human being. No one was ever bored talking to her . . . She amazed me with the short skirt and the sex. Oh, the sex, the sex, the sex. She told me the whole story about the way she and David fell in love and them doing it. On the ship she would say the same thing—'Lovely dinner but you'll have to excuse us but David and I are in a loving mood.' She was not actually sexy-looking. It was like making love to an ironing board. She really played it to the hilt, about this sex with him. She must have known what he liked, no doubt about it. It kept the marriage together. I think she knew that's how she was going to keep him."

Levitt watched Helen cater to her man, defer to him often, and stay ever vigilant to David's moods. "He had a dark side. No doubt about it. On the boat, sometimes he would sit watching the sea and stare. He wanted quiet time, absolutely. But she respected that and didn't make him feel like 'C'mon, David, join the crowd.'

"Interestingly enough—even though she was sex oriented—she really was a woman's friend. She never made me feel like I wasn't important because I wasn't a man that was going to make a pass at her. She talked to me like I was the only person in the room. She was fully interested in me—at least it appeared to me. She asked me so many questions, always. But I believed she really took every human being really seriously.

She was not a superficial person at all and she really felt that everyone had something great to offer."

ALICE MASON, ON SOCIAL GRACES

After thirty years of giving her exclusive and storied dinners in her Upper East Side apartment, Alice Mason lives alone, quite contentedly, she says, with her tiny dog. As real estate broker to the mighty, she has been in—and sold and resold—every posh urban castle in the right parts of town. While working on a huge memoir that she has decided not to publish, she sat down and did the math: "Mostly in the seventies and eighties I had a dinner nine times a year—that's sixty people nine times a year, five hundred settings a year, and I did it for like thirty years." It was a rule that she separated married couples at different tables and in different rooms. "It wasn't about friendship. Ever. It was about who was important in New York. It was introducing everybody to everybody. When you came, everybody was famous. I put Malcolm Forbes at my table, Norman Mailer, and always, Barbara Walters. I never had Helen or David at my table. Ever. I never gave David and Helen especially great tables."

Helen was generally sent to the gulag of boring spouses, even though Mason says that she did not fall into that category. "Helen was very tolerant of sitting with anybody. Once she sat down at dinner, she was quite comfortable. She never minded. Most people do mind. I would mind." The Browns, polite and unassuming, were the vital interstitial tissue—congenial by nature, and pleased as heck to be there.

"The Browns were regulars at the dinners, for about twenty years, right until when I stopped giving them." Unlike many who acknowl-edged the trophy invitations over the years with crisp, pro forma notes, the Browns always returned the honor in kind, and then some. "I knew David and Helen many years, intimately. Helen called me for lunch once a month. She was always easy to talk to because she had no pretensions. And what had she done? She wrote a book about sex, it was a big success. But Helen worked very hard, right to the end. That's what she loved. They [Hearst] should have been nice, because she made that magazine, she saved the company. Her whole life was work.

"I don't think they entertained anyone as much as me because they came to so many dinners that I gave. They both always made an effort. They always had a car. But they were never overly impressed with themselves. They took me with my daughter. We mainly went to dinner but they took me to the theater. Helen always ordered but she didn't eat very much. She always exercised so much and she even carried that mat with her. She exercised twice a day. I thought it was very sad in the end because there she was . . . well, fat. Of all the things she hated.

"I had a million letters from Helen Brown, every time they came to dinner. They never took it for granted. David would write wonderful letters. David was a better writer than she was. Helen was a very cozy writer. Yes, sometimes she called me pussycat."

LIZ SMITH, ON BEING SPOKESWOMAN

Swear to God, says Liz Smith, if one more person in this, the ninth decade of her life, asks what Helen Gurley Brown was *really* like, they'll get baptized with this nice tart margarita. For nearly half a century, Smith has been the quotable media Font of HGB, cannot count the Brown-related items she tucked into thirty-three continuous years of columns in the New York *Daily News*, the *New York Post*, and *Newsday*. Lizzie, aka Honey to Helen, *dear* Lizzie, official HGB roaster and toaster, arranger of birthday parties, joke *Cosmo* covers, endless prezzies. And yes, damn it, eulogizer. Helen's archives hold plenty of Lizzie speeches but perhaps the best HGB encomium is the tersest: "She's our adorable fanatic."

Helen was always most satisfying one-on-one, and it was to her that Smith confessed her sorrow and rage when Rupert Murdoch's News Corp fired her as columnist and spoiled her fine long run. She and Helen had their ups and downs and always forgave—at least Smith did. Though it would have been nice if the fancy foundation doling out the Browns' fortune had found a bequest for her Literacy Partners charity. "She left me some fruit plates. I think like all people who live a long time, she had a lot of china she didn't know what to do with. Because she didn't really entertain. All the time they lived on Central Park West, I went there once. To a party they had for Woody Allen.

"I used to say to Helen: What are you gonna do with all this fucking money? If David dies, take a yacht and go around and take all your girlfriends and we'll have a great time. Even if he *doesn't* die you should do that. She would just laugh."

LOIS CAHALL, ON BEING "LOIS ANN"

Lois Cahall was living on Cape Cod, the divorced mother of two girls, when, sometime in the disco eighties, she was in New York and first saw HGB at Studio 54, a vision in leopard pumps and micro-miniskirt. She went home and later reread *Having It All*; like so many other women, she wrote Helen a thank-you note. HGB invited her to visit the next time she was in Manhattan; so began a close friendship of more than two decades. Helen insisted on calling her Lois Ann; only her late mother had called her that.

"We called each other every week. 'Is this a good time?' was always my opening line—something advised from her book. When we didn't speak, we wrote to each other, long old-fashioned letters, me from my computer in Cape Cod, her from her old typewriter on her pink pussy-cat stationery in Manhattan. Thousands of letters, ranging from her invalid sister, the loss of my mother, gossip, her hurt at being 'ousted at *Cosmo*' after creating its empire. Helen taught me to 'just get on with it, Lois Ann.'"

For the decade that Cahall lived in New York as the partner and fiancée of the screenwriter Stephen Schiff, the Browns came to weekly dinners at their apartment. On Sunday nights, she saw them off with David toting a Tupperware container of leftovers. He was very fond of Cahall's stuffed peppers and her wiseacre daughter Maxine, who wrote a paper on women in politics titled "From Helen to Hillary."

"Maxine curled up on the sofa in Helen's office as she dispensed wisdom on everything from bosoms to boardrooms. History was re-peating itself. When I sent her a copy of the paper with the A my daughter received, Helen declared it 'quite sparkly! She can *write!*'"

On one of her final visits to Helen after David's death, Cahall was speaking generally of m-e-n and her own recent love troubles, as they had so often and deeply over a quarter century. During the afternoon,

Helen had been in and out of the present. Cahall asked her, "Helen, you've spent your lifetime telling us how to *please* men but you never told us what to do when it goes wrong. You taught me 'I love you, I miss you, but I gotta go.' But what happens after the woman goes? Where do we go?"

HGB shrugged. "Maybe it's time for another magazine."

JOAN RIVERS, ON SEX, PLASTIC SURGERY, AND BEING
AMERICA'S "LAST" GUEST

A few months before her death during a surgical procedure in September 2014, Joan Rivers called from the road to talk about her friend Helen; she was at "some hotel in Virginia or God knows where," working, of course, at eighty-one. Rivers was at the Browns' home only once, at a rare dinner party ("someone else must have canceled"), but she and Helen had plenty of TV and beauty adventures together. Once, Rivers recalled, she drove all over Atlantic City—don't even *ask* why they were there, who the *hell* remembers—to find Helen an emergency wig. She could only find "a hooker wig," but Helen was glad to have it. "She burned her hair on a radiator."

What?

"Don't ask."

They didn't really lunch and they didn't hang out at each other's glamorous Manhattan homes. Home was sanctuary to both women, but since they were always working, their relationship solidified in Johnny Carson's Burbank studio. They were wicked co-conspirators when Johnny was away and Rivers took over as guest host. She had made her comic chops scurrying around that stage like a goldfish bumping against the bowl, bubbling out unlovely one-liners: *My best birth control now is just to leave the lights on. I wish I had a twin so I could know what I'd look like without plastic surgery.*

Badum-bum.

Could it be that as well-known cosmetic surgery junkies, theirs was a sisterhood of sutures? Can we talk about it? Did they? "The plastic surgery? Oh sure, we talked about it. A lot. That was during my heyday with it—you know what I'm saying? And it was considered so private and it was considered so . . . well, it was a dirty little secret. You know, the joke was always you can talk about your sex life but you won't say you had your face done. Helen was such an advocate of it and that was wonderful. We would discuss who the good doctors were in those days. You went to [Dr. Michael] Gurdin first. And then when Gurdin began to fade you went to [Dr. Jeffrey] Hoefflin. She was very frank about it and very open about it.

"I think her whole life was the office. I remember very early on, Marty Erlichman, who was then my manager—he's still Barbra Streisand's manager—called me with a story. Helen wanted to do something with Barbra [for *Cosmo*]. Marty was a young man then at that point. Helen said, 'We'll meet up in my office.' And she was having her hair colored while Marty went in to talk to her. He was in shock. He said, 'Can you believe it? I went into her office and there they were, dyeing her hair and she was talking to me. Oh my God. She had the paste all over her hair.'"

Rivers had a very different reaction: "I thought, 'How smart is that?'" She laughed. "She's not letting time go by. How smart. She's still running the magazine."

Rivers wrote for *Cosmo* from time to time, and Helen also ran pieces about this fearless female comic. Rivers appreciated the exposure; likewise, she was a great Helen booster on *The Tonight Show* when she guest hosted. They were good together. That was before Johnny got wind that Rivers was getting her own late-night show and banned the uppity, traitorous *c*-word forevermore. Both women understood their places in that late-night man cave, and did their best. The key to Helen's ubiquity there, Rivers said, was her humility. She could roll with anything and kept her expectations low. During commercial breaks, Rivers would find her in the greenroom, watching the monitor and the clock, assessing her odds of actually getting on if the marquee guests ran long. When the production team did each night's lineup for guest spots, Helen was always at the bottom of the batting order.

"She was a great, not a major. The first guest was usually the movie star or the big comic. And the main guest was the one that you pulled across midnight so nobody changed the channel. That would be when they had Bob Hope or Gwyneth Paltrow, you know what I'm saying? The last guest was always the writer, the author, the magazine person, and that's who Helen was. And she was always very good. But Helen was never the first guest. She was the last guest."

And she was damned glad to be there. Every time she was on *The Tonight Show*, Helen sent a gushy, grateful note to the makeup man Bob Oysterman, who always did right by her. He sent her out to take her place on the sofa, still warm from a twinkly starlet in a tube dress, and made Helen feel she had a right to be there. Rivers said that Bob was a sweetheart. He understood.

"Helen was never pretty. She made herself into the most glamorous woman, a New York glamour girl. Of course she was insecure or she wouldn't be not eating at the age of seventy, and she wouldn't be wearing a minidress. You know . . . to the very end she wanted to be a sex symbol."

My God, the woman was stubborn about some things. Cheap? Don't get Rivers started. She recalled a day when she was in a cab and noticed Helen at a bus stop, trying to juggle overstuffed work satchels. Rivers rolled down her window and hollered at her:

"Helen, calm down and take a cab! Your husband made *Jaws*!"

Epilogue: "Take Me to the Ozarks"

Helen didn't tell women how they had to be. She offered them a choice. With a cherry on top, a push-up bra, an often overlooked pragmatism, and plain good horse sense.
—Liz Smith, at HGB's memorial service

"HAVE YOU HEARD? Helen is coming home."

There was some talk in Osage in the fall of 2012 when two new tombstones popped up in the Sisco cemetery. Nothing else happened until the spring of 2013. The local potter Newton "Newt" Lale can generally see and hear the funeral home's backhoe from Osage Clayworks, his store and studio, if the machine is chewing up turf in the Sisco plot. But there had been no activity to indicate an imminent burial. He asked Jim Smith of the Smith funeral home, the family firm that had received David's ashes two years earlier. Smith told Lale that he just drove out one day and dug the small hole himself to accommodate Helen's ashes, spading up the turf just feet from the resting places of Cleo and Mary.

The Sisco family home where the Gurley girls spent their summers had been torn down for general decrepitude and its appeal to feral cats. While it was still standing empty, Helen paid the late Frank Stamps, who owned the adjoining property, to keep the yard mowed.

By arrangement, Stamps sent her pictures of the finished work before she sent his check. Helen still insisted on Value.

The family cemetery is a well-shaded, peaceful plot defined by a neat stone wall that separates it from undulant fields and the winding two-lane road, Arkansas 103. There is a barn up the hill and on a quiet day, when the uphill grind of semis hauling poultry feed subsides, the bleat of livestock drifts down. When she brought Mary and Cleo here from Oklahoma, where they died, she had them laid side by side near Cleo's parents, Alfred and Jennie Sisco.

None of the many Brown friends interviewed for this book, save Liz Smith; David's production partner, Kit Golden; and Alex Birnbaum knew where the mortal remains of two New Yorkers honored as Manhattan "Living Landmarks" were laid to rest.

On such matters, Helen and David had remained as private as ever—sort of. They didn't discuss their final marriage bed with others, but of course one of them wrote about it. The decision to rest here was made sometime before 1990, the year David mentioned it in his memoir. He remembered it this way: "In a macabre exchange, Helen wanted to know whether I would agree to be buried with her in the hills of the Ozarks in Arkansas, where I've never been. Or, she asked lovingly—what a loving girl she is—would I prefer to be buried in Southampton, Long Island . . . No, I replied, take me to the Ozarks. I want to be wherever you are, and besides, I've always liked to go to new places."

A while after David's funeral, Kit Golden was back in the office, working at winding up loose ends. "I remember there being some discussion of sending David's ashes out. Someone said, 'Well, you're going to fly them out first class, right? David would have insisted.' It's hard to imagine him in Arkansas but where else would he be? He's got to be with her." Alex Birnbaum was surprised to find that the gentleman's remains had already left New York. "I went to Frank Campbell to see to David's ashes after the funeral and someone had already come and taken them—some cousin or someone."

David, a kinless New Yorker raised on concrete, preferred to avoid the subject of interment entirely. Helen knew the old ways; you lie down where you have people and mingle your shared DNA back into the loam and chickweed. In 2000, the Browns went to Arkansas together to have a look. They stopped first in Little Rock. Helen had made their visit known beforehand. When they arrived, they were met by a woman holding the elected office that Ira Gurley had decided to run for just before his death. Secretary of State Sharon Priest, previously the first female mayor of Little Rock, welcomed them to the Capitol Building.

Secretary Priest had a packet for Helen containing photocopies of the two acts sponsored by Ira, as well as photos of him from his service in the Forty-Second through Forty-Sixth General Assemblies. The secretary then produced Governor Mike Huckabee himself, who came out to the Capitol steps to welcome the native daughter home. Had she known the governor's Neanderthal views on women's reproductive rights, Helen just might have knocked him down those stairs. Priest remembered the visit well, but she was unsure whether she heard one thing correctly. "I could swear they said they were looking at gravesites—that was the reason for their trip," she said. "Could that be?"

There was a rare May snow on the day that a procession of black livery cars arrived at the Sisco cemetery in 2013; Newt Lale knew they were Hearst people from New York, because after the private graveside service a bunch of them stopped by and asked to use his restroom. The caravan then disappeared back up the road, leaving Helen to her people.

Ira Gurley lies alone beneath a small marker in the Glenwood Cemetery in Green Forest; even his parents abandoned the substantial Gurley monument erected near Ira's small flat stone to rest together in Alpena. In Osage, the Sisco family plot has been looked after by Carolyn Clayton, the widow of Helen's cousin Wayne Bell. According to Lale, Clayton was working as a greeter at Walmart; her son Jerrit Bell keeps the cemetery grass mowed. The graves are adorned in the local custom with sprays of plastic flowers; many bloom in colors not found in nature's paint box. "They know you're in town," Lale said of Helen's remaining kin; he was not surprised that they might be keeping out of sight during a nosy stranger's visit.

The floral tributes for Helen and David are modest and subdued, just a couple of small pink and white faux carnations. Helen's stone is pink granite, with a five-inch rendition of Lovey, her pussycat logo, etched at its center; David's gray marker bears an etched Oscar statuette. The back of Helen's stone is fully inscribed with the name of her husband as well as the full, three-generation Sisco pedigree. It barely fits. David's reads just this:

MARRIED TO HELEN GURLEY BROWN

Notes

ABBREVIATIONS USED IN THE NOTES
Archival citations and privately held HGB interview material provided to the author are represented in the Notes section with the following abbreviations:

DAP — Audiotapes of interview of HGB by Dr. David Allyn for his book *Make Love Not War: The Sexual Revolution: An Unfettered History* (New York: Little, Brown, 2000), in the David Allyn Papers, held in the LGBT Community Center National History Archive in New York City.

DBP-AHC — The David Brown Papers, American Heritage Collection, University of Wyoming, Laramie.

DBP-SWC — The Don Belding Papers, 1872–1987 and undated, Southwest Collection/Special Collections Library, Texas Tech University, Lubbock, Texas.

CKVP — The Charlotte Kelly Veal papers, privately held.

HGB-SSC — Helen Gurley Brown Papers, Sophia Smith Collection, Smith College, Northampton, Massachusetts.

LSP-UTA — Memorabilia and correspondence between Liz Smith and Helen Gurley Brown, loaned privately by Liz Smith and now archived as the Liz Smith Papers at the Briscoe Center for American History, the University of Texas at Austin.

Published books by Helen and David will be referred to by their authors and titles in chapter notes; full citations are below.

DAVID BROWN

Brown's Guide to the Good Life Without Tears, Fears or Boredom. Fort Lee, NJ: Barricade, 2006.

Let Me Entertain You. Beverly Hills, CA: New Millennium, 2001; originally published in 1990 by William Morrow, New York.

The Rest of Your Life Is the Best of Your Life: David Brown's Guide to Growing Gray (Disgracefully). Fort Lee, NJ: Barricade Books, 1991; originally published in 1987 by Delacorte Press, New York.

HELEN GURLEY BROWN

Dear Pussycat: Mash Notes and Missives from the Desk of Cosmopolitan's *Legendary Editor*. New York: St. Martin's, 2004.

Having It All: Love, Success, Sex, Money, Even If You're Starting with Nothing. New York: Linden Press, 1982.

Helen Gurley Brown's Outrageous Opinions. New York: Avon, 1982.

I'm Wild Again: Snippets from My Life and a Few Brazen Thoughts. New York: St. Martin's, 2000.

Sex and the New Single Girl. New York: B. Geis Associates; distributed by the World Pub., 1970.

Sex and the Single Girl. Fort Lee, NJ: Barricade Books, 2003; originally published in 1962 by Bernard Geis Associates, New York.

Sex and the Office. New York: Barnes & Noble, 2005; originally published in 1964 by Bernard Geis Associates, New York.

Helen Gurley Brown's Single Girl's Cookbook. Greenwich, CT: Fawcett Publications, 1972.

The Late Show: A Semiwild but Practical Survival Plan for Women over 50. New York: William Morrow, 1993.

The Writer's Rules: The Power of Positive Prose—How to Create It and Get It Published. New York: William Morrow, 1998.

PREFACE: THE TROUBLE WITH HELEN

xi *"I embrace the label of bad feminist"*: Roxane Gay, *Bad Feminist* (New York: Harper Perennial, 2015), xi.

xii *Long before she was famous*: Unnamed persons referred to in this section are Don Belding, General Omar Bradley, and Jack Dempsey; citations for them are in chaps. 9 and 10.

xiii *The composer Irving Berlin so adored Helen*: Brown, *Let Me Entertain You*, 4–41; depression discussion with Mike Wallace and Art Buchwald, HGB, *The Late Show*, 32.

xiv *Let it be understood at the outset*: Information on number of foreign editions of *Cosmo* as of January 2015 from Kate Dries, "Cosmo Is Taking Over the World, One International Website at a Time," *Jezebel*, January 12, 2015, http://jezebel .com/cosmo-is-taking-over-the-world-one-international-websi-1679015736.

xiv *Today's* Cosmopolitan, *using its "mega DAM"*: Citations on *Cosmo*'s digital presence from Garett Sloane, "Cosmo Is Getting 3 Million Readers a Day on Snapchat," *Digiday,* http://digiday.com/platforms/cosmo-says-getting-3-million-readers -snapchat-discover/; "Nifty at Fifty: The Never-Aging, Always-Rocking *Cosmopolitan* Magazine, *Mr. Magazine,* March 5, 2015, https://mrmagazine.wordpress .com/2015/03/05/nifty-at-fifty-the-never-aging-always-rocking-cosmopolitan -magazine-the-mr-magazine-interview-with-donna-kalajian-lagani-senior-vice -president-publishing-director-chief-revenue-of/.

xiv *"Perhaps you will reconsider"*: HGB, *Sex and the Single Girl,* 257.

xv *As the late Joan Rivers told me*: Author's interview with Joan Rivers.

xvi *"this* global *editor?"*: Quoted in author's interview with Lyn Tornabene.

xvii *what* Forbes *magazine termed "do-me feminism"*: Helaine Olen, "Helen Gurley Brown and the Failure of Do-Me Feminism," *Forbes,* August 14, 2012, www .forbes.com/sites/helaineolen/2012/08/14/helen-gurley-brown-and-the-failure -of-do-me-feminism/.

xvii *full-page ads in* The New York Times *ballyhooed*: Ad appeared on the last page of *The New York Times* business section, October 12, 2015.

xvii *And her legacy as pop/cult muse*: See Weiner quote at http://flavorwire.com /510877/its-about-class-matthew-weiner-and-mad-mens-cast-on-the-shows -final-episodes. "Bananas" reference from the introduction to Lena Dunham's *Not That Kind of Girl.* Reference to *Sex and the Single Girl* in Marc Myers, "Review of 'Matthew Weiner's Mad Men' at the Museum of the Moving Image: 'Clothes Made the Men,'" *The Wall Street Journal,* April 1, 2015, www.wsj.com/articles /review-of-matthew-weiners-mad-men-at-the-museum-of-the-moving-image -1427925433; Elizabeth Wagmeister, "HBO Orders 1960s Feminist Comedy Pilot from Lena Dunham & 'Girls' Team," *Variety,* October 13, 2015, http://variety .com/2015/tv/news/hbo-max-series-lena-dunham-lisa-joyce-magazine -comedy-1201617081/.

xviii *A study in the online magazine*: See http://www.slate.com/blogs/xx_factor /2013/10/15/_am_i_pretty_or_ugly_youtube_videos_alarming_or_maybe_ok .html.

xviii *Thrilled by the invitation*: Helen began sending her material to Smith College in 1974. Letter from HGB to Cleo, HGB, *Dear Pussycat,* 330.

xx *Smith College has physical possession*: From permissions section of the Finding Guide for HGB-SSC, at smith.edu.

xxi *Many questions have been raised*: Katherine Rosman, "Who Owns Helen Gurley Brown's Legacy?," *The New York Times,* August 23, 2015.

xxi *Helen still prattles online*: See "Helen Gurley Brown—Lessons in Love—07— How to Love a Man if You Aren't Pretty, www.youtube.com/watch?v=mY7 _hz6G6Vk—6:16; "Helen Gurley Brown Interview Clips," www.youtube.com /watch?v=5HYgMF8Jb2Q—5:26.

xiii *So I was madly grateful*: James Landers, *The Improbable First Century of* Cosmopolitan *Magazine* (Columbia: University of Missouri Press, 2010).

xxiv *It brought to mind*: Lyrics from Bob Dylan's "Leopard-Skin Pill-Box Hat," Sony Music Entertainment, from Bob Dylan's *Blonde on Blonde*, release date 1966.

PROLOGUE: THAT WOMAN

3 *The house that Randy High's parents rented*: Author's interviews with Randy High by phone and at the Carroll County Historical Society, Berryville, Arkansas. Observations from research trip to Arkansas, summer of 2014.

5 *On July 6, 1971*: Article, "Helen Gurley Brown Visits" by J. E. Dunlap, Jr., *Harrison Daily Times*, July 7, 1971.

6 *Their mother-daughter relationship*: Helen's answers to the "Proust Questionnaire" feature, *Vanity Fair*, August 2007.

6 *"had about as much insight as a waffle"*: HGB, "Memories of Mother and Early Life in Little Rock," unpublished memoir, HGB-SSC, Box 35, Folder 11, hereinafter "Memories of Mother."

6 *"You can't understand a single thing"*: Author's interview with Simone Levitt.

PART ONE: ARKANSAS

7 *"I'm sure this is very clichéd"*: HGB in *Somewhere Apart*, "My Favorite Place in Arkansas." Compiled by the staff of the *Arkansas Times* and the staff of the University of Arkansas Press, Fayetteville, AR, 1997.

1. CLEO'S LAMENT

9 *"It was a terrible life"*: *Vanity Fair*, "Proust Questionnaire," August 1977 issue.

9 *Born in 1893, Cleo Fred Sisco was the first*: Helen has alternately said that her mother was one of nine or ten siblings. The ten Sisco siblings recorded in genealogies held in the Carroll County Historical Society in Berryville, Arkansas, include: Cleo (b. 1893), Jennie Gladys Sisco (b. 1895), Henry Booker Sisco (b. 1897), Jessie Willie Sisco (b. 1899), Charlie Burton Sisco (b. 1903), Carl Wilson Sisco (b. 1903), Mary Louise Sisco (b. 1905), Thelma Ruth Sisco (b. 1908), Virginia Helen Sisco (b. 1914), and Jack Harvey Sisco (b. 1918). All were live births and survived well into adulthood.

Genealogical and cemetery records read "Jennie" for the name of Helen's grandmother; Helen's writings refer to her as Jinny and Ginny, which was possibly the family pronunciation.

Genealogies cited: *The Siscos of Carroll County, AR*, compiled by George R. Sisco (April 1992; 2nd revision, January 1993). Also: *Families of Thomas F. Sisco Sr. and Nancy Miller Sisco*, compiled by Gene Roberts (1989). Birth and death dates from genealogies were compared and matched with those on tombstones in the Sisco family graveyard on Route 412, Osage, Arkansas, as well as the Sneed family graveyard, also on Route 412 in Osage. Additional Sisco family information, including history, land records, and military service, also drawn from *Carroll County Families: These Were the First* (Carroll County Historical and Genealogical Society, 1996).

9   *For a time, Alfred ran the general store*: The store referred to was later known as the Stamps Store, on what is now Route 412 in Osage, currently on the National Register of Historic Places and owned by Newton Lale, potter and resident. The building is now operated as Osage Clayworks. Information on the family cemeteries, burials of Helen and David there, and routes taken through surrounding land by Native Americans traveling the Trail of Tears, from author's interview with Lale at his store.

9   *It was understood that the eldest child*: HGB, "Memories of Mother," HGB-SSC. See also Helen's letter to Cleo, October 10, 1978, in HGB, *Dear Pussycat*.

10   *"she was nursemaid"*: HGB, "Memories of Mother," HGB-SSC.

10   *"Smart kid"*: Ibid.

10   *As graduation approached*: Ibid.

10   *In later life, Cleo would tell her daughters*: Historical information on the university as well as Cleo Fred Sisco's matriculation dates provided in e-mail exchanges with Steve Voorhies, manager of media relations, and by the Registrar's Office at the University of Arkansas, Fayetteville. Further historical information from the university's website, http://uark.edu/about/history.php.

11   *earn a salary of about thirty dollars*: Approximate teacher salaries from interview with Randy High, Carroll County Historical Society.

11   *Every weekday morning*: HGB, "Memories of Mother," HGB-SSC.

11   *Her students numbered*: Interviews with Randy High, July 27 and October 15, 2014. Additional information on Rule from http://carrollcountyar.com/sources.php.

12   *In cold weather*: Information on one-room schoolhouses in rural Arkansas from interview with Randy High and tour of classroom replica with original desks, books, and photographs (including Ira Gurley as a teacher) in the Carroll County Historical Society, July 26, 2014.

12   *Jennie Seitz's family*: Genealogical information from Carroll County Historical Society.

13   *The Osage, originally from*: History of the Osage Indians in Arkansas from *The WPA Guide to 1930s Arkansas* (Lawrence, KS: University Press of Kansas, 1987), 30–32; originally published in 1941 by Hastings House as *Arkansas: A Guide to the State*.

13   *Throughout the 1830s*: Routes and history of the Trail of Tears progress through northwestern Arkansas from http://trailofthetrail.blogspot.com/2009/10/trail-of-tears-in-northwest-arkansas.html.

13   *Charles's last will and testament*: Copy and typescript of original document on file at Carroll Country Historical Society. Helen also provided a copy for her papers archived at Smith College, HGB-SSC, Box 13, Folder 11.

14   *The ensuing war years*: For information on how the Civil War impacted areas of Carroll County, see "Berryville in the Civil War," entry for Berryville at

arkansascities.com. Also, Jim Lair, *An Outlander's History of Carroll County, Arkansas, 1830–1983* (Berryville, AR: Carroll County Historical and Genealogical Society, 1983); "Carroll County," *The Encyclopedia of Arkansas History and Culture* (Little Rock: Central Arkansas Library System), www.encyclopediaofarkansas .net/encyclopedia/entry-detail.aspx?entryID=752; and Lt. Col. Leo Huff, "Guerillas, Jayhawkers and Bushwackers in Northern Arkansas During the Civil War," *Arkansas Historical Quarterly* 24, no. 2 (Summer 1965): 127–48.

14   *Charles Sneed's pretty homestead*: From genealogy in CCHS and author visit to Sneed cemetery on Route 412 in Osage, Arkansas.

15   *Ira was born*: On Ira's parentage: listing in genealogy at Carroll County Historical Society: 1. Cedella Melvin LIPPS was born 31 OCT 1855 in Carroll County, Arkansas, and died 10 DEC 1924 in Boone County, Arkansas. She was the daughter of 2. James Harrison LIPPS and 3. Elizabeth ANN. She married John Henry GURLEY 10 FEB 1881 in Boone County, Arkansas. He was born 28 SEP 1860 in Gadiston, Georgia, and died 10 FEB 1940 in Alpena, Boone County, Arkansas.

15   *Ira had three sisters*: Ira Gurley obituary. "Ira Gurley Dies in Elevator Mishap," *North Arkansas Star*, June 23, 1932.

15   *law degree from Cumberland University*: Ira Gurley's matriculation and graduation records provided by Cumberland University, Lebanon, Tennessee, as follows: "According to our files in the Stockton Archives, Ira Marvin Gurley from Alpena Pass, Ark. graduated from the Cumberland University School of Law in June 1916. His name is listed in the 1916 Phoenix Yearbook as well as the Cumberland University Bulletin 1916–1917. Ira is also mentioned in other yearbooks viewable on the following links, which also contain information on tuition and coursework in the School of Law during that era: The link for the 1916 yearbook is: https://archive.org/details/phoenix1916cumb. The link for the bulletin is: https://archive.org/details/cumberlanduniver1917cumb."

16   *Helen was horrified*: HGB, "Memories of Mother," HGB-SSC. The appellation "caveman Gurley" from Cleo's letter to Helen, June 1962, HGB-SSC, Box 6, Folder 5.

17   *In the fall of 1918*: Details on campaign and election results in *North Arkansas Star*, November 1, 1918, and November 6, 1918.

17   *By the time the next election neared*: John Wells, paid commentary, "Ira Gurley's Record in the Legislature," *North Arkansas Star*, October 29, 1920, followed by Ira's "Dear Sir" challenge, November 5, 1920; election returns in the same newspaper on November 13, 1920.

18   *Archival records of the session suggest*: Research conducted by Jane Wilkerson, archival manager, Arkansas History Commission, yielded this information: The legislature that Ira Gurley participated in was in session from January 13, 1919, to March 13, 1919. He sponsored three bills that session. One of them became Act 151 of 1919.

18   *"In the matter of the bill"*: Paid commentary supporting Ira Gurley after his defeat in *North Arkansas Star*, November 5, 1920.

19   *"Cleo also told me a hundred times"*: HGB, *I'm Wild Again*, 78.

20   *"She didn't ruin my life"*: HGB, "Memories of Mother," HGB-SSC.

2. DADDY'S GIRL

21   *"I'm just a little girl from Little Rock"*: lyric from the score of Broadway adaptation of Anita Loos's 1925 bestselling book, *Gentlemen Prefer Blondes: The Intimate Diary of a Professional Lady*.

21   *it was first christened Pulaski Heights*: Illustrated history of the neighborhood by Cheryl Griffith Nichols and Sandra Taylor Smith, *Hillcrest: The History and Architectural Heritage of Little Rock's Streetcar Suburb* (Little Rock: Arkansas Historic Preservation Program, 1990). See also "Pulaski Heights," *Encyclopedia of Arkansas History and Culture*, www.encyclopediaofarkansas.net/encyclopedia /entry-detail.aspx?entryID=6575.

22   *at 404 North Spruce Street*: Site visited and locations confirmed on author's trip to Little Rock to the neighborhood once known as Pulaski Heights.

22   *The whole family could hop*: HGB, "Memories of Mother," HGB-SSC. Company history of Franke's in Little Rock at frankescafeteria.com.

22   *How the couple treated each other*: Helen describes her mother, Cleo, as not a sexual person in an interview about her own sexual history with Dr. David Allyn, DAP.

23   *German measles*: HGB, "Memories of Mother," HGB-SSC.

23   *My father was a very affectionate man*: From a short Father's Day piece that Helen wrote for *Good Housekeeping*, 1975.

23   *Ira took the girls*: Information on the state fairs the Gurleys attended from *The WPA Guide to 1930s Arkansas*, 169.

23   *Cleo "poured all her frustration"*: HGB, "Memories of Mother."

24   *One of Cleo's clients*: Ibid.

25   *Ira moved steadily*: Record of Ira Gurley's various positions held from *Historical Report of the Secretary of State, 2008* (Little Rock, AR: Office of the Secretary of State).

25   *"She thought I was not pretty"*: Helen speaks of her mother's statements or implications of her not being "pretty enough" on many occasions, in many published writings. One example, from *I'm Wild Again* (p. 276): "my mother pretty much convinced me I wasn't (beautiful enough) and would need to use whatever brain I had to attract life's blessings . . . I wish she hadn't done that . . . you spend years trying to be more smashing without ever feeling you've smashed!"

25   *Ann was a perfect doll*: HGB, "Memories of Mother," HGB-SSC.

26   *Neither could recall*: Letter from Elizabeth Jessup Bilheimer to Helen, HGB-SSC, Box 6, Folder 8.

27   *"Our darling mother"*: HGB, *The Late Show*, 157.

27   *Much of the state's population was still reeling*: "The Ten Costliest Floods in American History," *The Atlantic*, May 23, 2011; *The WPA Guide to 1930s Arkansas*, 43; and John M. Barry, *Rising Tide: The Great Mississippi Flood of 1927 and*

How It Changed America (New York: Simon & Schuster, 1997); as well as the account in "Green Forest (Carroll County)," *Encyclopedia of Arkansas History and Culture*, www.encyclopediaofarkansas.net/encyclopedia/entry-detail.aspx ?entryID=844.

27   *Worthen Bank*: History of the Worthen Bank in "William Booker Worthen," *Encyclopedia of Arkansas History and Culture*, www.encyclopediaofarkansas .net/encyclopedia/entry-detail.aspx?entryID=2438.

27   *On Christmas Day 1930*: Letter from HGB to Elvin MacDonald, editor at *House Beautiful*, April 8, 1976, HGB-SSC, Box 35, Folder 5.

28   *rather Proustian raptures*: HGB letter to Schneider, HGB-SSC, Box 13, Folder 11.

28   *Patsy was designed by*: Andy Port, "Dollmaker Played Papa," *Newsday* syndicate, *Milwaukee Journal*, January 23, 1974; Patricia N. Schoonmaker, *Patsy Doll Family Encyclopedia* (Cumberland, MD: Hobby House Press, 1992); history of the Americana doll company Effanbee at http://patsyann.net/patsy-anns-story-pictures/.

29   *that was all too dear for Ira's*: Salary approximations from the 1929 Acts of Arkansas for the Game and Fish budget, listed as follows: Secretary $1,200, Bookkeeper $4,200, Fish Culturist $3,000, Game Breeder $2,400, Boat Mechanic $1,500, One Clerk $1,800, One Stenographer $1,800.

29   *415 North Monroe Street*: Copy of warranty deed obtained from Pulaski County Clerk's office listing Grantors, JS and Leelah Bailey to Ira M and Cleo Gurley.

29   *In the summer of 1932*: Intent of Ira to run for secretary of state from interview with Sharon Priest, former secretary of state for Arkansas, per her meeting with HGB. Further details of his office routine from tour of state house premises and site of elevator accident with Dr. David Ware, capitol historian, in Little Rock on July 27, 2014. Accounts of the accident: "Ira Gurley Dies in Elevator Mishap," *North Arkansas Star*, June 23, 1932; "Injury in Elevator Fatal to Ira Gurley," *The Harrison Times*, June 23, 1932.

31   *Her memories of that day*: HGB, "Memories of Mother," HGB-SSC.

32   *The first came just weeks after*: Ibid.

32   *Afterward, Cleo would often refer to*: Ibid.

32   *Helen remembered the amount*: Helen's memory of the settlement amount for her father's death was deemed excessive by capitol historian David Ware, during author's interview at Arkansas State Capitol building on July 27, 2014.

3. FEAR ITSELF

34   *"So, first of all"*: From Franklin Delano Roosevelt's first inauguration speech in 1933.

34   *In the first months after Ira's death*: Helen's letter to Cleo, HGB, *Dear Pussycat*, 337–43. Also, HGB, "Memories of Mother," HGB-SSC.

34   *The motion picture business*: Information on the origins and deployment of the Motion Picture Code as well as Max Factor's work with Jean Harlow from Fred E. Basten, *Max Factor: The Man Who Changed the Faces of the World* (New York: Skyhorse Publishing, 2013). Also, information on his work with Jean

Harlow at Max Factor's website: http://maxfactor-international.com/heritage
/iconic-look/jean-harlow.

35   *When they were in the fifth grade*: HGB, "Memories of Mother."

36   *The eruption was over*: Ibid.

37   *Helen was ecstatic*: Ibid.

37   *The four-hundred-acre fairgrounds*: Helen and Cleo's trip through the fair draws
from HGB, *The Writer's Rules*, xiv, and HGB, "Memories of Mother," HGB-SSC;
from descriptions of fair attractions and controversies in the fair's official book-
let at https://archive.org/stream/officialguideboo00centrich/officialguideboo00
centrich_djvu.txt; and in a comprehensive analysis of the 1933 fair, Sally Rand,
and women's issues at the time in Cheryl R. Ganz, *The 1933 Chicago World's Fair:
A Century of Progress* (Urbana: University of Illinois Press, 2008), especially
chap. 1, "Sally Rand and the Midway," and chap. 5, "Women's Spaces at the Fair."

39   *First Lady Eleanor Roosevelt did speak*: On Roosevelt's appearance at the fair, see
Paul Bernstein, *Letters to Eleanor: Voices of the Great Depression* (Bloomington,
IN: AuthorHouse, 2004), xxviii.

39   *called herself Sally Rand*: Ganz, *The 1933 Chicago World's Fair*, 9–27. Additional
information on Max Factor from Mathis Chazanov, "Museum of Beauty Rescued
from Ugly Prospect of Closure," *Los Angeles Times*, December 10, 1992; Silviane
Gold, "The Figure Behind the Fan: Celebrating Sally Rand," *The New York Times*,
June 27, 2004; footage of Rand dancing at the 1934 fair at www.youtube.com
/watch?v=QTEIWK9CaEs; Helen's letter to Mary about Sally Rand from HGB,
The Writer's Rules, xiv.

42   *Helen talked about her sexual awakenings*: DAP.

43   *"I never liked the looks of"*: Helen, on distancing herself from her relatives in
Osage, in HGB, *Having It All*, 39.

43   *Her teenage uncle shadowed her*: DAP.

4. ROADS TO NOWHERE

44   *"The excursion is the same"*: Eudora Welty in "The Wide Net."

44   *thousand-room Hotel Cleveland*: History and location of the hotel from the
Cleveland Historical Society, http://clevelandhistorical.org/items/show/465#
.VInrWWTF8i4.

45   *Helen was confused*: HGB, "Memories of Mother," HGB-SSC.

46   *Oaklawn Park Race Track*: History and location of the racetrack from *WPA
Guide to 1930s Arkansas* (Lawrence, KS: University Press of Kansas, 1987), x, liii,
and 163–63. Helen's recollections of the trips there from HGB, "Memories of
Mother."

46   *The Jessup house was a lively spot*: On Aleta Jessup's attentions to Helen and
other young people: letter to HGB from Elizabeth Jessup Bilheimer, HGB-SSC,
Box 6, Folder 8, letter from Helen to Aleta Jessup reprinted in Helen's collection
of letters, HGB, *Dear Pussycat*, 317.

47   *Helen did not recall being envious*: HGB, "Memories of Mother," HGB-SSC.

48 *the southern states would see outbreaks*: Kathryn Black, *In the Shadow of Polio: A Personal and Social History* (Reading, MA: Addison-Wesley, 1996), 39–40, 80–83.

48 *Freed was gently, briefly mourned*: In December 1989, Elizabeth Jessup Bilheimer wrote a long letter to Helen, structured on "The Twelve Days of Christmas," and reminiscing about many aspects of their childhood together. HGB-SSC, Box 6, Folder 8.

48 *Helen had a brush with their feral groping*: DAP.

48 *She traced her curiosity about sexual matters*: HGB, *I'm Wild Again*, 54.

49 *Tangee was their brand*: For history and manufacture of lipstick, see Jessica Pallingston, *Lipstick: A Celebration of the World's Favorite Cosmetic* (New York: St. Martins, 1999). For reproductions of Tangee lipstick advertising from the period, see www.cosmeticsandskin.com/cdc/indelible.php. Statistics and comments from Leonard Lauder in Kay Schaefer, "Hard Times but Your Lips Look Great," *The New York Times*, May 1, 2008.

50 *"Having babies isn't all there is"*: This, and information on Cleo hedging her bets again, in HGB, "Memories of Mother," HGB-SSC.

50 *"In my home-economics class"*: HGB, *The Late Show*, 157.

50 *"I couldn't have had a more repressed"*: DAP.

51 *"She was terrified that my sister"*: Ibid.

51 *That year, Pontiac laid out its most aggressive*: A video of the film Pontiac made for its sales force regarding the model that Cleo Gurley bought is at www.youtube.com/watch?v=-tiT5S2f7Ws. For gas prices in 1935, see http://energy.gov/eere/vehicles/fact-835-august-25-average-annual-gasoline-pump-price-1929-2013.

52 *The girls thought the car stunning*: HGB, "Memories of Mother," HGB-SSC.

52 *"Gloria Hibiscus"*: Helen's series of car names from HGB, *Helen Gurley Brown's Outrageous Opinions*, 28.

52 *Her logic for choosing that distant and unknown city*: HGB, "Memories of Mother," HGB-SSC.

53 *She was ready in the summer of 1936*: Ibid.

PART TWO: LOS ANGELES

55 *"Good times were the"*: Joan Didion, *Where I Was From* (New York: Alfred A. Knopf, 2003), 129.

5. WHAT FRESH HELL

57 *"My shrink says"*: HGB, *Having It All*, 450.

57 *One of her roommates*: HGB, "Memories of Mother," HGB-SSC.

57 *John and his wife, Nita*: The 1940 census for Los Angeles township lists John Gurley and his wife, Nita.

58 *Helen was out in the yard*: HGB, *I'm Wild Again*, 5.

58 *While Mary struggled through*: Ibid.

58 *Orthopaedic Institute for Children*: On Dr. Lowman and his pioneering work at

the institute, see Cecilia Rasmussen, "A Medical Pioneer for Children," *Los Angeles Times*, November 9, 1997.

58   *Though the paralytic disease had been seen*: Kathryn Black, *In the Shadow of Polio: A Personal and Social History* (Reading, MA: Addison-Wesley, 1996), 24.

59   *Helen sat down and wrote*: HGB, *Helen Gurley Brown's Outrageous Opinions*, 233.

59   *run-down spa/resort in Warm Springs*: Black, *In the Shadow of Polio*, 24–25.

59   *"Thank you with all my heart"*: HGB, *Dear Pussycat*, 2.

59   *forgettable sophomore year at Belmont High*: HGB, *Dear Pussycat*, 145.

59   *"Sometimes she [Cleo]"*: HGB, *The Late Show*, 32.

60   *these were hardly joyrides*: Ibid.

60   *"smeared with strawberry jam"*: HGB, *I'm Wild Again*, 6.

60   *"At that time the medical profession"*: Ibid. Acne Vulgaris information from Guy F. Webster, "Acne Vulgaris," *BMJ* (*British Medical Journal*) 325 (August 31, 2002): 475–79.

60   *At "Poly," they were already calling the Arkansas import*: HGB, *I'm Wild Again*, 6.

60   *Poly, the second-oldest high school*: Helen's two years at Polytechnic High School are reconstructed with information from a variety of sources, including correspondence with Ari Bennett, current principal of Polytechnic High School, now located in Sun Valley, California, a January 22, 2015, interview with John Blau, Polytechnic High historian and teacher, retired, and author's correspondence with Chi-Sun Chang, student advisor to the school newspaper, *The Poly Optimist*, who provided copies of articles from back issues. Also consulted: 1939 graduation program and clippings from both *The Optimist* and school yearbooks, HGB-SSC, Box 1, Folder 4, as well as Helen's mentions of her high school years in "autobiographical work," HGB-SSC, Box 35, Folders 9 and 10. For further history of the school, see "Famed Poly High Finds Valley Home," *Los Angeles Times*, October 14, 1956.

61   *.04-percent population*: Statistics on population by race from www.city-data .com/city/Green-Forest-Arkansas.html.

61   *"Would you believe"*: HGB, *I'm Wild Again*, 5–7.

62   *"So, what does a sixteen-year-old"*: HGB, *I'm Wild Again*, 6.

62   *"I willed myself to become more outgoing"*: Brown/Tornabene tapes, HGB-SSC, Box 36A.

62   *number-two apple polisher*: Clippings from the Polytechnic newspaper, *The Poly Optimist*, HGB-SSC, Box 1, Folder 4.

62   *Recalling her best Poly teachers*: Article on Helen's favorite teachers written for *Teachers Make a Difference*, Harrison County Department of Education publication, Harrison, AR, 1987. HGB-SSC, Box 35.

63   *writing quick skits*: HGB, *I'm Wild Again*, 6.

63   *She joined a clutch of Poly's fifty clubs*: Clippings from *The Poly Optimist*, HGB-SSC, Box 1, Folder 4.

63   *On that day, she wrote to "Tabby"*: Correspondence with Little Rock friends, HGB-SSC, Box 13, Folder 10.

63   *"I wasn't a belle"*: HGB, *I'm Wild Again*, 6.

63   *who would remain her ardent admirer*: Love letters and poems, letters to and from Bob Brown in service, HGB-SSC, Box 6, Folder 9.

64   *"My theory from high school on"*: HGB, *I'm Wild Again*, 6.

64   *Helen maintained that there was nothing hot and heavy*: DAP.

64   *"I would now say they were homosexual"*: HGB, *I'm Wild Again*, 7.

65   *She reported to Betty Tabb*: High school correspondence to and from Betty Tabb, HGB-SSC, Box 13, Folder 10.

65   *Cleo had discovered the racing scene*: Santa Anita track history from its website, www.santaanita.com/discover/history/; Braven Dyer and Frank Finch, "The Story of Santa Anita," *Sport* magazine, www.sportthemagazine.com/1947/01/the -story-of-santa-anita/.

65   *New Year's resolutions*: Helen's handwritten 1939 resolutions, HGB-SSC, Box 1, Folder 4.

66   *She would be voted third most popular girl*: Clippings from *The Poly Optimist*, HGB-SSC, Box 1, Folder 4.

66   *a five-day information program*: Ibid.

66   *"Thoughts at Eventide"*: Ibid.

66   *Senior Prom was on St. Patrick's Day*: Ibid.

67   *"It wasn't because he considered me a wallflower"*: HGB, *I'm Wild Again*, p. 7.

67   *Still living in California*: Hal Holker answered questions on his old flame through his daughter Janet Kessler in June 2014. He died in November 2014 at the age of ninety-four. Biographical information on Holker from author correspondence with Janet Kessler.

67   *on March 23, 1939*: Certificate of marriage No. 3346, filed on March 23, 1939, in Los Angeles County Clerk's Office. The license was obtained there the previous day.

68   *"embarrassing and ineffectual"*: HGB, *I'm Wild Again*, 9.

68   *On Thursday evening, June 22, 1939*: Poly Graduation Program, HGB-SSC, Box 1, Folder 4.

68   *"Some of the best smooching"*: HGB, *I'm Wild Again*, 7.

69   *the spring semester at Texas State*: Brown/Tornabene tapes, HGB-SSC.

70   *Cleo had forced herself*: HGB, *I'm Wild Again*, 8–9.

6. SINKING IN

71   *"Nobody likes a poor girl"*: HGB, *Sex and the Single Girl*, 104.

71   *"The Super Chief or something went by"*: HGB, *Sex and the Single Girl*, 276–77.

71   *The Super Chief was the glamour liner*: Information on period Santa Fe train schedules and track locations courtesy of Eric A. Bowen, a railroad historian who documents timetables and routes on the site streamlinerschedules.com.

72   *"You could hear the little bastards"*: HGB to writer Margy Rochlin in "Bad, Bad Gurley Brown," *LA Weekly*, June 6, 2001. Most thorough description of the infestation is in HGB, *I'm Wild Again*, 8.

72   *"shy to the point of verbal paralysis"*: HGB, *I'm Wild Again*, 8–9 (on both Cleo's and Mary's jobs).

73   *"somehow got beyond the sads"*: Ibid., 8.

73   *her afternoon job at the radio station KHJ*: Accounts of that job taken from HGB, *I'm Wild Again*, 7–8, and *Sex and the Office*, 284–86.

74   *"The place was loaded with men"*: HGB, *Sex and the Office*, 285.

76   *One such incident unfolded right on the Sunset Strip*: Author's interviews with Lyn Tornabene.

76   *"You are beautiful enough"*: HGB, *I'm Wild Again*, 276.

76   *"In my own life later"*: Ibid., 277.

76   *The proof is indeed in the photos*: Snapshots of Helen in that time period provided by the family of Hal Holker, along with an excerpt of a note praising Helen from Hal's sister.

77   *Helen's resolve to avoid such wounds*: Brown/Tornabene tapes, HGB-SSC.

77   *Helen charted a plan*: Ibid.

77   *Sinking in would become her signature skill*: Ibid. Helen speaks of sinking in when describing how to capture a man's attentions if one is not a stunner, but her use of the phrase predated the taped conversations with Tornabene and would expand throughout her life and career. Sinking in would become a leitmotif in Helen's magazine writing and in her books; the phrase was often used to convey a quiet perseverance to attain the desired goal/job/man.

78   *Helen had thoroughly enjoyed testing the powers of temptation*: HGB, *I'm Wild Again*, 9.

78   *She described "the deflowering"*: DAP.

79   *"The first time I had intercourse"*: Ibid.

79   *The terrible fear of pregnancy*: Ibid.

80   *"I had hoped to marry somebody wealthy"*: HGB, *The Late Show*, 282.

80   *"Oh well he's got that je ne sais quoi"*: Poetry snippet from HGB miscellaneous writings, HGB-SSC, Box 36, Folder 12.

80   *A few years into Cleo's second marriage*: HGB, *I'm Wild Again*, 9, 11.

80   *"Those visits to him in the Los Angeles County Hospital"*: Ibid.

80   *All citizens of Los Angeles had a right to the jitters*: Information on wartime Los Angeles and coastal California from the following sources: "Battle of Los Angeles," www.militarymuseum.org/BattleofLA.html; "Army Says Alarm Real: Roaring Guns Mark Blackout," *Los Angeles Times*, front page, February 26, 1942; report of news coverage of the event during that blackout, *Los Angeles Times*, December 11, 1941, http://framework.latimes.com/2012/12/11/times-editors-working-during-first-world-war-ii-blackout/; account of the event at www.sott.net/article/132795-Eyewitness-to-History-The-Battle-of-Los-Angeles.

81   *war had driven the Thoroughbreds away*: Alison Bell, "Santa Anita Racetrack Played a Role in Japanese Internment," *Los Angeles Times*, November 8, 2009. See also the ongoing, publicly funded history of Japanese in wartime America, http://encyclopedia.densho.org/Santa_Anita_(detention_facility)/.

81   *Helen assumed that she would be working directly*: Helen's descriptions of life at MCA on her first tour of duty there in HGB, *Sex and the Office*, 287–89.

82   *MCA's founder, Jules Stein, was a former eye surgeon*: Biographical information on Stein from Peter Kihiss, "Jules Stein, 85, Founder of MCA, Dies," *The New York Times*, April 30, 1981.

83   *A long letter to the happy couple*: Helen's letter to the newly married Bilheimers, "four days after the merge," in early January 1943, HGB-SSC, Box 6, Folder 8.

7. NOT PRETTY ENOUGH

85   *professional portrait she had taken*: Photograph, HGB-SSC, Box 5, Folders 2 and 3; see also caption, photo insert in HGB, *I'm Wild Again*.

86   *Perma-Lift "bullet bras"*: Vintage ad for Perma-Lift, www.google.com/search?q =bullet+bra+1940s&espv=2&biw=1287&bih=717&tbm=isch&imgil=tJxwUK1S MEtY1M%253A%253B3HgHAOBVWGZiSM%253B.

86   *An active-duty snapshot of Brown*: Photograph, correspondence in HGB-SSC, Box 6, Folder 9.

86   *"I learned how it felt to be very, very popular!"*: HGB, *Sex and the Office*, 290.

86   *her Wednesday evening trips to dance with patients*: speech with comment about Helen's war volunteering in CKVP, undated.

86   *On June 28, as more war casualties continued*: Death record for William Leigh Bryan, California Death Index 1905 to 1997.

86–87   *"Cleo slept with a total of two men in her life"*: HGB, *The Late Show*, 276.

87   *struggling with what she termed daddy issues*: CVP.

87   *"In 1944, I went to a therapist"*: DAP.

87   *asked, nastily, whether her mother "put out"*: HGB, *The Late Show*, 276.

87   *"I think I went through psychiatrists"*: Brown/Tornabene tapes, HGB-SSC.

88   *Helen was a brave and eager analytic subject*: Drawn from multiple references to Helen's therapy in books (HGB, *The Late Show*, *I'm Wild Again*, *Having It All*) and in interviews with Liz Smith and Helen's New York friend, Faith Stewart-Gordon.

88   *"I was always attracted to psychiatry"*: Author's interviews with Lyn Tornabene.

88   *Yvonne Rich*: Interview by author with Yvonne Rich, then Yvonne Findling.

89   *fishnet stockings would become an HGB signifier*: Multiple interviews by author with friends and former *Cosmopolitan* employees all mention the ubiquitous stockings, often bagging at the knees and, toward the end of Helen's tenure at Hearst, often torn.

89   *She was secretary to Mickey Rockford*: Helen names Citron as her lover in *Dear Pussycat*, 169. Further details on the affair are in HGB, *I'm Wild Again*, 17–18, and in Brown/Tornabene tapes, HGB-SSC.

90   *On the hunt for profitable clients*: Description of Citron as the Iceman in Melville Shavelson, *How to Make a Jewish Movie* (Englewood Cliffs, NJ: Prentice-Hall, 1971).

91   *"sex is power"*: Helen's use of the phrase and wishing to create a Broadway production number around it in author's interviews with Tornabene. Examples of Helen's frequent sexual boasting in author's interview with Tornabene and

in Nora Ephron, "If You're a Little Mouseburger, Come with Me. I Was a Mouse-burger and I Will Help You," originally published in *Esquire* and reprinted in Ephron's anthology *Wallflower at the Orgy* (New York: Viking, 1967).

92   *"one of the biggest swordsmen in Hollywood"*: Discussions of Helen's relationship with Walter Pidgeon from author's interview with Lyn Tornabene.

92   *Marvin the Gag Writer*: HGB, *Sex and the Office*, 289–90.

92   *"Gurley! Come over here!"*: Ibid.

8. THE KEPTIVE

94   *"A secretary offers"*: From LP, *Lessons in Love*, recorded by HGB in 1963 on the Cascade label. Available online at www.youtube.com/watch?v=n1C1NqLEDAo— 3:05 "Helen Gurley Brown—Lessons In Love—03—Getting The Most From Your Secretary."

94   *She generally cannot remember their names*: Author's interview with Yvonne Rich.

94   *He was from Chicago*: Information on Paul Ziffren's Chicago background and Los Angeles career from Dennis McDougal's biography of Lew Wasserman, *The Last Mogul* (New York: Crown, 1998), 141, 183, 278. When McDougal's book came out in 2001, Helen wrote to him, effusive in her praise for his reporting and calling it a masterpiece. She mentions her affair with Citron, but there is no reference to Ziffren or the material contained in this passage from the book. For her letter praising the book and discussing her adventures at MCA with Mickey Rockford and Herman Citron, see HGB, *Dear Pussycat*, 169–70.

94   *Helen's boss at yet another showbiz job*: HGB, *Sex and the Office*, 289–90.

94   *"I hated legal work"*: Ibid., 290.

94   *On her first day of work*: Ibid.

95   *"I was frequently a* metastasized *case"*: Helen's quote, as well as Paul Ziffren's quote comparing her to Atlas, from HGB, *The Late Show*, 342.

95   *when Ziffren was terminally ill*: Letter from Helen to Paul Ziffren, June 20, 1988, published in HGB, *Dear Pussycat*, 31–33.

95   *"In every work of genius"*: Ralph Waldo Emerson, *Essays, First Series, 1841, Essay II, Self Reliance*. Note: this is the correct version of the sentence; Helen mis-quoted it slightly in her letter to Paul Ziffren.

97   *Ziffren would also be known*: McDougal, *The Last Mogul*, 278.

97   *"Who knows who left whom?"*: HGB, *Sex and the Office*, 290.

97   *"Cleo's separating me from them"*: HGB, *I'm Wild Again*, 10.

97   *She closed the door on the rodent-plagued house*: Addresses for Helen's various single-girl residences are taken from her accounts in *Sex and the Office* and *I'm Wild Again*. Descriptions of these apartment buildings or houses and their neighborhoods are provided in part by Google maps of those still standing. Helen revisited some of these addresses with the journalist Margy Rochlin for her article "Bad, Bad Gurley Brown," *LA Weekly*, June 6, 2001.

98   *fifteenth job in six years*: Various writings mix the order of some of Helen's secre-tarial jobs; in others, she confesses to not remembering one or two. There is some

conflict in terms of boss pseudonyms and order. The most complete accounting is in the appendix to HGB, *Sex and the Office*; all versions have been compared and cross-referenced.

98 *She had been looking for a sugar daddy*: Rochlin, "Bad, Bad Gurley Brown." Other mentions of Helen's relationship with Mason Miller can be found in HGB, *Sex and the Office* and *I'm Wild Again*, but under different pseudonyms.

98–99 *He and his wife took frequent trips to Europe*: Details on the married life of Mason Miller are taken from HGB, *I'm Wild Again*, 14–21, and Brown/Tornabene tapes, HGB-SSC.

99 *"Pretty hip advice for 1947"*: Brown/Tornabene tapes, HGB-SSC.

99 *Helen's tax return*: HGB-SSC, Box 4, Folder 6.

99 *In* I'm Wild Again: HGB, *I'm Wild Again*, 12–22.

100 *an almost anthropological fascination*: Brown/Tornabene tapes, HGB-SSC.

101 *Mary had warned her*: Helen used the term "hillbilly" and mentioned her sister's sanctions at an author's luncheon at Stanford, HGB-SSC, Box 37, Folder 4.

101 *Helen's "at homes" featured*: Author's interview with Yvonne Rich.

101 *"In Little Rock, where I grew up"*: Helen's musings on the morality of staying with a rabid anti-Semite and learning to "identify" Jews by physical characteristics are discussed in HGB, *I'm Wild Again*, 18–20.

102 *She explained to Helen*: Author's interview with Lyn Tornabene.

103 *She devoted a paragraph to the dilemma*: HGB, *I'm Wild Again*, 19.

103 *"He actually said"*: Reference to the plot of land near Ginger Rogers and why she never got it in HGB, *I'm Wild Again*, 19.

104 *By then it was not making love*: Ibid., 15.

104 *Tucked amid Helen's unpublished writings*: Retellings in much of Helen's writing, published and unpublished, deal with the men she was involved with in her single years. Much of the writing bears resemblance to actual relationships. See HGB-SSC, Box 35, Folder 12, listed as "short stories and notes 1944–74," and Box 36, Folder 13, listed as "fiction: short stories, notes and fragments."

105 *"I very carefully picked my predators"*: Brown/Tornabene tapes, HGC-SSC.

105 *"I don't remember gulping in pain"*: HGB, *I'm Wild Again*, 21.

105 *forest-green Buick station wagon*: Ibid., 22.

9. DEAR MR. B . . .

107 *"It was exciting"*: HGB, *Sex and the Office*, 299.

107 *On a Saturday morning just after her twenty-sixth birthday*: Accounts of Helen's working years at Foote, Cone & Belding (FC&B) are taken from Helen's own descriptions in "The Perils of Little Helen," the appendix to HGB, *Sex and the Office*, as well as from personal letters, memos, press clippings, and telegrams contained in DBP-SWC, Box 2, Folder 103. Those materials include: letter from HGB to Alice Belding, August 5, 1964; birthday note from HGB to Don Belding, undated; memo on Don Belding stationery listing his five secretaries at Foote,

Cone & Belding, undated; secretarial correspondence, letters, and telegrams from HGB to the traveling Don Belding, November 5, 1956.

Additional detail on Helen's work at FC&B is drawn from author's interviews with Lyn Tornabene, and from CKVP.

108 *The man in the chair did have a rather forbidding mien*: Description of the interview at FC&B with Don Belding from HGB, *Sex and the Office*, 294–95. Biographical information drawn directly from Belding's papers is mostly cited from Jeanne Marie Knapp, "Don Belding: Advertising America," thesis submitted to and accepted by the Graduate Faculty of Texas Tech University, 1983, DBP-SWC.

110 *In an undated letter to Belding*: DBP-SWC.

110 *"It was like finding a haven"*: Helen Gurley Brown letter to Alice Belding, August 5, 1964, DPB-SWC. Description of the Beldings' ranch from "The Ranch," typed notes, HGB-SSC, Box 35, Folder 12.

111 *"I was living just an adorable career-girl life"*: Brown/Tornabene tapes, HGB-SSC.

111 *Helen rarely knew what to expect*: Tales of clients, HGB, *Sex and the Office*, 296–98.

111 *no FC&B client was as furtive as Howard Hughes*: Ibid., 298.

112 *Belding was a civic and political dynamo*: Information on the origins of the Freedoms Foundation and Belding's role cited from "The History of Freedoms Foundation" on its website, www.freedomsfoundation.org/ourhistory.

112 *Don Belding was hell on commies*: Verification of Belding's service as vice president for operations on the Citizens Food Committee, also known as the Luckman Committee, documented in an official report at www.columbia.edu/cu/lweb/digital/collections/rbml/lehman/pdfs/0571/ldpd_leh_0571_0014.pdf. Regarding Belding's participation in RKO's *Letter to a Rebel*, see Knapp, "Don Belding: Advertising America."

113 *Wrestling, albeit briefly, with her Democratic*: HGB, *Sex and the Office*, 11–12.

114 *The effects of this immersion*: HGB, *Sex and the Office*, 296–99.

115 *In 1949, Helen hired*: Helen's hiring of Charlotte Kelly; background on Kelly's family tragedy; life at FC&B; speech on their long relationship, undated; biographical information, including clippings from *The Tonapah Daily Bonanza*, 1916, and grandparents' death certificates after their murder, all from CKVP.

117 *"I felt like the blackballed freshman"*: Circumstances around Helen's entering the *Glamour* contest, HGB, *Sex and the Single Girl*, 226, 265; author's interview with Yvonne Rich.

118 *Belding was always on the hunt for good copywriters*: Don Belding's written account recalling his wife's urging to promote Helen, dated May 19, 1969, DBP-SWC, Box 103, Folder 2. Helen's quote about always being able to write from James Landers, *The Improbable First Century of* Cosmopolitan *Magazine* (Columbia: University of Missouri Press, 2010), 222.

119 *One morning, while Yvonne Rich was in the kitchen with her baby*: Author's interview with Yvonne Rich.

120 *Every now and again, she "borrowed" a little girl*: Brown/Tornabene tapes, HGB-SSC.

120 *She could barely manage*: Charlotte Kelly's recall of Helen's goldfish from a speech given in HGB's honor in the mid-1990s, CKVP. On getting her Siamese kitten, Spam, jottings and typed fragments from HGB-SSC, Box 35, Folder 12.

121 *Outside the FC&B office*: Author's interview with Yvonne Rich.

122 *"I've never been a revolutionary"*: DAP.

122 *They relished their liberties*: Accounts of discussion among Helen's friends about their experiences and the difficulties getting abortions, and Helen's care of friends having had the procedure, are taken from DAP, author's interviews with Lyn Tornabene. Helen's recounting of her roommate's abortion from "The *Playboy* Interview," *Playboy*, April 1963.

123 *"I'm going to give you to the boys tomorrow"*: First accounts of Helen's work for General Bradley and his aides appear in HGB, *Sex and the Office*; there is no reference to her sexual relationships with two of those aides. Details and identities from Brown/Tornabene tapes and author's interviews with Lyn Tornabene. Helen sent an obituary of one of the men, General Chester "Ted" Clifton, Jr., to be added to her papers in the Sophia Smith Collection, Smith College, with the folder designation "beaux."

Details of Clifton's military career are drawn from "Gen. Chester Clifton, Jr., 78, Dies; Was Military Aide to 2 Presidents," *The New York Times*, December 28, 1991. Information on Clifton drafting MacArthur's dismissal note from Stanley Weintraub, *MacArthur's War: Korea and the Undoing of an American Hero* (New York: Free Press, 2000), 335.

126 *Here was the silly little secret*: Helen discussed the evolution and uses of her sexual prowess in DAP; also in author's interview with Lyn Tornabene.

126 *"Business I could rely on"*: Brown/Tornabene tapes, HGB-SSC.

10. HOW EVER DID SHE DO IT?

127 *"She is a feeling being"*: From a job performance evaluation prepared for Foote, Cone & Belding by the Runner Corporation of Golden Colorado, titled "Report: to Foote, Cone & Belding . . . Regarding: Helen Marie Gurley," prepared in February 1957, HGB-SSC, Box 4, Folder 4.

127 *On a frosty evening in January 1953*: Descriptions of Helen's *Glamour* contest and trip from her published descriptions in *Sex and the Office*, *I'm Wild Again*, *A Writer's Rules*, and *Sex and the Single Girl*, as well as the relevant articles in *Glamour* (May 1953) and an unpublished account of the visit to New York, undated manuscript, HGB-SSC, Box 35. Also, author's interview with Yvonne Rich, and news clippings: "Miss Helen Gurley, Former Arkansan, Honored by Glamour," *Arkansas Gazette*, March 15, 1953; GIRL WITH GOOD TASTE, photograph, *Honolulu Star Bulletin*, August 5, 1953; GOOD TASTE, photograph, *San Francisco News*, August 12, 1953.

128 *How ever did she do it?*: Helen's account of how she put her 1953 contest entry

together is in typed notes, HGB-SSC, Box 35, Folder 12. The photograph for her entry is reproduced in HGB, *I'm Wild Again*; information on the photographer John Engstead's career from his book, *Star Shots* (New York: E. P Dutton, 1978).

129 *That August, Mr. Cyril Magnin*: Article on winning contestants' activities, *Glamour*, May 1953. Photo and caption with Magnin, *San Francisco News*, August 12, 1953.

129 *the values of women's professional organizations*: On women's networking: various clippings of Helen's activities in Los Angeles women's professional organizations, HGB-SSC, Box 1, Folder 4. Personnel manager's doubts on promotion, Brown/Tornabene tapes, HGB-SSC.

130 *"I was utterly terrified"*: HGB, *Sex and the Office*, 51.

130 *At thirty-one, Helen had come to know*: Helen took Pyribenzamine, an early antihistamine, for the hives and discovered that its tendency to induce drowsiness was also helpful with her insomnia, as she describes in a letter (HGB, *Dear Pussycat*, 132). Helen's quote about colitis from Brown/Tornabene tapes, HGB-SSC.

130 *She also recognized her cyclical susceptibility*: From "notes and papers," HGB-SSC, Box 35, Folder 15.

131 *much to congratulate herself for*: Helen's duties as a copywriter at FC&B are described in HGB, *Sex and the Office*, 303–309, as well as in FC&B press releases on her award-winning campaigns and correspondence in DBP-SWC, Box 2, Folder 103. On the experience chaperoning Hillevi Rombin, HGB, *Sex and the Office*, 305–306. On selling swimsuits in department stores, HGB, "Four Weeks Behind the Counter," *Western Advertising*, n.d., HGB-SSC, Box 1, Folder 4.

132 *It was sometime during this period*: Portions of Helen's solo trip to Europe are referenced in HGB, *I'm Wild Again*, 208, and in a travel "diary" that consists of pages from a steno notebook, HGB-SSC, Box 36, Folder 15; those pages contain another verification that she did indeed have a tryst with General Clifton there at the Plaza Athénée, the same event referenced in chap. 9 and in her book *Having It All*.

135 *The performance evaluation*: Job evaluation for FC&B done by the Runner Associates, Golden, Colorado, HGB-SSC.

135–36 *"I have never worked anywhere"*: HGB, *Having It All*, 51.

136 *Helen was hot professionally*: Information on Helen's professional awards for campaigns for FC&B drawn from newspaper and advertising journals and FC&B press releases in DBP-SWC.

136 *Feeling somewhat established*: Descriptions of the decorating of Helen's apartment and her entertaining there appear in HGB, *Sex and the Single Girl*, 126–28. On décor challenges, Jerry Talmer, "At Home with Helen Gurley Brown," *New York Post*, April 1, 1972.

137 *Once the lair was completed and the stage set*: Helen spoke of her entertaining at brunches in *Sex and the Single Girl*, and in *Helen Gurley Brown's Single Girl's Cookbook*. More on brunches in author's interview with Yvonne Rich.

137 *Her romantic flings effervesced*: Author's interviews with Lyn Tornabene; HGB,

Having It All, Sex and the Office, Sex and the Single Girl; Brown/Tornabene tapes, HGB-SSC; and DAP. Additional details on the Swiss lover Freddy in *Sex and the Office*, 301.

139 *"I remember splendid years"*: HGB, *Having It All*, 203.

139 *She had a brief affair with an art director*: Author's interview with Lyn Tornabene.

139 *As is often the plotline*: "Don Juan" appears in most of Helen's books, sometimes under a pseudonym or as "DJ." Additional information from author's interviews with Lyn Tornabene, as well as from CKVP, which confirm his real identity. On DJ's bad behavior, see also HGB, *Sex and the Office*, 302–303. Given Helen's tendency to provide various versions of certain memories, her statements regarding Don Juan are remarkably consistent, as are Helen's detailed fictional accounts, HGB-SSC. One manuscript is an outline for a novel to be titled "The Girls of Beverly Hills." In an accompanying letter to Bernie Geis, Helen admits that one main sketch is based on Helen's own experience with Don Juan, HGB-SSC.

140 *The villain is nearly always referred to as Don Juan*: There were actually two men that Helen termed "Don Juans." One affair began as soon as Helen joined FC&B and lasted a few months. The man she very much wanted to marry, an executive at another ad agency, is referred to as "Allen" in *Sex and the Office* and simply as "Don Juan" elsewhere. Helen identified him by his actual name in her taped conversations with Lyn Tornabene. More on the relationship is drawn from her published accounts in HGB, *I'm Wild Again*; HGB, "autobiographical work," HGB-SSC, Box 35, Folders 9 and 10; and in Helen's letter to him in *Dear Pussycat*. Letters to Helen by the man identified as Don Juan are contained in CKVP, along with HGB commentary.

140 *"He was very romantic"*: DAP.

141 *Charlotte Kelly took Helen's sobbing phone calls*: Recollections about the bad relationship with DJ from a speech in CKVP.

142 *she confessed some serious anger issues*: Brown/Tornabene tapes, HGB-SSC. More examples, including hiding DJ's car and the blond model, in CKVP.

142 *"Whatever the emotional problems"*: DAP.

142 *She left DJ many times*: Helen's romance with Dempsey is detailed in HGB, *Sex and the Office*, 301–302; HGB, *I'm Wild Again*, 26; and Walter Winchell, "Man About Town" column, New York *Daily Mirror*, n.d., HGB-SSC, Box 1, Folder 4. Details on Dempsey's life and boxing career from Victor Mather, "With One Boxer Dominating, the Heavyweight Division Seems Light," *The New York Times*, April 23, 2015.

11. THE CURES

145 *"I believe psychiatry helps"*: from HGB, *Helen Gurley Brown's Outrageous Opinions*, 249.

145 *The meeting space of the group psychotherapy practice*: Having begun therapy at age twenty-two, Helen saw a shifting cast of psychotherapists in Los Angeles and New York. Information on those treatments is drawn from HGB, *Having It All, I'm Wild Again*, and *The Late Show*, as well as from her syndicated *Los Angeles Times* column, "A Woman Alone," collected in book form as *Helen Gurley Brown's Outrageous Opinions*. Additional information from author's interviews with Liz Smith and Faith Stewart-Gordon, friends of Helen's with whom she discussed such matters. Descriptions of the group and private therapy sessions with Charles Cooke are drawn from several sources: DAP, which also covers her interest in Albert Ellis, and from author's interviews with Lyn Tornabene.

See also C. E. Cooke and A. E. Van Vogt, *The Hypnotism Handbook* (Alhambra, CA: Borden, 1965); and Charles E. Cooke and Eleanore Ross, *Sex Can Be an Art!* (Los Angeles: Sherbourne Press, 1964).

146 *"Depression is waiting for you"*: HGB, *Helen Gurley Brown's Outrageous Opinions*, 254.

146 *"It's such a dull, ordinary"*: Ibid., 256.

146 *"I sort of expiated the pain"*: DAP.

147 *"He [Cooke] said"*: Ibid.

147 *"The sex urge is as strong"*: Cooke and Ross, *Sex Can Be an Art!*, 14.

148 *Kinsey's report was shocking at the time*: Overview of national reactions to the study in David Halberstam, *The Fifties* (New York: Villard Books, 1993), 276–81. Albert Kinsey, *Sexual Behavior in the Human Female* (Bloomington: Indiana University Press, 1998; originally published in 1953). Also "The Kinsey Report: Media Reaction to Sexual Behavior in the Human Female," report on the Kinsey Institute (at Indiana University) website at http://kinseyinstitute.org/services /2003/media-reaction.html.

149 *"I would always bring along a little something"*: Incident with the fellow patient breaking his hand in a speech that Helen gave to the American Society of Magazine Editors on August 9, 1980. HGB-SSC, Box 15.

149 *Helen Gurley was nothing but a* slut!: Brown/Tornabene tapes, HGB-SSC.

150 *Slut-shaming is an ancient*: See Monica Lewinsky TED talk at www.ted.com /talks/monica_lewinsky_the_price_of_shame?language=en.

151 *Austen confessed in a letter*: Jane Austen's fascination with Don Juan is mentioned in a September 1813 letter to her sister, Cassandra. Deirdre Le Faye, ed., *Jane Austen's Letters* (New York: Oxford University Press, 1995), 219, 221.

151 *"He almost took the fun out of it"*: DAP.

151 *Helen made herself do it*: Helen described the nude exercise in Brown/Tornabene tapes, HGB-SSC, as well as in an undated fiction fragment, HGB-SSC, Box 35, Folder 12.

152 *Burnouts were common in the trade*: Helen's account of male coworkers complaining from HGB, *I'm Wild Again*, 114.

153 *"pressing for news of dating"*: HGB, *Sex and the Single Girl*, 168–71. More on her work with Miss Universe in HGB, *Sex and the Office*, 305–306, and in unpublished jottings in HGB-SSC, Box 35, Folder 12.

153 *Helen took her place in line*: Helen's meeting and relationship with Gladys Lindberg are in HGB, *The Late Show*, 158; *Sex and the Single Girl*; *Sex and the Office*; and a book written by Gladys Lindberg's daughter: Judy Lindberg McFarland, *Aging Without Growing Old* (Lake Mary, FL: Siloam Press, 2003), xv–xx.

154 *Given more energy, she began to exercise*: Helen's earliest exhortations on fitness appear in HGB, *Sex and the Single Girl*. Also in "Look Ma, I'm a Yogi," originally appearing as a "Woman Alone" column, *Los Angeles Times*, and reprinted in HGB, *Helen Gurley Brown's Outrageous Opinions*.

154 *Thinking that she might feel safe*: Helen's car names, HGB, *Helen Gurley Brown's Outrageous Opinions*, 28. Helen's misgivings after her impulsive Mercedes purchase is a tale retold in nearly all of her books and in a nonfiction fragment, HGB-SSC, Box 35, Folder 12. Her extreme distress is also recounted by her friend Charlotte Kelly in a speech, CKVP.

155 *Just as she settled into*: Don Belding's version of Helen's wooing by a rival agency is from an undated speech contained in his papers; DBP-SWC, Box 2, Folder 103. Helen's difficulty in making the decision to leave FC&B from CKVP.

155 *"They needed to staff up"*: The description of her beginnings at Kenyon & Eckhardt and her work on the Max Factor account, as well as information on the strange methods of Mr. Gross, are drawn from Helen's version, in *Sex and the Office*, 306–307.

156 *The agency was reeling*: Additional information on the Edsel disaster from the Foote, Cone & Belding history in the online *AdAge Encyclopedia* compiled by *Advertising Age*, http://adage.com/article/adage-encyclopedia/foote-cone-belding -fcb-worldwide/98467/.

156 *Helen applied her adjectival wizardry*: Samples of Helen's ad copy and promotional ideas for Max Factor, HGB-SSC, Box 35, Folder 2. Her observations and complaints about her treatment at K&E and its mismanagement are contained in HGB, *Sex and the Office*, as well as an article titled "Top Ad Woman to Tell Woes of Copywriter," in University of Southern California newspaper, *The Trojan Owl*, March 16, 1959. More details in a talk to the Los Angeles Copy Club in October 1962, as reported in "Sins of Creative Directors Revealed by Helen Gurley Brown," *Media Agencies Clients* (trade publication). Helen's description of the women copywriters' office at Kenyon & Eckhardt, HGB, *Sex and the Office*, 46. Her complaints regarding treatment of the three female copywriters are also described in HGB, *The Writer's Rules*, 81–82.

158 *"David came to me presold"*: Brown/Tornabene tapes, HGB-SSC.

12. THE MARRIAGE PLOT

159 *"Helen wants to marry"*: From Jean Walker, "Marriage? Three Modern Misses Discuss an Up-To-Date Dilemma," *Los Angeles Mirror News*, May 5, 1959.

159 *Helen was willing to play the long game*: Courtship details have been drawn and cross-checked from David's first memoir, *Let Me Entertain You* (including a section in that book given over to Helen's version of the story, pp. 38–40), as well as in Helen's *I'm Wild Again*, 25–27, *Sex and the Single Girl*, 3–4, and *The Late Show*, 52–54. David's quote about his premarital dating in California from Cindy Adams, "He Made Her a Married Woman," *Pageant*, December 1963. Additional details from Judy Bachrach's "Couples" profile, *People*, November 1, 1982.

The subject of Helen's "sinking in" to her intended was discussed in author's interviews with Lyn Tornabene. Helen used the term throughout her writing life. An example in HGB, *Sex and the Single Girl*, 204, as well as a section titled "Sinking In" in HGB, *Having It All*, 266.

161 *He was born into*: Early biographical facts are drawn chiefly from Brown, *Let Me Entertain You*, as well as Brown's recounting of the years growing up on Long Island in "Long Island and the Single Boy," *On the Sound*, August 1972; and Andrew Goldman's account of Brown's long friendship with Ernest Lehman, "The Producers," *The New Yorker*, March 4, 2002. Additional information from Brown's other two books, *The Best of Your Life Is the Rest of Your Life* and *Brown's Guide to the Good Life*.

Further details on Brown's magazine career, William Randolph Hearst, and the state of *Cosmopolitan* magazine in the mid-forties are contained in Herbert R. Mayes, *The Magazine Maze: A Prejudiced Perspective* (New York: Doubleday, 1980), and James Landers, *The Improbable First Century of Cosmopolitan Magazine* (Columbia: University of Missouri Press, 2010).

Information on David Brown's first two marriages, to Liberty LeGacy and Wayne Clark, from Brown, *Let Me Entertain You*; plus author's interviews with Lyn Tornabene, the author Judith Krantz, and Alex Mayes Birnbaum, daughter of David's *Cosmopolitan* boss Herb Mayes, who first met Brown when he was a child and remained a close friend until his death, and with Marc Haefele, a former friend and college roommate of David's son, Bruce Brown. David Brown's domestic arrangements prior to marrying Helen—particularly in terms of the home itself and Helen's observations of the housekeeper, dog, and Bruce Brown—are detailed in HGB, *I'm Wild Again*; HGB, "autobiographical work," HGB-SSC, Box 35, Folders 9 and 10; as well as in Brown/Tornabene tapes, HGB-SSC.

13. LET THE GAMES BEGIN

169 *"I wish I was a woman of about"*: Daphne du Maurier, *Rebecca* (New York: Little, Brown, 2013), e-book.

169 *Finally, it was time*: Ruth Schandorf's invitation to David Brown from Joanne Kaufman, "Starting Over," *Vanity Fair*, October 1988. Information on the courtship and wedding from HGB, *I'm Wild Again*, 25–27; and the section Helen authored in Brown, *Let Me Entertain You*, 38–40. See also Helen's letter to Ernest

Lehman in HGB, *Dear Pussycat*, 303, and HGB, "autobiographical work," HGB-SSC, Box 35, Folders 9 and 10.

170 *deployed the soon-legendary HGB Eye Lock*: Many sources interviewed for this book, most of them male, commented on Helen's intense and sometimes mesmerizing stare during one-on-one conversations. For a humorous description of the phenomenon, see James Kaplan, "The Mouseburger That Roared," *Vanity Fair*, June 1990.

170 *This Helen believed*: Helen's books are filled with how-tos on hooking a man with sex. She also suggested a musical number for her proposed Broadway show titled "Sex Is Power." HGB-SSC, Box 36, Folders 2 and 3.

171 *Helen considered a change in birth control*: DAP.

171 *David was still dating others*: David's avid interest in the novelist Rona Jaffe, as well as his dating her, is discussed in Helen's section of Brown, *Let Me Entertain You*, 109. Jaffe biographical facts from "Rona Jaffe, Author of Popular Novels, Is Dead at 74," *The New York Times*, December 31, 2005; and theater review, Ben Brantley, "'The Best of Everything,' Based on Rona Jaffe's Novel," *The New York Times*, October 7, 2012. Jaffe's comments from her foreword and text of *The Best of Everything* (New York: Penguin, 2005; originally published by Simon & Schuster, 1958).

173 *He had long admired a certain flock*: Brown, *Let Me Entertain You*, 33–34.

174 *David infuriated Helen by suggesting*: Author's interview with Lyn Tornabene on Helen's frustrations getting David to consider her as a wife, and Brown/Tornabene tapes, HGB-SSC, Box 36A.

175 *a soupçon of what she called "latent revenge sex"*: Helen's brief fling with Jean Ronald Getty in 1959 is discussed in HGB, "autobiographical work," HGB-SSC.

175 *Something snapped in Helen*: Description of Mrs. Neale, housekeeper, and the argument in Brown, *Let Me Entertain You*, 39; and HGB, "autobiographical work," HGB-SSC.

177 *One dreadful night he pushed back*: HGB, "autobiographical work," HGB-SSC, and in Helen's account of their courtship, Brown, *Let Me Entertain You*, 38–40.

177 *Cleo, out for a visit*: HGB, "autobiographical work," HGB-SSC.

177 *He finally agreed to set a date*: Helen's version of the wedding secrecy from author's interview with HGB for "Popping the Question," New York *Daily News Magazine*, April 16, 1978. Also, Brown, *Let Me Entertain You*, 40.

178 *Helen ordered her wedding dress*: Description of dress from photograph in Brown, *Let Me Entertain You*. Information on Helen's favorite designer and the design of her wedding dress from "Life with the Jax Pack," *Sports Illustrated*, www.si.com/vault/1967/07/10/619989/life-with-the-jax-pack.

179 *The things she carried*: What Helen brought to her new home, HGB, *Sex and the Single Girl*, 9.

179 *Congratulatory wires*: HGB, "autobiographical work," HGB-SSC.

14. WHISKEY SOURS WITH CARL SANDBURG

180 *"Unlike Madame Bovary"*: HGB, *Sex and the Single Girl*, 9.

180 *Helen surveyed her new domain*: Accounts of the beginning of the Browns' marriage at 515 Radcliffe Avenue are taken from HGB, "autobiographical work," HGB-SSC, Box 35, Folders 9 and 10; Brown, *Let Me Entertain You*; author's interview with Yvonne Rich; and Brown/Tornabene tapes, HGB-SSC. Details on Helen's friendship with Charlotte Kelly from speakers at the memorial service for Charlotte Kelly Veal at St. Peter's church, New York City, November 2013, and from CKVP.

Material on Bruce Brown and his behavioral problems from HGB, "autobiographical work," HGB-SSC, and a fragment of writing, undated, HGB-SSC, Box 35, as well as from author's interviews and correspondence with Marc Haefele, Bruce Brown's roommate at New York University in the early 1960s. Information on the Browns' friendship with Herbert and Grace Mayes from author's interview with their daughter Alex Mayes Birnbaum and from Herbert R. Mayes, *The Magazine Maze: A Prejudiced Perspective* (New York: Doubleday, 1980).

Descriptions of David's stalker, Nadine, in HGB, "autobiographical work," HGB-SSC.

182 *Despite the difficulties at home*: Commentary on Helen's dining habits from author's interviews with Lyn Tornabene, Faith Stewart-Gordon, Barbara Walters, Liz Smith, Alex Mayes Birnbaum, Yvonne Rich, and others. Helen's early exercise regimes are described in HGB, *Sex and the Single Girl*, 180–85.

182 *"A plague on hostesses"*: HGB, *I'm Wild Again*, 160.

183 *By the beginning of 1960*: Account of the trip to Chicago to woo Carl Sandburg and Stevens's quote in Brown, *Let Me Entertain You*, 194–95. Helen's recollection of Sandburg's visit to their home in HGB, "autobiographical work," HGB-SSC.

185 *In the Brown home, another wave of intrusions*: HGB, "autobiographical work," HGB-SSC.

185 *"We've lost Buddy"*: David's account of Buddy Adler's death and funeral in Brown, *Let Me Entertain You*, 50–53, 130.

186 *The choice rested with the studio head*: Biographical information on Spyros Skouras from ibid., 177–79.

186 *One humdrum day, Helen was summoned*: Account of her salary cut at K&E from HGB, "autobiographical work," HGB-SSC.

15. FOR ALL THE SINGLE LADIES . . .

188 *"In those days, the only people"*: Renata Adler, *Pitch Dark* (New York: New York Review of Books Classics, 1983), 13.

188 *"I guess it was a pippy-poo little book"*: Brown/Tornabene tapes, HGB-SSC, Box 36A.

188 *David was searching for something in a storage room*: Helen's notation about David's finding her correspondence with the Chicagoan Bill Peters is attached to the letters between them, HGB-SSC, Box 9, Folder 4.

190 *"You have a delightful writing style"*: Helen's recollection of their conversation from her participation in a *"Playboy* Interview," *Playboy*, April 1963.

190 *"My God, that's my book, that's my book!"*: Ibid. Helen's version of the book's origin also from Brown, *Let Me Entertain You*, 103–107.

190 *"They would have said, 'To hell with it!'"*: Brown/Tornabene tapes, HGB-SSC.

191 *"I got into something more personal"*: Ibid.

191 *She was still fuming*: The article that incensed Helen: Eleanor Harris, "Women Without Men," *Look*, July 5, 1960, 43–46. Statistics for women working during and after World War II and quotes from Dorothy Thompson from Mary P. Ryan, *Womanhood in America: From Colonial Times to the Present* (New York: New Viewpoints, 1975), 315–20.

192 *"There is a tidal wave"*: HGB, *Sex and the Single Girl*, 4.

192 *"I think a single woman's"*: Ibid.

193 *"Make voyages"*: Ibid., 266.

193 *"It's one of the regrets"*: Brown/Tornabene tapes, HGB-SSC.

193 *"This then is not a study"*: HGB, *Sex and the Single Girl*, 11.

193 *She worked on the book all day*: For the Browns' accounts of the publication process: HGB-SSC, Box 19, letters between Helen and David Brown and Berney Geis and Letty Cottin Pogrebin, as well as from author's interview with Letty Pogrebin.

194 *"I am not beautiful or even pretty"*: HGB, *Sex and the Single Girl*, 3.

195 *"most of the advice givers"*: HGB in Brown, *Let Me Entertain You*, 106.

195 *There would be much to admire*: Page references for the following quotes, in order of appearance in this text, are: from HGB, *Sex and the Office*, "chinning bar," 44; from HGB, *Sex and the Single Girl*, "Give the man who showers," 137; "Negotiate with," 107; "Try to like kidneys," 111; "I know that everybody is always tugging," 266; "Perhaps you will reconsider," 257; "I needn't remind you," 103; "Creep up on decorating," 131; "There is a catch," 8, "I think marriage is insurance," 8.

198 *"There apparently aren't many men who"*: HGB in Brown, *Let Me Entertain You*, 105.

198 *"I never would have been me now"*: Ibid.

16. WE HAVE LIFTOFF!

199 *"We stand today"*: JFK speech accepting Democratic nomination, delivered in Los Angeles, July 15, 1960, available at www.presidency.ucsb.edu/ws/?pid =25966.

199 *"You can fail in your brazenry"*: HGB, *Sex and the Single Girl*, 248.

199 *Helen made some bold aesthetic adjustments*: David Brown's description of Helen as he first met her mentions her salt and pepper hair, in Brown, *Let Me Entertain You*, 38.

200 *"Plastic surgery is admittedly expensive"*: Helen's account of having her nose revised appears in HGB, *Sex and the Single Girl*, 222. See also "Dr. Michael M.

Gurdin; Leader of Plastic Surgery Societies," *Los Angeles Times*, January 26, 1994.

201   *With peace came a sharp decline*: For the history of plastic surgery, Elizabeth Haiken, *Venus Envy: A History of Cosmetic Surgery* (Baltimore, MD: Johns Hopkins University Press, 1997).

201   *Americans even saw themselves differently*: Basic facts on the space race, the rise of color television, and the approval of the Pill for contraceptive use from David Halberstam, *The Fifties* (New York: Villard Books, 1993).

202   *Being a habitual early adopter*: Helen's dating her use of the Pill from a letter to her cosmetic surgeon Dr. Norman Orentreich, HGB-SSC, Box 9, Folder 3.

202   *As the next election cycle churned*: Don Belding's work with Richard Nixon's political campaign and that of his wife, Alice, are described in Belding's memo "My Contacts with Nixon," DBP-SWC. Helen confesses to switching parties in DAP, which also contains a history of her voting records in several presidential elections, along with the reasons behind her choices.

202   *When the Beldings gave a party for the Nixons*: Belding, "My Contacts with Nixon," DBP-SWC.

203   *As David Brown settled into his new role*: Helen's description of the continued difficulties with Bruce Brown in HGB, "autobiographical work," HGB-SSC, Box 35, Folders 9 and 10. Information and dates on Bruce's life in New York City and his college years from author's interview with his college roommate Marc Haefele.

203   *"David and I both felt that whoever"*: Brown, *Let Me Entertain You*, 105. The publishing backdrop for the selling of *Sex and the Single Girl* was drawn from these sources: Dick Schaap, "How to Succeed in Publishing Without Really Publishing," *The New York Times Book Review*, August 13, 1967; Douglas Martin, "Oscar Dystel, Who Saved Bantam Books, Dies at 101," *The New York Times*, May 2, 2014; and the section on Bernard Geis (chap. 22, "Berney and Company") in Barbara Seaman, *Lovely Me: The Life of Jacqueline Susann* (New York: William Morrow, 1987). Also author's interview with Letty Cottin Pogrebin; and Brown/Tornabene tapes, HGB-SSC, Box 36A. Details on Geis's life story and spending patterns from Riva Davis, "Bernard Geis, Celebrity Publisher, Dies at 91," *The New York Times*, January 10, 2001.

205   *The deal was structured*: 1961–63 correspondence between David and Helen Brown and Berney Geis, and Lucy Kroll, Helen's agent, HGB-SSC, Box 19, Folder 1.

206   *"when he crossed out or rewrote"*: From Helen's account of her writing process in Brown, *Let Me Entertain You*, 106; author's interviews with Letty Cottin Pogrebin. Comparison of the final book was done against a copy of the original edited manuscript, HGB-SSC, Box 20. Helen's accounts of Geis's excisions from her description of the edit process in "The *Playboy* Interview," *Playboy*, April 1963.

206   *"I'm sure your problems"*: Helen's quotes on lesbians and gay men, HGB, *Sex and the Single Girl*, 30–31.

207 *"Babies, rump roasts"*: Ibid., 235.

207 *characterized the era as "optimistic philoprogenitive"*: Halberstam, *The Fifties*, 587.

207 *"I could never bring myself"*: HGB, *Sex and the Single Girl*, 4, 5.

207 *The "ticking biological clock"*: Childbearing information from Sharon E. Kirmeyer and Brady E. Hamilton, "Childbearing Differences Among Three Generations of U.S. Women," U.S. Department of Health and Human Services (National Center for Health Statistics), NCHS Data Brief, no. 68, August 2011.

207 *"I guess if you've gotta foal"*: HGB, *Sex and the Single Girl*, 91.

208 *"Letty Pogrebin is an impish"*: Schaap, "How to Succeed in Publishing." Quotes and background from author's interview with Letty Cottin Pogrebin.

209 *Months before the publication date*: Account of coaching Helen for opposition on her publicity tour, author's interview with Letty Cottin Pogrebin.

17. ROADSHOW

211 *"I understand that if I do not feel"*: Geis guarantee in ad for the book. Original ad obtained on eBay.

211 *As publication grew near*: The preparations for launching *Sex and the Single Girl* draw upon correspondence between Helen and David Brown and Bernard Geis and Letty Cottin Pogrebin, HGB-SSC, Box 19. Letter on author photo from Geis to HGB, December 26, 1961. Further details on marketing from author's interview with Pogrebin. The copy of the condensation of *Sex and the Single Girl* by *The American Weekly* was published by Hearst on June 2, 1962. All information from an existing copy of that issue as it ran in the *Seattle Post-Intelligencer*.

The sale of the movie rights was the subject of Shana Alexander, "Single Girl's Success," *Life* magazine, March 1, 1963. Comments in *Variety* on the difficulties with her book from November 12, 1963, issue. Quote from Jack Warner from Charlotte Pagni's academic study of sexology and film, "Does She or Doesn't She? Sexology and Female Sexuality in Sex and the Single Girl," *The USC Spectator* (University of Southern California journal of film and television criticism), n.d.

214 *Despite all the good news*: The dread Helen felt in sending the galleys to her mother and father-in-law, and their reactions, are detailed in Brown/Tornabene tapes, HGB-SSC, Box 36A, and in two letters from Cleo to Helen, HGB-SSC, Box 6, Folder 5. Quote on married men from HGB, *Sex and the Single Girl*, 24.

214 *Cleo's first blast was devastating*: Cleo's reaction to reading the manuscript of *Sex and the Single Girl* from her May 3, 1962, letter to Helen, HGB-SSC, Box 6, Folder 5. In June, Cleo would write a more conciliatory note professing great hopes for its success. Helen discussed her own reaction to Cleo's first letter and her belief that Cleo deluded herself into thinking Helen was still a virgin in Brown/Tornabene tapes, HGB-SSC, Box 36A.

214 *There had been no loud and notorious female*: Carry Nation's brief settlement in

Alpena Pass, her shelter and school in nearby Eureka Springs, Arkansas, and her death are recounted in Fran Grace, *Carry A. Nation: Retelling the Life* (Bloomington: University of Illinois Press, 2001), 265–74.

215 *In Berney Geis's hive*: In addition to the correspondence noted above among Geis, Pogrebin, and the Browns, information on Hearst's Sunday magazine *The American Weekly*, with circulation figures, from Glen W. Peter's study "The American Weekly," *Journalism Quarterly* (Autumn 1971). Newsstand statistics from Gary M. Stern, "Are New York's Newsstands Facing Oblivion?" *The Observer*, September 3, 2014.

216 *A bit of fishing on eBay*: Copies of original ad for *Sex and the Single Girl* (with Joan Crawford quote and Berney Geis's guarantee) and the issue of *The American Weekly* devoted to the excerpt obtained by author.

216 *Team Helen did not rest*: Detail on continued promotion from Geis/Pogrebin/Brown correspondence, HGB-SSC, Box 19, Folder 5, and author's interview with Letty Cottin Pogrebin.

217 *Germany would move energetically*: Letters documenting the German government's intent to have the book banned from HGB-SSC, Box 20, Folder 1.

217 *"She was fantastic"*: Author's interview with Letty Cottin Pogrebin.

218 *In New York City*: Ibid.

218–19 *Joan Ganz Cooney, who would go on*: Author's interview with Cooney.

219 *Mr. Kirsch may have thought he did his best*: Details of the column's origins in the introduction to HGB, *Helen Gurley Brown's Outrageous Opinions*. Contract detail from HGB-SSC, Box 31, Folder 11.

220 *Cleo had calmed down*: Conciliatory letter from Cleo to Helen in June 1962 while she was on tour, HGB-SSC, Box 6, Folder 5.

220 *As Helen continued her triumphant march*: The circumstances that led to David Brown's firing from 20th Century Fox in late 1962 are detailed in his memoir *Let Me Entertain You*, 73–77. A more complete version of the *Cleopatra* debacle and its damage to the studio is documented in David Kamp, "When Liz Met Dick," *Vanity Fair*, April 2011, as well as in Peter Lev, *20th Century Fox: The Zanuck-Skouras Years, 1935–65* (Austin: University of Texas Press, 2013).

222 *It was no small consolation*: Correspondence between David Brown and Berney Geis on the subject of renegotiating Helen's deal, as well as between Geis and Helen on the subject of her next book for his company, from HGB-SSC, Box 20.

222 *Helen had been working up a few ideas*: In March 1962, before publication of *Sex and the Single Girl*, Helen wrote to Berney Geis about an idea on lesbians; he wrote back discouraging the project. Letter from Geis to HGB, March 14, 1962, HGB-SSC, Box 20.

223 *Gene Norman, a Los Angeles producer*: Details on Norman and the LP from WFMU radio blog, http://blog.wfmu.org/freeform/2011/09/helen-gurley-brown -and-lessons-in-love.html; and Margalit Fox, "Gene Norman, Music Producer with an Ear for Jazz, Dies at 93," *The New York Times*, November 13, 2015.

223 *"As for naughty words"*: From *Lessons in Love* LP, online at www.youtube.com /watch?v=pl4FM5kX-2A.

223 *By November 1962*: Helen's account of her officemates' departures from HGB, *Sex and the Office*, 83.

18. MEET THE PRESS

225 *"It's hard to stop me"*: HGB, *The Writer's Rules*, xiii.

225 *In early February 1963*: Correspondence between David and Bruce Brown and Kathy Ames from HGB-SSC, Box 4, Folder 9. Like Helen, David Brown often kept carbons of his voluminous personal correspondence, which is held in the David Brown Papers, American Heritage Collection at the University of Wyoming, Laramie (DBP-AHC). Additional letters to Bruce Brown from his father, in that collection.

225 *Bruce had been living in an apartment*: Information about Bruce Brown's college years from author's interviews with his roommate Marc Haefele and with professors familiar with Bruce Brown's only published book, *Marx, Freud, and the Critique of Everyday Life* (New York: Monthly Review Press, 1973, 2009). Background on two of Bruce Brown's teachers from Richard Bernstein, "Sidney Hook, Political Philosopher, Is Dead at 86," *The New York Times*, July 14, 1989; and William H. Honan, "William Barrett, 78, a Professor and Interpreter of Existentialism," *The New York Times*, September 10, 1992. Further information on Bruce Brown's higher education from alumni organizations and graduation programs at NYU and Washington University, and from correspondence between father and son, as cited above.

228 *The third Mrs. Brown*: Shana Alexander, "Singular Girl's Success," *Life*, March 1, 1963.

229 *Within days of the* Life *story*: Quotes from Helen's *"Playboy* Interview," *Playboy*, April 1963, 53–61. Introduction to the article also mentions Geis's early sale of *Sex and the Office* to Pocket Books. Listings of other women interviewees and confirmation of Helen's being *Playboy*'s first female interviewee provided by the research department at *Playboy*.

230 *In a subsequent issue*: Helen wrote of the humiliation in a November 1972 letter to the self-help writer Dr. David Reuben, HGB-SSC, Box 9, Folder 7.

231 *She asked Letty Pogrebin*: Return letter from Pogrebin to Helen, HGB-SSC, Box 22.

231 *While Helen may have been personally stung*: Work on TV ideas began after Helen's first book tour. David Brown, who was out of work by November 1962, had time on his hands to help. Proposals for all of Helen's television ideas from HGB-SSC, Box 35. Additional notes and proposal information in correspondence between the Browns and Lucy Kroll, HGB-SSC, Boxes 19 and 35. Details on the Finkbine case from "Mrs. Finkbine Undergoes Abortion in Sweden; Surgeon Asserts Unborn Child Was Deformed," *The New York Times*, August 19, 1962.

PART THREE: NEW YORK

235   *"Give me such shows"*: Walt Whitman, "Give Me the Splendid, Silent Sun," in *Drum-Taps* (New York, 1865).

19. SHE'LL TAKE MANHATTAN

237   *"New York, I soon recognized"*: HGB, *I'm Wild Again*, 38.

237   *In the early spring of 1963*: Travel description from Brown, *Let Me Entertain You*, 254.

237   *"Helen became—may I say?"*: Ibid., 255.

238   *The secretarial work was*: Charlotte Kelly's accounts of working at the job David helped her get with David O. Selznick in unpublished manuscript, CKVP. Background on Helen's long and close friendship with Charlotte Kelly, later Charlotte Veal, from author's interviews with Veal's friends, among them Betsy Carter, Nancy Megan, and the attorney Robin LoGuidice, who later acted as her conservator and executor.

239   *One column read as a book review of sorts*: Column titles from HGB, *Helen Gurley Brown's Outrageous Opinions*. Quotes on *The Feminine Mystique* from manuscript of Betty Friedan column, "Envy Anyone?" that never ran, in HGB-SSC, Box 31, Folder 12.

240   *Friedan could speak as one of them*: Betty Friedan, *The Feminine Mystique* (New York: W. W. Norton, 1963; 50th anniversary ed., 2013); for critiques of Friedan's book and biographical details, see also Louis Menand, "Books as Bombs," *The New Yorker*, January 24, 2011.

242   *Not long after the Browns*: Helen's account of running into the Mansfields from Barbara Seaman, *Lovely Me: The Life of Jacqueline Susann* (New York: William Morrow, 1987), 282–83. Jackie's domestic arrangement and the contents of the Mansfields' hotel refrigerator from author's interview with Michael Korda.

243   *"Did Helen Gurley Brown do that?"*: Seaman, *Lovely Me*, 283.

244   Sex and the Office *was a financial success*: From introduction to HGB's "*Playboy* Interview," *Playboy*, April 1963, 53–61.

244   *"He [Geis] thought it might hurt sales"*: Ibid.

244   *The kinky vignettes*: All quotes from HGB, *Sex and the Office*, chap. 13, "Three Little Bedtime Stories." Helen's disputes with Bernard Geis from comparing draft and final version of *Sex and the Office*, HGB-SSC, Box 22, as well as from correspondence between them, Box 19. In her "*Playboy* Interview," Helen describes the frustrations of her publisher's censorship of *Sex and the Single Girl*. Letty Cottin Pogrebin did agree with Geis on excising contraception references in *Sex and the Office*; see her letter to Helen in HGB-SSG, Box 19.

245   *Cleo arrived in New York for a visit*: HGB's reference to swatting Cleo from HGB, "autobiographical work," HGB-SSC, Box 35, Folders 9 and 10, and from author's interview with Lyn Tornabene.

246   *A draft of a will*: HGB-SSC, Box 4, Folder 5.

247   *Mary Gurley had married*: HGB, *I'm Wild Again*, 10–11. Helen's efforts to help Mary and her brother-in-law, George Alford, from *I'm Wild Again*, 68.

20. "HOW DARE YOU, HELEN GURLEY BROWN?"

249   *"I just want to say"*: Quote from anonymous caller to radio show on Helen's *Sex and the Office* tour, as reported by Joan Didion in "Bosses Make Lousy Lovers," *Saturday Evening Post*, January 30, 1965.

249   *"We are getting overexposure signals"*: Letter from Letty Pogrebin to the Browns, HGB-SSC, Box 22, Folder 1.

249   *As Letty Pogrebin began lining up the publicity campaign*: Letter to Browns from Letty Pogrebin, HGB-SSC, Box 22, Folder 1.

249   *Pogrebin was able to book Helen*: Description of Helen's ordeal on *The Mike Douglas Show* from author's interview with the show runner in 1964, Forrest "Woody" Fraser, and Brown/Tornabene tapes, HGB-SSC, Box 36A. Letter from HGB to Roger Ailes, HGB-SSC, Box 6, Folder 6. Description of the early days on *The Mike Douglas Show* also from Gabriel Sherman, *The Loudest Voice in the Room: How the Brilliant, Bombastic Roger Ailes Built Fox News—and Divided a Country* (New York: Random House, 2014), 18–21.

254   *As you settle in*: Recording of the Joe Pyne radio show, episode 3, with Helen Gurley Brown promoting *Sex and the Office*, held by the Paley Center for Media, New York City.

255   *One reporter, as slim and bird-boned*: Joan Didion, "Bosses Make Lousy Lovers," *The Saturday Evening Post*, January 30, 1965. Information on Didion's California heritage and her contest entry for *Vogue* from her book *Where I Was From* (New York: Alfred A. Knopf, 2003), 204–17. More on Didion's life, especially her guest editorships at *Mademoiselle* and *Vogue*, from Tracy Daugherty, *The Last Love Song: A Biography of Joan Didion* (New York: St. Martin's, 2015). See also Meghan Daum, "The Elitist Lure of Joan Didion," *The Atlantic*, September 2015; and Michelle Green, "Becoming Joan Didion," *The Awl*, May 23, 2012, www .theawl.com/2012/05/becoming-joan-didion.

256   *There was one crucial nexus*: On guest editorships: Meg Wolitzer, "My Mademoiselle Summer," *The New York Times*, July 19, 2013. Further details on the history of the magazine's guest editorships in Lynn Peril, *College Girls: Bluestockings, Sex Kittens, and Co-Eds, Then and Now* (New York: W. W. Norton, 2006), 135–37. See also Alex Witchel, "After 'The Bell Jar,' Life Went On," *The New York Times*, June 22, 2003.

259   *"They can't put me off"*: HGB quotes in this section from Didion, "Bosses Make Lousy Lovers."

260   *"While Helen doesn't show it"*: David Brown letter to Berney Geis, HGB-SSC, Box 22, Folder 1.

260   *Helen was already on it*: Account of Helen's job interview for a copywriter job from author's interview with Mary Wells Lawrence. Information on Lawrence's career and specific campaigns from her autobiography, *A Big Life (in Advertising)* (New York: Alfred A. Knopf, 2003), and from Ginia Bellafante, "A Pioneer in a Mad Man's World," *The New York Times*, June 8, 2012. Helen's musing on Lawrence's vulnerability from author's interview with Lyn Tornabene.

21. IN WHICH *COSMOPOLITAN* GETS A MAKEOVER

264 *"In those days,* Cosmopolitan *was a failing horror"*: Author's interview with Lyn Tornabene.

264 *In the winter of 1964*: Descriptions of working on the proposal for *Femme* from Brown, *Let Me Entertain You*, 111. Also, author's interviews with Lyn Tornabene.

264 *Helen's mock-up cover for* Femme: *Femme* cover and proposal, HGB-SSC, Box 37.

265 *"We decided it would have to appeal"*: Brown, *Let Me Entertain You*, 111.

266 *Many subjects of interest*: *Femme* basic tenets as quoted in James Landers, *The Improbable First Century of* Cosmopolitan *Magazine* (Columbia: University of Missouri Press, 2010), 223.

266 *"It was all loving hands at home"*: Brown/Tornabene tapes, HGB-SSC, Box 36A.

266 *The risqué ads*: Charlotte Pagni, "Does She or Doesn't She? Sexology and Female Sexuality in *Sex and the Single Girl*," *The USC Spectator* (University of Southern California journal of film and television criticism), n.d.

267 *"A new slanguage"*: Ibid.

267 *Helen's positively dreamiest prezzie*: Account of the crowds at New York theaters as well as A. H. Weiler, "Movie Review: Sex and the Single Girl," *The New York Times*, December 26, 1964.

268 *"I thought the movie was"*: Pagni, "Does She or Doesn't She?"

268 *Deems was frank in his distaste*: David's account of pitching *Femme* from Brown, *Let Me Entertain You*, 111–13.

269 *Helen and David both went*: Ibid., 112.

269 *David knew all too well*: Information and dates on *Cosmopolitan*'s decline and internal comments on Helen's appointment from Herbert R. Mayes, *The Magazine Maze: A Prejudiced Perspective* (New York: Doubleday, 1980); Landers, *The Improbable First Century*, 218–24; and Helen's account of her start there in Brown, *Let Me Entertain You*, along with author's interviews with Lyn Tornabene, who had been an editor at both *Good Housekeeping* and *Cosmopolitan* before Helen's arrival.

Salinger incident from author's interview with Lyn Tornabene and from PBS *American Masters* interview with A. E. Hotchner, a former editor at *Cosmopolitan* who faced Salinger's wrath after his story title was changed without his knowledge or permission. Viewable at www.pbs.org/wnet/americanmasters /episodes/jd-salinger/film-excerpt-salingers-last-story-in-cosmopolitan-blue -melody/2836/.

270 *David negotiated*: Correspondence between HGB and Richard Deems, HGB-SSC, Box 39, Folder 7.

271 *"Helen Gurley Brown, that ad agency"*: Mayes, *The Magazine Maze*, 29.

272 *Helen was due to take over the magazine*: Accounts of Helen's anxieties as she prepared to take over the magazine from author's interviews with Lyn Tornabene;

author's interview with the Browns' friend Faith Stewart-Gordon; and Helen's account in Brown, *Let Me Entertain You*, 107–10.

273 *"I go in for our meeting"*: Author's interview with Lyn Tornabene.

274 *"She had a self-deprecating Arkansas charm"*: Liz Smith, *Natural Blonde* (New York: Hyperion, 2000), 216; author's interviews with Smith.

274 *Reed rewound back to his days*: Author's interview with Rex Reed.

276 *Soon after Smith told Rex Reed of the change*: Helen's schedule for March 25, 1965, the day she interviewed Rex Reed, HGB-SSC, Box 3, containing datebooks. Reed's account of that meeting and subsequent events from author's interview with Reed.

277 *"You must converse with your reader"*: Helen's comments on her writerly guidelines from Landers, *The Improbable First Century*, 238.

278 *"Hello, I'm* Cosmopolitan's *new editor"*: HGB, first editorial column, "Step into My Parlor," *Cosmopolitan*, July 1965.

278 *Her inaugural main feature*: Information on the Supreme Court decisions regarding contraception from Mark Tushnet, *I Dissent: Great Opposing Opinions in Landmark Supreme Court Cases* (Boston: Beacon Press, 2008), 179–90. Details of contraception cases also from U.S. Supreme Court website, https://supreme.justia.com/cases/federal/us/381/479/ (Griswold) and https://supreme.justia.com/cases/federal/us/405/438/ (Eisenstadt). Details on the benefits of the Pill as explained in "Oh, What a Lovely Pill!" *Cosmopolitan*, July 1965, 33–37.

22. WEEKDAYS IN THE PARK WITH DAVID

280 *"A man must feel he runs things"*: Jacqueline Susann, *Valley of the Dolls* (New York: Grove Press, 1997; original copyright 1966 by Tiger, Inc.).

281 *Dr. William Appleton, a Boston psychotherapist*: Author's interview with Dr. Appleton.

281 *In her first three years*: Circulation and ad statistics from James Landers, *The Improbable First Century of* Cosmopolitan *Magazine* (Columbia: University of Missouri Press, 2010), 225. Executive commentary from Richard Deems in memos from HGB-SSC, Box 39, Folder 7.

281 *The sales appeal lay in Helen's editorial mix*: Titles listed from the contents pages from back issues of *Cosmopolitan* held in the New York Public Library and in HGB-SSC.

281 *"There's always the basics"*: Landers, *The Improbable First Century*, 285.

283 *"We'd ride around Central Park in a taxi"*: Brown, *Let Me Entertain You*, 113.

283 *She had some insider's tips*: Details of the book publicity and movie deal for *Valley of the Dolls* and Geis and David Brown's involvement in Barbara Seaman, *Lovely Me: The Life of Jacqueline Susann* (New York: William Morrow, 1987), 300–303, 332; and Amy Fine Collins, "Once Was Never Enough," *Vanity Fair*, January 2000, www.vanityfair.com/culture/2000/01/jacqueline-susann-valley-of-the-dolls-books.

285 *In the year of* Dolls's *release*: Movie grosses from imdb.com at www.imdb.com/title/tt0062430/business; other financial info from Seaman, *Lovely Me*, 302.

285 *Helen did suffer one brief and public stumble*: Account of HGB's daytime TV show and interview, Judy Klemesrud, "Mrs. Brown, Your Subject Is Showing," *The New York Times*, December 31, 1967.

287 *The Browns and the Mansfields grew closer*: Details on celebratory dinner and Susann's illness from Seaman, *Lovely Me*, 332.

287 *even at Wyntoon*: Hearst's extravagance on Wyntoon at the expense of his companies, Landers, *The Improbable First Century*, 174. Details of the stay in Helen's letter to her friends Larry Baldwin and John Clerk-Scott, HGB-SSC, Box 6, Folder 7.

287 *Back in New York, she put in seventy*: Landers, *The Improbable First Century*, 265.

288 Cosmo *readers were exceptionally loyal*: Ibid., 271.

288 *her numbers were also buoyed by a demographic tsunami*: "A Century of Change: The U.S. Labor Force, 1950–2050," *Monthly Labor Review*, U.S. Department of Labor, Bureau of Labor Statistics, May 2002, www.bls.gov/opub/mlr/2002/05/art2full.pdf; and *Historical Statistics of the United States: Colonial Times to 1970*, bicentennial ed. (Washington, DC: U.S. Dept. of Commerce, Bureau of the Census, 1975).

289 *The* New York Times *reviewer*: Alan F. Guttmacher, "Clinical Analysis," *The New York Times*, May 29, 1966.

290 *In* Re-Making Love: Barbara Ehrenreich, Elizabeth Hess, Gloria Jacobs, *Re-Making Love: The Feminization of Sex* (New York: Anchor/Doubleday, 1986), 39–43.

290 *In 1969, two-thirds*: Changing *Cosmo* demographics, Landers, *The Improbable First Century*, 291–92.

290 *at Hearst, she was still on a short leash*: Letters to HGB from Richard Deems and Richard Berlin, HGB-SSC, Box 39, Folder 3. See also ibid., 260, on bonus requests and salary.

291 *Instead, she traded shameless editorial mentions*: On TWA flight, "Step into My Parlor," *Cosmopolitan*, September 1966.

291 *Helen would also receive a demoralizing note*: Letter from Richard Berlin to Helen, HGB-SSC, Box 39.

23. RECIPE FOR SUCCESS

292 *"It is better to get hollandaise"*: Helen Gurley Brown's *Single Girl's Cookbook* (Greenwich, CT: Fawcett Publications, 1969). Originally published by Bernard Geis Associates, 1969.

292 *Helen did not let up, not for a second*: Helen's handwritten list of items on her daily food regime, HGB-SSC, Box 4, Folder 7.

293 *Thus the* Cosmo *girl was a fairly oblivious*: Article subjects and titles from *Cosmo*'s tables of contents and reader mail page, "Dear Cosmo," in the late 1960s.

294 *When necessary, she took writers to lunch*: Entries from Helen's office datebooks,

1965–70, HGB-SSC, Box 3. Commentary on Helen's lunch habits from author's interviews with Faith Stewart-Gordon, Peter Rogers, and Judith Krantz. Additional details in letters from the Liz Smith–HGB correspondence, LSP-UTA.

295 *One day, when she was sorting*: Quotations from Mimi Sheraton, *The Seducer's Cookbook* (New York: Random House, 1963). Also from author's interview with Mimi Sheraton.

296 *Success did usher in a ruthless*: Helen's lifetime Jell-O obsession is detailed in a letter to the president of General Mills, HGB-SSC, Box 13, Folder 9.

297 *Besides, David liked her skinny*: Brown, *The Rest of Your Life Is the Best of Your Life*, 47.

297 *The Browns relied on*: Note to the housekeeper Anna Freimanis in *Dear Pussycat*, 38.

297 *This was a woman who made salads*: Author's interview with Lyn Tornabene.

297 *The book was fried by critics*: Robert Glasgow, "Helen Gurley Brown: The Fanny Farmer of the Boudoir," *Los Angeles* magazine, February 1963.

298 *Here is Gloria Steinem*: From "Six Current (but perennial) Fascinators," *Cosmopolitan*, February 1966.

298 *Nora Ephron was game for nearly anything*: Interview with Ephron (2001) provided by the journalist Margy Rochlin, who spoke to Ephron for a story about HGB for *LA Weekly*. Ephron's *Cosmo* contributions include "*Women's Wear Daily* Unclothed," January 1968; "Starting a Conversation," December 1968; and "Makeover: The Short Unglamorous Saga of a New Glamorous Me," May 1968.

299 *"Some little bitch"*: On controversy over breast memo leaked to *WWD*, see HGB profile in Nora Ephron, *Wallflower at the Orgy* (New York: Ace/Viking, 1973), 48–49.

300 *"Italian men! They are so quaint"*: Tom Wolfe, "Life of a Teenage London Society Girl," reprinted in *Cosmopolitan*, February 1967.

300 *Gail Sheehy, she of the multi-book*: Sheehy's early *Cosmo* articles included "She Works While He Studies," "Portrait of a Divorce," and "What Your Sleep Habits Reveal."

300 *Gael Greene did not trifle*: Author's interview with Gael Greene. Also Greene's memoir, *Insatiable: Tales from a Life of Delicious Excess* (New York: Warner Books, 2006), 78–81.

301 *Myrna Blyth was a married young mother*: Author's interview with Myrna Blyth.

301 *Given the fact that*: Readership demographics from James Landers, *The Improbable First Century of Cosmopolitan Magazine* (Columbia: University of Missouri Press, 2010), 274.

302 *Regardless of Helen's alleged blind spots*: Roster of famous authors from 1965 to 1975 from *Cosmo* tables of contents and editor's columns. Special men's issue was the subject of Helen's February 1966 "Step into My Parlor" column, with note on Oriana Fallaci.

24. BIG SISTER AND THE YOUTHQUAKE

303 *"Wanted: Keeno, diggo, coolo"*: Classified ad in the September 1968 issue of *Eye* magazine.

303 *"You had to come up with ideas"*: Harriet LaBarre, an editor at Helen's *Cosmo*, in James Landers, *The Improbable First Century of* Cosmopolitan *Magazine* (Columbia: University of Missouri Press, 2010), 240.

303 *Though she was happy to have the writing assignments*: Author's interview with Lyn Tornabene.

304 *"My name cannot go on"*: Unsent letter to HGB from Liz Smith, LSP-UTA.

304 *For months, at the beginning of Tornabene's*: Author's interview with Lyn Torna- bene.

306 *Helen and Gloria, the Arkie and the heiress*: On their meeting, author's interview with Liz Smith. Helen's complaint that Vanderbilt would not talk about the for- ties in Los Angeles in letter to friends Larry Baldwin and John Clerk-Scott, HGB-SSC, Box 6, Folder 7. The couple were friends of both HGB and Vanderbilt in those years.

306 *"We danced all night there"*: Author's interview with Peter Rogers.

307 *She met her husband, Steve*: Author's interview with Judith Krantz.

308 *Hearst executives felt that Helen needed*: Author's interview with Jeanette Sarki- sian Wagner.

309 *"Flies or bees bothering you?"*: Collected tips for *Cosmo*, list from Helen in CKVP.

310 *Helen would be paid*: Letters to Richard Deems on compensation for work at *Eye*, HGB-SSC, Box 39, Folder 7.

310 *"She called me up and asked if I was interested"*: Author's interview with Susan Edmiston.

311 *Contributing editors included*: Details on the editorial content of *Eye* magazine from author's interview with Edmiston, and from old copies of *Eye*. Sheila Weller quote from her article "Betsey Johnson: A Role Model, Still," *The New York Times*, February 13, 2015. Quote on the death of the art director Judy Parker from Sheila Weller, *Girls Like Us: Carole King, Joni Mitchell, Carly Simon—and the Journey of a Generation* (New York: Washington Square Press, 2008), 265.

312 *There had never been good chemistry*: Author's interview with Jeanette Sarkisian Wagner.

25. A MARCH FORWARD, A FEW STEPS BACK

314 *"The feminists attacked me"*: David Brown, quoting HGB, unpublished writing, HGB-SSC, Box 35.

314 *Mary Alford's home companion*: Letter to Helen from Teresa Rowton, Shawnee, Oklahoma, HGB-SSC, Box 9, Folder 7.

314 *Life just wasn't getting any better*: Helen's account of her efforts to help George Alford in HGB, *I'm Wild Again*, 67–68. Letters to and from HGB and Oral Rob- erts, HGB-SSC, Box 9, Folder 6.

315 *Nature's implacable cruelty*: From correspondence in HGB-SSC and CKVP, it is

evident that Helen sent the clovers to many friends and associates in dire straits. Origin of the clovers in a note from HGB to Charlotte Veal, CKVP.

315 *David, working at Fox in tandem*: Brown, *Let Me Entertain You*, 128–29.

316 *Helen was fighting trim*: Helen's measurements from HGB-SSC, Box 4, Folder 7.

316 *David's son and daughter-in-law*: Author's interview and e-mail correspondence with Bill Kortum, who knew Bruce Brown at WBAI radio in New York City. Also, author's correspondence with Spencer Sunshine, assistant editor of *Monthly Review*, Bruce Brown's book publisher. Kathy Brown's employment history from her writings, from program for Helen Gurley Brown memorial service and from author's interview with Amy Levin Cooper, former editor in chief of *Mademoiselle*.

316 *"I felt tensions building up"*: Brown, *Let Me Entertain You*, 189–90.

317 *She wrote about it in her editor's column*: HGB, "Step into My Parlor," *Cosmopolitan*, May 1970.

317 *During that office invasion, Helen got off easy*: Account of sit-in at *Ladies' Home Journal*, Grace Lichtenstein, "Feminists Demand 'Liberation' in *Ladies' Home Journal* Sit-in," *The New York Times*, March 19, 1970.

318 *"What is all that crap about"*: Vivian Gornick, "The Women's Liberation Movement!" *Cosmopolitan*, April 1970.

319 *a very long and trying day*: "Leading Feminist Puts Hairdo Before Strike," *The New York Times*, August 27, 1970. See also Linda Charlton, "Women March Down Fifth for Equality," *The New York Times*, August 27, 1970.

319–20 *Helen and Friedan were miles apart*: Roger Chapman, ed., *Culture Wars: An Encyclopedia of Issues, Viewpoints, and Voices* (Armonk, NY: M. E. Sharpe, 2010), 73.

Despite the criticism from Friedan, Helen remained a supporter of her work. Friedan relates the phone call from Helen soliciting the second article in "Where Are Women in 1978?" in the May issue of that year.

321 *"I've never read such rave reviews"*: HGB, "Step into My Parlor," *Cosmopolitan*, October 1970.

322 *Her interviewer was a writer*: Nora Ephron, "If You're a Little Mouseburger, Come with Me. I Was a Mouseburger and I Will Help You," originally published in *Esquire* and reprinted in Ephron's anthology *Wallflower at the Orgy* (New York: Ace/Viking, 1973).

322 *Helen gave Ephron*: From Ephron's 2001 interview with the journalist Margy Rochlin about HGB.

323 *the word "penis" appeared*: Landers, *The Improbable First Century*, 258.

323 *Lovey was the last good thing*: David Brown's recounting of his firing from Fox and his reaction in Brown, *Let Me Entertain You*, 128–29. Introduction of Lovey, HGB, "Step into My Parlor," *Cosmopolitan*, November 1970.

324 *an expensive series of lurid disasters*: David's account of the making of *Beyond the Valley of the Dolls*, Brown, *Let Me Entertain You*, 128–29. The settlement of the Mansfields' lawsuit against Fox and *Beyond* was reached after Jacqueline Susann's death. See "Mansfield Wins Lawsuit," *The New York Times*, August 2, 1975.

324 *"Failure is always at your heels"*: Brown, *Let Me Entertain You*, 131.

324 *"My darling's depressions"*: HGB, *The Late Show*, 51.

325 *"a dog-eared manuscript"*: Letter from Harper Lee in letters column, "Dear Cosmo," *Cosmopolitan*, March 1971.

326 *"I told him to think of sensational things"*: Author's interview with Liz Smith.

326 *Judy Krantz called Helen*: Author's interview with Judith Krantz.

26. *COSMO* GOES TO HARVARD

328 The Tonight Show *flickered onscreen*: Information on the making of the *Harvard Lampoon Cosmo* parody from author's interviews with Eric Rayman and Patricia Marx. See also Philip K. Dougherty's *New York Times* advertising column, "Cosmopolitan Barb," which included an interview with Rayman, June 7, 1972. On the choice of Burt Reynolds and Helen's expectations, see Burt Reynolds's recollections from his two memoirs, *My Life* (New York: Hyperion, 1994) and *But Enough About Me* (New York: G. P. Putnam, 2015).

328 *staffers were having difficulty choosing a victim*: History of the *Lampoon*'s magazine parodies from Jim Downey and Eric Rayman, eds., *100 Years of Harvard Lampoon Parodies* (Cambridge, MA: Harvard Lampoon, 1970).

331 *Even the conservative moral arbiter*: William F. Buckley, "You Are the More Cupcakeable for Being a *Cosmopolitan* Girl," *National Review*, September 22, 1970, 999–1000.

332 *In a priceless memo*: From HGB to Richard Deems, December 4, 1968, HGB-SSC, Box 39, Folder 7. Helen also discussed her disappointment with the Coburn photos in Nora Ephron, "If You're a Little Mouseburger, Come with Me. I Was a Mouseburger and I Will Help You," originally published in *Esquire* and reprinted in Ephron's anthology *Wallflower at the Orgy* (New York: Ace/Viking, 1973).

332 *"Helen didn't have to talk me into it"*: Reynolds, *But Enough About Me*, 92.

333 *In the months following the centerfold issue*: James Landers, *The Improbable First Century of* Cosmopolitan *Magazine* (Columbia: University of Missouri Press, 2010), 229.

334 *The* Lampoon *staff had rented*: Author's interviews with Eric Rayman and Patricia Marx; and Bryan Marquard, "Iven DeVore, Celebrated Harvard Anthropologist, Dies at 79," *The Boston Globe*, September 29, 2014.

334 *While the children were having their fun*: Letter from HGB to Eric Rayman in HGB, *Dear Pussycat*, 191.

334 *"Untamed Va-jay-jays"*: Cover line from *Cosmopolitan*, May 2010.

335 *In the years from 1965 to 1972*: Landers, *The Improbable First Century*, 229.

335 *Before she left for Arkansas*: Gael Greene's account of her experiences with Burt Reynolds from author's interview with Greene and from her memoir, *Insatiable: Tales from a Life of Delicious Excess* (New York: Warner Books, 2006). Burt Reynolds's recollections from Reynolds, *My Life* and *But Enough About Me*.

27. ISN'T SHE LOVELY?

338 "*'Beauty' is a word*": Francesco Scavullo in William Norwich, "Francesco Scavullo Showed There Was No Surface in the Public Arena That Couldn't Be
Polished," *The Observer*, October 13, 1997.

339 *At Helen's insistence, cover shoots were minimalist*: Details on the process of creating
a *Cosmo* cover in Francesco Scavullo's studio from author's interviews with the
models Beverly Johnson, Brooke Shields, and Karen Bjornson Macdonald, and
with Scavullo's former studio manager Bob Cass and hairdresser Harry King.

339 *Her most important dictate was this*: Memo regarding art format to staff editors
from HGB, HGB-SSC, Box 41, Folder 8.

339 *Helen also relied heavily on*: Author's interview with Nick Piazza.

28. HIGH TIDE

345 *"Start the shark!"*: Author's interview with Carl Gottlieb, cowriter of the *Jaws*
screenplay.

345 *One afternoon in mid-May*: David Brown's description of his father's death and
infidelities from Brown, *Let Me Entertain You*, 62–64.

346 *Headlines screamed the horrors*: The series of shark attacks—historic in their
ferocity and clustering—occurred from July 1 to 12, 1916. This time period
coincided with the final two weeks of Lillian Brown's pregnancy. See "Shark
Kills Bather Off Jersey Beach," *The New York Times*, July 7, 1916. The most
comprehensive history of the attacks is Michael Capuzzo, *Close to Shore: A
True Story of Terror in an Age of Innocence* (New York: Broadway Books,
2001). Capuzzo drew his conclusion that "Peter Benchley invoked the shark as
the role model for his fictional white shark" after extensive discussions with
the ichthyologist George Burgess, a shark expert also quoted in Megan Gam-
bino, "The Shark Attacks That Were the Inspiration for *Jaws*," *Smithsonian*,
August 6, 2012.

Years after his success with both *Jaws* and *Jaws II*, Peter Benchley denied that
the Jersey attacks—unique in history—were the model for his horror scenarios.
Benchley rued the massive shark hunting endangering the species and became a
spokesman for the Oceans Program in the National Council of Environmental
Defense.

346 *In the wake of their banishment*: Description of how Brown and Zanuck ran the
company on both coasts from author's interview with Carl Gottlieb.

347 *Enter Lyn Tornabene*: Author's interviews with Lyn Tornabene. Information on
Norman Darer from CBS report to stockholders, 1973.

347 *Having read the manuscript*: Background on the making of *Jaws* from author's
interview with Carl Gottlieb, and from his book *The Jaws Log* (New York: New-
market, 1975).

348 *Around Thanksgiving of that year*: Letter about the comet to HGB from Mary,
HGB-SSC, Box 6, Folder 2.

349 *Within the film industry*: On David trying to game the bestseller system, author's interview with Carl Gottlieb.

349 *In April 1974*: Supreme Court decision and the arts from David A. Cook, *Lost Illusions: American Cinema in the Shadow of Watergate and Vietnam* (Berkeley: University of California Press, 2002), 282. On Helen and Jackie Susann at the panel, Barbara Seaman, *Lovely Me: The Life of Jacqueline Susann* (New York: William Morrow, 1987), 443, 449. David on Susann's death, Brown, *Let Me Entertain You*, 165–66.

350 *"Dick and David had innocently assumed"*: Gottlieb, *The Jaws Log*, chaps. 7–12 for accounts of filming mishaps. See also *Reader's Digest*, www.rd.com/culture /jaws-movie-trivia-facts/.

351 *"it happened before!"*: From *Jaws*, screenplay by Peter Benchley and Carl Gottlieb, 1975.

351 *Oscar Dystel and David Brown reveled*: Photographs of all *Jaws* merchandising in Gottlieb, *The Jaws Log* (photo insert), show the full panoply of *Jaws*-related products, including the Bantam paperback's illustration on movie posters, T-shirts, and the lot. Production and revenue information from "*Jaws*: How 'Massive' Promotion Built a Summer Blockbuster," *The Hollywood Reporter*, June 9, 2015, www.hollywoodreporter.com/news/jaws-how-massive-promotion-built -799579.

351 *Worldwide grosses to date*: The original *Jaws* movie, released June 20, 1975, grossed $260,000,000 domestically and $210,653,00 foreign, according to www .boxofficemojo.com/franchises/chart/?id=jaws.htm.

352 *"I always have, always"*: HGB, *The Late Show*, 285.

352 *"So when the millions were pouring in"*: Author's interview with Carl Gottlieb.

352 *"I'm getting these phone calls"*: Author's interviews with Lyn Tornabene.

353 *In 1976, Alice Mason, a prominent*: Author's interview with Alice Mason.

353 *"It was supposed to be tacky over there"*: Olivia Barker, "'Cosmo' Editor Elevates Retro Chic to Classic," *USA Today*, February 8, 2007.

353 *Alice Mason was the sort of broker*: Author's interview with Alice Mason.

353 *Penthouse 22D*: Real estate specs from listing of the Brown apartment by Sotheby's in late 2015. The Browns gave a house tour, with photographs, to *USA Today* in 2007: Barker, "'Cosmo' Editor Elevates Chic to Classic."

353 *He was certainly in a position*: David's portfolio and earnings discussed in Steven Flax, "A Boffo, Socko Portfolio," *Forbes*, April 13, 1981.

354 *The architectural critic Paul Goldberger*: Author's interview with Paul Goldberger. See also Goldberger's column "Design Notebook," *The New York Times*, February 16, 1978; and Micki Goldberg, "Gurley Show," *New York Post*, January 25, 2007.

355 *The Browns were well settled*: HGB, "Step into My Parlor," November 1976.

356 *The turn of the year brought another Oscar race*: John Corry's society column, "New Yorkers, etc.," *The New York Times*, March 30, 1977.

29. VICTORY LAP

357 "My only previous exposure": Author's interview with Bobbe Stultz.

357 *Mary Alford watched from her front door*: Helen's Holiday Inn perks, letters to Holiday Inn proprietors, HGB-SSC, Box 13, Folder 8. Description of the Alfords' problems, HGB letter to Elizabeth Bilheimer, HGB-SSC, Box 6, Folder 8.

358 *When Cleo turned eighty-five*: Letter from HGB to Cleo in HGB, *Dear Pussycat*, 337–42.

358 *She had written a very different letter to Mary*: HGB to Mary Alford, HGB-SSC, Box 6, Folder 2.

359 *At 2:00 p.m. on Halloween*: Obituary of Cleo Fred Sisco Gurley Bryan, *Carroll County Tribute*, October 29, 1980. Also, author's interview with Randy High, associate with the Nelson Funeral Service, Berryville, Arkansas.

359 *Joni Evans, an editor*: Author's interviews with Joni Evans.

360 *The* Cosmo *juggernaut was growing*: Rise in subscriptions, James Landers, *The Improbable First Century of* Cosmopolitan *Magazine* (Columbia: University of Missouri Press, 2010), 288.

360 *"Flick your tongue around"*: HGB, *Having It All*, 225.

360 *The language in the magazine*: Landers, *The Improbable First Century*, 266.

360 *In January 1980,* Cosmo *had invited*: Survey findings as presented in Linda Wolfe, *The Cosmo Report: Female Sexual Behavior* (New York: Arbor House, 1981).

361 *"It was her idea"*: Author's interviews with Joni Evans and Michael Korda.

362 *Having seen the splashy* New York *magazine*: Jesse Kornbluth, "The Queen of the Mouseburgers," *New York* magazine, September 27, 1982.

362 *She shot Deems a long note*: Letters and notes between Richard Deems and HGB, dated only 1982, HGB-SSC, Box 39, Folder 7.

362 *Neither party brought up*: Exchange with Steinem, ibid. Also, CKVP.

363 *Perhaps fancying herself*: Information on the day-to-day running of *Cosmopolitan*, its personnel, and fees from author's interviews with Cindy Spengler, Bobbe Stultz, Betty Sargent, John Searles, Judi Drogin-Feldman, Jeanette Sarkisian Wagner, and Claudia Payne.

364 *Cindy Spengler has vivid memories*: Author's interviews with Cindy Spengler.

30. THIN ICE

367 "It's bad enough": Elizabeth Taylor, from the website for her AIDS foundation at http://elizabethtayloraidsfoundation.org/.

367 *Helen had certainly heard the news*: "Way Bandy, Makeup Artist and Best-Selling Writer, Dies," *The New York Times*, August 15, 1986; on Carangi, Justine Elias, "A Chic Heroine but Not a Pretty Story," *The New York Times Magazine*, January 25, 1998. Scavullo quote and memorial service information from Steven Fried, *Thing of Beauty: The Tragedy of Supermodel Gia* (New York: Pocket Books, 1993), 389. Scene with Angelina Jolie in 1998 HBO movie *Gia*. Further details in Alana Nash, "The Model Who Invented Heroin Chic," *The New York Times*, September 7, 1997.

368 *Her thinking was woefully uninformed*: Some early mentions and articles on
AIDS in *Cosmopolitan* include a brief mention in the "Your Body" column,
August 1983; "Is There Gay Life After AIDS?," December 1985; "Crucial Sexual
Dilemmas of the 1980s," January 1986; "Whatever Happened to Great Sex?,"
August 1987; and "What's Everybody Doing About Sex?," April 1988.

368 *"Don't be one of those women"*: Section on friends' reactions to Helen's AIDS
ignorance from author's interviews with Liz Smith, Judith Krantz, and Alex
Mayes Birnbaum.

369 *Helen wouldn't let it rest*: Quotations and assertions from Dr. Robert E. Gould,
"Reassuring News About AIDS: A Doctor Tells You Why You May Not Be at
Risk," *Cosmopolitan*, January 1988.

370 *Soon after the article hit the stands*: Interview with Maxine Wolfe, ACT UP
member who planned and participated in the *Cosmo* protest. Video of event,
along with video of the Phil Donohue and *Nightline* segments devoted to the
controversy, is archived at the Lesbian Herstory Museum in Brooklyn. See also
documentary on the *Cosmo* AIDS protests, *Doctors, Liars and Women: AIDS
Activists Say No to Cosmo* (produced by Jean Carlomusto and Maria Maggenti,
1988).

371 *"We have come so far in relieving women"*: HGB on *Nightline*, January 21, 1988.
Article including some transcript from that broadcast, Jeff Cohen and Norman
Solomon, "Cosmo's Deadly Advice to Women About AIDS," *Seattle Times*,
July 30, 1993. Letter to HGB from Surgeon General C. Everett Koop, HGB-SSC,
Box 8, Folder 6.

372 *In* Cosmo, *the contretemps*: HGB, "Step into My Parlor," April 1988.

372 *she would even refuse* : HGB, *Dear Pussycat*, 291.

372 *There was another, more personal disruption*: The Brown/Zanuck split details
and David's commentary are drawn from Joanne Kaufman, "Starting Over,"
Vanity Fair, October 1988; and Marlys J. Harris, *The Zanucks of Hollywood: The
Dark Legacy of an American Dynasty* (New York: Crown, 1989), 295–96. Also,
on Helen's attitude toward Lili Fini Zanuck, author's interview with Lois Cahall,
a personal friend of Helen's.

373 *"I am a very complicated older man"*: Kaufman, "Starting Over."

373 *The former* Time *managing editor Henry Grunwald*: Author's interview with
Louise Grunwald on party details and the Grunwalds' relationship with the
Browns.

374 *"I've concluded that Helen is like Salome"*: Richard Deems remarks from a program from Helen's twenty-fifth anniversary party, LSP-UTA. Photos of the event
from twenty-fifth anniversary issue, HGB-SSC, Box 44, Folder 7.

374 *That night David Brown and Richard Zanuck*: Information on Thalberg Award
and past recipients at www.oscars.org/governors/thalberg.

374 *"Abelardo dear"*: Letter to Abelardo Menendez in HGB, *Dear Pussycat*, 240.

375 *It wasn't as bad as the AIDS debacle*: HGB, "At Work, Sexual Electricity Sparks
Creativity," *The Wall Street Journal*, October 29, 1991.

375 *She welcomed her newly hired*: Author's interview with Betty Sargent.

376 *"a girl who really knows her onions"*: Letter to HGB from composer Irving Berlin, HGB-SSC, Box 6, Folder 7.

31: A SORT OF CRISIS

377 *"It's not true that"*: Brown, *Brown's Guide to the Good Life*, 5.

377 *In October 1993, David Brown*: Death record of Bruce Brown from Social Security Death Index, 1935–2014. Two women close to David Brown—his longtime friend Alex Mayes Birnbaum and his production partner Kit Golden—did confirm in interviews that Bruce Brown died of AIDS in Philadelphia, but both were unsure of the date. Kit Golden recalls mailing checks for Bruce's care to an address in Philadelphia. Both stated that David Brown was in Canada when the call came. Further discussion of the silence around the death from author's interviews with Marc Haefele, Bill Kortum, and Amy Levin Cooper. Marc Haefele's blog post on the occasion of Helen's death and the mystery around Bruce is at www.scpr.org/blogs/offramp/2012/08/29/9615/helen-gurley-browns-deleted-stepson/.

378 *There is only one potential clue*: HGB, *The Late Show*, 163.

379 *Besides a smart, scholarly book*: Bruce Brown, *Marx, Freud, and the Critique of Everyday Life* (New York: Monthly Review Press, 1973, reprinted in 2009). Mentions of Bruce Brown's death: "The birth of my first and only son," from Brown, *Let Me Entertain You*, 81; and "Not having children pains me," from Brown, *Brown's Guide to the Good Life*, 35.

379 *"I did know that David had a son"*: Author's interview with Michael Korda.

380 *"There's a side to David"*: Author's interview with Gloria Vanderbilt.

32. THE POLITBURO MUST FALL

381 *"Someone asked me"*: Liz Smith remarks from a "roast" of HGB, LSP-UTA.

381 *some pretty young woman*: HGB, *The Late Show*, 12.

381 *"Shrink listened"*: Ibid., 14.

382 *"1,400 people turned out for our press"*: HGB letter to Liz Smith, May 3, 1994, from LSP-UTA. Details on George Green's launch of a Russian edition of *Cosmo* in Jean Rosenthal, "Can You Say 'Cosmo' in Russian?" *Yale Insights*, Yale School of Management, April 28, 2009, http://insights.som.yale.edu/insights/can-you-say-cosmo-russian. See also Margaret Shapiro's "Post-Communist Cosmo Girl," *The Washington Post*, April 29, 1994; and "Sex Please, We're Russian," *The Economist*, May 7, 1994. Helen's note, with a clipping of the article from David's copy of *The Economist*, from CKVP.

384 *The international ad/editorial partnerships*: Author's interview with Jeanette Sarkisian Wagner.

385 *But she did make time to deal with*: Author's interview with Robin LoGuidice, friend and later attorney and executor of Charlotte Kelly Veal.

385 *There was nothing Helen could do*: Account of Charlotte Veal's firing from Robin

LoGuidice and from "Carlotta," a long poem Helen wrote about her friend, in CKVP.

385   *"The body was in shape"*: Veal manuscript on getting face-lift, ibid. Also, correspondence in CKVP between Dr. Helen Colen and Veal, between HGB and Colen, and Helen's letter with terms of agreement for the free face-lift to Dr. Colen, reprinted in HGB, *Dear Pussycat*, 98.

386   *"I quit that"*: HGB, *The Late Show*, 147.

386   *"Jesus, the things you do"*: HGB, *Having It All*, 181. Discussions of Helen's breast enlargement, David's regretting it, and the uses of Crisco for surgical scars in HGB, *I'm Wild Again*, 128–31.

386   *Helen was displaying her new*: Author's interview with John Searles.

386   *Increasingly, there were signs*: Helen's various public fits of anger from author's interview with Alex Birnbaum; upending tray on airplane, HGB, *I'm Wild Again*, 200; screaming-baby incident from HGB, *The Late Show*, 30. Police report from San Antonio and description of arrest, LSP-UTA and draft of column item.

388   *Gil Maurer had invited*: Author's interview with Bonnie Fuller. See also Carl Swanson, "What Makes Bonnie Run?" *New York* magazine, July 14, 2003.

390   *"Probably the best interview"*: HGB, *I'm Wild Again*, 37.

390   *Not that Helen was downplaying the devastation*: Ibid., 29–31.

390   *Friends of the Browns*: Author's interview with Alex Witchel.

390   *She told Liz Smith*: Letter from HGB to Liz Smith, LSP-UTA.

390   *There was a fudge brownie cake*: Party details in Helen's thank-you letter for her party, and photos, LSP-UTA.

391   *"Helen, if you'll cut a tape"*: HGB, *I'm Wild Again*, 30.

391   *The dual transitioning*: Author's interview with Bonnie Fuller.

391   *"I would see her as regularly"*: Author's interview with Cathie Black, who had just taken over as chief of Hearst magazines.

391   *Atoosa Rubenstein*: Author's interview with Atoosa Rubenstein.

392   *Helen had jumped all over her*: Faith Stewart-Gordon, *The Russian Tea Room: A Love Story* (New York: Scribner, 1999), as well as author's interview with Stewart-Gordon.

392   *She allowed herself a bit of bragging*: Helen's final editor's column, *Cosmopolitan*, February 1997.

392   *Mary Gurley Alford had died*: Letter from HGB to Liz Smith, LSP-UTA, and letter from HGB to former coworker Berna Linden in HGB, *Dear Pussycat*, 21–22.

392   *In July 1998, Helen was diagnosed*: Helen's accounts of her breast cancer experience in HGB, *I'm Wild Again*, 138, 151 (quotes); *Dear Pussycat*, 134 (letter to her surgeon).

393   *Fuller's successor, Kate White*: Author's interviews with Kate White.

394   *Helen's stash of four-leaf*: Author's interview with Erica Jong. Letter about sympathy for Joyce Maynard, CKVP; to Steve Rubell, HGB-SSC, Box 9, Folder 7; to Lizzie Grubman, HGB, *Dear Pussycat*, 28–29. Thank-you notes to

and from Browns and Woody Allen and Soon-Yi Previn, HGB-SSC, Box 6, Folder 6.

395 *In the electronic media*: Episode of the BBC show *Where's Elvis This Week?* online at www.youtube.com/watch?v=yoEc7eFArqw. First aired on October 13, 1996.

395 *At seventy-six, a time when an arthritic shoulder*: CKVP, correspondence with HGB, including a clipping of "No Wallflowers in Dance Heaven," by Sandee Brawarsky, *The New York Times*, August 25, 2000. Also, letter from Eve Ensler to HGB and author's interview with Ensler.

33. "WHAT THE HELL, WE'RE OFF TO KOREA!"

396 *"Find out what you can still do"*: HGB to interviewer in the same video that shows her doing the tango. Unaired. Online at www.youtube.com/watch?v=jg162 A9oq-8.

396 *Helen left her penthouse*: News clipping about Danse Elegante from CKVP.

396 *In cold weather*: Author's interview with Kit Golden.

397 *"What the hell, we're off"*: Author's interview with Jamie Brickhouse.

397 *In June 2001*: Margy Rochlin, "Bad, Bad Gurley Brown," *LA Weekly*, June 6, 2001; and author's interview with Rochlin.

398 *Helen had written another iteration of her Book again*: Author's interviews with the editors Sally Richardson and Elizabeth Beier at St. Martin's Press, and with the then publicist Jamie Brickhouse.

398 *For decades, Helen had been writing*: Author's interviews with Nancy Megan, friend of Charlotte Veal, and Robin LoGuidice, Veal's friend, attorney, and executor. Letters and e-mails regarding the disposition of Helen's papers from CKVP.

399 *When the wealthy financier Pete Peterson*: Author's interviews with Pete Peterson and Joan Ganz Cooney.

400 *To those who knew about her divertissements*: Author's interviews with Robin LoGuidice, Nancy Megan, Lyn Tornabene, and Simone Levitt. Also in CKVP.

400 *After his death, Helen put information*: HGB-SSC.

400 *David Brown heard rumors about his wife*: Brown, *The Rest of Your Life Is the Best of Your Life*, 30.

400 *There may be a simple reason*: Brown, *Let Me Entertain You*, 70.

401 *When I wanted to borrow her flat*: Excerpt from "Carlotta," poem written for her friend, in CKVP.

401 *"Why are we (not me)"*: HGB, *I'm Wild Again*, 52.

401 *For years, until well into the 2000s*: Letters from DJ to HGB in CKVP, along with commentary by HGB; letter to "Sweetiepie" in HGB, *Dear Pussycat*, 354–56. Also, letters to Don Juan in her papers at Smith.

402 *Two years after Helen's experiment*: Author's interview with Eve Ensler; letter from Ensler to HGB, 2000; Helen's monologue later performed onstage excerpted from Ensler's book *The Good Body* (New York: Villard, 2004), 11–14.

404 *The dreaded things*: On David's broken hips, two letters from HGB to Liz Smith, LSP-UTA.

405 *"They were very nice"*: Author's interview with the Four Seasons' co-owner Julian Niccolini.

405 *"We were the downstairs people"*: Author's interview with David Patrick Columbia.

34. THE LONG GOODBYE

406 *"please don't die"*: Bit of poetry from random and undated HGB writings, HGB-SSC, Box 39.

406 *On February 1, 2010*: Details on the illness and death of David Brown and Helen's reaction to it from author's interviews with Alex Mayes Birnbaum, Liz Smith, Kit Golden, and Lois Cahall.

408 *The first person to speak was*: Recording of the speakers at David Brown's memorial provided by a friend of the family in attendance.

409 *"Well, I haven't coped too well"*: Radio interview of HGB by Scott Spears, and author's e-mail with him.

409 *"She was told she could not come over"*: Author's interviews with Robin LoGuidice and Charlotte Veal's friend Nancy Megan. Additional testimony on the difficulty of old friends visiting from author's interview with Lois Cahall.

410 *"We ended up with a partnership"*: Author's interview with Nicholas Lemann.

410 *But she was not a brick-and-mortar*: Information on HGB's bequests and the controversy on control of her legacy from Katharine Rosman, "Who Owns Helen Gurley Brown's Legacy?," *The New York Times*, August 22, 2015.

411 *The obituary writer, Margalit Fox*: Margalit Fox, "Helen Gurley Brown, Who Gave 'Single Girl' a Life in Full, Dies at 90," *The New York Times*, August 13, 2012.

411 *The Hearst send-off*: Memorial service details from the program and handouts given at the event, LSP-UTA and from interviews with Liz Smith and Brooke Shields.

35. THE WOMEN: CAN WE TALK?

412 *"A best girlfriend is like Mentholatum:"* HGB in *I'm Wild Again*, 224. For this chapter, author's interviews conducted with Gloria Vanderbilt, Barbara Walters, Simone Levitt, Liz Smith, Lois Cahall, and Joan Rivers. Additional material from Lois Cahall's unpublished memoir. On Simone Levitt, biographical material from Rich Levin, "La Belle Simone," *New York* magazine, November 10, 2013. After Joan Rivers's death, some of her one-liners were posted at www.people.com/article/joan-rivers-best-quotes-one-liners. Also in Rivers section, HGB letter to the makeup artist Robert Oysterman, HGB-SSC, Box 9, Folder 3.

EPILOGUE: "TAKE ME TO THE OZARKS"

425 *"Have you heard?"*: Author's interview with Newton "Newt" Lale at Osage Clayworks, near Sisco family cemetery. Also author's conversation with Kathy Smith of Smith Family Funeral Home, Green Forest, Arkansas, about the Browns' interment.

425 *While it was still standing empty*: Author's interview with the reporter Cyd King, and King's article "*Cosmo* Editor Called Home in End," *Arkansas Online*, November 29, 2012. Also, author's notes and photographs of Sisco family cemetery, gathered in July 2014.

426 *He remembered it this way*: Brown, *Let Me Entertain You*, 259.

426 *A while after David's funeral*: Author's interview with Kit Golden.

427 *When they arrived, they were met*: Author's interview with Sharon Priest, former secretary of state of Arkansas; and HGB's letter to Priest, HGB, *Dear Pussycat*, 80.

427 *Ira Gurley lies alone*: Author's interview with Randy High; author's photographs of Greenwood Cemetery in Green Forest, Arkansas.

427 *In Osage, the Sisco family plot*: Author's interviews with Newt Lale and Kathy Smith.

428 *Married to Helen Gurley Brown*: Grave inscriptions for both Browns from author's photographs.

Acknowledgments

This book began where much of it was written, in the New York Society Library on East Seventy-Ninth Street. One morning, I ran into Betsy Carter, friend, editor, fine writer, and longtime denizen of the library's Hornblower Room, where a robust portion of Manhattan writers find sanctuary, Wi-Fi, and civility. Knowing that I was casting about for a book idea, Betsy said, "Why not Helen Gurley Brown? It's a great story. Think about it." I would never blame Betsy for the special torments of the ensuing three years; I do thank her, so very much, for her support, for sharing her own HGB encounters and insights, and for her boundless patience in abiding my escalating whines. As I looked up from my keyboard all those months and saw her curly head bent—with joy!—over new fiction, Betsy was a reassuring polestar. She's right: we *are* fortunate to do this crazy thing for a living.

As ever, the next step was up to my beloved friend and agent, Flip Brophy, who knew exactly where to place this project, and with whom. For the first time, I got to see the process firsthand; she closed the deal as we convened at a borrowed house on the Jersey shore. For the aspiring author, it was nerve-racking and impressive; by lunchtime, Flip had made another perfect match, with Sarah Crichton Books at Farrar, Straus and Giroux. Sarah Crichton is the increasingly rare *working* editor who gets into it up to her elbows, gently tamps down author excess, leaves no footprints, and always makes it better. It was a wild ride at times; I am so grateful for Sarah's faith, humor, constancy, and calm. Many thanks to her quicksilver assistant, Marsha Sasmor, who was never too busy to counsel a cyber-klutz and was too polite to laugh.

I am one lucky dog to have had the keen eyes and sensibilities of copy editor Lisa Silverman and production editor Frieda Duggan, who coddled, triple-checked, and fine-tuned my copy. All the way through, as I was researching and writing, and during the close vetting of this book, I simply could not have persevered without the sound judgment and boundless patience of the attorney Eric Rayman. So many people in publishing told me, "You have *Eric*? You're lucky." Amen.

At the outset of my research, more good fortune led me to Chloe Boxer, then a whip-smart recent Vassar grad who agreed to sign on as a part-time researcher. She dove in with enthusiasm and with cyber skills far superior to mine; no one can massage a search engine like Chloe. It was inevitable that she would land an excellent "real job." I've missed her, and how. But given the material she turned up and the organization she imposed on the digital mountain of documents and transcripts, Chloe was with me the whole way home.

The incomparable Ms. Lizzie Smith has been a generous source, conduit, and sounding board since my days at *The Washington Post*. For this book about her close friend Helen, Liz opened up her mammoth HGB correspondence and her heart and dispensed a few timely doses of Texas pragmatism that generally ended with: "Honey, just get *on* with it. Would you like a margarita?" A deep curtsy to Mary Jo McDonough, who wrangles Liz's vast network, archives, and pesky seekers like me with grace, professionalism, and warp speed.

When corporate restrictions limited use of some of Helen's richest material, other journalists and friends stepped up to share HGB interviews and encounters. My thanks to Alice Baer for permission to quote the correspondence of the late Bernard Geis from Bernard Geis Associates. Lyn Tornabene is a fine journalist with clear, granular recall and the generosity to share and elaborate on her remarkable set of interviews with Helen. Lyn was also a gracious and unflappable hostess at her gorgeous desert home in Arizona; an hour after my arrival she hauled me to an urgent care facility after this city girl's close encounter with a scorpion. After all we've been through, I am fortunate to call her a friend.

My deep thanks to David Allyn for access to the full version of his remarkable talk with Helen on her "sexual awakenings," when he spoke with her for his book *Make Love, Not War: The Sexual Revolution: An Unfettered History*. Rich Wardell, an archivist at the LGBT Community Center National History Archive, kindly retrieved the cassettes from storage and had them digitized for me. In 2001, the writer Margy Rochlin had the brilliant notion to invite the seventy-nine-year-old HGB on a tour of her single girl homes for *LA Weekly*; thanks to Margy for recounting that memorable road trip and for sharing her interview with Nora Ephron about Helen. Eve Ensler gave me permission to quote the bravura HGB monologue she brought to print and the stage in *The Good Body*; she also spoke to me about her surprising relationship with Helen. I thank her for providing the vibrant and touching coda in Helen's own words. My debt to the research and analysis of James Landers is detailed in the preface; I thank him again here for his kindness in sharing the "outtakes" of his interactions with Helen and Hearst. Lois Cahall gave her all—photos, memories, and tender sections of her unpublished memoir—which provided an intimate look at Helen's love for her women friends and her last days with David Brown. Just when I thought I was done with research, Katie Rosman's deftly reported *New York Times* article, "Who Owns Helen Gurley Brown's Legacy?," motivated some concerned close friends and associates of the Browns to speak with me. Connecting with Robin LoGuidice, friend, attorney, and executor of the late Charlotte Veal Kelly, Helen's BFF since 1948, was a huge and unexpected game-changer. I cannot thank her enough for recounting her own, often hilarious adventures with Helen and "Carlotta" and for granting me access to Charlotte's "deep dish" papers. Bringing that friendship to life—with the additional help of Charlotte's friend Nancy Megan—sharpened my perspective and the narrative immeasurably.

In Los Angeles: At Polytechnic High School, the current incarnation of Helen's alma mater, John H. Francis Polytechnic High School, I had the generous assistance of its principal, Ari Bennett; the former school historian John Blau; teacher and year-book advisor Chi-Sun Chang; and Michelle Elias, co-advisor for the school yearbook, *The Optimist*.

In Arkansas: Many thanks to Randy High, a Carroll County native son who was so helpful during my visit to the historical museum there and during our talks and e-mails thereafter. Newt Lale, a talented potter and unofficial historian of Helen's home place in Osage, proved to be a generous repository of local doings, from Helen's very quiet burial to the ghastly historical details of the Trail of Tears as it wound through the area in the nineteenth century. The reporter Cyd King of the *Arkansas Democrat-Gazette* wrote the first story about the Browns' final resting place; she kindly brought me up to speed before my trip south. The former Arkansas secretary of state Sharon Priest dug into her records and her memories to detail Helen and David Brown's visit to the state capitol. In Little Rock, Dr. David Ware, capitol historian, conducted an informative tour of Ira Gurley's workplace, the capitol building, including the spot where he met his death. I'm most grateful to another Carroll County native, Jane A. Wilkerson, archival manager at the Arkansas History Commission in Little Rock, who guided my research in the state archives there, answered my many questions in subsequent months, then graciously read and commented on the Arkansas chapters of the manuscript.

At Smith College in Northampton, Massachusetts: What a privilege it was—and what fun—to have the collegial help and guidance of the archivists at the Sophia Smith Collection, which holds the Helen Gurley Brown papers. Special blessings to the professional and compassionate Kathleen Nutter. Thanks also to Elizabeth Myers, Director of Special Collections; Amy Hague, who helped me through the permissions thicket; and Nichole Calero, who kept apace of my frantic digital orders with calm and good cheer.

My thanks to Mark Ekman for his welcome to the research services at the Paley Center for Media, and for walking me over to meet the manager of research there, Jane Klain, explaining, "This is someone you absolutely need to know." And how. Thank you, Jane, for your persistence in helping me track the early HGB on TV and radio and helping me get to the bottom of "the shaming in Cleveland."

The information age is a boon for churning up experts on all things; I was so glad to have research help from the railroad historian Eric A. Bowen and the musical theater expert John Kenrick. Bill Kortum, formerly of WBAI radio, went far beyond the call in canvassing former colleagues on the subject of Bruce Brown and his work at the station. At *Playboy* magazine, Theresa Hennessey and Stephanie Worth researched Helen's appearance as the "first woman" to do the *Playboy* interview and provided a roster of those who followed soon after.

Helen Gurley Brown touched so many lives. In my efforts to toss the net as widely as possible, I wrote too darned much; there was a surfeit of rich material and fabulous anecdotes that simply wouldn't fit. Cutting any of it was agony. With gratitude and contrition, I beg the forgiveness of my sources whose contributions are no less valuable as background. To those who helped despite corporate prohibitions and preferred not to be named, I salute your integrity and goodwill. For swelling the HGB chorus with their interviews and by making key introductions, my gratitude to: Dr. William S. Appleton, Elizabeth Beier, Alexandra Mayes Birnbaum, Cathie Black, Myrna Blyth, Jamie Brickhouse, Lois Cahall, Bob Cass, Dick Cavett, David Patrick Columbia, Joan Ganz Cooney, Amy Levin Cooper, Susan Edmiston, Joni Evans, Judi Drogin Feldman, Forrest "Woody" Fraser, Bonnie Fuller, Paul Goldberger, Kit Golden, Carl Gottlieb, Gael Greene, Louise Grunwald, Marc Haefele, the late Hal H. Holker and his daughter Janet Kessler, Beverly Johnson, Erica Jong, Harry King, Michael Korda, Judith Krantz, Mary Wells Lawrence, Nicholas Lemann, Steve Leveen, Karen Macdonald, Bill Manville, Patty Marx, Alice Mason, Nancy Megan, Michael Musto, Julian Niccolini, Claudia Payne, Mitzi Perdue, Pete Peterson, Nicholas Piazza, Letty Cottin Pogrebin, Sharon Priest, Rex Reed, Yvonne Rich, Sally Richardson, Alan Richman, the late Joan Rivers, Peter Rogers, Katherine Rosman, Atoosa Rubenstein, Diane Salvatore, Betty Sargent, Rhonda Schwartz, John Searles, Mimi Sheraton, Brooke Shields, Patty Sicular, Scott Spears, Faith Stewart-Gordon, Bobbe Stultz, Spencer Sunshine, Gloria Vanderbilt, Jeanette Sarkisian Wagner, Barbara Walters, Dr. David Ware, Kate White, Alex Witchel, Maxine Wolfe.

How I have sorely tried my friends, and how forgiving they have been. My apologies, love, and thanks to our ad hoc urban family:

We met David and Michaelyn Mitchell in Lamaze class, but it seems—thank heaven—that they have always been there for us. So have John and Zoe Eisenberg, Mark Gallogly and Lise Strickler and the nine (!!) children we herded to New Year's Eve fireworks in Central Park. Lisa Henricksson and Jim Kelly conferred advice, introductions, restorative dinners, miles of park walks, and the always engaging (yes!) company of their son, Luke. Like HGB, I have always found girlfriends essential, "soothing as Mentholatum," and ever so much fun. Here's to that stalwart girl group: Sally Boyd, Marilyn Healy, Marnie Henricksson, Sali Masters, Sue Mittenthal, Ellen Weyrauch, and Joellen Winter. Special blessings to Jane Leavy, who gave a married pair of twitchy writers the gift of quiet and beauty in off-season Truro; those six weeks could have played out like *The Shining* but for the generous spirit that inhabits her home there.

Three generations of the Spiegel family have made us welcome as part of their extraordinary West Eighty-Third Street community; we mourn the recent passing of the building elders Helen and Aaron who first welcomed us, and take comfort in living amid the remarkable and loving clan they left behind. Cindy, you're right; this building is a book. But it would take a village . . .

I won the in-law lottery, big time, when I married Jeanie and Gary Zwonitzer's eldest son and got two superb brothers, Scot and Mike; our nieces, AJ and Arin; and a sweet, roiling pack of rescue dogs. Despite the vexing geography, they are always with us. So many times, upon turning up another delectable HGB anecdote, I wished that I could have shared it with my brothers, Don and Harland, both wry connoisseurs of Old Weird America. I miss them so. My mother, Rose, has watched me operate in a world quite alien to her, but her quiet lessons in compassion and respect have helped me snare the toughest interviews and harvest the best stories—the kind conferred by mutual trust. At ninety-one, Mom is still an exemplar of How to Treat People. My sister Barbara—my rock—has steadied me with a sweet equanimity I only wish were genetic. Navigating the last few difficult years in our family would have been impossible without the resilience, hard labors, and wicked humor of her husband, Robert, and their sons, Robert and Christian. Thank you, gentlemen, with all my heart.

Our children, Sam and Lila, could not be more different from each other, but they are equally loving, quietly astonishing, and always restorative when they put their feet back under our dinner table. They are the mightiest of so many joys that followed meeting my husband, Mark. For nearly thirty years, he has never quit promising, "It will get better." It has. It will, because of you—only and ever *you*.

Index

A NOTE ABOUT THE AUTHOR

For more than thirty years, Gerri Hirshey has worked as a features writer, columnist, reporter, and essayist at *The Washington Post*, *The New York Times Magazine*, *Vanity Fair*, *GQ*, *Esquire*, and *New York*, among other publications. She has also written for *O, The Oprah Magazine*, *More*, *The Nation*, and *Food & Wine*. Beginning in the 1980s, Hirshey was the first female contributing editor to *Rolling Stone*—she wrote celebrity profiles of numerous artists, musicians, actors, authors, and fashion designers. She is the author of several books, including *Nowhere to Run: The Story of Soul Music*, which is now in its seventh reprint incarnation, and *We Gotta Get Out of This Place: The True, Tough Story of Women in Rock*. Hirshey also collaborated with ex-Ronette Ronnie Spector on Spector's one-woman cabaret show "Beyond the Beehive." Hirshey lives in New York City with her husband, Mark Zwonitzer, a writer and documentary filmmaker; they have two young adult children.